AFTER EDEN

The Gender Study Team
Back Row, left to right: Kate Miller (team secretary), Annelies Knoppers, Douglas Schuurman, Mary Stewart Van Leeuwen, Helen Sterk (and daughter); *Middle Row:* Margaret Koch, Diane Marshall (adjunct fellow), Margaret Dokter (adjunct fellow), Ruth Tucker (adjunct fellow), Rebecca Flietstra (student fellow); *Front Row:* Natalie Hart (student fellow), Stephanie Dorner (student fellow)

AFTER EDEN

Facing the Challenge of Gender Reconciliation

by

Mary Stewart Van Leeuwen
Project Coordinator and Editor

Annelies Knoppers

Margaret L. Koch

Douglas J. Schuurman

Helen M. Sterk

WILLIAM B. EERDMANS PUBLISHING COMPANY
GRAND RAPIDS, MICHIGAN

THE PATERNOSTER PRESS
CARLISLE

Copyright © 1993 by Wm. B. Eerdmans Publishing Co.
255 Jefferson Ave. S.E., Grand Rapids, Mich. 49503
All rights reserved

First published 1993 jointly by Wm. B. Eerdmans Publishing Co. and
The Paternoster Press Ltd.
P.O. Box 300, Carlisle, Cumbria CA3 0QS England

Printed in the United States of America

Library of Congress Cataloging-in-Publication Data

After Eden: facing the challenge of gender reconciliation /
by Mary Stewart Van Leeuwen ... [et al.].
p.   cm.
Includes bibliographical references and index.
ISBN 0-8028-0646-5 (paper)
1. Sex role. 2. Sex role — Religious aspects — Christianity.
3. Feminism. 4. Feminism — Religious aspects — Christianity.
I. Van Leeuwen, Mary Stewart, 1943–   .
HQ1075.A3   1993
305.3 — dc20   93-18020
                                                    CIP

British Library Cataloguing in Publication Data

Leeuwen, Mary Stewart Van
After Eden: Facing the Challenge of Gender Reconciliation
I. Title
261.8
ISBN 0-85364-554-X

CONTENTS

PART I: HISTORICAL AND CROSS-CULTURAL PERSPECTIVES ON GENDER RELATIONS

PART II: THEOLOGICAL AND RHETORICAL PERSPECTIVES ON GENDER RELATIONS

PART IV: SOCIAL INSTITUTIONS AND GENDER RELATIONS

CONCLUSION

PREFACE

In the academic year 1989-90 an interdisciplinary team of scholars assembled at the Calvin Center for Christian Scholarship to study and write together on a topic whose official title was "Gender Roles: Stability and Change within the Context of a Christian Worldview." Twelve groups of scholars had preceded us annually at the Calvin Center, whose purpose is "to promote rigorous, creative and articulately Christian scholarship addressed to the solution of important theoretical and practical issues." At this study center, housed and supported by Calvin College in Grand Rapids, Michigan, books have been written on a variety of topics that are important to all Christians, but especially to those who share the Reformed Christian conviction that all of life — not simply an isolated, individualized, moral-spiritual part of it — is to be redeemed in Christ.

The topics studied by previous C.C.C.S. teams bear witness, along with our own, to the strength of this shared conviction. Books emerging from the study center have covered subjects such as Christian stewardship of natural resources, faith and rationality, public justice and educational equity, the search for a responsible technology, and the relationship of Christian faith to health and medical practice. Obviously such topics are existentially as well as intellectually involving for the scholars working on them, and it is likely that the topic of gender relations — especially at this point in history — is among the most personally involving of all. There is not a person alive who does not participate in shaping and being shaped by gender roles and relationships, and there is arguably not a single aspect of our lives that is not influenced by the results of that shaping. Child-raising practices, education, language, law, health care, dress, work, worship — these and all other areas of our lives are variously nuanced, enriched, and distorted by our assumptions about gender and the practices that result.

But even in a year-long residency shared by five full-time and three adjunct scholars, plus three student members and two support staffers, we could not hope to explore all the areas where Christian faith and life intersect with the topic of gender. Consequently, our book represents an attempt to wed the strengths of our various specialties together with several enduring — and currently very urgent — questions about gender relations. A brief summary of those specialties may help orient readers as they work through the book. A summary of the main issues that unite the book will be included in Chapter One.

Here are the five persons who made up our writing team and the specialties they brought to it. Annelies Knoppers, until recently a professor in the sociology of gender and sport at Michigan State University, was also one of the architects of that institution's Women's Studies Program. In this volume she has concentrated on a critical-theoretical analysis of gender relations and on topics such as the gendering of the human body and gender relations in the spheres of domestic and waged work. Margaret Lindley Koch, a historian from Bethel College in St. Paul, Minnesota, brought fieldwork experience as well as academic expertise to the topic of gender relations in the Third World, and more specifically to the impact of modernization on women and their activities. She has also written on the history of feminism. Douglas Schuurman, a theologian and ethicist at St. Olaf College in Northfield, Minnesota, examined the tensions and compatibilities between feminist and more traditionally Reformed theologies. He also helped the rest of us enrich our more practical theologies with an appreciation for some of the formal aspects of his discipline. Helen Sterk, a professor of communication and rhetorical studies at Marquette University in Milwaukee, Wisconsin, concentrated on topics such as language and gender, the shifting norms of gender relations as revealed in dress, and the way in which rhetoric and narrative function to maintain certain assumptions about gender in the church. Our final full-time scholar, Mary Stewart Van Leeuwen, holds a cross-disciplinary appointment in psychology and philosophy at Calvin College. She wrote the proposal that enabled the study team to come together, coordinated team members' activities during their year together, and edited the resulting volume in the months afterward. Her topics in the book include a survey of contemporary feminist theories and a critique of the public/private dichotomy as it affects gender relations.

Readers will soon notice that the focus of this book is on gender relations especially as they concern *women*. Men are always included in our discussions, but often on the periphery, or in terms of their impact on women. Why have we chosen this approach rather than giving "equal time" to women *and* men? We hope that the answer is obvious: there is a long-standing asymmetry in the relationship between men and women, especially in the Western world, such that men have almost always spoken for and about women, on the presumption that what is male is "standardly human," while what is female is "residue" that requires explanation, or even "deviance" that requires control. We do not believe that such asymmetry and the injustice following from it are always the result of conscious conspiracy on the part of men toward women — any more than asymmetries in race relations are always the result of conscious conspiracy on the part of the racially dominant group in a given society. Nevertheless, these asymmetries of power continue — sometimes all the *more* powerful for being unconsciously taken for granted as "just the way things are." It is the "taken for grantedness" of this state of affairs that we critically challenge. We acknowledge that race and class are equally important factors in the construction of human power-relations; we also acknowledge that male power comes in complex gradations, such that a given man may be dominant in some situations and quite subordinate in others. Nevertheless, we have chosen in this book to highlight gender relations and the voice of women in particular, simply because the latter have been publicly voiceless for so long.

Having said all this, we should also mention that in a number of places we have quoted older sources that use the so-called generic masculine on the presumption that women will assume themselves to be included. There is now abundant research criticizing this assumption and its behavioral effects (some of which we refer to in Chapter Eleven). However, rather than burden the reader with repeated interruptions to the text in the form of *[sic]*, we have left such quotations intact, while supporting in our own writing the more inclusive language that is now the norm.

The five full-time team members mentioned above had primary responsibility for this book, and a note at the beginning of each chapter indicates the main author (or authors) of that chapter. However, both our year together and the resulting volume were greatly enriched by input and encouragement from our adjunct and student scholars. Our adjunct scholars included social worker Margaret Exoo Dokter, now a student in the Master of Divinity program at Calvin Theological Seminary; therapist Diane Marshall, who is associate clinical director at the Institute of Family Living in Toronto, Ontario; and historian Ruth Tucker, a seasoned author and independent scholar who has taught both at Calvin College and at Trinity Evangelical Divinity School in Deerfield, Illinois. Our student team members, all seniors at Calvin College during our year together, were psychology major Stephanie Dorner, biology major Rebecca Flietstra, and Natalie Hart, who was majoring jointly in English and philosophy. These part-time team members gave generously of their labor and knowledge as their schedules permitted, among other things pulling the full-time scholars firmly back to the real world when our analysis was in danger of degenerating into the overly abstract.

For such reminders we were grateful, since all of us are committed to the goals of feminist scholarship. Those goals include a determination to relate our theoretical reflections to the concrete lives of ordinary women and men, and consequently to make this a volume that is accessible to lay as well as academic audiences. Our readers will have to judge our success in realizing that goal throughout the book, but we want them to know in advance that our intentions were honorable. We also want to thank the many persons from our families, our classes, our circles of friends, and our public lecture audiences who helped us work toward that goal. Readers will notice that we have included the comments and experiences of a wide variety of people to help enliven the text, so in a very real sense this book belongs to a much larger "cloud of witnesses" than those who served formally on the Calvin Center "gender team." We hope that their inclusion has helped mitigate the fact that this team, although not lacking in international experience, was still entirely white and entirely middle-class.

Mediating our residency at Calvin and the final published volume were several supporting team members whose work and personal commitment to the project smoothed our way during the year together and kept us on target to get the book done after we had dispersed. These

include, first and foremost, our secretaries Kate Miller and Donna Ro-
manowski, who "job-shared" so efficiently and cooperatively that they
(and their husbands) became living examples of what is possible in terms
of combining waged work with the parenting of young children. Rodger
Rice, the Director of the Calvin Center, kept us largely free of administrative hassles during our time together, and his successor, Ron Wells,
gave us both administrative and moral support in the editing stages of
the book. Finally, Mary Hietbrink and Jon Pott at Eerdmans saw to it
that the final editing and production proceeded smoothly and on
schedule. To all of these indispensable helpers we tender our fervent
thanks.

Because this book is about sources of gender brokenness and the
hope for gender reconciliation, some final remarks should be shared
about our own experience of working together on this project. As we
sought to become a small community of colleagues, we needed — and
sought — the love of Christ to help us hold fast the bonds of peace even
as we tried to speak the truth in love. We did not always agree with each
other, our shared Christian and feminist commitments notwithstanding.
We represented a variety of Christian denominations, social strata, work
and life experiences, family histories, and theoretical allegiances. Some
of us were parents, others single. Some were, or had been, single parents.
Nevertheless, we sought to share our lives with one another as we
struggled to understand and express the challenge that faces all of us in
the healing of gender relations.

Our personal histories took us well beyond the mere citation of
statistics and the creation of theoretical models. Some of us had had
"traditional" fathers who were breadwinners and mothers who were
domestic workers; others had parents who, for a variety of reasons, did
not embrace that model of family life even a generation ago. Our histories included the experiences of rape, sexual abuse, sexual harassment,
physical violence, discrimination in housing and waged work due to
femaleness, singleness, or single-parent status, and the struggle of having
to deal with problem pregnancies. However, our life histories also included the joy of reconciliation with estranged family members, the
stability of supportive marriages and friendships, and the satisfaction of
seeing children grow in wisdom and stature. They included the empowering experiences of effecting political change at the local level and
of working in women-friendly organizations. We knew what it meant
to be creatively and happily single, to have the love of loyal friends, and

to have the privilege of pursuing meaningful work. In these respects our lives countered many of the stereotypes and statistical trends we studied.

Because we sought to hear each others' stories, because we met and spoke with many groups of students, church members, and colleagues, and drew on stories from friends, family, and clients, we came to see how much the silencing of women's voices has distorted gender relations and made true community more the exception than the rule, even among Christians. In seeking to understand the Western world and our own place in it, we also looked at the critique of Western "civilization" and Western feminism leveled by women from the Two-Thirds World and by women from our own communities of color. We were challenged by the various survival strategies of women throughout the world, and realized again and again that despite their often marginalized status, women display the agency and creativity that is part of the image of God in all human beings. Far from being perpetual victims, women throughout history have been amazingly adaptive, tough, and resilient as they sought to realize their own visions of vocation, community, and justice. In many places throughout the book we use a narrative form to make the stories of such women come alive, recognizing that we ourselves, as followers of Jesus Christ, participate in God's ongoing narrative of creation, fall, redemption, and future hope.

It is our hope that in the process of becoming a small community we have produced a book that will help others work out the biblical vision of *shalom* as it applies to gender relations. We pray that the fruit of our joint labors will help our readers live out their commitment to be a "new creation" and so to live out the gospel call to be a reconciled and reconciling people.

CHAPTER 1

Living between the Times: Bad News and Good News about Gender Relations

"It was the best of times; it was the worst of times." That was how Charles Dickens began his *Tale of Two Cities*, which traces the involvement of an Englishman, Sydney Carton, in the nineteenth-century aftermath of the French Revolution. The "tale" that we try to tell in this book is not about two cities but about two genders — women and men — and what might be called the ongoing revolution in their relations with each other.[1]

Dickens's words are an apt beginning to a volume titled *After Eden*, for they express a tension that is intrinsic to the authors' view of gender

---

1. In this book we adhere to the now-prevalent distinction between *sex* and *gender*. The former term is used to refer to biological differences as well as to issues pertaining to sexuality — as in the phrase "sexual harassment." The term *gender* refers to the social construction of what, in any given culture, is taken to be properly masculine or feminine. *Gender* can thus be used as a verb, an adjective, or a noun. When people participate in the construction of certain ideas about what men and women should be like, they are "gendering." The result of their efforts will be that culture's "gender ideology" and a group of women and men who "have gender." Chapter Eight develops these ideas more fully.

All of the full-time team members contributed to this chapter.

1

relations. As scholars who are also Christians working in the Reformed tradition, we see all human institutions and activities in terms of what has often been called "salvation history." Its detailed application to gender relations will come later in this chapter, but the basic idea begins with this: God created our world, its creatures, and its potential as "good" — even "very good" (cf. Gen. 1:10, 12, 21, 25, 31). And to this day the goodness of that creation shines through all human and superhuman attempts to distort it. Creational goodness is present in the beauty of the earth and in human attempts to do artistic justice to it. It is present when we responsibly and freely (as opposed to selfishly and compulsively) appropriate God's gifts of food, drink, rest, and love. It is present whenever there are just and faithful relationships between generations, nations, and other groups. It is present in the wholehearted worship of God, in the responsible stewardship of God's earth, and in a host of other activities and things too numerous to mention. To the degree that such creational goodness characterizes human life, we indeed live in "the best of times."

Good News and Bad in the Biblical Drama

But salvation history only begins with the good acts of God's creation. Human beings, in their desire to "be like God, knowing good and evil" (Gen. 3:5) have inherited very ambiguous tendencies. Both individually and institutionally, we are capable of great sinfulness toward God and our neighbors. We do not live *in* but *after* Eden. The result is that we approach life not just as if we were looking "in a mirror, dimly" (1 Cor. 13:12) but also as if we were looking "in a mirror, distortedly." People's ambivalent attraction to a distorting mirror comes from the realization that what they see reflected therein both *is* and *isn't* themselves. There is enough of our original image and mannerisms reflected to make us recognize ourselves, but the accompanying distortions can be truly disturbing.

And so it is with every human being and every human institution: creational goodness is present, yet marred, and gender relations are no exception. Because our society has so systematically romanticized sexual attraction, marriage, and family life, we all too easily view such institutions as "havens in a heartless world" that should somehow solve all our problems. But a theology that is properly Reformed will have none of

2

this. Like everything else on earth, these institutions are both creationally good *and* fallen. They are thus to be compared less to safe "havens of rest" than to the mercurial little girl of nursery-rhyme fame: "when she was good, she was very, very good, but when she was bad she was horrid." And to the extent that we struggle with the "horror" of distorted creation — in race, class, gender, or other relations — we indeed live in "the worst of times."

But our struggles are not without hope. If the first act of salvation history concerns God's good creation, and the second humankind's rebellion against God and its consequences, the third and climactic act concerns the One who, in the words of the Nicene Creed, "for us . . . and for our salvation, came down from heaven." Those who confess Christ, the apostle Paul writes, have become "a new creation: everything old has passed away; see, everything has become new" (2 Cor. 5:17). This being the case, he continues, "God, who reconciled us to himself through Christ, . . . has given us the ministry of reconciliation" (v. 19). Through the power of the Holy Spirit, we can be reconciled to God and work toward a "re-creation" of just and right relationships among individuals and groups — and the healing of gender relations is part of this task.

We do not mean to be utopian when we say this. Part of our Christian confession is that we live not yet in the new heaven and the new earth but in "the time between the times." Christ indeed "breaks the power of cancelled sin," in the words of an old hymn, but sin's dying body continues to thrash and flail in our lives, causing much residual distortion. Our final healing awaits God's full inauguration of the new heaven and earth at the end of salvation history, and thus we must be cautious about the claims we make for any solution to the brokenness of gender (and other) relationships. Unlike classical Marxists, Christians can never claim that human beings can perfect society on their own, armed only with good intentions, the right theory, and the opportune moment in history.

Nevertheless, substantial healing *is* possible. Created in God's image and thus possessing agency and self-consciousness, human beings can reinterpret the past and re-envision the future, even given the very real constraints that biology and history place upon us. This is a theme of hope and empowerment that runs through the whole of this volume. In particular, those who confess Christ should feel more rather than less free to acknowledge past errors and sins, knowing that sin is common to all of us, that through Christ we share in the renewing power of the Holy Spirit, and that our God is ever "the God of the second chance."

Today we are witnessing white, South African, Reformed Christians — raised in an atmosphere steeped with the theological defense of apartheid — showing their determination to dismantle that political and social system and replace it with one which is racially more just. Can Reformed and other Christians the world over do less for the cause of just gender relations? In either case, it is true, we cannot predict all the consequences of our reforms: recall the problems wrought by the reconstructionist era after the American Civil War and the official dismantling of slavery as an institution. But lack of omniscience about the future cannot be used as an excuse to preserve an unjust status quo. We must simply begin with a clear understanding of the current state of affairs, compare it with the vision for *shalom* called for in Scripture, and take whatever risks may attend our actions as we strive to close the gap.

A careful documentation of the state of gender relations in the recent past and in the present, in the home and in the waged workplace, in the church and in the academy, in the language of professional journals and in the language of popular culture — that is the primary aim of this book. And where we feel competent to do so, we point to concrete possibilities for reform. But is the state of gender relations really that bad? Even if we do subscribe to the Calvinist doctrine of pervasive depravity, is it not possible that we are seeing things in too gloomy a light? Let us briefly consider this question before we return to the contours of the biblical drama and its more detailed implications for gender relations.

Good News and Bad in
Contemporary Gender Relations

According to some analysts, the world has all but completed the task of shaping just gender relations. Have we not had recent female heads of state in countries as diverse as Iceland, Pakistan, Israel, Great Britain, India, Nicaragua, and the Philippines? Are women not entering professions such as law and medicine, fields previously restricted almost entirely to men, in greater and greater numbers? Have we not, especially in the West, largely dismantled the sexual double standard that required the strictest chastity of "decent" women while allowing men to "sow wild oats"? And on the North American educational front, writes columnist John Leo, "We have more to do, but we have come a very long way

4

in a very short time. Our textbooks and expectations have changed; sex differences on [standardized] tests are narrowing; females generally get better grades than males, go to college in greater numbers, get more M.A. degrees and are catching up on the Ph.D. level."[2]

All of this is true; but there is another side to the story. Despite her educational and professional attainments, a woman in the waged work force in America still averages only 71 cents to every dollar earned by the average man. It is true that three-fifths of the 23 million new jobs created since 1970 have gone to women; but most have been low-wage jobs with few benefits and little security.[3] And the decline of the sexual double standard has been a very mixed blessing for women, for it is now widely assumed that they will be sexually available on men's terms. In a recent study of the MTV network, the generic viewer was found to be a male between the ages of twelve and twenty-five, and the most prevalent theme of the videos was "woman as nymphomaniac."[4]

Could there be a connection between this media behavior and the fact that one in six women college students reports having been the victim of date rape? Or that an estimated one in ten families is involved in incestuous abuse? Or that close to a quarter of all American couples have experienced physical violence in their relationship?[5] Whatever the causal connections, it is clear that there is still as much "bad news" as "good news" in contemporary gender relations.[6] Moreover, this "bad

2. Leo, "Sexism in the Schoolhouse," *U.S. News and World Report,* 9 March 1992, p. 22.

3. Sarah Kuhn and Barry Bluestone, "Economic Restructuring and the Female Labor Market: The Impact of Industrial Change on Women," in *Women, Households, and the Economy,* ed. Lourdes Benaria and Catherine R. Stimpson (New Brunswick, N.J.: Rutgers University Press, 1987).

4. Sut Jhally, "Dreamworlds: Desire/Sex/Power in Rock Video" (Amherst, Mass.: Dept. of Communications videocassette, University of Massachusetts, 1990).

5. See Diana E. H. Russell's *Secret Trauma: Incest in the Lives of Girls and Women* (New York: Basic Books, 1986); and Murray A. Strauss and Richard Gelles's "Societal Change and Change in Family Violence from 1975 to 1985 as Revealed by Two National Surveys," *Journal of Marriage and the Family* 48 (August 1986): 465-79.

6. See also Susan Faludi's *Backlash: The Undeclared War against American Women* (New York: Crown Publications, 1991). Although not without some factual errors, Faludi's book — winner of the 1991 nonfiction award from the National Book Critics Circle — is generally solid in its documentation of how far women *haven't* come, even given the gains of second-wave feminism.

news" is not limited to the unchurched—nor would we expect it to be, given our allegiance to the doctrine of sin and sin's pervasiveness. For example, in the same denomination whose college sponsored the writing of this book, a 1990 survey showed that reported prevalence rates of physical, psychological, and sexual abuse were within the same ranges typically found in studies of North Americans at large. And as in more general studies, the denominational study found that the perpetrators of abuse were mostly adult males while victims were largely women and children.[7]

Gender Relations and the Biblical Drama

Our hope is that this book will help to heal broken gender relations. It is our conviction that God's purpose for gender relations aims at mutuality and equality between women and men in marriage, the church, and society. Most of the chapters that follow assume but do not explicitly elaborate this conviction. In the rest of this chapter, therefore, we set forth our understanding of God's will for gender relations. Until recently, much writing on this topic has focused narrowly on the issue of women's ordination to church office and on a few biblical texts relating to this theme. We choose instead to show the basis of a broader vision, and we invite readers to follow along.

Stated most broadly, the Christian is called to share God's intentions and to participate in God's redemptive mission. This vocation is rooted in God's grace and calling, which empower persons to carry out God's mission for creation. Moreover, the theme of gender relations is

7. Calvin College Social Research Center, "A Survey of Abuse in the Christian Reformed Church" (Grand Rapids: Calvin College, 1990). We mention this study because it appears to be the first systematic survey of abuse ever to be done on a random sample of an entire denomination. Other churches—most notably the Roman Catholics—have focused their research and efforts at change on abuse problems within the church hierarchy. See, for example, Peter Steinfels's "Inquiry in Chicago Breaks Silence on Sex Abuse by Catholic Priests," *New York Times,* 24 February 1992, pp. A-1, A-8; and Andrew Greeley's "Priestly Silence on Pedophilia," *New York Times,* 13 March 1992, p. A-15. See also Angela Bonavoglia's "Sacred Secret," *Ms.,* March/April 1992, pp. 40-45.

For a good introduction to the research literature on these topics, see *Abuse and Religion: When Praying Isn't Enough,* ed. Anne L. Horton and Judith A. Williamson (Lexington, Mass.: D. C. Heath, 1988).

a significant one in the biblical account of God's actions and intentions
toward creation. A developed account of Christian vocation will certainly not resolve all the difficulties facing men and women who are
trying to live responsibly in contemporary society—in addition, we
need discernment concerning the details of gender brokenness in our
lives and motivation and power to restructure our lives according to
God's plan. Nevertheless, a biblical understanding of vocation can provide a perspective that shapes Christian identity. It can help point us
toward decisions, attitudes, and practices that are more faithful to the
gospel of Jesus Christ.

Creation, Fall, and Gender Relations

God created men and women to be covenant partners—to image God
together, to be co-stewards of creation's vast potential, and to share in
the abundance of God's provision from the earth (Gen. 1:26-31).
Whatever differences there were between the sexes were sources of
delight and mutual help, a source of enrichment to each and to the
covenant partnership. There is no mention of the man "ruling" the
woman before the Fall; there are no rigid role-assignments along the
lines of a gendered public/private split; there is no devaluation or
competition in the relationship. Instead, the man delights in the woman
as "the helper corresponding to him" (Gen. 2:18),[8] and together they
begin the venture for which God created them.

But then sin comes, and because of sin, the subordination of
woman, the dominance of man, and the resulting perversion of their
reproductive and stewardly responsibilities (Gen. 3:16-19). Human history becomes in large part a story of the fallenness of gender relations.
It is a story of rape, lust, seduction, adultery, fear, sexual competition,
polygamy, dominance, and submission. We have already noted some
of the ways in which this fallenness mars our society today. There are
many who groan in travail under the burden of this sin, including rape
victims, abused children, and emotionally and physically wounded
wives. There are also those who seek eternal life through their careers,
those who are addicted to their sexual desires, and those whose capaci-

8. The translation is Phyllis Trible's. See her book entitled *God and the Rhetoric
of Sexuality* (Philadelphia: Fortress Press, 1978), p. 92.

7

ties for life and service have been stunted by the effects of others' sexual sin.[9]

Ultimately these struggles are not just against flesh and blood but against principalities and powers, spiritual forces of evil at work in a fallen world (Eph. 6:12). "We know," Paul writes, "that the whole creation has been groaning in labor pains until now; and not only the creation, but we ourselves, who have the first fruits of the Spirit, groan inwardly while we wait for adoption, the redemption of our bodies" (Rom. 8:22-23).

The Redeemer and Gender Reconciliation

But God would not let sin and evil triumph in the destruction of creation. Although in this fallen world only sparks of the image of God are discernible in gender relations, it is the Creator's will that male and female once again display the divine glory. God chose to save the world from sin and its results. God's redemptive purpose is most clearly revealed in the person and work of Jesus Christ. In Christ we can see what humanity ought to be; in Christ we can see the face of God as it is turned toward fallen creation. What does Jesus' life and teaching reveal about God's will for gender relations?

According to Luke's gospel, Jesus began his public ministry with these words: "'The Spirit of the Lord is upon me, because he has anointed me to bring good news to the poor. He has sent me to proclaim release to the captives and recovery of sight to the blind, to let the oppressed go free, to proclaim the year of the Lord's favor'" (4:18-19). The ministry of Jesus focuses on freedom from sin, the forgiveness of sins, lifting up those who are bent beneath the burden of sin, and casting down the mighty. In Jesus we see God's compassion for victims of disease and social injustice, and we see God's power to remove sin and its effects.

With regard to gender relations, we see that Jesus elevated the status of women and subverted the structures supporting male privilege and superiority. For example, in the Palestine of Jesus' day, women were not taught the Law. Rabbi Eliezer wrote, "Rather should the words of the Torah be burned than entrusted to a woman. . . . Whoever teaches

9. For a more detailed analysis, see in particular Patrick Carnes's *Don't Call It Love: Recovery from Sexual Addiction* (New York: Bantam, 1991).

his daughter the Torah is like one who teaches her lasciviousness."[10] By contrast, Jesus praised Mary of Bethany for listening to his teaching rather than following the typical woman's role of serving the meal (Luke 10:38-41). He revealed himself as the Messiah to the doubly marginalized Samaritan woman (John 4:5-26) and included many women among his disciples (Luke 8:1-3).

According to Jewish law at the time of Jesus, women were not permitted to be witnesses in legal proceedings. But the resurrected Jesus appeared first to women, whom he then commissioned to be his witnesses to others (John 20:11-18; Matt. 28:9-10; Mark 16:9-11). When the crowd wanted to stone to death a woman caught in adultery (one wonders why her male partner was not included), Jesus exposed the hypocrisy of her accusers, and rather than condemning the woman simply told her to "sin no more" (John 8:2-11, KJV). Jewish law also allowed men to be polygamous, denied women the right to a divorce, and permitted husbands to divorce their wives for even frivolous reasons. By contrast, Jesus insisted on monogamy and assigned the same rights and responsibilities to both husbands and wives (Mark 10:2-10; Matt. 19:3-9).

In Jesus' day, women's value and identity rested largely in their role as wives and mothers. But when a woman in a crowd cried out, "Blessed is the womb that bore you and the breasts that nursed you!" Jesus replied, "Blessed rather are those who hear the word of God and obey it!" (Luke 11:27-28). And we should also note that the men whom Jesus called to follow him left their occupations; Jesus thus associated with both men and women who had low status in the eyes of society.

---

10. *Mishna*, Sota 3,4. The citation is from Leonard Swidler's *Yeshua: A Model for Moderns* (New York: Sheed & Ward, 1988), p. 79. See also Swidler's *Biblical Affirmations of Women* (Philadelphia: Westminster Press, 1979); Elisabeth Schüssler Fiorenza's *In Memory of Her* (New York: Crossroad, 1985); and Phillip Segal's "Elements of Male Chauvinism in Classical Halakhah," *Judaism: A Quarterly Journal of Jewish Life and Thought* 24 (Spring 1975): 226-44. Some Jewish and Christian feminists are concerned that the contrast between the "sexist" Jewish culture and the "feminist" Jesus both derives from and contributes to anti-Semitism — see, for example, Rosemary Radford Ruether's *Sexism and God-Talk: Toward a Feminist Theology* (Boston: Beacon Press, 1983), and *Womanspirit Rising*, ed. Carol Christ and Judith Plaskow (San Francisco: Harper & Row, 1979). While the contrast can be drawn too sharply, it is undeniably present. However, in light of the patriarchal practices of the Christian church over the past two millennia, Christianity hardly compares favorably with Judaism on the treatment of women.

Gender Relations in the Early Church

In light of Jesus' elevation of women's status, it comes as no surprise that the apostle Peter interpreted the outpouring of the Holy Spirit on women and men at Pentecost as the fulfillment of Joel's prophecy: "'In the last days it will be, God declares, that I will pour out my Spirit upon all flesh, and your sons and your daughters shall prophesy.... Even upon my slaves, both men and women, in those days I will pour out my Spirit; and they shall prophesy'" (Acts 2:17-18). Membership in the body of Christ comes by baptism and faith, not by race, class, or gender. Through the waters of baptism, "There is no longer Jew or Greek, there is no longer slave or free, there is no longer male and female; for all of you are one in Christ Jesus" (Gal. 3:28).

Furthermore, in the New Testament church, gifts and functions are not distributed along gender lines; rather, they are "activated by one and the same Spirit, who allots to each one individually just as the Spirit chooses" (1 Cor. 12:11). Women not only listen to the teaching of others (1 Tim. 2:11); they also prophesy (1 Cor. 11:5; Acts 21:9), function as deacons (Rom. 16:1-16), and are "prominent among the apostles" (Rom. 16:7).[11] Although these egalitarian teachings and practices disappeared early in church history—to be ignored or suppressed for almost two thousand years—they have left an indelible stamp in the New Testament record.

When we recall Jesus' disregard for wealth and social status, it comes as no surprise that the Spirit also empowers people of little worth in society's eyes. Thus Paul writes to the Christians at Corinth, "Consider your call, brothers and sisters: not many of you were wise by human standards, not many were powerful, not many were of noble birth. But God chose what is foolish in the world to shame the wise; God chose

---

11. It is significant that the New Testament "deacons" not only cared for the physical needs of the community but also preached. One of the first deacons, Stephen, was actually martyred because of his preaching of the gospel (Acts 6–7). Since a number of women were deacons, it follows that they also preached. And although some translations and interpretations of Romans 16:7 change the name "Junia" to the masculine "Junias" or "Junianus," this change lacks textual support and reflects instead a patriarchal bias. For a discussion of this text and related others, see Schüssler Fiorenza's *In Memory of Her*, and *Women Priests: A Catholic Commentary on the Vatican Declaration*, ed. Leonard and Arlene Swidler (New York: Paulist Press, 1977), pp. 141-44.

10

what is weak in the world to shame the strong; God chose what is low and despised in the world . . . so that no one might boast in the presence of God" (1 Cor. 1:26-29).[12]

To summarize, differences of class, race, and gender — on which the human sense of superiority and inferiority is based — are first relativized in the body of Christ by the waters of baptism, then transformed into unique and valued contributions to the common good. There is no room for envy or superiority in the body of Christ, for "we were all made to drink of one Spirit" (1 Cor. 12:13). There is also no room for an attitude of self-sufficiency, for even the apparently weaker members of the body "are indispensable" (1 Cor. 12:22). Differences within the inclusive mutuality of the body of Christ become occasions for healthy interdependence, mutual vulnerability, and even delight.

The trenchant social inequalities of the culture surrounding the New Testament church were thus undermined and transformed by the grace and calling of Christ.[13] Inequality and subordination based on race, class, and sex were undermined in principle and subverted in practice. The gospel called neither for a social revolution nor for a passive acceptance of the status quo. Rather, it initiated a transformation of social relations toward equality, mutuality, and positive interdependence.

The Continuing Call to Mutuality

The life and teachings of Jesus as revealed in the Gospels and the account of his continuing work through the Holy Spirit in the New Testament church display God's will for gender relations. It is God's desire to oppose societal patterns that elevate some persons over others and that harm, demean, subordinate, and oppress various women and

12. Note that this is a pervasive theme in both the Old and New Testaments: Jacob was chosen, not Esau; Joseph, not his older brothers; Israel, not Egypt; Nazareth, not Jerusalem; and so on.

13. In *The Great Reversal: Ethics in the New Testament* (Grand Rapids: William B. Eerdmans, 1984), Allen Verhey argues that the New Testament authors transformed social relations in light of the gospel not by overthrowing them overtly but rather by undermining their attitudinal foundations. For a similar analysis, see also Victor P. Furnish's *Moral Teaching of Paul: Selected Issues,* rev. ed. (Nashville: Abingdon, 1985); and Abraham Kuyper's *Lectures on Calvinism* (Grand Rapids: William B. Eerdmans, 1975), especially pp. 27-28.

11

men. It is God's will to restore gender relations to the mutuality and equality that characterized the covenant partnership of woman and man in creation. Christ was sent by God the Father and anointed with the Spirit to initiate, among other things, this redemption of gender relations.

For us at the end of the twentieth century, Jesus' revelation of God's will stands against the temptation to absolutize career, social status, or money above all other values. A man's worth is to be judged not by his income or job status but by his response to God in Christ. A woman's worth is to be judged not by her relationship to her father, husband, or son — or alternately, by her career achievements or lack of same — but by her response to God's call. In the perspective of Christian vocation, intellectual activity is not more noble than manual activity, church work more significant than "secular" work, professional accomplishments more important than domestic accomplishments. Although our society places supreme value on wealth and professional achievement, the God who calls us out of this world does not.

All Christians share Christ's mission and Christ's anointing. For example, the Heidelberg Catechism asks the question "But why are you called a Christian?" and answers as follows: "Because by faith I am a member of Christ and so I share in his anointing. I am anointed to confess his name, to present myself to him as a living sacrifice of thanks, to strive with a good conscience against sin and the devil in this life, and afterward to reign with Christ over all creation and all eternity."[14] However they may differ in terms of gifts and callings, all Christians are anointed with the energies of the Holy Spirit so that they can fulfill the prophetic, priestly, and kingly functions referred to in that answer.

It does not take a great deal of imagination to apply these functions to our present-day concerns about gender relations. Can any person "anointed to confess [Christ's] name" bow mindlessly to any human lord — whether that "lord" be a husband, parent, boss, general, monarch, or president? Can anyone who confesses Christ as Lord use his or her power and privilege to lord it over others? God forbid! It is to be hoped that every one of Christ's anointed will instead prophetically denounce whatever contradicts God's purposes for this world and its people. Can anyone anointed to be "a living sacrifice of thanks" permit himself or herself to be physically, sexually, or emotionally abused, or to be an

14. Lord's Day 12, from *The Heidelberg Catechism* (Grand Rapids: CRC Publications, 1975).

12

abuser? On the contrary, just as Christ shed his own blood for us all, so too should each of his followers be willing to spend much effort working for healing, justice, and *shalom* in gender relations.

More specifically, the biblical revelation of God's mission calls Christians to resist the oppression and subjugation of women. The fact that gender relations are prominently mentioned in the biblical accounts of creation, fall, and redemption strongly implies that Christians should not dismiss concern for gender relations as trivial in comparison with other kingdom causes, whether evangelistic or social. Through the wisdom and power of God's word and Spirit, Christians are called to speak and work against rape, incest, wife abuse, the objectification and devaluation of women, and the subtle mechanisms that promote such evils. Christians must also resist defining a man's worth by his income or job status, by his ability to control others, or by his blind willingness to die in any war to which his society assigns him. It is God's will that men and women live as covenant partners and as stewards of God's gifts and callings. Faith, hope, and love require this. It was and is the way of Jesus Christ.

Looking Ahead

The biblical vision sketched in the preceding section provides a kind of orienting "North Star" to guide Christian participation in God's mission for gender relations. However, additional insights are needed if we are to relate this vision to concrete strategies and actions. We must first uncover the dynamics of gender brokenness if we are to be effective reformers of gender relations. In the same way that accurate and discerning knowledge of the causes of poverty and disease is needed to advance God's mission in these areas, so also Christians need an analysis of the mechanisms of sexism if they are to work successfully for the healing of gender relations.

Feminists have wrestled with issues of gender relations for many years now, some with a broad scope of concern and a profound depth of insight. In an effort to move beyond Protestantism's usual preoccupation with the ordination of women, we devote the first section of our book to an account of various feminist approaches to gender relations. Our aim here is to introduce readers to some of the complexity and diversity of feminist analysis, both Western and non-Western. In the

13

second section we focus more specifically on feminist theology, both descriptively and in terms of its import for Christian (and more especially Reformed Christian) worldviews. We also apply this analysis to the case study of a Reformed church grappling with the issue of women's place in the church.

In the third and fourth parts of the volume we examine significant aspects of culture and society, with a view to showing some ways in which gender relations are shaped, distorted, and redeemed. We analyze how values relating to our bodies and clothing express gendered attitudes, practices, and power relationships. We examine language: how it reflects, perpetuates, and occasionally helps to change existing gender relations. Because of the profound impact wrought by the gendering of the split between public and private life, we devote two chapters to an analysis and assessment of this pervasive aspect of our society. We follow this with some case studies on women in India and Egypt, in order to show both similarities to and differences from the West in women's strategies for coping with modernization. Finally, we return to the Western world with an examination of the ways in which gender structures and is structured by both domestic and waged work.

Throughout the chapters that follow, our aim has been to provide some new tools for Christians to use as they work toward the healing and renewal of gender relations. Vision from the biblical "North Star" combines with what we hope is thorough analysis and wise discernment of the times. But more is needed. Christian vision, analysis, and discernment by themselves cannot change individual hearts or interpersonal and societal relationships. The gracious power of God, revealed in Christ and operating by the Holy Spirit, is indispensable to any attempt at reform and renewal.

Lights at the End of the Tunnel

For this power in abundance we continue to pray. Moreover, we do see evidence of that power at work. Consider, for example, the case of Rita Milla, a devout young Catholic woman from Los Angeles who from the age of sixteen on was coerced into sexual activity with her much-trusted priest and six of his colleagues. After being impregnated by one of them and nearly dying of ensuing complications, she attempted to tell her story to the bishop, only to be brushed aside. When she decided to sue

14

the church with the help of an experienced feminist lawyer, the priests named in the suit mysteriously disappeared, and archdiocesan officials claimed to know nothing of their whereabouts.

That might have been the unresolved ending of the tale — except that seven years later, in 1991, the original priest who seduced Rita returned to Los Angeles on his own initiative (from the Philippines, where his superiors had sent him) and made a public apology to Rita and her family. "As a priest," he acknowledged, "I had Rita's full trust and confidence. Yet, I got sexually involved.... I admit my fault.... I am truly sorry for the pain, the anxieties, and the sufferings she has endured all these years." Furthermore, he released supporting documentation regarding the archdiocesan cover-up of the matter seven years previously.[15] Breaking silence about abuse — and breaking ranks with those who collude in hiding it — requires monumental courage on the part of survivors and perpetrators alike. We believe that the power of the Holy Spirit is evidenced in such courageous attempts to seek gender justice and reconciliation.

Or consider the following reflections from one of our own team members:

> When I was young I watched a lot of movies. I was always enchanted by the image of a woman wearing a man's shirt and nothing else. Doris Day especially. The shirt was always huge on her, emphasizing her smallness in relation to him. My fantasy was that I'd marry a big man, certainly one bigger than me. Instead, I fell in love with Mark, a man only marginally taller than me, and about the same weight, whose feet were no longer (only they are wider!).
>
> It's been hard for me to shelve the fantasy, but I know I have a better marriage with Mark than I would have had with any of Doris Day's leading men! We wear the same size sweatshirts. We give them to each other. People who do that aren't living in a fantasy world of big and small, masculine and feminine, "wearing the pants" and "wearing the skirts." We're living in a reality of mutuality, co-operation, sharing, and flexibility. Isn't it ironic that *this* is not the relationship fantasy fed to American teenagers? We'd probably have healthier marriages if it were.

Stories such as this one show that none of us (gender studies specialists included!) is exempt from the distorting effects of gender-role sociali-

15. Quoted by Bonavoglia in "The Sacred Secret," p. 42.

15

zation, that the healing of gender brokenness is an ongoing process, and —best of all—that there are positive surprises in store for those who take up the challenge. We believe that the Spirit of Christ enables such healing and bestows the happy surprises that come in its wake.

Consider, finally, the comments of a Reformed church delegate to a synod still debating whether or not to open up all church offices to women. The denomination's official form for the public profession of faith, he pointed out, concludes by welcoming all new confessing members "to *all* the privileges of full communion . . . to full participation in the life of the church . . . to its responsibilities, its joys, and its sufferings."[16] But, he continued, in light of the church's continued practice of not letting women be elders or pastors, such words turned to dust in his mouth—especially when speaking to someone as gifted as his wife.[17]

The implication was clear: either the church should change the words of the profession of faith form to reflect the different practices regarding men and women coming into the church, or it should change its practice to reflect what is promised in the words of the form— namely, a welcoming of *all* new members to *all* the privileges of full communion. For the many women who heard—but could never participate in—synodical discussions regarding their own future in the church, this male delegate was a courageous mentor and spokesman on their behalf.

Historians and social scientists tell us that groups which hold a monopoly on any kind of power never give it up voluntarily. Yet that same synod of one hundred men voted a few days later to eliminate the clause in the denomination's church order which restricted the offices of elder and pastor to men. When such events take place, it is the power of Christ's Spirit that prevails, as surely as it does in South Africa when voters in an all-white referendum affirm their determination to dismantle white racial privilege.

As readers attend to our assessments of gender relations in the chapters which follow, it is our hope that Christ's Spirit will continue to be present, pointing the way to a new creation.

16. Form for the Public Profession of Faith, *Psalter Hymnal of the Christian Reformed Church in North America* (Grand Rapids: CRC Publications, 1987), p. 964 (our italics).

17. Taped proceedings of the Synod of the Christian Reformed Church in North America, Calvin College, Grand Rapids, Mich., 18 June 1990.

PART I

HISTORICAL AND CROSS-CULTURAL PERSPECTIVES ON GENDER RELATIONS

CHAPTER 2

Feminism and Christian Vision:
Lessons from the Past

I f you lived in the United States of the 1950s, or even if you have just read about that era, you may know what is suggested by the term *McCarthyism.* Joseph R. McCarthy was a U.S. senator who dominated the early 1950s with sensational but unproven charges of communist subversion in a variety of public spheres. Working both alone and as head of a Senate subcommittee, McCarthy was the architect of a nationwide anticommunist crusade that damaged the reputations — and sometimes the entire careers — of artists, civil servants, politicians, and military personnel. Although finally censured by his Senate colleagues for witchhunting cloaked in the language of patriotism, he managed for a time to turn the mere suggestion of communist sympathies into a recipe for possible ruin. The term *communist,* like the term *witch* in earlier times, became a linguistic silencer: whether the word was specifically or (more often) vaguely defined, nobody wanted to be publicly tarred by it for fear of being socially ostracized and perhaps even professionally and financially ruined.

It would be inaccurate to say that the term *feminism* has become

The primary authors of this chapter are Margaret Koch and Mary Stewart Van Leeuwen.

the linguistic equivalent of the term *communism* in 1950s America. But in some circles (including some Christian circles) it comes close to being just that. For example, one of our study-team members recently taught a summer course on the psychology of women at a graduate school for Christian studies. Arriving the weekend before the course began, she happened to meet one of the summer-school students in the residence hall. Unacquainted with her course, the student asked her what it included. But as he listened to her description, he began glancing around as if to make sure that no one else was within earshot. Finally he moved several inches closer, lowered his voice, and queried her nervously: "But you wouldn't go so far as to call yourself a . . . *feminist,* would you?" The study-team member replied that she did indeed consider herself a *biblical* feminist and did not regard this as a contradiction in terms.[1] But she didn't get very far with her explanation because the student excused himself and walked quickly away, almost as if she had just announced that she had an infectious disease.

Feminism, like McCarthy's *communism,* is a term that many people use imprecisely and very emotionally. And to an extent this is understandable: when new social movements threaten old categorical certainties, it is tempting to dismiss them with a sweeping, pejorative label whose negativity, it is hoped, will persuade movement members to revert to the status quo or at least keep quiet. Nor is this merely a tendency of the less educated: it is not uncommon for recognized intellectuals to write best-selling books that decry the supposed effects of "feminism" without acknowledging its different expressions or even defining their own use of the term.[2]

It is, however, a little puzzling to observe the extent to which

1. Throughout this volume we will use the terms "biblical feminist" and "Christian feminist" interchangeably, reflecting the biblical-theological position we laid out in Chapter One. See also Chapter Five for elaboration.

2. See, for example, Allan Bloom's *Closing of the American Mind: How Higher Education Has Failed Democracy and Impoverished the Souls of Today's Students* (New York: Simon & Schuster, 1987), and George Gilder's *Men and Marriage* (Gretna, La.: Pelican Publishing, 1987). Bloom's book topped the *New York Times* nonfiction best-seller list throughout the summer of its publication. Bloom blames "feminism" both for undermining the prestige of traditional, male-authored classics and for contributing to the decline of the family. For a critique of Bloom, see Susan Moller Okin's *Justice, Gender, and the Family* (New York: Basic Books, 1989), especially chapter 2. For a critique of Gilder, see Mary Stewart Van Leeuwen's "Selective Sociobiology and Other Follies," *Reformed Journal* 38 (February 1980): 24-28.

Christians take part in such unreflective name-calling. For most Christians, if they are more than merely nominal Christians, know what it is like to be placed in a negative category that makes no distinctions among them — which assumes, for example, that all evangelicals necessarily support the financial irresponsibility of a Jim Bakker, or that all Catholics turn a blind eye to the criminal activities of the Mafia. In such situations Christians rightly wonder why their critics have made no effort to understand the complexity of historical and contemporary Christianity — why they don't recognize that Anabaptists are in many ways different from Calvinists, Dispensationalists from Pentecostals, African Methodist Episcopalians from Southern Baptists, and so on. Yet many of these same Christians have not made any effort to understand the various faces of feminism before using the term as dismissively as some secularists use the term *Christian*.[3]

We hope that these analogies, along with the material presented in Chapter One, have convinced readers of the need to understand the history and various expressions of feminism before presuming to judge it. To that end, in this and the following chapter we will present and defend our working definition of feminism, then review the history of Anglo-American feminism, a movement that has developed from the late eighteenth century through the twentieth century. We focus primarily on Anglo-American feminists because in sheer numbers as well as in published output they have been the most conspicuous. In this chapter we will concentrate on the beginning of Western feminism from just before 1800 until the end of World War II. In Chapter Three we will take a more detailed look at contemporary Anglo-American feminism. In Chapter Four, however, we will see that white, middle-class, English-speaking feminists have gradually been learning to hear the concerns of white working-class women, women of color in the West, and Third World women.

How We Define Feminism

There are Christians who, like the student who scuttled away from our study-team member, apparently believe that "Christian feminism" is a

---

3. See, for example, John Piper and Wayne Grudem's book entitled *Recovering Biblical Manhood and Womanhood: A Response to Evangelical Feminism* (Westchester, Ill.: Crossway Books, 1991).

contradiction in terms. We do not agree. Indeed, as we will see later in this chapter, there are forms of feminism that have been strongly motivated by Christian compassion and Christian principles. How, then, might we craft a definition of feminism that would be compatible with a Christian worldview?

To begin with, as Christian feminists we hold that all persons are made in the image of God and therefore deserve the dignity and respect that this implies. Thus our definition of feminism will be one that is committed to the ultimate welfare of both men and women, although giving greater emphasis to the situations and needs of women. For we also hold that the fallenness of humankind has so affected gender relations that serious work is needed to restore justice between the sexes, particularly where women are concerned. This is not to say that men are inherently more sinful than women, but it is to say that distortions in gender relations are endemic to the human condition, and that in general (as the record of history makes clear) women as a group suffer devaluation and injustice in gender relations more than men do.

Finally, because we see in Christ's salvation the promise of a restored creation, we believe that we *can* work with some success toward reconciliation in gender relations. We do not aim to be utopian or triumphalistic when we say this. As people living in the "time between the times" — between Christ's resurrection and the final realization of the new heaven and earth — we acknowledge that all healing is partial and subject to reversals, because even though we are "made new" in Christ we still carry the scars of our sinful tendencies. Nevertheless, as biblical feminists we affirm that substantial healing is possible and that we are called to participate in its achievement.[4]

With these considerations in mind, we offer the following working definition: A feminist is a person of either sex who works to restore social, economic, and political justice between women and men in a given society. This work is motivated by the conviction that the devaluation of women and their activities as compared with the valuation of men and their activities is wrong, and that the systematic disempowering of

4. For a further treatment of gender relations in the context of the biblical drama of creation, fall, and redemption, see, for example, Gilbert Bilezikian's *Beyond Sex Roles* (Grand Rapids: Baker Book House, 1985); *Images of God and Gender Models,* ed. Kari E. Børresen (Stockholm: Solum Forlag, 1991); and Mary Stewart Van Leeuwen's *Gender and Grace: Love, Work and Parenting in a Changing World* (Downers Grove, Ill.: InterVarsity Press, 1990).

women in relation to men is unjust. Feminist activity thus focuses on the situation and needs of women, even though it may eventually benefit people of both sexes. It assumes that men and women share a common humanity, but also that their different experiences must be taken into account.[5]

Our definition anticipates the historical survey of this and the next chapter. That survey will show that three currents of feminist thought — which we call the liberal, the relational, and the socialist — tend to recur in varying forms in both nineteenth- and twentieth-century feminism. We believe that aspects of all three are compatible with our Christian-based definition of feminism. For example, in assuming a common humanity and the need to achieve gender justice in society, our definition draws on a feminist tradition, rooted in Enlightenment thought, which takes the individual human being, regardless of sex, as its basic unit of analysis. This tradition has focused on the attainment of individual rights. It has generally been uneasy with talk about differences between the sexes because historically such "differences" have tended to be translated into "deficits" on the part of women and used as reasons for restricting them further. This current of thought, sensitive to individual rights while downplaying gender differences, is often known as liberal feminism. In the words of historian Karen Offen,

> [Liberal feminism] emphasize[s] more abstract concepts of individual human rights and celebrate[s] the quest for personal independence (or autonomy) in all aspects of life, while downplaying, deprecating, or dismissing as insignificant all socially-defined roles and minimizing discussions of sex-linked qualities or contributions, including childbearing and its attendant responsibilities.[6]

But our definition also refers to the *different experiences* of women and men and the need to strive for a society in which they benefit together. Sometimes known as relational feminism, this current of thought believes that an acknowledgment of some complementary dif-

---

5. This definition is adapted from Karen Offen's "Defining Feminism: A Comparative Historical Approach," *Signs* 14, no. 1 (1988): 119-57. It should be noted that this is not a definition with which all feminists — particularly secular feminists — will agree. According to some definitions, only *women* can be feminists; according to others, the welfare of men is a matter of comparative indifference.

6. Ibid., p. 136 (shift to present tense ours).

ferences between men and women is not only permissible but necessary to adequate feminist theory and practice. Appearing in slightly different forms in nineteenth- and twentieth-century Western feminism, as well as in the feminism of contemporary Third World women and Western women of color, relational feminism, according to Offen, "emphasize[s] women's rights *as women* (defined principally by their childbearing and/or nurturing capacities) in relation to men. It insist[s] on *women's* distinctive contributions in these roles to the broader society and make[s] claims on the commonwealth on the basis of these contributions."[7]

Relational feminism has often appealed to Christians who wish to emphasize that God created humankind "male *and* female" (Gen. 1:27). And until recently it has been relational feminists of various kinds who have most seriously tackled gender issues directly, rather than trying to subsume them under some other rubric. Liberal feminists have adopted the strategy of focusing on the *common humanness* of men and women, while Marxist and early socialist feminists held that gender issues were mostly reducible to questions of *economic class.* Relational feminists have refused both of these positions, which they see as evasions. They insist that gender is too important as an explanatory concept to be reduced to "mere humanness" or "mere economics."

But relational feminist analysis also has its dangers, as we will see in this and the next two chapters. For one thing, it pays scant attention to women who, for whatever reasons, do *not* live with men and may not have primary nurturing responsibility for children. Moreover, if the activities assigned to women who do live with men are effectively stripped of social, economic, and political power, then women are vulnerable to overt or subtle abuse, with few options for redress. Finally, relational feminism in the hands of the economically privileged tends to degenerate into a "cult of domesticity," in which women's supposed differences from men get translated into weaknesses, thus justifying restrictions on their work and movement. For example, as men acquire more wealth, one way of advertising their new status is to have their wives and daughters conspicuously leisured at home. This may be quite bearable (at least in the short run) for economically privileged women, provided they *do* remain economically secure in their families and are not subject to other kinds of abuse. But it is a disastrous standard of femininity to hold up to most of the world's women, for whom sheer

7. Ibid., p. 136 (emphases Offen's; shift to present tense ours).

24

physical survival has always meant hard work, both within the household and outside it. Indeed, it is often these women who for poor wages do the work that frees up their more privileged sisters to concentrate on being exaggeratedly "feminine."

For this as well as other reasons, our definition of feminism includes an emphasis on political, social, and economic justice — a justice, moreover, that is meant to take class as well as gender into account. This emphasis also has a distinguished history in feminist thought, beginning with the nineteenth-century socialist critiques of emerging capitalist, industrial society and continuing in the Marxist and (neo-)socialist feminism of today. It is a tradition which recognizes that gender reconciliation cannot be simply a matter of individual rights or of getting gender roles properly defined and protected within one's own economic, religious, or cultural group. Rather, it proclaims that certain larger societal structures need to be changed before justice can be achieved in class or gender relations.

Some Further Theological Reflections

As Christian feminists, we believe that insights in all three feminist traditions need to be recognized. The very notion of the individual person (so dear to the hearts of liberal feminists) is a profoundly Christian one, dating back to the early church's efforts to express the nature of God and the Trinity. In both Greek and Roman thought, the word we know as *person* (*prosopon* in Greek; *persona* in Latin) referred to the "part below the cranium" (i.e., the eyes) *masked* in a dramatic production. In classic Greek tragedy the characters attempt to assert themselves against the necessary, fixed reality of the universe, and their final failure to do so is precisely the nature of their tragedy. The characters rebel against fate, thereby learning what it means to be a unique and free "person," but in the end fate still has its way in their lives. The masked actors take on a temporary personhood (as we know it) behind their masks, but by the play's end they are still the pawns of necessity.

It was in their struggle to understand the freedom and unconstrained love of God, as well as the freedom and interdependence of all members of the Trinity, that the early church fathers developed the notion of personhood. And having clarified the personhood of God (in contrast to the Greek notion of ontological necessity, to which even

25

God was bound), they also came to assert the uniqueness and freedom of each person made in God's image.[8] Thus, in many respects, the tradition of liberal feminism is a secular continuation of the historic Christian proclamation that all human beings are equally bearers of God's image, equally called to exercise their vocations within God's kingdom community.

At the same time, the Christian faith is profoundly relational. It affirms that female and male, while created as separate beings, jointly image God and need each other to carry out God's will for human life. This does not mean that all men and women have to marry in order to be fully human. Indeed, Christianity, unlike many religions and cultural traditions, has a high regard for singleness as a vital and respected calling. Its theology of singleness has admittedly been allowed to languish in recent times, but it is a theology that Christians can and should take seriously, for it affirms that one does not have to marry in order to be a fully contributing human member of society. Moreover, in the New Testament church the married couple and their children, while still an acknowledged creational unit, become part of the larger and more important "kingdom family" in which every individual's welfare is the concern of all.

The German theologian Dietrich Bonhoeffer captured this tension between the individual and the relational aspects of Christianity in his little book entitled *Life Together,* which he wrote on the eve of World War II while he taught in an underground seminary:

> *Let him who cannot be alone beware of community.* He will only do harm to himself and to the community. Alone you stood before God when he called you; alone you had to struggle and pray; and alone you will die and give an account to God. You cannot escape from yourself; for God has singled you out. If you refuse to be alone [i.e., to be an individual] you are rejecting Christ's call to you, and you can have no part in the community of those who are called. "The challenge of death comes to us all, and no one can die for another. Everyone must fight his own battle with death by himself, alone.... I will not be with you then, nor you with me" (Luther).
>
> But the reverse is also true: *Let him who is not in community beware of*

8. John D. Zizioulas, *Being as Communion: Studies in Personhood and the Church* (Crestwood, N.Y.: St. Vladimir's Seminary Press, 1985). See also J. N. D. Kelly's *Early Christian Doctrines* (London: A. & C. Black, 1958).

26

being alone. Into the community you were called, the call was not meant for you alone; in the community of the called you bear your cross, you struggle, you pray. You are not alone, even in death, and on the Last Day you will be only one member of the great congregation before Jesus Christ. If you scorn the fellowship of the brethren, you reject the call of Jesus Christ, and thus your solitude can only be hurtful to you. "If I die, then I am not alone in death; if I suffer they [the fellowship] suffer with me" (Luther).[9]

Finally, a fully orbed biblical feminism must take economic as well as other kinds of justice into account. What we have in mind is more than the economic justice that is the focus of Marxist and socialist thought. We appeal rather to the vision of *shalom* proclaimed by the Old Testament prophets, poets, and crafters of proverbs and affirmed in the New Testament as well. This *shalom,* while including economic justice, goes well beyond it:

> Shalom is the human being dwelling at peace in all his or her relationships: with God, with self, with fellows, with nature.... The peace which is shalom is not merely the absence of hostility, not merely being in right relationship. Shalom at its highest is *enjoyment* in one's relationships. A nation may be at peace with all its neighbors and yet be miserable in its poverty. To dwell in shalom is to *enjoy* living before God, to *enjoy* living in one's physical surroundings, to *enjoy* living with one's fellows, to *enjoy* life with oneself.[10]

Living under biblical *shalom* means being able to delight in creational diversity — among individuals, between the sexes, among cultural traditions — without turning differences into deficits. It is not an easy goal to reach in a fallen world. But it is the vision we want readers to keep in mind as they read about the history of Western feminism in this and the next chapter, and the feminism of Third World women and Western women of color in the chapter after that.

Before we embark on our overview of feminist history, one more qualifier is in order. What follows is necessarily a very cursory outline of the history of feminism, mainly in its Anglo-American forms.

9. Bonhoeffer, *Life Together,* trans. John W. Doberstein (London: SCM Press, 1954), pp. 57-58.
10. Nicholas Wolterstorff, *Until Justice and Peace Embrace* (Grand Rapids: William B. Eerdmans, 1983), pp. 69-70.

Women's studies and gender studies have become burgeoning academic fields in the past quarter century — so much so that by 1990 approximately 30,000 university-level courses were being taught in these areas in the United States alone. Included in this outpouring of scholarship are thousands of books, journals, and articles on the history of feminism. In this chapter we can only introduce readers to this wealth of scholarly research and invite them to consult our bibliography as a door to a more comprehensive understanding.

Roots of Contemporary Feminism — The "First Wave"

It is common to speak of two different waves of activity in the history of feminism: a "first wave," from about the end of the eighteenth century until the attainment of women's suffrage in the major English-speaking countries, and a "second wave" from the early 1960s up to the present. Our historical overview will adhere to this distinction: we will discuss the "first wave" in this chapter and the "second wave" in the following chapter.

Three major "first wave" currents have fed contemporary feminism.[11] The liberal current, rooted in Enlightenment understanding, focused on the rights of individual women. This perspective has consistently pressed for women's right to join the main currents of society as the rational equals of men. The second, more relational current of the evangelical reformers proclaimed that the individual — whether man or woman, slave or free — had dignity and worth because Christ had died for all people. Rather than emphasizing women's right to join the larger society, this tradition produced reformers committed to rooting out social evils that damaged women where they already were. The third current, the socialist, has emphasized the need to emancipate women,

---

11. In adopting this tripartite perspective, we are following the perspective of historian Nancy Cott in *The Grounding of Modern Feminism* (New Haven: Yale University Press, 1987) and of sociologist Olive Banks in *Faces of Feminism: A Study of Feminism as a Social Movement* (New York: St. Martin's Press, 1981). Recent work on feminism identifies as many as seven different currents feeding contemporary feminism, even without moving beyond the perspectives developed by white, middle-class, Western women. See, for example, Rosemarie Tong's *Feminist Thought: A Comprehensive Introduction* (Boulder, Colo.: Westview Press, 1989).

along with men, from socio-economic structures and conventions that undermine human life. According to this perspective, if things were to be well with women, the society itself would need restructuring from its economic base upward.

We will begin by exploring the different direction each current took in articulating its defense of women. But the similarities among them are equally important. Each was firmly grounded in the Western cultural tradition, each spoke in the context of emerging, modern, industrialized society, and each mounted a defense of women suffering from institutionalized injustice. As modern Western feminist perspectives, they share a concern for justice in society, an optimism about the possibility of reform, and an insistence that individual women be protected as dignity-bearing human beings. But from their different conceptions of the just society, the means of attaining it, and the ways of protecting women within it, three distinct currents of feminist thought emerged.

Liberal Thought

Throughout this book we will see that classical liberal thought is under attack by various kinds of contemporary feminists. Nevertheless, the great strains of Enlightenment thought have served the interests of women in many ways. This uniquely modern Western perspective begins with a commitment to the dignity and freedom of human individuals, who have too often been crippled by the whim of aristocratic governments, bound by social traditions, or blinded by superstitions passed off as religion. As creatures of reason, the liberal argument goes, human beings have "natural rights" to an autonomy that should be protected by law. Man's capacity for reason, that which separates him from the "brute creation," equips him to assert his freedom from all of these shackles. In the initial articulation, "man" meant quite specifically "men," not humankind in general.

British feminist Mary Wollstonecraft was one of the persons who inserted the inevitable protest from women into the process of liberal discourse in the late eighteenth century.[12] If reason and freedom make

12. A brief introduction to early feminists who predated Wollstonecraft, such as Mary Astell, Mary Wortley Montagu, Catherine Macaulay, and Mary Hays, can

one human, and women are denied both, can women be human? As she analyzed the ways in which society crippled women, Wollstonecraft argued that "liberty is the mother of virtue, and if women be, by their very constitution, slaves, and not allowed to breathe the sharp invigorating air of freedom, they must ever languish like exotics, and be reckoned beautiful flaws in nature."[13] Stripped of the virtues that might arise from reason, women were encouraged to cultivate the artificial, to display emotions that could give them a "short-lived tyranny" over lovers, to become "insignificant objects of desire — mere propagators of fools."[14]

Within the terms of Enlightenment discourse, Wollstonecraft's argument is a masterpiece. One cannot read it today without being painfully aware that the more things change, the more they stay the same. But even as Wollstonecraft highlighted major injustices to women, she accepted assumptions of Enlightenment discourse that devalued many people, women among them. The Enlightenment sought equality for all human beings who were essentially "the same," and Wollstonecraft tailored her argument accordingly. Acknowledging and championing the differences between men and women, which were the cause of both pain and pride, were beyond the vision of feminists like Wollstonecraft. Arguments crafted on Enlightenment terms left women, whose lives were in some ways different from those of men, in an unfortunate bind.

"Free," rational men of property, classically educated, defined humanity in Enlightenment thought. The British in India may have taught that all men deserved to be self-governing, but they *meant* that all men who thought and acted like Britishers should be self-governing. If "all men are created equal," then to extend this argument beyond the circle of white, property-owning males, one must argue that black men, that non-property owners, that black and white women are *like* the males originally assumed in the argument. Thus Wollstonecraft was forced to argue that if reason, character, and virtue define a man, then surely all "*rational* men" would "wish with me, that they [women] may every day

---

be found in *Feminist Theorists: Three Centuries of Key Women Thinkers,* ed. Dale Spender (New York: Pantheon, 1983).

13. Wollstonecraft, *A Vindication of the Rights of Woman* (London, 1792). The text cited here is a reprint of the second London edition edited by Carol H. Poston (New York: W. W. Norton, 1975), p. 37.

14. Ibid., p. 11.

grow more and more masculine."[15] Because differences between men and women, like the differences between men of different cultures, could easily be twisted into evidence of a failure to meet the mark of full humanity, the liberal feminist emphasis was on equality.

The argument is clean, straightforward, and powerful. Women are human, fully human. Women are the equals of men because in all the ways that matter, women are the same as men. Later feminist challenges which acknowledge difference have sometimes been twisted in ways that sharply limit women. But liberalism's strong, stable argument has consistently been used to open doors for some women into the increasingly impersonal, male-dominated social institutions that shape modern life. As historian Nancy Cott notes, it is the argument that allows women to "join" the society. But in its clean lines, it fails to capture the complex ways in which the experiences of men and women create differences between them. It fails as well to address the ways in which Western cultural and social structures may devalue the work, lives, and thought of many women.

Evangelical Reform: A Relational Expression of Feminism

The nineteenth-century evangelical reformers were as firmly convinced as their Enlightenment predecessors that women were fully human. The roots of this common humanity were, however, seen quite differently. It was the heart of the evangelical gospel — God's claim on the life of the individual — that proclaimed the worth of each individual person. Each person for whom Christ died had a value that transcended the distinctions between male and female, the free person and the slave, the gentry and the lower classes, the clever and the slow-witted. It was the individual person who would live forever with Christ — and at the foot of the cross no man or woman could claim to stand taller than another.

According to historian Olive Banks, this powerful sense of the dignity of each human being resulted not only in a "drive to save souls" but also in "a crusade to stamp out sin." Moral reform societies, led by

---

15. Ibid., pp. 8, 11 (her italics). But Wollstonecraft still went to some length to disarm those who might accuse her of arguing for "masculine women." She herself would "join the cry" against women with a passion for "hunting, shooting and gaming."

31

women, flourished on both sides of the Atlantic, sparked by the religious awakening of the early nineteenth century and its successive revivalist waves. One strong voice in defense of women was raised by Hannah More, a popular evangelical Anglican who wrote during the same period as Mary Wollstonecraft.[16] In the company of reformers such as abolitionist parliamentarian William Wilberforce, More launched a defense of women that matched Wollstonecraft's in commitment, if not in style and content.

The differences between these two apologists for women can be seen in their approaches to the common concern of "female education." Wollstonecraft argued that women should have the opportunity to cultivate the human grandeur of reason. By contrast, More fought for the ability of women to support themselves economically. Educating a woman as a dilettante who could dance, speak a bit of French, and sketch a landscape would leave her with no tools to support herself and no independent sense of herself. As historian Shirley Mullen has written, "More deplored the plight of the woman who, after all the artifice had been removed, after all the spectators had disappeared, was left with nothing."[17] Thus More's practical concern led her to establish schools for poor children and their mothers, to set up cooperative village ovens, and to organize pools of funds through which women could support themselves in times of unemployment.

Yet paradoxically, this accomplished woman of letters who herself never married argued that the "proper" sphere of women's activity was that of home, family, and charity. Hannah More hated — and feared — the concept of individual rights and equality that lay beneath the excesses of the "atheistic" French Revolution. As Mullen explains, More believed that the "women's question" could be addressed only in the

16. See Shirley Mullen's "Women's History and Hannah More," *Fides et Historia* 19 (February 1987): 5. Leonore Davidoff and Catherine Hall have recently set More's work within the larger context of social and cultural change in *Family Fortunes: Men and Women of the English Middle Class, 1780-1850*, ed. Catharine R. Stimpson (Chicago: University of Chicago Press, 1987); see especially pp. 167-72. The *Works of Hannah More* were published in London by H. Bohn in 1853-54. M. G. Johnes has written the most recent full-length biography entitled simply *Hannah More* (Cambridge: Cambridge University Press, 1952). According to Mullen, "Nineteenth-century Britons consumed More's writings in sufficient quantity to merit five editions of her complete works between 1801 and 1864."

17. Mullen, "Women's History and Hannah More," p. 12.

context of a vision "for total national reform and renewal. . . . The women's question was a matter of tangible everyday concern, insepa- rable from the real women among whom More labored, and inextricably linked to the living social organism of which these women were a vital part."[18]

Nevertheless, despite the number of practical advances More spearheaded, she was in some ways blinded by her own comfortable social position as an educated and independent woman of means: she articulated a romanticized social vision that failed to take seriously the abuses to which gendered power imbalance could lead. Her vision also failed to take account of the ways in which industrial society was trans- forming "home." In a nutshell, the home was rapidly changing from a place where women and men had jointly worked and parented to a place from which men, and almost all money-producing activity, were being steadily withdrawn, leaving women socially isolated and economically vulnerable in its shrunken sphere.

To contemporary readers, More's stance might seem to be an example of "anti-feminist" thinking. For example, in her work on the history of the women's movement in America,[19] Aileen Kraditor sets the Enlightenment-based appeal to "justice" against the evangelical re- formist appeal to "expediency." But in fact the Enlightenment argument sidestepped many social realities by assuming that when rational in- dividuals were free and educated, a just society would naturally emerge. By contrast, the nineteenth-century evangelical reformers did not sub- scribe to such a utopian ideal; they stepped into muddy social realities. And whether their agenda was reforming education for women, enabling working-class women to support their families, or fighting for temper- ance to curtail domestic violence, evangelical reformers took for granted the existence of social differences between men and women.

The best Kraditor can say for the evangelical approach is that in some social movements it has been "expedient" (whether one believed in it or not) for making certain arguments about women: for instance, women should be educated so they could be better mothers, or they should be given the vote because their largely pacifist tendencies would

18. Ibid., p. 9.
19. Kraditor, "Introduction," in *Up from the Pedestal: Selected Writings in the History of American Feminism* (New York: Quadrangle/The New York Times Book Co., 1968).

help to curb warfare. This "expediency argument" was at times given a racist twist: women should be given the vote to undercut the power of blacks in the South, or to undercut the votes of immigrant Catholics in the city slums of the North.[20] But Kraditor is skeptical about any use of an "expedient" argument that presumes differences between men and women. She is skeptical because when the reformers spoke about women's social condition in ways that assumed stereotypical differences between men and women, their rhetoric fed into the emerging "cult of domesticity" that was progressively restricting the lives of women in a rapidly changing, more mobile society. And in the historical context of the industrializing Western world, the presumption of such differences seemed to justify the further restriction and devaluation of women.

But more recent historical research suggests that a feminism which accepts a relational view of men and women in society *can* motivate social changes that are highly beneficial to women.[21] With this in mind, let us examine Hannah More's position a bit more closely.

More's defense of women offered several advantages that eluded theorists like Wollstonecraft, who was forced to argue that women be given the opportunity to become more like men in order to be accepted as fully and autonomously human. By contrast, More's social vision allowed her to argue that what were dismissed as "women's concerns" were in fact primary *human* concerns. Rather than speaking of autonomous individuals, More located persons in relationship to each other in society. Moreover, she wanted to help women develop an "internal" independence that would free them from a concern with audience and allow them to concentrate on the pursuit of goodness. Rather than elevating reason as the paramount human quality, she celebrated the "peculiar excellences" of womanly sensitivity and emotion as being equally human. Several decades ago historian Ray Strachey wrote of More, "Without the least intending to do so, she was making out a new sphere for the young women of the middle classes, and their revolt against their own narrow and futile lives followed as a matter of course."[22]

20. Ibid., pp. 253-66.
21. Olive Banks and Nancy Cott outline the story and provide the bibliography to trace these feminist arguments in England and America. For a wider European perspective, see Karen Offen's "Defining Feminism: A Comparative Historical Approach."
22. Strachey, quoted in Davidoff and Hall's *Family Fortunes,* p. 172.

34

Maintaining a larger social vision was a strength in this line of argument. That social vision, like all others to this point, recognized some differences between men and women. The fate of this vision demonstrates why people concerned for justice in gender relations become nervous about the presumption of differences between men and women. In the hands of the wealthy, whose women could retreat from the dislocations of the Industrial Revolution into comfortable domesticity, the ideology of "separate spheres" ended up dramatically restricting the work and denigrating the womanhood of those who stepped out of the idealized, domestic "woman's sphere" into any other life-supporting labor.

Nevertheless, among those with the leisure and financial security to participate in the women's organizations to which this ideology gave rise, women's power and value achieved institutional expression. Nancy Cott writes that "the language of moral reform evoked women's power: power to avenge, power to control and reform."[23] One may or may not accept Cott's thesis that activity in such specifically female organizations later led to the emergence of other forms of feminism.[24] But the point remains that women who shared this perspective did create a positive women's culture.[25] Those who led the women's missionary and temperance societies of the nineteenth century accomplished no mean feat. The "female power" of strong women's organizations provided at least a "moral economy of resistance" to the social changes that were marginalizing women by separating the "private" sphere of home from the "public" sphere of economic, civic, and other activities.[26]

23. Cott, *The Grounding of Modern Feminism,* p. 153.

24. Cott, *The Bonds of Womanhood: "Woman's Sphere" in New England, 1780-1835* (New Haven: Yale University Press, 1977).

25. For a historiographic review of the use of the term "separate spheres," see Linda K. Kerber's "Separate Spheres, Female Worlds, Women's Place: The Rhetoric of Women's History," *Journal of American History* 75 (June 1988): 9-39. Kerber makes the important point that the metaphor was often used interchangeably to refer to "an ideology *imposed on* women, a culture *created by* women, a set of boundaries *expected to be observed by women*" (p. 17).

26. Jane Jaquette makes this point about "separate spheres" in Third World settings in "Women and Modernization Theory: A Decade of Feminist Criticism," *Women's Studies Quarterly* 15 (Fall 1986): 281. The reference is to James Scott's thesis in *The Moral Economy of the Peasant: Rebellion and Subsistence in Southeast Asia* (New Haven: Yale University Press, 1976). Scott tried to demonstrate how the peasants'

Beyond this, the evangelical concern for "moral reform" gave birth to organizations that anticipated the contemporary feminist agenda, though they approached that agenda quite differently. For example, the temperance movement fought to curtail drunkenness, which was seen as the root of wife abuse. Josephine Butler, an English reformer active in the late nineteenth century who believed that prostitutes were victims of women's economic position and "the double standard of morality that enabled men to sin with impunity," spoke out against legislation that she believed reinforced this double standard: the Contagious Diseases Acts.

The Contagious Diseases Acts were designed "to protect soldiers and sailors from venereal disease, not by making prostitution illegal, but by checking prostitutes. . . . Any woman suspected of being a prostitute was required to undergo a regular medical examination to detect and then to treat VD."[27] The legislation embodied in the Contagious Diseases Acts was put into force in the 1860s and applied to all British towns that had high concentrations of armed forces personnel.

In 1869, when it seemed that these acts would be applied to the entire country, a group of Christian men approached Josephine Butler to spearhead a campaign for their repeal. Butler was already an active supporter of women's education and suffrage, and having worked with prostitutes, she understood the relationship between poverty and prostitution. As she saw it, prostitutes were primarily victims of a double standard that was both economic and sexual. Consequently, she willingly and successfully campaigned against the Contagious Diseases Acts. She argued that the law embodied in those acts simply allowed men to sin without sanctions while it forced prostitutes to accept the humiliation of periodic examination.[28] In her campaign she had the full support of her clergyman husband, even though he knew as well as she that her activism might jeopardize his standing in the church. (It did.)

Thus, at their best, the arguments and activities of the evangelical reformers led to cultural ideals and institutions that allowed women to

---

nonresistance was a way of coping with the status quo; similarly, a study of separate spheres may not be a "rationalization of the present" but rather an attempt to show "women's stake in the existing distribution of power."

27. Elaine Storkey, *What's Right with Feminism* (Grand Rapids: William B. Eerdmans, 1986), p. 146.

28. Banks, *Faces of Feminism,* p. 65. See also Storkey's *What's Right with Feminism,* especially chap. 12.

use their strengths for the transformation of society. At its worst, the reformist ideology of "separate spheres" for women and men fossilized and romanticized a pattern of gender relations that acquired quite different meanings as nineteenth-century industry and commerce transformed society.

The Socialist Vision

Feminist-leaning Enlightenment thinkers defended a view of women as fundamentally the same as men and so argued for their right to participate fully in society. Evangelical reformers called women and men in their different ways to work for the moral transformation of society. The socialist vision assumed that the well-being of men and women would automatically follow from changes in society's economic ground rules. This socialist perspective shared with Enlightenment thought a confidence that there were no really critical differences between women and men. And it shared with the evangelical reformers a vision for a better society. But as we have seen, the positive social Christian vision often ended up romanticizing the societal status quo of separate spheres, purged of individual sin with the help of the emerging "women's institutions." By contrast, the socialist vision proclaimed that women would be free only when the *entire society* was radically restructured from the economic base up. Institutions, not just individuals, were in need of purifying change.

Neither the liberal thinkers of the Enlightenment nor the middle-class Christian reformers were prepared to criticize the industrial, capitalist society emerging in the nineteenth century. Enlightenment thinkers assumed that free individuals would automatically create the good society. Middle-class Christian reformers *did* challenge the institutional injustice of slavery and the economic abuses of the early factory system. But in the long run they found it easier to sustain focus and attract a following by appealing to personal moral issues such as sexual purity and temperance. By contrast, the early utopian socialists, followed by Marx and Engels, expected no fundamental righting of the wrongs against women apart from a restructuring of competitive, capitalist society.

As communist regimes crumble in Europe and Westerners congratulate themselves on their precocious clearheadedness, the insights of this socialist perspective are hardly in vogue. But in the midst of this self-congratulation both secular and Christian voices are bemoaning the rampant individualism of American life and calling for a renewed commitment to community and family. Hence we have good reason to listen to those who first dreamed of overcoming the individualism and social fragmentation of Western industrial, commercial society.

Saint-Simon (1760-1825) was an early utopian socialist who combined the teachings of Jesus with ideas of science and industrialism. Although he had little to say about women per se, his disciples fleshed out the feminist implications of his thought. Among these disciples was Anna Wheeler, a feminist writer and lecturer. Socialist William Thompson acknowledged his heavy debt to Wheeler when he wrote his *Appeal of One Half of the Human Race*, which in 1825 was "the first book ever written with the express purpose of advocating the grant of the parliamentary vote to women."[29] But Wheeler's vision was far bigger than this. She dreamed of a world

> where restless and anxious individual competition shall give place to mutual co-operation and joint possession; where individuals in large numbers, male and female, forming voluntary associations, shall become a mutual guarantee to each other for the supply of all useful wants, and form an unsalaried insurance company where perfect freedom of opinion and perfect equality will reign.[30]

An implication of this argument was that if cooperation replaced competition, men might be morally elevated, and women's "equality" with men might then become an advantage to them. But for the interim, as Wheeler saw things, the interests of men and women could best be served by rejecting marriage and all the institutions "which turned women into mere instruments of men's arbitrary will [and] perpetuated the selfishness and ignorance of the entire race."[31]

Thus the early communitarian phase of socialism produced radical experiments in relations between men and women. Groups ranging from the anti-religious New Harmony community established by Welsh socialist Robert Owen (1771-1858) to the religiously inspired Oneida Com-

29. Banks, *Faces of Feminism*, p. 48.
30. Richard Pankhurst, "Anna Wheeler: A Pioneer Socialist and Feminist," *The Political Quarterly* 25 (April-June 1954): 136.
31. Ibid., p. 137.

munity shared the vision of a perfect society in which harmony and cooperation would replace competition and conflict. These communitarian socialists realized that the inequalities inherent in modern industrial society extended to male-female relationships. The more humane alternative required thorough societal revision, from industrial production to the reproductive life of families. In these experimental communities domestic work and child raising were often carried out communally. Where marriage was retained, it was to be based on mutual choice and freed from the coercive economic considerations to which private, male-dominated property gave rise.

Marxist thought grew out of and radically reshaped this early utopian socialism. Friedrich Engels, who wrote more on the subject than Marx, argued that male control of private property in the family was the root of women's subordination. Anxious to establish legitimate heirs of their own property, Engels theorized, men at some point in history began to restrict women's sexuality. He then argued that women's freedom could be attained only through — and indeed would follow automatically from — the elimination of privately controlled property.

These early insights might lead one to expect an easy marriage of socialism and feminism. The reality has been less heartening. Early female trade unionists, for example, were often silenced and ostracized by their male counterparts, who shared the larger society's disapproval of working women. Women who worked for wages were seen as competing for "men's jobs" and neglecting their children. Thus these women, who in fact worked to support their families, were often deliberately excluded from trade union struggles and settlements. And these women had concerns of their own. How would they care for their children when their working hours were so long? With uncertain, low-paid work, would they be able to maintain a stable home? Would the long hours of working on their feet at exhausting jobs reduce their ability to bear and raise children? These concerns rarely reached the agendas of male union organizers. The cry of working-class women, "Give us bread, but give us roses," reflected their stubborn determination to define themselves not only as workers but as *women* workers.[32]

Because Marxists located the root of women's oppression in private

32. Sarah Eisenstein, *Give Us Bread, But Give Us Roses: Working Women's Consciousness in the United States, 1890 to the First World War* (Boston: Routledge & Kegan Paul, 1983).

property, any discussion of issues pertaining specifically to women was often dismissed as tangential. While the Bolsheviks welcomed women who shared their contempt for "mere feminism," they regarded activities aimed specifically at women with suspicion.[33] For example, Russian feminist Clara Zetkin wrote of being taken to task by Lenin for spending time with women comrades discussing sexual problems and historical forms of marriage. "I ask you," Lenin queried: "Is now the time to amuse proletarian women with discussions of how one loves and is loved, how one marries and is married?"[34]

Similarly, Ding Ling, a later Chinese revolutionary hero, confronted the dilemmas faced by women in the Communist-held province of Yanan. The traditional pressure to marry continued, but once female party leaders married, they were pressured to give up their political careers. Yet if they yielded to these pressures and stayed home with their children, they were sneered at as "Noras who came home." Because she highlighted the difficulties of women in this "new order," Ding Ling was removed from her journalistic duties and sent to study with the peasantry.[35]

Thus, while the socialist vision held forth equality between men and women as an ideal in revolutionary society, it was ill-equipped to deal with the differing concerns of women and men — before or after the revolution.

Toward a Dynamic Concept of Gender Relations

Each current of first-wave Western feminism has proven politically important. The strong Enlightenment emphasis on the sameness of men and women was crucial for the admission of women to universities and

33. See, for example, Richard Stites's *The Women's Liberation Movement in Russia: Feminism, Nihilism, and Bolshevism, 1860-1930* (Princeton: Princeton University Press, 1978), pp. 233-77.

34. Zetkin, *Reminiscences of Lenin* (New York: International Publishers, 1934), p. 46.

35. Jonathan Spence, *The Gate of Heavenly Peace: The Chinese and Their Revolution, 1895-1980* (New York: Viking Press, 1981), pp. 288-95. The reference to "Noras" is possibly an allusion to *A Doll's House* by Henrik Ibsen. Nora, the play's main female character, is a thoroughly domesticated, nineteenth-century middle-class wife who, by the end of the play, leaves her husband in order to find herself.

the professions. In many of the battles that led to women's suffrage, the liberal and reformist arguments came together. For example, the women's rights convention of 1848 held at Seneca Falls produced a declaration that restated the liberal doctrines of the Declaration of Independence to include women. The meeting that produced this document grew out of conversations in London between American reformer Susan B. Anthony and Quaker preacher Lucretia Mott when both were barred as delegates to a meeting of the International Anti-Slavery Society because they were women. Thus, although it is possible to draw an intellectual contrast between liberal and evangelical reformist arguments, politically they often operated together.

Recent historians have shown how these two perspectives, which seemed to embrace contradictory appeals to "sameness" and "difference," in fact complemented each other in the decades prior to the attainment of women's suffrage.[36] As Nancy Cott points out, the struggle for voting rights for women lent itself to arguments from both perspectives because "it was an equal rights goal that enabled women to make special contributions; it sought to give women the same capacity as men so they could express their differences; it was a just end in itself but it was also an expedient means to other ends."[37]

The complexity of these negotiations and activities on behalf of women's suffrage leads us to note an important theological and methodological point. Both in the past and in the present, it has been all too easy to reduce the discussion of gender to talk about women's or men's "proper place" — or, in the jargon of recent social science, to men's and women's respective "roles." In social science, as in the theater, a "role" refers to a prescribed set of actions — that is, behaviors and their supporting attitudes — expected of people who occupy a certain social position. And the concept of roles has been implicitly attractive to many Christians, especially to those who wish to stress that God, both in creation and in redemption, has a "blueprint" or plan for human life toward which we should all be striving.

We have already affirmed our commitment to the biblical vision of

36. See, for example, Nancy Cott's *Grounding of Modern Feminism* and Dale Spender's *Feminist Theorists.*

37. Cott, "Feminist Theory and Feminist Movements: The Past Before Us," in *What Is Feminism? A Re-examination,* ed. Juliet Mitchell and Ann Oakley (New York: Pantheon Books, 1986), pp. 53-54.

shalom as that plan for human life on earth. But what Christians have often too quickly assumed is that *shalom* will be achieved when we have figured out, once and for all, the correct "roles" or "scripts" that women and men should follow. But speaking as both Christians and feminists, we regard this as far too simple an analysis. The concept of "role" is a fairly static one: it suggests an unchanging set of behaviors — actual or ideal — that a person adopts without much question and with only minimal room for interpretation. Such an analysis underrates both the complex history of gender relations and the agency of human beings created in God's image. Part of that imaging of God involves both the freedom and the responsibility to care for the earth and each other in ways that are creative, flexible, and mindful of individual needs, changing times, and varying locations.

As the historical example of the women's suffrage campaign indicates, gender is much more a matter of active negotiation than it is of static roles. Using their respective social and material resources, men and women debated the theoretical and practical merits of "sameness" versus "difference" and ultimately worked toward women's suffrage in a complex set of alliances that allowed for both. One cannot capture the rich texture of that historical movement by appealing strictly to men's and women's roles and ignoring their interaction — any more than one can understand the phenomenon of hand-clapping by analyzing each of a pair of hands in isolation without attending to their actions in relation to one another.

Thus, as Christian feminists concerned to give human agency and relationality their due, we agree with the social scientists who have made these observations:

> The conception of gender as a set of socially constructed relationships which are produced and reproduced through people's actions is central. Such a view highlights social interaction rather than the unidirectional processes of socialization, adaptation, and/or oppression. This emphasis suggests that we appreciate women as the active creators of their own destinies within certain constraints, rather than as passive victims or objects. At the same time, this suggests that feminist scholars must avoid analyzing men as one-dimensional, omnipotent oppressors. Male behavior and consciousness emerge from a complex interaction with women as they at times initiate and control, while at other times co-operate [with] or resist the action of women.[38]

38. Judith M. Gerson and Kathy Peiss, "Boundaries, Negotiation, Consciousness: Reconceptualizing Gender Relations," *Social Problems* 32 (April 1985): 327.

These concepts of reciprocal agency, negotiation, and dynamic change are central to an adequate understanding of gender, as we have already seen in our survey of "first wave" feminism, and as we will see in our treatment of all other topics throughout the rest of the book. For the moment, however, we continue with our historical survey of feminism, with a view to its elaboration in the second half of the twentieth century.

CHAPTER 3

Western Feminism since the 1960s:
Lessons from the Present

From the 1860s onward, the massive "first wave" of the feminist movement focused more and more specifically on the issue of women's suffrage. But after women won the vote in Britain and North America, concern with feminist issues — whether from a liberal, relational, or socialist perspective — faded dramatically. Part of the reason for this was the coming of World War II, hard on the heels of the Great Depression. During World War II, women were recruited into industrial and manufacturing jobs to replace men who were in the armed services. But after the war, in the push to restore "normal" family life and to insure jobs for returning veterans, waged women workers were pressured in various ways to return to domesticity. The 1950s was the decade of the postwar baby boom, the suburban tract home, the commuter-father and the stay-at-home wife and mother. Consequently, when the "second wave" of feminism began in the 1960s, its terms of discourse were quite different from those of the first wave.

By the 1960s the earlier evangelical reformist impulse had definitely lost its feminist edge. In the nineteenth century Christian feminists

---

The primary author of this chapter is Mary Stewart Van Leeuwen.

of a relational bent, such as Angelina Grimké, had argued that women possessed special talents and values associated with their work as mothers and homemakers, as a result of which they were peculiarly suited to lead the reform of society. This was a feminism that took for granted certain differences between the sexes. But it did not translate these differences into an ideology of separate spheres that would leave women socially isolated, economically marginalized, and often intellectually un-derchallenged in the home while men spent most of their time away from it. By the mid-twentieth century, however, Christians and secular-ists alike had bought into just such an ideology: the "ideal woman" was now restricted largely to the home while her husband toiled daily for a family wage, usually in an office or a factory too far away to allow a return home even for a noon meal. A group of evangelical Christian journalists, gently satirizing what it was like to "grow up born again" in the 1950s, reminisced in the 1980s about their parents' respective roles:

> The born again father is most certainly in charge of family discipline. He's head of the house and he's not running a democracy. . . . Most often, Mother is the one to discover your acts of disobedience. She handles minor infractions of the rules with scolding, mouth washings, or by sending you to your room. Major infractions elicit the dread pronouncement, "Wait till your father gets home." The rest of the day you're miserable, dreading what will happen when Dad gets home. . . .
> Born again mothers are also "peculiar" in the eyes of the world. [They] look like mothers—not like older sisters. . . . A born again mother is in the kitchen when you get home from school. She's not out playing tennis at some country club. If fathers are the authority figures in Christian homes, representing God the Father, mothers are like the Holy Spirit—the source of love and comfort. Born again mothers are very good at being mothers. They are fruitful vines.[1]

Liberal Feminism Revisited

Whatever the rigidities of "born again" parental roles, these families at least had the advantage of being lodged within a larger, meaningful

1. Patricia Klein et al., *Growing Up Born Again: A Whimsical Look at the Blessings and Tribulations of Growing Up Born Again* (Old Tappan, N.J.: Fleming H. Revell, 1987), pp. 17-20.

church community. But in general the restrictive ideology of gendered, separate spheres took a heavy toll on middle-class, educated women. Some of them began to wonder if domestic isolation and economic dependence weren't too high a price to have paid for their postwar vision of a home in the suburbs and a husband and children around whom to center their lives.

These women had everything that the "experts" told them they needed in order to be happy, yet they were *not* happy. And by the early 1960s a feminist writer in the liberal tradition had re-emerged to pass judgment on this "problem with no name" and on the socially constructed cult of domesticity that lay at the root of it. At least one of us can remember cutting her feminist teeth on the first edition of Betty Friedan's *The Feminine Mystique* — a book that is now perhaps best remembered as the one which naively suggested that middle-class women could "have it all."[2]

Friedan's prescription for understimulated suburban housewives was to enter the full-time public work force. Rather than choosing marriage and parenthood instead of careers (a choice not forced on their husbands), they should be able to choose *both* options in the interests of their own development, their children's independence, and the health of their marriages. Friedan argued that a woman could discharge all of her wifely, motherly, and professional obligations with a minimum of outside help because she lived in a modern, technologically sophisticated society. All that was needed was an equalizing of legal, educational, and occupational opportunities — goals that still comprise the agenda of the National Organization of Women (NOW), the liberal feminist organization that Friedan helped to launch in the United States.

The continuity of this argument with first-wave liberal feminism is clear: women are the rational equals of men; therefore, both justice and social efficiency demand that they be allowed to exercise their gifts

2. Friedan, *The Feminine Mystique* (New York: W. W. Norton, 1963). Another analyst has suggested that men's growing dissatisfaction with being the primary wage-earners also contributed to the "problem with no name" in middle-class American homes, a dissatisfaction vocalized a decade prior to Friedan's book in the launching of *Playboy* magazine. The lead article of the first issue of *Playboy* was a diatribe against the concept of alimony in particular and money-hungry wives in general. It was titled "Miss Gold-Digger of 1953." For a more detailed analysis, see Barbara Ehrenreich's book entitled *The Hearts of Men: American Dreams and the Flight from Commitment* (Garden City, N.Y.: Doubleday–Anchor, 1984).

in the public domain alongside men. Since the 1960s, it has been liberal feminists who have campaigned to get women into public office. They have worked to change laws and customs that have limited women's entrance into certain schools, organizations, and occupations. They have mounted campaigns against gender stereotyping in the media and in school textbooks. Liberal feminists have also helped to bring about other changes in schools, such as the gender desegregation of home economics and woodworking classes and the expansion of girls' opportunities in athletics. In the United States they have worked for the passage of the Equal Rights Amendment (ERA), which would require state and federal governments to enforce equality of rights under the law for both sexes. To this day even the harshest critics of liberal feminism routinely preface their judgments by giving credit where it is due. "For all its limitations, its strengths are undeniable," writes philosopher Rosemarie Tong:

> It is doubtful that without liberal feminists' efforts, so many women could have attained their newfound professional and occupational stature. To be sure, there is more to feminism than educational and legal reforms aimed primarily at increasing women's professional and occupational position. But such reforms are to be neither trivialized nor memorialized as *past* accomplishments. Liberal feminists still have much more work to do before *all* women's educational, legal, and professional/occupational gains are entirely secure.[3]

But Tong's last remark hints at an important criticism of liberal feminism — one that has been growing steadily since the 1960s. For all its accomplishments, liberal feminism has remained largely an individualist-oriented, white, middle-class movement. And despite the idealized images of family life projected by post–World War II media, there were always plenty of women who didn't even *have* the choice to be isolated and bored in suburbia: single women, women of color, women with little education, and women with husbands who earned low wages. For such women, waged work, generally of the unglamorous, low-paid variety, was simply what they had to do to survive. In addition, those who had families usually worked a "double day" or "second shift," coming home from the office or factory to a round of domestic duties from which

3. Tong, *Feminist Thought: A Comprehensive Introduction* (Boulder, Colo.: Westview Press, 1989), p. 38. See also Alison M. Jaggar's *Feminist Politics and Human Nature* (Totowa, N.J.: Rowman & Allanheld, 1983), especially chaps. 3 and 7.

47

custom largely exempted their husbands — if indeed they had husbands, which some did not.

The liberal feminist was generally blind to such "second shift" problems until she herself started juggling a two-career marriage with child raising and household management. Finding that her husband and children continued to assume homemaking was "her" responsibility, with which they might occasionally "help out," she began to realize that "having it all" was more elusive than Betty Friedan had predicted, even given the economic advantages of a middle-class, intact marriage.[4] And with their added economic burdens, it is hardly surprising that working-class women have proved resistant to liberal feminist discourse, seeing it as irrelevant or even antagonistic to their concerns. Economist Sylvia Hewlett remembers her own awakening as a sometime-liberal feminist when she canvassed on behalf of the ERA among women workers in a small textile plant in Georgia during the late 1970s. She recounts an exchange between her and a young black woman whom she attempted to give some ERA literature:

> "You know, I've heard of you 'libbers' and your ERA. . . . Equal rights for women is a bad deal because we would lose a whole lot. Like us girls get an extra break in the shift, the management can't force us to work overtime the way they force the men." As she warmed to her theme, her voice rose. "You should try working in this lousy factory week in and week out and I bet you would want all the benefits you could get."
>
> I attempted a comeback: "You know the ERA wouldn't necessarily take job benefits away from women; the ones that mean anything would be extended to men. If women need special benefits, so do men."
>
> This factory worker was now really angry. "If you think life's fair you're crazy," she snapped. "I've got two kids under five and a husband who doesn't lift a finger. What's fair about that? Why shouldn't I get some breaks on the job?" She flung my pamphlets into the gutter and stalked off to the bus stop. . . . I felt cowed and uncomfortable. It was the last time I canvassed for the ERA.[5]

4. For a sociological analysis, see Arlie Hochschild's *The Second Shift: Working Parents and the Revolution at Home* (New York: Viking Press, 1989).

5. Hewlett, *A Lesser Life: The Myth of Women's Liberation in America* (New York: William Morrow, 1986), pp. 202-3.

Marxist Feminism: A Class-Based Analysis

This anecdote helps us to contrast the concerns of Marxist feminists with those of their liberal counterparts. To begin with, whereas liberal discourse considers rationality and the drive for autonomy to be central human characteristics, Marxism asserts that what makes us human is our ability to transform and manipulate nature in order to meet our subsistence needs. Of course, this demands human mental capacities far more complex than those underlying the instinctual behaviors of animals — Marxist, liberal, and Christian theorists of human nature would surely agree on this point. But Marxists differ from both Christians and liberals in their emphasis on the *collective and material* determinants of human thought. For liberals it is the ideas and values of individuals that account for social and historical change. For Marxists it is almost the opposite: it is material forces — our collective ways of producing and reproducing — that condition how we think. Known as "historical materialism," this doctrine was summarized by Karl Marx when he wrote that "the mode of production of material life conditions the general process of social, political, and intellectual life. It is not the consciousness of men that determines their existence, but their social existence that determines their consciousness."[6]

Thus Marxists would point out to both traditional male and modern feminist liberals that their stress on individual freedom and equality of opportunity is *not* (as liberals assume) the result of objective, rational reflection about human nature and social justice. Instead, liberals value freedom and equality because of the vested bourgeois interest they have in a capitalist mode of production — one that concentrates ownership of the means of production in the hands of a few and dooms all others to sell their labor for less than it is worth in a market which is usually overstocked with workers.

It is doubtful that Hewlett's young African-American interviewee was a card-carrying Marxist, but Marxist analysis certainly helps us understand her heated response to Hewlett's individualist-oriented promotion of the ERA. Structurally, there is little likelihood that this worker would benefit from the ERA. Its passage would not alter the fact that her unskilled labor commanded a low wage in a one-factory town. Of

6. Marx, *A Contribution to the Critique of Political Economy* (1859; rpt. New York: International Publishers, 1972), pp. 20-21.

more immediate value to her would be legislation raising the minimum wage, an issue that concerns liberal feminists only if pay scales are systematically different for women and men in the same job. Better still from a Marxist point of view would be a strong trade union, linked to an international workers' movement, which could gradually gain leverage over managers and owners, first at the local level but ultimately in a global, revolutionary replacement of capitalism with a pure communist state. Under the latter system (at least according to Marxist ideals), workers are neither exploited nor alienated, because the means of production are collectively owned rather than concentrated in the hands of an exploiting few.

Women as Producers and Reproducers

Although the Marxist vision is now undergoing progressive modification in the Eastern bloc nations, this should not lead us to dismiss it completely. When liberal *or* Christian feminists ignore class-structure issues of the sort that Marxists care about, they prompt understandably cynical responses from poor people of both sexes throughout the world. But what has a specifically *feminist* contemporary Marxism to offer our young woman worker? How does Marxist feminism put gender together with class in its analysis of history, politics, and economics?

In our earlier overview of first-wave feminism, we saw that Friedrich Engels traced the problem of women's subordination to the emergence of male control over private property in the family. Determined that only their own descendants would inherit their property, men began to regulate women's reproductive life. Engels argued that women's subordination would thus end with the elimination of privately owned property, at least at the level of large-scale public production. Now a moment's reflection shows that this is not a foregone conclusion, for Engels's historical-materialist analysis does not tell us why it was *men*, rather than women, who gained control of property and family-naming procedures in the first place. Nor does his solution guarantee that largely male control of the means of production wouldn't simply be transferred from a capitalist to a socialist state. It is just such omissions that have prompted radical feminists (whom we will discuss shortly) to insist that patriarchal oppression is *more* fundamental than class oppression in explaining women's social and economic position.

50

The Family under Capitalism

By contrast, because Marxist feminists are committed to historical materialism as their fundamental explanatory category, they have tended to focus almost exclusively on women's *work-related* concerns. It is their thesis that the nature and function of women's work under capitalism is the root cause of their oppression. The resulting analysis, while far from complete, is one that is worth considering. For example, Marxist feminists have helped to clarify the relationship of the family to capitalism. In pre-capitalist, subsistence-oriented times, productive and reproductive activities took place together under the umbrella of the household, which often consisted not just of a nuclear family but of an extended family, all of whose members engaged in economically significant activity. With industrialization the production of goods was transferred increasingly to the waged public workplace, to be done largely by men, aided as time went on by underpaid single women. Hence married women, to the extent that they remained consumers and reproducers at home, came to be regarded as "nonproductive" in contrast to their "productive" (i.e., wage-earning) husbands.

Even Engels realized that this is a false dichotomy, underrating as it does the importance of domestic work and child care to the general productivity of a society.[7] Indeed, the peculiarly modern separation of domesticity from waged productive work *has* marginalized women homemakers, isolating them from adult fellowship in the home as well as taking away a large share of their productive labor. Dorothy Sayers, writing not as a Marxist but as a Christian in the 1940s, recognized as much when she wrote the following in her witty essay entitled "Are Women Human?":

> It is a formidable list of jobs [which women had in the Middle Ages]: the whole of the spinning industry, the whole of the weaving industry, the whole catering industry and . . . the whole of the nation's brewing and distilling. All the preserving, pickling and bottling industry, all the bacon-curing, and . . . a very large share in the management of

7. See Engels, *The Origin of the Family, Private Property and the State* (1884; rpt. New York: International Publishers, 1972), pp. 71-72. See also Heidi Hartmann, "The Family as the Locus of Gender, Class, and Political Struggle: The Example of Housework," in *Feminism and Methodology,* ed. Sandra Harding (Bloomington: Indiana University Press, 1987), pp. 109-34.

landed estates. Here are the women's jobs — but modern civilization has taken all these pleasant and profitable activities out of the home, where the women looked after them, and handed them over to big industry, to be directed and organized by men at the head of large factories. Even the dairy-maid in her simple bonnet has gone, to be replaced by a male mechanic in charge of a mechanical milking plant.[8]

Of course, in her analysis Sayers omits mentioning the continued importance of women's child-care activities in the industrial-era home — perhaps because Sayers was a scholar and author who, although married for a time, chose to do no primary nurturing of children herself.[9] She did, however, point out that even if a couple earnestly wanted many children, they now lacked both the space and the income to raise them, living quarters having shrunk with urbanization and children having ceased to be the economic asset they once were as workers in a home-based business. And she did recognize that no human being — male or female — could make a lifetime vocation of parenting. Hence her conclusion about the relationship of industrialization to feminism: "It is perfectly idiotic to take away a woman's traditional occupations and then complain because she looks for new ones. Every woman is a human being ... and a human being *must* have occupation, if he or she is not to become a nuisance to the world."[10]

Housework: Socialized or Home-Waged?

Some Marxist feminists respond to this dilemma by advocating the socialization of both housework and child care, thereby freeing women to join the paid work force without the added problems of a "second shift" of

8. Sayers, "Are Women Human?" in *Are Women Human?* (Downers Grove, Ill.: InterVarsity Press, 1971), p. 24.
9. For an honest yet sympathetic account of Sayers's (fairly successful) attempt to raise her out-of-wedlock son in secret by using the home of a cousin, see James Brabazon's *Dorothy L. Sayers: A Biography* (New York: Charles Scribner's Sons, 1981). In the context of the quotation from Sayers, it is worth wondering if the growing popularity of home schooling among Christians (and others) is not an attempt to reinvest women's homemaking with some of the intellectual stimulation and social significance it lost when the Industrial Revolution gained momentum in the capitalist West.
10. Sayers, "Are Women Human?" p. 25.

domestic responsibilities. Under such a system, young children would be cared for in state-funded nurseries and families would live in accommodations where both cleaning and meal preparation would be done by waged, full-time staff. Moreover, Marxist feminists claim, making such tasks adequately *paid* tasks would signal their importance to the entire society and perhaps even induce men to take a larger part in them. Yet even in socialist countries, the rhetoric of gender equality notwithstanding, public funding of both child care and domestic work is routinely upstaged by industrial, military, and other budgets, leaving women workers with the continuing burden of the "second shift." Such developments strongly suggest that male domination — whether at home or on the job — is not merely an incidental fallout of capitalism but a primary problem in itself.[11]

Many critics of Marxism have taken its recommendations to presume the breakup of the nuclear family. But in point of fact Marxists have long acknowledged the importance of the working-class family as a locus of resistance to middle-class capitalist values. Consequently, most have advocated the demise of the nuclear family only as an *economic* institution, not as a committed *emotional* unit.[12]

Some Marxist feminists have suggested that instead of having housework socialized, women homemakers *themselves* should get a wage for housework, either through compulsory deductions from their husbands' paychecks or through the levying of a more general tax such as the one that supports education. This move, they say, would clearly show just how much capitalism relies on the "invisible" labor of women to produce the labor power of men and children.[13] Perhaps only a coordinated general strike by housewives would bring this change about, but some Marxist feminists see precursors of such action already:

> Whenever a woman divorces her husband she is "refusing the work" that goes along with having a husband around the house. Similarly, when a woman practices contraception or abortion, she is refusing to take on

11. See, for example, Hilda Scott, *Working Your Way to the Bottom* (London: Pandora Press, 1984).
12. For an introductory survey to this debate, see Michele Barrett and Mary McIntosh's *The Anti-Social Family* (London: New Left Books, 1982).
13. See, for example, *The Power of Women and the Subversion of Community*, ed. Mariarosa Dalla Costa and Selma James (Bristol, U.K.: Falling Wall Press, 1972), and *All Work and No Pay*, ed. Wendy Edmond and Suzie Fleming (London: Power of Women Collective and Falling Wall Press, 1975).

the extra work a large family would bring. Finally, when a secretary says "no" to making coffee, or a teacher says "no" to taking her students on extra field trips, or a nurse says "no" to working eighteen-hour shifts, she is refusing to work "for love"—that is, for free. Such rebellions on the part of women have revolutionary potential.[14]

The "Comparable Worth" Campaign

Of course, the "wages for housework" solution does not solve the problem of women's domestic isolation, nor the problem that Sayers noted —that of the industrial, male takeover of what were previously some of women's most creative economic tasks. And by reducing women's economic incentive to work outside the household (and men's incentive to undertake domestic tasks, including child care) a wages-for-housework policy would simply ossify an already questionable division of labor between the sexes. Accordingly, Marxist feminists who are concerned about the inequitably *gendered* nature of work tend to concentrate on a third issue—that of "comparable worth" in the public workplace. They note that even when women do enter the public arena, their work (a) tends to be an extension of domestic labor (e.g., nursing, cleaning, cooking, social work, teaching young children) and (b) is clearly undervalued, as witnessed by the fact that in most workplaces even today a woman's average salary is less than two-thirds what a man would get with comparable training, experience, and responsibility.

We will deal with the topic of work and gender in more detail in a later chapter. But for now we note that one does not have to be a Marxist in order to support comparable worth reforms. Indeed, at least two American states (Washington and Minnesota) and one Canadian province (Ontario) have recently instituted job-evaluation procedures aimed at eliminating the inequitable wages that result from job segregation by sex. Why, for example, should truck drivers (most of whom are male) routinely get higher pay than secretaries (most of whom are female), or animal keepers (mostly male) be paid more than nursery-school teachers (mostly female)? It is hard to escape the conclusion that in North America, as in almost all other societies, it is simply the case that whatever men happen to do is valued more than whatever women

14. Tong, *Feminist Thought*, p. 55.

happen to do, even in cases where job responsibility and job-training requirements are the same.[15]

Conservative critics of comparable worth procedures have often argued that it is impossible to create measurements which could adequately compare the worth of various jobs — it would be like trying to compare apples and oranges, they say. Yet we have implicitly been comparing "apples and oranges" for years when it comes to traditionally *male* jobs: few would question that, on the basis of education, skills, and responsibility, male brain surgeons should be paid more than male truck drivers. Why, then, is it so impossible to make similar judgments across the traditionally gendered job divide?

The Marxist notion of "ideology" — the entrenchment of a value system and worldview that serves the material interests of a ruling class — is helpful in understanding this inconsistency. Either it is the case that all women, due to some innate, ineradicable inferiority, really do perform in a less economically valuable way than all men in all occupations, or else it is the case that some people (Marxists would say male capitalists and the women who benefit from association with them) have a vested interest in promoting this theory, as well as the related theory that women "just naturally" want to work for love more than for money. But one does not have to be a thoroughgoing Marxist to appreciate the fact that real economic injustice has been done to women through the traditional practice of gendered job segregation, a topic to which we will return in our chapter on gender and work.[16]

Radical Feminism: A Form of Contemporary Relational Feminism

In our summary of the "first wave" of feminism, we identified relational feminism as a current of thought that acknowledges certain complemen-

---

15. For a further discussion of the question of women's and men's social value in various pre-industrial cultures, see *Women, Culture and Society*, ed. Michelle Zimbalist Rosaldo and Louise Lamphere (Stanford: Stanford University Press, 1974).

16. For a further discussion of the concept and implementation of comparable worth, see *Comparable Worth and Wage Discrimination: Technical Possibilities and Political Realities*, ed. Helen Remick (Philadelphia: Temple University Press, 1984). For a more specifically Marxist slant, see Teresa Amott and Julie Matthaei's "Comparable Worth, Incomparable Pay," *Radical America* 18 (September/October 1984): 21-28.

tary differences between women and men and focuses on women's child-bearing and nurturing capacities in relation to men and children. Radical feminism, which faults classical Marxist analysis for its reduction of gender problems to economic class problems, is in many ways a current version of relational feminism. We say "in many ways" because many contemporary radical feminists are more concerned with improving the bonding of women with other women than they with shoring up and improving heterosexual relations, which was the agenda of earlier relational feminists. Even so, most radical feminists celebrate what they see as unique *women's* strengths, rather than downplaying or marginalizing these, as liberal or Marxist feminists have done. In this respect they are in the relational tradition.

Two other types of feminism that are broadly relational in their focus are those we will label "psychoanalytic" feminism and "philosophical" feminism. The first of these emphasizes the roots of boys' and girls' differing emotional development and their consequences for adult "masculine" and "feminine" personality. The second focuses more on the differences between women's and men's styles of thinking and making moral decisions, without trying to settle the question about whether such differences originate in biology, socialization, or both. At this point we will look only at some contemporary expressions of radical feminism, returning to the more specialized foci of psychoanalytic and philosophical feminism in Chapter Twelve.

Without a doubt, radical feminism is among the most difficult forms of feminist thought to summarize neatly. What unites all types of radical feminists, as we have already hinted, is their conviction that women's oppression is the *most fundamental form* of human oppression — one that precedes, outstrips, and perhaps even explains oppression based on class, race, military might, or any other type of power. Beyond this, radical feminists have a great diversity of interests. Some of them focus on art or religion, others on ecology, sexuality, or reproduction and/or mothering. In each of these areas radical feminists wish to retrieve what previously silenced or marginalized women have contributed and to advance these specifically female contributions in the future, freed from the problems of male domination. Of all types of feminism, radical feminism is the most consistently and pointedly "woman-centered."

Shulamith Firestone, a radical feminist writing in the late 1960s, reformulated Engels's historical materialism to assert that it is *sex* class rather than gender-blind economic class — the relations of *reproduction* rather than production — which constitutes the prime moving force in human history. In other words, women are subordinate to men first and foremost for *biological* reasons, not economic reasons. The very first division of labor was that of men's and women's differing roles in reproduction, Firestone argued. As a result, she concluded, only a reproductive revolution could bring about gender equality. Such a revolution would include all possible reproductive technologies, up to and including the *in vitro* union of ova and sperm and the gestation of the resulting embryos in artificial wombs. The offspring of such technologically monitored unions would ideally be nurtured by a variety of caring adults of both sexes. Thus relieved of their differing roles in the reproductive drama (other than the donation of ova or sperm), women and men would gradually shed all other limiting and oppressive gender roles.[17]

The Radical Feminist Retrieval of Mothering

For the most part, however, latter-day radical feminists do not follow Firestone's lead. Not only have they become somewhat cynical about the liberating potential of reproductive technology, which they see as largely male-created and male-controlled for male benefit; they also do not wish to dismiss the unique satisfactions (along with the burdens) of female childbearing and child raising. For radical feminists, our culture's feelings of repulsion toward menstruation, childbirth, nursing, and general bodily care are the legacy of liberal "somatophobia" — that is, the devaluation of the necessary and recurrent functions of the body as compared with the "higher" and "timeless" life of the mind.[18]

It is quite true that in identifying the capacity for reason with true humanness, liberal thought — and, indeed, the Western philosophical

17. Firestone, *The Dialectic of Sex: The Case for Feminist Revolution* (New York: William Morrow, 1970). For a feminist science-fiction scenario that builds on Firestone's work, see Marge Piercy's *Woman on the Edge of Time* (New York: Fawcett–Crescent Books, 1976). For more comprehensive surveys of radical feminism, see chaps. 5 and 9 of Alison Jaggar's *Feminist Politics and Human Nature* and chaps. 3 and 4 of Rosemarie Tong's *Feminist Thought.*

18. "Somatophobia" is a term coined by philosopher Elizabeth V. Spelman. See her essay entitled "Woman as Body: Ancient and Contemporary Views," *Feminist Studies* 8 (Spring 1982): 109-31. See also chap. 7 of Alison Jaggar's *Feminist Politics and Human Nature.*

tradition more generally — has routinely denigrated or ignored the significance of the physical for the maintenance of human life. From a Marxist perspective, this somatophobic attitude contributes to class divisions in a capitalist society. Those who own the means of production (or are close to those who do) are given the mental work of inventing, planning, and managing, and they are paid well for doing it. Those who have only their physical labor to sell get to do atomized, uncreative jobs with low wages and little responsibility.

Radical feminists have taken this critique of somatophobia a step further by exposing its gendered aspects. The mental/physical distinction, they point out, has been used not only by capitalists to control workers but also and even more basically by men to control women. Western thought has historically identified women with the "lower" life of the body and men with the "higher" life of the mind. This dichotomy has been further used both to exclude women from activities deemed "rational" (e.g., assuming the responsibilities of citizenship, engaging in scholarship) and to define their traditional work of birthing and nurturing as "nonrational," "animal-like," and unworthy of serious scientific study. Even in the twentieth century, which has seen the extension of science into the "womanly" activities of birthing, child raising, and food preparation, women have too often been the controlled rather than the controllers. In Alison Jaggar's words, "Men appropriated the 'mental' labor of developing theories about nutrition, medicine, child development, psychotherapy and obstetrics, while women were assigned the 'manual' labor of following the male experts' advice."[19]

For many radical feminists, the solution to such dichotomies lies not in women's *rejecting* childbearing and child raising but rather in their *regaining control* of both — in deciding for themselves "who, how, when and where to mother"[20] rather than submitting to the dictates of male partners and/or "experts" in these matters. In her book titled *Of Woman Born*, Adrienne Rich points out that such a solution would advantage not only mothers and their daughters but their sons as well. In a patriarchal society, she observes, men too often want sons for the wrong reasons: as heirs to their name and property, as apprentice workers, as expendable

---

19. Jaggar, *Feminist Politics and Human Nature*, pp. 187-88. See also Evelyn Fox Keller's *Reflections on Gender and Science* (New Haven: Yale University Press, 1985), and Genevieve Lloyd's *Man of Reason: "Male" and "Female" in Western Philosophy* (London: Methuen, 1984).

20. Tong, *Feminist Thought*, p. 87.

warriors in causes dictated by their elders, as extensions of their own egos. By retrieving motherhood on their own terms, Rich concludes, women can both enjoy it more and at the same time raise children of both sexes with feminist values. (We will present a more detailed treatment of this retrieval of "maternal thinking" in Chapter Twelve.)[21]

The Radical Feminist Rejection of Femininity and the Retrieval of Sexuality

Radical feminist discourse does not stop with the concern to reform reproduction and mothering. Just as important are the questions about how women can be freed from male gender-role expectations — in other words, from "the cage of femininity" — and how they can be freed from male-dominated sexual practices such as rape, pornography, prostitution, and physical abuse.

With regard to the question of gender roles — as with the question about whether women should reject or reform reproduction and mothering — there has been an earlier, more "androgynous" answer and a later, more explicitly "woman-celebrating" answer. Writing in the late 1960s, radical feminist Kate Millett argued that patriarchal ideology has exaggerated biological differences between women and men in order to keep women subordinate in all social institutions — the academy, the political forum, the church, the family, and so on. Having been socialized to see themselves as emotional, nonaggressive, and hypersensitive, Millett argued, most women have come to consent to the very terms of their marginalization and oppression. Her solution to this problem was to eliminate the "sex/gender system" — that is, any and all practices that reinforce stereotypical masculinity and femininity — and to replace it with androgynous ideals and practices. This would mean the equal valuation of the best of stereotypically masculine *and* stereotypically feminine traits, and their encouragement in children and adults of both sexes.[22]

The androgynous ideal is a clear step away from traditionally liberal-feminist aspirations. As radical feminists have pointed out, the

---

21. Rich, *Of Woman Born* (New York: W. W. Norton, 1976). For a less separatist treatment of the value of mothering, see, for example, Sara Ruddick's *Maternal Thinking: Toward a Politics of Peace* (Boston: Beacon Press, 1989).
22. Millett, *Sexual Politics* (Garden City, N.Y.: Doubleday, 1970).

59

physical and the feminine, being seen as inferior, have usually been assigned to the "private" or domestic realm, well away from the public arena where rationality holds sway. And liberal feminists have generally not questioned this dichotomization of public/male/rational/superior from domestic/female/physical/inferior. Rather than challenging the very terms of the dichotomy — for example, by contrasting constructive, domestic feminine nurturance with destructive, public masculine war-mongering — they have demanded, with Henry Higgins of *My Fair Lady*, "Why can't a woman be more like a man?" Unlike Higgins, who concluded that women were constitutionally incapable of acting and thinking like men, liberal feminists have implicitly answered, "Just let us try, and we'll show you!" By contrast, the androgynous ideal calls for men to develop the best of traditionally feminine traits just as it calls for women to develop the best of traditionally masculine traits.

But even this apparently more evenhanded goal is now being questioned by radical feminists. Some assert that the very *dichotomy* between masculinity and femininity is a male invention, and prefer instead to focus on a more "woman-celebrating" response to the problem of down-graded female traits. They conclude that strong, authentic womanhood will be achieved only when women separate from men and allow to flourish the very traits men have traditionally castigated them for: volcanic emotion, bluntness, an unsculptured, natural body, even witch-like repugnance and power. The resulting "elemental woman," as Mary Daly has called her, will be so powerful that no patriarchal system will ever hold her back again.[23] This is a form of radical feminism which comes close to suggesting that male sexism is the original sin and that woman — or a particular kind of unreconstructed, elemental woman — is the new, redeemed creation. As such, it is the most "spiritually" oriented of the second-wave feminisms we have encountered thus far. Whereas Marxist feminism dismisses religion as a case of false consciousness in a purely material universe, and liberal feminism relegates religion to the realm of private preference along with all other "nonrational" activities, this particular form of radical feminism celebrates a woman-centered, woman-defined spirituality.[24]

23. Daly, *Gyn/Ecology: The Metaethics of Radical Feminism* (Boston: Beacon Press, 1978). See also her book entitled *Pure Lust: Elemental Feminist Philosophy* (Boston: Beacon Press, 1984).

24. For a more detailed survey and bibliography, see chap. 4 of Tong's *Feminist Thought*.

We will defer our theological reflection on this point until later in this chapter. In the meantime, to conclude our survey of radical feminism, we need to say a little about its treatment of genital sexuality. Just as male-defined gender roles and reproductive demands constrict women's potential as persons and mothers, so, according to radical feminists, male-defined sexual demands constrict women's capacity to recognize and fulfill their own sexual desires. Central to this problem, in radical feminist analysis, is the normalization of men's dominance and violence in their sexual relations with women, and the expectation that women will passively submit. "Boys will be boys," we are taught, and it's up to women to accommodate them dutifully and nonjudgmentally, if not enthusiastically. That sexual pleasure is largely unreciprocal between men and women can be seen, according to radical feminists, in the institutionalized male practices of rape, pornography, prostitution, sexual harassment, and battering. In each case it is overwhelmingly men whose preferences and power are affirmed, and it is women (and mostly female children) who are victimized.[25]

Radical feminists have mounted a range of programs to deal with such problems. They were among the first to open up shelters for women victimized by rape and physical assault and to set up support groups for incest survivors. They have mounted legal campaigns against pornography, either on the grounds that its consumption leads to actual sexual violence against women or on the grounds that women's civil rights and freedom of movement are constricted by the demeaning attitudes pornography provokes.[26] They have organized grass-roots campaigns to "take back the night," insisting that city streets be made at least as safe and accessible to women as they are to men at all times of day. To justify their drawing of public attention to such previously unmentionable sexual issues, radical feminists have routinely invoked the slogan that "the personal is political." Classically liberal feminists relegate not just religion but also sexuality to the realm of private life and mutual consent, insisting that it be neither socially judged nor legally regulated. By

25. See, for example, Andrea Dworkin's *Woman Hating: A Radical Look at Sexuality* (New York: E. P. Dutton, 1974), and also her book entitled *Our Blood: Prophecies and Discourses on Sexual Politics* (New York: G. P. Putnam, 1981).
26. See, for example, Catharine MacKinnon's *Feminism Unmodified: Discourses on Life and Law* (Cambridge: Harvard University Press, 1987). For a more complete discussion of the feminist debate on pornography, see chap. 4 of Tong's *Feminist Thought.*

contrast, radical feminists have exposed the extent to which real, flesh-and-blood women are damaged by the privatization of sexual activity in particular and domestic life in general, a theme to which we will return in Chapter Twelve.

Some Theological Observations

To the extent that Christians understand the different expressions of feminism, it is radical feminism which seems to offend them most. Apparently they are particularly put off by the physical/sexual emphasis of radical feminism. But the biblical view of persons stresses *both* the unity of mind and body *and* the value of the the the latter, as expressed in the incarnation of Jesus and the promise that we will be resurrected *as bodies.* And although the Bible realistically portrays the abuses to which genital sexuality can lead, it is by no means antisexual, any more than it is antifemale. Yet Christians, marching to the drumbeat of their sinful surroundings more than they realize, have tended to fear or denigrate the body and to turn a blind eye to misogyny (the devaluation of women) and even to sexual abuse within their own ranks. Indeed, a recent survey of the denomination to which several of us belong has shown prevalence rates for physical, psychological, and sexual abuse that are essentially the same as those found in surveys of the general North American population.[27] And it is questionable whether Christians' growing concern for victims of physical and sexual violence would have arisen without the groundwork laid by "strident" radical feminists. (Have we forgotten that the Old Testament prophets were also criticized by their society for "stridently" calling attention to prevalent kinds of abuse?) Just as we grant that liberal feminists are legitimately concerned about equal rights and that Marxist feminists are legitimately concerned about class-based

27. Calvin College Social Research Center, "A Survey of Abuse in the Christian Reformed Church" (Grand Rapids: Calvin College, 1990). See also the following: James Alsdurf and Phyllis Alsdurf's *Battered into Submission: The Tragedy of Wife Abuse in the Christian Home* (Downers Grove, Ill.: InterVarsity Press, 1989); Marie M. Fortune's *Sexual Violence: The Unmentionable Sin* (New York: Pilgrim Press, 1983); Maxine Hancock and Karen Burton Mains's *Child Sexual Abuse: The Hope for Healing* (Wheaton, Ill.: Harold Shaw, 1986); and Mary Stewart Van Leeuwen's *Gender and Grace: Love, Work and Parenting in a Changing World* (Downers Grove, Ill.: InterVarsity Press, 1990), especially chaps. 9 and 12.

injustice, we need to give radical feminists due credit for their insistence that the personal is in many ways political.

Recent Developments:
Socialist and Postmodern Feminism

Our overview of the second wave shows that feminist theories have gradually deepened and broadened even as they have built on the foundations laid by the first wave of the eighteenth and nineteenth centuries. But because neither liberal, Marxist, nor radical feminism can give a full account of women's oppression, we should not be surprised to discover that a "hybrid" form of feminism — combining Marxist, radical, and sometimes psychological insights — has arisen in recent years. Known as socialist feminism (but not to be confused with its nineteenth-century precursor), its adherents speak of the "overdetermination" of women's subordination. By this they mean that various forces, such as capitalism, patriarchy, and internal psychological factors, *combine* to keep women "in their place." Most socialist feminists try to unify aspects of Marxist and radical feminist thought, although at least one early work — Juliet Mitchell's *Psychoanalysis and Feminism* — tries to give due credit to psychological factors as well.[28]

One socialist feminist, Alison Jaggar, uses the concept of "gendered alienation" to unify Marxist and radical feminist insights. "Alienation" is a classical Marxist concept describing the sense of fragmentation and meaninglessness that workers under capitalism feel when they have no say over what they produce or how they produce it. It is also used to describe the feelings of separation produced between different classes and between members of the same class who must compete for a limited number of jobs. Jaggar extends this concept to show how women are alienated *as women* — not only alienated as generic workers from capital-driven, waged labor but also alienated as women from their bodies, from each other, and from the children they bear. Women, for example, must sculpt and beautify their bodies in ways not demanded of men. They are forced to compete with each other for "scarce" husbandly resources. They are told when and how many children to bear, sometimes having more than they can humanly care for and sometimes being forced

28. Mitchell, *Psychoanalysis and Feminism* (New York: Vintage Books, 1974).

to abort when they would rather not. In all of these ways, says Jaggar, capitalism and patriarchy dovetail in the oppression of women. And because women's subordination is overdetermined, no single program — economic, social, or psychological — will end it. Change will be required on all fronts at once.[29]

In later chapters we will return to an aspect of contemporary socialist feminism known as *critical theory*. Like other socialist feminists, critical theorists take seriously the "overdetermination" of women's subordination in particular and of gender relations in general. In other words, they recognize that individual, interpersonal, *and* social-structural factors must be taken into account when we try to understand or change gender relations. But in addition to recognizing the social and psychological forces impinging on women and men, critical theorists also take human freedom seriously. As they see it, marginal groups — women, blacks, gays, and other minorities — are not only "passive victims" but at times assertive fighters who find ways to "contest the system." That is, they find ways, individually and collectively, to maximize their own comfort, freedom, and dignity within the system and sometimes even find ways to change the ground rules of the system itself.

This "double awareness" — of the forces that shape us *and* of our ability to contest and reroute them for other purposes — is important to us for two reasons. It is important *theologically* because the biblical concept of personhood affirms that we are *both* "dust of the earth" *and* "imagers of God." As dust of the earth we cannot escape our embeddedness in the material world. We *are* affected by material, economic, social, and psychological forces, and whatever personhood and community we achieve must be achieved within the parameters of such forces. At the same time, as imagers of God, we *can* to a degree transcend the limitations of these forces — indeed, we are *called* to do so as stewards of the earth and as God's agents of reconciliation. Although we are the products of our past, we confess as Christians that God works redemptively *through* and *beyond* our past history and present circumstances, calling us constantly to be more than we once were.

But this paradox of human freedom within material limits is important to us as *feminists* as well. For if it were true that women have been nothing but "victims" of male oppression, then on what grounds could we argue for their present liberation? If women always and every-

---

29. See Jaggar, *Feminist Politics and Human Nature*, especially chaps. 6 and 10.

where took whatever was handed out to them without being able to shape their circumstances even to their own limited advantage, then they could hardly be classified as accountable human agents capable of handling more freedom and responsibility *now*. But as we will see in subsequent chapters, women, like other marginal groups, *do* contest the accepted norms of gender relations. In doing so, they sometimes succeed in making life only a little more tolerable for themselves and their dependents. At other times, like the present, entire systems of rules governing gender relations begin to shift in response to their efforts and the efforts of sympathetic others.

Our point is simply this: a viable social theory that is both Christian and feminist requires us to acknowledge agency, in addition to the effects of material forces, in both women and men. Subsequent chapters will apply this insight to various areas of gendered activity — such as work, dress, and the construction of ideals of "masculine" and "feminine" bodies.

Postmodern Feminism: The Challenge of Deconstructionism

Although socialist feminists combine insights from a variety of sources, they remain confident that a unified theory of women's subordination and a prescription for its cure will eventually emerge. But ironically, after so much work has gone into second-wave feminist theorizing (or perhaps precisely *because* so much work has been done), other feminists have begun to doubt that it is even possible to create theories that apply to *all* women. In a sense, one could see this coming. Liberal feminism began by making a case for the simple, generic humanness of women and men. Relational feminists of various sorts then countered with the insistence that women have unique concerns and capacities, rooted in nature, nurture, or a combination of both. In turn, some radical feminists have asserted that heterosexual and lesbian women cannot be lumped together in one category. Socialist feminists have added that one must also take class into account: for example, a working-class man may oppress his wife, but in turn be oppressed in a different way by the wife of his boss.

In other words, gradually we have seen more and more qualifiers added to the generic notion of "women's oppression." And if the women who are being oppressed vary so much by class, race, ethnicity, and sexual orientation, can we even claim that there *is* such a thing as *the* common experience of being a woman? Philosopher Elizabeth Spelman offers this comment:

> What is it to think of a woman "as a woman"? Is it really possible for us to think of a woman's "womanness" in abstraction from the fact that she is a particular woman, whether she is a middle-class Black woman living in North America or a poor white woman living in France in the seventeenth century? . . . One's gender identity is not related to one's racial and class identity as the parts of pop-bead necklaces are related, separable and insertable in other "strands" with different racial and class "parts."[30]

However, it is important to note that these concerns were brought to the fore in international women's gatherings, where Western feminists were confronted by other women who articulated their problems differently and who challenged Western feminism's truisms. Thus the challenge to Western feminism was not primarily launched by deconstructionist theorists, although they have undertaken the work of deconstructing the notions that have come under attack.

It is concerns such as these that occupy feminists of a "postmodern" or "deconstructionist" bent. In dismantling, or deconstructing, the idea of generic womanness, they are in part concerned to "give difference its due." They realize that there is a certain false humility at work when middle-class white feminists say things like "Underneath our exteriors we are all really alike." Examined closely, such thinking is apt to mean, in Spelman's words, that "the womanness underneath a Black woman's skin is a white woman's, and deep down inside the Latina woman is an Anglo woman waiting to burst through an obscuring cultural shroud."[31] As a result of all this, many contemporary feminists are anxious to cast off residual colonial attitudes and acquire a truer humility of culture, race, class, and even sexual orientation. That such an exercise is long overdue will become abundantly clear in the following chapter, which reviews the critique of Western feminism leveled by non-Western feminists and Western women of color.

But another motive in deconstructing the idea of generic woman-

30. Spelman, *Inessential Woman: Problems of Exclusion in Feminist Thought* (Boston: Beacon Press, 1988), chaps. 13 and 15.
31. Ibid., p. 13.

hood is, ironically, a desire to be *more* feminist. The very notion that there has to be a single, true vision of reality is, on this account, a "phallocentric" or male way of thinking. It is male philosophers, feminist deconstructionists claim, who insist on "positive" knowledge, who believe that everything is categorizable and reducible to a fixed "essence." It is male thought that likes to dichotomize — culture from nature, mind from body, activity from passivity, male from female — rather than give particularity and change their due. Women, by contrast, remain more fluid in their thinking, their writing, and their relationships with each other and the environment. "By refusing to center, congeal, and separate their thoughts into a unified truth too inflexible to change," Rosemarie Tong points out, "feminists resist patriarchal dogma."[32]

Postmodern feminists recognize that taking such a stance may be a recipe for continued marginalization in our modern, scientized, technocratic society. But, they now ask, what is so terrible about being marginalized? Is it not the disadvantaged, the rejected, the "wretched of the earth" who accurately see the complexities of reality from which the privileged, in their single-mindedness, are protected? Unlike liberal feminists, who wish to make a place for women among the elite, postmodern feminists have adopted, in secularized form, the stance of Old Testament prophets, who denounced the follies and injustices of their society at whatever cost to their own comfort. At the same time, however, postmodernism has become a fashionable trend in many university departments. So it remains to be seen whether postmodern feminists' prophetic critique can survive the comforts of becoming part of the intellectual mainstream.

What Price Pluralism?
Problems and New Possibilities

Deconstructionist thought is supported in part by postmodern epistemology, which rejects the notion that all people share a reliable "foundation" for truth — such as the evidence of their senses, or certain

---

32. Tong, *Feminist Thought*, p. 7. For a more complete review and bibliography, see chap. 8 of Tong's book. Works by prominent feminist deconstructionists include Helene Cixous's "Castration or Decapitation?" *Signs* 7, no. 1 (1981): 41-55; Luce Irigaray's *This Sex Which Is Not One*, trans. Catherine Porter (Ithaca, N.Y.: Cornell University Press, 1985); and Julie Kristeva's *Revolution in Poetic Languages*, trans. Leon Roudiez (New York: Columbia University Press, 1984).

self-evident "first principles" from which all other truths logically flow. Deconstructionism also draws on developments in literature and linguistics which hold that words and texts do not have meanings that can be pinned down once and for all by the application of formal methods of analysis. And there are aspects of the deconstructionist, postmodern project that Christians can welcome. For example, the postmodern recognition that "objective" observation and formal logic are not neatly separable from "subjective" feelings, values, and beliefs has helped to restore the intellectual respectability of religious conviction, rooted in revelation, as a grounding for knowledge and moral action.[33]

On the level of feminist discourse, as we have seen, the deconstructionist project embraces pluralism and rejects the idea of a single common female experience. But to be consistent, such pluralism must acknowledge that if "being a woman" is inseparable from being Afro-American, working class, or lesbian, then for many women it is *also* inseparable from being Christian, or Jewish, or Moslem. Although slow to take hold in feminist circles, this concession represents quite a change from the liberal feminist consignment of religion to the realm of the private and subjective, from the Marxist rejection of religion as an illusion, and from the radical feminist dismissal of religion as one more example of the patriarchal control of women. Indeed, this concession has even helped Christians like ourselves to feel less marginalized and more attentively listened to at scholarly gatherings of feminists. For example, British and American feminist historians are now slower to dismiss the religious views of nineteenth-century evangelical women as a case of false, prefeminist consciousness. In the words of Lyndal Roper, a professor of history at the University of London, "Today we are facing up to the fact that many [nineteenth-century Western] women were passionate evangelicals. It doesn't do any good to convict them of error without thinking about what attracted them to evangelicalism."[34]

33. See, for example, Nicholas Wolterstorff's *Reason within the Bounds of Religion* (Grand Rapids: William B. Eerdmans, 1976). See also Mary Stewart Van Leeuwen's "Psychology's Two Cultures: A Christian Analysis," *Christian Scholar's Review* 17 (June 1988): 406-24; and Kelly J. Clark's *Return to Reason: A Critique of Enlightenment Evidentialism and a Defense of Reason and Belief in God* (Grand Rapids: William B. Eerdmans, 1990).

34. Roper, as quoted in Karen J. Winkler's article entitled "Scholars of Women's History Fear the Field Has Lost Its Identity," *Chronicle of Higher Education* 36 (July 1990): A-6.

But among adamantly secular feminists there is a price to be paid for this gain in humility and respect for diversity. For it is one thing to admit that one's own perspective as a white, middle-class, liberal, American feminist is not the privileged foundation for truth and justice that one naively used to think it was. It is quite another thing to conclude that racial, class, ethnic, religious, and other diversities prevent human beings from *ever* knowing what is true and just and acting accordingly. In other words, postmodern feminism risks undercutting the entire feminist project. For if there is only diversity and pluralism, who can dare say what is "right" and "true" for all women? If all thought and values are relative to one's race, class, sexual orientation, religion, and time in history, who can even say that oppressive patriarchy, as a worldview, is any less valid than a feminist vision of mutuality and gender justice?

It would be naive to assume that Christian feminists have all the resources — intellectual, theological, and evangelistic — to rescue their feminist colleagues from this relativistic bind. But we are at least able to give an accounting for the hope that is in us (1 Pet. 3:15). Christian faith, particularly in its Reformed expression, recognizes that religious commitment of some sort grounds all people's quest for truth. It also recognizes that all people, as imagers of God called to fill and manage the earth, must have *some* common means of recognizing what truth is. It would have been strange indeed for God to have given humankind a mandate to unfold the potential of creation but at the same time to have given us no possibility of a common sense of truth and justice — transcending conditions of race, class, gender, and so on — as a yardstick against which to measure our progress.[35] That corporate sense is indeed limited by our finiteness and distorted by sin. But it is still there, and we confess as Christian feminists that the Old Testament and New Testament visions of *shalom* bear witness to it. As we proceed in the following chapter to examine the feminism of Third World women and Western women of color, the need to proclaim that vision of *shalom* will continue to guide us.

35. This conviction leads many Christian philosophers to be "critical realists" in their epistemology. For a further explanation, see Del Ratzsch's *Philosophy of Science: The Natural Sciences in Christian Perspective* (Downers Grove, Ill.: InterVarsity Press, 1986).

CHAPTER 4

A Cross-Cultural Critique
of Western Feminism

In his celebrated *History of India,* published in 1818, James Mills stated what is still the received wisdom in Western culture: "Among rude people the women are generally degraded; among civilized people they are exalted. . . . As society refines upon its enjoyments, and advances into the state of civilization, . . . the condition of the weaker sex is gradually improved."[1] Westerners may hotly debate what is good or bad about "feminism," but feminist and anti-feminist alike share a pride in the respect that our culture has shown for women. It would be hard to find anyone who would argue for reversing the gains Western women have achieved in the last two hundred years — the right to higher education, the right to own property and to vote, access to the professions and to public office. The common assumption is that, if they are fortunate, the rest of the world's women will follow Western women down this hard-won path.

---

1. Mills, quoted by Ghulam Murshid in *Reluctant Debutante: Response of Bengali Women to Modernization, 1849-1905* (Rajshahi University, Rajshahi, Bangladesh: Sahitya Samsad, 1983), p. 23.

The primary author for this chapter is Margaret Koch.

70

Ethnocentrism, the assumption that one's own culture "has it right," is a recurring human perspective. The story is told of a scholar from China in the nineteenth century who was asked, "What do you think of Western civilization?" "I think," he replied, "that it would be a good idea." But China paid a high price for the blind spots created by its appropriation of Western ethnocentrism. Accordingly, in a discussion of gender relations it is well to listen when, despite the obvious privileges of Western women, non-Western women ask this blunt question: "Is it not possible that Western women gave birth to feminism because in some ways modern, industrial society makes the lives of women harder?"

Since the mid-1970s various voices from outside the white, middle-class feminist mainstream have developed a critique of English-speaking Western feminism. It is these voices that we will attempt to understand in this chapter.

Challenges to White Western Feminism

The rich range of international feminist voices defies easy categorization. Like Western feminists, women in other parts of the world have launched a variety of challenges to beliefs and practices that hurt women. A growing body of literature catalogs the critiques of Arab, Indian, Latin American, and African feminists, critiques aimed at abuses against women that their societies accept as normal. Since we are Westerners whose challenge has been to understand gender injustice in our own society, we must admit that these intracultural critiques have remained largely beyond our scope.

However, during the United Nations Decade on Women (1975-85), women from the Southern hemisphere insisted that the wealthier women of the North come to recognize that women's issues are part of global issues. They charged that the luxuries which Western women enjoy blind them to the realities of less privileged women around the world. This in turn has distorted feminist theory. Explanatory theories that Western feminists assume to be universal have not always rung true for other cultures.

It is certainly possible to find in any country feminist voices that sound remarkably like their Western counterparts. For example, in the introduction to one of her books Lourdes Beneria, a leading Latin American feminist, lists the goals of feminist politics as "equality before the law, women's economic and psychological self-reliance, the abolition of a gender-based division of labor, women's control over their sexuality and reproductive capacity, and the eradication of male violence and coercion over women."[2] This is a list with which most Western feminists would feel entirely comfortable. The interests of women around the world clearly overlap, as do the injustices they face. In fact, the very ease of locating cruelty to women around the world has contributed to some of the glib universalizing of Western feminism. However, international feminist critiques have begun to expose crucial blind spots within Western feminism. Nevertheless, while quarreling with feminist theory as it exists, these critics share with all feminists a commitment to the defense of women. This should not be forgotten as we focus on three areas of difference — first, in the understanding of autonomy; second, in a commitment to social solidarity; and third, in a greater reluctance to abandon cultural traditions.

Autonomy, Development, and Class

When Aileen Kraditor wrote the introduction to her classic collection of American feminist documents, she searched for and tried to describe the common thread that held the diverse perspectives together as "feminist" voices:

> This fundamental something can perhaps be designated by the term "autonomy." ... The grievance behind the demand has always seemed to be that women have been regarded not as people but as female relatives of people. And the feminists' desire has, consequently, been for women to be recognized, in the economic, political, and/or social realms, as individuals in their own right.[3]

Although they vary in their understanding of the nature of this autonomy, Western feminists seem to agree with Kraditor that autonomy is a

2. Beneria and Martha Roldan, *The Crossroads of Class and Gender: Industrial Homework, Subcontracting, and Household Dynamics in Mexico City* (Chicago: University of Chicago Press, 1987), p. 12.

3. Kraditor, introduction to *Up from the Pedestal: Selected Writings in the History of American Feminism* (New York: Quadrangle/New York Times Book Co., 1968), p. 8.

central feminist claim. Socialist feminist Zillah Eisenstein argues that "all feminism is liberal at its root in that the universal feminist claim that woman is an independent being (from man) is premised on the eighteenth-century liberal conception of the independent and autonomous self."[4] The Combahee River Collective, the group who penned the influential document titled "A Black Feminist Statement," seem to concur when they write, "Above all else, our politics initially sprang from the shared belief that Black women are inherently valuable, that our liberation is a necessity not as an adjunct to somebody else's but because of our need as persons for autonomy."[5] From whatever root it springs, the feminist voice cries, "Women are people too."

But as non-Western women begin to articulate a feminism of their own, it is increasingly evident that Western feminists have twisted this universal endorsement of autonomy into a peculiar shape. Not only the heritage of ideas about the value of all individuals but also the economic and political structures of modern industrial, bureaucratic society have shaped Western feminist understandings. Beyond this, the peculiar flavor of American individualism has left American feminists with a parochial understanding of human equality about which they have tended to assume universal agreement.

The understanding of autonomy articulated by Indian sociologist Rama Mehta illustrates nuances that are missing from most Western feminism. She based her award-winning novel, *Inside the Haveli,* on her experience as a young educated woman from south India who married into an upper-class family from north India that still observed an extreme form of purdah, the seclusion of women. With tears and shivers the main character, Geeta, enters the family mansion, or *haveli,* where the women greet her with a scolding question: "Where do you come from that you show your face to the world?" This is seemingly a feminist dystopia in which women enter the public sections of the house only to serve food. Every movement of the young bride is prescribed, and she

4. Eisenstein, *The Radical Future of Liberal Feminism* (New York: Longman, 1981), p. 5. She goes on to argue that "all feminism is also radically feminist in that women's identity as a sexual class underlies this claim." What this book argues is that both the history and the present formulation of liberal feminism are more complicated than the usual and perfunctory description the term elicits.

5. Combahee River Collective, "A Black Feminist Statement," in *This Bridge Called My Back,* ed. Cherrie Moraga and Gloria Anzaldua (New York: Kitchen Press, 1984), p. 212.

73

feels imprisoned: "There were many times when she felt the crushing weight of the walls that shut off the outside world. The chatter of the maids, the gossip that floated into the courtyard, were amusing distractions, but not sufficient to be really satisfying."[6] Yet as Mehta explores this loss of personal autonomy during the crumbling of the *haveli* as an institution, she uncovers other meanings of freedom, not all of them good.

To begin with, Mehta points out that the strict purdah of Oswal women in Mewar (Udaipur) in northern India began when Oswal men were employed as administrators in a court strongly influenced by centuries of Mughal rule, in which purdah was the norm for women of the ruling class. The segregation of women was thus a matter of court etiquette, a condition of employment.[7] Oswals in other parts of India did not observe purdah as did the Oswals in Mewar. With the birth of independent India, the court system collapsed, and a revolution began in the lives of women. Surely the autonomy granted women by the destruction of this repressive system is cause for feminist rejoicing. And Mehta, as both character and author, clearly joins in this celebration. But she also reveals an ambivalence often missing in Western perspectives on autonomy.

First, she sees not only the limitations but also the power that women enjoy within the *haveli*. Geeta's mother-in-law is the capable administrator of a large establishment that supports the life of many people; the oldest maid also enjoys enormous authority, based on her knowledge of and commitment to the *haveli*. Others have responsibilities according to age and rank. Women negotiate the marriages that serve as economic and political links in the community and are thus not without access to public power. Living closely with many different women and apart from men, women in the *haveli* become aware of their own capabilities and power.

Second, the autonomy given to individuals as the *haveli* disintegrates comes at a cost. Mehta points out, for example, that in the emerging new order some servants can "earn a hundred to two hundred rupees

---

6. Mehta, *Inside the Haveli* (New Delhi: Arnold Heineman, 1977), p. 70.
7. Mehta, "From Purdah to Modernity," in *Indian Women from Purdah to Modernity*, ed. B. R. Nanda (New Delhi: Vikas, 1976), pp. 113-28; and "Purdah among the Oswals of Mewar," in *Separate Worlds: Studies of Purdah in South Asia*, ed. Hanna Papanek and Gail Minault (Columbia, Mo.: South Asia Books, 1982), pp. 139-63.

for just eight hours of work a day."[8] This possibility allows others to charge their employers with "exploitation," shortens the supply of servants, and introduces the idea of waged employment as opposed to lifelong service, with its complex set of mutual obligations between servant and master. But only a few will find their way to a better life. A mass of unprotected poor exists in present-day India, demonstrating the cost of eliminating a social safety net woven from the interchange of services within a network of human relationships. Women of the wealthy class clearly do enjoy greater autonomy. But for most people what accompanies the individualization of modern life under capitalist development is hardly a positive notion of "freedom."

Often it has meant destitute isolation from old networks of support. For an example we can look at the impact of the Green Revolution on women in India.[9] Its introduction of high-yielding varieties of seeds and fertilizers and of irrigation by motorized pumps has indeed increased overall agricultural production. But it has done so at the price of making farmers increasingly dependent on materials that must be purchased with cash, and this has dramatically changed the shape of agriculture in India. Although a small number of farmers have increased production, many others have lost access to the land from which their predecessors wrested a living within a network of patron-client relationships. One of the consequences is a large number of unemployed men, and where there are many unemployed men, women employed as day laborers can only find work which is so poorly paid that men will not take it. And the "lucky" woman whose family has retained their land may now find herself working a "double day" — as a waged laborer under a capital-intensive farming system, and as a domestic worker who bears half a dozen children, prepares food from scratch, and forages continually for firewood.

Furthermore, in the global economy the so-called autonomy of individuals has disproportionately served the interests of Western women and men. Poor women who receive far less than a living wage for smocking children's clothes in the Philippines or assembling VCRs and CD players in Mexico keep our closets and entertainment centers full.[10] Furthermore, this "liberation" has allowed Western men cheap

8. Mehta, *Inside the Haveli*, p. 107.
9. Gita Sen, "Women Workers and the Green Revolution," in *Women and Development*, ed. Lourdes Beneria (New York: Praeger, 1982), pp. 1-28.
10. See, for example, *Women, Men, and the International Division of Labor*, ed.

access not only to labor for multinational corporations but also to the bodies of the world's poor women. Most of Bangkok's estimated 200,000 prostitutes come from its poorest provinces in the north and the northeast. As the region has been integrated into the international market, farmers have lost access to individualized forestry, crafts, and mining, all of which helped them remain solvent in hard times. The one regional product that commands a steady price in the global economy is young women's bodies. German businessmen can sample the "wares" of "sex tours" advertised in magazines with promotional copy like this: "Thailand is a world full of extremes and the possibilities are unlimited. Anything goes in this exotic country, especially when it comes to girls.... For the first time in history you can book a trip to Thailand with exotic pleasures included in the price."[11] Japanese and American businessmen have also responded in droves to buy the bodies of young Thai women who go to the cities to earn the cash their families need. What these girls experience is hardly a liberation for which most women would fight.

Finally, Geeta's view from the *haveli* shows the cost of autonomy to children and indirectly to women as well. It is when she watches her daughter thriving in the network of care that surrounds *haveli* children, those of owners and servants alike, that Geeta first begins to see the value of the institution. "Where else in the world would you find this kind of devotion?" she asks.[12] As Mehta's sociological essays make clear, the relationship of women and children changes dramatically when this carefully joined world splits apart. Upper-class professional women who work in cities must rely on servants with no long-standing relationship to the family. The more fortunate lower-class people who find regular employment in factories or households find that a new, high wall divides the once-integrated work of caring for children and supporting the family economically.

June Nash and Maria Patricia Fernandez-Kelly (Albany, N.Y.: SUNY Press, 1983); and *Daughters in Industry: Work Skills and Consciousness of Women Workers in Asia,* ed. Noeleen Heyzer (Kuala Lumpur: Asian and Pacific Development Center, 1988). A telling juxtaposition of the views of those who own the factories and those who work in them is found in the film titled *The Global Assembly Line.*

11. German Rosie Reisen (Rosie Travels) advertisement, cited by Pasuk Phongpaichit in "Bangkok Masseuses: Holding Up the Family Sky," *Southeast Asia Chronicle* 78 (1984): 15-23. Phongpaichit's complete study was published as *Rural Women of Thailand: From Peasant Girls to Bangkok Masseuses* (Geneva: ILO, 1981).

12. Mehta, *Inside the Haveli,* p. 107.

Mehta's work reflects a complex and ambivalent understanding of progress that is decidedly unfamiliar to modern, Western thought. Westerners like to think that the political and economic dislocations of the "Third World" are merely temporary setbacks on the road to progress. The wealth and power of the democratic West, seemingly confirmed by recent events in Eastern Europe, in fact reflect an optimistic, nineteenth-century view of progress. The Western ideal of "development" still assumes, as have both classical Marxist economics and liberal economics, that the rest of the world is simply on lower rungs of a historic ladder which it can progressively ascend until all have the wealth and well-being now enjoyed in the West. Even the long-standing international debt crisis with its harsh global impact seems hardly to have dented this optimistic perspective. If those "behind us" on the ladder are steadily climbing upward, there is no particular reason to look backward, except perhaps to lend a hand.

But in fact, global commerce and industry have made the lives of many far more difficult. It is the rare country in which the harsh impact of these social changes is only a short-term glitch on the way to the happy results enjoyed in leading capitalist countries. Moreover, two decades of research in the field known as "Women and Development" show that the economic "liberation" accompanying Western ideals of "freedom" has made life especially difficult for many women.[13] If feminist "autonomy" loses sight of the many ways in which human life is sustained, it will speak only for the fortunate few who not only can survive alone but also can survive and thrive — at least economically. For most of the world's women and men, "autonomy" means not "breaking the shackles which bind" but rather "having one's world come unglued." If we do not understand this, we may be tempted to interpret resistance to the Western feminist celebration of "autonomy" as antifeminist.

The solidarity that upper-class women in places such as Egypt, Turkey, and India feel with their Western feminist sisters has often been

13. Ester Boserup's classic exploration entitled *Women's Role in Economic Development* (London: George Allen & Unwin, 1970) spurred a wave of global research on the impact of development on women. A brief bibliography of this literature is found in "Women in Development: Courses and Curriculum Integration," *Women's Studies Quarterly* 24 (Fall/Winter 1986): 21-28. For a recent, more complete treatment, see Irene Tinker's *Persistent Inequalities: Women and World Development* (New York: Oxford University Press, 1990).

seen as a spillover of Western ideals. Ideals concerning the dignity of all people indeed fed earlier revolutions against colonial governments, and they continue to provide a foundation for many feminists abroad.[14] But it is also true that the concept and attainment of "autonomy" has best served societies' privileged. Elite women had a great deal to lose if they did not gain an autonomy that paralleled that of their husbands. Upper-class women in many pre-industrial societies had enjoyed a complementary power to that of their fathers, brothers, and husbands, despite restrictions on their sexuality and movement. But as modern political reorganization and commercial development moved power from domestic and kinship networks to bureaucratic, impersonal ones, elite women lost a great deal. Consequently, to regain their position of status and power these women had to break out of the now sharply constricted world of "home" and begin to move independently to participate in the wider societal activities that came to define status and power.

Nineteenth-century colonial officials thought that simply removing restrictions on women's movement and encouraging their education would lead all "native" women to the same liberation their Western sisters were beginning to enjoy. But the changes inaugurated by colonial governments, like those brought by modern industry, often undermined the kinds of power women once enjoyed. The switch to individualized land ownership, the fact that only men had access to technical knowledge, the movement of political and economic power away from kinship networks — all of these changes, however unintentionally, pushed women further from the mainstream of the society. What lower-class women lost often threatened their very lives, because these changes isolated them from the mainstream of income-generating resources and revived old images of women being burdens to their kin groups.

Western feminists have too often regarded the establishment of autonomy by upper-class women as the signal of the liberation of all women. Examples include Huda Sha'arwi, first among upper-class Egyptian women to throw off her veil, the millions of Turkish and Indian women well-established in professions, and liberal feminists pushing, like Betty Friedan, through "the feminine mystique" to careers outside the home. This autonomy is made possible and necessary by a particular

14. For a historical exploration of the interaction of feminism and nationalism in a number of different countries, see Kumari Jayawardena's *Feminism and Nationalism in the Third World* (London: Zed Books, 1986).

social organization, access to which has indeed been crucial for elite women. Yet the reorganization of society around industry based outside the home and government bureaucracies that bypass kinship networks has also brought to many women and men an unwelcome social isolation. Moreover, the "absolute freedom" of some has too often come at high cost to others, who for low pay not only do field and factory work but also do the cleaning, maintenance, and child care that allow elite men and women to "shape their own destinies."

Social Solidarity: Within the Family, with Women, and with Men

This "view from the bottom" has led us to reflect on the multiple meanings of autonomy. In addition, as we will see subsequently, women who are not white, middle class, and Western have different perspectives on social solidarity — within the family, with other women, and with men.

Solidarity within the Family

The several expressions of Western feminism are hardly united in their views about family life. Liberal feminists, concerned mainly for equality in work, politics, and law, have had little to say about the family until recently. Socialist, radical, and psychoanalytic feminists have offered different and sometimes complementary theories about the ways in which gender discrimination is rooted in family. To paint all feminists as "anti-family" is to overlook abusive realities within families, which feminists have rightly exposed. But feminist voices within other cultures have also complained about the Western feminist bias *against* family, a bias that oversimplifies reality and limits feminism's political appeal. If we are concerned with the defense of women and the development of healthy gender relations, we must listen to these voices.[15]

15. That some feminists have also been listening to Western critics can be seen in Judith Stacey's "Are Feminists Afraid to Leave Home? The Challenge of Conservative Pro-family Feminism," in *What Is Feminism? A Re-examination*, ed. Juliet Mitchell and Ann Oakley (New York: Pantheon Books, 1986), pp. 208-37; in comments in Linda Gordon's "Why Nineteenth-Century Feminists Did Not Support Birth Control and Twentieth-Century Feminists Do: Feminism, Reproduction and the Family," in *Rethinking the Family: Some Feminist Questions*, ed. Barrie Thorne and Marilyn Yalom (New York: Longman, 1982), pp. 40-54; and in Lesley Caldwell's

Black feminist bell hooks has continually tried to mediate between mainstream feminists and black women who feel alienated from feminism. Although she is convinced that feminist theory is politically essential, hooks minces no words in challenging the class-based distortions and ethnocentrism that muddy the thinking of white feminists. In her critique are included feminist perspectives on the family:

> Contemporary feminist analyses of family often implied that a successful feminist movement would either begin with or lead to the abolition of family. This suggestion was terribly threatening to many women, especially nonwhite women. While there are white women activists who may experience family primarily as an oppressive institution, (it may be the social structure wherein they have experienced grave abuse and exploitation) many black women find the family the least oppressive institution. Despite sexism in the context of family, we may experience dignity, self-worth, and a humanization that is not experienced in the outside world wherein we confront all forms of oppression. We know from our lived experiences that families are not just households composed of husband, wife, and children or even blood relations; we also know that destructive patterns generated by belief in sexism abound in varied family structures. We wish to affirm the primacy of family life because we know that family ties are the only sustained support system for exploited and oppressed peoples. We wish to rid family life of the abusive dimensions created by sexist oppression without devaluing it.[16]

Hooks's perception that the positive side of family is left out of white feminist analysis is echoed in many international critiques. Valerie Amos and Pratibha Parmar see Western feminism as practicing a theoretical imperialism that makes rejection of family synonymous with feminism.[17] Kum-Kum Bhavnani and Margaret Coulson show that an important feminist challenge for women of color in Great Britain is that of holding a family together in the face of racist immigration policies. They charge

---

review article entitled "Feminism and 'The Family,'" *Feminist Review* 16 (April 1984): 88-96.

16. hooks, *Feminist Theory: From Margin to Center* (Boston: South End Press, 1984), p. 37. It should be noted that bell hooks prefers to use only lower-case letters in the spelling of her name.

17. Amos and Parmar, "Challenging Imperial Feminism," *Feminist Review* 17 (July 1984): 3-19.

that "the state's practices in terms of the ideology of family unity are pretty contradictory in relation to black people."[18] Do white feminists, they ask, know what it is like to get a family of color together in Britain in the face of racist immigration laws? Judy Kimble and Elaine Unterhalter make a related point. Those who highlight the abuses of family life, they charge, seem to forget the pain inflicted on nonwhites in South Africa, where the destruction of "normal family life" (for example, by requiring black male miners to live and work away from their families) has been a central crime of successive governments committed to apartheid.[19]

To middle-class white women experiencing the changes resulting from the industrial and commercial revolutions, the family has often seemed the most visible barrier locking them out of the mainstream of society. For example, Zillah Eisenstein speaks of a "sex-class analysis," which she traces well back into the history of liberal feminist thought. This central feminist insight roots women's oppression in families, where women were made a subordinate class by the male control of reproduction. As far back as the mid-nineteenth century, liberal feminist Elizabeth Cady Stanton wrote,

> The influence the Catholic Church has had on religious free thought, that monarchies have had on political free thought, that serfdom has had upon free labor, have all been cumulative in the family upon women.... Taught that the fruits of her industry belonged to others, she has seen man enter into every avocation most suitable to her while she, the uncomplaining drudge of the household, condemned to the severest labor, has been systematically robbed of her earnings, which have gone to build up her master's power, and she has found herself in the condition of the slave, deprived of the results of her own labor.[20]

We readily admit that finding global evidence of the abuse of women in families — as in most social institutions — is not difficult. Nevertheless, making generalizations about the family based on its mod-

---

18. Bhavnani and Coulson, "Transforming Socialist Feminism: The Challenge of Racism," *Feminist Review* 23 (June 1986): 86.
    19. Kimble and Unterhalter, cited by Sheila Rowbotham in "What Do Women Want? Women-Centered Values and the World as It Is," *Feminist Review* 20 (June 1985): 49.
    20. Eisenstein, *The Radical Future of Liberal Feminism*, p. 158.

ern, middle-class, Western expression creates serious analytical distortions. The world in which Stanton began to write about the abuses of family life was one in which the "fruits of industry" belonged to individuals, not collectivities — a description that still applies today. It is also a world in which a wage economy devalues domestic work into "shadow support" behind the "real" work that yields cash. It is a middle-class world in which women are, in a quite individualistic sense, "separate." It is a very modern Western world in which the reproduction of life is marginalized from, or even seen as a hindrance to, the main task of producing things.

For many women around the world and even within our own society, the experience of family is quite different. First, the family, though often the site of *gender-based* oppression, may also be the site of resistance to *other* forms of oppression. Women of color may work together to decrease domestic violence but assert that "at the same time the black family is a source of support in the context of harassment and attacks from white people."[21] One of the recurring themes in a volume called *The Empire Strikes Back* is the way in which family has served in colonial and Western societies to shelter victims of racism and oppression. In the essay she contributed to this volume, Hazel Carby argues that "during slavery, periods of colonialism and under the present authoritarian state, the black family has been a site of political and cultural resistance to racism."[22] Another critic, Mina Davis Caulfield, has argued that non-Western people have good reason to see an attack on family as part of a larger strategy of "divide and rule" on the part of the dominant group.[23] Personal, kin-based networks provide an alternate base of power in the face of impersonal, bureaucratic, and seemingly totalitarian institutions.

Family networks also provide a base for resistance to the isolation of each individual worker in capitalist production. The shift from communal to individual ownership of land and the employment of uprooted laborers by plantations and factories have weakened kinship networks of mutual support. Yet it is through these networks that many people develop strategies for economic survival. While Western feminists focus

21. Bhavnani and Coulson, "Transforming Socialist Feminism," p. 88.
22. Carby, "White Woman Listen! Black Feminism and the Boundaries of Sisterhood," in *The Empire Strikes Back: Race and Racism in 70s Britain,* ed. by the Centre for Contemporary Cultural Studies (London: Hutchinson, 1982), p. 214.
23. Caulfield, "Imperialism, the Family, and Cultures of Resistance," *Socialist Revolution* 20 (October 1974): 67-85.

on the abuses of extended and nuclear family life, many non-Westerners, newly isolated in nuclear households, see more clearly the losses resulting from the breakup of family and work groups and are anxious to hang on to the remaining threads of these older networks.

Kinship networks are especially crucial for those trying to survive on the bottom of the society. Where do you sleep when the gas is turned off? Who helps your son find a job when he migrates to find waged labor in a city slum? The editors of the Indian journal *Manushi,* who focus on abuses that occur under the cover of "family," still acknowledge that "for the present, the family is the only source of social and emotional support available to most women in India."[24] Carol Stack's work on black communities demonstrates that "an extended cluster of kinsmen related chiefly through children but also through marriage and friendship" provides a crucial support network.[25] And networking is not limited to kinship links. To repeat an assertion quoted from bell hooks, marginalized people "know from [their] lived experiences that families are not just households composed of husband, wife, and children or even blood relations." Whoever helps you survive becomes "like family." Ties not just of kin but also of locality form the basis of such networks. In the Calcutta slums or the ghettos of New York, where biological and adoptive kinship help people survive against the odds, an analysis that sees the family only in terms of oppression is never likely to ring true.

Solidarity with Other Women

Historian Nancy Cott expressed one paradox of feminism in this way: "It aims for individual freedoms by mobilizing sex solidarity. It acknowledges diversity among women while positing that women recognize their unity. It requires gender consciousness for its basis, yet calls for the elimination of prescribed gender roles."[26] But Cott is writing about

---

24. Madhu Kishwar, introduction to *In Search of Answers: Indian Women's Voices from Manushi,* ed. Madhu Kishwar and Ruth Vanita (London: Zed Books, 1984).

25. Stack, "Sex Roles and Survival Strategies in an Urban Black Community," in *Woman, Culture and Society,* ed. Michelle Zimbalist Rosaldo and Louise Lamphere (Stanford: Stanford University Press, 1974), pp. 113-28; see also Nancy Tanner's "Matrifocality in Indonesia and Africa and among Black Americans," in *Woman, Culture and Society,* pp. 150-56.

26. Cott, "Feminist Theory and Feminist Movements: The Past before Us," in *What Is Feminism? A Re-examination,* p. 49.

Western feminists, for whom solidarity with other women had ceased to be a given and had to be re-created. By contrast, many women around the world grow up with an awareness of the powers of women and of their capacity to help each other in oppressive circumstances, as the following examples show.

Leila Ahmed makes this comment about Saudi Arabian women, who live in a sharply segregated female world:

> I have never seen in any other culture, including America, women whose self-perceptions were so singularly impervious to the assertions of the dominant ideology regarding their "natural" inferiority and "natural" subservience, and who clearly perceived that ideology as part of a system whose object is to legitimize, mystify, and further entrench those in power. . . . Arabian women . . . have from within that exclusively female space developed strengths and skills and analytical and imaginative resources that it would perhaps take centuries to develop again.[27]

Few white, Western women have known anything like this, as bell hooks noted when she began taking courses in women's studies at Stanford University in the 1970s. The white women in the classes found that being together and discussing women's issues was "an important, momentous occasion." Hooks, a black American woman, "had not known a life where women had not been together, where women had not helped, protected, and loved one another deeply."[28] In writing about black author Alice Walker, Diane Sadoff draws attention to the powerfully interconnected, affirming communities that women friends and relatives form across the generations within the larger black communities of which Walker writes.[29]

Within white Western social contexts, it was feminists, particularly radical feminists, who led in the crucial "rediscovery" of solidarity among women. What women in other cultures may take for granted had to be reborn in the West as feminists led the way in establishing shelters for abused women, quality child care for working mothers, and rape crisis

27. Ahmed, "Western Ethnocentrism and Perceptions of the Harem," *Feminist Studies* 8 (Fall 1982): 530-31.
28. hooks, *Feminist Theory*, p. 11.
29. Sadoff, "Black Matrilineage: The Case of Alice Walker and Zora Neale Hurston," *Signs* 11, no. 1 (1985): 5-12.

centers that took the victim's voice seriously. The isolation of white, Western women had to be unlearned in "consciousness-raising" sessions, where women spoke of concerns they had never discussed before in a group of women.[30] Our first point, then, is that modern white feminist theory has developed in a world where women's cross-generational experience with other women is minimal. And if solidarity with other women is discovered only in the context of feminist experience, it will have only a limited range of meanings.

A second point is that many black and Third World women seem less hesitant to embrace motherhood as part of their identity. This perspective highlights the dilemma of motherhood for middle-class Western women. In other societies, motherhood may indeed increase women's burdens, but it often gradually increases their authority too. In Western society, mothering means a dramatic and often permanent constriction in a woman's range of activities and a parallel rise in dependence. In modern industrial society, "home" offers women few of the economic options available in other societies. For example, the traditional Bedouin wife may appear powerless, but her contribution to the wealth and status of the household is recognized to be substantial, since she is the one who raises the children, organizes the weaving done by older girls inside the tent, and maintains social networks. Mothers in Western society find it very difficult to have their mothering recognized as "real work," and it is a rare thing for persons — male or female — to be able to care for their own children and maintain a mainstream career as well.

It is not surprising, then, that Western women have been ambivalent about motherhood. But to women in other societies, this has often seemed

---

30. Veena Das also makes the point that Western women must compete with each other in a way that Indian women do not: "The pattern of courtship in Western societies, which is relatively recent in their history, imposes severe strains on the relations between women, since they are set up in competition against each other. Even women as closely related as sisters are often seen in a relation of competition in popular English fiction. What is more, this serious division between women does not end at marriage, due to the entire cultural notion that the moral justification of a marriage lies in continued romantic interest between a man and a woman. This, coupled with the institution of monogamy, makes it imperative for a wife to ensure that her husband does not fall in love with a younger, or a more attractive girl" ("Indian Women: Work, Power, and Status," in *Indian Women: From Purdah to Modernity*, p. 145).

odd. Nigerian feminist Buchi Emecheta, whose novel entitled *The Joys of Motherhood* acknowledges the ambivalent nature of mothering, writes, "The Western woman should go back to re-learn how to be a woman, because at the moment she has so undervalued herself that she is groping in the dark."[31] In some settings mothering is still a source of considerable power. A woman political leader in Sierra Leone states, "We give birth to men so in a way we own them." African women have been able to use their importance as mothers and food producers to assert their interests, not only by using "pressure or coercion but also by praising the virtues and powers of motherhood and food production."[32]

By contrast, Indian sociologist Veena Das perceptively summarizes the central problems of gender relations in the West, where women have been segregated in a home that is isolated from the main currents of the society, "not on grounds of custom, but on grounds of efficiency and rationalization." Writes Das,

> The rigid segregation of roles between men and women and the decreasing participation of each in the roles of others; the pattern of courtship which divides women permanently from each other, are surely unique developments in human history. They go a long way in explaining the principal targets of attack by Western feminists: the isolation of women in the narrow world of domestic life and the use of women as primarily sex symbols.[33]

Solidarity with other women, combined with the different experience of mothering, creates a unique feminist understanding in other societies. Indeed, one African woman has commented, "The very language and style of the women's movement of the West is an admission of the women's belief that they are inferior to men."[34] Perhaps it is in reaction to the progressive marginalization and devaluation of women that the emphasis of white Western feminists on separation from men has come to seem pragmatically, if not philosophically, essential.

---

31. Emecheta, "Education — United States," *Women: A World Report* (New York: Oxford University Press, 1985), p. 218.

32. Filomina Chioma Steady, "The Black Woman Cross-Culturally: An Overview," in *The Black Woman Cross-Culturally,* ed. Filomina Chioma Steady (Cambridge, Mass.: Schenkman Publishing, 1981), p. 34.

33. Das, "Indian Women," p. 145.

34. Steady, "The Black Woman Cross-Culturally," p. 34.

Solidarity with Men

The crucial importance of family and community to many nonwhite women means that in their feminist theorizing they have shown a greater reluctance to identify men as "the enemy." As Chilla Bulbeck has noted, "for women of colour to leave the side of their men is to leave the side of an oppressed, as well as oppressive, group."[35] Black feminists do recognize the reality of black male sexism. But, in the words of bell hooks, "many of us do not believe we will combat sexism or woman-hating by attacking black men or responding to them in kind."[36] Another example of this differing perspective is illustrated in an incident related by Alice Walker, a situation in which a student asked her a question about how to express her feminist viewpoint and Walker responded frankly:

> Well, black and third-world women always seem connected to some man. Since I am a separatist, this means I can't work with them. What do you suggest I do?
>
> Personally, I'm not giving up Stevie Wonder and John Lennon, no matter what, I reply, but you should do whatever you want to do, which obviously is not to work with black and third-world women.[37]

Many black women, who experience the same humiliations their men face, do not feel the pressure that white women do to "catch up" with white men. More than this, black women know that in working against stiff odds to protect their community in a racist society, black men and women need each other. In like fashion, native North American women have searched for ways to confront domestic violence without further undermining the way their male partners feel about themselves.[38] Even black lesbians have hesitated to embrace the separatism advocated

35. Bulbeck, *One World Women's Movement* (London: Pluto Press, 1988), p. 85. This is also discussed by bell hooks in *Feminist Theory*, p. 69. See as well the essay by Bernice Johnson Reagon entitled "Coalition Politics: Turning the Century," in *Home Girls: A Black Feminist Anthology*, ed. Barbara Smith (New York: Kitchen Table/Women of Color Press, 1983), pp. 356-68.

36. hooks, *Feminist Theory*, p. 69.

37. Walker, "Breaking Chains and Encouraging Life," in *In Search of Our Mothers' Gardens*, ed. Alice Walker (New York: Harcourt Brace Jovanovich, 1984), p. 279.

38. Anecdotal information from work done by therapist Diane Marshall.

by some of their white feminist counterparts. One of their widely circulated documents puts it this way: "Although we are feminists and lesbians, we feel solidarity with progressive Black men and do not advocate the fractionalization that white women who are separatists demand. We struggle together with Black men against racism, while we also struggle with Black men about sexism."[39]

Thus an alliance with black men, who share with them the realities of racism, has seemed to black women far more trustworthy than an alliance with white, middle-class feminists, who often find it convenient to ignore the contrast between their own lives and the lives of those who clean their houses and care for their children. According to bell hooks, white women have identified all men as "oppressors" and all women as "oppressed" in order to press their case for "equality." But in reality, she claims, white women have not been interested in equality with working-class men (or women) of color, but rather in sharing the power of the "white supremacist, capitalist, patriarchal class."[40] In the process they have seemed not to notice that equality with men oppressed by present ghetto conditions was not the goal sought by black women. In the words of Bobby Sykes, a movement that could attract black women must "have built into it a means for the black community to gain *real* power and control and this must be available not only to black women but particularly to black men."[41]

The concern of bell hooks that feminist theory not alienate black women has led her to remind white feminists that many women want to be with men. Calls for separatism, she has argued, alienate women who support most of the feminist agenda but feel solidarity with men as well.

39. Combahee River Collective, "A Black Feminist Statement," p. 213.

40. hooks, "Racism and Feminism: The Issue of Accountability," in *Ain't I a Woman: Black Women and Feminism* (Boston: South End Press, 1981), pp. 119-58.

41. Sykes, cited by Christine Jennett in "The Feminist Enterprise," in *Three Worlds of Inequality: Race, Class and Gender,* ed. Christine Jennett and Randall G. Stewart (Melbourne: Macmillan, 1987), p. 369. The concern for solidarity with men who share the same race and class oppression echoes protests against "bourgeois feminism" by Marxists decades before. Theorist Alexandra Kollantai wrote that women of the proletariat "do not see men as the enemy or oppressor. For them, the men of the working class are comrades who share the same joyless existence, they are loyal fighters in the struggle for a better future. The same social conditions oppress both the women and their male comrades, the same chains of capitalism weigh on them and darken their lives" (from *Selected Writings of Alexandra Kollontai,* trans. Alix Holt [Westport, Conn.: Lawrence Hill & Co., 1977], pp. 51-52).

In her words, "Feminism will never appeal to a mass-based group of women in our society who are heterosexual if they think that they will be looked down upon or seen as doing something wrong." According to hooks, the blanket identification of men as the enemy has also alienated men who might have been the allies of feminism: "Had feminist activists called attention to the relationship between ruling class men and the vast majority of men, who are socialized to perpetuate and maintain sexism and sexist oppression even as they reap no life-affirming benefits, these men might have been motivated to examine the impact of sexism in their lives."[42]

Feminist theory is now coming to terms with the fact that solidarity with men is a given for most women. Radical feminism has offered women unity with other women, but Western feminism in general has been less successful in proposing a vision toward which men and women can struggle together. Third World women and black women in particular are looking for such a vision, one that embraces men in the context of a common cultural tradition.

Emancipation from Tradition

So far we have examined how black American and international feminists have challenged Western feminist perspectives on autonomy and on social solidarity within the family, with other women, and with men. We now consider how black and international feminists have protested ill-informed attacks on their cultural traditions, attacks that have often verged on a blindness to their cultures' very existence. White feminist theory has had a strong tendency to universalize from the cultural experience of Western women. Where does this arrogant universalizing leave women of color? Alice Walker describes the way in which white feminist language participates in the cultural dominance so sharply criticized in its male form:

> It is, apparently, inconvenient, if not downright mind straining, for white women scholars to think of black women as women, perhaps because "women" (like "man" among white males) is a name they are claiming for themselves, and themselves alone. Racism decrees that if they are now women (years ago they were ladies, but fashions change)

42. hooks, *Feminist Theory*, p. 75.

89

then black women must, perforce, be something else. (While they were "ladies" black women could be "women" and so on.)[43]

A subgroup of Western feminists have in fact seriously studied non-Western cultures, albeit with their own presuppositions and agendas.[44] But to many nonwhite feminists, the Enlightenment and socialist roots of Western feminist discourse seem to imply that if women are to enjoy full human autonomy, traditional cultures must be "overcome." It is true that the societies in which women enjoy the greatest measure of freedom, education, and comfort are white, individualistic Western cultures. The roots of this lie to a large extent in the global economic privilege of the West. But Western feminists have often assumed that their own liberation has resulted from a Western individualism that required people to shed "traditional" cultural constraints. The question then becomes this: If feminism celebrates, or is even predicated on, dismantling cultural and social traditions apparently rooted in patriarchy, can a non-Westerner be a feminist?

The complaint inherent in this question arises in its simplest form because Western feminists have looked too superficially among world cultures for evidence of women's oppression. They have not expected to find and thus rarely have found evidence of strength and wisdom in nonwhite women. For example, in an open letter to Mary Daly, black feminist Audre Lorde asks why Daly, in her book entitled *Gyn/Ecology*, never explores old African cultural expressions of female power. Instead,

43. Walker, "One Child of One's Own: A Meaningful Digression within the Work(s)," in *The Writer on Her Work,* ed. Janet Sternburg (New York: W. W. Norton, 1980), pp. 133-34. Trinh T. Minh-ha echoes Walker, commenting, "*Wo-* appended to *man* in existing contexts is not unlike *Third World, Third, Minority* or *Colour* affixed to *Woman* in pseudo-feminist contexts. Yearning for universality, the generic *woman,* like its counterpart, the generic *man,* tends to efface difference within itself" (from her article entitled "Difference: 'A Special Third World Women Issue,'" *Feminist Review* 25 [March 1987]: 16).

44. Two classics of Western feminist explorations in the 1970s are *Woman, Culture and Society,* ed. Michelle Zimbalist Rosaldo and Louise Lamphere (Stanford: Stanford University Press, 1974); and *Toward an Anthropology of Women,* ed. Rayna Reiter (New York: Monthly Review Press, 1975). Much of the sophisticated and seminal work in these volumes springs from a search for a universal root of patriarchy. While these cross-cultural explorations generated insights that are still important to feminist thought, critics have since shown how the Western political and intellectual agenda that motivated the work hid other crucial realities.

90

Daly introduces non-European women "as victims and preyers upon each other." Lorde explains her response to Daly's focus:

> I began to feel my history and my mythic background distorted by the absence of any images of my foremothers in power. Your inclusion of African genital mutilation was an important and necessary piece in any consideration of female ecology, and too little has been written about it. But to imply, however, that all women suffer the same oppression simply because we are women, is to lose sight of the many varied tools of patriarchy. It is to ignore how those tools are used by women without awareness against each other.

Lorde challenges Daly not "to deny the fountain of non-European female strength and power that nurtures each of our visions," and to enrich her own understandings with "the old traditions of power and strength and nurturance found in the female bonding of African women."[45] Echoing these sentiments, a Latina feminist wonders why there is such a ready acceptance of "the very male view of Latin American culture as consisting simply of macho males and Catholic priests?" Why do feminists continue to ignore the "scores of strong women" in Latin American history and society?[46] This complaint emerges because liberal, socialist, and even radical feminists all share the Enlightenment assumption that the good life results only when individuals are freed from the weights of social tradition, religious superstition, and unjust laws. As Hazel Carby puts it,

> The "feminist" version of this ideology presents Asian women as being in need of liberation, not in terms of their own herstory and needs, but *into* the "progressive" social mores and customs of the metropolitan West. The actual struggles that Asian women are involved in are ignored in favour of applying theories from the point of view of a more "advanced," more "progressive" outside observer.[47]

Thus Western feminists have often assumed that if women are to enjoy full human autonomy, their cultures will necessarily become increasingly

---

45. Lorde, "An Open Letter to Mary Daly," in *Sister Outsider* (Trumansburg, N.Y.: The Crossing Press, 1984), pp. 66-71.
46. Moschkovich, " — But I Know You, American Woman," in *This Bridge Called My Back*, p. 82.
47. Carby, "White Woman Listen!" p. 216.

Western. Judit Moschkovich, a Jewish, Latin American immigrant, voices her angry response to such assumptions:

> My Latin culture means many things to me: the food I like to eat, the music I love, . . . how I am used to kissing and hugging people when I greet them, etc., etc., etc. . . . I could go on forever. It also means the things I'd like to change in Latin culture and I'm not speaking of changing men, but of changing *systems* of oppression. As a result of these changes I do not forsee a culture-less vacuum because "all cultures are bad so I don't want any of them." That culture-less vacuum proposed would actually be the American culture of French Fries and Hamburgers (or soyburgers), American music on the radio (even if it's American women's music on a feminist radio show), not kissing and hugging every time you greet someone, etc. And it would ultimately still be the culture of exploitation of other countries/cultures combined with ignorance about them.[48]

Western culture thus produces a profound ambivalence in many people from other cultures. In the wake of colonial rule, non-Westerners have often fought hard to recover a strong pride in their own cultural heritage. Certainly throughout history various cultures have adapted in the process of interaction with other cultures. But borrowing from the Western heritage is at best a mixed blessing for non-Western women. It is true that Pakistani women lawyers who are working to protect the eroding public rights of women owe a debt to the Enlightenment and the British Raj. And Korean women at the university must trace their educational opportunities to the efforts of Western Christian missionaries. Still, these liberating privileges came mixed together with colonial political rule and economic exploitation, both of which either undermined or fossilized traditional cultures. As colonial governments put their economic, political, and military force behind certain social groups, the interests of local ruling elites turned from traditional, reciprocal relations within their society toward an alliance with their European overlords. In this context, "tradition" often lost its historic fluidity, because both allies and critics of the Europeans used an ossified understanding of "tradition" as a weapon in their power struggle. Reclaiming a fuller understanding of their own traditions has thus been a primary concern of formerly colonized peoples.

48. Moschkovich, " — But I Know You, American Woman," p. 80.

This project has been doubly complicated for women. Women in non-Western cultures are facing the social dislocations that Western women first experienced with industrialization and the expansion of international markets. Yet women are still identified with "traditional" cultural values symbolized by "home." If conservative anti-feminist rhetoric in the West plays on our hunger for a "haven in a heartless world," what is the double burden of non-Western, recently colonized women? An Algerian novelist describes the plight thus:

> The woman, traditionally the guardian of the past, became (increasingly) passive in her role. The Algerian man, at this time, was colonized in the street, in his work, obliged to speak a language that was not his own outside. [H]e found his real life at home, in his house, with his wife. The house was still the sacred place, which the foreigner never entered.[49]

Thus those concerned with the defense of women in a neo-colonized world must be sensitive to "the issue of remaining loyal to one's culture, of, although 'modern' and 'European' in one's outlook, not betraying one's society's (and one's own) cultural identity."[50]

The struggle of non-Western women is, in summary, to retain roots and identity within their own cultures while confronting oppressive patriarchy and looking for women's "cultures of resistance" within it. When Leila Ahmed and Veena Das attempt to show Westerners the powers of women in their cultural traditions, they are not interested in romanticizing "traditional" culture. First of all, both know that their cultural traditions are not static but are instead rich and complex historical realities that have adapted to all sorts of change over the centuries. Incorporating feminist understandings from the West in the Middle East or India is simply a continuation of the centuries-old practice of borrowing from whatever has flowed through these great civilizations. "Traditionalism" may be a current social force to be reckoned with, but these traditions have proven their flexibility.

Second, those confronting the oppression of women around the world share the feminist goal of redressing the balance of power be-

49. Cited by Ahmed in "Feminism and Feminist Movements in the Middle East—A Preliminary Exploration: Turkey, Egypt, Algeria, People's Democratic Republic of Yemen," *Women's Studies International Forum* 5, no. 2 (1982): 164.
50. Ahmed, "Feminism and Feminist Movements in the Middle East," p. 162.

tween men and women. Although we have focused mainly on their areas of disagreement with Western feminist theory, their areas of common concern are also important. They may not face the same problems that Western women face in rampant pornography, the social devaluation of mothering, and a skyrocketing incidence of rape. But women around the world face their own demons in "machismo" culture in Latin America, the excruciating choice between an unwanted marriage and social isolation, and in the fact that a bright young girl is less likely to be sent to school than her less competent brother. Non-Western feminists confront these issues within the terms of their respective cultures. As Westerners come to understand these perspectives, they may even have to ask if, in attacking Western traditional religion, feminists threw out not only patriarchy but also social and cultural resources that might have been used against it.

The Decentering of Feminism

We have seen how the international feminist dialogue has challenged the terms of Western feminism. Gradually a significant question has begun to emerge: Has feminism, which has understood itself to be the voice of all suffering women, unconsciously created its own hegemonic voice that has excluded realities crucial to many women? Many white feminists have begun to acknowledge that their analysis presumed a woman who was white, Western, and privileged. And Western feminism has indeed had a head start in dealing with gender issues that face the economically privileged in the context of modern industrial societies. Feminist scholarship in the West has provided new tools for understanding the way that gender relations operate. But bedrock feminist understandings no longer seem so clear or so simple.

French feminism, historically more comfortable with accepting differences between men and women, has given birth to a feminist theory that takes difference as its starting point. French "deconstructionist" philosophers have attempted to analyze the ways in which the structure of all kinds of "discourses" are defined in the interest of those in power, and the ways in which challenges to the discourse are framed in the network of language. This postmodern philosophical tradition, in addition to the political challenges of international feminism, has contributed to a burgeoning feminist literature of deconstruction.

As we saw in Chapter Three, deconstructionism works to "keep us honest" and has made it possible to embrace crucial elements of the cross-cultural feminist critique. There is a growing sensitivity to the ways in which Western feminist discourse has been "hegemonic," ignoring differences of race and class. Feminism is also coming to terms with the ongoing agency of women in social networks, as opposed to the merely passive victimization of women. Like radical feminism, deconstructionism has created a "safe place" in which to explore difference. Radical feminism depends on a philosophical or pragmatic separatism from men so that women are protected from attempts to co-opt women-defined differences into oppressive patriarchal ideology. Deconstructionism, in a backhanded undercutting of gender differentiation, so insistently embraces diversity in a phenomenological exploration of the women's experience that generalization is impossible.

The Advantage: A New Humility

This shaking of confidence in received feminist understandings has brought a much-needed breeze of humility into recent feminist scholarship. In the past, many have found the "missionary" character of Western feminism unattractive. But the pitfalls of being a feminist "missionary" should be understandable to Christians. Feminists, like Christians, believe that they have a crucial understanding of truth which needs to be heard. Without this truth, people suffer and sometimes die. And so, in an alien environment that is hostile to this truth in some ways, the missionary — whether feminist, Christian, or both — speaks out. But certain modes of speaking make listening difficult. An Egyptian Christian once suggested that much of Christian mission in his country had at one time looked like this:

> Christians huddle together in a fortress castle. Outside, they see the surrounding hordes. Their main work is to protect themselves, and also preach as much as possible. A few brave souls go outside, find a disgruntled member of the local society and draw him inside the castle walls. He tells the Christians about his awful life on the outside, and how wonderful it feels to be inside. His story confirms the Christians' perspective, and makes them feel so good that they bestow a halo on him, and surround him with a warm glow which makes him break all

ties with the outside which might have created a bridge between two understandings of reality.[51]

Feminists have often been as certain of their truth as Christians have been of theirs. And each group has welcomed like-minded converts inside its fortress. Purity has thus been protected, and the message has been made immune to most outside influences. Feminists, like Christians, have seen themselves committed to a life-preserving truth and thus have often listened little while speaking courageously. Just how those who refused the message heard it or evaluated it was seldom known. Corked tightly in too small a bottle, grains of truth fermented into untruth.

Just as local churches in areas previously dominated by missionaries have brought new perspectives on Christianity, so the lively currents of international feminist debate have "uncorked" Western feminism. With the Western ideological grip thus loosened, a far wider range of data is finding its way into feminist analysis. In recent years, both class and cultural differences among women have figured more prominently in feminist theorizing. Black and international feminists have highlighted blind spots in Western (as well as in non-Western) societies.

Many Western women have opposed the feminist movement or regularly prefaced quite feminist remarks with the comment "I'm not a feminist, but. . . ." These reactions, in addition to more than a decade of cross-cultural dialogue, have made an increasing number of feminists ready to consider the experiences of a wider range of women and men rather than assuming the problem is in the ear of the listener. It is now clear, for example, that it was not just working-class women's ignorance which kept them from embracing feminism but also partly the fact that their life experiences were not taken into account by middle-class feminist analyses. The privileged are likely to find exciting work and good care for their children. The less privileged are likely to find tedious work at low pay and child care of minimal quality. Feminist theory must take into account both realities.

Cross-cultural perspectives have also highlighted the particular gender problems that Westerners face. Women suffer most harshly when they are in families isolated from larger social networks, when they are distanced from productive resources, when domestic work is devalued,

51. This image was drawn by an Egyptian Christian at the Lausanne II Congress held in Manila in 1989.

and when they lack access to bureaucratized institutions of power. Accordingly, if the daughters of the socially privileged groups are to have any of the power and status guaranteed earlier through channels such as kinship, they must have access to the individual skills and mobility necessary to success in industrial society. But if the daughters of the less privileged, whose husbands must now find work away from the fields and the activities of the household, are simply to do what most women have always had to do — support and care for their children — they too must have access to paid employment outside the home and help with their children.

It has also become clear that, in some ways, "the feminine" has been uniquely devalued in modern Western society. The work of women has been marginalized, alienated from community networks, and not even counted as part of the gross national product of industrialized nations.[52] Mothering in our society pushes women toward painful choices without the empowerment that accompanied it at other times and in other places. At the same time, our definitions of manhood have been narrowed to exclude care for others, the love of poetry, or the communal storytelling celebrated as ideals of masculinity in other cultures. Our gender relations are shaped by narrrowed, degrading media images of women as sex objects and of men as distant, powerful earners or (in times of conflict) as expendable warriors. Much of Western life precludes opportunities for ongoing, face-to-face relationships between real men and women who are both weak *and* strong.

White feminists have taken the centrality of gender oppression as its starting point. But feminists of color have challenged white feminists to rethink the central categories of feminist theory "from margin to center," making plain the ways in which race and class hierarchies interact with those of gender.[53] This perspective clearly challenges the interests of many white women, for feminists of color are not looking for a token acknowledgment of race or a confession of individual preju-

---

52. Marilyn Waring, *If Women Counted: A New Feminist Economics* (San Francisco: Harper & Row, 1989).

53. The phrase is taken from the title of bell hooks's book entitled *Feminist Theory: From Margin to Center*. To sample the voluminous literature in which women of color articulate their concerns, Western feminists attempt to incorporate these concerns, and non-Westerners respond, see Chilla Bulbeck's *One World Women's Movement* and essays by Dorothy Broom, Helen Hill, and Christine Jennett in *Three Worlds of Inequality: Race, Class and Gender*.

dice. As feminists should know from their study of gender, the essential issue of racism is *not* individual prejudice but institutional domination.[54]

Feminist journals provide evidence that Western — particularly American — theoretical hegemony is becoming a thing of the past. Growing numbers of Arab women are studying their own societies. Aboriginal women of Australia and slum organizers from Nicaragua are getting their life stories into print. Historical currents of European "relational" feminism, previously dismissed as irrelevant, are being retrieved and discussed. All of this exciting new data suddenly makes the entire feminist project much more complicated. What, if anything, is common in the oppression of women? How do we understand the relationship between what women say they want and what is "good for them"? How are we to view family structures and cultural traditions that sustain patriarchy but are nevertheless valued by women? If the freedom of the individual from all external, "traditional" constraints is *not* to define the feminist agenda, what will?

To put it more bluntly, if all ideas about universal justice and humanity are dismissed as part of a hegemonic, masculinist, Enlightenment project, and if all traditions and forms of gender relations are equally embraced, against what — if any — common standard can feminist claims be judged? To pursue an earlier analogy, if the missionaries inside the fortress lose the conviction that they have any truth worth telling, any injustice worth battling, what is to keep them from simply opening the gates, changing their clothes, and taking in the local sights? This leads us to a consideration of the *disadvantage* inherent in the deconstructionist and international feminist projects, a disadvantage we have already noted briefly in Chapter Three.

The Disadvantage: Loss of Moral Grounding for the Feminist Project

We have said that a decrease in Western and particularly American ethnocentrism is crucial to the development of feminist theory. But the end point for which feminists around the world strive is *not* merely a celebration of quaint differences in gender relations. Women's lives are restricted, their work devalued, their ways of expressing themselves

---

54. See bell hooks's *Talking Back: Thinking Feminist, Thinking Black* (Boston: South End Press, 1989), p. 119.

trivialized, their activities marginalized. The mistreatment of women can even be life-threatening. The goal of feminist theory must be to identify the sources of this oppression so that it can be challenged and dismantled. The biases of class, race, and culture of white Western feminist theory have sometimes led to theory that does not ring true in other contexts and thus is not politically compelling. But if the needed correctives to this feminist ethnocentrism occur in the absence of a common moral grounding, the entire feminist project is on shaky ground.

The growing respectability of feminist scholarship has created a veritable industry of deconstructionism. The deconstructionists are like a team of lumberjacks set loose with buzz saws who see all trees as fair candidates for felling. With no remaining moral map of the forest, even the Enlightenment assumptions beneath the Western feminist agenda are bared to the blade. Indeed, Marxist critiques have highlighted this hazard. Writing in *New Left Review,* Sabina Lovibond gave this pointed critique of deconstructionism:

> What, then, are we to make of suggestions that the project has run out of steam and that the moment has passed for remaking society on rational, egalitarian lines? It would be only natural for anyone placed at the sharp end of one or more of the existing power structures (gender, race, capitalist class . . .) to feel a pang of disappointment at this news. But wouldn't it also be in order to feel *suspicion?* How can anyone ask me to say goodbye to "emancipatory metanarratives" when my own emancipation is still such a patchy, hit-and-miss affair?[55]

This concern is echoed by Nancy Hartsock, who ponders why it is that "just when we are talking about the changes we want, ideas of progress and the possibility of systemically and rationally organizing human society become dubious and suspect."[56] The relativizing of all moral truth — a logical end point of the deconstructionist project — simply is not in the interest of anyone committed to the defense of women.

55. Lovibond, "Feminism and Postmodernism," *New Left Review,* November/December 1989, p. 12. We are indebted to philosopher Carol Pass for acquainting us with philosophical and feminist deconstructionism and its critics. See also Elizabeth Fox-Genovese's *Feminism without Illusions: A Critique of Individualism* (Chapel Hill: University of North Carolina Press, 1991).

56. Hartsock, "Foucault on Power: A Theory for Women?" in *Feminism and Postmodernism,* ed. Linda Nicholson (London: Routledge & Kegan Paul, 1990), pp. 163-64.

International feminists, like deconstructionists, have challenged the boundaries of Western feminist understandings. But they have their own reasons for resisting the full implications of the deconstructionist project. Many women around the world have only begun to face cultural patriarchy in their traditions, all the while wrestling with the problems created for women by modern industrial society. In this setting, a consistent feminist ethic is crucial. For example, while Turkish feminist Marnia Lazreg attacks Western feminist ethnocentrism, she also quarrels with the relativism that undercuts any moral grounding for the feminist. If all differences are to be embraced and tolerated, she asks, how is injustice to be identified? "The rejection of humanism and its universalistic character in discourse analysis and deconstruction deprives the proponents of difference of any basis for understanding the relationship between the varieties of modes of being different in the world. Difference becomes essentialized."[57]

Complete moral relativism can never be a place of comfort for a feminist. We are involved not in mere intellectual parrying but in working to protect real women. "Survival," in Audre Lorde's words, "is not an academic skill."[58] The world's privileged may be able to toy with puzzles of the symbolic order, but the problems facing most of the world's women demand more concrete solutions. In the end, the driving force behind feminism has been a concern with the injustices that hurt women in society. By contrast, deconstructionism, in its extreme form, allows the focus to shift to an analysis of the symbolic order that does not even require listening to the voices of flesh-and-blood women. When this infatuation with verbal games has passed, what will motivate the feminist project? Surely this is an issue about which Christian feminists should have something to say.

A Christian Perspective on Difference

Women of color have pressed Western feminists toward an understanding of gender relations that offers no easy solutions — not faith in the

57. Lazreg, "Feminism and Difference: The Perils of Writing as a Woman on Women in Algeria," *Feminist Studies* 14 (Spring 1988): 97.
58. Lorde, "The Master's Tools Will Never Dismantle the Master's House," in *This Bridge Called My Back*, p. 99.

virtues of autonomy, or in a private "women's world," or in a social overhaul that destroys valued traditions and kinship networks. But even as we admit the complexity of the problem, we have seen that it is not enough simply to "celebrate diversity." *Some* traditions and *some* kinship structures promote injustice and require challenge. Living with diversity, particularly if one has strong convictions about justice, is thus a complex, taxing project, both personally and socially.

The world has seen as much interreligious and interethnic strife as it has tolerant plurality. Must we then choose between a humility that allows cross-cultural perspectives to challenge received notions and a commitment to whatever universal truth is needed to confront injustice? Deconstructionism seems to poise feminism on the edge of a relativistic humility that may undercut the entire feminist project. At the other end of the spectrum are many Christians, quite comfortable with the notion of absolute truth, who have waged war to protect versions of truth later unmasked as self-interest. Can Christianity provide the universal ethical grounding from which to judged the myriad forms of gender injustice in all cultures and societies, including our own? As Christians, we are confident of God's truth as revealed in Christ. As Christian feminists, we are also aware of the ways in which Christian tradition has been used to defend slavery and apartheid, to promote war and imprison women. The shift of Christianity's demographic and moral center away from the West to Africa, Latin America, and Asia offers a far richer prism through which to see Christian truth. With Christians from around the world, we find the grounding for our feminist project in the powerful vision of *shalom,* in which God acts to restore the beauty, peace, and justice of the creation.

As Christians, we understand that both men and women are created in God's image, and that both are the subjects of redemption history. Thus men and women are fundamentally equal. Yet the Creator, whose appreciation of diversity vibrates throughout creation, made both men and women as human beings embodied differently and thus bound to experience the creation in certain unique ways. Accordingly, equality and diversity are at the heart of creation, and at the center of the human community.

But with the entry of sin into the world, differences were no longer simply an expression of God's creativity and the basis for human mutuality. Since the Fall, difference has become the foundation on which we have built prejudice, discrimination, and oppression. Differences between men and women have served as a basis for discrimination, as have differences between married and single people, between peach and olive people, between cultures that celebrate with drums and those that celebrate with flutes. Instead of building an imaginative playground on the foundation of difference, human beings have erected the structures of power over others.

The ongoing misuse of difference to harm some groups and concentrate power in the hands of others gives feminists a realistic reason to be wary of *any* discussion of difference. American feminists in particular have expressed an understandable fear and anger when discussions of the differences between men and women have arisen in any context besides the "safe places" created by radical and deconstructionist feminism. There is good reason to fear any emphasis on difference which rigidly compartmentalizes women from men, for

> the very theme of difference, whatever the differences are represented to be, is useful to the oppressing group. . . . Any allegedly natural feature attributed to an oppressed group is used to imprison this group within the boundaries of a Nature which, since the group is oppressed, ideological confusion labels "nature of oppressed person." . . . To demand the right to Difference without analysing its social character is to give back the enemy an effective weapon.[59]

Alice Walker, who has confronted this weapon of "difference" in its forms of gender, class, and race, points out, "Man [*sic*], like all the other animals, fears and is repelled by that which he does not understand, and mere difference is apt to connote something malign."[60] We therefore walk a very tricky tightrope in attempting to call attention to difference without laying the groundwork for future discrimination.[61] For example, can we argue for any special considerations for women who carry heavier child-care burdens without undercutting the insistence that men and women together are responsible for raising the next generation? Is it possible, in other words, to embrace the possibility of differences between men and women without these differences becoming deficits?

59. Trinh, "Difference," p. 18.
60. Walker, "What White Publishers Won't Print," in *I Love Myself When I Am Laughing—A Zora Neale Hurston Reader*, ed. Alice Walker (New York: Feminist Press, 1979), p. 169.
61. This dangerous tightrope is very much in evidence in Elizabeth H. Wolgast's *Equality and the Rights of Women* (Ithaca: Cornell University Press, 1980).

Whatever the hazards, we cannot address the issues before us without cautiously embracing the discussion of difference again in some new form. Arguments based on the sameness of men and women can take us only so far toward just gender relations. Individualistic solutions, as we have seen again and again, are likely to work well only for the privileged. They cannot unravel the complexities of gender, for in the end gender is not about individual men and women but about the differences that emerge when men and women are *in relationship* in human communities. To understand and attempt to correct the injustices of gender relations, we must explore the dynamics of men and women in relationship with each other.

By the same token, utopian social visions that suppress the problem of ongoing gender relations cannot provide us with the map we need. Both the biblical drama and the wisdom of those rooted in older cultures remind us that, like death and taxes, problems in gender relations are with us for the long haul. As Christians we set before us a vision of kingdom *shalom*, but we are also realistic, recognizing that working toward healthy gender relations will always be just that: work. As historian Joan Scott has wisely noted, "Power is constructed on and so must be challenged from the ground of difference."[62] Our strategy must begin with a realization that difference, in one form or another, is here to stay. And difference will always be a potential rationalization for discrimination.

When we are willing to explore the differences that emerge in relationships between men and women in community, we create both possibilities and dangers. Legal scholar Martha Minow, in analyzing the "difference dilemma"[63] in bilingual education, suggests some of the quandaries that arise when gender theorizing acknowledges difference. First, she points out that those in power are best placed to ignore difference. Because of the privileges they enjoy, they are not likely to "see"

62. Scott, "Deconstructing Equality-versus-Difference: or, The Uses of Post-structuralist Theory for Feminism," *Feminist Studies* 14 (Spring 1988): 33-50.

63. Minow, "Learning to Live with the Dilemma of Difference: Bilingual and Special Education," *Law and Contemporary Problems* 48, no. 2 (1984): 157-211. Joan Scott first used Minow's perspective to explore the ways in which arguments offered by historians Alice Kessler-Harris and Rosalind Rosenberg were used in the sex discrimination suit brought against Sears in 1979. See Scott's essay entitled "Deconstructing Equality-versus-Difference," pp. 33-50. Related questions are explored by Paul Marshall in "Individualism, Groups and the Charter," unpublished manuscript, Institute for Christian Studies, Toronto, 1987.

the differences that are obvious to the less privileged. Those who speak the dominant language may be totally unaware that some of their hearers are struggling to understand. So too, feminist theory shaped by privileged women long ignored issues of class and race. When black feminists began to write, they called attention to social dynamics that were obvious to them but that had been invisible to white feminists. By ignoring differences that are obvious from the bottom, dominant groups retain a faulty sense of their own neutrality.

But if focusing on difference can unmask a hierarchy in which one group subordinates another, it can also serve, in Minow's words, to "underscore the stigma of deviance." Highlighting difference, like ignoring it, can contribute to the perpetuation of hierarchy. Where women are not assimilated into a male-defined world, they may be ghettoized in a woman's world. Women, like ethnic minorities, must indeed come together to develop some sense of independent identity apart from that assigned to them by the dominant group. But if either women or ethnic groups struggle toward self-definition only in their own ghettos, they may continue to be stigmatized as inferior and will thus be unable to confront intergroup misunderstandings.

This tension is the heritage of a fallen creation in which differences in gender and in race, initially part of the creation celebration, now serve as the basis for hierarchies that preserve the privileges of some while dehumanizing others. Difference and equality were never intended to be at opposite poles. The multiplicity of cultures around the world bears testimony to the creativity of people made in the image of God. Different cultures have at times peacefully coexisted, trading goods and cross-fertilizing each other with new ideas and technological innovations. But just as often cultures specializing in the arts of war have crushed cultures specializing in the arts of peace. On the basis of differences have been erected the hierarchies of slavery, gender, class, and caste.

A Christian perspective requires us to resist the use of difference as a basis for hierarchy. It also requires us to recognize our own participation in any group which, by its dominant position in the social order, is unlikely to "see" and value the rich creational diversity in the human community. In an urban culture, for example, city dwellers are apt to ignore the concerns of rural life. Where families dominate, the perspectives of single people may go unheard. Where youth is king, the voices of the old may have no value. As Christians, part of our work in the human community is to see, celebrate, and create space for the diversity of human life. And this requires renouncing the use of difference to consolidate power for ourselves and the groups to which we may belong. When we use difference — whether on the basis of locality, kinship, gender, ethnicity, or religion — as a grounds to exalt "mine" over "yours," we are not moving toward the kingdom of God but supporting the discriminatory practices of a fallen world.

In the Western historical setting, the problems of negotiating gender differences are complicated by both the structure and the scale of our social institutions. Work and home life are often separated by major physical and cultural distances. Cultural stereotypes about gender are writ large in the media. As a result, while individual Western women have far more choices than most women around the world, they are denied the opportunity to negotiate the subtleties of gender differences. It is hard for Westerners to balance, according to the needs of various situations, playful accentuation of such differences with a careful muting of them. Instead, both the emphasis of differences and the denial of them are writ large and unyielding in law and public rhetoric, and both extremes tend to ossify the situation as often as they clarify it.

But however risky it is, we seem to have no choice but to acknowledge the existence of gender differences while continually keeping in mind that their meanings are shaped by particular social contexts. And as we begin to make room for arguments that acknowledge difference, a crucial perspective will be that of poor women. Historically, the upper classes have emphasized differences between men and women as an indicator of "conspicuous leisure." Removing women from manual work in the fields and elaborating the rituals of domesticity have served as indicators of social status. In return for enjoying such comforts, women have often accepted limitations on their mobility and an exaggeration of their weakness and dependence. By contrast, in settings where every person is crucial to survival, differences are more likely to highlight the strengths of *both* men and women rather than exaggerate a falsely ascribed weakness in women.

Toward a Christian Feminist Vision
That Embraces Women and Men

In a sense, the wide circle of feminist thought in the last centuries has brought us full cycle. As we saw in Chapter Two, early feminist discussions assumed some differences between men and women. Although this voice has continued to be heard, it has been muted in the second wave of feminist theory, which we outlined in Chapter Three. But a renewed emphasis on difference in recent Western feminist discourse has combined with the international feminist insistence that women's issues be discussed in the context of larger community concerns. These two movements have brought feminism back to a focus on gender relations. This is both a heartening and a frightening development.

It is heartening because the goal of feminism at its best has always been a better human community, not just a defense of women. We grant that focus on women as individuals and on women without men has contributed to the clarity and vitality of Western feminist theorizing. It is easier to name injustice as injustice when one is limited neither by a dependence on nor a love for the oppressor. But as Christians we cannot stop with either individualistic solutions that work only for privileged women or radical solutions that settle for the empowerment of women in communities completely without men.

Feminists have gained something in theoretical clarity by focusing on oppression without attending to gender relationships. But this again has often been offset by a lack of attention to the deep value most people place on relationships across gender lines. Women of color have reminded white feminists that only a minority of people are willing to suspend the agenda of harmonious relations between the sexes until justice is achieved for women. And the recognition of this old truth has led to renewed scholarship on neglected European feminists, who rejected the individualistic currents of Anglo-American feminism and posited, within a relational feminist framework, quite radical agendas that had "an explicit acknowledgement of differences in women's and men's sexual functions in society (or, to use Catharine MacKinnon's apt phrase, the 'difference difference makes')."[64] Thus, while the accept-

64. Karen Offen, "Defining Feminism: A Comparative Historical Approach," *Signs* 14, no. 1 (1988): 139. Offen, for instance, argues that French feminism has characteristically resisted individualist feminist arguments because "sexual dimorphism was a fundamental ingredient of French social and political thought and the family — not the individual — continues to compose the core unit in their thinking. The structure of French society, as historian Louis Tilly notes, gave rise quite naturally to this perspective. According to Tilly, 'It was the family's continuing role as an economic productive unit for peasants and craftsmen, and its continuing role as economic resource for propertied and wage earning persons, that makes the family

ability of discussing "difference" in mainstream feminism may appear new, the discussion itself is in fact an important part of feminist history.

Yet the movement toward a more relational feminist understanding is also frightening. Historically, the most enduring defense of women has been the one that sees women as individuals, and some of the most trenchant abuses against women have been defended in the name of women's "unique calling." Thus the project of working out gender justice in the context of ongoing social relations with men, while acknowledging some difference between men and women, seems to be like stepping into a minefield, for as Christians we enter this minefield with a dual understanding. The new feminist emphasis on the dynamic of gender relations is consonant with our goal as Christians: to work toward harmonious relations between women and men. As Christians we know that God created men and women to be in relationship with one another in human society. Yet we have no romantic illusions about achieving fully healthy gender relations in a fallen world. Both ethnocentrism and the desire for a quick solution have sidetracked a thoroughgoing analysis. We welcome the increasingly careful, ongoing analysis of gender relations for the insights it can yield into what really happens between men and women in a fallen world.

But as Christians, we begin such explorations with the assumption that we will discover not only "difference" embraced as variety but also "difference" that can be marked as "right" or "wrong." Some things destroy individual life and violate the God-ordained vision of *shalom* in a community. These we do not hesitate to call sin. Yet we are aware that as human beings our understanding is limited by time, space, and our tendency to read even the Bible in a way that serves our own interests. Thus it is often difficult to see and even harder to work against evil that serves our own immediate interests. American feminists have needed those outside the culture to highlight the individualism and materialism inherent in much of our analysis. Likewise, white Christians "see" and fight all too little the racism of American society.

---

so central in understanding French social relations and French women's collective action'" (p. 145). Recent scholarship has taken a new look at the work of Swedish feminist Ellen Key. In "Motherhood at Center: Ellen Key's Social Vision" (*Women's Studies International Forum* 5 [1982]: 599-610), Cheri Register suggests that the misuse of an ideology of "motherhood" in Nazi Germany and Stalinist Russia has left Europeans "incapable of imagining a highly valued motherhood that is not simply expedient to patriarchy," thereby leading them to neglect or misinterpret the work of important early feminists.

It should not be surprising, then, to discover a feminist vision that embraces both men and women in community which is set forth not by the privileged but by the less privileged — by black "womanists." Both literary critic Chikwenye Okonjo Ogunyemi[65] and author Alice Walker have found in black women's culture a perspective that commits the "womanist" to the "survival and wholeness of entire people, male and female."[66] Black women's experience, whether in racist America or hungry Africa, requires black women not to tackle questions "limited to issues defined by their femaleness but . . . to tackle questions raised by their humanity."[67] Women who give and sustain life against the onslaughts of poverty and racism must release their full powers not only for the protection of women but also for the benefit of the community. Thus the "womanist" is marked by an audacity born of desperate realities. Alice Walker defines the womanist as one who, like the slave daughter and her mother, is ready to make this kind of statement: "'Mama, I'm walking to Canada and I'm taking you and a bunch of other slaves with me.' Reply: 'It wouldn't be the first time.'"[68] A womanist celebrates the strength and "emotional flexibility" of women's culture and harnesses these toward the protection of the community.

The problems addressed in this powerful relational feminist vision are enormous. The "womanist" is called to confront not only sexism but also racism and economic injustice. Michelle Wallace once remarked that black women may be reluctant to identify themselves as feminists "because, being on the bottom, we would have to do what no one else has done: we would have to fight the world."[69] Wallace speaks from a knowledge of historical realities: it has taken black women *and* men to confront racism in white society. It has taken women of *all* colors to confront sexism.

65. Ogunyemi, "Womanism: The Dynamics of the Contemporary Black Female Novel in English," *Signs* 11, no. 11 (1985): 63-80.

66. Walker, "Womanist," in *In Search of Our Mothers' Gardens,* p. xi. A similar perspective is found in Filomina Chioma Steady's "The Black Woman Cross-Culturally: An Overview," p. 34.

67. Ogunyemi, "Womanism," p. 68.

68. Walker, "Womanist," p. xi.

69. Wallace, "A Black Feminist's Search for Sisterhood," in *All the Women Are White, All the Blacks Are Men, But Some of Us Are Brave: Black Women's Studies,* ed. Gloria T. Hull, Patricia Bell Scott, and Barbara Smith (Old Westbury, N.Y.: Feminist Press, 1982), p. 12.

But in spite of historical realities, all Christians are called to challenge injustice within the human community. The issues addressed are not simply those of cultural difference. They are matters of right and wrong, and as such, they are the responsibility of all Christians. The history of racism in American society is not, after all, the history of black America. It is the history of white America. The story of oppression against women is not finally a woman's story but the story of men in relationship with women. Christian feminism, then, challenges both women and men to work toward God's vision of *shalom* in the human community.

German Christians in Nazi Germany, Christian men in America or the Philippines, and white women in America are accountable not only to their culture's immediate standards but also to God's standards of right and wrong, justice and injustice. And discerning the right and the wrong in any of these situations requires listening to those one could normally avoid, to those locked out of the more privileged levels of the society. Whether or not particular Christians have themselves been on the receiving end of gender injustice, God's standards of *shalom* call them to work to restore social, economic, and political justice between women and men, aiming to benefit people of both sexes, while being aware of their differences.[70]

Black women's experience of oppression, their lack of resources needed to survive, and their struggle for survival and dignity against great odds — all this has nourished a womanist vision. Filomina Steady argues that one cannot even be a feminist without this experience.[71] Similarly, Chikwenye Okonjo Ogunyemi asserts that only a black woman can be a womanist. However, Alice Walker hedges somewhat by defining the womanist as "traditionally universalist, as in: 'Mama, why are we brown, pink, and yellow, and our cousins are white, beige, and black?' ans. 'Well, you know the colored race is just like a flower garden, with every color flower represented.'"[72] Walker locates the power of black Southern writing in the clarity of vision given by "parents who refused to diminish themselves as human beings by succumbing to racism."[73] In this womanist vision, "a compassion for the earth, a trust in humanity

---

70. This owes much to Karen Offen's "Defining Feminism."
71. Steady, "The Black Woman Cross-Culturally," pp. 35-36.
72. Walker, "Womanist," p. xi.
73. Walker, "The Black Writer and the Southern Experience," in *In Search of Our Mothers' Gardens,* p. 19.

beyond our knowledge of evil, [and] an abiding love of justice" reflect much of the Christian vision of *shalom*.

By contrast, when privileged groups have adopted a relational feminism, their vision has rarely gone beyond the embrace of their own community, and herein lies the danger. The fate of the evangelical reformers' vision in the hands of white middle-class and working-class women suggests both the possibilities and the limits of the relational perspective. (See Chapter Two.) On the positive side, the themes that historian Deborah Valenze finds in the preaching of nineteenth-century Methodist women preachers from the lower class[74] echo the ideas of "womanism." The Female Revivalist Hymnal, like the audacious womanist, "vigorously encourage[d] loud complaint."[75] Communities and families were being torn asunder by shifts in commercial agriculture and the demands of urban industrial production. Hymns catalogued grievances. Women preachers ministered in the tents or makeshift homes of displaced wanderers. They held before the migrants and wayfarers a vision of "home" in which men and women resisted the mobile isolation of industrial labor and a segmented life ruled by the factory clock. In this situation lower-class white women who lived in a society on the verge of industrialization shared a vision of mutuality which paralleled that of other marginalized women around the world.

In the hands of the middle class, however, the relational perspective turned all too easily into the "cult of domesticity." Its language celebrated women's peculiar gifts to humanity. But instead of proclaiming the strengths of all women, it became a vision in which "good" women — those who were "pure, clean, sexually repressed, and physically fragile" — were set apart and protected at home from the work and knowledge of "dirty, licentious, physically strong" women who earned their own livelihood.[76] The life-style of middle-class women depended on underpaid household help and the sweat of factory workers, but the

74. Valenze, *Prophetic Sons and Daughters: Female Preaching and Popular Religion in Industrial England* (Princeton: Princeton University Press, 1985). See also the article by Ruth L. Smith and Deborah Valenze entitled "Mutuality and Marginality: Liberal Moral Theory and Working-Class Women in Nineteenth-Century England," *Signs* 13, no. 2 (1988): 277-98.
75. Valenze, *Prophetic Sons and Daughters,* pp. 199-200.
76. Phyllis Marynick Palmer, "White Women/Black Women: The Dualism of Female Identity and Experience in the United States," *Feminist Studies* 9 (Spring 1983): 157.

"cult of true womanhood" provided a cloak within which privilege could be protected — and the strength of women entombed.

Thus the relational argument is a two-edged sword, used sometimes to empower women and sometimes to paralyze them. White women have used it to identify negative qualities with other kinds of women or with men, while denying these qualities in themselves. Fannie Lou Hamer said of white women,

> You thought you was *more* because you was a woman, and especially a white woman, you had this kind of angel feeling that you were untouchable. . . . But coming to the realization of the thing, her freedom is shackled in chains to mine, and she realizes for the first time that she is not free until I am free.[77]

Consequently, a white feminist perspective can share in the life-giving, community-embracing strains found in "womanism" only to the extent that white people loosen their hold on economic power and material comfort, let go of their claim to intellectual superiority, and begin to absorb into their vision and their lives the experiences of the less privileged.

White Western women and men cannot share this vision of *shalom* without paying a price. They will be challenged to carry, rather than pass on to others, their share of the underside of life. Reconciliation in gender relations requires starting with the common creaturely limitations and challenges that women and men of all races and classes share — the shortsightedness of our personal vision, an aging parent's need to be washed and fed, a child's need to have his stories heard and remembered, the importance of celebrating a friend's retirement or of mourning a community tragedy. An educated refocusing on the needs of all members of the community may also show white men and women how to transform the privileges inherent in their race. They may then be able to work with others to reshape social structures that hurt not only white, middle-class women but men and women of other races and classes as well. They may learn from those who do not benefit from current economic and social structures a way of restructuring society that embraces "womanness," and with it a shared humanity.

77. Hamer, quoted by Palmer in ibid., p. 167.

Conclusion

Contemporary Christian perspectives on gender have too seldom reflected the analysis laid out in the past three chapters of this book. And thus, as we move toward the *shalom* vision of mutual, caring relations between men and women, we will do well to incorporate features from each of the three historic strands of feminism.

First, the Enlightenment strand has presented most clearly the need for individual justice. In the context of abusive homes, societies where elders still stifle all choice, and places where women are kept from earning a livelihood in the name of tradition, Enlightenment arguments are crucial. When we confront such harsh realities, an emphasis on the "rights" of human beings seems almost too weak to bring to the surface cries that run so deep. For often what is being violated is not an abstract "right" but a woman herself.

Second, the possibilities of a revised relational feminism are suggested by black womanism. From their subordinated position, black women have avoided some of the blind spots of white feminism, including the naive notion that "difference" might make no difference. At the same time, where men and women are involved in a struggle for economic and/or ethnic survival, the strengths of both men and women are more likely to be tapped. This "view from the bottom," which embraces gender unity and difference in a common human struggle, offers some hope to those who are unwilling to put the goal of harmonious gender relations indefinitely on hold.

Third, the socialist perspective reminds us that an ideology of relational feminism in the hands of the industrialized middle class can cripple women. Where industrial labor and domestic work are radically separated and where class differences are dramatic, the interests of men and women and of women in different classes often pull in radically different directions. We must dismiss as romantic gibberish any vision of gender unity and diversity that does not directly confront social structures which make mutuality almost impossible.

Each of these three perspectives can be useful in the ongoing struggle toward gender justice and reconciliation. This remains true despite the fact that the original three strands of argument continue to branch out with growing theoretical sophistication, sometimes distancing themselves from the reality of the struggle. Feminist arguments birthed in the optimism of the nineteenth century have been necessarily chastened. As Sheila Rowbotham puts it, "Patterns of subordination and power pummelled firmly into shape in one quarter have a disturbing capacity to pop up round the corner clad in a new outfit and bright as a daisy, or turn inside out and alternate their colours."[78] Thus we cannot expect problems in gender relations to go away any time soon. We are hunkering down for the long haul. But, armed with a renewed Christian vision of *shalom*, a fresh humility, and chastened feminist insights about the way gender relations work in a fallen world, we dare to reach into the core of human suffering, grab the twisted knot of gender relations, and begin to knead it back into its creational shape.

78. Rowbotham, "What Do Women Want?" p. 53.

PART II

THEOLOGICAL AND RHETORICAL PERSPECTIVES ON GENDER RELATIONS

CHAPTER 5

Reformed Christianity and Feminism: Collision or Correlation?

Christians throughout the world are reexamining their behavior and their theology in light of challenges posed by the feminist movement. Gender-related topics used to receive limited treatment in systematic theology under the rubric of the doctrine of creation and in moral theology under the rubric of sexual ethics. But gender as a topic has recently grown and become more significant, and it now helps to shape the fundamental aim and nature of Christian theology. The changes occurring in this shift have arisen out of much more than mere speculative curiosity. They represent an attempt to respond to the rising awareness that our culture — its economic system, social practices, legal systems, socialization processes, family dynamics, language, theory, and educational curricula — creates and perpetuates both the subordination and the oppression of women. Such awareness now spans national, economic, racial, and denominational boundaries: more and more people are questioning traditional patterns of gender relations in marriage, family, church, and workplace. As a result, new challenges have emerged for Christians wishing to live in ways that are faithful to the call of Jesus as it meets us within this new context.

The primary author of this chapter is Douglas Schuurman.

Christians from Reformed traditions have been slow to respond to this new challenge. In recent years, however, several responses have emerged from Reformed communities. Some criticize feminism; some affirm it at key points; some merely aim to inform.[1] These responses express diverse understandings of Christianity, of feminism, and of how to relate the two. Moreover, because Christians disagree about central claims and emphases in their confession, and because feminists disagree among themselves regarding the nature, causes, and cures of patriarchy, we are in danger of oversimplifying the issues when addressing a topic like "Reformed and Feminist Worldviews."

Hoping to avoid such dangers, we will limit our sketch of Calvinism and feminism to several basic themes drawn from their respective worldviews. We concentrate on Calvinism because the faith of most of the members of our team was nurtured through that tradition and because we find it a particularly fruitful intellectual tradition. Our focus on the Reformed tradition, however, is not meant to exclude members of other Christian traditions. We have selected themes and issues that are crucial to other traditions as well. We hope our effort to locate mutually critical correlations between Calvinism and feminism will help other Christians to reexamine their lives, their beliefs, and their traditions in light of feminism, even as we have been helped to do so by representatives of non-Reformed traditions. The feminism we concentrate on in this and the following chapter is being wrestled with by Christian

---

1. For Reformed responses that are highly critical of feminist theology, see Donald G. Bloesch's *Is the Bible Sexist?* (Westchester, Ill.: Crossway, 1982); Elizabeth Achtemeier's "Female Language for God: Should the Church Adopt It?" in *The Hermeneutical Quest*, ed. Donald G. Miller (Allison Park, Pa.: Pickwick Publications, 1986), pp. 97-114, and her essay entitled "The Impossible Possibility: Evaluating the Feminist Approach to Bible and Theology," *Interpretation* 42 (January 1988). Cynthia Campbell is more irenic, aiming to inform rather than to criticize, in her *Theologies Written from Feminist Perspectives: An Introductory Study* (New York: Office of the General Assembly of the Presbyterian Church [U. S. A.], 1987). For more sympathetic responses, see Mark Kline Taylor's *Remembering Esperanza: A Cultural-Political Theology for North American Praxis* (Maryknoll, N.Y.: Orbis Books, 1990); Brian Wren's *What Language Shall I Borrow? God-Talk in Worship: A Male Response to Feminist Theology* (New York: Crossroads, 1990); Johanna W. H. van Wijk-Bos's *Reformed and Feminist: A Challenge to the Church* (Louisville: Westminster/John Knox Press, 1991); Mary Stewart Van Leeuwen's *Gender and Grace: Love, Work and Parenting in a Changing World* (Downers Grove, Ill.: InterVarsity Press, 1990); and Elaine Storkey's *What's Right with Feminism* (Grand Rapids: William B. Eerdmans, 1986).

118

theologians who are trying to forge or, alternately, to avoid or destroy a Christian-feminist synthesis.

Our procedure is to identify several significant theological topics. Under each of these topics we will selectively explore central claims of Calvinists and feminists, with a view to sorting out conflicts and correlations between the two systems of thought.

In this chapter we concentrate on defining some key terms (such as what we mean by *Calvinism, feminism, patriarchy, oppression,* and *worldview*), and on making a general comparison of Reformed and feminist approaches to Christian life and thought. This comparison centers on three basic issues: the relationship of Christian faith to worldly activity, the role of experience in Christian life and thought, and the interpretation and use of Scripture. Having established this methodological foundation, we will use the chapter following this one to compare Reformed and feminist thinking on three specific theological topics — namely, God, humanity, and world. The third and final chapter in this section of the book will apply some insights from these first two chapters, along with an analysis based on a rhetorical methodology, to the current debate about gender relations in one specific Reformed denomination.

Basically, we hold that Reformed and feminist worldviews stand in a creative tension with each other. They are not locked in mortal combat; but neither are they capable of an easy compatibility. Many but not all of the deepest aspirations of feminism are contained in the Christian gospel, and particularly in the Reformed experience and understanding of that gospel. In what follows we will develop these claims by analyzing themes that are important to Reformed and feminist worldviews respectively.

Definitions and Restrictions of Scope

When we use the terms *Calvinism* and *Reformed,* we refer to thought and practice that traces its roots back to John Calvin. We will refer particularly to Dutch Calvinists, who try to work out the socially transformative impulses and perspectives of the Christian faith. We recognize that there have been and are socially conservative strands of the Reformed tradition, but in our retrieval we will attempt to locate and utilize elements from the transformative strands of Calvinism. These Calvinists attempt to construct a comprehensive world-and-life view based upon their

119

Christian confession.[2] We use the term *feminism* as we defined it in Chapter Two: the theoretical worldview and liberation movement for cultural, social, and ecclesiastical change toward a way of thinking and living that is inclusive of women and men. Unless otherwise indicated, the adjective *feminist* refers to Christian feminists — that is, to women and men who are trying to be self-consciously Christian *and* feminist. Among Reformed thinkers, we focus particularly on the writings of those who either reject feminism or are trying to forge a critical synthesis of Christianity and feminism.

Within Christian feminism there are three groups that we can differentiate. One group is the "post-Christian" or "revolutionary" religious feminists. These theologians, including people like Mary Daly and Starhawk, have forsaken the Christian faith because they judge it to be essentially and irremediably contrary to feminist perspectives. However, they remain "religious," unlike their secular counterparts, and try to revive goddess traditions and other religious traditions in order to fashion a new religion.

The other two groups have supplied the primary resources for Christian feminism as we understand it in this chapter. These are "reformist" or "mainline" feminists and "evangelical" or "biblical" feminists. To date, most evangelical feminism has focused on biblical studies, the neglected role of women in church history, and the question of women's ordination. Recently, however, evangelical feminists have expanded their scope to include theological, ethical, psychological, and social issues. "Mainline" Christian feminists are a theologically diverse group who usually come from Catholic, Anglican, Baptist, Presbyterian, Lutheran, and other so-called mainline Christian traditions. Some lean more toward the post-Christian camp; others lean more toward the evangelical feminist camp. Thus far, mainline feminists have treated the systematic theological, philosophical, ethical, and social dimensions of feminism more extensively than have the evangelical feminists.

2. For a study of the socially transforming impact of Calvinism on modern political life, see Michael Walzer's *Revolution of the Saints: A Study in the Origins of Radical Politics* (Cambridge: Harvard University Press, 1965). In *Dutch Calvinism in Modern America* (Grand Rapids: William B. Eerdmans, 1984), James D. Bratt provides an illuminating study of varied forms of Dutch Calvinism; and in *Until Justice and Peace Embrace* (Grand Rapids: William B. Eerdmans, 1983), Nicholas Wolterstorff attempts to carry forward this transformative Reformed approach in his analysis of pressing social problems today.

When we refer to "feminists" without qualification, we mean to include both mainline and evangelical feminists. If there is an issue on which the two camps tend to divide, then we will refer to the specific subgroups. When the claims we discuss are advanced by the "post-Christian" religious feminists, we will also identify them. In an overview like this one we must neglect much of the diversity among Christian feminists and among Calvinists. However, we hope that losses due to oversimplification will be compensated by gains that result as we highlight issues requiring further Calvinist-feminist dialogue.

Other terms we use include *androcentrism, patriarchy, oppression,* and *subordination.* These terms refer to the disadvantaged position of women relative to men in culture and society, and to the structural, systemic character of the mechanisms that keep women in this position. *Androcentrism* means "male-centered" — that is, descriptively and normatively defining humanity in terms of men. An androcentric worldview sees men as the bearers of authority, power, and value to the relative or complete exclusion of women.[3] Women are thus always defined in relation to men, while men are not correspondingly defined in relation to women. We use the term *patriarchy* in the way in which Elisabeth Schüssler Fiorenza does in *Bread Not Stone,* "[not] in the loose sense of 'all men dominating all women equally,' but in the classical Aristotelian sense. Patriarchy as a male pyramid of graded subordinations and exploitations specifies women's oppression in terms of the class, race, country, or religion of the men to whom [they] 'belong.'"[4] Although patriarchy includes androcentrism, it involves more than that, for it points more directly to the sociopolitical mechanisms creating and sustaining the oppression of women.[5]

We use the terms *subordination* and *oppression* as historian Gerda Lerner defines them. Subordination "marks a dominance relation, includes the possibility of a voluntary acceptance of subordination in exchange for protection and/or privilege, and does not imply that there is always evil intent on the part of the dominators." Oppression implies "forceful subordination with victimization of the oppressed."[6] Thus op-

3. See Campbell, *Theologies Written from Feminist Perspectives,* p. 11.

4. Schüssler Fiorenza, *Bread Not Stone: The Challenge of Feminist Biblical Interpretation* (Boston: Beacon Press, 1984), p. xiv.

5. Ibid., p. 5.

6. Lerner, *The Creation of Patriarchy* (New York: Oxford University Press, 1986), as summarized by Wren in *What Language Shall I Borrow?* p. 22.

121

pression is a specific kind of subordination, one in which there is less collaboration, less freedom, and more grievous harm on the part of the victim, and in which there is more knowledge and freedom on the part of the oppressor. Although the distinction is important, we will often use the terms *subordination* and *oppression* together to refer to the harms suffered by women in society.

We use the term *worldview* in the loose sense of "a framework or set of fundamental beliefs through which we view the world and our calling and future within it."[7] Worldviews both reflect and shape our experience of ourselves, our world, and God. Worldviews are especially important for human action. As philosopher Albert Wolters puts it, a worldview "orients us in the world at large, gives us a sense of what is up and what is down, what is right and what is wrong in the confusion of events and phenomena that confronts us."[8] Worldviews help to answer certain fundamental questions. Why do we and the world exist? What is finally wrong with us and our world? Who are we and what are we to become? How does all this fit together? Worldviews tend to be comprehensive in scope; they shape a person's approach to reality in its parts and in its totality.

Comparing Reformed and feminist worldviews is a daunting challenge because of the great diversity within Calvinism and within feminism. Some scholars who have surveyed the variety of perspectives within feminism even worry that the diversity and conflicts are so great that we cannot speak of feminism as a coherent set of ideas and practices.[9] As women of color and colonized women enter the discussions, the diversity increases, a point that we developed in Chapter Four.[10] Because of this diversity, we will limit our discussion of Reformed and feminist worldviews to certain basic themes, theological and ethical. We will try to develop these themes in ways that will be fruitful for all

7. James H. Olthuis, "On Worldviews," in *Stained Glass: Worldviews and Social Science,* ed. Paul A. Marshall, Sander Griffioen, and Richard J. Mouw (Lanham, Md.: University Press of America, 1989), p. 29.

8. Wolters, *Creation Regained: Biblical Basics for a Reformational Worldview* (Grand Rapids: William B. Eerdmans, 1985), p. 4.

9. For an introductory survey of various secular feminist views, see Rosemarie Tong's *Feminist Thought: A Comprehensive Introduction* (Boulder, Colo.: Westview Press, 1989).

10. See also Susan Thistlethwaite's *Sex, Race, and God: Christian Feminism in Black and White* (New York: Crossroad, 1989).

Christians, not just for those who are Reformed or whose disciplinary interests are theological.

Basic Approaches to Christian Life and Thought

The vision of Christianity emerging in feminist theology shares many of the concerns and perspectives of Calvinism. These similarities are often overlooked, partly because so much feminist theology begins by criticizing "traditional" theology, and partly because so many theologians who represent mainline Christian traditions are critical of feminist theology. So let us begin by comparing Reformed and feminist approaches to Christian life and thought. Although there are important differences between them, they agree (1) that Christianity should be world-formative, (2) that experience is and ought to be important for Christian life and thought, and (3) that the interpretation and use of Scripture should be governed by theological/ethical norms.

The Affirmation of World-Formative Christianity

Philosopher Nicholas Wolterstorff distinguishes between *world-avertive* and *world-formative* versions of Christianity. World-avertive Christianity is "otherworldly." According to this view, the world in which we now live is alien to us, "a reality ultimately unworthy of us, the inferior of another reality to which we have access — the world of the eternal, the immutable, the incorruptible, the imperishable."[11] Wolterstorff sees medieval Christianity as having been predominantly world-avertive. It construed all reality in terms of a "great chain of being" that was hierarchically ordered, with each entity having beings "above" and "below" it on the chain. According to this view, human society mirrors (or should *aim* to mirror) this hierarchical chain of being, since persons are created unequally to fit into different social positions.

11. Wolterstorff, *Until Justice and Peace Embrace*, p. 4. Wolterstorff's interpretation of Calvinist in relation to medieval understandings of God and the social order follows that of Ernst Troeltsch (*The Social Teaching of the Christian Churches*, trans. O. Wyon, 2 vols. [New York: Harper-Torchbooks, 1960], 2: 515-660) and Michael Walzer (*The Revolution of the Saints*, especially pp. 1-113).

Individuals attain their various positions — as serfs, nobles, lords, and so on — purely by heredity, both biological and social. Since this hierarchical structure was presumably ordained by God, it followed that a Christian's vocation is not to *challenge* the social order or even as an individual to *forsake* his or her position in search of another. Rather, according to the world-avertive view, Christians are called to *submit* to the duties defined by their "places" within society while they await their true destiny in eternity.[12]

By contrast, world-formative Christianity, of which Calvinism is one expression, is "this-worldly." It holds Christians responsible, Wolterstorff says, "for the structure of the social world in which they find themselves. That structure is not simply part of the order of nature; to the contrary, it is the result of human decision, and by concerted effort it can be altered. Indeed, it *should* be altered, for it is a fallen structure, in need of reform."[13] According to this view, Christians are called to serve God and the common good through their various positions in society. But if a person's position does *not* promote the common good, or if a person can better serve others by finding a different position in society, then she or he must either *reshape* the position so that it better serves the common good or *change* to a position that has greater possibilities for such service. World-formative Christianity holds that Christians are not merely "passing through" this world; God created us *for* this world — not as it often is, corrupt and corrupting, but as it ought to be in God's *shalom*.

Such a view resists easy acceptance of the status quo and instead encourages a prophetic critique of society. The words of Allan Boesak, a black Reformed South African pastor, convey the heart of this Calvinist conviction:

> For the black church, Jesus Christ is Lord. He is Lord over all of life.... Our loyalty and obedience are to him alone.... Our allegiance is ultimately not to the laws of the state, or to the laws of self-preservation, but to the commands of the living God. Our loyalty is to Christ. Our criteria are the demands of his kingdom. We shall have to learn not to be dictated to by the demands of the status quo, however intimidating; or by the demands of any ideology, however tempting. Our faith in Jesus Christ and the liberating power of his

12. Wolterstorff, *Until Justice and Peace Embrace*, pp. 4-8.
13. Ibid., p. 3.

gospel must form the basis upon which we offer ourselves as a humble servant in the world.[14]

Like Calvinists, feminists reject a faith that applies only to persons but not to social structures, or applies mainly to the future or eternal realm but not to this world. This refusal to insulate faith from any part of experience, and particularly from social and cultural patterns, is a pervasive theme in feminist theology. Rosemary Radford Ruether's understanding of the prophetic character of feminist theology is a good example of this basic theme:

> The God-language of the prophetic tradition is destabilizing toward the existing social order and its hierarchies of power — religious, social, and economic. Its understanding of salvation is neither conformist or privatistic. Rather it is a vision of an alternative future, a new "deal" of peace and justice that will arise when the present systems of injustice have been overthrown.[15]

The world-formative character of feminist theology is also evident in its similarity to the liberation theologies crafted by African-Americans and various colonized peoples. Central to these theologies is the claim that sin and salvation encompass *social* as well as *individual* reality. Affirming this theme, Letty Russell focuses on the transforming, thisworldly character of salvation:

> Without denying that salvation includes the message of individual deliverance from sin and death (Rom., chs. 5 to 7) [liberation theologians] nevertheless place emphasis on the total goal of salvation (Rom., ch. 8) which is the gift of shalom (complete social and physical wholeness and harmony). And Gustavo Gutierrez says: "Salvation is not something otherworldly, in regard to which the present life is merely a test. Salvation — the communion of . . . [people] with God and the communion of . . . [people] among themselves — is something which embraces all human reality, transforms it, and leads it to its fullness in Christ."[16]

14. Boesak, *Black and Reformed: Apartheid, Liberation and the Calvinist Tradition*, ed. Leonard Sweetman (Maryknoll, N.Y.: Orbis Books, 1984), p. 28.

15. Ruether, *Sexism and God-Talk: Toward a Feminist Theology* (Boston: Beacon Press, 1983), p. 26.

16. Russell, *Human Liberation in a Feminist Perspective — A Theology* (Philadel-

Thus both Calvinism and feminism hold to a faith that demands the reformation of both individuals *and* societal/cultural patterns. This reformation involves exposing the ways in which sin has *distorted* all of life and discovering ways in which salvation and redemption *reshape* life according to the goal and will of God. Feminism thus exhibits the "totalism" or wholistic analysis that also characterizes Calvinism.[17] In particular, feminist theology shows how an oppressive gender system has distorted our world and harmed women and men. Calvinism has shown great concern for *other* forms of injustice and idolatry — for example, those that are "economic" and "political" in the traditional sense. But it has either overlooked the theme of gender or muted its importance. In spite of this, both Calvinism and feminism stress the truth and importance of world-formative Christianity.

The Importance of Experience for Christian Life and Thought

Calvinism and feminism also agree that human experience plays a normative role in creating, shaping, and sustaining a Christian view of God, humanity, and world. The normative role of experience in Calvinist thought has often been denied or muted by "Orthodox" and "Neo-Orthodox" Reformed theologians: these scholars understandably have wanted to distance themselves from liberal Protestants who dismissed parts of the Bible in the name of either "experience" or "scientific reason." There is no denying, however, that *believers' experience* of God's sovereign grace, of the testimony of the Holy Spirit, and of the fellowship of the forgiven all play a decisive and normative role in Reformed thought and life.

For example, Abraham Kuyper, the turn-of-the-century Dutch statesman and theologian, locates the "mother-thought" of Calvinism *in* experience:

Thanks to this work of God in the heart [the work of the Spirit bringing assurance of eternal salvation], the persuasion that the whole

---

phia: Westminster Press, 1974), p. 110. She is citing Gustavo Gutiérrez's *Theology of Liberation: History, Politics and Salvation* (Maryknoll, N.Y.: Orbis Books, 1973), p. 151.

17. In *Until Justice and Peace Embrace,* Wolterstorff describes Calvinist totalism as an "insistence that there is nothing at all in our experience that is not — so far as is necessary and possible — to be subjected to the will of God" (p. 10). See also "On Christian Learning," in *Stained Glass,* pp. 65-66.

of a man's life is to be lived as *in the Divine Presence* has become the fundamental thought of Calvinism. By this decisive idea, or rather by this mighty fact, it has allowed itself to be controlled in every department of its entire domain. It is from this mother-thought that the all-embracing life system of Calvinism sprang.[18]

For Kuyper this experience or "mighty fact" is certainly not brought about without the Bible; in this fallen world the Bible is the light without which we would be groping about in darkness.[19] But when the question is "How should we organize and systematize Christian insights and claims about God?" Kuyper would answer, "In accordance with their relation to the mother-thought and originating experience of Calvinism; namely, assurance of pardon leading to the conviction that all of life should be permeated with God's presence."

Kuyper also ascribes a kind of primacy to experience when he describes the dynamics leading to the formation of the Reformed worldview:

18. Kuyper, *Lectures on Calvinism* (Grand Rapids: William B. Eerdmans, 1931; rpt. 1976), pp. 25-26.

19. Kuyper understands the Bible in terms of its relation to a superior revelation that was lost in the Fall and that will be regained in the Eschaton. "In Paradise, before the Fall, there was no Bible, and there will be no Bible in the future Paradise of glory. When the transparent light, kindled by Nature, addresses us directly, and the inner word of God sounds in our heart in its original clearness, and all human words are sincere, and the function of our inner ear is perfectly performed, why should we need a Bible? What mother loses herself in a treatise upon the "love of our children" the very moment that her own dear ones are playing about her knee, and God allows her to drink in their love with full draughts? But, in our present condition, this immediate communion with God by means of nature, and of our own heart is lost. Sin brought separation instead, and the opposition which is manifest nowadays against the authority of the Holy Scriptures is based on nothing else than the false supposition that, our condition being still normal, our religion need not be soteriological. For of course, in that case, the Bible is not wanted, it becomes, indeed, a hindrance, and grates upon your feelings, since it interposes a book between God and your heart. . . . When the sun shines in your house, bright and clear, you turn off the electric light, but when the sun disappears below the horizon, you feel the *necessitas luminis artificiosi*, i.e., the need of artificial light, and the artificial light is kindled in every dwelling. . . . When history, experience and consciousness all unite in stating the fact that the pure and full light of Heaven has disappeared, and that we are groping about in the dark, then, a different, or if you will, an artificial light *must* be kindled for us, — and such a light God has kindled for us in His Holy Word" (ibid., pp. 56-57).

Calvinism is rooted in a form of religion which was peculiarly its own, and from this specific religious consciousness there was developed first a peculiar theology, then a special church-order, and then a given form for political and social life, for the interpretation of the moral world-order, for the relation between nature and grace, between Christianity and the world, between church and state, and finally for art and science.[20]

Thus, according to Kuyper, the development of a person's faith proceeds from the experience of God's assurance of pardon (a "specific religious consciousness"), to theological articulation, to church polity, to politics and society, to a comprehensive system or worldview. We need not agree with Kuyper on the succession of stages in this process in order to affirm his basic point: the experience of assurance of salvation (and the related conviction that all of life belongs to God) is the unifying impulse of Christian vision and action. As such, it exerts a normative influence throughout Christian life and thought.[21] Thus the "antithesis" between believers and unbelievers depends as much upon whether or not a person has experienced this assurance as it does upon whether one knows what is in the Bible.

Feminist theologians make analogous claims about the importance of experience for Christian thought and life.[22] But for most feminists the central experience is not the assurance of eternal life communicated to the guilty sinner by a righteous but forgiving God. In most feminist theology the emphasis rests upon how one stands relative to *other people* rather than upon how one stands relative to *God*. More specifically, feminist theologians tend to emphasize women's experience of God's grace in the struggle for liberation from patriarchy and for the affirmation of women as women. Thus the problem of central concern in most feminist theology is not the need for individual pardon but the need for

20. Ibid., p. 17; see also pp. 171, 194.
21. Kuyper here follows an organizing principle patterned after the Heidelberg Catechism rather than the Belgic Confession. The latter document, after introductory sections about revelation and God, organizes the Christian confession along the lines of the biblical narrative of creation-fall-redemption-consummation.
22. For an introduction to some of the more important issues and literature, see Ruether's *Sexism and God-Talk*, pp. 12-16; Judith Plaskow's *Sex, Sin and Grace: Women's Experience and the Theologies of Reinhold Niebuhr and Paul Tillich* (Washington: University Press of America, 1980), pp. 29-50; and *Feminist Interpretation of the Bible*, ed. Letty Russell (Philadelphia: Westminster Press, 1985).

the victims of sexism to be free from their oppressors and the need of those who perpetuate sexism to repent. According to this view, the revelation of God occurs in the community of Christians struggling *against* patriarchy and *for* a new way of thinking and living inclusive of women and men.

Some Christian feminists speak of their coming to awareness of the oppressive, patriarchal system as a sudden and decisive "conversion" experience;[23] others describe the process as a more gradual turning, a slow but steadily growing awareness. Moreover, just as new converts to Christianity often feel compelled to point out every sign of sin and hypocrisy they see, so too many feminists struggle to control their spontaneous desire to correct all instances of patriarchy. Some also cry tears of joy when they finally hear a woman preach or pray to God as "Mother." All gain a new understanding of themselves as image bearers of God and full members by baptism in the body of Christ. They testify to finding new energy for developing their spirituality, their professional lives, and their friendships. The shift is not a minor one; it is a deep and total turning from something old toward something new.[24]

There are two closely related aspects of women's experience that unify Christian feminist thought and life. The first is the struggle against patriarchy and for a new humanity on the part of women and of men who share their cause. Thus, for example, Elisabeth Schüssler Fiorenza says,

> The spiritual authority of women-church rests on the experience of *God's sustaining grace and liberating presence* in the midst of our struggles for justice, freedom, and wholeness of all [my emphasis]. It rests not simply on the "experience of women" but on the experience of women struggling for liberation from patriarchal oppression.[25]

23. Some gatherings we participated in reminded us of "testimony time" in many fundamentalist and evangelical churches. People were very eager to give testimonies about how their consciousness was raised, how they became "feminist," and how they still struggled with the pervasive powers of sexism. It also often seemed that having such an experience was a prerequisite for becoming a full-fledged member of the group.

24. See Beverly W. Harrison's "Keeping Faith in a Sexist Church: Not for Women Only," in *Making the Connections: Essays in Feminist Social Ethics,* ed. Carol S. Robb (Boston: Beacon Press, 1986), pp. 206-34.

25. Schüssler Fiorenza, *Bread Not Stone,* p. xvi. See also Campbell's *Theologies Written from Feminist Perspectives,* pp. 21-24.

This experience of becoming aware of women's oppression, of the structural strategies that support this oppression, and of the possibility of struggle against it in the name of a new humanity can be called the "oppression-liberation" aspect of women's experience.

The second aspect of women's experience that unifies feminist life and thought is the "affirmation of women-as-women" aspect. This concerns the various ways in which women may be different from men. These differences include women's social subordination and oppression but also their distinctive bodily processes (menstruation, pregnancy, giving birth, breast-feeding, etc.) as well as their connectedness with other women and their distinctive emotional and cognitive tendencies. Insofar as the gender system causes both men and women to devalue and even despise these differences, much feminist theology seeks to affirm them. Some feminist theologians omit this aspect or clearly subordinate it to the experience of women's struggle for liberation.[26] In other feminist theological writings, this women-affirming aspect is given the same importance as the struggle against patriarchy. Sallie McFague, for example, identifies both aspects as crucial for understanding patriarchy and for revising Christian theology.[27]

The unifying principle for this experience-based feminist theology

26. In this respect feminist theologians show the same diversity as feminist theoreticians in general (see Chapters Two and Three). Elisabeth Schüssler Fiorenza and Rosemary Ruether tend to emphasize the theme of liberation, subordinating that of women's difference to it. However, the two themes are linked in that the concern for liberation *presupposes* that uniquely "feminine" experiences are suppressed by patriarchy and need to be reaffirmed in a new society; hence the distinctions between them are often not made clearly. Feminist theologians are often wary of emphasizing the "difference" theme because of the ways in which sex/gender differences are used to justify the subordination of women.

27. McFague, *Metaphorical Theology: Models of God in Religious Language* (Philadelphia: Fortress Press, 1982), p. 155. At the moment it seems that Christian feminists are less prone to emphasize women's differences from men than are secular feminists. It is difficult to know whether the Christian concern for similarity derives from intrinsically Christian perspectives on women and men (as sharing the same image of God, the same fall into sin, the same faith and baptism, etc.) or from theologians' tendency to lag a bit behind secular theorists. Feminists, Christian or not, are sometimes fearful that highlighting the differences between women and men will only augment women's oppression. Men in power have used dimorphic and androgynous understandings of the genders to oppress women: androgynous definitions of "human" have excluded women, and dimorphic understandings have ascribed less value to the stereotypical feminine attributes than to the masculine ones.

is a vision of God and of a "new heaven and earth" that requires rejection of anything which devalues or harms women, and the promotion of a "new humanity" which includes women as fully as men. Thus both Calvinism and feminism have a unifying coherence, and both identify the experience of God as the source of this unity.

The content of this experience reflects a concern for God and for humanity in both feminism and Calvinism. In Calvinism the human need for assurance of pardon reflects a vision of Christ's Lordship over every inch of creation. In feminism the human need for liberation and affirmation reflects a vision of God as Liberator and Promisor of a new creation and a new humanity in which women are affirmed. In Calvinism there is a deep awareness of the sovereignty of God as experienced both in the grace of individual pardon and in the Lordship of Christ over all of life. In the Calvinist analysis, the freedom of God, especially in the grace of forgiveness, gives rise to a profound gratitude that motivates Christian obedience in every area of life. In most feminist theology, however, these impulses — to see oneself as sinful, as an undeserving recipient of pardon from a free and sovereign God, and therefore to be profoundly grateful — are missing or muted.

Although these differences between Calvinists and feminists ought not be overlooked, the fact that both unify thought and life around a principle based on an experience of God is important. To accuse feminist Christians, for example, of being "unbiblical," as though the central issue were one of accepting or rejecting the authority of the Bible, fails to reckon with the profound ways in which experience shapes Calvinist uses of the Bible. It also fails to reckon with the distressingly pervasive way in which the Bible has been *misused* to keep certain people "in their place" — whether those people be slaves, the poor, those of other races, or women. This brings us to a third theme that Calvinist and feminist theologians have in common.

The Importance of Interpreting and Using Scripture according to Theological/Ethical Norms

Feminists and Calvinists share the conviction that Scripture, as well as experience, is crucial for creating, testing, and sustaining worldviews.[28]

28. In *Creation Regained,* Al Wolters emphasizes the role of Scripture in shaping

However, Reformed thinkers have often criticized feminists for *displacing* the authority of Scripture with the authority of experience, while feminists have accused Reformed thinkers of using the slogan *sola scriptura* ("Scripture alone") to conceal and justify their own sexist biases. Although there are important conflicts here that ought not be glossed over, there are also similarities between feminism and Calvinism regarding the normative role of Scripture for Christian thought and life. Because our aim is to define the lines of compatibility between Calvinism and feminism, we will highlight the similarities. These include the recognition (1) that theological and ethical principles govern interpretation and use of the Bible, and (2) that the Bible, properly interpreted, becomes a source of criticism to be applied to tradition, church, and society.

Calvinist Biblical Interpretation

One of the distinctive features of the Protestant Reformation was its emphasis on the authority of the Bible for Christian faith and life. Over against the appeals to experience made by the enthusiasts and the appeals to tradition made by Roman Catholics, the Protestant Reformers declared that the Bible is the final authority in matters of doctrine and morals. Where experience, tradition, and reason did not conflict with the Bible, Christians were free to follow their lead. But where there was a conflict between those things and the Bible, particularly when the issue concerned God and God's relation to humanity and the world, the Bible alone was the supreme authority. Thus *sola scriptura* became one of the key phrases of the Reformation.

But as the Reformers interpreted the Bible, they made judgments concerning the relationship of its central message to the faith and life of their communities. Eventually these judgments were articulated in the Protestant confessions.[29] Although in theory the Reformers subordinated the authority of these confessions to the authority of the Bible, in practice they permitted the confessions to *govern* much of their use of the Bible for the theology and life of the churches. As Calvinists

---

and testing a worldview (p. 6). In "On Worldviews," James Olthuis stresses that life experience is as important for worldview as is revelation (p. 32).

    29. Some of the more important confessions are the Belgic Confession, the Heidelberg Catechism, the Canons of Dordt, the Westminster Confession, and the Helvitic Confession.

found it necessary to distinguish themselves from Roman Catholics, Lutherans, and Anabaptists—who likewise appealed to the Bible to support their ideas and practices—the practical authority of the confessions was augmented.

Calvin himself recognized that a person's interpretation of Scripture is governed by discernment of a set of theological/ethical principles. This is evident in his brief preface to the 1559 edition of the *Institutes*.

> It has been my purpose in this labor to prepare and instruct candidates in sacred theology for the reading of the divine Word, in order that they may be able both to have easy access to it and to advance in it without stumbling. For I believe I have so embraced the sum of religion in all its parts, and have arranged it in such an order, that if anyone rightly grasps it, it will not be difficult for him to determine what he ought especially to seek in Scripture, and to what end he ought to relate its contents.[30]

As Calvin saw it, proper interpretation of Scripture not only requires careful attention to such matters as language, authorial intent, and the situation of the original recipients of the biblical books; it also requires a clear understanding of the Bible's theological/ethical core.

What Calvin called his "rule of sobriety" also reflects this recognition that readers bring to the Bible a prior understanding of God that governs their interpretation. Calvin himself follows the rules of "modesty and soberness" when reflecting on any religious doctrine. He recommends that in obscure matters we "not . . . speak or think, or even long to know, more than the Word of God has delivered" and that "in reading the Scriptures we should constantly direct our inquiries and meditations to those things which tend to edification, not indulge in curiosity, or in studying things of no use."[31]

To understand Calvin's view of what themes "tend to edification," we must consider what he means by *piety*—the source and goal of all genuine theological knowledge, according to Calvin. Calvin defines piety as "that reverence joined with love of God which the knowledge of his benefits induces. For until men recognize that they owe everything to

30. Calvin, "John Calvin to the Reader," in *Calvin: Institutes of the Christian Religion*, Library of Christian Classics, vol. 20, ed. John T. McNeill, trans. Ford Lewis Battles (Philadelphia: Westminster Press, 1960), p. 4.
31. Ibid., 1.14.4.

God, that they are nourished by his fatherly care, that he is the Author of their every good, that they should seek nothing beyond him — they will never yield him willing service."[32] For Calvin, true piety is the result of faith. But he also says that a person's "heart is not aroused to faith at every word of God." Consequently, he tries to identify just what faith looks to in the Bible. Calvin finally focuses on the promises of God's benevolence and mercy, fully revealed in Christ, as the core of the Bible to which faith looks. Although faith subscribes to every word of God's truth "whenever and whatever and however it speaks," the part of the Bible that most interests Calvin is the promise of grace. Thus he defines faith as "a firm and certain knowledge of God's benevolence toward us, founded upon the truth of the freely given promise in Christ, both revealed to our minds and sealed upon our hearts through the Holy Spirit."[33]

For Calvin, then, not all Scripture is on equal footing when it comes to the Christian community. All of Scripture is the Word of God. But some parts of this Word are obscure or very remotely related to its promissory core. Calvin's theological judgments about *what* contributes to true faith and piety shape his treatments of Scripture and his treatment of traditional topics in theology. In his commentaries these judgments shape his treatment of Old and New Testament books; in his more systematic works they shape the structure and content of nearly

32. Ibid., 1.2.1.
33. Ibid., 3.2.7. Augustine follows a similar procedure. For him the basic concern is the movement of the soul, either in charity toward God and neighbor or in cupidity toward self and world. Interpretations that encouraged cupidity were wrong, even though they might be entirely adequate in terms of their grammatical, literary, and historical exegeses. Interpretations that encouraged charity were right, even if they might be based on false grammatical, literary, and historical exegeses. Thus he says, "Whoever, therefore, thinks that he understands the divine Scriptures or any part of them so that it does not build the double love of God and of our neighbor does not understand it at all. Whoever finds a lesson there useful to the building of charity, even though he has not said what the author may be shown to have intended in that place, has not been deceived, nor is he lying in any way" (*On Christian Doctrine*, trans. D. W. Robertson, Jr., Library of Liberal Arts, no. 80 (Indianapolis: Bobbs-Merrill Educational Publishing, 1958), bk. 1, sec. 36, par. 40, p. 30; see also bk. 3, secs. 10-16. Augustine compares such an interpreter to a person who wanders from the path only to meet it again later. Although Augustine acknowledges that charity-producing interpretations are right, he recommends interpretations that *both* express the authors' intentions *and* encourage charity.

everything he says. As such they have normative force for his entire worldview.

For Calvin and for Calvinism, when Scripture is rightly interpreted, it is truly the power of God for salvation: it both assures sinful people of God's grace and challenges impieties and injustices in the world. The conflict between the biblical vision for creation and the injustices and idolatry of the present world gives rise to the reforming impulse that characterizes Calvinism. Thus for Calvinism the Bible provides the vantage point for a critique of tradition and of contemporary society, and the source for a vision of a new social order.[34]

Feminist Biblical Interpretation

Feminist theologians as well are very much aware of the ways in which theological and ethical interests govern the interpretation and use of the Bible. This sharp awareness is partly due to the ways in which the Bible has been used to support the oppression and subordination of women. As Elisabeth Schüssler Fiorenza puts it, "Whenever women protest against political discrimination, economic exploitation, sexual violence, or our secondary status in biblical religion, the Bible is invoked against us."[35] Such awareness is also due to the fact that the Bible does not actually contain a direct and sustained critique of the oppression or subordination of women; it even seems to support patriarchy, not only in the Old Testament but also in the New. Thus many Christian feminists see the "spectacles" of Scripture as dark and clouded, blinding those who wear them so that they cannot see the wrongness of our patriarchal world.

34. Wolterstorff describes the importance of the Bible for Calvinist social reform as follows: "But first, why were the Calvinists so persuaded that the social structures as presented to us are fallen? And where did they get their guidelines for reform? What was the root of their radical social critique? The answer is clear: it is the Word of God, presented to us in the Bible, that shows up for us the corruption of our social order. And it is that same Word of God that provides us with our fundamental pattern for reform. The reformation of society according to the Word of God: this was the Calvinist goal" (*Until Justice and Peace Embrace*, p. 18).

35. Schüssler Fiorenza, *Bread Not Stone*, p. 8. See also Willard M. Swartley's *Slavery, Sabbath, War, and Women: Case Issues in Biblical Interpretation* (Scottdale, Pa.: Herald Press, 1983), esp. pp. 152-91; and Elizabeth Cady Stanton's introduction to *The Original Feminist Attack on the Bible: The Woman's Bible: Part 1*, ed. Elizabeth Cady Stanton et al. (1898; rpt. New York: Arno Press, 1974), pp. 7-13.

To post-Christian feminists, for example, the Bible is irretrievably patriarchal, and they have accordingly forsaken the Bible and the Judeo-Christian heritage.[36] As Winsome Munro points out, during the nineteenth and early twentieth century, the church used the Bible, and especially passages like 1 Corinthians 14:33-35, to silence women who publicly advocated the abolition of slavery and the universal suffrage of women. By contrast, in the second half of the twentieth century, "It is the Bible and the church that have become the butt of feminist accusations for being the main culprits for the development and preservation of western patriarchy. Now the same texts previously used against women have come to be used with great effect against western religious tradition."[37]

Feminists who wish to remain Christian choose to reinterpret Scripture and establish principles of interpretation to oppose its abuses. These feminists vary widely in terms of critical methodology, denominational background, and willingness to dismiss certain parts of the Bible.[38] In the same way that Luther was eager to throw the Epistle of James out of the canon because it seemed to teach works-righteousness, so too some feminists are ready to dismiss several of the Pauline letters because they seem to teach patriarchy. Most feminists agree, however, that the Bible, properly understood, supports the liberation and affirmation of women. Thus one of the central tasks of feminist theology is

36. For introductions to debates between post-Christian and mainline Christian feminists on whether the Bible should be rejected or reinterpreted, see Rosemary Ruether's "A Religion for Women: Sources and Strategies," *Christianity and Crisis* 39 (10 December 1979): 307-11; and *Womanspirit Rising,* ed. Carol P. Christ and Judith Plaskow (San Francisco: Harper & Row, 1979).

37. Munro, "Women, Text and the Canon: The Strange Case of 1 Corinthians 14:33-35," in *Biblical Theology Bulletin* 18 (January 1988): 27.

38. Two important biblical studies by mainline Christian feminists are Elisabeth Schüssler Fiorenza's *In Memory of Her: A Feminist Theological Reconstruction of Christian Origins* (New York: Crossroad, 1985); and Phyllis Trible's *God and the Rhetoric of Sexuality* (Philadelphia: Fortress Press, 1978). Schüssler Fiorenza's work is especially influential for New Testament studies that utilize historical-critical scholarship; Trible's work lacks the comprehensive scope of Schüssler Fiorenza's, but her feminist reinterpretation of selected Old Testament passages has stimulated many discussions for those using literary-critical approaches to biblical interpretation. For a sampling of hermeneutical debates among Christian feminists, see *Feminist Interpretation of the Bible,* ed. Letty Russell. For a concise overview of feminist approaches to biblical authority, with special reference to Pauline materials, see Winsome Munro's article entitled "Women, Text and the Canon."

to reconstruct the Christian tradition, Scripture included, to expose its patriarchal bias and emphasize its liberating possibilities.

Like Calvin, feminists make plain their own "rule of sobriety" in treating Scripture and theology. This reflects their own recognition of the importance of theological/ethical norms for proper interpretation. In an often-cited passage, Rosemary Ruether defines the overarching principle of feminist theology as follows:

> The critical principle of feminist theology is the promotion of the full humanity of women. Whatever denies, diminishes, or distorts the full humanity of women is, therefore, appraised as not redemptive. Theologically speaking, whatever diminishes or denies the full humanity of women must be presumed not to reflect the divine or an authentic relation to the divine, or to reflect the authentic nature of things or to be the message or work of an authentic redeemer or a community of redemption.

Ruether goes on to note the positive principle implied by this negative one — namely, that whatever *does* promote the full humanity of women "is of the Holy, it does reflect true relation to the divine, it is the true nature of things, the authentic message of redemption and the mission of the redemptive community."[39]

The extent to which the Bible itself contradicts this central principle of feminist theology is a matter of rigorous debate among feminists.[40]

---

39. Ruether, *Sexism and God-Talk*, pp. 18-19.

40. Although Ruether does find her critical principle expressed and supported in various parts of the Bible, she argues that the Bible is thoroughly permeated with patriarchy. She says that the Bible teaches that God is male (with some female attributes); that its monotheism is an ideology supporting the male ruling class; that Genesis 1 reveals God as a deified Patriarch and Genesis 2 is a "patriarchal reversal myth," since Eve is born of the man; and that the subordination of woman in Genesis 3 is presented as a just punishment for her sin. She argues that much of the New Testament betrays the egalitarian impulse of the Gospel. In her litany entitled "Exorcism of Patriarchal Texts," Ruether casts out the clearly patriarchal passages (Lev. 12:1-5; Exod. 19:1, 7-9, 14-15; Judg. 19; Eph. 5:21-23; 1 Tim. 2:11-15; 1 Pet. 2:18-20) in a way that evangelical and reformed feminists will find objectionable: "These texts and all oppressive texts have lost their power over our lives. We no longer need to apologize for them or try to interpret them as words of truth, but we cast out their oppressive message as expressions of evil and justifications of evil" (in *Women-Church: Theology and Practice of Feminist Liturgical Communities* [San Francisco: Harper & Row, 1986], p. 137). Nicholas John Ansell provides perceptive

Those who see only "remnants" of a nonpatriarchal Christian ethos in the Bible tend to take note of passages teaching the subordination of women but deny their authority for Christians today. Thus Elisabeth Schüssler Fiorenza, for example, notes that Ephesians 5:21-33 affirms, with only slight modifications, the patriarchal submission of wife to husband. She writes, "The 'gospel of peace' has transformed the relationship of gentiles and Jews, but not the social roles of wives and slaves within the household of God. On the contrary, the cultural-social structures of domination are theologized and thereby reinforced."[41] Rather than try to harmonize Ephesians 5:21-33 with other parts of the New Testament that seem to overthrow this patriarchal pattern, Schüssler Fiorenza is content to reject the authority of this passage on the grounds that it reflects a "Pauline trajectory" which ought not have authority for the church.

By contrast, those who see much or all of the Bible as supportive of the liberation and affirmation of women tend to argue that such passages are not really advocating subordination. Nancy Hardesty and Letha Scanzoni, for example, contrast the view of marriage in Ephesians 5 with the patriarchal pattern found in the Old Testament and in the Roman culture of the church at Ephesus. They argue that in Ephesians 5 the marriage relation is marked by reciprocity and mutuality rather than by hierarchical subordination of the wife to her husband.[42] In the case of texts clearly reflecting patriarchal perspectives (e.g., 1 Tim. 2), an effort is made to show how these perspectives are culturally conditioned, reflective of an earlier period and other perspectives in the history of God's revelation (e.g., the perspective on polygamy in the Old Testament), or descriptive of the fallen character of human history rather than prescriptive of God's will for humanity (e.g., Gen. 3:15). These efforts reflect the feminist assumption

analysis and evangelical critique of Ruether's view of Scripture and tradition in his master's thesis entitled "'The Woman Will Overcome the Warrior': A Dialogue with the Feminist Theology of Rosemary Radford Ruether" (Institute for Christian Studies, Toronto, 1990), pp. 34-111.

41. Schüssler Fiorenza, *In Memory of Her*, p. 270.

42. Scanzoni and Hardesty, *All We're Meant to Be* (Waco, Tex.: Word Books, 1974), pp. 119-26. For analogous debates relating to Genesis 1-3, compare Rosemary Radford Ruether's *Womanguides: Readings toward a Feminist Theology* (Boston: Beacon Press, 1985), p. 62, and her book entitled *New Woman/New Earth: Sexist Ideologies and Human Liberation* (New York: Seabury Press, 1975), pp. 14ff., 148, with Trible's *God and the Rhetoric of Sexuality*. Ruether argues that these chapters express and promote patriarchy; Trible argues that they convey feminist perspectives on gender relations.

that the Bible has a theological and ethical core which supports women's struggle for liberation and identity, a core to which the "non-core" parts must be subordinated in some way.

Feminists also differ regarding which *parts* of the Bible express its liberative, authoritative core. Letty Russell and Rosemary Ruether identify specific traditions and texts within the Bible that they believe are genuinely liberative for women. In other words, the revelation of God experienced in the present struggle for gender justice finds a correlate within the ancient biblical text. Russell believes that the "Bible has authority because it witnesses to God's liberating action on behalf of God's creation."[43] She examines many themes from the Old and New Testaments, arguing for their connection with the universality and liberated nature of God's future kingdom. For Russell, therefore, the eschatological promise of a new heaven and a new earth is the liberative center of the Bible, and as such it shapes her interpretation and highlighting of biblical texts.[44]

Rosemary Ruether, on the other hand, identifies the prophetic critical principle as the authoritative core of the Bible. According to this core principle, just as Jesus and the prophets denounced the religious, economic, and political powers of their day, so we must denounce the patriarchal system (among others) of our day. Although Jesus and the prophets did not directly denounce the patriarchal system, their *pattern* of prophetic critique encourages and justifies the feminist critique. It is also on the basis of this biblical principle that Ruether dismisses and denounces the patriarchal parts of the Bible:

> Feminist readings of the Bible can discern a norm within Biblical faith by which the Biblical texts themselves can be criticized. To the extent to which Biblical texts reflect this normative principle, they are regarded as authoritative. On this basis many aspects of the Bible are to be frankly set aside and rejected.[45]

Thus, just as Jesus and the apostles set aside the Hebrew ritual law in the name of the gospel, so today feminist theologians should set aside

43. Russell, cited by Schüssler Fiorenza in *Bread Not Stone,* p. 13.

44. See Russell's essay entitled "Feminist Critique: Opportunity for Cooperation," *Journal for the Study of the Old Testament* 22 (1982): 54-66; and her book entitled *Human Liberation in a Feminist Perspective,* esp. pp. 27-33 and 56-58.

45. Schüssler Fiorenza, *Sexism and God-Talk,* p. 23.

patriarchal texts by appealing to the Bible's more central, prophetic, and liberating message. Because this process of prophetic critique and revision is exemplified within the Bible itself, argues Ruether, when we do likewise we are being biblical in the deepest sense.

A third feminist theologian, Schüssler Fiorenza, is critical of *any* approach that identifies all or some parts of the Bible as authoritative. In her view such approaches treat the Bible as an "archetype" rather than as a "prototype," which creates critical difficulties: "As mythical archetype the Bible can be either accepted or rejected, but not critically evaluated. A mythical archetype takes historically limited experiences and texts and posits them as universals, which then become authoritative and normative for all times and cultures."[46] Schüssler Fiorenza objects to this approach for three reasons. First, it fails to take seriously the androcentric nature of biblical language and the "patriarchal stamp of all biblical traditions." Second, in distinguishing between language and content, patriarchal expression and liberating tradition, it relies "on an untenable linguistic-philosophical position that divides form and content, linguistic expression and revelatory truth." And third, by choosing one text, tradition, or dynamic, this approach "is in danger of advocating a reductionist method of theological critique and of relinquishing the historical richness of biblical experience."[47]

Schüssler Fiorenza claims that the Bible should be seen as a "prototype" rather than as an "archetype." In this approach the source of authority is not the Bible but rather the present community that struggles against racism, sexism, and poverty. For this community

> [the Bible is] a formative root-model of biblical faith and life. [The community's] vision of liberation and salvation is informed by the biblical prototype but is not derived from it. It places biblical texts under the authority of feminist experience insofar as it maintains that revelation is ongoing and takes place "for the sake of our salvation." It does not seek identification with certain biblical texts and traditions, but rather solidarity with women in biblical religion. As the church of women, we are called not to reproduce biblical structures and traditions but to remember and transform our biblical heritage.[48]

46. Schüssler Fiorenza, *Bread Not Stone*, p. 10.
47. Ibid., p. 13.
48. Ibid., p. 15. For an exchange between Douglas Schuurman, the primary author of this chapter, and Allen Verhey on this and related issues in hermeneutics,

Schüssler Fiorenza might find some authorization for her approach in the example of the biblical authors themselves. Those authors selected, omitted, and rewrote Old Testament and Jesus traditions because they felt compelled to illuminate or censure the beliefs and praxis of their communities. According to this account, we must do the same with the various traditions available to us. Given her earlier statement, however, Schüssler Fiorenza realizes that this might be misconstrued as treating the biblical authors' pattern of creative revision as an archetype. Thus she finds authorization for her approach *not* primarily in the example of the biblical authors but rather in the contemporary community of women, and men who identify with women, who struggle for salvation and liberation.

It is clear that various feminists differ on whether a given passage or biblical teaching is patriarchal and differ on which traditions within the Bible express its liberative core. They do not, however, differ with each other about whether patriarchal passages and themes per se have normative status for Christian faith and life. All agree that the theological and ethical core of Christian faith supports the liberation and affirmation of women. It is this core that functions normatively for feminist interpretation and use of the Bible, just as John Calvin's emphasis on God's promise of grace served as his interpretive core.

Thus for Christian feminists the Bible, properly interpreted, becomes a source of criticism for tradition, church, and society. Letty Russell, for example, measures the poverty, racism, and sexism of our society against the biblical vision of a new heaven and a new earth. According to this perspective, the contrast between what now is and what God will bring to pass should generate criticism and transformation of society. Insofar as the teaching and practice of the church and of tradition have contributed instead to oppression, Russell critically revises traditional theology and calls for new practices leading to liberation.[49]

A Reformed Response

Some Reformed thinkers are extremely critical of Christian feminist approaches to the Bible and its authority. For example, Elizabeth Achte-

---

see Douglas Schuurman's "The Great Reversal: Ethics and the New Testament — A Critical Assessment" and Allen Verhey's "A Response to Douglas Schuurman," both in *The Calvin Theological Journal* 23 (November 1988): 222-37.

49. See Russell's *Human Liberation in a Feminist Perspective*.

meier rejects the cavalier way in which many feminist theologians seem to distort and dismiss parts of the Bible. She rejects feminists' invocation of experience: "When our own experience is the criterion, what overcomes our tendencies to self-interest, to pride, to rationalization, and to sin? What becomes the measure of what is just and unjust? What determines what is true and untrue?"[50] Because all human experience is fallen experience, Achtemeier is saying, it should not be the norm for Christian thought and life. Neither should any part of Scripture be rejected: "The Word of God, mediated through the Bible, creates in our lives that of which it speaks," she asserts, "and when we abandon any portion of that Word, Christian life and hope are distorted and cannot be sustained."[51] And because Scripture speaks of Christ as Lord, we must accept him as such, something many feminists reject: "Many [feminists] do not want to trust a Lord — that basic requirement of the Christian faith. The Lordship of Jesus Christ, in whose service is perfect freedom, smacks too much to them of a hierarchical domination." Achtemeier accuses feminists of reducing Christ to "just a 'paradigm,' a 'model of liberated humanity.'" In doing so they "have vitiated the Christian faith and left themselves without an ethic and indeed without empowerment."[52] As she sees it, feminist claims about experience and the Bible are both theologically wrong and practically unworkable.

Achtemeier's criticisms certainly capture Reformed convictions about the fallenness of humanity, the sovereignty of God in Christ, and the supreme importance of the Bible. However, her criticisms apply to the more radical end of the mainline feminist spectrum and not to many other mainline and evangelical feminists. Except for this more radical group, most feminists do not cavalierly dismiss entire sections of the Bible.

Even so, there are weaknesses in Achtemeier's critique, and these weaknesses reflect issues that Calvinists should attend to more carefully than they have in the past.

The first issue involves the need for Reformed Christians to acknowledge the ways in which *their own* confessional traditions shape their interpretations of the Bible. It is true that in theory Calvinism does not

50. Achtemeier, "The Impossible Impossibility," p. 51.
51. Ibid., p. 52.
52. Ibid., p. 54.

"abandon" any portion of the Bible. However, as we noted earlier, Calvinists regularly function with a confessionally defined core in their use of the Bible and their doing of theology. Consequently, those parts of the Bible that seem to conflict with the accepted core are suppressed or subordinated through interpretation. Calvinists should be more honest about this aspect of their interpretation and use of the Bible.

The second issue concerns sin and its effects upon appeals to authority. Achtemeier correctly points out that the sinful character of human beings infects appeals to experience; however, she neglects to point out that it also infects appeals to *Scripture*. Achtemeier fails to reckon adequately with the fact that often *both* the oppressed *and* the oppressors appeal to the Bible to support their stance. The Reformed tradition has reflected deeply and critically about wicked political rulers who use texts like Romans 13:1 to demand submission to evil laws and practices,[53] but it has generally neglected the ways in which biblical texts have been used to sustain or ignore abuse against women.[54] For example,

53. For a helpful historical survey of the politically revolutionary strands of the Calvinist tradition, see Michael Walzer's *Revolution of the Saints.* The pastors and theologians supporting the resistance of apartheid in South Africa provide the most recent examples of this long and impressive Reformed tradition of resistance. It is significant that Allan Boesak and other anti-apartheid theologians do not identify appeal or nonappeal to Scripture as the central issue in their struggle. Boesak writes, "When, precisely, do the actions of a government collide with the demands of the word of God? In deciding this, the church should be led by the word itself, knowing the demands for justice and peace, and also by the actual experience of the people. It is in the concrete situations of actual human experience that the word of God shows itself alive and more powerful and sharper than any two-edged sword." This excerpt is taken from "Divine Obedience: A Letter to the Minister of Justice," in *Black and Reformed: Apartheid, Liberation and the Calvinist Tradition,* p. 38. See also "The Confession 1982" (officially adopted by the Synod of the Dutch Reformed Mission Church) in *A Moment of Truth: The Confession of the Dutch Reformed Mission Church,* ed. G. D. Cloete and D. J. Smit (Grand Rapids: William B. Eerdmans, 1984), pp. 1-6, and the excellent essay by D. J. Smit in that volume entitled "What Does *Status Confessionis* Mean?" pp. 7-32.

54. In his sermon on Deuteronomy 23, Calvin describes the sensible wife as follows: "Since God has given me such a condition that I be subject to my husband, there is no question of my raising my head like a deer, and that I reject the yoke: for I shall not disobey a mortal man, I won't even offend him, in that I gave him my word, to be subject and obedient to him, and I am doing the very opposite; but I will offend the one who subjected me to him: it is God who gave me into the hands of my husband, and who wants me to be more subject to him than to father or mother" ("Marriage in Calvin's Sermons," trans. Claude-Marie Baldwin, in *Calvin-*

the tyrannical "Christian" husband or father who uses Ephesians 5:22 and 6:1 to bludgeon his wife or children into submission to his inordinate or perverse demands certainly "appeals" to Scripture — but in a profoundly inappropriate way.[55] The Tempter also appealed to Scripture in his unsuccessful efforts to thwart the Messiah. The words of false prophets may conform perfectly to words found in the Bible, and yet they may be deceptively and destructively untrue. In what sense, then, is the Bible the *only* norm? Although there is indeed an unbelieving rejection of Scripture closely related to the rejection of Jesus Christ as

---

iana: Ideas and Influence of Jean Calvin, vol. 10: *Sixteenth-Century Essays and Studies,* ed. Robert V. Schnucker [Kirksville, Mo.: Sixteenth-Century Journal Publications, 1988]). One case that came before the Consistory at Geneva involved a woman, Martinaz, who was being beaten by her husband, lumberjack Claude Soutiez. Although Claude beat Martinaz so severely that he put out one of her eyes, the Council only called him to promise not to "irritate" *(corroser)* his wife and ordered him to appear before the Small Council. The Consistory enjoined Martinaz to obey and live peacefully with her husband, and required her also to promise not to irritate her husband. (This information came from a letter dated 3 April 1990 from Jeff Watt, History Department, University of Mississippi, to Dr. Richard Gamble, Director, Meeter Center for Calvin Studies.) In his letter to an abused woman, Calvin counsels almost total submission: "We have a special sympathy for poor women who are evilly and roughly treated by their husbands, because of the roughness and cruelty of the tyranny and captivity which is their lot. We do not find ourselves permitted by the Word of God, however, to advise a woman to leave her husband, except by force of necessity; and we do not understand this force to be operative when a husband behaves roughly and uses threats to his wife, nor even when he beats her, but when there is imminent peril to her life, whether from persecution by the husband or by his conspiring with the enemies of the truth, or from some other source.... We exhort her ... to bear with patience the cross which God has seen fit to place upon her; and meanwhile not to deviate from the duty which she has before God to please her husband, but to be faithful whatever happens" (cited by Jane Dempsey Douglass in "Women and the Continental Reformation," in *Religion and Sexism: Images of Woman in the Jewish and Christian Traditions,* ed. Rosemary Radford Ruether [New York: Simon & Schuster, 1974], pp. 300-301). Although some of Calvin's writings contain calls for analogous submission to princes and kings, the basis for resistance to them is clearer than that for wives to resist abusive husbands. The Reformed tradition has augmented the glimmerings for *political* resistance provided by Calvin, but it has rarely developed the strands in Calvin's writings that might have provided a basis for domestic resistance.

55. For a social-historical study of family violence, with special attention to its regulation among the Puritans of Massachusetts, see Elizabeth Pleck's *Domestic Tyranny: The Making of American Social Policy against Family Violence from Colonial Times to the Present* (New York: Oxford University Press, 1987).

Lord, there is also an equally dangerous abuse of the Bible in the service of injustice that is easily concealed by the slogan *sola scriptura.* Think, for example, of the so-called biblical grounds for the long-standing defense of apartheid by white South African Reformed churches, or of the "biblical" arguments in favor of slavery made by American pastors and governors little more than a century ago.[56] It is *fallen* human beings who decide how to interpret and apply the Bible. Appeals to the Bible as well as to experience must be governed by God's purposes in this world if they are to resist the insidious influences of sin.

We agree that Achtemeier's scathing criticisms do apply to the more radical feminist theologians. Those who, in the name of experience, make intentional and avowedly ideological use of Scripture need to learn from the Reformed principle of *listening* to Scripture. Nevertheless, on the two issues just outlined, Calvinists can learn a great deal from the more moderate mainline and evangelical feminist theologians.[57]

Conclusion

As the preceding discussion indicates, Reformed and feminist worldviews have certain themes in common. Within both groups of thinkers we have seen a strong concern that the Christian faith be "world-formative" — that is, concerned with institutional reform and not merely with "personalized" religion. We have also seen that both groups give experience an important role to play in Christian life and thought — although feminists appear to have been more honest about this than many Calvinists. Finally, we have seen that neither group simply "lets the plain truth of the Bible speak for itself" — indeed, we are convinced that this is *never* possible. Instead (like all Christian groups who claim to have a high regard for Scripture), both Calvinists and feminists approach and organize the Bible in terms of a confessionally defined core of issues that each group sees to be of greatest importance. In the case of Calvinists, God's sovereignty and God's promises are important themes. Among

56. See Swartley's *Slavery, Sabbath, War, and Women,* esp. pp. 31-66.

57. The book by van Wijk-Bos, *Reformed and Feminist,* does take these issues seriously. Although she recognizes the patriarchal character of the Bible, van Wijk-Bos experiences God's redemption and verification as communicated by the Bible. Her reflections on biblical authority and her interpretations of Old Testament texts exemplify the kind of Reformed feminism that we think is needful.

feminist theologians, the full humanity of women and their equal partnership with men are the themes used to judge what is central and what is peripheral in Scripture.

In the following chapter we will build upon this foundational comparison by looking at three more specific theological topics that are important to both feminists and Calvinists — namely, the nature of God, the nature of humanity, and the nature of the created world — as well as the relationships among all three.

CHAPTER 6

God, Humanity, and the World in Reformed and Feminist Perspectives

In the previous chapter we compared Calvinism and feminism on their basic approaches to Christian thought and life. In this chapter, as promised, we compare them on three more specific theological topics important to both traditions — namely, God, humanity, and the world. As in the previous chapter, we will find both commonalities and conflicts between the two groups. Where there is a genuine conflict between Calvinist and feminist perspectives, Calvinist feminists must be *mutually critical* — at one juncture requiting or revising a Calvinist theme; at another juncture rejecting or revising a feminist theme. Adopting this method, as opposed to clinging to an ideological Calvinism or feminism, will take us one step closer to creative fidelity to the gospel of Christ in our day.

God

The conflict between feminism and Calvinism is probably more intense regarding the doctrine of God than any other aspect of Christian the-

---

The primary author of this chapter is Douglas Schuurman.

ology. Feminists have criticized the doctrine of God's sovereignty on the grounds that it undermines human responsibility for social and ecological problems and reflects a dangerous, male understanding of the God-world relationship — one in which God is essentially independent of the world and hierarchically rules over it. This in turn is said to encourage oppressive relations between men and women and between other dominant and subordinate groups as well as the exploitation of nature.[1] Many feminists also reject the traditional trinitarian formula for God as Father, Son, and Spirit.[2] They reject both its predominantly male imagery and its hierarchical subordination of the Son to the Father and the Spirit to both the Father and the Son. Many feminists even question the salvific efficacy of a male Christ and the need to bow before Christ as Lord. Appealing to the wide variety of imagery for God in the Bible and to women's experience of God amid oppression and liberation, feminists are proposing that God be described as feminine, immanent, dynamic, gender-surpassing, and mysterious. Within the feminist camp, debates also abound concerning the criteria for determining appropriate God-language (shall we invoke Scripture? tradition? experience?) and which attributes of God should be advanced or abandoned.[3]

We cannot begin to do justice to the many theological issues implied by these claims. Accordingly, we will examine feminist claims relating to two particular issues related to the doctrine of God, issues

1. See, for example, Dorothee Soelle's *To Work and To Love* (Minneapolis: Augsburg, 1984), esp. pp. 13-29; and Sallie McFague's *Models of God: Theology for an Ecological, Nuclear Age* (Philadelphia: Fortress Press, 1987), pp. 14-21.

2. See, for example, Rosemary Ruether's *Sexism and God-Talk: Toward a Feminist Theology* (Boston: Beacon Press, 1983), p. 60.

3. Some feminists wish to continue to give "Father" imagery a central place but insist upon redefining fatherhood in ways that emphasize God's care for and intimacy with us. For examples of this approach, see Diane Tennis's *Is God the Only Reliable Father?* (Philadelphia: Westminster Press, 1985), and Nancy Hardesty's "'Whosoever Surely Meaneth Me': Inclusive Language and the Gospel," *Christian Scholar's Review* 17, no. 3 (1988): 231-40. Others propose a ban on "Father" imagery because of its recent hegemony and the contemporary need for other imagery (see McFague's *Models of God*, p. 13), or because of the "kerygmatic reason" that Christians have "an obligation to bear faithful witness to the complex reality *of God*" rather than reinforce an idolatrous constriction of God as Father (see Mary Potter Engel's "Tambourines to the Glory of God: From the Monarchy of God the Father to the Monotheism of God the Great Mysterious," *Word and World* 7, no. 2 [1987]: 153-66). Still others propose that "Father" imagery continue to be used, but only as one among many kinds of diverse biblical names and images for God.

that we introduced in the previous chapter. Then we will develop a Reformed response to these feminist claims. The *first* issue concerns the feminist critique of the ways in which traditional God-language supports the oppression of women and the exploitation of nature. The *second* issue concerns feminist proposals for a God-language inclusive of feminine characteristics and concerns.

The Feminist Critique of Traditional God-Language

One focus of the feminist critique of the dominance of masculine God-language is deeply theological. Some feminists argue that if God is Holy Mystery, pure Spirit, unnameable YHWH, then using exclusively or primarily one set of images is idolatrous. Thus Mary Potter Engel says, "Those who claim Father as *the* title or *the* divinely revealed name of God, according it a special status beyond that of all 'humanly constructed' images, would do well to remember the warning of the fiery bush that God is the Unnameable One, the Uncontrollable One. Unless one keeps this in mind, the use of Father as the name for God is blasphemy."[4] Similarly, Sister Sandra M. Schneiders affirms that not only is it permissible to imagine God as a woman, "it's necessary if we wish to have a healthy, balanced image of God operating in our spirituality. God is spirit, neither male nor female." Schneiders believes that we need to keep many metaphors of God active simultaneously to keep ourselves aware that "none of them is adequate to the Holy Mystery who is God" and so to avoid idolatry.[5] Nancy Hardesty recognizes the profound significance of God's nature for inclusive language. For her, however, the central theological issue is the inclusive nature of the gospel. "The clear teaching of Scripture is that God's love, Christ's redemption, is inclusive. . . . Inclusive language is simply a concrete expression of what we say we believe theologically — that all human beings are made in God's image."[6]

Feminist criticism of traditional God-language also focuses on the way in which masculine God-language legitimizes the oppression of

4. Engel, "Tambourines to the Glory of God," p. 162.
5. "God Is More Than Two Men and a Bird," interview with Sandra M. Schneiders, I.H.M., *U.S. Catholic,* May 1990, pp. 20-21.
6. Hardesty, "'Whosoever Surely Meaneth Me,'" p. 237.

women and the exploitation of the environment. In our culture, according to Marchiene Rienstra, "women still suffer, as they have in the past, the oppressive effects of stereotyping, of dehumanizing expectations, of confused and inferior self-images, of great odds when they try to make it in what is yet a man's world, of attacks on their femininity when they are too successful."[7] Moreover, a high percentage of women in our society are victims of domestic or sexual abuse (25 percent is a modest estimate),[8] usually at the hands of men they know and once trusted. Much of the feminist criticism of masculine God-language grows out of a pastoral concern for women's struggle with these realities.

Although logically and theologically false, Mary Daly's infamous aphorism, "Since God is male, the male is God," accurately captures certain social and psychological abuses of masculine God-language.[9] According to Daly,

> [The] symbol of the Father God, spawned in the human imagination and sustained as plausible by patriarchy, has in turn rendered service to this type of society by making its mechanisms for the oppression of women appear right and fitting. If God in "his" heaven is a father ruling "his" people, then it is in the "nature" of things and according to divine plan and the order of the universe that society be male-dominated.[10]

Male God-language, she claims, creates a "mystification of roles" so that "the husband dominating his wife represents God 'himself.'"[11] The dom-

---

7. Rienstra, "God's Freedom for Women," *Reformed Journal* 27 (September 1977): 11.

8. Susan Thistlethwaite estimates that one in two women is a victim of sexual or domestic abuse, usually at the hands of someone close to them; see *Sex, Race, and God: Christian Feminism in Black and White* (New York: Crossroad, 1989), p. 24. The most conservative estimate is that one in six women is a victim of sexual or physical abuse; see Mary Stewart Van Leeuwen's *Gender and Grace: Love, Work and Parenting in a Changing World* (Downers Grove, Ill.: InterVarsity Press, 1990). See also *Abuse and Religion: When Praying Isn't Enough,* ed. Anne L. Horton and Judith A. Williamson (Lexington: D. C. Heath, 1988).

9. Daly, "The Qualitative Leap beyond Patriarchal Religion," *Quest* 1 (1974): 21.

10. Daly, *Beyond God the Father: Toward a Philosophy of Women's Liberation* (Boston: Beacon Press, 1973), p. 13.

11. Ibid. Rosemary Ruether likewise says, "Male monotheism reinforces the social hierarchy of patriarchal rule through its religious system in a way that was not the case with the paired images of God and Goddess. God is modeled after the

inance of masculine names, similes, and metaphors for God too easily slides into an idolatrous equation of God with males. When this idolatry occurs, it perpetuates tangible harm and injustice against women as well as more subtle forms of women's subordination to men.

Feminists also criticize the ways in which masculine God-language sanctions and promotes the exploitation of nature. Sallie McFague poses the problem in terms of the traditional theological emphasis on God's independence from and God's supreme power over the world:

> The primary metaphors in the tradition are hierarchical, imperialistic, and dualistic, stressing the distance between God and the world and the total reliance of the world on God. Thus, the metaphors of God as king, ruler, lord, master, and governor, and the concepts that accompany them of God as absolute, complete, transcendent, and omnipotent permit no sense of mutuality, shared responsibility, reciprocity, and love (except in the sense of gratitude).[12]

According to McFague, "Father," the primary metaphor for God, *might* in principle allow for a more relational and interdependent view of God and the world. But this metaphor "has been so qualified by being associated with the metaphors of king and lord (as, for instance, in the phrase, 'almighty Father') that its potential as an expression of a unified, interdependent view of God and the world is undercut."[13]

A key question in relation to this feminist critique is whether the biblical and traditional language for God *naturally* and *inevitably* leads to the oppression of women and the exploitation of nature, or whether these admittedly tragic effects result from the *abuse* of biblical and traditional God-language. After all, many good things can be perverted to serve

---

patriarchal ruling class and is seen as addressing this class of males directly, adopting them as his 'sons.' They are his representatives, the responsible partners of the covenant with him. Women as wives now become symbolically repressed as the dependent servant class. Wives, along with children and servants, represent those ruled over and owned by the patriarchal class. They relate to man as he relates to God. A symbolic hierarchy is set up: God-male-female. Women no longer stand in direct relation to God; they are connected to God secondarily, through the male. This hierarchical order is evident in the structure of patriarchal law in the Old Testament. . . . In the New Testament this hierarchical 'order' appears as a cosmic principle" (*Sexism and God-Talk*, p. 53).

12. McFague, *Models of God*, p. 19.
13. Ibid.

wicked ends. As the medievals used to say, the abuse of a doctrine or claim does not destroy its legitimacy and proper use. Evangelical feminists usually say that it is the abuse of biblical language that is the problem, showing how what they call a truly biblical understanding of God resists such abuses.[14] They then use this biblical view to criticize contemporary and traditional Christian God-language. Thus Marchiene Rienstra says that women have experienced the Reformed doctrine of God

> as excessively masculine, with its preoccupation with his forceful power, his absolute control, his sovereign rule, his anger at sin as an offense to his honor and rebellion against his authority. In the process, the scriptural teachings, just as numerous and weighty, which describe God's omnipotence as a love which conquers all obstacles; his providence as loving care for his children and creation; his omnipresence as his constant nurturing, teaching, enabling Presence in our lives; his irresistible grace as a love which wins through a compelling force which does not destroy freedom; his omniscience as his capacity for awareness and ability to meet all needs and opportunities for loving; his anger at sin as based upon the fact that sin destroys his beloved children and creation — all these aspects have received too little attention.[15]

However, mainline Christian feminists usually say that the problem goes much deeper than a mere masculine overemphasis in our use of biblical and traditional God-language. Oppressive distortions are thought to be nearly inevitable, either because biblical and traditional God-language is irredeemably patriarchal,[16] or because the modern situation is such that this language will inevitably be abused.[17]

14. See Hardesty's "'Whosoever Surely Meaneth Me'" and her book entitled *Inclusive Language in the Church* (Philadelphia: John Knox Press, 1987).

15. Rienstra, "God's Freedom for Women (3)," *Reformed Journal* 27 (November 1977): 26.

16. This seems to be the position that Ruether takes in *Sexism and God-Talk*. Mary Daly is aware of the fact that for a theologically informed Christian, God is neither male nor female but transcends both genders. But she complains that "even when the basic assumptions of God-language appear to be nonsexist, and when language is somewhat purified of fixation upon maleness, it is damaging and implicitly compatible with sexism if it encourages detachment from the reality of the human struggle against oppression in its concrete manifestations. That is, the lack of explicit relevance of intellection to the fact of oppression in its precise forms, such as sexual hierarchy, is itself oppressive" (*Beyond God the Father*, p. 20).

17. Thus Sallie McFague says, "Language that supports hierarchical, dualistic,

152

Differences on this point lead to different proposals for revising God language. Evangelical feminists generally try to retain biblical imagery but give greater place to feminine biblical imagery alongside the traditionally emphasized masculine imagery. In this way they emphasize the more feminine aspects of God. (See also Chapter Eleven.) Some mainline feminists follow the evangelical feminist pattern; others create new imagery for God, tending to reject masculine imagery rather than revising its content. This leads to a second theme that emerges from feminist concerns about the doctrine of God.

Imaging God: Feminist Alternatives

This second theme relates to the "affirmation of women-as-women" aspect of feminist experience, which was introduced in the previous chapter. Here the effort is to arrive at new images, metaphors, and models for God that will function as alternatives to traditional God-language. The hope is that these will help to reverse the social and psychological oppression of women and also lead to a responsible ecological ethic. The proposals vary widely, but broadly they fall into four groups: (1) proposals calling for a female deity, (2) proposals calling for inclusion of feminine imagery with masculine imagery for God, (3) proposals calling for non-gender-related imagery, and (4) proposals calling for a great variety of imagery, both gendered and nongendered. The general direction of all four proposals, however, is toward a view of God that emphasizes God's immanence, mysteriousness, relationality, liberating power, and nurturing capacity more than most previous theologizing has.

With regard to the first of these proposals, post-Christian religious feminists call for a *female* deity to *replace* the traditional male deity. Naomi Goldenberg, Carol Christ, and Mary Daly all agree that "a female deity or divine principle is necessary if women's experience is to be included in a religious world view."[18] The goddess, according to Sallie McFague,

external, unchanging, atomistic, anthropocentric, and deterministic ways of understanding these relationships [between God and the world and between humanity and the world] is not appropriate *for our time*, whatever its appropriateness might have been for other times" (*Models of God*, p. 13).

18. This claim is explored by Sallie McFague in *Metaphorical Theology: Models of God in Religious Language* (Philadelphia: Fortress Press, 1982), p. 156. McFague is examining, not advocating, such post-Christian feminist claims.

frees women to look to the female principle in herself and in other women as the sustaining and saving power [and here she quotes Carol Christ]: "The simplest and most basic meaning of the symbol of Goddess is the acknowledgment of the legitimacy of female power as a beneficent and independent power." A woman who echoes Ntozake Shange's dramatic statement, "I found God in myself and I loved her fiercely," is saying "Female power is strong and creative."[19]

By contrast, mainline and evangelical feminists reject the post-Christian proposal for a female deity on the grounds that it is unbiblical, that it depends upon limiting stereotypical feminine traits, and that it lacks a self-critical dimension when it gives women the status of savior to both themselves and the world.[20] Instead, these feminists support the other three proposals previously mentioned. Those who propose that masculine imagery for God should be complemented by feminine imagery often make use of biblical materials. Thus Phyllis Trible discerns a feminist perspective even within the Old Testament, though she is careful to distinguish it from the post-Christian perspective: "This perspective is, however, unlike that of the Goddess religions, for while God is imagined in masculine as well as in feminine metaphors, the divine is neither male nor female but embraces and transcends both."[21] Nancy Hardesty argues for a renewed emphasis on the maternal images for God in the Bible — such as Isaiah's descriptions of God as a woman in labor (42:14), as a woman giving birth (46:3-4), and as a mother who would never forget her "sucking child" or "have no compassion on the [child] of her womb" (49:15, RSV), and Hosea's picture of God as "a bear robbed of her cubs" (13:8).[22]

The third group of proposals leads partially or totally *away* from familial and gender-related imagery. Rosemary Ruether rejects the title "Mother-Father God" because it "suggests a kind of permanent parent-child relationship to God."[23] By calling God "God/ess" and "Primal Matrix," Ruether attempts to retain feminine aspects of God but avoid

19. Ibid., p. 158.
20. Evangelical feminists emphasize that a Goddess religion is unbiblical. Sallie McFague, a mainline feminist, rejects it for all three reasons given above. (See her *Metaphorical Theology*, pp. 152-92.)
21. Ibid., p. 168. McFague is describing Phyllis Trible's view as found in "Depatriarchialism in Biblical Interpretation," *Journal of the American Academy of Religion* 41 (March 1973): 34.
22. Hardesty, "'Whosoever Surely Meaneth Me,'" pp. 234-35.
23. Ruether, *Sexism and God-Talk*, p. 69.

stereotypic ways of thinking about gender. With this naming she moves away somewhat from gender-related imagery.

Sallie McFague argues that gendered images, which are usually paternal or maternal, need to be balanced by the gender-neutral metaphor of God as "friend." She also says that parental images "cannot express mutuality, maturity, cooperation, responsibility, or reciprocity," and that they neglect the public and political dimensions of relationships.[24] In her book entitled *Models of God*, McFague develops the model of God as "friend" in a way that still respects the inequality of states between God and humanity. Her proposal is feminist in the broad sense of emphasizing the relatedness of God to the world and the reciprocity that exists between them.[25]

Other feminists such as Sister Sandra Schneiders say that we shouldn't settle for very long on *any* image or name for God, be it father, mother, friend, or Primal Matrix:

> Such images of God as mother, father, shepherd, sower, and baker are very useful, but so are such nonhuman images as lamb, lamp, gate, and water. What we need to do is get all of these images into the Christian imagination and experience so that they constantly play off one another and keep any one single image from being idolized. The mystics have always known this.[26]

Mary Potter Engel appeals to God's own nature as the basis for variety in terminology. She writes, "I am opposed to any name or title for God, including Mother, and instead favor the use of a variety of images for God. . . . If God is not a thing to be described but a limit we experience, every image will distract us away from as well as point us toward that reality."[27]

Feminists are quick to emphasize the analogical or metaphorical character of *all* God-language. Thus Sallie McFague speaks of "models" or "metaphors" for God and explains how they function:

24. McFague, *Metaphorical Theology*, pp. 178-79.

25. Richard J. Mouw approves of McFague's efforts to retain God's transcendence within feminism. See his book entitled *The God Who Commands* (Notre Dame: University of Notre Dame Press, 1990), p. 163. One of the central tenets of Mouw's "Calvinist feminism" is the establishment of egalitarian, intrahuman relations upon a hierarchical divine-human relation (pp. 161-69).

26. "God Is More Than Two Men and a Bird," p. 21.

27. Engel, "Tambourines to the Glory of God," pp. 162-63.

To say that "God is mother" is not to identify God with mother, but to understand God in light of some of the characteristics associated with mothering. It is, then, also to say, "God is not mother," or, to combine the positive and negative aspects of metaphorical assertion, "God is/is not mother," or yet again, "God as mother."[28]

Feminist theology of God is thus marked by images, models, paradigms, similes, and metaphors rather than by reified "names" and syllogistic thought.[29] The great variety of biblical imagery for God challenges the hegemony of masculine imagery and serves as an invitation to envision God in new ways. The creative revisioning of God that is seen to be biblically and theologically mandated is also considered necessary for ministering to the needs of women and men in the church.

God-Language: A Reformed Response

Reformed faith, along with feminism, condemns the abuse of God-language in the service of women's oppression and the exploitation of nature. To Reformed sensibilities, such abuse is sheer idolatry — the conceptualization and utilization of God to serve the interests of oneself or one's own group. By the light of Reformed faith, the living God does *not* sanction social oppression of any kind; the living God does *not* desire the exploitation of nature. The living God instead smashes idols, demands love and justice in society, and cherishes creation. Although these themes are often distorted by Calvinists, they run deep throughout the history of the tradition.

The Reformed tradition emphasizes God's transcendence, but in its better expressions it does not do so at the expense of human responsibility or God's concern for the cries of the poor and the groaning of the earth. On the contrary, the God revealed in Christ resists oppression of every kind.[30] Thus Allan Boesak declares,

28. McFague, *Models of God*, pp. 22-23.
29. See Donald K. McKim's "Hearkening to the Voices: What Women Theologians Are Saying," *Reformed Journal* 35 (January 1985): 9.
30. Richard Mouw charts the course of "Calvinist feminism" between the two extremes of "the long-standing oppressive teaching that a male-ruling-female hierarchy is the only appropriate way to mirror the God-ruling-humankind hierarchy, and the more recent heterodoxy that a healthy intrahuman egalitarianism can only

The God of the Bible is the God of Jesus Christ who took upon himself the condition of oppression and poverty. Jesus Christ sides with the poor and the weak. He speaks of himself as a "servant." Jesus becomes one of the *'am ha-aretz,* the poor of the land. He is a man without majesty, a man of sorrows and familiar with suffering, whose life reflects so much of the life of oppressed peoples today.[31]

In the same vein, Abraham Kuyper says of the influence of Christ and the church, "Slavery was broken at its root, and underwent a moral criticism which demolished it as an institution. Men began to be concerned about the care of the poor and of orphans. . . . Higher and lower classes approached each other on a footing of freer association."[32]

But even though Reformed thinkers agree with feminists that the God of the Bible resists all idolatry and injustice, they do *not* locate the problem in the doctrine of God's sovereignty and power. Perhaps more than any other major Christian tradition, the Reformed tradition has emphasized the transcendence of God and the distinction between Creator and creature. This emphasis is due in part to the Reformed experience of God's sovereignty in grace, to which we referred in the last chapter.[33] It is also due to Reformed sensitivity to the temptations of

---

be sustained by a kind of immanentistic God-human egalitarianism" (*The God Who Commands,* p. 164). According to Mouw, the way to avoid these extremes is to explore the ways in which the theme of God's sovereign rule over humans can function as a basis for nonhierarchical relations among human beings (pp. 165-67). Mouw believes that God's assignment of accountable dominion (hierarchical relation) is to be accepted equally by women and men (nonhierarchical relation). Mary Stewart Van Leeuwen follows a similar line of reasoning in *Gender and Grace,* pp. 33-53, expanding the scope of her discussion to include creation, fall, and redemption.

31. Boesak, *Black and Reformed: Apartheid, Liberation and the Calvinist Tradition,* ed. Leonard Sweetman (Maryknoll, N.Y.: Orbis Books, 1984), p. 73.

32. Kuyper, *Christianity and the Class Struggle,* trans. Dirk Jellema (Grand Rapids: Piet Hein Publishers, 1950), p. 31.

33. Mary Potter Engel revises our understanding of God's transcendence in a way that is amenable to Reformed experience. After admonishing feminists for neglecting divine transcendence, she calls for "a renewed emphasis upon the transcending God that rises up out of our awareness of ourselves as frail and finite, dependent creatures pushing up against the limits of a reality that is powerful, incomprehensible, and uncontrollable; out of our recognition that the reality we call God is unfathomable, impenetrable, unreachable, existing beyond all our imagings, desires, needs, hopes, feelings, thoughts, actions, and expectations; out of our acknowledgment that the Life Dwelling in the Many that is ever near to us and

157

idolatry and the related critique of social injustices that flow from idolatry. Calvinism is indeed a "theocentric" rather than an "anthropocentric" theological tradition.[34]

Yet it is the very omnipotence of God that *gives* Calvinists the confidence and courage to resist the oppressor, even to the point of death. Thus Allan Boesak says,

> It is my conviction that, for a Christian, obedience to the state or any earthly authority is always linked to our obedience to God. That is to say, obedience to human institutions (and to human beings) is always relative. The human institution can never have the same authority as God, and human laws must always be subordinate to the word of God. . . . Even God does not expect blind servility; Christians cannot even think of giving unconditional obedience to a government.[35]

Christ is Lord, and there is no other — that is the heart of Calvinism's ethic. This theme is supported by affirmations of God's sovereignty and the need for sinful human beings to surrender to the will of God. Some feminists share the Calvinist affirmation of divine transcendence;[36] others reject it as finally serving oppressive, patriarchal ends. Still others acknowledge the importance of divine transcendence — as a needed reference point for social criticism (Rosemary Ruether) or as necessary for affirmation of God's mystery (Mary Potter Engel) — but resist

---

heedful of us is also the One Who Dwells in Glory that is inaccessible to us" ("Tambourines to the Glory of God," pp. 160-61). The central difference between Kuyper and Calvin on the one hand and Potter Engel on the other is that Kuyper and Calvin finally rest awareness of God's transcendence on awareness of human sin and divine grace, whereas Potter Engel rests this awareness upon human finitude and divine mystery.

34. For a discussion of this sensitivity, see Nicholas Wolterstorff's *Until Justice and Peace Embrace* (Grand Rapids: William B. Eerdmans, 1983), pp. 54, 64-66; see also James M. Gustafson's *Ethics from a Theocentric Perspective*, vol. 1: *Theology and Ethics* (Chicago: University of Chicago Press, 1981), esp. pp. 88-99, 163-87.

35. Boesak, *Black and Reformed*, p. 35. Note the contrast between Boesak's position and John Calvin's (cited in Chapter Five, note 54), in which almost unconditional obedience of wives to husbands is enjoined.

36. Rosemary Radford Ruether, Mary Potter Engel, Anne Carr, Sallie McFague, and Elisabeth Schüssler Fiorenza all argue that to eliminate transcendence in the name of immanence is wrong. Accordingly, they all revise the concept of divine transcendence in ways aimed at preventing its abuse by those concepts and structures that are anti-creation and anti-woman.

making hierarchical understandings of the God-human relation the *prevailing* view of God. This remains one of the fundamental differences between feminist and Reformed visions of God.[37] Calvinists should reject the feminist claim that God's transcendence inevitably leads to injustice, and affirm those feminist efforts to revise our understanding of transcendence.

At its best, the Reformed tradition also rejects any understanding of God that sanctions the exploitation of nature. In Reformed thought all of creation belongs to God and mirrors God.[38] Calvin says, "Wherever you cast your eyes there is no spot in the universe wherein you cannot discern at least some sparks of [God's] glory. You cannot in one glance survey this most vast and beautiful system of the universe, in its wide expanse, without being completely overwhelmed by the boundless force of its brightness."[39] So much does the creation display the glory of God that Calvin confesses "that it can be said reverently, provided that it proceeds from a reverent mind, that nature is God."[40] For Calvin, the deepest motive behind human spoilage of nature is the desire to destroy God, to remove all reminders of God from a universe which faithfully mirrors God. In a Reformed perspective, then, to spoil, pollute, or plot to destroy creation is to sin directly against God.

Thus, insofar as feminist theology challenges idolatry and its re-

37. For strong polemical indictments of the dominance of hierarchical construals of the divine-human relation in the Protestant tradition, see Beverly Wildung Harrison's essay entitled "Human Sexuality and Mutuality," in *Christian Feminism: Visions of a New Humanity*, ed. Judith L. Weidman (San Francisco: Harper & Row, 1984), pp. 141-57, and her essay entitled "Sexism and the Language of Christian Ethics," in *Making the Connections: Essays in Feminist Social Ethics*, ed. Carol S. Robb (Boston: Beacon Press, 1986), pp. 22-41. Although Mouw makes room for feminist views of God, his own Calvinist "divine command theory" retains the dominance of hierarchical imagery that is so central in the Reformed tradition. For a description and some critical questioning of this aspect of Mouw's Calvinist feminism, see Douglas Schuurman's review of Mouw's book in the *Journal of Religion*, forthcoming.

38. Calvin, *Institutes*, 1.1.1-3.

39. Calvin, *Institutes*, 1.5.1.

40. Calvin, *Institutes*, 1.5.5. Calvin qualifies his remark as follows: "but because it is a harsh and improper saying, since nature is rather the order prescribed by God, it is harmful in such weighty matters, in which special devotion is due, to involve God confusedly in the inferior course of his works."

sultant social oppression and ecological exploitation, Reformed thought is in agreement with it. But the two perspectives differ in that the Reformed tradition, by and large, has not directly criticized (and has often sanctioned) *women's* oppression, and in that it does not see the sovereignty of God as being the problem.[41] For Reformed faith, the problem is the sinful tendency of human beings to lapse into an idolatry that will distort *any* language for God — masculine or feminine — in pursuit of their own evil ends.

The conflict between Reformed and feminist understandings of God is more severe on the issue of feminine language for God than on the issue of challenging abuses of masculine God-language. This is due

41. Abraham Kuyper argued against granting women the right to vote. His argument reflects his acceptance of stereotypical views of men as designed for "public" life and women as designed for "private" life. "The woman who longs for the voting booth, in order to act politically like the man, acknowledges *the inferiority* of her feminine nature. If only she could become like a man! And if not completely, then at least half! The woman who has God resting in her, on the other hand, establishes her honor in precisely the opposite way, by remaining a woman. Not by imitating the man in clothing and manners, but by helping to unfold all the glorious riches of the female nature, of the feminine gifts, and of the female being." (See "The Woman's Position of Honor," 11 June 1914, trans. Irene Konyndyk, unpublished manuscript, Calvin College 1990, p. 30. An analysis of this document is contained in Mary Stewart Van Leeuwen's "Abraham Kuyper and the Cult of True Womanhood," paper given at the 25th Anniversary Conference of the Institute for Christian Studies, Toronto, June 1992.) In his exemplarish biblical study, *Women of the Old Testament* (6th ed., trans. Henry Zylstra [Grand Rapids: Zondervan Publishing Co., 1934], a book brought to our attention by Theda McBryde), Kuyper says that Eve's sin was less profound than was Adam's (p. 7), that women are more susceptible to sin and to faith than are men (p. 5), that the subordination of woman to man was a pre-Fall creation ordinance (p. 172), that if Bathsheba had been "appropriately modest" and not "presented herself nudely," David would "never have become guilty of such an outrageous disgrace" (p. 114), that "genuine, feminine fullness" is best depicted by one "no longer a girl and yet not quite a woman" (p. 80), that Samson's "prodigious masculine energy so completely mastered him that he could not purge himself of this weakness [sleeping with harlots]" (p. 86), and that women are more susceptible to the occult than are men (pp. 119-20, 165). There are glimmerings of a deeper Christian vision of gender relations when Kuyper praises the midwives in Egypt for not obeying Pharaoh's decree and Vashti for refusing to obey her husband's summons to display her beauty before his friends. "Every Christian wife knows that she need not and may not obey her husband in what opposes God's laws, and in what infringes upon her feminine pride" (p. 172). Unfortunately, this more biblical perspective on divine transcendence and gender relations is at best only a minor theme in Kuyper's writings and in the Reformed tradition.

partly to the Reformed emphasis on God's sovereignty and partly to Reformed respect for the normative role of Scripture in choosing God-language. Even here, however, we think that a case can be made for *some* feminist proposals in the direction of a more "feminine" view of God.

Certain Reformed theologians are highly critical of proposals for feminine God-language on the grounds that these proposals undermine the distinction between Creator and creation and thus lead inevitably to pantheism. For example, Elizabeth Achtemeier claims that feminine God-language inevitably leads to the imagery of God giving birth to the world. She then argues that "if a female deity gives birth to the universe, . . . it follows that all things participate in the life or in the substance and divinity of that deity—in short, that *the creator is indissolubly bound up with the creation.*" Accordingly, Achtemeier warns, "The church cannot and it must not accede to feminist demands that language about God be changed to feminine, for then the church will have lost that God in whom it truly lives and moves and has its being."[42]

Another major criticism from Reformed circles is that feminist proposals for God-language fail to reckon with the uniqueness of "Father" and "Lord" as divine *names.* One reason that these names are thought to be unique is the sheer frequency of their usage in the Bible; the other reason is that they are said to designate the being of God in a more strict and nonnegotiable sense than other similes, symbols, and images. Thus Donald Bloesch says,

> I concur with Barth and Berkhof that the words "Father" and "Lord" in reference to God and Christ respectively are not merely figurative. They are not simply symbols of a power or essence which is beyond fatherhood and personality (as in Tillich and Mary Daly). They are analogies that contain a univocal meaning. The univocal in this case is not just the personal, as Paul Jewett implies; it also embraces the element of omnipotent or absolute power which is a masculine, not a feminine, attribute.[43]

According to Bloesch, it is legitimate to say that God is *like* a mother but not that God *is* mother; however, Bloesch believes that God both *is like*

42. Achtemeier, "Female Language for God: Should the Church Adopt It?" in *The Hermeneutical Quest*, ed. Donald G. Miller (Allison Park, Pa: Pickwick Publications, 1986), pp. 100, 109.
43. Bloesch, *Is the Bible Sexist?* (Westchester, Ill.: Crossway, 1982), p. 76.

and *is* father.[44] He argues that this difference faithfully reflects the biblical view of God, in which God is *primarily* transcendent and masculine and only *secondarily* immanent and feminine.

How might a Calvinist reply to these criticisms directed at feminist proposals about God-language?

First, it is important to note that Achtemeier's criticisms are valid when their target is the extreme feminist proposal that a goddess be substituted for God. But what of the more moderate proposals for balanced emphases upon God as "feminine" and "masculine" and for non-gender-related God-language? Since Achtemeier and Bloesch, like so many critics of feminist theology, focus upon the more radical proposals, it is not easy to discern what their criticisms imply for mainline and evangelical feminist proposals. Nevertheless, we offer the following observations.

To begin with, Achtemeier's thesis that feminine imagery leads to pantheism is both logically and theologically false. Pantheism, as well as the idolatrous divinization of creation that accompanies it, is as much a temptation for *masculine* as for *feminine* God-language. The Old Testament condemns worship of the (male) Baals as well as of the (female) Ashteroth. Calling Jesus "Lord" can lead to the deification of a monarch, just as calling God "Mother" can lead to the divinization of motherhood. And the Bible *does* freely use feminine imagery for God, even though it does so less frequently than it uses masculine imagery. The Bible *does* declare that female and male are both created in the image and likeness of God. Furthermore, the imagery of God giving birth to the world or to the people of God no more divinizes creation than the imagery of God as "our Rock" divinizes granite. Are we not born anew by the Spirit of God? Yet this need not result in the affirmation that we are God! It is true that sinful human beings do make idols and that they do confuse God with creation. The proper response to these failings, however, is not to rob the church of the feminine imagery found in the Bible and the Christian tradition; rather, the proper response is to remind the church that *all* our language for God is analogical and to *diversify* our God-language, both theologically and liturgically.

Second, recall Bloesch's thesis that God "is" Father but only "is

---

44. Ibid., p. 121n.38. For a similar argument, see John W. Cooper's "God Is Not Father and Mother," *The Banner*, 30 April 1990, pp. 8-11.

like" a mother. This argument neglects the fact that in saying "God-language is analogical," the theological tradition affirms *both* a "univocal" *and* an "equivocal" component to *all* our God-language. In other words, God is both like *and* unlike what we know as fatherhood, motherhood, wisdom, water, fire, and so on. And the significance of God as "Father" is *not* primarily God's transcendence and certainly not God's maleness, but rather *God's relationship with Jesus Christ.* Who is the God of Israel and the church? Not just any God but *this* God, who sent Jesus of Nazareth into the world and whose power raised Jesus from death itself to usher in the new creation. According to the gospel, that — and not some masculinizing of God — is the true theological significance of God as Father.

Nor can it be claimed that words like "Father" and "Lord" name God or Christ in a categorically unique manner, for such a claim inadequately reflects what the Bible says about God and Christ. When Moses asked God what he should say to those who ask who sent him, God replied,

> "I AM who I AM." He said further, "Thus you shall say to the Israelites, 'I AM has sent me to you.'" God also said to Moses, "Thus you shall say to the Israelites, 'The Lord, the God of your ancestors, the God of Abraham, the God of Isaac, and the God of Jacob, has sent me to you': This is my name forever, and this is my title for all generations." (Exod. 3:14-15)

If "Father" is a name that designates God's being univocally and uniquely, then what about these names? If Christ has only "Lord" as his "name," and other descriptions are merely metaphors or titles, then Isaiah misspoke himself when he said, "For a child has been born for us, a son given to us; authority rests upon his shoulders; and he is *named* Wonderful Counselor, Mighty God, Everlasting Father, Prince of Peace" (Isa. 9:6, our emphasis). It seems that the Spirit of God in the biblical word has failed to observe present-day scholastic distinctions among names, titles, and metaphors!

Calvinism at its best keeps God's transcendence and God's immanence in a balanced tension. Whether in creation, providence, or redemption, it sees God as free and sovereign on the one hand and as loving, loyal, and involved on the other. Although some have argued that the sovereignty of God *is* the most important theme for Calvin's theology, the central images for God in Calvin's *Institutes* are in fact "Source of every good gift" and caring, nurturant "Father." Hence the Christian life is a life of gratitude (the proper response to God as Bestower of gifts) and a life of filial obedience (the proper response to God as Father). And for Calvin it is only through faith in Jesus Christ, as revealed in the Bible, that anyone can come to know God as Gift-giver and as Father. Although Calvin certainly uses the name "Father" for God, his central emphasis is *not* God's masculinity; it is rather God's tender, loving, steadfast care.

For all of these reasons, Calvinism can legitimately support the mainline and evangelical feminist proposals to make God-language more inclusive, whether by using imagery that is overtly feminine or by diversifying imagery for God. Because God is distinct from creation, none of our language or thoughts ever fully expresses God's nature. But because God's glory is mirrored in creation, our language and thoughts can partially reflect God. Insofar as Calvin does favor masculine language for God as "Father," his central concern is for God's nurturant, loving, sustaining relationship to humanity and the world. This brings us to the second and third theological themes that we wish to examine in this chapter.

Humanity and the World

Even Reformed thinkers who are wary of feminist proposals for God-language will be able to accept much feminist thinking about humanity and the world. For example, Elizabeth Achtemeier, though extremely critical of inclusive God-language, affirms the following about humanity:

> The Christian faith proclaims that both male and female are made in the image of God (Gen. 1:27), that husband and wife are to join flesh in a marital union of mutual helpfulness (Gen. 2:18), that the ancient enmity between the sexes and the subordination of women are a result of human sin (Gen. 3), that the sinful enmity and subordination have been overcome by the death and resurrection of Jesus Christ (Gal. 3:28), and that all women and men alike are called to equal discipleship in the service of their risen Lord.[45]

45. Achtemeier, "Female Language for God," p. 97.

Although Calvinism converges with feminism on many central themes relating to humanity and the world, there are some important areas of conflict. We will trace both the conflicts and the agreements in three areas: (1) the critique of dualism and the affirmation of an interdependent wholism, (2) the fallenness of humanity and the world, and (3) the equality and inequality of women and men.

The Critique of Dualism and the Affirmation of Wholism

One of the hallmarks of feminist thought, religious and secular, is a rejection of dualisms. Those who mount this critique accuse male thinking in general, and male theological thinking in particular, of separating reality into various pairs of spheres, which are then put into conflict with each other so that one finally "rules" the other. Thus Dorothee Soelle criticizes the theological tradition for separating and polarizing God and world, humanity and nature, men and women, soul and body, reason and passion/emotion, culture and nature, sacred and secular, public and private.[46] Feminist theologians allege that each sphere tends to be made independent of the other and put in conflict with the other. They also allege that male theology subordinates the second aspect of each pair to the first. For example, as God "rules" the world, so culture must "rule" nature, men must "rule" women, soul must "rule" body, and so forth. Moreover, the ruled part is always judged to be inferior, ontologically and ethically, to the part that rules. In addition, the first member of each pair is generally seen as "active," the second as "passive." Finally, the various pairs mutually reinforce each other, so that to challenge the dualism of one pair is implicitly to challenge them all. However, unless challenged, these dualisms combine to support the oppression of women (who are always associated with the second, subordinated sphere) and the exploitation of the natural environment.

As a constructive alternative to this binary, conflictual, and hierarchical model of reality, feminist theologians develop models that are unitary, mutual, and egalitarian. It is the relatedness of all things that particularly interests feminist theologians. Thus they emphasize the interdependence, connectedness, equal value, and mutual need that char-

46. Soelle, *To Work and To Love*, pp. 13-14, 23-25, 77. See also Rosemary Ruether's *Sexism and God-Talk*, esp. pp. 72-82.

acterize the world and God, nature and humanity, women and men, body and soul, and so on. A central interest in this new emphasis is the creation of a new social and cultural order that both fully includes women and sustains a positive ecological ethic.

However, there is one dualism that sometimes remains in feminist theology — namely, a dualism between men and women. For example, in her later writings Mary Daly presents men as ontologically evil and women as ontologically good. But most mainline and evangelical feminists criticize this description of the sexes on the grounds that it too is dualistic.[47]

There is much in the critique of dualism and the related affirmation of wholism that is also central to Calvinism. Abraham Kuyper, for example, sought to extend the significance of faith to all domains of life. More recently, Albert Wolters has asserted that one of the distinctive features of a Reformed worldview is its resistance to dualism. He writes,

> All other Christian worldviews . . . restrict the scope of each of these terms [creation, fall, reconciliation, kingdom of God] in one way or other. Each is understood to apply to only one delimited area of the universe of our experience, usually named the "religious" or "sacred" realm. Everything falling outside this delimited area is called the "worldly," or "secular," or "natural," or "profane" realm. All of these "two-realm" theories, as they are called, are variations of a basically *dualistic* worldview, as opposed to the *integral* perspective of the reformational worldview.[48]

Thus Reformed "totalism," like feminist theology, presses its worldview toward "wholism" and an "integral" view of reality, and thus away from dualism.

Both Reformed and feminist thinkers criticize dualism in the name of wholism, but the basic motive for this opposition is different for each group. Feminists oppose dualism (1) because it is allegedly a "masculine"

---

47. For a critical assessment of Daly on this point, see Mary Ellen Ross's "Feminism and the Problem of Moral Character," *Journal of Feminist Studies in Religion* 5 (Fall 1989), esp. pp. 54-60.

48. Wolters, *Creation Regained: Biblical Basics for a Reformational Worldview* (Grand Rapids: William B. Eerdmans, 1985), p. 10. Wolters also explicitly rejects nature/culture and public/private dualisms (pp. 14, 30).

rather than a "feminine" way of doing theory and practice, and (2) because it is complicit both in the gender-system's oppression of women and in the rape of the earth. Calvinists, by contrast, oppose dualism (1) because it expresses a gnostic tendency to devalue creation, and (2) because it conflicts with the all-encompassing scope of God's works of creation and redemption, and the all-encompassing scope of human sin and of God's law for humanity and the world.[49]

For example, there is a saying among contemporary Calvinists to the effect that "all of life is religious"—a saying that contains come curious echoes of the feminist declaration that "the personal is political." The saying is meant to embody a summary rejection of all unbiblical dualisms regarding creation, fall, and redemption. It is a rejection of the nature/grace split that carves out a limited sphere of life for Christian obedience (e.g., personal morality, religious observance, or theological reflection) and labels other areas (e.g., intellectual, political, or cultural life) as neutral or unimportant. It is a rejection of the tendency to see some spheres of life (e.g., that of family or the church) as exempt from the effects of the Fall while others (e.g., sexuality) are made somehow responsible for it. It is finally a rejection of the suggestion that some things are inherently irredeemable (e.g., the business world or popular culture), while others (such as drug problems or sexual aberrations) are open to a spiritual "quick fix" that ignores the physical, social, and psychological realities which led to them. The Reformed emphasis on the Lordship of Christ thus results in a suspicion of any dualisms that exempt some spheres of life from the goodness of creation, or from the effects of sin, or from the reach of God's lordship and saving activity.

Yet despite this rejection of dualisms shared by feminists and Calvinists, the latter have been slow to admit that perhaps a residual male/female dualism in their own thinking has kept them from developing a concern for the harms and systemic injustices that dualist thought encourages specifically toward women. For example, Kuyper's view of "sphere sovereignty" supported his argument against women's suffrage by reinforcing the "public-private" dualism in his thinking, and his swallowing of culturally stereotypical definitions of masculine and feminine traits likewise reinforced his dualistic understanding of men's "public"

---

49. Wolters's development of these objections in *Creation Regained* is typical of Calvinism's primary concern with dualism.

167

and women's "private" domains.[50] (We will develop a more detailed critique of this public-private dichotomy in Chapter Twelve.)

In addition to the basic differences already noted, Calvinism differs from feminism in denying that the "God-world" distinction is the originator and perpetuator of all other dualisms. For most feminists, the vision of God as one who creates the world *ex nihilo*, who is sovereignly free to create or not to create, who will continue to endure though the world be annihilated, who fashions the world as a potter fashions clay — all of this adds up to a dualistic vision that underlies all other dualisms they criticize.[51] But for Calvinists the view of God just summarized is crucial to a biblical and Reformed faith.[52]

As we see it, Calvinists need to learn from feminists about the ways in which various dualisms support the subordination and oppression of women. Even though they have been aware of the hazards of dualisms in other areas of life and thought, Calvinists have generally not thought through the implications of dualism in a society that harms women. But Calvinists should not do this at the expense of their other critiques of dualism or at the cost of rejecting a sharp distinction between God and the world. They must continue to affirm the sovereign power and freedom of God, and not only for theological and biblical reasons. A high view of God's freedom and sovereignty provides a secure vantage point from which to criticize the social order and work for its reform. It also safeguards us against falling into either a despairing pessimism (which forgets that God's justice *will* ultimately prevail) or a utopian optimism (which overestimates human freedom and forgets that God's ends are achieved in God's own time and way). In their development of these themes, Reformed thinkers will get much assistance from those Christian feminists — like Rosemary Ruether, Sallie McFague, and Mary Potter Engel — who reaffirm God's transcendence with a view to re-establishing *shalom* in gender relations.

50. See Kuyper's essay entitled "The Woman's Position of Honor" and his book entitled *Women of the Old Testament*, both cited and commented on in n. 40. For an illuminating critique and attempt to arrive at a more adequate Reformed, feminist perspective, see also Van Leeuwen's *Gender and Grace*, chaps. 7 and 8, and also Elaine Storkey's *What's Right with Feminism* (Grand Rapids: William B. Eerdmans, 1986).
51. See Dorothee Soelle's *To Work and To Love*, esp. pp. 13-49.
52. For a recent articulation of these Reformed themes with special reference to feminist and other criticisms of "hierarchical" thinking, see Richard Mouw's book entitled *The God Who Commands*.

The Fallenness of Humanity and the World

Two themes recur in feminist theology concerning the fallenness of humanity and the world. These themes also reflect the two aspects of feminist experience identified in an earlier chapter. Corresponding to the "oppression-liberation" aspect of feminist experience is a focus on the systemic, structural character of sin. Corresponding to the "affirmation of women-as-women" aspect is a feminist distinction between the primary temptation and sin of women as distinct from that of men.

With regard to the first of these, sin is perceived by feminist theologians as not merely a private, personal matter. The social and cultural milieu is also marred by sin. Thus Rosemary Ruether writes,

> Once a breach in the wall of sexist ideology and depersonalization of woman is made, the entire ideological and social superstructure built up over thousands of years of sexism and justification of sexism is open to question. Every aspect of male privilege loses its authority as natural and divine right and is reevaluated as sin and evil. . . . More than that, women have to suspect that the entire symbolic universe that surrounds them, which has socialized them to their roles, is deeply tainted by hostility to their humanity. This touches on all their most intimate relations, to mother and father, ministers and teachers, husband, male and female children. An entire social and symbolic universe crumbles within and outside them.[53]

According to this view, if women are to be free from abuse, devaluation, restrictive stereotyping, and poverty, then the entire edifice of society and culture must be challenged. Moreover, feminist theologians not only denounce the structures of oppression; they also call for positive analyses — political, economic, psychological, and social — to undergird a praxis that resists oppression and aims to reform the world.

Earlier feminist thought focused on the need for legal and political reforms that would enable women, like men, to enter the professions of their choice, to vote and hold political office, to obtain higher education, and to receive equal pay for equal work. While these liberal feminist concerns continue, there is now an effort afoot to analyze and overcome many other problems as well. These include the ways in which women's oppression and subordination are supported by language, marriage, and

53. Ruether, *Sexism and God-Talk*, p. 173.

parenting roles, psychological dependencies, economic inferiority, patterns of reasoning, and more. The general criticism is that our culture is *androcentric,* so that women are defined only in relation to men and are valued less than men; *hierarchical,* so that women are always subordinated to men in terms of power and value; and *oppressive,* so that women are victims, in a way that men are not, of harms and injustices systemically sustained in our society and culture.

The second theme in feminist development of the doctrine of sin focuses on the differences between typically "male" and "female" sins. Valerie Saiving Goldstein argues that most doctrines of sin developed by twentieth-century Protestant theologians *neglect* and even *harm* women.[54] According to Goldstein, these (male) theologians identify the generic "human" problem as the temptation to abuse the freedom intended for creativity. They see the anxiety attaching to freedom as giving rise to the sins of selfishness and pride, where one turns everything to selfish purposes and rebels against the rule of God. These theologians then see the solution to this problem as the self-sacrificial love, or *agape,* which turns the self to God and others in service. Goldstein acknowledges that selfishness and pride might be central problems for men, but she argues that women have quite a different problem. For women the temptation is to succumb to their dependence upon others for identity. This temptation in turn spawns typically "feminine" sins such as exaggerated self-abnegation, the loss of self in socially directed roles, and the refusal to develop one's gifts in service to God and others. Thus, according to Goldstein, the call to agapic, self-sacrificial love only aggravates women's central problem. Women generally require not self-sacrifice but self-affirmation.

Barbara Andolsen, in a later essay in which she develops Goldstein's thesis, suggests that for women the solution is love-as-mutuality rather than love-as-self-sacrifice. Such love includes both the individual self-affirmation of women and the corporate affirmation of women, and it challenges women to develop themselves rather than lose themselves in the identity of others.[55] In a similar vein, Mary Stewart Van Leeuwen

54. Goldstein, "The Human Situation: A Feminine View," in *Womanspirit Rising: A Feminist Reader in Religion,* ed. Carol P. Christ and Judith Plaskow (San Francisco: Harper & Row, 1979), pp. 25-42. This essay, which originally appeared as an article in the *Journal of Religion* in April 1960, is seen as the landmark article on this topic for feminist theology.

55. Andolsen, "Agape in Feminist Ethics," in *Journal of Religious Ethics* 9 (Spring 1981): 69-83.

argues that the fundamental sin for women is "enmeshment" within social relations; their basic challenge is thus learning to exercise faithful, accountable "dominion." Conversely, for men the basic sin is "domination" within social relations, and their challenge is to develop their "relatedness" to others.[56]

Feminists' focus on the social-structural aspects of sin has inclined them to see women more as victims of the sins of others than as sinners in need of repentance. From their perspective, it is men who oppress women and who need to repent of their sins. When feminists have acknowledged women's guilt, that guilt has usually been attached to their failure to resist oppression and develop their own gifts. But as we saw in Chapter Four, more recent feminist theory (which is only more recently being incorporated into feminist theology) integrates concerns for class and race into the concerns about gender relations, and in doing so it begins to acknowledge that women do in fact oppress others. Thus Susan Thistlethwaite confesses that she (and, by implication, many feminists) are "recovering racists" who have exercised an exclusivist, hegemonic power over women of color and colonized women. Even this kind of confession, however, is often qualified: women's racism and classism, like their tendency to self-sacrifice, are seen as flaws that they "couldn't help" acquiring. Thistlethwaite writes,

> One of my greatest fears is that in putting forth this argument certain proof-texts will be abused to further the liberal guilt of white women or, even worse, as an undeserved put-down of post-Christian feminism. In traveling around the country to speak on the subject of the difference race makes for white feminist theology, I have been struck by how difficult it is to own one's own racism as the *inevitable product* of socialization in a racist culture.[57]

56. Van Leeuwen, *Gender and Grace,* pp. 42-48. Unlike Valerie Saiving Goldstein and Barbara Andolsen, Van Leeuwen bases her claims on exegetical as well as on sociological and psychological grounds. Of particular import is Genesis 3:16b — "yet your desire shall be for your husband, and he shall rule over you." She argues that men are especially prone to distort creationally given capacities for "dominion" into abusive "domination" ("and he shall *rule* over you"), and that women are especially prone to distort their creationally given capacities for "sociability" into "enmeshment" ("your *desire* shall be for your husband"). Rather than following Augustine, who takes "desire" here to mean "desire to usurp" the authority of men, Van Leeuwen follows Gilbert Bilezikian, taking "desire" to mean "desire for intimacy."

57. Thistlethwaite, *Sex, Race, and God,* p. 7 (our emphasis).

Calvinists will have mixed responses to feminist revisions of the doctrine of sin. They would agree strongly that social structures, not just individual people, are distorted by sin and are thus in need of reformation. But there are two themes in Calvinism that separate it from feminism at this point. The first theme concerns a theological reading of history as a struggle between belief and unbelief rather than between oppressor and oppressed. Nicholas Wolterstorff notes that this perspective is especially characteristic of "second-generation" Dutch neo-Calvinism:

> Here the cries of the wretched of the earth are not given voice. Here there is little talk of oppression, and consequently little of liberation from oppression; the talk is more of "authority structures." And here there are no reflections on violence (which, incidentally, makes neo-Calvinism significantly different also from early Calvinism). There is indeed talk of conflict in society, but it is the religious conflict between believer and idolater and not the social conflict between oppressor and oppressed that is discussed.[58]

Wolterstorff does find Kuyper and early Calvinism attentive to oppression. But for Calvin himself and for many Calvinists, the story of fallen history is at bottom a story of belief versus unbelief. Hence idolatry can motivate both oppression and resistance to oppression. From this viewpoint, patriarchalism is certainly both oppressive and idolatrous, but so is any form of feminism that worships the human creature rather than the creator-God. Thus Calvinists, in addition to resisting the power of the oppressor, resist the excessive confidence in human beings that is characteristic of Marxism and other utopian social movements, including some forms of feminism.

Even so, Calvinists call for Christians to resist injustice wherever it is found, because love requires it and because God wills it. For this reason the Reformed concern about oppression is intense, and Reformed awareness of the need for social change is acute. Thus the Reformed concern about systemic, structural evil is correlated with and shaped by its concern about the antithesis between faith and idolatry. The primary concern of most feminists is whether one is male or female and how this difference shapes the rest of life and thought. By contrast, the primary concern of most Calvinists is whether one is a believer or an

58. Wolterstorff, *Until Justice and Peace Embrace*, p. 53.

172

unbeliever and how this difference shapes the rest of life and thought. Yet, since both Reformed and feminist thinkers relate, in varying degrees, social oppression to religious orientation, the difference is mostly one of emphasis.

There is a second point at which Calvinists will resist the feminist understanding of the structural character of sin. It relates to the Reformed emphasis on the "ambiguity" of the world as "created-but-fallen." Wolterstorff focuses on the "fallen" character of social structures and shows that there is a deep strand in the Reformed tradition to support his emphasis.[59] But there is another strand in Calvinism which emphasizes that social structures, like all the world, are "*created*-but-fallen" — that is, these social structures express not only human sin and miscreation but also God's provident sustaining of the life of creation. Feminists agree with Wolterstorff about the fallenness of worldly social structures, but they often disagree with the other part of Calvinism that emphasizes the "created good" aspect of the created-but-fallen world. Feminists resist emphases upon the "goodness" or "ambiguity" of the world because of the ways in which traditional theology has abused the doctrine of creation to sanction inequalities in the social order, and because feminists are interested in radical social change.

Calvinists who emphasize the *good* side of our ambiguous world are concerned theologically to avoid gnostic devaluation of the world and politically to avoid the revolutionary and utopian strategies of the French Revolution and Marxism. Accordingly, they emphasize that our world *is* essentially good, and that sin is a secondary perversion of the good creation. This being the case, only judicious reform, never total revolution, is justified. In this connection, Calvinists commonly distinguish between "structure" and "direction." According to this distinction, although the aim and motive of human activity (directional features) are radically distorted by the Fall, the laws of nature and the basic norms and patterns for cultural life (structural features) are left relatively intact.

Thus abuses of law and authority do not destroy the fundamental goodness of the human institutions they represent.[60] For example, marriage, politics, education, and so forth can be so distorted as to destroy life. But they are in essence rooted in the good creation, even though in history these structures are corrupt and in need of reform. The Re-

59. Wolterstorff, *Until Justice and Peace Embrace,* esp. pp. 7-22.
60. See Wolters, *Creation Regained,* p. 43.

formed assumption seems to be that the real danger lies in the deeply entrenched human tendency to blame one part of society for all the ills of the world, and then to hope in utopian fashion that the removal of this part will solve the human problem. (An example would be the early radical feminist deprecation of childbearing and the ensuing claim that the "technologizing" of reproduction would eliminate women's oppression.) By contrast, as Albert Wolters points out, the Reformed distinction between structure and direction leads to "reformism" rather than to "revolutionism," "consecration," or "conservatism."[61] Mainline and evangelical feminists, in their rejection of post-Christian feminism as revolutionary, would likely agree with the Reformed rejection of revolutionism, though for different reasons.[62]

Where one goes with this emphasis on the "fallenness" or the "ambiguity" of social structures depends upon whether one sees conservatism or revolutionism to be the bigger social problem. Those Calvinists who emphasize the essential goodness of the world usually judge revolutionism to be the more dangerous problem.[63] But those Calvinists who emphasize the fallenness of social structures see conservative affirmation of the status quo as the more dangerous problem.[64] Feminists

---

61. Ibid., pp. 51, 72-78. Wolters argues that the biblical view of reformation rejects "consecration" or a "setting apart" of some parts of life for religious purposes because this suggests an external (rather than an internal) connection with the sacred (p. 74). He also says that the biblical view of reformation demands "progressive renewal" rather than "revolution," where the latter involves "(1) necessary violence, (2) the complete removal of every aspect of the established system, and (3) the construction of an entirely different societal order according to a theoretical ideal" (p. 77). The biblical view, according to Wolters, also rejects quietistic conservation of the status quo, since it demands drastic reorientation of "directional" features of life (p. 78).

62. See Rosemary Radford Ruether's critical challenge to Naomi Goldenberg, and to others in the feminist spirituality movement who reject the Judeo-Christian tradition in favor of Goddess religion, in her article entitled "A Religion for Women: Sources and Strategies," *Christianity and Crisis* 39 (10 December 1979): 307-11.

63. That this emphasis runs deep, especially in Dutch Calvinism, is seen in the title of the early Dutch Calvinist party — the Anti-revolutionary Party.

64. Thus Wolterstorff identifies "that most insufferable of all human beings" as "the triumphalist Calvinist, the one who believes that the revolution instituting the holy commonwealth has already occurred and that his or her task is simply to keep it in place. Of these triumphalist Calvinists the United States and Holland have both had their share. South Africa today provides them in their purest form" (*Until Justice and Peace Embrace*, p. 21).

174

wouldn't agree with those Calvinists wary of revolutionism, but they would agree with those Calvinists who discern that the need to change the status quo is more pressing than the need to avoid revolution.

A closely related matter is whether one reads the movement of history as an evolutionary "differentiation" of the original creation or as a more revolutionary, "conflictual" pattern between oppressors and oppressed. The former stance usually correlates with the Reformed emphasis on the world as ambiguous yet essentially good (and also correlates with those more conservative sociological theories of society labeled "structural-functional"). The latter stance usually correlates with an emphasis on the world as fallen and in need of strong change (and also resonates with what are known as the more radical "conflict theories" of society). A final related issue is whether one sees the basic problem to be the deeply entrenched tendency to blame one part of creation for all the ills of the world (resulting in an anti-revolutionary stance)[65] or the deeply entrenched human tendency toward willful ignorance and blindness to one's own power and to the ideologies that justify it (resulting in a selectively pro-revolutionary stance).[66]

We can hardly resolve these complex and profound matters in a single chapter.[67] Our modest point here is that there is at least *one* major strand of Calvinism which is very much in agreement with the feminist emphasis upon the structural, systemic character of sin. We contend that although Calvinists (and, indeed, all Christians) should avoid the one-sided ingratitude which so often accompanies revolutionary critiques of society, they must still reckon with the prophetic indictments of society and culture found in feminist theology and in certain strands of the Reformed tradition.

65. See Wolters, *Creation Regained*, p. 51.

66. Feminists emphasize this aspect of the human problem. In his preface to *Until Justice and Peace Embrace*, Wolterstorff says that the main problem in regard to poverty is that people refuse to do anything about it, even though they know there is a problem and have resources with which to remedy it. In allowing this perspective to shape his approach to world poverty, Wolterstorff follows a pattern similar to that of many feminists who criticize structural problems of sexism.

67. Douglas Schuurman analyzes the bearing of creation and eschaton upon these and other related issues, with special reference to Emil Brunner and Jürgen Moltmann, in *Creation, Eschaton, and Ethics: The Ethical Significance of the Creation-Eschaton Relation in Emil Brunner and Jürgen Moltmann* (New York: Peter Lang Press, 1991).

In related fashion, Calvinist conceptions of sin both agree and disagree with the feminist thesis that the primary temptation for women is different from that of men. Calvinists have certainly criticized the view of agapic love that was prevalent in twentieth-century Protestant theology, especially as developed by scholars such as Anders Nygren and Reinhold Niebuhr. Henry Stob, for example, argues that Nygren's view posits an unjustified opposition between agapic love and the natural, erotic forms of love that undergird self-love, romantic love, and friendship.[68] The Reformed tradition also sees sin as involving acts of omission as well as acts of commission: the vice of sloth as well as that of pride, failure to heed God's call to service as well as actively resisting that call.[69] Insofar as feminism revives awareness of such sins of omission, it comports very well with the Reformed "double emphasis" that we have just summarized.

But in claiming that women are more prone than men to sins of omission, feminists are making a novel claim. Calvinists believe that *all* people are guilty of *both* kinds of sins. On the passive side, all fail to give thanks and to be responsible before God; on the active side, all reject God and rebel against God's will. Another major difference between Calvinism and feminism on this point is that Calvinism sees self-sacrifice as crucial; indeed, Calvin sums up the Christian life as a life of self-sacrifice:

> We are not our own: let not our reason nor our will, therefore, sway our plans and deeds. . . . We are not our own: insofar as we can, let us therefore forget ourselves and all that is ours. . . . From this also follows this second point: that, almost forgetful of ourselves, surely subordinating our self-concern, we try faithfully to devote our zeal to God and his commandments.[70]

For Calvin and the Protestant Reformers generally, sin is the tendency to be "curved in upon one's self," and salvation involves movement away

---

68. Stob, *Ethical Reflections: Essays on Moral Themes* (Grand Rapids: William B. Eerdmans, 1978), pp. 114-20.

69. See Karl Barth's powerful discussions of pride and sloth in his *Church Dogmatics*, vol. 4, no. 1, trans. G. W. Bromiley (New York: Charles Scribner's Sons, 1956), pp. 413-78; and his *Church Dogmatics* 4, no. 2, trans. G. W. Bromiley (Edinburgh: T. & T. Clark, 1958), pp. 378-489.

70. Calvin, *Institutes*, 3.7.1-2.

from selfishness to the service of God and neighbor. The feminist imperative of self-love clashes with this Reformed view of the human condition. As Karl Barth put it, "'God will never think of blowing on this fire, which is bright enough already.'"[71] Self-affirmation is not a legitimate end in itself; it is justified only where it serves God and neighbor.[72] On this issue, then, classical Calvinism is at odds with the feminist analysis of sin's different effect on women and men.

Equality and Inequality of Women and Men

Feminists' awareness of the subordination and oppression of women within an androcentric and patriarchal culture and their desire for liberation lead them to emphasize the fundamental and thoroughgoing equality of women and men. Thus Mary Stewart Van Leeuwen defines a Christian feminist as a "person of either sex who sees women and men as *equally* saved, *equally* Spirit-filled and *equally* sent."[73] Cynthia Campbell says, "To be a feminist is to affirm the dignity and worth of women in God's design for creation and to repudiate anything which degrades, devalues, or relegates women to a secondary or subordinate status."[74] And Letty Russell defines a feminist as anyone who is "actively engaged in advocating the equality and partnership of women and men in church and society."[75] For feminist theologians, all of this leads to a critique of traditions that support women's subordination and oppression. It also leads to a retrieval of any traditions that support gender equality.

71. Barth, cited by Gene Outka in *Agape: An Ethical Analysis* (New Haven: Yale University Press, 1972), p. 221.

72. Paul Ramsey's way of legitimizing self-concern is typical: "Some definition of legitimate concern for the self must be given, even if only as a secondary and derivative part of Christian Ethics. For certainly as a part of vocational service grounded in Christian love for the neighbor, an individual has great responsibility for the development and use of all his [sic] natural capacities, or else he takes responsibility for rashly throwing them away" (*Basic Christian Ethics* [New York: Charles Scribner's Sons, 1953], p. 159).

73. Van Leeuwen, *Gender and Grace*, p. 36.

74. Campbell, *Theologies Written from Feminist Perspectives: An Introductory Study* (New York: Office of the General Assembly of the Presbyterian Church [U.S.A.], 1987), p. 22.

75. Russell, *Human Liberation in a Feminist Perspective — A Theology* (Philadelphia: Westminster Press, 1974), p. 19.

For evangelical feminists and most mainline feminists, the retrieval begins with the biblical accounts of creation and fall. Evangelical feminists are nearly unanimous in affirming that Genesis 1 and 2 teach that women and men are equal — equally made in the image of God, equally created for dominion, equally gifted by God, equally dependent upon each other, equally participants in the Fall. Inequality is seen to be a result of the Fall, since the penalty that God imposed upon the woman included her subjection to man (Gen. 3:16). But Jesus Christ was sent to remove sin and its effects, and the New Testament testifies to the equality of men and women in God. Jesus respects women as image bearers of God and as disciples, rejecting their subordination in the Old Testament and in Judaism. The Holy Spirit is poured out upon women and men, and the prophesying of women is identified by Peter as a sign of the new age (Acts 2:17-18). Through baptism, believers join the body of Christ, in which "there is longer Jew or Greek, there is no longer slave or free, there is no longer male and female" (Gal. 3:28). Women prophesy regularly at Corinth, and the Pauline letters frequently mention women in leadership positions in the church.

A central and obvious problem for evangelical feminists is how to understand the Pauline materials in the New Testament that seem to conflict with this reading of the Bible — passages that seem to endorse a "benevolent subordination" of women to men in marriage, church, and society (e.g., 1 Tim. 2:11-15; 1 Cor. 14:33b-36 and 11:7-16; Eph. 5:21-33; Col. 3:18-19). Mainline feminists reject the normative force of these apparently subordinationist passages either on the grounds that these passages were not really written by Paul and so are of no authority, or on the grounds that they conflict with the normative core of the Christian faith. Although many evangelical feminists also follow mainline feminists here, they, more than mainline feminists, try to show that these "apparently" subordinationist passages are really advocating equalitarian gender relations.[76]

Feminists thus re-examine the theological as well as the biblical tradition, critically rejecting subordinationist themes and retrieving the more egalitarian ones. These rejected (and historically common) theological traditions include the following: that women do not image God as fully as men; that women lack the spiritual, moral, or intellectual capacities of men; that though women image God as fully as men do

76. See Chapter Five, n. 42.

and share in all men's capacities, they are consigned to social subordination by arbitrary divine ordinance.[77]

However, although all feminist theologians claim that women and men are equal, they do not all affirm women's "sameness" with men. Some do emphasize sameness because they fear that an emphasis upon differences will lead to a renewed subordination of women to men.[78] But others stress the ways in which women are different from men and assert that these differences should in no way lead to the social subordination of women by men.[79] Still others combine sameness and difference in such a way that an affirmation of difference does not cancel out the many important ways in which women and men are alike.[80] The relationship of sameness to difference and of both to equality and inequality is currently a matter of intense debate in both secular feminist and Christian feminist literature.[81]

Where does Calvinism stand on the issue of female-male equality? Although on the one hand Calvinism has declared that all Christians are prophets, priests, and kings, it has on the other hand largely failed to apply this insight to women. Indeed, in his sermon on 1 Timothy 2:12-14, Calvin says,

> As God created man out of his free goodness so he endowed him with the superiority that he has above woman. Contrariwise, he willed that woman be subject.... If the woman should ask: And why should man have preeminence? The answer is: God willed it.... What ingratitude it would be if the woman were not content to be in this *middle rank* where God had placed her. The brute beasts if they would talk would not be so ungrateful.[82]

77. See Ruether's *Sexism and God-Talk,* pp. 94-99, for a brief summary of these "patriarchal anthropologies." For ways in which Abraham Kuyper's statements about women reflect the sexist status quo of his time, see n. 40 in this chapter.

78. See, for example, Mary Daly's *The Church and the Second Sex* (New York: Harper & Row, 1968), Letty Russell's *Human Liberation in a Feminist Perspective,* and Rosemary Ruether's *Sexism and God-Talk.*

79. See Thistlethwaite's book entitled *Sex, Race, and God* and Beverly Wildung Harrison's essay entitled "Sexism and the Language of Christian Ethics" in *Making the Connections.*

80. This is Mary Stewart Van Leeuwen's approach in *Gender and Grace.*

81. For a recent attempt to evaluate debates among secular and post-Christian feminists on this issue from a more mainline Christian perspective, see Mary Ellen Ross's "Feminism and the Problem of Moral Character," pp. 47-64.

82. Calvin, cited by Marian Battles in "Birthday Celebration, July 10, 1985, John Calvin," address delivered at Calvin College.

Calvinist scholar Jane Dempsey Douglass argues that Calvin saw women's exclusion from ecclesiastical office as an accommodation to human law and custom rather than as something required by God's eternal commandment.[83] Nevertheless, those seeking a rapprochement between Reformed and feminist worldviews would hope for a less equivocal record from Calvin on this point.[84]

Although many of Abraham Kuyper's statements about women simply accommodate the sexist status quo of his generation,[85] he still offers valuable resources for people trying to retrieve elements from the Reformed tradition that are conducive to gender reconciliation. He discerns that various worldviews either weaken or accentuate the differences (man/woman, rich/poor, talented/less talented) that exist among human beings. According to Kuyper, pantheistic systems result in a social caste system where the so-called more "godlike" people are privileged over the "godless" ones. Islam, Kuyper suggests, lets sensuality usurp public authority, so that "the woman is the slave of man." Roman Catholicism structures differences within a social hierarchy. Modernism, by contrast, "kills life by placing it under the ban of uniformity."[86]

Over against these worldviews, Kuyper describes Calvinism as follows:

> If Calvinism places our entire human life immediately before God, then it follows that all men or women, rich or poor, weak or strong, dull or talented, as creatures of God, and as lost sinners, have no claim whatsoever to lord over one another, and that we stand as equals before God, and consequently equal as man to man. Hence we cannot recognize any distinction among men, save such as have been imposed by God Himself, in that He gave one authority over the other, or enriched one with more talents than the other, in order that the man

---

83. Douglass, *Women, Freedom, and Calvin* (Philadelphia: Westminster Press, 1985).

84. See *Renaissance, Reformation, Resurgence,* papers and responses from the Colloquium on Calvin and Calvin Studies held at Calvin Theological Seminary, 22-23 April 1976 (Grand Rapids: Peter De Klerk, 1976). For an informative and balanced study of the ways in which the Reformation improved and failed to improve the condition of women, see also Steven Ozment's *When Fathers Ruled: Family Life in Reformation Europe* (Cambridge: Harvard University Press, 1983).

85. See n. 40.

86. Kuyper, *Lectures on Calvinism* (1931; rpt. Grand Rapids: William B. Eerdmans, 1976), pp. 26-27.

of more talents should serve the man with less, and in him serve his God. Hence Calvinism condemns not merely all open slavery and systems of caste, but all covert slavery of woman and of the poor; it is opposed to all hierarchy among men; it tolerates no aristocracy save such as is able, either in person or in family, by the grace of God, to exhibit superiority of character or talent, and to show that it does not claim this superiority for self-aggrandizement or ambitious pride, but for the sake of spending it in the service of God. So Calvinism was bound to find its utterance in the democratic interpretation of life; to proclaim the liberty of nations; and not to rest until both politically and socially every man, simply because he is man, should be recognized, respected and dealt with as a creature created after the Divine likeness.[87]

For Kuyper, then, experiencing the assurance of God's pardon ideally has the effect of creating social equality that does not fall into social uniformity. Thus he says that "the immortal glory which incontestably belongs to Calvinism" is that it "placed man on a footing of equality with man." The main difference between Calvinism and the "wild dream of equality of the French Revolution is that while in Paris it was one action in concert *against* God, here all, rich and poor, were on their knees *before* God, consumed with a common zeal for the glory of His Name."[88] Kuyper in fact praises the United States (relative to other Western countries at the turn of the century) for displaying the equalitarian fruit of Calvinism in the autonomy and decentralization of its local governments and for "the esteem in which woman is held among you."[89] This equality should not dissolve difference into a bland uniformity; it should allow room for differences among people. But these differences are expressed in the larger context of equality and mutual service.

Given this egalitarian impulse, why then did early Calvinism not utterly level the hierarchical medieval structures from which it emerged? Kuyper responds,

Even as in its early stage Christianity did not abolish slavery, but undermined it by a moral judgment, so Calvinism allowed the pro-

87. Ibid., p. 27.
88. Ibid., p. 28.
89. Ibid., p. 193.

visional continuance of the conditions of hierarchy and aristocracy as traditions belonging to the Middle Ages.... But inwardly Calvinism has modified the structure of society, not by the envying of classes, nor by an undue esteem for the possessions of the rich, but by a more serious interpretation of life.... And from this holy fear of God and this united stand before the face of God a holier democratic idea has developed itself, and has continually gained ground.[90]

These insights of Kuyper, even though not applied systematically to the oppression and subordination of women, are very compatible with feminist views on the equality of women. They also suggest an interpretive strategy for the New Testament and for the Reformed tradition. As Kuyper sees it, though Paul and the New Testament did not abolish slavery, they undermined it in principle. Eventually the leaven of Christian faith did abolish slavery. In a parallel manner, although early Calvinism did not overtly topple medieval hierarchicalism in political and ecclesiastical life, in principle it did so. The result was that Kuyper's time, the nineteenth century, saw the effect of this leaven of Reformed faith. And from our twentieth-century vantage point, we might say that although neither the New Testament nor Calvin nor Kuyper abolished patriarchy, they undermined it in principle. And our day is experiencing the fruit of these leavening powers of the Christian gospel.

In Calvinism, then, the emphasis must rest upon the basic equality of women and men. Men and women are similar in so many important ways — as persons created in God's image, as sinners fallen from our intended state, as redeemed, as called to participate in God's mission in this world. These truths do not abolish the complementarity between women and men. Rather, they imply that whatever differences exist are to be directed to the purposes of the God who created and redeemed us and who calls us to service.

Conclusion

Calvinists should be eager to enter discussions with feminists. Many sisters and brothers from other Christian traditions, and even some within Reformed ranks, have already begun such a dialogue. But honest and

90. Ibid., pp. 27-28.

open participation will be a risky business, for the feminist critique and alternatives quickly draw us into the most sensitive areas of life and thought. Conflicts will remain, but if the discussions are carried forward in the right spirit, both Calvinists and feminists (not to mention Calvinist feminists!) will be the richer, not only for the correlations but also for the conflicts. This participation requires a spirit sensitive to the wounds of the world, a spirit of bold confidence born of trust in a living God. It also requires the sort of creative appropriation of tradition that we find in Abraham Kuyper's work. According to Kuyper, "what the descendants of the old Dutch Calvinists as well as of the Pilgrim fathers have to do, is not to copy the past, as if Calvinism were a petrifaction, but to go back to the living root of the Calvinist plant, to clean and to water it, and so to cause it to bud and to blossom once more, now fully in accordance with our actual life in these modern times, and with the demands of the times to come."[91] In that Spirit, Calvinists may proclaim the fruit of their baptism, in which there is "no longer Jew or Greek, there is no longer slave or free, there is no longer male and female, for all . . . are one in Christ Jesus" (Gal. 3:28).

91. Ibid., p. 171.

183

CHAPTER 7

Gender Relations and Narrative
in a Reformed Church Setting

As children, many Christians memorized John 3:16, the verse that reads, "For God so loved the world that he gave his only Son, so that everyone who believes in him may not perish but may have eternal life." John 3:16 is also a key verse directed to adult inquirers who have little or no background in the Christian faith. From this verse both children of the church and those seeking to become part of it learn the liberating word that Jesus came to save all people — female, male, adult, teen, child, and so on. However, in many Protestant denominations, as well as in the Roman Catholic Church, female Christians often find that once they have *made* their Christian commitment, the appropriate memory verse for them is not *John* 3:16 but *Genesis* 3:16: "To the woman [God] said, 'I will greatly increase your pangs in childbearing; in pain you shall bring forth children, yet your desire shall be for your husband, and he shall rule over you.'"

Many churches find it difficult to reconcile these two texts for women. All recognize that salvation applies equally to women and men, but many remain closed to the possibility of equal service here on earth. Implicitly, they grant the Genesis text from the Fall narrative more

---

The primary author of this chapter is Helen Sterk.

power to interpret and direct action than the John text from the redemption story. While women are welcomed into the body of Christ, once in they are sent to the heart and hands of that body rather than to the head and feet.

In important ways, Christians live the life of faith informed by stories such as those of creation and fall as well as those of Christ's work. On one level, they know the basic story of the Bible — human beings were created by God and, through sin, fell away from God's grace. God called a chosen people, Israel, to redemption. In Christ's death and resurrection that redemption was extended to all people. All are called to live a life of faith — looking forward to Christ's return, which will usher in a new heaven and a new earth. This is the *core story* or *grand drama* of biblical salvation. But on another level, within the larger sweep of the biblical drama, *particular* stories are told, each one being heard and understood in relation to its place within the larger story. For Christians in the pews, these stories are shaped and given meaning by church doctrine, ritual, music, and social practice, and they constitute not only the milk but much of the meat of Christian nurture.

From the stories of Eve and Adam, Abraham and Sarah, Elijah, Elisha, Ruth, Esther, Job and so many others, believers learn models for living. Within these stories, or narratives, characters take on unique personalities through their actions and the motives that prompt them. Actions, too, take on "character" when they cause certain things to happen. Daniel's faithful prayers to God, which he continued to offer despite the king's command to pray only to him, caused Daniel to be cast into a den of ravenous lions. Because of Daniel's faithfulness, God protected him by closing the lions' mouths. In the end, the king too rewarded Daniel's faith when he rescinded his earlier order and replaced it with a command to worship Daniel's God. Believers nurtured on such stories of faith draw conclusions about how God wants them to live, and they try to fulfill God's perceived mandate. While biblical stories certainly are not the *only* means for guiding Christians, they are a crucial means.

The Importance of Narrative
for Gender Relations

Scholars from many fields — rhetoric, philosophy, theology, and psychology, to name only a few — now are attending closely to the effects of narrative on human belief and action. They are finding that people learn from and live by not only principles and rules but also stories. Furthermore, important insights into gender relations can be made through studying narrative.

The study of narrative form and content is important to gender studies in at least two ways. First, research shows that women find stories exceptionally congenial forms of expression, well suited to preserving and passing on knowledge. In her research Carol Gilligan discovered that women tend to *think* narratively — balancing characters' actions alongside their motives, relating demands of character and plot to those of situation.[1] In her work on public speakers, Kathleen Hall Jamieson found that women in general told stories more effectively than men. Linking this to the stories that mothers pass on to children, Jamieson observes, "In both primitive and advanced cultures, women are the repositories of parable-like dramatic vignettes, concise stories that transmit the common wisdom from woman to woman and generation to generation."[2] Similarly, Sara Ruddick sees stories as mothers' ways of helping children make sense of their worlds. Ruddick concludes that the cardinal virtues of mothers' stories are "realism, compassion, and delight."[3]

Studying stories that comment on some way on gender relations provides a second link to gender studies. In general, stories provide models for action. Both psychoanalyst Bruno Bettelheim and philosopher Alasdair MacIntyre argue that traditions passed from generation to generation through stories such as myth and fairy tale shape people's understanding of what it means to be a hero or a heroine, a mother or a father, the lover or the beloved.[4] So, taken together, the form and content of stories have powerful potential for showing how people think and what communities as well as individuals will think about.

In the context of this book, it seems particularly appropriate to study

1. Carol Gilligan, *In a Different Voice: Psychological Theory and Women's Development* (Cambridge: Harvard University Press, 1982). See especially the last chapter.

2. Jamieson, "The 'Effeminate' Style," in *Eloquence in an Electronic Age* (New York: Oxford University Press, 1988), p. 83.

3. Ruddick, *Maternal Thinking: Toward a Politics of Peace* (New York: Ballantine Books, 1989), p. 98.

4. Bettelheim, *The Uses of Enchantment* (New York: Alfred A. Knopf, 1976); and MacIntyre, *After Virtue: A Study in Moral Theory* (Notre Dame: University of Notre Dame Press, 1980).

at least briefly how biblical narratives may shape gender relations among Christians. In the previous two chapters, we summarized the theological commonalities, as well as some differences, between Calvinist and feminist thinkers. Much of the tension between these two groups lies in the differing answers they have given to the following question: "What is the basic story of gender relations in the Bible — one of enduring hierarchy, or one of progressively restored equal partnership?" The past two chapters have dealt with that question in terms of both theological method and substantive theological questions. In this chapter we want to apply some insights from those chapters to a particular church-based case study, and to do so using a rhetorical rather than a theological approach. We will consider how the shape and interpretation given to one particular biblical story of gender relations can both affect and be affected by church policy. In so doing, we will see narrative form and content interacting to influence women's and men's lives and their relations to one another and God.

As just mentioned, the analysis that follows is rhetorical rather than theological. While we indirectly address theological issues, our main concern in this chapter is the persuasive impact of one biblical story — that of human creation. Rhetorical criticism focuses upon public documents, especially those containing policy deliberations whose outcome affects a specific audience. The public documents chosen for this analysis are drawn from the deliberations of the Synod, or annual "parliament," of one modest-sized Protestant denomination, the Christian Reformed Church in North America.[5] These deliberations (whose outcomes have binding authority in the church) are published annually as the *Acts of Synod*. Our primary documents are not theological articles or books written and read by a highly trained group of theological scholars, but rather those authored and endorsed, for the most part, by ministers and elders representing the various classes (regional bodies) of the Christian Reformed Church. These texts affect the lives of every person in the denomination. Not only do they reflect policy, but also when the pastors involved in crafting them return home to their pulpits, their subsequent

5. This chapter was written in the summer of 1990 and reflects decisions made by the Christian Reformed Church Synod up to that time. Since then, the Synod of 1992 has met and decided *not* to ratify the 1990 decision to open all offices within the church to women. Instead, it struck a compromise: to leave the office of deacon open to both women and men, but to close the offices of elder and minister to women. Women may *expound* the Scriptures from CRC pulpits, but they may not *exhort*. Exhortation is a job reserved for men only.

187

preaching and discussion with parishioners is affected by these texts. For reasons of economy this chapter includes just one denomination, but the story that unfolds may well find an echo among readers from other conservative evangelical communities.

In what follows, we will analyze two distinct tellings of the same scriptural story of human creation, showing their impact on women's and men's experience of themselves in relation to each other and God. Before we get to that point, however, we will lay some necessary groundwork, first discussing the role of creation stories in general, and then the function of narrative in believers' religious experience. Next, we will turn to a brief history of the role played by the creation story in policy deliberations of the Christian Reformed Church. And finally, two tellings of the same creation story will be contrasted and assessed for their value in creating spiritually healthy relations between women and men within the church community.

The Creation Story as a Fundamental and Rhetorical Narrative

One of the ways humans enact community is through creating a shared identity. Identity is forged through actions — when people choose to live near each other, for example, or to share holiday rituals. Identity is also forged through symbols. Shared language and history, shared ritual, doctrine, and dogma, shared forms of dress, shared hymns and songs, and shared sacred stories represent only some of the many ways a community develops its identity symbolically. Sacred stories in particular carry normative principles and moral imperatives. They are seen as containing the principles that should be embodied in action. The major Christian source for such sacred stories is the Bible. At times Bible stories motivate listeners to right action. For example, within the Bible itself the Exodus story is repeated often to the Israelites to remind them that they too once were slaves and so should be hospitable to strangers and grateful to God for their own deliverance. On the other hand, stories like the one about Samson (Judg. 13–16) may indicate how *not* to act by showing the negative consequences of disobedience. They may also expose the evil motives of some seemingly good actions, as does the story of Ananias and Sapphira (Acts 5). The relations of story to imperative are numerous and diverse.

In the previous two chapters we demonstrated that faith communities never treat all parts of the Bible as equally relevant, but instead build their theology and doctrines around a confessionally based "core" of Scripture. A similar kind of selectivity is at work with regard to biblical narratives. While Christians regard all of the Bible's stories as inspired by God and therefore true and trustworthy, not all of these stories find equal "place" within a given faith community. In some communities the Exodus story may be seen as the most crucial; in others it will be God's choosing of Abraham and Sarah as the parents of Israel. Some may emphasize Christ's crucifixion, while others may emphasize his resurrection, the event of Pentecost, or what will happen in the "last days" yet to come. Whichever story (or set of stories) gets priority becomes like a lens through which all others are viewed: its perspectives, characters, and emphases suggest how other biblical stories are to be ranked in relation to it. Believers do not — in fact, *cannot* — give every story in the Bible equal status. In a text as long and complex as the Bible, some stories necessarily are chosen as emblematic and used to interpret others.[6]

One of the key stories told by faith communities is the story of how the world and humans came to be. Any story of origins gives humans a sense of place, personal identity, gender identity, relationship to God (or to the powers of the universe), relationship to each other, and purpose for human existence. As told within a community, stories of origins have often justified male dominance not only in more formal social relationships but also in more personal relationships. Moreover, these stories often privilege people of one color over those of another.[7]

Any story of origins also imposes order on chaos, whether it is a story of the "big bang" followed by evolution, or of God creating Adam and Eve to care for the Garden. The story of origins a community chooses to tell affects not only its view of the past but also its view of the future. In its privileged form (the one told by the persons in power), a story of origins

6. Northrop Frye, *The Great Code* (New York: Harcourt Brace Jovanovich, 1982); and Mary Stewart Van Leeuwen, *Gender and Grace: Love, Work and Parenting in a Changing World* (Downers Grove, Ill.: InterVarsity Press, 1990), chap. 2.

7. An African folktale has God commissioning a painter to paint the dolls that will become people. The painter lavishes color on the first doll, but gradually runs out of pigment and ends up creating pale people last (from the story told by Tejumola Ologboni at Marquette University, Milwaukee, Wisconsin, 22 October 1990).

189

sets the parameters for right action. In effect the storytellers say, "If this is what God *intended* for the world and its inhabitants, then we must do all we can to preserve it." The preferred creation story imprints upon a community a sense of "right" or "wrong" actions.

The creation story told in Genesis 1–3 could be called up as a commentary on many topics — astronomy, evolution, care of the environment, and so on. It has most certainly been used to frame many Christian discussions of gender relations. As many feminists have pointed out, authors since the time of Christ have used the creation story to portray women as less than men — intellectually, physically, and morally.[8] The story as it is traditionally told emphasizes Adam's temporal priority (translating it into the greater value of men as compared to women), Adam's naming of Eve, and Eve's sinning first, then tempting Adam.[9]

In the traditional telling, the first human is male and the first relation between the sexes is hierarchical, with the male by nature and/or

8. Mary Daly, *The Church and the Second Sex* (New York: Harper & Row, 1968), chap. 2; and Phyllis Trible, *God and the Rhetoric of Sexuality* (Philadelphia: Fortress Press, 1978), chap. 4. In *Adam, Eve, and Serpent* (New York: Random House, 1988), Elaine Pagels offers her account of how Augustine's interpretation of the creation story became normative for the early church, thus becoming the standard by which other tellings were judged. In light of Augustine's structure and shading of the story, humans became the center of the universe — separate, distinct from and superior to other creatures; humans took on hierarchical relations to one another; humans could be held responsible for their actions; and sex and death as they are presently experienced were a result of the Fall rather than part of God's created order. Pagels argues that Augustine's narration of the creation story more closely fit the mores and norms of his day than did Julian of Eclanum's telling of it. For that reason, Augustine was able to get Julian branded as a heretic and get his own narration accepted as canonical (pp. 144ff.).

9. In its general outlines, this narration is endorsed by theologians such as Calvin, Luther, and Kuyper (although Luther held that women and men were equal in status at creation and that subordination entered at the time of the Fall). See *Women and Religion: A Feminist Sourcebook of Christian Thought*, ed. Elizabeth Clark and Herbert Richardson (New York: Harper & Row, 1977), p. 144. Currently, many evangelicals endorse this telling too. (See, for example, "The Danvers Statement" by the Council on Biblical Manhood and Womanhood in *Christianity Today*, 13 January 1989, pp. 40-41). Given the history behind it, this creation story will hereafter be called the "traditional" story. While there are always a plurality of tellings in any tradition, our use of the term *traditional* refers to the dominant telling of the creation story.

by God's creation order in authority over the female. The male is said to be the "head" of the female, in the sense of having authority over her rather than in the sense of being her place of origin. Accordingly, the male is the original human, the female the secondary human, and the proper relationship between them — in domestic and, by implication, in public settings — is one of male leadership, if not domination. With this rendering of the creation story as a warrant, Christian husbands have demanded obedience of wives (e.g., in traditional marriage vows), wives' confinement to the home, and male priority in domestic, civic, and ecclesiastical life.

Traditional emphases presume the authority of male tellings, tellings which have become so entrenched that they are seen as the basic, unvarnished, and true story itself. Women hearing the traditional creation story must more or less suspend their identity as women in order to enter into the story. Mary Ann Tolbert observes that "in order simply to follow the story line . . . we must . . . imagine ourselves as male in order to fulfill the conventional role of reader."[10] However, as that telling has been enacted and tested by people in their everyday lives, *its* authority has been challenged, even as the authority of the *scriptural* narrative has remained intact.

How Narrative Shapes Religious Experience

Spiritual life and religious experience are formed by a variety of means — shared confessions, doctrines, dogma, ritual, sermons, Bible study groups, Sunday School lessons, and personal as well as family devotions. We have chosen *narrative* as this chapter's lens on religious life. How narrative form and content affect our relations with God and each other deserves scrutiny because narrative gives presence to what goes on *in* the believer. This perspective approaches religious life from a personal angle.

In this section we will see how a narrative dynamic operates within religious life. Several major aspects emerge. First, the storyteller has tremendous power. The storyteller's point of view informs both *how* and *what* a hearer thinks. Second, stories present characters who act out of

10. Tolbert, "Protestant Feminists and the Bible: On the Horns of a Dilemma," *Union Seminary Quarterly Review* 43, no. 14 (1989): 13.

certain motives. Hearers are encouraged to enact those roles, to avoid bad motives, and to integrate good motives into their lives. Third, the relation between story and audience is interactive — audiences not only *hear* but also *act out* stories. Each enactment tests the value of the story. And fourth, the stories operate on two levels — the *sacred* (the true and foundational level) and the *mundane* (the level of being told, which is inevitably located within a given time and culture, with all of the limitations and potential for distortion that this suggests).

Narrative embeds unique human characters in personal relationships and concrete situations, and shows those characters to be guided by motives revealed through various processes. Because it can give coherent shape to human events and make human actions understandable, narrative form helps people to feel that they understand their world. Human beings call upon the narrative form when they need to present a meaningful account of experience to themselves and others.

Because these accounts become the symbolic "stuff" that holds a community together, the role of storyteller is a crucial one. Whoever is authorized to tell stories can set the parameters for what is known, thought, done, and considered worth doing. Furthermore, the characters who enliven the stories become models for action in the community. Where would Christians of any era be if there were no stories of Abraham, Ruth, David, Mary, or Jesus? Theological concepts alone do not move a community.

Stories can thus be powerful social tools. Those who get to tell the stories shape communal memory, and hence a community's identity. For example, American identity is now being altered as stories other than those told by powerful white males come to the fore. African-Americans tell a story of slavery and of a marginal life quite different from that of Anglo-Americans. Native American stories show Sacajawea as more heroic than Lewis and Clark. Women tell stories about giving birth quite different from those of male doctors. Whoever gets to tell the story in its most respected and widespread form determines the perspective from which the entire community tends to view a certain set of experiences.

The available *character roles* also shape communal existence. If the main roles for women are the fairy-tale roles of princess or wicked stepmother, what does that mean for women's lives? If Bible stories are told about Abraham but not Sarah, David but not Tamar, or Jesus but not Mary, the lives of Christian women are impoverished. Stories affect the kind of lives that people can normally live within a community.

In *Human Communication as Narration,* Walter Fisher maintains that human beings negotiate values by means of stories rather than arguments. Stories go to the heart of human motives, including motives for ordering gender relations. Narratives are not merely stories we tell for personal enjoyment and enrichment; they also function "rhetorically, in a mode of social influence."[11] So whoever gets to tell such stories publicly holds substantial power over what ideas will be considered valid.

Narrative form knits events together, connecting them from beginning to middle to end, creating a seamless sense of purpose and coherence. In a tantalizingly ambiguous statement, Stephen Crites says this of the power of narrative: "Narrative alone can contain the full temporality of experience in a unity of form."[12] Purpose may not be apparent in overt behavior, but framing human actions in story form creates the assurance of unity, coherence, and purpose. "The full temporality of experience" is captured in narrative form because it moves the reader or hearer through time, ordering events in time. Neither essay nor formal argument nor poetry (in most of its forms) relies on time for its sense. These genres are released from time, from the "and this happened, and then because of that, this happened" form. Only narrative requires a sense of time.

Knitting events together in time effectively unites past to present and future. In the narratives held in common by a community, the order of past events affects present action and future policies, for narratives present possibilities and suggest courses of action. Alasdair MacIntyre sees this function of narrative playing out in the way *tradition* operates within a given community. He observes that "an adequate sense of tradition manifests itself in a grasp of those future possibilities which the past has made available to the present."[13] A community with a shared tradition and therefore with a communal sense of "self" enacts that tradition through the stories it chooses to tell and retell. Since those stories suggest model actions for the community, members find themselves turning to shared narratives for wisdom and direction.

Here again we see the social power of narrative. A community

---

11. Fisher, *Human Communication as Narration: Toward a Philosophy of Reason, Value, and Action* (Columbia, S.C.: University of South Carolina Press, 1987), p. 90.

12. Crites, "The Narrative Quality of Experience," in *Why Narrative? Readings in Narrative Theology,* ed. Stanley Hauerwas and L. Gregory Jones (Grand Rapids: William B. Eerdmans, 1989), p. 78.

13. MacIntyre, "The Virtues, the Unity of a Human Life, and the Concept of a Tradition," in *Why Narrative?* p. 108.

refers to its stories for guidance about what course of action to take. If the available stories include mainly those told by "white guys in suits,"[14] then almost certainly the valued characters will be white males, the valued roles masculine, and the valued policies ones that favor middle-class or upper-middle-class men. Narrative is thus no innocent, value-free medium.[15] It serves those who are empowered to tell stories within a community.

In bringing the past to bear on the present, narratives also unite generations. Walter Brueggemann, writing about the use of the Bible in communities of believers, says that "memory and vision" pass from one generation to another by means of key repeated stories.[16] Within one community of believers, such as the Jewish community, the Exodus account in the Old Testament may be the story seen as encapsulating the faith. That story of God's intervention and redemption becomes emblematic of God's relationship to the faith community. Children who are told this story, as Jewish children are every year during the Seder meal of Passover, receive a sense of their place among a people who bear a particular relation to God. In Brueggemann's view, the Exodus account is also the key story from the Old Testament for Protestant communities of believers. However, for Protestants the story of Christ is paramount in the New Testament. Exodus emphasizes God's ongoing, liberating agency in the life of the chosen *people*, while Christ's story emphasizes God's intimate, saving agency in *individual* human lives. In Protestant communities of believers, the continuity between these two stories (God's redemptive activity) overshadows the contrast (the Old Testament's focus on a people and the New Testament's on individuals).

Such is not the case for Jewish believers. In explaining why devout Jews have such trouble accepting the Jesus of the New Testament, Michael Goldberg invokes a narrative reason. For Jews, he argues, the contrast overwhelms the continuity between the two stories. For Jewish

14. Parker Palmer, keynote address of the Conference on Communication and Christianity, Marquette University, Milwaukee, Wisconsin, June 1990.

15. In chapter 13 of *Justice, Gender, and the Family* (New York: Basic Books, 1989), Susan Moller Okin criticizes MacIntyre for his blindness to women's enforced silence due to their absence from communal narratives. If few communal stories feature women, and those that do portray women negatively, the "tradition" is hospitable only to those whose purposes are served by such stories.

16. Brueggemann, *The Bible Makes Sense* (Winona, Minn.: Saint Mary's Press, 1985), p. 25.

believers, Exodus is the single paradigmatic story, in that it lays out the covenantal nature of the relationship of God to humanity. The Exodus narrative shows that God expects reciprocal action from Israel in effecting its own salvation. Such an interpretation of the Exodus story, Goldberg maintains, makes it impossible for Jews to envision the New Testament Christ as the Messiah. The New Testament Christ, presented in the biblical narrative as being himself God, did not require salvific action from humans. Goldberg says, "For in attempting to effect salvation in the very person of Jesus of Nazareth, God would have in essence been playing both parts — his own and that of humanity — consequently usurping the role previously accorded, for better or worse, to humankind alone."[17] From the perspective of Judaism, the person of Christ does not fit the narrative logic set forth in the Exodus story and carried out in the rest of the Old Testament. Therefore, says Goldberg, the narrative does not allow Jews to accept Jesus as the Messiah without a radical reordering of their entire religious worldview.

These two examples point directly to the interactive quality of narrative. When a given narrative is owned by a community, that narrative has life within the community. Members will call it up to explain things that happen, to point to appropriate behavior, to indicate what should be done in the future. From these examples, one can see at least part of the reason why *community* matters so much to Jews and *personhood* matters so much to Christians.

Narrative "life" unfolds in at least two ways — first, the narrative is *enacted* by community members, and second, the narrative is *tested* through each enactment for truth and coherence. According to Fisher, enactment is a key distinguishing feature of the way narrative works in people's lives. They may *accept* an argument, but they will *own* (or cease or refuse to own) a narrative. They will "creatively read and evaluate the texts of life and literature. . . . Viewing human communication narratively stresses that people are full participants in the making of messages, whether they are agents (authors) or audience members (co-authors)."[18] Furthermore, people do not simply tell and pass on narratives; they *live out* narratives, replaying them in the same way that actors enact scripts. For Stanley Hauerwas, the identifying mark of a "live" narrative is that people take it

17. Goldberg, "God, Action, and Narrative: *Which* Narrative? *Which* Action? *Which* God?" in *Why Narrative?* p. 363.
18. Fisher, *Human Communication as Narration,* p. 18.

seriously enough not just to hear and tell it but to *do* it: "For internal to the story itself is the claim that we cannot know the story simply by hearing it, but only by learning to imitate those who are now the continuation of the story."[19] Thus, ownership of a narrative demands hearing, understanding, and then ordering one's life in accord with those demands. And for a sense of what the narrative means, we look not only to our own understanding of the narrative text but also to people who are perceived as already living out the narrative. In this way, narratives are literally embodied by a community.

However, neither Fisher nor Hauerwas explicitly recognizes one crucial implication of this analysis. For someone to "enact a narrative," there must be a role for that person to play. Insofar as passive roles are given to women, with active roles largely reserved for men, women are left out of enactment. Not only are women not *telling* public stories; they are not even given many roles to play in the stories that *are* told.

Consider, for example, the Bible study guide called *A Woman and Her World*, meant to be used specifically by groups of women in a neighborhood church outreach ministry. The lesson on friendship features the story of David and Jonathan, not that of Ruth and Naomi. The parenting story features Abraham and Isaac rather than Mary and Jesus. The narrative of the virtuous woman of Proverbs 31 does not appear in the lesson on money management. Each lesson is followed by a page of quotations from secular and religious authorities in which women are again conspicuous by their absence. Even though the Bible contains stories featuring women, these were not chosen for inclusion in the study guide. Instead, the authors chose the male-dominated stories traditionally associated with the various topics.[20] As this guide illustrates, women are seldom given visibility within the religious tradition, even when their stories do exist and are fitting. What this means is that women must usually take on a male perspective when hearing the stories of faith. When women are not telling the stories, they are forced, however awkwardly, to enact men's stories.

It is no surprise that narrative is fundamental to communities because it is fundamental to human nature. According to Fisher, human rationality is "determined by the nature of persons as narrative beings — their inherent awareness of *narrative probability*, what constitutes a

19. Hauerwas, *A Community of Character: Toward a Constructive Christian Social Ethic* (Notre Dame: University of Notre Dame Press, 1981), p. 152.
20. *A Woman and Her World* (Grand Rapids: CRC Publications, n.d.).

coherent story, and their constant habit of testing *narrative fidelity,* whether or not the stories they know [are] true in their lives."[21] Live narratives are not "settled." They respond to the life circumstances of a community, which is one of the ways they affect present life and give frameworks — what Stephen Crites calls "anticipatory scenarios"[22] — for future action.

Narratives die when they no longer reflect the lived experience of the community. Hauerwas calls "truthful" those narratives that remain "open to challenge from new experience."[23] For example, in contemporary America, the Horatio Alger stories of self-made men no longer ring true: in an era of shrinking resources, young people's economic good fortune is no longer perceived as depending solely upon hard work and pluck. Alasdair MacIntyre points out that not only is a narrative dead when it no longer is open to testing, but that the tradition itself, "when vital, embod[ies] continuities of conflict. Indeed when a tradition [avoids conflict], it is always dying or dead."[24] Conflict is a necessary result of people actually living out the implications of narratives, and it is the mark of narrative testing. When people cease to see narratives as having consequences in their lives, not only the narratives but the traditions from which they grow cease to matter. In effect, then, both narrative and tradition decay. Narratives draw whatever life they have from the consent and enactment of their communities.

It is important to recognize that while any actual narrative may wither from lack of consent and enactment, usually the narrative *form* upon which it is based reappears in another telling. The concept of narrative has at least two levels of articulation in it. These levels have been labeled formal and actual, or "sacred" and "mundane,"[25] "mythic" and "actual,"[26] "primal" and "historical,"[27] "primordial" and "historical."[28]

21. Fisher, *Human Communication as Narration,* p. 5.
22. Crites, "The Narrative Quality of Experience," p. 77.
23. Hauerwas, *A Community of Character,* p. 151.
24. MacIntyre, "The Virtues, the Unity of a Human Life, and the Concept of a Tradition," p. 107.
25. Crites, "The Narrative Quality of Experience," p. 71.
26. Fisher implicitly privileges basic story forms over the various institutions of those forms when he says, "The most compelling, persuasive stories are mythic in form, stories reflective of 'public dreams,' that give meaning and significance to life" (*Human Communication as Narration,* p. 76).
27. Brueggemann, *The Bible Makes Sense,* p. 46.
28. Bruce Gronbeck, "Communication and Community: Mythic Conceptions

Whatever the terms, the idea is this: certain narrative frameworks are foundational, and on their frames different tellings, or narrations, are constructed. In *The Great Code*, Northrop Frye argues that all the basic narrative frameworks of Western literature — including comedy, quest, and romance — can be found in the Bible. But Christians take this much more seriously than Frye does, in effect uniting Frye's perspective with the idea of enactment. Not only do they see the sacred story-types as formulas for carrying various plots; they also see them as the frameworks for human living.[29] No community's *actual* telling of a story captures the complete essence of the underlying sacred story; rather, each telling *attempts* to capture its structure and meaning.

So, in response to the questions "Who am I?" "Who made me?" and "Where do I belong?" we turn to our sacred stories, telling them in old and new ways, trying to capture the sacred story's essence, but never quite succeeding. These stories, which Christians confess as being inspired by the Holy Spirit, matter so desperately to us because they orient us in relation to time, to God, to each other, and to ourselves. Our communal sacred stories "create" us by allowing us to glimpse human potential and its limits, to glimpse God's nature and relation to us, and to glimpse our purpose for living. Narrative, especially sacred narrative, is an important source of knowing; through it, our identity is communicated *to* us and structured *by* us.

Nevertheless, this form of communication is inherently ambiguous. Unlike argument, narrative works by implication, not assertion. Gordon Fee and Douglas Stuart find it significant that God did not choose clear propositional language as the major medium of biblical revelation. God spoke instead through "the particular circumstances and events of human history."[30] God used all sorts of nonpropositional forms, "narrative history, genealogies, chronicles, laws of all kinds, poetry, riddles, drama, biographical sketches, parables, letters, sermons,

---

of Self and Society," paper delivered at the Central States Communication Association Conference, Detroit, 1990, p. 1.

29. Again, Stephen Crites sees this clearly: "For these are the stories that orient the life of a people through time, their life-time, their individual and corporate experience, and their sense of style [the way in which life should be lived], to the great powers that established the reality of their world" ("The Narrative Quality of Experience," p. 70).

30. Fee and Stuart, *How to Read the Bible for All Its Worth* (Grand Rapids: Zondervan, 1982), p. 19.

and apocalypses,"[31] with narrative forms predominating. Within the Christian community, the sacred narratives of creation, liberation, salvation, and service are filtered through the simpler stories told in Sunday School and through sermons, hymns, homilies, theological interpretations, and narrative warrants for church policy.

None of these can capture fully the import and impact of the sacred narrative; they can only approach it. Led by the Holy Spirit, faith communities evaluate mundane tellings on the basis of their fidelity to the deep structure of the story and their "life" for the community. Recognizing the two levels of narrative articulation makes one aware that this side of heaven no human can fully tell any sacred story. It can only be approximated. Humility requires Christian communities to be open to new insights on how to tell the sacred stories.

A Story of Gender Relations

By looking at a case study of narrative in action, we put flesh and blood on theoretical bones. For many religious traditions — Jewish, Roman Catholic, and Protestant — the creation story has provided keys for understanding and enacting gender relations. Believers seem to feel that if they could just know *for sure* what God intended women and men to be and do before sin entered the world, they would know how to structure gender relations *now* — at home, in church, and in society. However, if any sacred story exhibits the characteristics of ambiguity, it is the story of human creation.

Several factors veil our understanding of the sacred story. First, there are two creation accounts. In Genesis 1 woman and man are represented as being created at the same time, equally sharing in God's image and in the mandates to be fruitful and have dominion over the rest of creation. In

---

31. Ibid., p. 20. Walter Brueggemann expands upon this point by delineating the characteristics of a "Covenantal-historical" view of Christianity. According to this view, biblical faith is concrete, founded on (1) "concrete acts of power and mercy," (2) "precise historical memory," (3) "special expectation for the future and a dynamic which lets that promised future come among us," and (4) "[a definition of] human existence in terms of vocation" (*The Bible Makes Sense*, pp. 18-21). In other words, biblical narrative provides the "stuff" in which "acts of power and mercy" and "precise historical memory" are found. Narrative's interactive quality provides the flexible structure that allows a sense of future direction. And finally, the content of biblical narratives gives guidance on vocation.

the Genesis 2 account, man is created first, and *then* woman from man. Further, it seems that man named woman. It also seems that the woman sinned first and then persuaded the man to sin. These two accounts thus differ significantly. Second, the word *adam* as used in Genesis 1 and 2 may refer to a male person, a specific male person, or all of humankind.[32] Just which meaning is intended in which texts is not altogether clear. And third, few details are given regarding how Eve and Adam related to each other before the Fall. The Bible implies that they walked and talked with God on a regular basis; it also states (Gen. 2:25) that they were naked and not ashamed. But it does not specifically tell us what they did together. Certainly there are many factors that make it difficult to know how Adam and Eve lived before the Fall, and we have mentioned only a few. But they point to issues that are glossed over or (alternately) highlighted in any given telling of the creation story.

In order to anchor our discussion of the *use* of the creation story to influence gender relations within a given faith community, we now turn, as promised earlier, to the Christian Reformed Church. Over the past thirty-three years, the leaders of this church, all male, have been debating how women should fit into the church. These debates have been going on in congregations, classes (regional governing bodies filled with male elders and ministers and only the very occasional female deacon), and synods (the annual, international governing body in which only males have served as delegates). Committee after committee, each overwhelmingly male,[33] has been formed to determine, on biblical grounds, the right relation of women to men in the church.

32. Francis Brown, S. R. Driver, and Charles A. Briggs, *The New Brown-Driver-Briggs-Gesenius Hebrew and English Lexicon* (Peabody, Mass.: Hendrickson Publishers, 1979).

33. A 1957 committee deliberating on women's participation in church meetings was entirely male. A 1973 committee deliberating on women in office had one woman and six men; in 1975 the committee chosen to address that same issue had one woman and five men. The 1978 committee focusing on "hermeneutical principles regarding women in office" had no women. The 1981 committee reviewing the decision of the 1978 committee had one woman and seven men. The 1984 committee reporting on headship had two women and five men; the 1990 committee on headship had one woman and three men. Not only were few if any women included on these committees, but none had the theological credentials and standing of the Christian Reformed ministers and Calvin College and Seminary theologians who made up the rest of the committee. Combined, these factors made it all the more difficult for women's voices to be heard, let alone heeded.

As of this writing, the most recent committee was formed in 1987 to report to the Synod of 1990 on two questions: "Can headship be extended from marriage to church?" (the presumption being that male headship is to be taken for granted in the family), and "What are the implications of male headship for women in church office?" The resulting report reflects the impasse that the Christian Reformed Church faced in June 1990. The committee presented arguments for male headship, balanced with arguments against it, followed by a final section tellingly titled "Observations" rather than "Conclusions." In this section the committee refused to put the weight of their interpretation on one side or the other of the issue. While they found no biblical support for extending male headship from marriage to church, their language indicated a balance between the arguments: "While weighty arguments can be credibly adduced in [its] support, other weighty arguments can be raised against [it]."[34] The committee's recommendation was that Synod continue discussion on "perspectives, worldview, and hermeneutical assumptions"[35] as these relate to the questions of headship. In short, the committee recommended appointing yet another committee.

Keeping the question in committee was the course that had been followed in the Christian Reformed Church for the thirty-three years between 1957 and 1990, with only two small resulting actions: in 1957 congregational voting was opened to women, and in 1984 a modified form of the office of deacon was opened to women. Both of these were subject to the discretion of local churches and therefore were not binding on the denomination as a whole.[36] However, no committee has been able to find incontrovertible biblical grounds either for keeping women out of or for placing them in positions of leadership in the church. In the summer of 1990, the CRC Synod took the unexpected and unprecedented step of voting to change church order (the "Constitution" of the CRC) so that women could be ordained and serve individual churches,

34. "Report of the Committee to Study Headship," *Agenda and Acts of Synod* (Grand Rapids: Board of Publications of the CRC, 1990), p. 329.
35. Ibid., p. 330.
36. As of 1983, 29 percent of Christian Reformed Churches still permitted only confessing male members to vote in congregational meetings. By 1991, that figure was significantly lower: only an estimated 12 percent still adhered to this practice. However, by that same year, only an estimated 30 percent of the churches were ordaining women as deacons (Personal communication, Henry De Moor, Calvin Theological Seminary, December 1990).

not just as deacons but also as elders and ministers. However, this move was subject to ratification in 1992.

Over the thirty-three years, three lines of argument recur based on three narrative themes: (1) creation order and gender relations, (2) Christ's exercise of headship, and (3) Paul's reliance on creation norms to support the historical continuity of male dominance over females. A brief summary of the documents on women's place in the Christian Reformed Church will show how arguments over gender relations have focused more and more narrowly on the first of these lines of argument — namely, the story of creation, which has been used as a warrant for male dominance and female subordination. Over time, as other biblically based arguments were tested and found wanting, the synodical reports show a progressively greater reliance on the story of creation and fall, with its seemingly obvious assertion of male superiority and female submission.

We begin in 1957, when Synod acted on a recommendation that women be allowed to vote, subject to local option, in congregational meetings. Literally from beginning to end, the 1957 report emphasizes the male prerogative in telling the story of gender relations. The report begins with the words "Esteemed brethren" and concludes with the assertion that although women and men are created spiritually equal,

> the word of God teaches that there is a difference between man and woman, involving the headship of man, which is rooted in creation and which is not abrogated by redemption. In accordance with this principle rooted in creation and brought to bear on the life of the church by the apostle Paul, women would not be accorded a position of leadership in the church.[37]

The issue of women's place in the Christian Reformed Church then lay dormant until 1970. At that time, prompted by the 1966 decision of its Dutch sister church to open all offices to women,[38] the Christian Reformed Church established a study committee to report in 1973. That committee decided, on the grounds that women share humanity fully with men, that leadership was meant to be shared by women and men. The committee concluded that "the practice of excluding women from

---

37. "Women Suffrage in Ecclesiastical Meetings," Supplement 19, *Acts of Synod* (Grand Rapids: Board of Publications of the CRC, 1957), p. 313.
38. De Moor, personal communication, December 1990.

ecclesiastical office cannot be conclusively defended on biblical grounds."[39]

The 1973 report is noteworthy for its consistent stress on gender partnership in the Old and New Testaments. Its telling of the creation story underlined the fact that both women and men were created as image bearers of God and were meant to complement each other. While recognizing man's priority in the creation order and God's construction of woman as *ezer*—helpful companion—for man, this committee put the weight of its interpretation on the side of partnership between the sexes rather than on domination of the female by the male. Indeed, after reviewing the creation story, the committee concluded, "One might ask whether man may separate with respect to the offices of the church what God has joined together in the history of salvation."[40]

The report highlighted women's contributions as it traced the story of gender relations in the Old and New Testaments.[41] It argued that while order and decency are imperative within the church, each age needs to decide "what this call means in practical terms of social conditions and patterns of behavior"[42] between women and men. With a certain amount of surprise, the committee members admitted, "We also noticed that women, even in the most unfavorable situations, find ways and means to make an active contribution to the work Christ demands from all."[43] In short, the authors of the report found sufficient warrant in the biblical creation story, in Christ's example, and in Paul's epistles to recommend full acceptance of women as men's partners in the Christian Reformed Church.

39. "Women in Ecclesiastical Office," Supplement-Report 39, *Acts of Synod* (Grand Rapids: Board of Publications of the CRC, 1973), p. 587. This report was sent to a new committee that was mandated to evaluate and respond to it in 1975.

40. Ibid., p. 524.

41. Ibid. This report chronicles in careful detail the stories of Sarah, Rebekah, Leah and Rachel, Shiprah and Puah, the virtuous woman of Proverbs 31, Miriam, Huldah, and so on, showing women's agency in the story of the people of Israel. Interestingly, the report focuses on the Song of Solomon as well, showing the activity of the woman lover in pursuing and claiming her beloved (pp. 525ff.). From the New Testament, the report draws attention to Christ's many interactions with and parables featuring women, as well as the fact that the Samaritan woman was the first person commissioned by Jesus to preach to the Gentiles and women were the first witnesses of his birth, death, and resurrection. Further, the report takes note of Paul's many favorable mentions of women as co-workers (pp. 540ff.).

42. Ibid., p. 550.

43. Ibid., p. 586.

One member of that committee, however, submitted a dissenting minority statement. Peter Jonker took exception to the report's emphases in the creation story. He found in the story of creation sufficient grounds for limiting women's contributions to church life. He emphasized "the fact that woman was the first who fell in transgression," that "the Scriptures repeatedly stress the God-given order of submissiveness of the woman to her husband," and that "head" indicates a "position of authority and representation." He further argued that the authority of husband over wife justifies the authority of all men over all women.[44] Jonker explicitly rejected the majority's position that biblical principles need to be applied in ways appropriate to the age. He declared that the CRC cannot find its "norm in a changing society."[45]

Already in 1973, then, two tellings of the creation story emerge. One holds that gender partnership is the focal point of scriptural stories about human relationships. The other stresses the priority of male over female. The 1973 majority position viewed creation as only the beginning chapter in the ongoing narrative of God's care for all people, care that culminates in offering Christ as the means of salvation for women and men equally and the Spirit as the supporter of all Christian service. The minority position, by contrast, told a story of separate roles for women and men, arranged in a hierarchical relation in which women submit to men's God-given authority.

Subsequent reports on gender-related issues within the Christian Reformed Church's *Acts of Synod* recognize the existence of both interpretations of the Genesis creation story but privilege an interpretation of gender hierarchy over one of gender partnership. In 1975 another committee report was filed, this one evaluating the 1973 report and recommending that it *not* be upheld. The grounds given were that order must be maintained within the church and such "order" depends upon male authority in the home and in church. The report stated in summary that "if the present ordination of women to office would in any way undermine the church's insistence on maintaining the headship and authority of men in the home, then it should not be done."[46] Furthermore, the report demanded that women submit to men's *universal* au-

44. Postscript, ibid., pp. 589-93.
45. Postscript, ibid., p. 593.
46. "Women in Ecclesiastical Office," Supplement-Report 46, *Acts of Synod* (Grand Rapids: Board of Publications of the CRC, 1975), p. 572.

thority, on the grounds that "the basic or normative or abiding principle
. . . is not that of submission within the marriage relationship first of all,
but that of the submission of woman to man as indicated in 1 Corinthians 11 and 1 Timothy 2."[47] However, even this committee could not say
that the Bible was "in principle" against women holding "any office that
men may hold in the church."[48] Its report recommended opening the
office of deacon to women, provided such a move did not undermine
male authority, and indicated the need for further study of the other
offices.

The 1973 committee had done thorough spadework in reconstructing the full story of women's agency in both the Old and New Testaments (see n. 40). In light of this, subsequent committees were hard-
pressed to maintain the idea of female passivity or inferiority within the
broad sweep of the biblical story. As a result, they focused more and
more narrowly on the creation narrative, maintaining that male "headship" was a pre-Fall element of God's created order for the world and
not dependent on the merits of either sex. Committees were then
directed to report to the synods of 1981, 1984, and 1990 on the exact
nature of male headship.

Report 32, submitted to the Synod of 1981, noted the problem of
determining whether headship meant men's *power over* women or their
enabling of women's development. As a compromise, it recommended
redefining the office of deacon to distinguish it from the office of elder,
removing from the former any ruling function within the church and thus
opening it up to the exercise of women's as well as men's gifts.[49] In effect,
this report weighed in on the side of hierarchical gender relations, with
authority given to men and service (without authority) given to women.

---

47. Ibid., p. 573. This decision — that the passages in 1 Corinthians and in
1 Timothy refer to universal male headship rather than merely the headship of
husband over wife — is highly debatable. The words used in the Greek texts are
gune and *aner,* which could mean *either* "husband and wife" *or* "man and woman." Just
which is meant is not as clear as "Report 46" assumes.

48. Ibid., p. 593.

49. In a minority report, Henry Vander Kam argued that the three offices of
minister, elder, and deacon could not be broken up without doing damage to the creeds
of the church, so he recommended excluding women from *all* offices rather than
changing either the creeds or the church order ("Synodical Studies on Women in Office
and Decisions Pertaining to the Office of Deacon, Minority Report II," Report 32, *Acts
of Synod* [Grand Rapids: Board of Publications of the CRC, 1981], p. 530).

205

The Synod of 1984, however, faced a barrage of overtures from congregations and classes requesting a return to the pre-1975 status quo of male exclusivity in *all* church offices, including that of deacon. In response, Synod again focused on the meaning of headship. The 1984 report argued that male headship was instituted by God in creation and was not a result of humankind's fall from grace.[50] It effectively dismissed as unimportant women's contributions in the Old and New Testaments and deemed inferior women's work in the early church. In its explanation of the meaning of biblical words associated with women's work rather than men's, Report 33 found that *diakonos* meant "deacon" when applied to men and "helper" or "servant" when applied to women. It concluded that *prostatis* meant "ruler" for men but "helper" for women, and *synergos* meant "public preacher" for men but "private evangelist" for women.[51] (In their minority report, Willis De Boer, a theology professor at Calvin College, and Sarah Cook charged the committee's majority with sexism because of their reasoning that "if the word applies to women it must mean something lesser than [when applied to] men."[52]) In its recommendations, the 1984 report reaffirmed that male headship was creational but allowed that women could serve as deacons as long as they did not actually participate in church leadership and as long as churches were not *required* to consider women for diaconal office. Again, women's service was affirmed while their shared authority was denied.

Two significant minority reports were appended to Report 33, one (already mentioned) by Sarah Cook and Willis De Boer, and another by Thea B. Van Halsema, a professor at the Reformed Bible College in Grand Rapids. Van Halsema's report upheld the idea of universal male headship but argued against redefining the office of deacon on the basis that this would weaken the unity of the offices of minister, elder, and deacon. But what makes her contribution unique in the ongoing debate is that, out of all the reports submitted up to that time, hers alone recognizes that male headship depends upon women's *willingness* to support it. Male headship, she implied, is as much the result of a dynamic relationship as of a static creational given. Van Halsema pointed out that if headship were to work, women needed to take submission upon

---

50. "Committee on Headship in the Bible," Report 33, *Acts of Synod* (Grand Rapids: Board of Publications of the CRC, 1984), p. 295.

51. Ibid., pp. 320-21.

52. Ibid., pp. 367ff.

themselves, not have it thrust upon them by men. She also suggested that women be commissioned as official helpers of male office-bearers, assisting them in their work. Regressive as this may sound, Van Halsema alone among the authors of all the synodical reports suggested a way for *women's* service to be institutionalized in the church. Other authors took an all-or-nothing approach, which would have women work either completely in the shadows or, alternately, in the full light of ordination.

Cook and De Boer, on the opposite side of the debate, argued that the Bible's stories of creation and gender relations should be read in the light of the story of Pentecost, when the Holy Spirit was given to all believers. According to their reading, the nature of headship is not determined solely by the story of creation but is developed throughout Scripture, especially in the way Jesus worked to give power to others rather than keeping it for himself. Yet despite their differences, both minority reports responded to Scripture *as narrative,* recognizing its dynamic quality as expressed through enactment and testing.[53]

A year later the 1985 *Acts of Synod* was again filled with overtures from congregations and classes, protesting against opening even a modified diaconal office to women. The overtures appealed to "God's law," "order," "unity," and "the confessions," and pointed to the "clear," "obvious" "fact" of the "plain teaching of scripture" that men must be the sole rulers of the church and the family.[54] In response, Synod appointed yet another committee and asked it to report in 1990.

But the 1990 report on headship gave remarkably few grounds for progress in the debate. It presented arguments on what headship *could* mean lexically;[55] it also presented the case for the traditional view of headship as well as the case against it. In the case for the traditional view, the committee commented on Genesis 2, saying that the "male has a certain priority, a priority suggested by the fact that Adam was created before Eve (v. 22) and by Adam's responsibility to select a name for Eve

53. The minority reports by Van Halsema and by Cook and De Boer are found in ibid., pp. 337-75.

54. See Overtures 31-51, *Acts of Synod* (Grand Rapids: Board of Publications of the CRC, 1985), pp. 501-10.

55. This report rehearsed the case for interpreting the Greek word *kephale* (found in passages such as 1 Corinthian 11 that name the husband as "head of the wife as Christ is the head of the church") as meaning either "authority" or "source," giving a slight edge to the "source" interpretation. This in effect gives Adam no more power over Eve than the earth has over Adam.

(v. 23)."[56] In the case against the traditional view, the committee suggested a counterargument — namely, that "male firstness in the garden does not close possibilities of primary leadership to women."[57] At the same time, little effort was made to reframe the creation story in any significant way. While the report's rhetorical structuring of the two cases suggested a preference for understanding the relation between the genders as one of partnership, its conclusions did not. In fact, conclusions were replaced by mere "observations" and a call for still further study.

To summarize: the 1957 synodical report that allowed women to vote in consenting churches sounded two narrative themes which continued to play against each other throughout the next three decades. One was a reading of the creation story that assumed unchanging norms for gender roles and hierarchy in gender relations. The other was a narrative emphasizing women's equal calling and opportunity for service.

Those who were against opening church offices to women finally narrowed the basis for their case to an interpretation of Genesis 1–3 which claimed that women were secondary to men not only in the home but also in the church and sometimes even in the larger society. In reading the New Testament, they passed briefly over both Christ's behavior toward women and the inclusive outpouring of the Spirit at Pentecost, fixing instead on the Pauline epistles, where a creation-based gender hierarchy is occasionally proclaimed.[58] Genesis 3:16 was their implicit rallying point.

56. "Report of the Committee to Study Headship," *Agenda and Acts of Synod* (1990), p. 316.

57. Ibid., p. 323.

58. People who argue for a reading of Genesis 1–3 that emphasizes male priority often refer to 1 Corinthians 11:7-9, which reads, "For a man ought not to have his head veiled, since he is the image and reflection of God; but woman is the reflection of man. Indeed, man was not made from woman, but woman from man. Neither was man created for the sake of woman, but woman for the sake of man." Or they refer to 1 Timothy 2:13-14: "For Adam was formed first, then Eve; and Adam was not deceived, but the woman was deceived and became a transgressor." Such texts seem conclusive about what happened during creation. Yet people who fixate on these texts downplay other texts that seem to indicate quite the opposite. For example, Genesis 1:27 states, "So God created humankind in his image, in the image of God he created them; male and female he created them." Quite clearly, this verse states that *both* female and male are created in God's image. Further, if those who emphasize 1 Corinthians 11:7-9 would continue reading, they would find these assertions in verses 11-12: "Nevertheless, in the Lord woman is not independent of man or man independent of woman. For just as woman came from man,

Those who approved women's presence in all church offices framed the story of creation differently, placing it within the context of the entire sweep of Scripture. In their arguments, Christ's work — his death, resurrection, and offer of salvation to all — and Pentecost were placed squarely in the middle, with the more restrictive statements of the Pauline epistles accordingly marginalized. John 3:16 and Galatians 3:28 were their implicit rallying points.

An Alternative Story of Creational Norms for Gender Relations

Strikingly absent from the synodical reports discussed in the previous section is the clear sound of women's voices as authors, or even reference to a woman scholar.[59] Except for a passing mention of anthropologist Margaret Mead, no female authorities were ever named. One voice which would have been an asset is that of rhetorician and Old Testament scholar Phyllis Trible. In her book titled *God and the Rhetoric of Sexuality*, she analyzes the creation story found in Genesis 1–3. In the process she sheds new light on old tellings and may even nudge the tale somewhat closer to the sacred story.

We have chosen Trible's presentation of the creation story for three basic reasons. First, she meticulously grounds her reading of Genesis 1–3 in the original Hebrew, going as "straight to the source" as any human being can. In her reading, she carefully notes and evaluates semantic,

---

so man comes through woman; but all things come through God." These statements seem to take away the male prerogative given a few verses earlier. And in response to the text from 1 Timothy, consider what Paul says in Romans 5:12: "Therefore, just as sin came into the world through one *man,* and death came through sin . . ." (my emphasis). Here Eve is not singled out as the sole transgressor. If she is included in the "one man," it is as someone *equally* culpable.

59. Willis De Boer acknowledges that he found the work of some women biblical scholars helpful in his writing the Minority Report II to Synodical Report 33 (1984). He found Phyllis Trible's writings on the creation account particularly insightful. However, just as De Boer did not mention the names of the male theologians whose work he found useful, he didn't mention the names of the female theologians whose work he found helpful (letter to the author, 12 August 1991). In a personal conversation (in June 1990), DeBoer quipped that using the name of a recognized Dutch male theologian might have helped our case before Synod, but not using the names of women.

syntactic, and grammatical markers that necessarily escape the attention of someone reading a translation. She makes a deliberate effort to discover the sacred story that may be obscured by translations. Second, Trible's reading of creation provides a clear alternative to the one developed in the previous section, thereby throwing that reading into relief. But however distinct her interpretation may be, it is not eccentric. Her interpretive word choices lie within the realm of accepted scholarly opinion, and her conclusions are at least partially validated by sources as close to the Christian Reformed Church as the 1973 report and the 1984 opinion of Cook and De Boer. Third, her reading weds scholarly integrity with a woman's perspective. A main point in this chapter has been that the storyteller is crucially important to the story's shape and color. Trible's insights grow directly out of her recognition of herself as a gendered creature. While there may be other egalitarian perspectives on the creation story,[60] Phyllis Trible's is one of the most thorough, being concretely grounded in a verse-by-verse reading, in the original language, of Genesis 1–3.

Trible argues that the traditional male-filtered narrative of creation (echoed in almost all the study committees of the CRC and in many local and regional overtures to its synods)[61] routinely justifies

60. Two particularly accessible examples of egalitarian stories are Aida Besancon Spencer's *Beyond the Curse: Women Called to Ministry* (Nashville: Thomas Nelson Publishers, 1985), esp. chaps. 1 and 6; and Alvera Michelson's essay entitled "An Egalitarian View: There Is Neither Male nor Female in Christ," in *Women in Ministry: Four Views*, ed. Bonnidell Clouse and Robert G. Clouse (Downers Grove, Ill.: InterVarsity Press, 1989), pp. 173-206, esp. pp. 182-85.

61. Indeed, a reading of the overture to synod and letters to *The Banner*, the news and feature magazine of the Christian Reformed Church, would reveal how firmly the traditional male narrative of creation is held as sacred. For example, Classis Chatham maintains, "Scripture teaches that women ought to take a place of submissiveness in the church, not merely because of the historical-cultural situation of their time but because this is rooted in the order of creation (I Timothy 2:13), because of what the law says (I Corinthians 14:34), and because the woman was the first to fall into transgression (I Timothy 2:14)" ("Classis Chatham Appeals Decision of 1984 Synod re Women in Office," Protests and Appeals, *Acts of Synod* [1985], p. 513). This interpretation is repeated by Bakersfield Christian Reformed Church (p. 526), First Hanford Christian Reformed Church (p. 527), and others. In a 1983 letter to the editor of *The Banner*, Alfred Van Schepen of Ireton, Iowa, writes, "The Scriptures clearly imply that a woman is to play a role of submission in the church. Not that she is to be dominated over, which is sin, but that she should submit willingly, as that is how God intended it to be from the beginning of creation" ("Voices," *The Banner*, 7 March 1983, p. 3).

210

patriarchy. As this story is told, man was created before woman, so man literally takes priority over woman. Further, since God used man's rib to fashion woman, man could even be said to have given birth to woman. Having seen the woman, man named her and hence acquired further authority over her. When the serpent came to the Garden, the woman was the one tempted into sin. She then seduced man into sin, and thus was responsible for sin's entrance into the world. Woman consequently is cursed by pain in childbirth, yet she desires man, the one who impregnates her and is the indirect cause of her pain. Her desire leads her (quite rightly, on this account) to submit herself to man, and God gives man the further right to rule over her.[62]

But in working directly with the Hebrew text, Trible tells a rather different story, some elements of which appear, however fleetingly, in the CRC synodical reports favoring partnership between the sexes (such as Report 39 of 1973 and the third section of the 1990 report). According to Trible, the Genesis account of creation has three major sections: first, the human is created from the earth; second, man and woman are made as companions for each other; and third, together woman and man are responsible for sin.[63]

First, the human is created from the earth. According to Trible's reading of Genesis 1 and 2, the first human was neither male nor female but sexually undifferentiated. God took some earth *(ha'adama)* and made a person *(ha'adam)* from it. The equivalent pun in English would be "the human was made from humus." God tells this creature to care for the earth and to have dominion over the plants and animals.

One need not go as far as Trible does (all the way to androgyny) to see the point that before Eve's creation, "Adam" may not necessarily refer to a distinct male person. According to Leon Morris, who wrote the entry "Adam" in the *Evangelical Dictionary of Theology,* "many scholars hold that up to Genesis 4:25 all occurrences of 'Adam' should be understood to refer to 'man' [see Chapter Eleven for an explanation of the ambiguity of this term: it could refer to a human or to humankind] or 'the man.'"[64] *The New Brown-Driver-Briggs-Gesenius Hebrew and English Lexicon* offers further warrant for leeway in understanding Adam before

---

62. Trible, *God and the Rhetoric of Sexuality,* pp. 73ff.

63. This entire account can be found in ibid., pp. 80-133.

64. Morris, "Adam," in *Evangelical Dictionary of Theology,* ed. Walter A. Elwell (Grand Rapids: Baker Book House, 1984), p. 10.

Eve as more a human being than a man. For one thing, Genesis 1:27 "distinctly" identifies *adam* as including male and female. And even more tellingly, the account "seldom" refers to "man opp.[osite] woman."[65] In corroboration of this point, Leonard J. Coppes, in the *Theological Word-book of the Old Testament*, observes that *adam* "should be distinguished from *'ish* (man as opposite of woman, or as man distinguished in his manliness), *'enosh* (man as weak and vulnerable), and *geber* (man as mighty and noble).[66]

Perhaps the most balanced way to think of "adam" is as *potentially* male before Eve's creation. C. F. Keil and F. Delitzsch make this point in their *Commentary on the Old Testament*:

> Before the creation of the woman we must regard the man (Adam) as being "neither male, in the sense of complete sexual distinction, nor androgynous as though both sexes were combined in the one individual created at the first, but as created in anticipation of the future, with a preponderant tendency, a male in simple potentiality, out of which state he passed, the moment the woman stood by his side, when the mere *potentia* became an actual antithesis."[67]

The point is that both male and female are required before "humanity" can be considered to be complete.

The second major section of the story tells that man and woman were created to be companions. After a time, seeing that the creature finds no fit companion among the animals, God puts it to sleep and uses one of its own ribs as the building material to make its companion. The creature wakes up to a partner. In the Hebrew, two important grammatical changes suggest that this was the moment of sexual differentiation. Trible notes that "only after the surgery does this creature . . . identify itself as *male*." She also notes that pronouns for "he" *(ish)* and "she" *(ishshah)* come into use only after the surgery.[68] Moreover, the male creature does not at this

---

65. See the "Adam" entry in *The New Brown-Driver-Briggs-Gesenius Hebrew and English Lexicon.*

66. Coppes, "Adam," in *Theological Wordbook of the Old Testament*, vol. 1, ed. R. Laird Harris, Gleason L. Archer, Jr., and Bruce K. Waltke (Chicago: Moody Press, 1980), p. 10.

67. Ziegler, as quoted by Keil and Delitzsch in *Commentary on the Old Testament*, vol. 1, trans. James Martin (Grand Rapids: William B. Eerdmans, 1983), p. 88.

68. Trible, *God and the Rhetoric of Sexuality*, p. 98.

time *name* the female; instead he calls out to her in recognition:[69] "Bone of my bones and flesh of my flesh" (Gen. 2:23). This woman is a "companion corresponding to" the man.[70] Unlike the plants and animals, she is not a thing to be dominated, tilled, or kept. As can be seen when Genesis 1 is kept in tension with Genesis 2, man was given no creational power over woman: she and he were made as partners and jointly assigned the work of caring for each other and for the earth. And like the plants and animals, they were jointly to "be fruitful and multiply" (Gen. 1:28).

Trible finds rich evidence in the creation story for seeing woman and man as a united harmony of persons rather than two rigidly distinct sexes. For both woman and man, life comes directly from God rather than through any power of their own. No subordination inheres in the creation of one sex from the body and rib of the other, unless one also considers the original human subordinate to the earth from which it was made.[71] Trible also sees the creation of two sexes as the culmination of creation: God fashioned the original human from clay as a sculptor might and built the woman as an architectural artist might. Hands-on care went into the making of both the original human and the final, sex-differentiated pair.

When the male human awakes to find the female human, he bursts forth with a hymn of recognition: "This at last is bone of my bones and flesh of my flesh; this one shall be called Woman *[ishshah],* for out of Man *[ish]* this one was taken" (Gen. 2:23). Immediately following the hymn, the writer of Genesis comments on the primary purpose of sexuality, which is not procreation but oneness: "Therefore a man leaves his father and his mother and clings to his wife, and they become one flesh" (Gen. 2:24). Trible sees woman as "gift — God's gift of life."[72] The man and woman need each other for life, and both creation accounts emphasize their partnership.

69. Trible points out that in order to denote naming, the Hebrew verb for "call" must be followed by a name. Without the name ("Eve," for example) calling is not naming; it is merely recognizing (Ibid., p. 100).
70. Ibid., p. 90. In commenting on "Eve," H. M. Wolf observes that the elation between Adam and Eve suggested in Genesis 2 "occurs nowhere else in the O.T. The closest parallel . . . describes antiphonal choirs standing opposite one another and corresponding to one another (Neh. 12:24)" (*Evangelical Dictionary of Theology,* p. 384).
71. Trible, *God and the Rhetoric of Sexuality,* pp. 101-2.
72. Ibid., p. 104.

According to the third major section of the story, man and woman are together responsible for humankind's fall from grace. The original Hebrew account of the first sin, found in Genesis 3:6, is translated by Trible as follows: "She gave some to her husband, who was with her, and he ate it."[73] In other words, the serpent spoke to the woman *in the presence of the man*, tempting her to eat the fruit of the tree God had expressly forbidden to them. Both are responsible for the sin: she acted, but he failed to act. Instead, he passively responded to her offer of the fruit.[74]

When God comes to them after they have committed this sin and asks what they have done, the man blames God (and the woman God gave him), while the woman blames the serpent. In their confession the man and woman betray each other, shattering their harmonious relationship.[75] In retribution the serpent is cursed, and the earth is cursed because of the man's sin. Alone of the three, woman has no actual curse associated with her, only a judgment. The judgment placed on her warps God's original plan for sexuality,[76] multiplying her pain in childbirth and placing her under man's rule. Yet her desire for man continues, making sexuality a very mixed blessing.

After God's judgment, the man *does* name the woman (Gen. 3:20). And in naming her Eve, man takes power over her. In the Hebrew texts following the Fall, the term *ha'adam*, "man," takes on its full patriarchal meaning, rendering woman invisible. The early norm of creational unity between them remains only ambivalently present: the Fall distorts God's original intention for gender relations.

Trible's account of the Hebrew text suggests that *all* life comes

73. This is the way that both the New International Version and the New Revised Standard Version render the verse as well. The Revised Standard Version and the King James Version do not mention Adam's whereabouts, thereby absolving him of direct disobedience of God's command to the humans. Keil and Delitzsch also interpret the phrase "who was with her" as "who was present," but, oddly, still conclude that the man was tempted *by the woman*, as if he couldn't hear the serpent (Keil and Delitzsch, *Commentary on the Old Testament*, p. 95).

74. Although 1 Timothy 2:13-14 indicates that Adam was not deceived and that Eve was the transgressor, 1 Corinthians 15:22 makes it clear that Adam (whether Adam the man or Adam as humanity) is held responsible for sin: "For as all die in Adam, so all will be made alive in Christ." The Bible does not allow endless quibbling over whether the man or the woman committed the worse sin. Both sinned, and all humanity, through that act, was plunged into sin as a consequence.

75. Trible, *God and the Rhetoric of Sexuality*, p. 119.

76. Ibid., p. 129.

straight from God, who alone deserves the glory. No credit goes to the material that God used, whether that be the dust of the earth or the rib of a human creature. The power of sexual desire indicates how strongly humans yearn for the restoration of creational unity. That unity, not division, was God's intention for male and female. It is the post-Fall fragmentation of that unity which leads to man's domination over woman.

Evaluation of the Creation Stories

If both tellings of the creation story are human accounts aimed at representing a single foundational sacred story, how may they be assessed? By what criteria do we judge that one comes closer to the truth than the other? The argument in the preceding section showed how an egalitarian reading of the story of human creation can follow the original Hebrew text, remain sensitive to issues of biblical genre, and fall within the broader range of evangelical scholarship. Admittedly, it is not a mainstream reading, but Christ's example alone should be strong proof for Christians that truth is not always found in the mainstream. At times the Holy Spirit may choose to work against the grain of accepted tradition, showing that God's word speaks prophetically even today.

As stated earlier, the concern of this chapter lies much more with rhetorical than with theological issues. Reformed Christians may test a reading theologically by looking at the ways it comports with other Scripture passages, guided by presuppositions such as the following: that Scripture is God's communication to people; that the written word must be attended to as it was written; that one must look at both divine and historical revelation, weigh the unity and diversity of Scripture, and remember Scripture's redemptive focus.[77] However, when an issue is viewed from a rhetorical perspective, the question is not just one of fidelity to the text and its context but also of its effect on its audience. In a rhetorical analysis, the question regarding which telling of the creation story is most trustworthy cannot be answered simply by scriptural analysis and an appeal to theological sources. We must also look

77. These presuppositions are drawn from "Hermeneutical Principles Concerning Women in Ecclesiastical Office," Supplement-Report 31, *Acts of Synod* (Grand Rapids: Board of Publications of the CRC, 1978), pp. 491-94.

215

at what each perspective on the creation story *does* to women and men. To get at this point, it is useful to return to narrative theory.

Previously Stanley Hauerwas was quoted as saying that a story is truthful if it remains open to challenge.[78] A story that can accommodate challenge and yet remain in tune with its tradition will enable a community to adapt itself to new circumstances. The value of an egalitarian rendering such as Trible's is twofold: first, it is based on the original Hebrew texts rather than on translations that may obscure the underlying sacred story; second, it shows respect for God's sovereignty and for each member of the human pair. This respect is reinforced by the broad sweep of Scripture, which begins as a story of salvation for the restricted tribe of Israel but ends with the offer of salvation and the Spirit-filled life to all people. Trible's telling fits well within this redemptive-historical understanding of Scripture, in which God finally is seen as no respecter of persons. It is a rendering of the creation story that helps people enact mutually supportive rather than potentially adversarial gender relations. A possible weakness of Trible's reading is that it does not grow out of a specific religious community or tradition readily known to members of most churches.[79] Instead, it grows out of a fresh reading of the sacred text.

The value of the traditional telling is found in the very word *traditional*. Such a telling reflects a centuries-long proclamation, supported and passed on by communities well served by it. Its very survival is evidence of its importance in the life of a faith community. A hierarchical gender system has long used the traditional narrative to mold its initiates: male initiates have learned of their priority, and female initiates have learned submissiveness to the more highly valued males. By enacting the relations supposedly established at the time of creation, human beings could live in an ordered society where people's places were defined largely by their gender roles. But it is now clear that this order was maintained at great cost to the human spirit — *both* female and male. Domination of women by men diminishes each: men forget humil-

---

78. Hauerwas, *A Community of Character*, p. 151.

79. Trible does not clearly indicate that she speaks out of a particular tradition. However, there have been readings similar to hers — for example, those of Agrippa and Luther. See Ruth Tucker's *Daughters of the Church: Women and Ministry from New Testament Times to the Present* (Grand Rapids: Zondervan, 1987), pp. 172, 174-75. For more contemporary sources, see Mickelson's "An Egalitarian View" and Spencer's *Beyond the Curse*.

ity, and women forget their own dignity and responsibility as full imagers of God.[80] In summary, a hierarchical/patriarchal telling of the creation story limits possibilities for the future, while an egalitarian telling undermines reverence for the past.

Within the Christian Reformed Church those who stress the progressiveness of revelation endorse a creation story that enhances the possibilities for partnership between women and men. The 1973 report to Synod told the creation story as one of mutuality, using Galatians 3:28 as its focal point: "There is no longer Jew or Greek, there is no longer slave or free, there is no longer male and female; for all of you are one in Christ Jesus."[81] Cook's and De Boer's minority report of 1984 argued that creation must be understood in light of Pentecost, when the Holy Spirit was poured out on female as well as male believers, leading both to prophesy (Acts 2). In 1990, those questioning traditional notions of male headship pointed out that the character of headship should be seen in light of *eschaton,* the future fulfillment of God's kingdom:

> In sum, the overall sweep of Scripture is toward Christ's restoration of the original order of men and women living and working side by side, on a par, mutually supporting and ministering to each other in pursuit of their common task. This is the biblical sweep which contradicts the decision on headship adopted by Synod 1984 and Synod 1985 of the Christian Reformed Church.[82]

80. Barbara Hilkert Andolsen argues that the Western Christian tradition has viewed pride as humanity's besetting sin. She suggests that such an idea is peculiarly male, for women have struggled just to feel they *have* worth. Sacrifice of self is more likely women's sin. Andolsen links women's lack of self-esteem to men's urging sacrifice upon them as a key virtue ("Agape in Feminist Ethics," *Journal of Religious Ethics* 9 [Spring 1981]: 69-83). In addressing this idea, Elisabeth Schüssler Fiorenza has asserted, "While feminist theology advocates for men a 'theology of relinquishment,' it articulates for women a theology of 'self-affirmation'" (*Bread Not Stone* [Boston: Beacon Press, 1984], p. xv).

81. "Women in Ecclesiastical Office," Supplement-Report 39, *Acts of Synod* (1973), p. 577.

82. "Report of the Committee to Study Headship," *Agenda and Acts of Synod* (1990), p. 329. The 1978 report, "Hermeneutical Principles Regarding Women in Office," also emphasized the need to keep God's coming kingdom in mind, arguing that sometimes, "not only does the New Testament transcend the Old, but that the eschatologically new order transcends even the created order. . . . The church must ponder how the *eschaton* affects Christian life in the present" (p. 501).

A traditional orientation holds that the nature of gender relations was established once and for all at the time of creation. Reflecting this orientation was the flood of overtures to various CRC synods, and to the 1990 Synod in particular, aimed at maintaining the patriarchal status quo. In the name of "unity," "order," and the "clear teaching of scripture," these overtures insisted on a reaffirmation of male priority in the Christian Reformed Church. As one supporter of the traditionalist view put it, "Few of us question that God gave Adam headship over the family. The Israelites adhered to this throughout history. Why the cry for change?"[83]

However, choosing between these two positions is not simply like choosing between apples and oranges. The Christian community is founded upon a book that is filled with narratives guided by the master narrative of redemption in Jesus Christ. And for better or worse, each faith community needs to live within the parameters of narrative logic. A key component of narrative is its simultaneous presentation of a tradition and power to transform the future. People approach life in terms of their community's narratives. But if stories are to be *lived* by a community, they must be filled with value not only for the community as a whole but also for each of its members. The creation story favored by traditionalists sanctions the male restriction of female potential. It effectively denies women their full status as image bearers of God and members of the body of Christ. Furthermore, the traditional story as presently used closes off possibilities for change: it takes the sacred story as settled, as contained, as already told rather than still unfolding. Ironically, such a stance may contribute to the *dying* of the tradition, for if narratives are only enacted and not tested, the tradition ceases to meet the needs of an ever-changing community, and so will atrophy from lack of use and support.

It is significant that aspects of the traditionalist narrative of gender relations are already being tested *and* changed in light of an urgent, pastoral concern in the Christian Reformed Church. In 1989 one of the most conservative classes (districts) of the church recommended that Synod "appoint a study committee that includes women to research and provide recommendations to the churches on the subject of abuse (physical, sexual, or psychological) of children, spouses, the elderly or others."[84] The synodical gathering adopted this recommendation with

---

83. Walter Kruis, "Voices," *The Banner,* 5 March 1990, p. 3.

84. "Overture 2: Appoint Committee to Research Abuse," *Agenda and Acts of Synod* (Grand Rapids: Board of Publications of the CRC, 1989), pp. 309-10.

virtually no controversy and gave as one of its grounds for doing so that "the victims of abuse are often women and children, whereas the response of the church is ordinarily channelled through men."[85] The clear message from the (still all-male) Synod of 1989 was that all forms of interpersonal abuse are sinful, and that the church needs detailed advice in order to prevent it and heal its effects.

But as we saw in the chapter on Reformed and feminist worldviews, a *truly* traditionalist reading of gender relations would in fact allow Reformed Christian males to inflict a great deal of what we now call abuse upon women. Recall, for example, John Calvin's letter concerning a woman battered by her husband, in which he exhorts her to "bear with patience the cross which God has seen fit to place on her . . . to please her husband . . . [and] be faithful whatever happens" (see Chapter Five, n. 54). The present concern about abuse in the Christian Reformed Church suggests that even those of its members who retain some theological notion of male headship do not identify it with nearly the same degree of patriarchal power as their ancestors did. The implication seems to be that if male headship exists, it must take the form of servant leadership rather than punitive power-wielding.

The synodical committee appointed to study abuse commissioned, among other things, a thorough survey of the rates of physical, psychological, and sexual abuse within the denomination.[86] That the prevalence rates of all three types of abuse turned out to be no lower in the church than in the North American population at large became a source of both surprise and shame to many male church members. No one responded by mounting a theological defense of *any* form of abuse, John Calvin's advice notwithstanding! It is significant that the full report on abuse is scheduled for synodical consideration in the same year (1992) that the proposal to open up all church offices to women will or (will not) be ratified. At that time, will the all-male Synod of this church respond by *selectively* re-writing its narrative of gender relations? Will it endorse recommendations for the prevention

85. Ibid.
86. Calvin College Social Research Center, "A Survey of Abuse in the Christian Reformed Church" (Grand Rapids: Calvin College, 1990). It should be noted that some respondents to the survey questioned the boundary line between legitimate physical punishment of children and actual physical abuse. However, no respondents tried to make a similar distinction regarding "punishment" and "abuse" of women by men.

and treatment of abuse (most of which happens to women and children at the hands of men), while continuing to deny women full partnership with men in the church?

Conclusion

Certain questions are useful to ask of any story. Whose story is it? By whom is it told? To whom? For what purpose? In the case of the creation story, the root sacred story could be seen as one of human relations within the world and with God, told by God to humans to give us a sense of identity and purpose. From a patriarchal viewpoint, it becomes the story of male headship, told by powerful men to women and less powerful others with the purpose of maintaining male authority and priority in home and church, if not in the entire world. The story is told in a spirit of legalism and entrenchment rather than thoughtfulness and concern for the development of all.

If the creation story is to live as a narrative, it must be one that its hearers can enact and test, one that pays attention to tradition even as it turns its face to the future. Even as an egalitarian telling calls the tradition into question, it uses current insights to breathe new life into an old story. The particular egalitarian story that we have examined here is told from the perspective of a woman scholar reading the original Hebrew texts. It is told to women and men who believe in God and in the authority of Scripture, to help them understand who they originally were and perhaps could again become.

An egalitarian story of creation encourages humans to see themselves as partners, each person being free to choose how to act, making choices on the basis of mutual respect and deference rather than having choices forced on them on the basis of rules that presume the roles each must play.

It is like the difference between the human relations enacted while marching and those enacted while dancing. Marchers follow a leader, eyes front, locked in step, no deviation and no human eccentricity allowed. Marching isn't designed to help humans express humanity; it's intended to enforce conformity. A dance, however, is a wholly other thing. Ballet dancers, for example, relate to each other face to face, moving together and pulling away, but always swirling back toward each other. Dancing encourages creativity — the playful patterning of human

220

relations within a given set of forms. Which of these activities reflects the inspiration of a creative God?

In 1990 the Christian Reformed Church finally decided to align itself with a view of sacred narrative that affirms the full spiritual life and service of all its members. This decision has yet to be ratified. Nevertheless, by recommending that all church offices be opened up to women, Synod emphasized future possibilities over past absolutes. In doing so, Synod turned its face to the future, one in which women and men together sing, serve, and praise God. In a living faith community where the Holy Spirit is present and active, such efforts should be seen, as one speaker at Synod declared, not as "liberal" but as "liberated."[87]

87. Nelle Vander Ark, quoted by Galen Meyer in "Women in Office? Yes," *The Banner*, 2 July 1990, p. 7.

PART III

THE CULTURAL CONSTRUCTION OF GENDER RELATIONS

CHAPTER 8

A Critical Theory of Gender Relations

This is a chapter about theory — but please don't let that statement intimidate you! What we are going to do is describe a perspective that can help us understand the social dynamics of gender. In the 1960s and 1970s, theorizing about gender in the social sciences was often focused on individual behaviors and how these differed for females and males. It was a research tradition that centered on behavioral differences as opposed to behavioral similarities between men and women. A part of that tradition which received considerable attention in the social sciences was sex-role theory, which tried to define and explain the differences between so-called masculinity and femininity.[1]

We begin with a summary of the perspective of sex-role theory, after which we will offer an alternative approach, drawn from a tradition known as critical theory, which we consider to be more illuminating.

1. See Irene Frieze et al.'s *Women and Sex Roles: A Social-Psychological Perspective* (New York: W. W. Norton, 1978); and Janet T. Spence and Robert L. Helmreich's *Masculinity and Femininity: Their Psychological Dimensions, Correlates, and Antecedents* (Austin: University of Texas Press, 1978). For a review of the literature on sex roles, see Annelies Knoppers's article entitled "Androgyny: Another Look," *Quest* 32, no. 2 (1980): 184-91.

The primary author of this chapter is Annelies Knoppers.

225

Sex-Role Theory: An Overview

Popular Definitions of "Masculinity" and "Femininity"

What do we mean when we say, "She's so feminine?" or "He's a really masculine guy?" According to sex-role theory, people usually assign the word *masculine* to males who are "doers," breadwinners, and protectors; who are strong, independent, athletic, and active. People usually assign the word *feminine* to women who are physically attractive, gentle, nurturing, soft-spoken, somewhat dependent, and passive.

We assume that we behave in certain ways due to a combination of forces originating in nature and nurture. According to sex-role theory, we *learn* to behave in ways appropriate to our sex, primarily through the socialization process we undergo in childhood. This means that we learn as children to be masculine or feminine by imitating same-sex role models (often our parents and teachers), by listening to adults, by reading books and watching television, by responding to pressure (in the form of tangible or symbolic rewards and punishments) from parents and peers, and so on.[2] This "social learning" explanation for behavioral differences between males and females is an important component of sex-role theory. And although this theory may help to explain gendered behavior, we intend to show that it does so incompletely. Additional perspectives are needed for a more complete understanding of the dynamics of gender.

An implicit assumption of sex-role theory, often held by lay people too, is that the characteristics ascribed to each sex are valued equally and complement each other in a balanced way. For example, nurturing behavior is assumed to be valued as much as strong and stoic behavior, and those who are nurturant (women) presumably fit together in a mutually symbiotic way with those who are strong and stoic (men). The sexes are therefore assumed to complement each other. Females learn feminine behavior and males learn masculine behavior, and both encounter difficulties and benefits along the way. In other words, masculine and feminine sex roles are seen as equally constricting and equally advantageous.

Those who show characteristics considered inappropriate for their

2. See, for example, Irene Frieze et al.'s *Women and Sex Roles* and Lenore Weitzman's *Sex-Role Socialization* (Palo Alto, Calif.: Mayfield Publishing Co., 1979).

sex are labeled deviant or ill-adjusted. Boys who are not athletic or who are uninterested in sports are often called "effeminate" or "faggots," while girls who are very athletic and participate in team sports may be labeled "masculine," "lesbians," or "dykes."[3] There may also be people who show too much of a sex typed characteristic. Excessive sociability by women and excessive dominion by men have sometimes been ascribed to the fallen or sinful nature of human beings.[4]

A Critique of These Definitions

These and other traditional assumptions about masculinity and femininity by sex-role theorists have come under a great deal of criticism from social scientists in the 1980s. In the first place, the assumption that there is some kind of unchanging "essence" of femininity and masculinity fails to explain deviations within individuals and from person to person. Are atypical people those for whom socialization did not "take"? There are men who are not interested in sports and who walk away from or laugh at insults about their masculinity. There are some women who do not nurture, and others who are not even mothers. Two women can come from the same family and be taught the same popular definitions of femininity. One may join the police force, which is a male-dominated field, yet exemplify the stereotypical characteristics of femininity more than her sister, who as a secretary enters a female-dominated field. Which one is feminine? Is their femininity defined by their personal characteristics or by their jobs? Moreover, if our sex-role profile is something unchanging that we possess, like our eye color, would we not show it in a consistent manner? Sex-role theory fails to address an individual's behavioral differences in different situations. For example, the same secretary who is brusque and commanding in the typing pool

3. Mary Boutilier and Lucinda San Giovanni, *The Sporting Woman* (Champaign, Ill.: Human Kinetics Books, 1983).

4. See Judith Plaskow's *Sex, Sin and Grace: Women's Experience and the Theologies of Reinhold Niebuhr and Paul Tillich* (Washington: University Press of America, 1980); Valerie Saiving Goldstein's "The Human Situation: A Feminine View," in *Womanspirit Rising: A Feminist Reader in Religion,* ed. Carol P. Christ and Judith Plaskow (San Francisco: Harper & Row, 1979), pp. 25-42; and Mary Stewart VanLeeuwen's *Gender and Grace: Love, Work and Parenting in a Changing World* (Downers Grove, Ill.: InterVarsity Press, 1990).

may go home and engage in baby talk or smother-love with her pet iguana!

A second and major criticism of sex-role theory focuses on the assumption about the equal value of masculine and feminine traits. Most critics contend that traditional masculinity and femininity are *not* valued equally.[5] They argue that most of the characteristics and activities ascribed to males have greater cultural and economic value than those ascribed to females. Those things associated with females are often devalued relative to those things associated with males. At a young age, children have learned these differences; they already know which sex has greater value.

Listen to these responses from Michigan schoolchildren when they were asked this question: "If you woke up tomorrow and discovered that you were the other gender, how would your life be different?" The majority of boys were offended and appalled. Some envisioned taking their lives if they woke up and discovered they were girls:

"I would probably commit suicide."

"It would be dumb, stupid, sucky, and awful."

"I would stab myself in the heart fifty times with a dull butter knife. If I were still alive, I would run in front of a huge semi in eighteenth gear, and have my brains smashed to Jell-O. THAT would do it."

"Wouldn't want anyone to be my friend.... I'd take a whole bottle of aspirin."

Those boys who didn't mention killing themselves did mention what they saw as the drawbacks of being a girl:

5. See, for example, Robert W. Connell's *Gender and Power: Society, the Person and Sexual Politics* (Stanford: Stanford University Press, 1987); Arthur Brittan's *Masculinity and Power* (New York: Basil Blackwell, 1989); Tim Carrigan, Robert Connell, and John Lee's "Hard and Heavy: Toward a New Sociology of Masculinity," in *Beyond Patriarchy: Essays by Men on Pleasure, Power, and Change,* ed. Michael Kaufman (Toronto: Oxford University Press, 1987), pp. 139-92; and *The Making of Masculinities: The New Men's Studies,* ed. Harry Brod (Boston: Allen & Unwin, 1987). For a review of empirical studies demonstrating the greater social value of masculine stereotoypes, see Inge K. Broverman, Donald M. Broverman, Frank E. Clarkson, and Paul S. Rosenkrantz, "Sex-role Stereotypes: A Current Appraisal," *Journal of Social Issues* 28, no. 2 (1972): 59-78.

"I couldn't play any good sports and I wouldn't like any sports. All I could do would be to go roller-skating and I'd have to stay home."

"I wouldn't be able to play on the sports teams that I want to play like football, baseball, and wrestling, sports that only MEN can handle."

"Because I'm a war kind of person, I don't think I could join the Army, Navy, or Air Force or Marines."

"I'd be weak, a pansy, a wimp. All my friends would be little wimps."

Even though the girls said that they'd prefer to stay girls, most of them listed advantages to being a boy, primarily in terms of increased opportunities and decreased responsibilities:

"I'd have to get the firewood; shoot hoops after breakfast; be picked to demonstrate stuff, like in gym they get to show how to play a game."

"I'd hunt and fish with my Dad; have to act macho. I couldn't really cry or get upset, and I'd have to act tough all the time."

"I would start drinking beer, sitting back and burping. Beat my wife up and kick her out."[6]

Overall, the authors of this study concluded that these children, ranging from elementary to middle-school age, recognized that in our culture greater value is associated with being a boy than with being a girl. We see subtle signs of this difference in value at the adult level as well. Women are more often allowed to wear clothes considered masculine and do activities associated with males than men are allowed to wear clothes considered feminine and do activities associated with females. Why don't men wear comfortable dresses? In part because such clothing is associated with women, the less valued group. Similarly, as we will see in a later chapter, occupations that are female-dominated pay less and have lower social status than those that are male-dominated, even if these jobs require the same amount of education and responsibility. Clearly, what is associated with women has less value than what is

6. Office for Sex Equity in Education, "Influence of Gender Role Socialization upon the Perceptions of Children" (Michigan Department of Education, Lansing, Mich., 1989).

associated with men. And even though Christians proclaim that all groups are valued equally before God, societal evidence suggests that we do not practice this equal valuing. Currently, the assumption of equivalent value seems to exist primarily in theory, not in practice.

A third criticism of sex-role theory is that it does not adequately explain why and how certain characteristics became dichotomized and attached to men or women in the first place. It does not explain *why* boys are praised for not showing tears and girls for being pretty and slim. In addition, what we associate with masculinity and with femininity in our white Western culture may differ from the associations in other cultures or subcultures. The words *breadwinner* and *doer* not only describe men but also describe women of color and working-class women. When we define physical weakness, passivity, and dependency as "feminine," we ignore the many single women who parent and lower-class women who have always worked outside the home, often at physically demanding jobs that pay little. Clearly, sex-role theory is off the mark when it suggests that the essential definition of femininity is similar for both lower-class and upper-class women. In a similar way, black men may not define masculinity in the same way that white men do.[7]

Nor may different generations. For example, most of our great-grandparents thought it unfeminine for girls to wear pants and effeminate for boys to show an interest in cooking. By contrast, today's girls wear pants, and both girls and boys take cooking classes. Ideas about proper sex-roles vary across culture, race, class, and time. Thus important cross-cultural, intracultural, and generational differences are ignored when "femininity" is spoken of as an attribute that all women should possess in a similar manner, or when the same is said of masculinity and men.

A fourth and related criticism of sex-role theory focuses on the underlying assumption that gender forms the core of a person's identity.[8] This assumption, as we pointed out in an earlier chapter, ignores or at least greatly downplays how such things as race, ethnicity, class, and religion shape personal identity. Why do we give priority to gender above all other categories? We rarely talk about race roles, ethnic roles, religious roles, or class roles. Perhaps those of us who give such high

---

7. Kenneth Clatterbaugh, *Contemporary Perspectives on Masculinity: Men, Women and Politics in Modern Society* (Boulder, Colo.: Westview Press, 1990).

8. Brian Pronger, *The Arena of Masculinity: Sport, Homosexuality, and the Meaning of Sex* (New York: St. Martin's Press, 1990).

priority to gender are white and middle-to-upper class. Since our membership in these race and class categories (e.g., as "WASPS") brings us taken-for-granted privileges, we may falsely perceive gender as the salient category. And by universalizing the priority of gender, we ignore the realities of many people who feel that their race, class, or religion is a greater determinant of their identity than gender. For example, the poverty experienced by Third World women may make their class status more visible to them than their gender. Similarly, people of color in the U.S. may often be more conscious of their race than their gender. By universalizing the priority of gender, we may also be ignoring the manner in which God created us. We were created whole, not fragmented, human beings. It is in our total personhood that we image God, not in fragments defined by our membership in social categories — that is, not in our white or black identity, nor in our being male or female.[9]

This is not to say that our gender, race, or membership in other social categories never influences how we behave. We may through experience have developed a sensibility that comes from being male, from being female, from being black, from being Muslim, from being white, and so on. Brian Pronger argues that social categories are "modes of understanding and action that are variously appropriated and relinquished by human beings. The . . . categories are ways that people think of themselves and others in certain social spheres. These are ways of interpreting oneself in certain situations."[10] Consequently, a black

---

9. However, some Christians continue to maintain that masculinity and femininity are unchanging essences (which they claim are more fundamental than sex differences), that God is essentially "masculine" (even though not biologically "male"), and that for this reason men are created for headship over women and only men can be priests. Some hold this position, even though they admit that it cannot be exegetically produced from Scripture, because of their attraction to Platonic essentialism and/or certain pagan myths (e.g., about "earth mother" and "sky father") that they regard as vehicles of "general revelation" for Christians. Others do so because of their attraction to Carl Jung's notion of archetypes. See, for example, C. S. Lewis's essay called "Membership" in _Fern-seed and Elephants and Other Essays on Christianity_ (London: Collins, 1975), pp. 19-20; and his essay entitled "Priestesses in the Church?" in _God in the Dock: Essays on Theology and Ethics_, ed. Walter Hooper (Grand Rapids: William B. Eerdmans, 1970), pp. 234-39. See also Thomas Howard's essay entitled "A Note from Antiquity on Women's Ordination," _The Churchman_ 92, no. 4 (1978): 320-30; and Leanne Payne's _Crisis in Masculinity_ (Westchester, Ill.: Cornerstone Books, 1985).

10. Pronger, _The Arena of Masculinity_, pp. 93-94.

woman may be more aware of race when she is in a group of white women than when she is in a group of black women. Similarly, we may be more aware of gender when we are confronted with gendered expectations for a job, when we assign responsibility for child care or for pastoral care, or when we hear exclusive or inclusive language. A woman and man who are dating may behave differently when they are together than when each is with same-sex friends. In the first situation they may be very conscious of gender, in the second one less so. Thus to rely solely on sex-role theory to explain our behavior seems to privilege gender above all other social categories. It reduces people to only, or primarily, their gender.

A fifth criticism of sex-role theory centers on its apparent endorsement of passive learning. Sex-role theory seems to assume that we unreflectively imitate others and accept what we are told. In other words, it assumes that we end up being feminine or masculine in much the same way that a sponge soaks up water, and that we can explain our behavior by saying, "That's just what I learned to do." This may be partially true. Yet there is much evidence to show that we do *not* always become what we are socialized to be. For example, women's greater numerical presence in the areas of nursing, social work, and elementary-school teaching has been linked to women's socialization to be nurturant. Yet if this is true, then why is it that women do not dominate other fields that require nurturing skills, such as licensed psychological counseling, the ministry, or secondary-school teaching? It is assumed that women are socialized or trained for housework, yet when housework becomes paid work, women tend to disappear. For example, women comprise only a third of short-order cooks, dishwashers, and cleaning personnel.[11] Furthermore, if we look at the creation story, we see that despite their creaturely constraints, human beings were created to be agents, to be active in the world, not to be merely passive! Sex-role theory does not seem to allow much room for human agency; it makes us seem more like puppets than actors.

The assumption that masculine and feminine sex-roles can be equally constricting for both sexes has also been criticized. This assump-

11. Samuel Cohn, *The Process of Occupational Sex-Typing: The Feminization of Clerical Labor in Great Britain*, Women in the Political Economy series, ed. Ronnie J. Steinberg (Philadelphia: Temple University Press, 1985); see also the Bureau of Labor Statistics, 1987.

tion ignores the structural imbalance of power and the unequal access to resources between the sexes, and it fails to take into account the influence that this inequality has on behavior. For example, women who show "dependence" may do so because they are financially reliant on their husbands, fathers, or employers. By contrast, men may appear more "independent" than women because as men they often have easier access to high-paying jobs, to decision-making power in organizations, and to other kinds of authority.[12]

In summary, although sex-role theory may help explain our learning of gendered behavior, it cannot be the entire story. It seems to stress passivity over agency, suggests that masculinity and femininity are merely two sides of the same coin, overlooks differences in power and valuing, ignores the dynamic nature of gender and cultural specificity, and fails to take into account our creation as social beings who are always in relationship, not only with God but also with each other. We need a perspective that allows us to see people as whole, as relational, and as active rather than passive, and one that takes into account cultural context, historical period, and power differentials. Finally, we need a viewpoint that takes into account not only our status as imagers of God but also our fallenness.

Critical Theory as an Alternative to Sex-Role Theory: An Overview

Description

We can be helped toward this goal by a more recent tradition known as critical theory. This perspective looks at gender in its relational sense

---

12. See Brittan's *Masculinity and Power* and Connell's *Gender and Power*. This is not to suggest that *all* behaviors associated with women are constricting. For example, the association of nurturance with women often allows them to have more meaningful friendships than men. However, although women are "allowed" to be more relational, those relational skills are undervalued in a monied economy, as we shall see in a later chapter. Nor do we wish to suggest that the endorsement of characteristics associated with being an adult male and the employment of the attendant resources always occur without anxiety or cost. For a cross-cultural examination of the hurdles men must surmount to be associated with "real men," see David D. Gilmore's *Manhood in the Making: Cultural Concepts of Masculinity* (New Haven: Yale University Press, 1990).

and examines gendered and other social relationships in terms of power.[13] By *power* we mean the ability to make ideas stick, to make them the dominant ideas, and to have the resources for doing so. Power also involves the capacity to translate ideas into actions and embed them in institutional structures. Critical theorists examine how the power inequalities that mark social relations are embedded in social practices and cultural forms and how power is negotiated and reconstructed in varying situations.

What does this mean? By "social relations" critical theorists mean relationships among social groups (marked by race, class, gender, etc.) which are unequal in power — that is, which are characterized by domination/subordination. The focus of critical theorists, then, is not so much on the individual attributes of people in a social group but on the relationship between social groups. Thus they examine race relations, gender relations, class relations, and so on. For example, critical theorists could look at sport and ask, How does sport reproduce dominant ideas we have about race, and how does it provide new or alternative meanings? They could look at Christian schools and ask, What dominant ideas about social class remain embedded in the culture of these schools? Conversely, how are such ideas challenged, and what happens when these challenges occur?

Feminists who use critical theory look primarily at gender relations and examine social practices and cultural forms to see how each reproduces or contests dominant ideology about gender relations. Earlier in this chapter we heard girls and boys comment on what it would be like to be "the other gender." The dominant theme we heard was that what a boy is and does is more valued than what a girl is and does. Feminist theorists who use critical theory would explore where children *get* this idea and why and how some children *resist* this dominant idea. For example, according to the same children's study, there are some boys who *would* like to be girls so they could jump rope, play hopscotch, and

---

13. Theory building in this perspective has also been influenced by the "cultural studies" approach. This approach, which originated in the Centre for Contemporary Culture Studies in England, attempts to integrate ideas from sociology, literary theory, and social history. It is partly grounded in the work of Antonio Gramsci in *Selections from the Prison Notebooks* (London: Lawrence & Wishart, 1971). A key question asked by cultural studies theorists is, How does each social practice or cultural form (e.g., art, music, dress, etc.) both contribute to and act as a source of resistance to dominant ideology?

own Barbie dolls. How then does a certain idea about the relative value of each gender become dominant while others remain marginalized? This is the question we would like to explore next.

How Hegemony Works

Within each set of social relations there is an imbalance of power: one group (the dominant group, or "Doms") has more power than the other (the subordinate group, or "Subs"); that is, the "Doms" have more power to make their ideas stick than do the "Subs." How are the Doms able to do this? This inequality is maintained by *hegemony*. Hegemonic processes work to keep the dominant group in power by ensuring that others see the world the way those with power see it. The political hegemony that Hitler and the Nazis exercised over Germany was very efficiently crafted and is an obvious example of the imposition of hegemonic "groupthink" on a society. But rarely is the hegemony of dominant groups this blatant. What people receive instead are "symbolic eyeglasses" that cause them to see the world, often unconsciously, in a way that is most beneficial to the Doms.

A metaphor will help us to understand this better. Think of social reality or social life as a rope. Everyone is attached to that rope. In the Garden of Eden we probably all shared that rope and delighted in creating games to play with it; everyone would have had a just share in influencing how the games were to be played. Because of the Fall, however, people are polarized into unequal groups based on their gender, skin color, class, and so on. Within each of these classifications a game of rope tug is being played in which one group (the Doms) is always stronger than the other (the Subs). With respect to gender, the groups are divided into male (Doms) and females (Subs).

The group at one end of the rope is tied to the group at the other end. The groups are therefore in relationship to each other. Everyone pulls on the rope, with each side trying different things to move the other side. In this continuing game, the Doms also have the advantage of special tools to enhance their performance — shoes with cleats, special gloves, sweatbands, and so on — which are denied to the Subs. Since the Doms have more power than the Subs, the Doms could easily end the tug, but they need the Subs to continue, since without them there would be no game. The Doms give the Subs just enough power so that the latter often feel they have a chance and are "in" the game. In addition, the Subs, although they face much stress under these conditions, continually try to employ new tactics to change the way the game is being played so that the imbalance of power may lessen or disappear. In fact, many of the Subs and some of the Doms would like to change the nature of the game. Perhaps, for example, they would like to jump rope instead. Some of the Doms find it scary to think of giving away the equipment that has given them a historical advantage. (What if the other side used that equipment to *their* advantage?) Most of the Doms, however, do not even consider the possibility of giving up any of their power (let alone admit that it causes them anxiety) but simply want the game to stay as it is. So they continually devise new strategies to counteract the challenges of the Subs.

Although this metaphor may not apply completely, it should give us a glimpse into another way of looking at gender, a way of looking at it in relational terms. Keep the image of the rope tug in mind as we try to explain what we can learn from the critical theory perspective.

The degree of power a group has is determined by its access to and use of relevant resources which help make its ideas stick — that is, which ensure that people view the world through a specific type of "glasses." For example, those who own newspapers exert a great deal of influence by shaping editorial policy. In other words, a hegemonic group has the resources to get others to see the world the same way they do. As a result, the existing shape of gender (or race or class) relations is usually taken as normative and legitimate by those in the subordinate group as well as those in the dominant group.

To take another example, in pre–Civil War days the idea predominated that slavery was acceptable. When many white people read the Bible, what they *saw* through their "cultural glasses" was that the Bible supported slavery. Those against slavery, usually Afro-Americans, had little if any power to challenge that idea, and sometimes did not even have the support of other slaves. Similarly, Christians in the twentieth century often experience a "secularist hegemony" — that is, their Christian worldview may be dismissed as naive or prescientific by the dominant majority, whose cultural vision is not shaped by Scripture.

Let us look at an example of hegemony with respect to gender relations as portrayed in the electronic media. The mass media legitimate the actions of powerful men by focusing on their opinions, policies, and decisions. In a typical evening television broadcast we may be told what the

236

Russian head of state said to his Soviet congress. The meaning of that action will probably be explained by a male government official. George Bush may announce that the war on drugs will intensify, while the U.S. Congress may have voted to decrease the social services budget. Most of these newsclips depict the work and opinions of men. When we fail even to notice the absence of women, the absence of their work and their opinions and their concerns, hegemony has done its work. In other words, the glasses we are wearing do not allow us even to notice the invisibility of women.

Critical theorists do not mean to imply that hegemony is the result of an organized conspiracy or master plan by those in power, but only that those with power and privilege tend to do what they have to do to keep what they have.[14] Few people who have power and privilege are willing to share it or give it up. Thus the dominant group uses its existing power to stay in power and keep its privileges. The techniques for maintaining hegemony are many: economic sanctions, assertion of authority, persuasion, education, mass-media techniques, athletic and other recreational norms, state regulations, and so on. If all else fails, then coercion may be used, including the use of physical violence and appeals to people's *fear* of violence. Later in the chapter we will give more detailed examples of the dynamics of power retention by hegemonic groups.

Human Agency and Structural Constraints

At first glance critical theory may seem to regard people as passive, just as sex-role theory does. It seems to be saying that as a result of living at a certain time and in a certain culture, people receive a certain set of "social glasses" without having much choice about selecting another pair. But critical theory also assumes that people, regardless of their circumstances, are *not* stripped of their ability to "think critically" — that is, to redefine meanings. There may be "structural and ideological constraints around people's thoughts and actions, but these constraints do not fully determine the outcome. . . . People retain the ability to act as historical agents, thinking critically and acting transformatively."[15] The estab-

14. George Sage, *Power and Ideology in American Sport: A Critical Perspective* (Champaign, Ill.: Human Kinetics Books, 1990).
15. *Sport, Men, and the Gender Order: Critical Feminist Perspectives,* ed. Michael A. Messner and Donald F. Sabo (Champaign, Ill.: Human Kinetics Books, 1990), p. 8.

lishment of unions, the civil rights movement, the crumbling of the Iron Curtain, and the feminist movement are all examples of this collective resistance to or contesting of hegemony. We also see this challenge occurring at the individual level. For example, although in our culture the idea is dominant that women should take primary responsibility for child care and home care, we see some men challenging this idea by becoming homemakers or domestic workers. We also see women becoming pastors, even though they have been raised in churches where this was not sanctioned.

However, the agency of subordinates is often circumscribed by constraints set by the dominant group. For example, people who lived in East Germany during the era of the Berlin Wall may have recognized the weaknesses of their government but may also have been afraid to act upon that dissatisfaction. Similarly, the "choice" of a woman to leave a man who batters her may be constrained by economic dependency or fear of retaliatory violence. Such threats of violence are often used to keep subordinate groups in line. Usually the latter do not have an equivalent degree of power behind them. The way each group shows prejudice toward the other is a good example of this imbalance. Both the dominant and the subordinate groups may make prejudiced statements about and attribute negative qualities to each other, but there is a difference in how these play out. The important difference is that the subordinates do not have the power to bring about systemic societal inequality based on the stereotypes they apply to the dominant group. For example, black children tease white children about being "pale faces," but there is less institutional power behind those words than when white children call black children "chocolate drops."[16] We will return to the theme of hegemonic violence later.

But despite such constraints, the ability of human beings to think reflectively means that hegemony is never unchallenged. It is a process through which those in power must continually legitimate their ideas because their ideas are continually being contested. Thus, instead of seeing people as passive, the critical-theory approach sees them as being *both* actors *and* acted upon. In this respect it is consonant with the Christian confession that God has created human beings to be responsible actors in the world. The strength of the God-imaging human spirit and

16. Anja Meulenbelt, *De Ziekte Bestryden, Niet de Patient: Over Siksisme, Racisme en Klassisme* (Amsterdam: Van Gennep, 1986).

the hope that exists because the God of the Exodus is active in history enable us to exercise this agency. To be sure, our freedom was never absolute, and with the Fall both personal and structural sin have constrained us further. Nevertheless, critical theory is one of the few approaches that takes seriously both human agency and structural constraints on that agency.

How Sets of Social Relations Are Connected

What is the relationship among various sets of social relations? Is gender really the most important social category, as sex-role theory seems to imply? Many critical theorists disagree, maintaining that the various forms of social relations are arranged nonhierarchically. Michael Messner and Donald Sabo have used the image of a wheel to illustrate the perspective of critical theory on these relations. Here is an expansion of their metaphor. Think of a wheel with a hub, spokes, and ball bearings where the spokes meet the hub. The rim of the wheel represents today's society or social reality. Each of the spokes represents a set of social relations where domination or oppression occurs. In other words, one spoke stands for race oppression, another for class oppression, another for age oppression, another for gender oppression, and so on. All of these (and others) contribute to keeping society "rolling" in its present form. Depending on the culture and the period of time, other forms of oppression may also exist.

The hub that keeps the wheel in motion consists of the interaction of structural forces and human agency. As was pointed out earlier, the extent to which we are able to act is constrained by the degree of our access to resources. Think too of each spoke in the wheel having its own ball bearing. According to Messner and Sabo, this image is meant to suggest that each "form of domination has its own semi-autonomous dynamic of structural constraint and human agency. . . . A form of resistance against one form of domination may not necessarily constitute resistance against all domination; for example, there are some racist feminists, classist gay liberationists, and sexist Black power activists."[17]

Our image of the wheel clearly shows a nonhierarchical framework. This being the case, one might ask why we are writing a book that

17. *Sport, Men, and the Gender Order*, p. 247.

seems to privilege gender over other forms of social relations. We can offer an answer by quoting Messner and Sabo: "The role of theory . . . might be to identify which dynamic of structural constraint and human agency is most salient at a given historical moment without losing sight of the connections to other dynamics."[18] Our mandate for this book was to make gender salient. This does not mean that overall we privilege this form of relationship over others. We do try to show throughout this book the salience of gender in white Western culture, and sometimes in other cultures too. But although we focus on gender, nowhere do we wish to privilege gender over other social relations. These remain important subtexts in our analysis. With this qualifier in mind, let us examine the dynamic of gender relations.

Critical Theory and Gender Relations

Although gender relations are part of each culture and each period of history, they vary in shape and form. In other words, each culture has its own version of gender relations that also changes over time. We continue to label people and behaviors as feminine or masculine, yet our definition of each label has changed somewhat and continues to change. From this perspective, then, gender is seen not as an essential, inherent attribute but as something that we largely construct and to which we give meaning in a social context. In a sense, gender becomes a verb: that is, we gender. The nature of each culture's gender relations is most easily seen (1) in the structure of power (often called patriarchy), (2) in the division of labor between males and females, and (3) in the social organization of sexuality and attraction (often called cathexis).[19]

At the societal or collective level, gender relations (like all social relations) are marked by several features: (1) heterogeneity, (2) a power differential (commonly called oppression or domination/subordination), and (3) human agency. These features play out in different ways, each of which we will examine in turn.

18. Ibid., p. 11.
19. See Carrigan, Connell, and Lee's "Hard and Heavy"; Connell's *Gender and Power*; and Brittan's *Masculinity and Power*.

240

Heterogeneity

The critical-theory perspective also assumes that neither males nor females constitute a homogeneous group but instead that each consists of *groups* of "masculinities" or "femininities."[20] For example, men are not "mere" men: they also belong to other groups defined by social relations such as race, ethnicity, religion, class, age, and so on. And these groups differ in their definition of what it is to be female or male. Hispanic, white, and black men may each constitute a group in which masculinity is assigned a specific and different meaning.[21] Yet these constructions of masculinity do not have equal value on the societal level: men subordinated by class or race, for example, may find it difficult to discern where their experience as "men" stops and their experience as "laborers" or "Hispanics" starts. Women also belong to other societal groups. White, middle-to-upper-class women may be oppressed as women, but at the same time they may oppress people of other races and classes. Thus the net significance of each form of oppression is often hard to specify.

Domination/Subordination

One of the relational aspects of the gender system is domination/subordination, commonly called oppression. What then is meant by oppression? How does it manifest itself? It is a structure of societal inequality in which one group systematically dominates the other in very subtle ways and by means of interrelated social practices.[22] Oppression can be hard to pin down, since often it cannot be seen in one specific action or practice but can only be detected in the context of all societal structures and practices. Marilyn Frye's comparison of social barriers to the wires of a birdcage is helpful in understanding this:

> Cages. Consider a birdcage. If you look very closely at just one wire in the cage, you cannot see the other wires. If your conception of

20. See Carrigan, Connell, and Lee's "Hard and Heavy"; Connell's *Gender and Power*; and Brittan's *Masculinity and Power*.

21. Clatterbaugh, *Contemporary Perspectives on Masculinity*.

22. Marilyn Frye, *The Politics of Reality* (Freedom, Calif.: Crossing Press, 1983); and Meulenbelt, *De Ziekte Bestrijden, Niet de Patient*.

what is before you is determined by this myopic focus, you could look at that one wire, up and down the length of it, and be unable to see why a bird would not just fly around the wire any time it wanted to go somewhere. Furthermore, even if, one day at a time, you myopically inspected each wire, you still could not see why a bird would have trouble going past the wires to get anywhere. There is no physical property of any one wire, *nothing* that the closest scrutiny could discover, that will reveal how a bird could be inhibited or harmed by it except in the most accidental way. It is only when you step back, stop looking at the wires one by one, microscopically, and take a macroscopic view of the whole cage, that you can see why the bird does not go anywhere; and then you will see it in a moment. It will require no great subtlety of mental powers. It is perfectly *obvious* that the bird is surrounded by a network of systematically related barriers, no one of which would be the least hindrance to its flight, but which, by their relations to each other, are as confining as the solid walls of a dungeon.[23]

There are several features of oppression we should recognize. First, intent is usually not a factor in oppression. Rarely do well-meaning people dominate on purpose. The sinful, oppressive aspect of gender relations is so woven into the fabric of our lives and institutions that we often fail to "see" or "feel" it. We can engage in oppressive social practices without consciously intending to do so, since sin and shortsightedness permeate every individual practice and every social structure. Most of us think of ourselves as nice people who would not discriminate unfairly. But it is erroneous to think that because we do not do something intentionally, we therefore do not engage in that practice. Since we often sin without knowing it or meaning to, it follows that we can engage in unwitting oppression. For example, an institution or company can intend to be an equal opportunity employer and still end up employing men rather than women because men always turn out to be the "most qualified" people. Why? Because males construct the qualifications, which then seem to be the "obvious" or "natural" ones to consider. In other words, "most qualified" turns out, more often than not, to mean "most like us."

Just as oppression is systemic and can be engaged in unintentionally, so also people can be oppressed without feeling oppressed. For example, many women do not see themselves in the role of victim or want men to

23. Frye, *The Politics of Reality*, pp. 4-5.

feel sorry for them. They are proud of being women and do not *feel* oppressed. Why might some women not feel their oppression? First, in social relations marked by oppression, the self-esteem of the subordinate group tends to depend on the approval of the dominant group.[24] If the subordinates — in this case women — manage to get this approval (even though it is given according to terms dictated by the dominant group), they tend not to notice the power differential and therefore tend not to feel oppressed. Most women spend their lives with men: fathers, husbands, sons, brothers, colleagues, neighbors, and so on. These men may often be kind, gentle people whom women try to please. Thus, if women get approval from these men for being submissive or dependent, or if they receive a token amount of power, they may not feel oppressed.

Consider another example. One of us attended a meeting of Christian women who were trying to grapple with feminist theology. Most of the women were in their late sixties or older. Most had been, and still were, full-time domestic workers. Many said they were not oppressed and felt uncomfortable with that idea. Yet when they were asked about their work as homemakers, they all agreed that what bothered them so much about it was its taken-for-granted nature, its repetitive inevitability, and its undefined limits. If Johnny or Susan came home from school with a note saying they needed a costume for the school play, the mother was expected to sew or to scrounge together a costume. When these women were home with the children, it was considered normal, but when their husbands stayed home it was called "babysitting" and considered a task for which these women had to be grateful. These women were saying that they enjoyed homemaking but that they had little opportunity to define the job and that their husbands and children were always expected to come first. All the things they did were simply expected of them twenty-four hours a day without discussion. In other words, the demands of the job were nonnegotiable, taken-for-granted, and largely unrewarded by praise or appreciation. When it was pointed out to these women that "limited negotiability" and "inevitability" are marks of powerlessness, they began to see that their oppression had been real but subtle. They began to realize that while they had *some* power in the situation, the degree to which they could make choices was determined by their husbands and others.

24. Jean Baker Miller, *Towards a New Psychology of Women* (Boston: Beacon Press, 1976).

These women were certainly able to be agents, but they were constrained by the expectations that their husbands, children, other women, and the community had of full-time homemakers. Clearly, *being* oppressed may not necessarily mean *feeling* oppressed.

Some women may also not feel oppressed because they benefit from the status quo. Obviously there will be benefits accruing to *some* women under the current gender system, since those in power cannot alienate the powerless in *too* many ways or the chances of that power being contested will increase. Yet women who benefit from the status quo are still *women,* and because of this they are constantly under the threat of sexual assault, devaluation, and reduced economic security. Their male colleagues of the same social class or race will usually have more chances in the job market and have greater access to financial resources than they.

Lastly, women can be oppressed without feeling it because they may see gender as the most salient part of their identity. This is especially true for white, middle-to-upper-class women in Western culture.[25] Because of their race and class, these women enjoy certain privileges that accrue to dominant groups. They may take their privileged race and class so much for granted that they fail to notice these as parts of their identity in the same way that they notice gender. As a result, examining the construction of gender, which they may value as the major part of their identity, is a difficult thing for some women to do. In this way, too, women can be oppressed without consciously realizing it.

Another characteristic of oppression is that each member of a subordinate group gets defined as "other" rather than "one who is like me." Subordinate groups are then assigned negative stereotypes based on those characteristics that distinguish them from the dominant group, and their members and activities are assigned lower value than those of the dominant group.[26] Characteristics associated with being male are generally seen as more positive than those associated with being female.[27] We heard poignant testimony to this by those girls and boys who imagined what it would be like to wake up as members of the other sex.

25. Paula Rothenberg, "Teachable Truths: Connecting Race, Gender, Class," *Feminist Teacher,* vol. 3, pp. 1-3.

26. Meulenbelt, *De Ziekte Bestryden, Niet de Patient.*

27. Broverman et al., "Sex-role Stereotypes: A Current Appraisal," pp. 59-78.

Are Men Oppressed Because of Their Gender?

While we were working on this book, we constantly heard the refrain "But men are also oppressed. They also suffer because of the demands made on them as men." For example, men are "not allowed" to show much affection, and they have little choice about taking paid work as long as jobs are available. The idea that sexism is equally oppressive to men and women was exemplified in an issue of *Time* magazine (Fall 1990) that focused on women. In one article about the reactions of men to the changes in women brought about by the feminist movement, Sam Allis depicts the average man as being confused about the image he should portray.[28] Should he be Arnold Schwarzenegger? Alan Alda? Or something in between?[29] His company offers paternity leave. Should he take it, or will such an action jeopardize his career? If he supports affirmative action, will *he* reduce *his* chances of obtaining a job or a promotion? If he fails to work fifty to sixty hours a week because he is actively involved in parenting, will that hurt his paid career? The issues raised in this article echo the thesis of earlier sex-role theorists — namely, that sex roles are equally constricting for men and women.

We agree that men suffer because of sexism and that its elimination would enable them to live fuller and healthier lives. There is no doubt that the current nature of gender relations is detrimental to men, as the examples in the previous paragraph demonstrate. However, the argument for equal oppression is weak on several counts.

First and foremost, it ignores the imbalance of power between the two groups — that is, it overlooks the subordination of women to men. In current white Western culture, women as a group are not the dominant or valued gender. The "equality of oppression" argument ignores the subordination of women in the structuring of resources, work, and personal relationships. It overlooks the political and collective nature of gender. In

28. Allis, "What Do Men Really Want?" *Time,* Special Issue 136 (Fall 1990): 80-82.
29. In our team-taught course called "Perspectives on Gender," we had the students invent "genlets" — new words for previously undescribed, gendered experiences. One group of men coined the adjective "stallenesque," and explained that it described the pressures they felt from women to combine all the physical attributes of a Sylvester Stallone with all the emotional vulnerability of a Woody Allen! (The exercise took place before Woody Allen's questionable romantic liaison with his partner's adopted child in 1992.)

other words, it ignores the fact that the agency of women is more circumscribed than that of men because of women's relative lack of power. For example, most men do not commit sexual assault. Yet because some men do, all women are kept in a state of fear, and many men are empowered by taking on the role of women's "protector."[30] And recall the comments made by the girls and boys at the beginning of this chapter: *both* girls and boys showed an awareness of the privileges of being male and the costs of being female. The privileges of being men often outweigh the costs because men belong to the dominant gender group.

Second, men do not share equal oppression with women because, as both Marilyn Frye and Anja Meulenbelt argue, not every kind of pain is the result of oppression as we are using that term. Pain that comes from oppression is a function of *structural* inequality. An individual woman can make life miserable for her husband, which is certainly painful for him. But when a husband makes life miserable for his wife, there are more structural factors that come into play. Often she is economically dependent on him. In addition, the house may be in his name, the police may be lax about interfering in domestic disputes, and due to differences in physical size and acculturation, he is more likely to assault her in such a situation. Women often have no institutional power behind them in situations of conflict; men, on the other hand, have institutional power that they sometimes misuse, hurting themselves and especially others. As Michael Kaufman states,

> The very power relationships, the very social processes that give men power and privilege in a patriarchal society, cause men pain and hurt, cause a diminution and distortion of our human capabilities and capacities. Of course the two are not equal, they are not two balanced sides of the same coin — in patriarchal societies the relative power of men over women has more than compensated for any limitations accepted by men.... *In a male-dominated society men's experience of pain comes with a compensatory mechanism, which is the ongoing capacity to reassert personal power and self-worth over those who are not men (women), those who are not yet or never will be men (children) and, at least in the twentieth century, those who do not conform to the hegemonic forms of masculinity (gay men).*[31]

30. Jayne Schuiteman, "Self-Defense Training and Its Contributions to the Healing Process for Survivors of Sexual Abuse" (Ph.D. Dissertation, Michigan State University, 1990).

31. Michael Kaufman, "A Framework for Research on Men and Masculinity,"

As an individual, a man may not oppress the women he knows; he may share in the household and childraising tasks, never use the threat of violence, and be very nurturing. He may also risk being drafted to fight in wars, which is surely a painful prospect.[32] Yet if a man is white, heterosexual, and middle-to-upper class, he is still a member of the privileged, dominant group. As a "Dom," he still has easier access to resources and has privileges because of his gender. (Recall that in the game of rope tug, the Doms had the added advantages of cleats, gloves, and sweatbands.) What are some of the features of this power and privilege? They include being a member of the group that dominates the ranks of corporate executives, that decides whether or not to engage in war, that sets the welfare parameters for single mothers, that decides what the minimum wage will be, that decides if women in a denomi-nation are allowed to vote or hold church office, and so on.

True, many males do not have such decision-making responsibility, but the average male nevertheless enjoys certain perquisites of belonging to the dominant group. A male still enjoys such privileges whenever he picks up a textbook that centers primarily on males, when the church liturgy refers mainly to males and their experiences, when he earns more than a woman with a comparable job, when simply because he is a man people listen to him more readily than if he were a woman, when he can be "overweight" and not be discriminated against in the workplace, when he can walk across the street without being whistled at, when he can walk across town or step into an elevator at night and not worry about sexual assault, when he gains status by taking on the role of "women's protector" against sexual assault, when he does not have to be ultraconscious about his physical features, when he is not held re-sponsible for practicing birth control or having to worry about the side effects of such birth control on his body.[33] In addition, point out Sue

---

paper presented at the conference entitled "Re-Visioning Knowledge: Feminist Perspectives on the Curriculum," Michigan State University, East Lansing, Mich., 19-22 April 1990 (citation reflects our emphasis); forthcoming in *Men's Studies Review*.

32. For men of color, being drafted to fight in a war is part of *structural* oppression. For example, American men of color fought in the 1991 Gulf War in numbers disproportionate to their representation in the general population. This highlights issues of class and race as these intersect with gender.

33. See Carol Ehrlich, "The Reluctant Patriarchs," in *For Men against Sexism: A Book of Readings*, ed. Jon Snodgrass (Albion, Calif.: Times Change Press, 1977), pp. 141-45.

Wise and Liz Stanley, "We have no guarantees that even the most nicely mannered of men won't, in moments of exigency, fall back on the soft cushioning support of 'male reality' that is available to him as and when he wants."[34]

Thus white, middle-class, heterosexual men are not dominated as a group. They may have individual difficulties complying with the dominant form of masculinity, but considered as a social unit, they are not dominated in a systematic way. In fact, it is precisely many of these hegemonic males who set the terms for the subordination of all other groups.

This does not mean that men should feel guilty about being men. There will be little lessening of oppression if members of a dominant group are paralyzed by guilt because of their membership in that group. If, for example, men feel guilty because they are men, or white women feel guilty because they are white, they may depend even more on the subordinate group to make them feel good about being "male" or "white."[35] And this may lead to even greater dominance. If, on the other hand, a man feels comfortable with his body and with his maleness, he does not need to rely on a subordinated woman to give him his identity. Furthermore, we should point out that it can be healthy and productive for members of an oppressive group to feel guilty and repentant about their *position* over against subordinated groups. This guilt may then become an incentive to bring about change.

Human Agency

Oppression, as we noted, is never absolute because it does not completely eradicate the ability of subordinated people to think critically. Within their own situation, members of an oppressed group may cope by partially redefining certain social practices or engaging in others as a form of resistance. Earlier we gave examples of both individual women and groups of women who resisted dominant ideas about gender. We also saw attempts at redefinition in the example of the women who coped with their jobs as homemakers as best they could within circumstances defined by others. Their ways of resisting included claiming an hour a

34. Wise and Stanley, *Georgie Porgie: Sexual Harassment in Everyday Life* (London: Pandora Press, 1987), p. 125.
35. Meulenbelt, *De Ziekte Bestryden, Niet de Patient.*

day or a day a week for themselves (although they still had to arrange for babysitters and meals during their absence), negotiating with their husbands to do certain tasks, shaming their husbands ("Our neighbor gives his children baths; why can't you?"), and buying clothes that didn't have to be ironed. Within the constraints of their situation, these women were often reflective agents. As Sue Wise and Liz Stanley point out, women have always contested male domination. They have an awareness of male power, but their circumstances shape the ways in which they choose to resist it.[36]

To summarize: heterogeneity, oppression (or domination/subordination), and human agency are key features of gender relations, as well as of other social relations like race and class. This multifaceted nature of gender relations certainly increases the challenge of sorting out its dynamics.

Application of Critical Theory: "Masculinity" and "Femininity" Revisited

We can use other concepts of critical theory to examine the practices surrounding "masculinity" and "femininity" in the context of gender relations. How do we both construct and contest dominant definitions of what it means to be male and female in white, North American society? The concepts of hegemonic masculinity and privileged femininity will help us to answer this question.

Hegemonic Masculinity

Even though there are many forms of masculinity, there is one that is dominant in a given society at a given time. This version can be labeled *hegemonic masculinity*.[37] Hegemonic masculinity is, simply put, what men in the ruling class aspire to be like: emotionally controlled, financially independent, heterosexual, and so on. Hegemonic masculinity "is a question of how particular groups of men inhabit positions of power and wealth, and how they legitimate and reproduce the social relationships that generate

36. Wise and Stanley, *Georgie Porgie.*
37. Carrigan, Connell, and Lee, "Hard and Heavy."

249

their dominance. . . . Hegemonic masculinity is hegemonic so far as it embodies a successful strategy in relation to women."[38] Hegemonic masculinity is not a male "essence" or a male "role" equally applicable to all men, but rather a specific type of masculinity to which others are subordinated. Hegemonic masculinity thus excludes not only women but also men exhibiting "inferior masculinities": "Masculinities are constructed not just by power relations but by their interplay with a division of labor and with patterns of emotional attachment. . . . The ability to define a masculinity as subordinate is part of what we mean by hegemony."[39] Nevertheless, even those who exhibit a subordinate masculinity retain privileges as men with respect to the women of their particular social group.

Overall, there may be few men whose personalities actually fit that of hegemonic masculinity. Yet many men subscribe to the ideal of hegemonic masculinity because it legitimates institutionalized male dominance over women.[40] Michael Messner cites a cogent example of this. He describes a conversation with a male athlete who claimed that no woman could "take a hit" like those sustained by professional football players. As Messner points out, the athlete totally ignored the fact that most *men* can't "take" such hits either.[41] This athlete was endorsing a masculine ideal that many men believe but few men can attain; nevertheless, it helps maintain the myth of "womanly" weakness.

Although hegemonic masculinity may be muted in face-to-face relations, it has a form that is collectively and societally encoded, and this is what concerns us here. Think of your own situation at church or at work. What are the men like who have decision-making power and access to resources? Do they share an interest and skill in golf? Do they follow the stock market, wear suits, adhere to Roberts' Rules of Order, and have "traditional" families? If so, then this constellation of traits in part describes hegemonic masculinity within that context. In such a situation, the quiet, unmarried, working-class man who cuts the church lawn and never brings computer printouts to church board meetings exhibits a subordinated masculinity. He will probably speak less often and be taken less seriously than the men who conform to the dominant form of masculinity.

38. Ibid., p. 92.
39. Ibid., p. 90.
40. Ibid.; see also Connell, *Gender and Power*.
41. Messner, "Masculinities and Athletic Careers: Bonding and Status Differences," in *Sport, Men, and the Gender Order*, pp. 97-108.

The gendered nature of activities and task assignments and the structuring of power constitute other dimensions of hegemonic masculinity. What do hegemonic males do in your situation? Do they serve on school boards or work in day-care centers? Do they teach Sunday school or catechism? If we take a sampling across the country, we get some idea of the current form of American hegemonic masculinity.

How does one form of masculinity stay dominant? The dimensions of hegemonic masculinity get so embedded in all institutions that they come to be perceived as normal, legitimate, and common-sensical. Human perception, like human agency, is constrained by structural forces. Females and males may construct their sense of gender by "choosing" to behave in certain ways, but their choices are often constrained. One becomes a "masculine" male not just because of the influences of role models, the media, and education but also because of a combination of political, economic, and social privileges that accrue to those who act in certain male-defined ways. For example, we all know the "male" way and the "female" way of sitting, and we "choose" the appropriate way in situations where doing otherwise might bring us scorn or worse. Similarly, if a boy is afraid of being labeled gay, he will "choose" to behave in ways that deny the accuracy of that label. Homophobia and the threat of violence may play a large part in shaping his choice of certain behaviors.

Distorted Heterosexuality

A crucial legitimator of hegemonic masculinity is a way of thinking that often distorts relations between and within groups. To be a hegemonic male in our society, a man must not only be heterosexual but often prove that heterosexuality in distorted or questionable ways: by "capturing" a woman (one who is at least shorter and smaller than he is, and the more beautiful the better), by displaying sexual prowess, by objectifying women, and in general by being dominant in his relations with women. These flawed behaviors are given social sanction. The disparaging expression "She wears the pants in the family" has no husbandly counterpart!

As we shall see in a later chapter, sport is a primary way for boys and still-unmarried young men to show that they are heterosexual. The equation of sport with masculinity, and more specifically with heterosexuality, means that we often question the sexual orientation of boys

251

who show no interest in sports. We often call them "effeminate." The meaning of this term reveals much about our gender relations. *Webster's Third New International Dictionary* defines "effeminate" as referring to the "qualities more characteristic of and suited to women than to men." For a man to be "effeminate" and thus be suspected of being gay is for him to be like a woman, and with respect to men, women are a subordinate group. E. H. Thompson, C. Grisanti, and J. H. Pleck have argued that in today's society, manliness is confirmed by avoiding *all* female-associated behaviors. Since homophobia is in large part a rejection of the womanly, it is not surprising that more men than women have a disdain for or fear of homosexuals.[42]

We have just noted that with respect to gender relations, gay men are devalued, just as women are. It is no wonder then that manifestations of heterosexuality play such a large part in the construction of hegemonic masculinity. Young boys know this well. The boys in Gary Fine's study of Little Leaguers[43] and in Barrie Thorne's study of elementary schoolchildren[44] were quick to label any boy who did not like sports a "faggot." Those who aspire to be hegemonic males may try to distance themselves as far as possible from gay males, since their presence challenges the strongly heterosexual demand of hegemonic masculinity.[45] This self-conscious distancing of heterosexual men from gay men may help explain why male-led evangelical churches often fail to respond compassionately to the AIDS crisis. We have heard painful stories about the neglect of pastoral care obligations, the lack of compassion for HIV-positive males and their families, and the homophobic labeling of AIDS caregivers.

We do not wish to launch a debate about homosexuality itself,

---

42. Thompson, Grisanti, and Pleck, "Attitudes toward the Male Role and Their Correlates," *Sex Roles* 13 (1985): 413-27; E. Aguero, F. Bloch, and D. Byrne, "The Relationships among Sexual Beliefs, Attitudes, Experience, and Homophobia," *Journal of Homosexuality* 10 (1984): 95-107; Dana Brittan, "Homophobia and Homosociality: An Analysis of Boundary Maintenance," *Sociological Quarterly* 31 (1990): 423-39.

43. Fine, *With the Boys: Little League Baseball and Preadolescent Culture* (Chicago: University of Chicago Press, 1987).

44. Thorne, "Girls and Boys Together . . . But Mostly Apart: Gender Arrangements in Elementary Schools," in *Relationship and Development*, ed. W. Hartup and Z. Rubin (Hillsdale, N.J.: Lawrence Erlbaum Associates, 1986), pp. 167-84.

45. Connell, *Gender and Power*; Brittan, *Masculinity and Power*.

since the focus of this book is gender relations, not sexuality per se. We are merely pointing out how homophobia shores up hegemonic masculinity and reinforces a rigidly defined heterosexuality based on various distortions. The derogatory labeling of boys and young men who show no interest in sports or who are gentle and "soft" is such a distortion. Indeed, homophobia is a key aspect of hegemonic masculinity. Anyone who doubts its legitimating aspect for hegemonic masculinity should try to imagine what the world would be like without fear of or disdain for homosexuals. Might not the meanings we give to gender be less restrictive? Might not Christian males feel less obliged to immerse themselves in sports, or be less tempted to resort to violence to prove their manliness? Since taunts about masculinity or the lack of it would rarely be heard, calling a male a "faggot" or a "sissy" would have little power to provoke. In addition, AIDS-affected church members, their families, and their caregivers might feel less isolated in their grief and loss.

One feature of hegemonic masculinity is the power to demand "proof" of one's heterosexuality. It is as if one is guilty until proven innocent. But the hegemonic process is not exempt from attack. Human agency plays a role in contesting or challenging the gender order. Hegemonic masculinity repeatedly has to be "won and held": it is continually challenged and reconstructed.[46] It is true that at the individual level there are men who feel no need to prove their masculinity through their sexuality, who do not need to feel taller than their female partner or require her to be beautiful, who are true partners with the women in their lives, at home and at work. There are men who are gentle in both their home life and their career life, although they often encounter more criticism than support for being so. However, at the collective level, at this point in time, most of the challenge to hegemonic masculinity comes from feminist and gay sources.

But is there no such challenge from Christian men? One might expect there to be, since the fruits of the Spirit that Christians are supposed to exemplify are not usually identified with hegemonic masculinity in secular society. We might expect Christian men to counter the definition of hegemonic masculinity with one that is more consonant

46. Tim Carrigan, Robert Connell, and John Lee, "Toward a New Sociology of Masculinity," in *The Making of Masculinities*, pp. 63-100. See also Gilmore's *Manhood in the Making*.

with the New Testament. But there is little evidence that this has occurred on a large scale. Indeed, Christian men may sustain hegemonic masculinity both inside and outside the church because it helps to legitimate their dominance over women. They may reject (at least in theory) the subordination of other masculinities based on race or ethnicity but endorse the subordination of gay males and of women.[47] Thus they may be consciously or unconsciously selective in their endorsement of hegemonic masculinity. In other words, within Christian institutions there may be an ascendant masculinity which in part endorses that of the secular world and in part responds to its own social context.

Privileged Femininity

Unlike hegemonic masculinity, the femininity of a particular social group has no separate definition, since it is tied to hegemonic masculinity.[48] In other words, what is considered appropriate for women is defined in relation to what is hegemonically masculine. For example, if hegemonic masculinity requires men to endorse dominance over women, then women will be considered feminine if they are acquiescent in their relationships with men. If masculinity is defined as being a family provider, then femininity will be partly defined as earning less than one's husband or even not working for pay. Thus the definition of femininity depends on the meaning given to hegemonic masculinity in a certain culture at a specific period in time. In other chapters (e.g., the one on dress), we will examine this idea more fully.

Robert Connell suggests that we call the dominant form of femininity not hegemonic femininity but "emphasized" femininity. He defines this as a femininity performed especially for men, one constructed around compliance with and adaptation to male power. We think Connell is right about the theoretical impossibility of a hegemonic femininity. But we would argue that factors besides gender relations are more important to the dominant form of femininity than his definition sug-

47. We say "in theory" because in practice many churches who claim biblical authority for keeping women out of teaching ministries at home see no problem with allowing *white women* missionaries to have teaching authority over *black male* converts. Challenged with this inconsistency, a male member of one of our churches simply replied, "Oh, the women are fine for the natives." (This in 1990!)

48. Connell, *Gender and Power.*

gests. Class, race, and other social relations do play an important part in how a given femininity is constructed in relation to masculinity and to *other* femininities. Perhaps women who are sensitive to their oppression as women are more sensitive to other forms of oppression, but this is not necessarily so. A woman may fight against injustice to white, heterosexual, or middle-class women and at the same time ignore or accept the injustice encountered by black, lesbian, or working-class women. Nurturing and marginalizing behavior can coexist in the same person. The point is that in North America, women who are white and middle-to-upper class construct a femininity that becomes the standard for *all* women. Such femininity, constructed out of privilege, we call "privileged femininity."

Since privileged femininity is constructed to accommodate the interests and desires of hegemonic men, its central feature is attractiveness to men. This includes physical appearance, sociability, ego-stroking, management of emotions, and accepting certain "deals" both within marriage and within male-female relations on the job. We think it important to note that virtually all of the marks of this femininity center on the nurture of men and children. We do not mean to imply that nurturing others is a negative practice. In fact, we see it as a laudatory ideal for everyone. However, the current definition of nurturing in the context of gender relations often means that women receive less nurturance from men than they give to them.

Since hegemonic masculinity has distorted sexuality for men, it should come as no surprise that sexuality for women is distorted in different but complementary ways. Distorted heterosexuality means that a woman without a man is often seen as incomplete and sometimes as unfeminine. The word *spinster* traditionally has had more negative connotations than the word *bachelor*. In our culture we often assume that single women are spending their time waiting for the "right" man to come along, whereas bachelors are partying or dating several women, not able to decide on the right one or simply not ready to settle down. Frequently we assume that there is something wrong with a single woman because she is "unable to attract a man." Perhaps, we think, she is too interested in her career, too bossy, or too independent. In other words, she's not "feminine" enough. We fail to see that singleness is often a choice, and a choice we should respect.[49]

49. For a discussion of singleness from a Christian perspective, see Van

255

As with males and hegemonic masculinity, what women support as privileged femininity is not what actually characterizes most of them. Instead they use privileged females as their reference group, the group whose behavior they adopt as an ideal. This results in paying lip service to one creed while living by another. One of us had an experience that illustrates this practice. She returned to visit the congregation where she had been a member as a little girl. It was a church where male dominance and female submissiveness were loudly proclaimed by both women and men. Yet as she looked around in church that Sunday morning, she saw faces of women who showed immense strength in a variety of ways. There were women who worked side by side with their husbands to ensure family survival. There were women who worked in low-paying jobs to bring in money when their husbands were laid off or to ensure that their children could go to Christian schools. There were women who voiced their opinions very assertively at congregational meetings and during the church coffee-hour. If they had been *truly* quiet, timid, and submissive, their families would not have survived. Yet, though they were strong, active, and assertive in their daily lives, these women stressed submissiveness. They worked as equal partners with their husbands, yet in theory they endorsed male dominance. Similarly, a woman may publicly proclaim that she is not bothered by the comments her male colleagues make about her appearance because she regards the remarks as "harmless." Yet at the same time she may privately warn her daughters not to trust what their male dates say because "all men want is sex."[50]

Thus women, just like men, may endorse one type of femininity, marginalize those who do not display certain aspects of it, and at the same time not live up to it themselves. Homophobia also plays a role in keeping women from contesting privileged femininity. Women who through their actions or appearance do not seem to be endorsing privileged femininity are often labeled "lesbians." This label is frequently used to classify and disempower those who visibly contest male dominance: feminists, women athletes, single women, and so on.[51] This label-

Leeuwen's *Gender and Grace* and Mary Ellen Ashcroft's *Temptations Women Face: Honest Talk about Jealousy, Anger, Sex, Money, Food, Pride* (Downers Grove, Ill.: InterVarsity Press, 1991).

50. Wise and Stanley, *Georgie Porgie.*

51. Suzanne Pharr, *Homophobia: A Weapon of Sexism* (Inverness, Calif.: Chardon Press, 1988).

ing may partially explain why some women, especially in evangelical churches, shy away from calling themselves "feminist."

As we have already noted, there is no one form of femininity that includes all women. But the dominant form is marked by heterogeneity, as is the dominant form of masculinity. Moreover, groups that exhibit nonprivileged "femininities" are marginalized in order to prevent them from gaining legitimation. Such groups include women of color, women athletes, fat women, single women, and physically challenged women. However, this marginalization manifests itself differently from hegemonic masculinity's subordination of other masculinities. For example, members of the privileged feminine group rarely are physically violent toward nonprivileged women, though they may resort to verbal and emotional abuse.[52]

Human agency plays a part in the construction of femininity, as it does in the construction of masculinity. A woman's choice to enact or endorse behaviors that are part of privileged femininity will depend on a combination of personal, political, economic, religious, and social factors. We noted earlier that homophobia and the threat of violence strongly constrain men's choices. In the case of women, an additional factor — that of sheer economic vulnerability — affects the extent to which they may endorse and/or practice privileged femininity.

In summary, femininity and masculinity are not aspects of femaleness and maleness existing independently of each other as static entities. Femininity and masculinity are constructed and reconstructed in a relational manner. The hegemonic masculinity and privileged femininity that we have described are the dominant ways of living out gender relations in white Western culture at this time.

Application of Theory:
Continuing the Game of Rope Tug

Challenging the Game

According to critical theory, social relations marked by dominance/subordination are both enacted and contested in an ongoing fashion. The dominant group, which has the balance of power, works to protect the

52. Connell, *Gender and Power.*

status quo. But, regardless of circumstances, those in positions of less power do not lose their God-given ability to think reflectively and critically and act accordingly. And women are agents not just when they protest visibly (or loudly) against male domination. They are agentic whenever they find creative ways to cope *within* the framework of that domination. They are also agents when they choose to avoid potential danger by not going out at night or by not wearing specific types of clothes. Women are agentic when they accede to sexist practices in order to feel safe or to have access to resources. What is seen as "passive" behavior by women in the face of sexism is often a demonstration of agency. Women may *choose* to ignore insults, exclusive language, objectification, and other behaviors simply to save energy. If women challenged every act of sexism they encountered, they might be exhausted by the end of the day.[53]

Consequently, although in the following discussion we focus on the ways in which women contest the current nature of gender relations, we do not mean to imply that women who fail to engage in such challenges are passive. Gender relations, whatever their form, are always being contested. The feminist movement offers some good examples of this challenge at the collective level. Feminists of various kinds have made sexual violence visible, helped to establish houses for battered women, named and identified sexual harassment, drawn attention to pay inequities for similar but sex-segregated jobs, urged fathers to do more nurturing of children, and so on. Each of these has been of help to women; yet few changes have occurred in gender relations with respect to power. Why is this so?

As the nature of gender relations is challenged, those who have a vested interest in maintaining the status quo may use different tactics to maintain their power. These tactics include such things as violence, coercion, trivialization, co-optation (also known as muting), and reconstruction. What follows are examples of several such tactics.

Reactions to Challenges

Violence

An extreme response to the challenge of dominant rule is the use of violence to enforce the status quo. Within gender relations violence is

53. Wise and Stanley, *Georgie Porgie.*

258

the clearest expression of hegemonic male dominance and manifests itself in various ways, including sexual harassment, rape, incest, wife battering, and violent pornography.[54]

The evidence that this violence exists and is widespread in the United States is unequivocal. These are some of the sobering statistics: every fifteen seconds a woman is battered; every six minutes a woman is raped; one in four women will be sexually assaulted in her lifetime; battering is the most frequent cause of women's visits to hospital emergency rooms; survivors of wife-battering account for more than 50 percent of homeless women.[55] Overall, the U.S. outranks all other countries in its incidence of sexual assault, and this violence is inflicted on women not primarily by strangers but by men they *know*.[56]

Because this violence tends to occur in or near the home, for many women the home is not a "haven in a heartless world." Nor is wife abuse restricted to the lower classes. We know of one woman academic, divorced from a physically abusive husband, who used to teach evening courses at a Bible college in an inner-city setting only a few blocks from her home. When her colleagues discovered that she was in the habit of walking home after her classes, they chided her for "risking her life" in the black neighborhood and urged her to phone her husband for a ride instead. Ironically, she told us, she was never once harassed or harmed on her walks home. It was *after* she got home that her troubles began.

How is sexual violence related to the feminist challenge of the status quo in gender relations? First of all, the very existence of violence leads to a fear of violence. Recall how the fear of terrorism constrained the activities of people during the war in the Persian Gulf. Likewise, a woman may never actually be assaulted in her lifetime, but her knowledge that this happens to women and could happen to her may make her fearful, may make her curtail her activities, and may make her overly anxious to please men in order to prevent such violence from occurring.[57]

54. Michael Kaufman, "The Construction of Masculinity and the Triad of Men's Violence," in *Beyond Patriarchy*, pp. 1-29.

55. See *Ms.*, September/October 1990; and Katha Pollitt's "Georgie Porgie Is a Bully," *Time*, Special Issue 136 (Fall 1990): 24.

56. Jalna Hamner, "Men, Power and the Exploitation of Women," *Women's Studies International Forum* 13 (1990): 443-56.

57. Susan Griffin, *Rape: The Power of Consciousness* (San Francisco: Harper & Row, 1979). As indicated earlier, the fact that some men rape gives many men the powerful role of "protector."

This fear is based on reality: Katha Pollitt has shown that the rate of rape is increasing four times as fast as the overall crime rate in the U.S.[58] Jane Caputi and Diana Russell have argued that there has been a substantial increase in assaults on women since the 1960s, when the current wave of feminism began.[59] They attribute such changes not just to better reporting of crime statistics but also to a reaction to feminist challenges to male dominance. In other words, some males may be escalating violence toward women in order to reassert their perceived loss of authority.[60]

Despite feminist efforts to create rape crisis centers and shelters for abused woman, little has occurred on the societal level to alter the dynamics of gender relations with respect to sexual assault. We have often ignored the fact that sexual violence *is* about male dominance. We still excuse physical fighting among boys with the excuse "boys will be boys." Caputi and Russell have shown how little has been done to change the attitudes of males in ways that could reduce the frequency of assaults on females. In one recent study, 51 percent of college men said they would rape a woman if they knew they could get away with it;[61] in other such studies the reported rates vary from 30 percent to 60 percent.

Moreover, despite increased public awareness about the frequency of male sexual assault on women, the overwhelming public reaction still seems to be one of holding the victim responsible for the crime. For example, one of us worked at a large university where each occurrence of rape, especially stranger rape, was dutifully reported in the campus newspaper. Often the account of the incident was followed by advice from campus security officials about what women should do to be safe on campus: never walk alone after dark, walk in well-lighted areas, and so on. But never was this advice followed by parallel admonitions to men: stay home at night, do not attack women, and so on. When rape is framed

58. Pollitt, "Georgie Porgie Is a Bully."
59. Caputi and Russell, "'Femicide': Speaking the Unspeakable," *Ms.*, September/October 1990, pp. 34-37.
60. Caputi and Russell, "Femicide." Violence in male sports as well as spectator interest in those sports is also on the rise. The role of sport in gender relations will be discussed in the subsequent chapter.
61. This study was cited in *Ms.*, September/October 1990, p. 45. For a commentary on the way society tolerates sexual harassment even by young males, see Jerry Adler and Debra Rosenberg, "Must Boys Always Be Boys?" *Newsweek*, 19 October 1992, p. 77.

as a "women's problem," it leaves men's power to rape unchallenged. Acts of rape are still often seen as the fault of the women involved. ("She asked for it — by the way she dressed, by asking me to her apartment, by coming to my apartment, by letting me pay for an expensive dinner . . .")

If this technique of blaming the victim does not work, then alternatively, assaults on women may be interpreted as the isolated acts of disturbed men. Take as an example what happened at the University of Montreal on December 6, 1989. Fourteen women engineering students were killed by a man who did not even know them; he opened fire with a machine gun after announcing, "You're all a bunch of feminists, and I hate feminists." This incident occurred during the time we were working on this book at Calvin College, and it shocked us all. But among our male colleagues, in many churches, and in the national press the naming of this act as "femicide" was met with great resistance. The common assertion was "It wasn't a political act; it was an isolated shooting by a psycho." Yet if a white man had shot fourteen blacks after announcing his hostility to racial integration, would we not have named that a political act? If an anti-Semitic man had killed fourteen Jews, would we be so quick to label it solely as the isolated act of a psycho?

Our study team conjectured that such racist or anti-Semitic acts would be followed by a great deal of public examination of the political and social contexts that produce such killers and what we do to contribute to those contexts. Would we, as a result, hold blacks responsible for bringing about a decrease in racist attitudes and feelings? Would we lecture to them about "lynching prevention" the same way we lecture to women about rape prevention? Would we expect Jews to be primarily responsible for decreasing anti-Semitic behavior? Hopefully not, and probably not. Wouldn't we who are white Christians want to examine our social practices and take some responsibility for creating an environment where racism or anti-Semitism thrives? Hopefully so, and probably so.

But why do some men not take responsibility for such an act by one of their peers? According to Jalna Hamner, "Men are not accustomed to being held responsible for anything negative about themselves either individually or as a social group. . . . It seems to be unjustified to be attacked or criticized for one's . . . misuse of social power."[62] However,

62. Hamner, "Men, Power and the Exploitation of Women," p. 446.

as Christians we learn to reflect on our actions and to see all of them as potentially sin-tainted. That is what the famous (and much-misunderstood) Calvinist doctrine of "total depravity" is about. Given this belief system, shouldn't Christian men be better able than non-Christian men to recognize and assume some responsibility for decreasing male domination through sexual violence?

But what, in fact, has been the response of churches to violence against women? On the whole it has been negligible, even though women are as much at risk for battering in conservative religious families as in families in the population at large.[63] A few churches may co-sponsor "safe houses" or shelters for battered women, but what actual preaching is being done on this topic from the pulpit? Is there a message, or is there silence (which, after all, is also a message)? Sexual violence is in fact primarily about male behavior, and 95 percent of all spousal murders in the U.S. are committed by husbands. Will we begin to see the political meaning of such violence and begin to hold men accountable for it? If women are at risk at home, what are churches doing to make home a safe place? Are churches promoting a strong ethos of nonviolence, as well as one that sees all women as imagers of God? These are important questions to consider.

Certainly most men do not rape, commit incest, or assault women. Yet what responsibility do they take to ensure change in a culture where interpersonal violence thrives?[64] Think back to the children quoted at

63. See the following: Karen Burton Mains and Maxine Hancock, *Child Sexual Abuse: The Hope for Healing* (Wheaton, Ill.: Harold Shaw, 1986); James Alsdurf and Phyllis Alsdurf, *Battered into Submission: The Tragedy of Wife Abuse in the Christian Home* (Downers Grove, Ill.: InterVarsity Press, 1989); and Calvin College Social Research Center, "A Survey of Abuse in the Christian Reformed Church" (Grand Rapids: Calvin College, 1990).

64. An exception to this passivity is the Cambridge-based counseling group known as EMERGE, which deals with male batterers. EMERGE was set up in 1977 by pro-feminist men who acknowledged that woman-beating was a male, not a female problem, and that men therefore should be taking the initiative to resocialize other men away from such violence. A similar group in San Francisco, MOVE (Men Overcoming Violence), has been in existence since about 1980. In addition, the U.S. Catholic Bishops wrote its first official statement against spouse abuse in 1992, making it clear that violence against women is never justified and that the church should be a place where both abused women and battering men can come for help. See "When I Call for Help: A Pastoral Response to Domestic Violence against Women" (New York: Administrative Committee of the U.S. Catholic Bishops, 1992).

the beginning of this chapter. When the boys imagined being girls, they talked about committing violent acts. Will we raise our sons to respect women as human beings and as equal bearers of God's image? Will we teach them to be nonviolent and to pursue other ways of settling disagreements and frustrations? Will we insist that many heroes who promote male dominance, such as Rambo and many rock musicians, not be allowed a hearing? Will we encourage men to give up their "skin magazines, bimbo jokes, women-bashing rock and rap?"[65] As Christians we have an opportunity and a responsibility to be proactive and to ensure that challenges to male dominance are not met with further violent acts by males. Can we and will we take a leadership role to prevent such reactionary violence from occurring?

Muting

Dominant groups do not always resort to crude violence to stave off challenges by subordinates. They may instead co-opt or mute those challenges. Often this means that the dominant group will use advances made by subordinates to its own advantage. The dominant group may make superficial changes to accommodate the demands of marginalized groups, but in essence it is working to hold on to what it has, and little actual change occurs in its privilege and power. Muting is a common practice, and the following examples show its dynamics.

As a first example, consider the many women who work for pay in environments where they are continually bombarded with labels like "chairman," "manpower," and "spokesman." It has been our experience that when women have protested against the use of these words, the response has often been that these words are *not* sexist. Their complaints are often dismissed as "whiny" and insignificant. But what if these words were "chairwhite," "whitepower," and "spokeswhite"? Would we recognize them as being exclusionary and change them to be inclusive or racially neutral? Similarly, one woman who resisted being called a housewife ("I did not say 'I do' to a house, nor did I marry one!") was labeled "absurd." Despite such criticism, women have continued to resist such terms, and as a consequence they are now frequently changed to "chair," "workpower," "spokesperson," and "homemaker." However, most of these changes are made only when the words refer to women. Con-

---

65. Pollitt, "Georgie Porgie Is a Bully," p. 24.

sequently, the new words are still quite gender-linked. Thus a dominant group can stave off challenges by accommodating and then trivializing the concerns of the subordinate group.

As a second example, consider the struggle that feminist scholars have waged to obtain a place in academia for the study of women, in contrast to the usual academic focus on male thoughts, activities, and priorities. Now that women's studies has obtained such a place, some men are demanding inclusion by means of "men's studies" or "gender studies" programs. This dilution of women's studies may result in a loss of the radical, prophetic aspects of feminism. As Tim Carrigan and his coauthors point out, a great deal of the research on gender done by men obscures questions about privilege and power by focusing merely on the *negative* aspects of the male role.[66] Mary Evans further argues that using the phrase "gender studies" instead of "women's studies" implies the existence of two socially equal groups.[67] Feminism's challenge of male hegemony may thus get muted, especially if nonfeminist men are included in such programs.

As a third example, consider the struggles of many people who have worked hard to institutionalize the idea of "equal opportunity" so that women and people of color have access to activities and jobs previously denied to them. This provokes members of the dominant group, who are accustomed to using their power for "gatekeeping," or defining access to certain activities. Thus they may react indignantly, often appealing to the "equal opportunity" principle when they themselves are excluded from women-only activities or spaces.

For example, when we were in residence at Calvin College, we honored many of our Christian foremothers, using women's voices, in a chapel service held on International Women's Day. After the service, a male faculty member objected; he felt that male voices should have been included as well. Other faculty members and students wanted to know when International Men's Day would be held. Such challenges, like those to women's studies programs, simply overlook and in many ways sustain the continuing imbalance of institutional power between men and women.

Because men as the dominant group have power, they have the

66. Carrigan, Connell, and Lee, "Hard and Heavy."
67. Evans, "The Problem of Gender for Women's Studies," *Women's Studies International Forum* 13 (1990): 457-62.

ability, unless challenged, to "position the discourse" — that is, to distribute symbolic lenses which make people see reality the way men want them to. For example, when the feminist critique of nonnurturing men gained popular momentum, it was then turned around, with men castigating "selfish" *women* who left child care to their husbands (see, for example, the movies *Kramer vs. Kramer* and *Three Men and a Baby*).[68] Similarly, men are often given (by other men in the judicial system) joint custody of their children in divorce cases, even if they have not been greatly involved in raising their children.[69] Also, groups have sprung up to protect "men's rights," which suggests that feminism is only a question of *individual* "rights" and that men have been just as oppressed as women.[70] Thus, even though gender boundaries may shift, the power of men is still left largely intact through their ability to position the discourse.

In churches this practice of positioning the discourse has been used to stave off challenges to the proscription against women's ordination by endlessly pitting scriptural proof text against proof text or by appealing to the importance of church unity. Alternately, disagreements about gender concerns in the church are portrayed not as issues of injustice but as mere differences of opinion. The attitude then becomes, "If feminists don't like it here, they can leave." (Note that church unity usually becomes a concern only when *non*-feminists are unhappy.) It is hard to gain any real ground in this situation. When gender boundaries in one denomination were reconstructed so that women were "allowed" to be deacons, the job of deacon was more narrowly defined to ensure that it was different from that of (males-only) elders. Furthermore, within church periodicals Christian feminists are often labeled "radical" and "secular" by people who have read very little or very selectively in the feminist literature. When feminists make visible the practices that support male domination, their critique is quickly dismissed or trivialized as "male bashing." Do we call it "white bashing" when antiracist people point out ways in which we and the South African government contribute

68. Harry Brod, introduction to *The Making of Masculinities,* pp. 1-18.

69. For a discussion of the use of the law to mute challenges, see Carol Smart's *Feminism and the Power of Law* (New York: Routledge, 1989). We note that as of 1992 in the U.S., 70 percent of all men who used legal resources to try to obtain post-divorce custody of their children succeeded in doing so.

70. See *Beyond Patriarchy* and Clatterbaugh's *Contemporary Perspectives on Masculinity.*

to the oppression of blacks in South Africa? The frequent result of these practices is that Christian feminists, both women and men, continually have to struggle to make their voices heard, and often do so from a marginalized position.

A fourth example of "muting" pertains to the valuing of women and men. Throughout this chapter we have demonstrated that the current nature of gender relations is such that men and what they do are generally valued more than women and what they do. This "hierarchy of value," combined with the power that accrues to men because of their gender, makes it easy for them to co-opt or upstage women's agency. For example, if men are valued more than women, then the presence of men is assumed to give added credibility to any project or situation. We saw much evidence of this during our year of work at Calvin College. Prior to the project's beginning, many faculty members were anxious to make sure the research team was "gender-balanced"; otherwise, it was claimed, the project would be trivialized as the work of "the women's team." During our residency we celebrated International Women's Day, in part by creating and distributing buttons that read "Women: Celebrating God's Image." Some individuals would not buy a button (even though the price was a mere twenty-five cents) because it made no mention of men. At various times during our seminars and in reaction to certain bulletin-board displays, we would be asked, "Why do you always focus on women and not men?" Ironically, most of our work *did* include men, although the fact that we did not take for granted that "male" is the equivalent of "normative" may have led some people to conclude that men were being "neglected." By contrast, never once did we hear anyone ask, in response to displays in the college library of new books, all by male authors, "Why do they always focus on men?"

Another commonly posed question was, "Why do you only have one man on your study team?" Although this question may seem reasonable, it obscures the nature of the hegemonic male world. Decision-making groups of all kinds — church councils, governmental bodies, and so on — have always been composed primarily of men. Previous Calvin Center teams (with only one exception) were composed entirely of men. The work and decisions of such groups have legitimacy and credibility even when women are absent from them. Although we may bemoan the lack of attention paid to women in history books, we rarely think of these books as "lacking credibility" just because they focus primarily on the activities of men.

These several examples show how men, by demanding inclusion in activities that challenge their hegemony, can mute such challenges. This demand by men to be included whenever they deem it appropriate is also a sign of assumed privilege. Those in power usually have access on demand to whatever activities they wish to participate in. Their indignation when they are denied access reveals the extent to which they have taken this privilege for granted.

Although we could illustrate many other struggles to confirm or to change gender relations, the foregoing should give you a general idea of the dynamics of those relations. In a later chapter we will discuss ways of bringing about change. We note here, however, that there is no magical or painless way to do this. Asking people to give up power and privilege always brings resistance. The role of servant has always been a difficult one for those accustomed to power and authority.

CHAPTER 9

Using the Body to Endorse
Meanings about Gender

A ccording to James B. Nelson, "The way we think and feel about ourselves as bodies will always find expression in the way we think and feel about the world and about God. We experience the world only through our body selves."[1] This quotation highlights the importance of our bodies to our sense of self, God, and others. And our bodies affect not only our sense of ourselves but others' sense of us. From birth onward, we define bodies with and appraise bodies for characteristics that give us clues about class, sexuality, race, and gender. We dichotomize bodies (sometimes erroneously) into male and female, and in that process they are sexualized, and therefore alternately praised and punished. Although we create gendered meanings in many ways, the body is one place where we *visibly* create such meanings for ourselves, and where others create meanings on our behalf. And although it is important to remember that the embodiment of gender intersects with

1. Nelson, *Embodiment: An Approach to Sexuality and Christian Theology* (Minneapolis: Augsburg Publishing House, 1978), p. 20.

The primary author of this chapter is Annelies Knoppers.

class, race, and ethnicity, we will limit the following discussion to the white, middle-class, American body.

This discussion assumes that for people in white Western cultures, gender is a crucial part of one's identity.[2] The terms "femininity" and "masculinity" are the terms typically used to describe gender. What do such terms mean when applied to the body? What is a masculine body? A feminine body? Do all women look feminine because they are female? Are all men masculine? Do these words describe ways of doing things or essential being? What do we mean when we say, "He looks effeminate" or "She acts masculine"? In this chapter we will explore the popular meanings we have given to these terms with respect to the body. We will look at these terms in a societal context and attempt to show how masculinity and femininity, as currently constructed and given meaning through the body, can be dysfunctional.

Constructing the Female Body: Thin Is In

Being Thin Is No Sin

Today health and slimness seem to be almost synonymous. Fat people are seen as lazy, out-of-control individuals who "let themselves go."[3] Fatness is often viewed as a major obstacle to happiness and to the achievement of one's potential. Thinness is seen as healthy, fatness as unhealthy. This way of thinking has even found its way into religion. Some believers reason that if the body is the temple of God, then the ideal temple, especially for a woman, is a slim one! Since, on the average, women tend to have more body fat than men, it is not surprising that about 75 percent of American women think they are overweight and that 95 percent of the enrollees in weight-reduction programs are women. This emphasis on slimness also affects young girls. A study of girls in California indicated that 50 percent of the nine-year-olds and close to 80 percent of the ten- to eleven-year-olds were on diets because they thought they were too fat.[4]

2. Arthur Brittan, *Masculinity and Power* (New York: Basil Blackwell, 1989).
3. For a review of these perceptions, see Kim Chernin's *Fat Is a Feminist Issue* (London: Women's Press, 1981).
4. Roberta Pollack Seid, *Never Too Thin: Why Women Are at War with Their*

269

Males seem to have greater leeway with respect to these standards. A woman is usually considered fat if she is ten to fifteen pounds overweight; a man usually isn't considered fat unless he's more than thirty-five pounds overweight. Marcia Millman argues that having a fat body is less disturbing to men than to women. Being overweight may have health-related consequences for a man, but it does not affect every dimension of his life as it may for a woman. Few obese women are treated with the respect that many fat men still receive, especially if they are wealthy and/or powerful. Fat young boys can stave off taunts about their size by participating in sports. (If they aren't physically active, however, they may be ridiculed by their peers.) Indeed, heavy boys and young men are often encouraged to play football rather than to diet: heft on the playing field is considered a good thing. Men, it seems, are judged primarily on their accomplishments, not on their appearance.[5] It is primarily women for whom thinness is a lifelong requirement as part of privileged femininity. In contrast, slimness for men seems to be equated more with health and less with appearance and values associated with appearance.

Is a thin body really a "healthy temple," as some of the research suggests?[6] Not necessarily. More stress is placed on a body from constant dieting than from being twenty pounds overweight.[7] We need to be very cautious in interpreting the results of studies that show a significant negative relationship between excess weight and longevity. Often such studies assume a simplistic causality and do not take account of other factors such as class, race, nutritional practices, and activity patterns. Lower-class women, for example, may be heavier *and* die earlier than privileged women. But difference in longevity may be more a consequence of poverty, stress, and/or inadequate nutrition than of weight per se.

Bodies (New York: Prentice Hall Press, 1989); and Eva Aniko Szekely, *Never Too Thin* (Toronto: Women's Press, 1988).

5. Millman, *Such a Pretty Face: Being Fat in America* (New York: W. W. Norton, 1980).

6. See, for example, Theodore VanItallie's "Health Implications of Overweight and Obesity in the United States," *Annals of Internal Medicine* 103, no. 62 (1985): 983-88.

7. Laura Brown, "Women, Weight and Power: Feminist Theoretical and Therapeutic Issues," *Women & Therapy* 4 (Spring 1985): 61-71; Laura Brown, "Lesbians, Weight and Eating: New Analyses and Perspectives," in *Lesbian Psychologies: Explorations and Challenges*, ed. Boston Lesbian Psychologies Collective (Champaign, Ill.: University of Illinois Press, 1987), pp. 294-309; and Nicky Diamond, "Thin Is the Feminist Issue," *Feminist Review* 10 (1985): 45-64.

We are not recommending life-threatening or even health-risking obesity. All individuals should honor their bodies as gifts from God. However, we need to determine the health of that body not solely by its weight but also by its cholesterol level, its blood pressure, its heart rate while resting and while exercising, its lung capacity, its back strength, its flexibility, and so on.

Pathogenic Weight Control Behaviors

That the thinness ideal can be unhealthy for women has been recognized primarily in connection with pathogenic weight control behaviors — PWCB's — such as anorexia nervosa (starving oneself) and bulimia (binging and throwing up).[8] Approximately 1.6 per 100,000 girls and women suffer from these forms of eating disorders. Significantly, 95 percent of the females with bulimia and anorexia are white and live in Western countries. They become unable to maintain "normal" eating habits and have an intense fear of getting fat. Ironically, they have more access to food than many semi-starved people in non-Western countries. Laura Brown has called this state of mind "obesophobia."[9]

Laura Brumberg describes how PWCB's have been attributed to various physiological and (often conflicting) psychological causes: a hormonal imbalance, a fear of womanhood and pregnancy, an exaggerated desire to become a wife or mother, an attempt to gain control over oneself, a reaction to an over-controlling mother and/or other family dynamics.[10] With regard to obesity, the "addiction explanation" has also gained currency.[11] This theory suggests that people become addicted to food, especially in stressful situations. Obesity is consequently seen as a disease that manifests itself as an addiction. Thus groups which use the twelve-step approach, such as Overeaters Anonymous, have sprung up to help people to cope with their compulsive eating.

These theories, either individually or collectively, may explain

8. "Extreme eating disorder" (EED) is the more familiar term, but "pathogenic weight control behavior" (PWCB) is the more technically accurate term and the one that we will use throughout the rest of the chapter.
9. Brown, "Women, Weight and Power" and "Lesbians, Weight and Eating."
10. Brumberg, *Fasting Girls* (Cambridge: Harvard University Press, 1988).
11. Brown, "Women, Weight, and Power."

271

PWCB's partially but not completely. Calling eating an addiction risks giving the impression that it is necessarily destructive, requires abstention, and signals a person out of control. The addiction approach conveys the idea that women should *fear* feeding themselves and feeling well nourished instead of seeing these things as self-affirmations and indications of appropriate self-love.[12]

Most of the other psychological and physiological explanations of PWCB's are inadequate because they ignore the difference in rates of eating disorders across groups marked by different femininities. Laura Brown reports a lower incidence of eating disorders in the lesbian community than in the heterosexual community.[13] More lesbians are also "fat activists," although the relative number of "fat" heterosexuals and lesbians is the same. By pointing this out, we do not mean to imply that "fat oppression" does not exist in the lesbian community; it does, but so does fat activism. Similarly, eating disorders occur less frequently in minority and lower-class communities, although they are on the upswing there as well.[14]

These physiological and psychological theories, based mostly on correlational data, also fail to distinguish cause from effect. For example, does a hormonal imbalance cause the PWCB or does the PWCB cause a hormonal imbalance? In addition, the cultural and gender specificity of PWCB's has not received a great deal of attention. These theories do not explain why, for example, boys who may "fear masculinity" or be at odds with it rarely experience PWCB's. In fact, the chief weakness of these explanations is their inability to locate PWCB's in a gendered, societal context. These theories fail to explain why thinness is the ideal for privileged femininity instead of, say, fatness, muscularity, high fertility, or some other characteristic. They tend to focus the discussion on the individual women who experience PWCB's and obscure the extent to which PWCB's are symbolic of the social construction of privileged femininity. Indeed, Laura Brown contends that *everyone* who watches weight for non-health-related reasons has an eating disorder. For the sake of clarity, we have reserved the abbreviation PWCB for clearly pathogenic means of weight control such as bulimia and anorexia nervosa. And yet, as Brown points out,

12. Brown, "Women, Weight and Power" and "Lesbians, Weight and Eating."
13. Brown, "Women, Weight and Power."
14. Brumberg, *Fasting Girls;* Szekely, *Never Too Thin;* and L. K. George Hsu, "Are the Eating Disorders Becoming More Common among Blacks?" *International Journal of Eating Disorders* 6 (1987): 113-24.

Most women, at some point in their lives, spend significant amounts of time and energy hating themselves for the size and shape of their body, or some body part, and for the way they eat, and the nature and content of their food intake. For some women, the problem assumes a central place in life. These women define themselves as pathological because, and often only because, their eating and/or body size does not measure up to certain standards imposed on women.[15]

A Historical Perspective

To explain the roots of the slimness norm, we need to take into account historical processes. As the following chapter on dress indicates, the norms for body size and shape for privileged femininity have tended to change more than those for hegemonic masculinity. In the early twentieth century, however, certain social practices in middle-to-upper-class white Western society began to emerge that together helped to bring about today's definition of femininity. Roberta Seid has described these in great detail in her book entitled *Never Too Thin*. We will only summarize them here.

Traditionally, female beauty was equated with plumpness because it advertised a husband or father who was a good provider. (This is still the case in many poor societies.) Furthermore, in the nineteenth century the reproductive capability and the sexuality of women were seen as synonymous, so the roundness associated with fertility and childbearing were considered attractive. But in the twentieth century these gradually came to be seen as two separate entities. This separation of sexuality from reproduction was accompanied by a shift in the purpose of marriage from an economic and reproductive arrangement to an arrangement based on economics and sexual and emotional fulfillment. However, what in the previous chapter we called distorted heterosexuality remained a strong factor despite these changes, with the result that being attractive to men *increased* in relative importance for women. It was no longer enough for a woman to be a hard worker and to be fertile. She had to make her husband happy in a myriad of sexual and emotional ways.

In addition, whereas formerly a robust female body signaled a prosperous husband or father, now women's body size was used to signal

15. Brown, "Women, Weight and Power," pp. 62-63.

273

class differences. To distance themselves from the lower classes, middle- and upper-class women became thinner. (Hence Lady Astor's famous assertion "One can never be too rich or too thin.") This emphasis on thinness was enhanced by supposedly scientific discoveries of a link between obesity and decreased life-span, as well as by the increasing focus on physical fitness.

This emphasis on physical fitness, which escalated greatly in the 1970s, affected primarily middle- and upper-class adults.[16] Great emphasis was placed on the fact that the average woman had 37 percent body fat, and that a more desirable percentage would be about 25 percent. The activities recommended to achieve satisfactory fitness levels were jogging, cycling, and swimming. These activities were not as gender-stereotyped as many others, and they were accessible to many in the middle class. Thus few physically able women had an excuse for not looking fit. Aerobic dancing was soon added to the list and was geared especially toward women. Initially aerobics classes provided a safe, communal climate for exercising — one in which the body-as-object was de-emphasized. Women could disguise their bodies in sweats (impossible in swimming), get away from the judgmental eyes of males (difficult to do while jogging or cycling), and enjoy the camaraderie of other women.

Aerobics classes accomplished these goals to a certain extent, but their co-optation by the cosmetic and fashion industries soon transformed many classes into forums for females to work on heterosexual appeal.[17] Instructors were often hired more for their appearance and style than for their competence, and many classes seemed more like soft-porn sessions rather than exercise. This emphasis on heterosexual appeal was aided by such actors as Jane Fonda and Victoria Principal: by marketing videos and programs that equated fitness with beauty, they helped to distort heterosexuality.

One other social factor that deeply affected the current definition of the ideal physical type for privileged femininity was the second wave of feminism which began in the 1960s. With this wave came a critique of women as sex objects.[18] This critique pointed out a connection be-

16. Helen Lenskyj, *Out of Bounds: Women, Sport and Sexuality* (Toronto: Women's Press, 1986).

17. Ibid. This is another example of the process by which challenges to the status quo get muted or co-opted.

18. Wendy Chapkis, *Beauty Secrets: Women and the Politics of Appearance* (Boston: South End Press, 1986).

tween the emphasis on appearance and the use of beauty aids (e.g., makeup, girdles, etc.) on the one hand, and distorted heterosexuality on the other. Predictably, the cosmetic companies co-opted this feminist critique by beginning to market the "natural" look. The irony of women buying cosmetics to achieve the "natural" look should be obvious.

All of the foregoing dynamics have combined to produce a thematically consistent definition of privileged femininity for today. Its similarity to definitions of other historical periods lies in the fact that femininity is still primarily defined in terms of appearance that is attractive to men. The difference is in the nature of that desirable appearance. Today, women define themselves less in terms of how they dress and more in terms of body shape and condition. The next chapter on the history of dress shows the detailed progress of this definitional change.

These social changes have helped to reconstruct the gendered female body, especially for women who are white, Western, and privileged. If distorted heterosexuality is a prevalent part of the gender order, then women must continually try to make themselves attractive to men by whatever standards are current. This is not to suggest that women are always passive victims in these practices. In a climate of distorted heterosexuality, as Sue Wise and Liz Stanley have argued, women may appear to be conforming meekly to the current standard of privileged femininity while in fact they are actively using men's obsession with "female beauty" as a means of survival or even as a way to contest male dominance. Women know that if they conform to the current standards of privileged femininity, they may have an easier time of it than if they openly challenge those standards. Women can also use to advantage their knowledge that men's sexual orientation is suspect if they do not respond to beautiful women. (Thus by endorsing the demands of distorted heterosexuality, men are hoist by their own petard.) Nevertheless, life would be much easier for women if they did not have to cope with the impact of distorted heterosexuality in the first place.[19]

Moreover, if part of being attractive is being white, women of color will have a difficult time achieving the status of privileged femininity and may not even wish to enter the "contest."[20] Women who are

19. Wise and Stanley, *Georgie Porgie: Sexual Harassment in Everyday Life* (London: Pandora Press, 1987).
20. Chapkis, *Beauty Secrets*.

poor will also be unable to join the elite ranks of privileged femininity because of lack of time, money, and/or other resources.[21] They may simply accept their bodies, or alternately hate them. But for those who endorse the tenets of privileged femininity and/or aspire to join its ranks, being thin is a major part of a woman's identity, of being attractive to men.[22] We therefore need to ask what meaning slimness gives to this femininity.

Layers of Meaning of Slimness

According to Laura Brown, slimness has layers of meaning, which make it, rather than heaviness, a desirable characteristic of privileged femininity.[23] It will be helpful to briefly explore some of these thematic layers.

One such theme is that for a woman to be judged attractive and thus feminine, she has to have a small body that minimizes what are stereotypically regarded as her secondary sex characteristics — breasts, fat layers, hips, rounded belly and thighs. This is not to imply that a concept such as "female secondary sex characteristics" is biologically clear, or that such characteristics differentiate all females from all males. There are some men who have larger breasts, bellies, and hips than some women. There are also some boys who have more subcutaneous body fat than some girls. The main point we are trying to make is that women are urged to be as small as possible. Those who have large hips, breasts, and/or bellies and work in a male-dominated setting may feel pressure to reduce the very characteristics that most visibly mark them as female. Why might such a minimalist female body be considered beautiful? Part of the answer lies in social changes that led to a shift in the twentieth-century demographics of the work force.

In the nineteenth century, many lower-class women worked outside the home, primarily in female-dominated occupations and jobs. By the middle of the twentieth century, however, more middle-class white women began to work for pay, sometimes moving into male-dominated occupations. In these occupations, women have to appear competent,

21. Rita Freedman, *Beauty Bound* (Lexington, Mass.: D. C. Heath, 1986).
22. Szekely, *Never Too Thin,* and Seid, *Never Too Thin.*
23. Brown, "Women, Weight and Power" and "Lesbians, Weight and Eating."

often in male-defined ways — that is, they have to appear as similar to males as possible. Rosabeth Kanter, for example, has shown that those who are hired or promoted tend to be socially similar to those in power. "Keeping management positions in the hands of people of one's kind provides reinforcement for the belief that people like oneself actually deserve to have such authority," she points out. "So management positions . . . become easily closed to people who are different."[24] If this is an accurate portrayal of the male-dominated workplace, then when women's physical dissimilarities from men are very obvious, there will be direct or subtle pressure for women to minimize them as much as possible.[25] A woman who has big breasts, big hips, and/or is large may not be taken seriously. It is no wonder then that adolescent girls are at risk for PWCB's. Carol Gilligan and her associates found that the high-school girls they studied were ambivalent about maturational changes in their bodies. These girls realized that getting larger and developing more body fat — changes that their bodies were undergoing — were producing physical traits not highly valued in society. This contradiction between wanting to be "womanly" and wanting to be accepted led some of the girls to develop PWCB's.[26] Yet we surmise that girls who experience minimal physical changes are also ambivalent about their bodies, fearing they will not be seen as "adult" enough.

The "smallness" theme is reinforced through male-female relationship norms that characterize gender relations. Most women are smaller than their male partners. Although this may seem to be natural because the average woman *is* smaller than the average man, it overlooks the fact that the normal distribution for women's height has considerable overlap with that of men. Some women are taller than some men or as tall as others. Nevertheless, we continue to reinforce the myth that all males should be taller than all females. Playing out that myth requires tricks and deceptions. A woman who is the same height as her male partner will often wear low-heeled shoes or flats so that the man does not seem shorter. (Princess Diana is a very visible example.) Conversely, a man

24. Kanter, *Men and Women of the Corporation* (New York: Basic Books, 1977), p. 63.

25. Brumberg, *Fasting Girls.*

26. Catherine Steiner-Adair, "The Body Politic: Normal Female Adolescent Development and the Development of Eating Disorders," in *Making Connections: The Relational Worlds of Adolescent Girls at Emma Willard School,* ed. Carol Gilligan, Nona P. Lyons, and Trudy J. Hanmer (Troy, N.Y.: Emma Willard School, 1989), pp. 162-82.

may wear lifts in his shoes in order to appear taller. A perusal of many a pictorial church directory will show women in poses that make them appear shorter than their husbands. A woman who is taller than her husband told one of us that it is always a struggle to get photographers to understand that she will not stand a step lower or sit so that she will appear smaller than her husband. Such smallness supposedly makes her look more feminine, but she insists on challenging this particular part of the recipe for privileged femininity.

A minimalist body may bring a woman closer to the physical ideal of privileged femininity, but it also has drawbacks compared with a more substantial body. It takes up less space, is less visible, and more closely approximates the stereotypical body of a child than of a woman. Since children are not adults and hence do not always have to be taken seriously, the same can be presumed true for women with "child-like" bodies. The emphasis on youth thus intersects with desirable body shape to yield what is at best a mixed blessing.

An example from the sports world also illustrates the point. When women began to participate in sports in greater numbers, they were entering a male domain. Women's gymnastics in particular increased in popularity. However, over the past fifteen years the age and size of athletes in this sport has decreased to such an extent that girls rather than women are now winning gold medals. The participation and achievements of these athletes deserve respect, but at the same time their smallness and youth endorse privileged femininity and reduce any serious female challenge to the physical aspect of male dominance. Is it a coincidence that in college women athletes have a higher rate of PWCB's than do non-athletes?[27] Are such athletes at double risk by being women in a male-dominated culture and women in a male-dominated sports subculture?

A second theme related to slimness is the idea that women should be minimally muscular. They may have muscles, but these should not be too clearly defined. This is related to the assumption that women should be small and weak. It is interesting to note that the demand for sex-testing of women athletes in international events like the Olympics began only after big, strong women started to participate and win. After sex-testing programs had been established and big, strong women who had been "verified" as women continued to win, the validity of test

27. Lionel Rosen et al., "Pathogenic Weight Control Behavior in Female Athletes," *The Physician and Sportsmedicine* 14 (January 1986): 79-83, 86.

results was often questioned or, alternately, the women's muscularity was often attributed to steroid use. This example underscores our point that well-defined muscularity is currently not associated with privileged femininity. Another example is the controversy surrounding the ideal look for women bodybuilders, which focuses on strength and size.[28] Should these women be judged on their muscularity or their femininity (i.e., their weakness and smallness)? Currently they seem to be judged on an odd combination of the two.

Similarly, it would seem to be no coincidence that the first women's sports to receive widespread societal approval were gymnastics, figure skating, and tennis, sports in which the musculature of the athletes is usually not as clearly defined as it is in team sports or track and field. Diving and marathon running are two sports in which the significance of muscularity is currently downplayed. Sports commentators rarely mention the muscular strength that divers or marathoners need in order to compete successfully in their events, and this by implication makes them "suitable" for women.

Can women be muscular and still look feminine or attractive to hegemonic, white, middle-class men? The idea of muscular minimalism is related to the theme that women should be small. Thus a woman who is muscular can still be seen as feminine if she remains relatively "small." This emphasis on minimal muscularity combines with distorted heterosexuality to co-opt and sexualize even the physical activity of women who are nonathletes.[29] What we said earlier about aerobic dancing is a case in point.

According to Laura Brown, "to be beautiful and valuable, a woman must be physically weak,"[30] a cultural assumption that allows men to be seen as dominant. The standard is often enforced by labeling women who have clearly defined muscles, especially in the upper body, as "masculine," "unfeminine," or "dykes." It is interesting to note that when men are asked to evaluate other males, they indicate that they prize a strong upper body most.[31] Surely, then, it is not a coincidence that women with strong upper bodies are labeled as deviant.

28. Lenskyj, *Out of Bounds.*
29. Ibid.
30. Brown, "Women, Weight and Power," p. 64.
31. Marc Mishkind et al., "The Embodiment of Masculinity: Cultural, Psychological and Behavioral Dimensions," in *Changing Men: New Directions in Research on Men and Masculinity,* ed. Michael S. Kimmel (Newbury Park, Calif.: Sage Publications, 1987), pp. 37-52.

As we point out in the subsequent chapter on dress, the "beautiful and valuable equals physically weak" equation is reinforced through fashion. High-heeled shoes, narrow and/or short skirts, tight tops, and certain fashion accessories (such as girdles) restrain movement and thus limit the amount of muscle development that can occur in daily activities. Moreover, when women are weak, they are more vulnerable to sexual assault, which is also an act of male dominance.[32] A woman who walks in a nonassertive manner, who is clothed in restrictive attire, and who is small is a vulnerable target for assault. Even in a date-rape situation, a physically weaker woman has fewer chances of escaping than one who is physically strong.[33] Thus the promotion of the "small equals attractive, equals the ideal of privileged femininity" equation helps to reinforce hegemonic masculinity by keeping women physically subordinate to men.

The relationship between eating and body size also gives meaning to thinness. The women who are valued and considered "feminine" are those who nurture others, especially children and men. We should note at this juncture that the nurturing of others is truly a Christian calling and one that women have attempted to fulfill for many years. The nourishing of others through the preparation of meals is part of this nurturing, as the long tradition of Christian hospitality confirms:[34]

> Food . . . does what theology talks about. It nurtures and nourishes, it occasions celebration, and it mirrors how the human community divides up its resources. . . . Women give religious meaning to food. Sweet cakes, unleavened bread, and bitter herbs have ritual significance in various traditions.[35]

So being a source of nurturance is in itself a praiseworthy ideal; however, in its present form it implies that women should not employ those skills to nurture themselves and that men are largely exempt, in

32. Susan Griffin, "Rape: The All-American Crime," *Ramparts* 10 (September 1971): 26-35.

33. Pauline B. Bart and Patricia H. O'Brien, *Stopping Rape: Successful Survival Strategies* (New York: Pergamon Press, 1985).

34. The meanings given to food are also culturally determined. See, for example, a description of the significance of food to medieval women by Caroline Walker Bynum in *Holy Feast and Holy Fast: The Religious Significance of Food to Medieval Women* (Berkeley: University of California Press, 1987).

35. Mary Hunt, "Food, Glorious Food," *Waterwheel* 2, no. 3 (1989): 1.

practice if not in theory, from the call to nurture women and children in a more direct and comprehensive (as opposed to a merely income-earning) way.

Laura Brumberg points out that how, what, and how much women eat is often assumed to reveal something about their character.[36] Reflect on these phrases: "man-sized" portions, "hero" sandwiches, "manhandler" dinners.[37] What we associate with those phrases is quite different from the image implied by "ladies' portions." There is a historical basis for this kind of misguided labeling. Traditionally when women are in charge of cooking and resources are scarce, the best and largest portions go to the men. After that, the children must be well fed (particularly the male children), and only then is it women's turn to eat. Women are supposed to practice self-denial and not need much food because they supposedly do not work as hard as men. Yet women do two-thirds of the world's work and often have two jobs, one (usually inadequately) paid, the other unpaid. Women *do* work hard.[38]

Because self-feeding is a basic form of self-nurturing, it may seem to violate the principle of sacrificial love and other-nurturance that women have been taught. As a result, women often feel guilty when they enjoy food.[39] They may see self-feeding as inappropriate, betrayed and punished by a "fat" body. They may begin to hate and fear fat, and thus themselves. Maintaining this level of guilt reinforces a dislike for the body that prevents one from being empowered by it. If you are dissatisfied with your body, how can you rejoice in it and its capabilities?

Again, what most women support as the physical ideal of privileged femininity is not what they actually are, although they use privileged females as their reference group. We may think of Miss Universe as being beautiful, but our bodies do not match hers. Consequently, we are often ashamed of our bodies and judgmental about the bodies of other women. Many women punish themselves for violating the "no self-nurturance" rule by fasting, vomiting, counting calories, and so on. This leads to a very contradictory relationship with food, a contradiction that can easily lead

36. Brumberg, *Fasting Girls.*

37. Carol J. Adams, *The Sexual Politics of Meat: A Feminist-Vegetarian Critical Theory* (New York: Continuum Publishing Co., 1990).

38. Ibid. See also Gloria Steinem's *Outrageous Acts and Everyday Rebellions* (New York: Holt, Rinehart, & Winston, 1983).

39. Brown, "Women, Weight and Power"; and Nickie Charles and Marion Kerr, "Food for Feminist Thought," *Sociological Review* 34 (August 1986): 537-72.

to an obsession about eating and to PWCB's.[40] On the one hand, it would seem that Christian women might be more at risk for this guilt and obsession because they, more than secular women, tend to hear and heed the call to self-sacrifice. On the other hand, shouldn't Christian women be *less* at risk for developing obsessions with physical appearances because they know that God is concerned with the heart and the way of life that proceeds from the heart? It would be interesting to gather some statistics on the subject. Little research has been done in the Christian community to discern the extent to which slimness is an ideal in that context.[41]

In sum, the preoccupation of many American women with food and weight may be part of a struggle with cultural rules about power, size, and self-nurturing. This struggle, which leads in its extreme forms to PWCB's, will not subside until we begin to contest the nature of gender relations. And privileged femininity cannot be changed in isolation from hegemonic masculinity.

Challenging the Norm: Body Politics

There are various ways in which women may challenge the dominant norm of slimness. For example, big and heavy women violate all of the "rules" of attractiveness previously described. They are very visible, take up significant space, and have strong muscles as a result of moving their weight around. Football coaches recruit players such as William "The Refrigerator" Perry (of the Chicago Bears) in part because their bigness makes them strong and intimidating. But stereotypically these are positive attributes for men, not for women. The size of heavy women makes it seem as if they have engaged in self-nurturance (though research shows that heavy women on the average eat the same amount as other women), which is a clear and visible violation of the "you shall nurture only others" rule.[42] Strong and big women athletes, including women bodybuilders, may also be resisting privileged femininity in a visible manner. Their size and strength are intimidating and violate the themes of minimal size and weakness of privileged femininity. Thus heavy

40. Ibid.
41. But for an astute pastoral analysis of this problem, see Mary Ellen Ashcroft's *Temptations Women Face: Honest Talk about Jealousy, Anger, Sex, Money, Food, Pride* (Downers Grove, Ill.: InterVarsity Press, 1991).
42. Charles and Kerr, "Food for Feminist Thought."

women and big, strong women athletes resist and contest visible meanings of privileged femininity.[43]

Individual women can begin to challenge definitions of privileged femininity by contesting meanings attached to body size and creating others that are more empowering. One of the ways they can do this is by being sensitive to the meanings they give to weight loss. Think about the meaning of the remarks we make after someone has lost weight. "Oh, you've lost weight! You look *so* good!" Doesn't this statement convey that she looked terrible before the weight loss, and that if she regains this weight, she will not look "good" anymore? This statement also seems to imply that "looking good" means "looking slim." Why do we rarely compliment women on looking strong?

We also need to be sensitive to "body politics" and be ready to challenge norms that devalue women and their experiences.[44] Men's scars from violent activities (such as war) are often seen as badges of courage. Let's then value equally women's stretch marks and their scars from Caesarian sections. Not only are they badges of courage, but they also (unlike war scars) reflect nonviolent, procreative action. Women can also learn to celebrate the diversity of their bodies. They can learn to appreciate the beauteous curve of a non-flat stomach, or the pleasing definition of muscular arms and legs. They can aim for bodily strength and health without trying to attain the ideal of privileged femininity; they can see beauty in their diversity.

Another way we can contest meanings about privileged femininity is by encouraging girls and women to be physically active in vigorous sports. Women can be empowered if they participate in these sports because of the good feelings they generate (rather than because of their calorie-burning potential). As one woman who became physically active put it,

> I had the sense of well-being which comes from regular, strenuous exercise. I developed an agility in my movements and a resistance to fatigue and stress.... I began to feel like a person to be reckoned with, strong and competent. I began to feel powerful, emotionally and physically.[45]

43. If coaches or judges in bodybuilding contests accept such meanings, they may stress dieting and reducing body fat, possibly increasing the occurrence of PWCB's among their athletes.
44. Steinem, *Outrageous Acts and Everyday Rebellions.*
45. Linda Pearson, cited by Helen Lenskyj in *Out of Bounds,* p. 119.

This is the same kind of feeling that males get from sport, as we will see later. But for males it is also part of a lifelong process of learning and showing dominance. Thus participation by women in an activity that helps to construct male hegemony can also contest or challenge that hegemony.

Such newly gained strength and self-confidence may also be assets in resisting physical domination by males and in avoiding or getting out of sexual assault situations. Pauline Bart and Patricia O'Brien found that women who had a history of serious participation in team sports were more likely to be able to fight their way out of sexual assault situations than women with little athletic history.[46] Moreover, team-sport experiences often help women to bond emotionally. Experiencing such bonding in what has traditionally been a male-defined activity can strengthen women, perhaps more so than bonding in activities where women already predominate.[47]

Overall, then, while men's participation in team sports (as spectators or athletes) serves visibly to *maintain* hegemonic masculinity, women's participation in such sports can *contest* that hegemonic masculinity as well as contesting the meanings of privileged femininity.[48]

With respect to the meanings given to food and femininity, Laura Brown suggests that women need to develop "body wisdom," using their own standards of comfort and pleasure rather than those of hegemonic masculinity. They need to base their satisfaction with their physical selves on their energy level, health, and mobility, and on the pleasure they take in what they eat:

> A woman who self-nurtures with food, and who does so without guilt and self-hate, has broken the most basic of messages given women against feeling good and worthy of love and sustenance. A woman

46. Bart and O'Brien, *Stopping Rape.*
47. Roberta Bennet et al., "Changing the Rules of the Game: Reflections Toward a Feminist Analysis of Sport," *Women's Studies International Forum* 10, no. 4 (1987): 369-80.
48. Both Lynda Birke and Gail Vines in "A Sporting Chance: The Anatomy of Destiny?" (*Women's Studies International Forum* 10, no. 4 [1987]: 337-48) and Ruth Hubbard in her book entitled *The Politics of Women's Biology* (New Brunswick, N.J.: Rutgers University Press, 1990) have argued that personal biology and environment are constantly interacting. When women participate in strenuous sports, they may transform their personal biology. Many athletes have fewer periods and problems with premenstrual syndrome, tend to have an easier time in childbirth, and seem to be less at risk for breast and uterine cancer and diabetes.

who spends time and energy on her own pleasure by identifying the flavors that appeal to her, and who does not fall into the classic woman's role of cooking to please only the palates of those whose nurturance she is mandated to perform, but rather prepares foods that are nourishing to her own body and spirit has engaged in an act of quiet revolution. She has made her own nurturing needs equal to those of others at an extremely basic level.[49]

Women need to see that the emphasis on slimness is one "wire" in the cage of oppression that interacts with others to keep the cage closed. However, as we have already acknowledged, privileged femininity cannot be changed in isolation from hegemonic masculinity, because hegemonic masculinity defines privileged femininity. With this relational dynamic in mind, let us now examine how the *male* body becomes a site for the construction of hegemonic masculinity.

Constructing the Male Body: Big, Strong, and Aggressive

The "Ideal" Male Body

According to Robert Connell, the physical sense of maleness is not a simple thing.[50] It involves a man's size and shape, his habits of posture and movement, his possession of certain skills and lack of others. It also involves a man's image of his body, the way he presents it to other people, the ways they respond to it, and the way it functions in work and sexual relations. David Whitson points out that a boy does not automatically grow into manhood but has to learn to be a male — that is, "to project a physical presence that speaks of latent power . . . [to] develop body appearance and language that are suggestive of force and skill . . . to experience bodies and therefore themselves, in forceful, space-occupying, even dominating ways."[51]

49. Brown, "Women, Weight and Power," p. 65.
50. Connell, *Gender and Power: Society, the Person and Sexual Politics* (Stanford: Stanford University Press, 1987).
51. David Whitson, "Sport in the Social Construction of Masculinity," in *Sport, Men, and the Gender Order: Critical Feminist Perspectives,* ed. Michael A. Messner and Donald Sabo (Champaign, Ill.: Human Kinetics Books, 1990), p. 23. See also David

What does the ideal male look like? How can he use his body to prove that he endorses hegemonic masculinity? Researchers have found that most boys and men from five years old through college age want the "muscle man" look: a wide, well-developed chest, strong arms and shoulder muscles, and a tapering to a narrow waist.[52] A side note: it may not be a coincidence that the gender differences in upper-body strength are much-heralded, and that we rarely hear about the gender similarities in lower-body strength. It is through upper-body strength that males can differentiate themselves from females most easily and visibly.

Listen to what young men say about their bodies and the meaning they give to their bodies:

"The perfect man always has a good build, so it makes you feel more masculine. . . . And you know, it's always males that are supposed to be stronger."

"If I was walking in the mall in the summertime, wearing shorts and a T-shirt, I would feel most masculine by the fact that I could stand next to anybody, and I would probably dwarf them."

"It [a big body] makes you more masculine because people are intimidated by you and I guess it's kind of neat. . . . It makes you feel good. . . . Maybe they think I can kick their ass."

"I grew up on the West Coast . . . and who had the best-looking chicks? It was always the guy with the best build."[53]

As these comments indicate, the most desirable male body is big and strong-looking. The question we should ask is, Why are bigness and strength such key components of this desirable body? Why not shortness or a smaller body build? According to Robert Connell, bigness and body strength are "one of the main ways in which the power of men becomes 'naturalized,' i.e. seen as part of the order of nature. It is very important

---

Gilmore's *Manhood in the Making: Cultural Concepts of Masculinity* (New Haven: Yale University Press, 1990).

52. Mishkind et al., "The Embodiment of Masculinity."

53. Quoted by Tracy Olrich in "The Relationship of Male Identity, Mesomorphic Image and Anabolic Steroids in Body Building," unpublished thesis, Department of Physical Education and Exercise Science, Michigan State University, East Lansing, Mich., 1991, pp. 75-76.

in allowing belief in the superiority of men, and the oppressive practices that flow from it, to be sustained by men who in other respects have very little power."[54] Boys and men may also have learned that having a strong body provides security. Boys often settle disagreements with each other by means of physical aggression and are given tacit permission to do so. Michael Messner concludes that muscularity in men is seen as a sign of power over women and other men who exhibit different masculinities, in part because strength is linked with skill, aggression, and violence — that is, with hegemonic masculinity.[55] Nevertheless, for young boys and men, just having a strong body is often not sufficient to claim masculinity. Male ballet dancers also have strong bodies, yet people are not quick to endorse their masculinity. Men must also engage in appropriate activities to achieve this coveted label. These activities must be physically demanding (in order to support the idea of male physical superiority), must have clearly marked outcomes and goals, and must be competitive.[56]

A Historical Perspective

If this is so, then it is no wonder that our clearest images of hegemonic masculinity in American culture come from competitive sports, especially those that involve physical contact. How did this come about? Due to recent societal changes, many of the ways in which men traditionally affirmed hegemonic masculinity through physicality have become muted. The image of "man the warrior" used to be the chief feature of hegemonic masculinity,[57] although "man the hunter" and "man the farmer" were also prominent themes. These contributed to the image of men as being physically strong and active, an image that is now embodied primarily by males in sports, especially sports in which there is a great deal of physical contact.

This shift in masculine images became visible in the mid-to-late nineteenth century, when concern arose in North America about the

54. Connell, *Gender and Power,* p. 85.

55. Messner, "Sport and Male Domination: The Female Athlete as Contested Ideological Terrain," *Sociology of Sport Journal* 5 (1988): 197-211.

56. Donald Sabo, "Sport, Patriarchy and Male Identity: New Questions about Men and Sport," *Arena Review* 9 (1985): 1-30.

57. Brittan, *Masculinity and Power.*

feminization of society. In other words, the white, middle-class version of masculinity, with its supposed monopoly on strength and activity, was being challenged. This challenge came from several sources: the emerging women's movement of the late nineteenth century, the increase in the number of nonwhite immigrants, the decrease in male self-employment, and the increased routinization and mechanization of labor. The predominant response of white males to these forces consisted of "a masculinist effort to stem feminization."[58]

There was a fear that boys and men would become too soft, too much like women — that is, that they would no longer exhibit their difference from (i.e., superiority to) women. As a result, sport emerged as a context in which boys could be made into men and exhibit their manliness, in which they could show that they were different from women and girls. Since then sport has remained one of the primary ways for American men to counter the "feminization" of society.[59] It was thought that if boys didn't participate in sports, they "became womanlike, delicate and degenerate."[60] Of special concern was the perceived feminization of education. The supposition was that in school American boys fell too much under the influence of women and qualities traditionally ascribed to females such as compassion and expressiveness.[61] It is not surprising, given these historical conditions, to find that the United States and Canada are the only countries in the world where extensive sport programs are part of formal education and male athletes outnumber females two to one. The existence of such programs was and still is intended to counter the feminization of teaching and make men out of boys.

In addition, membership in many nineteenth-century Protestant churches consisted primarily of girls and women.[62] Here too the concern

58. Michael Kimmel, "Baseball and the Reconstitution of American Masculinity, 1880-1920," in *Sport, Men, and the Gender Order*, p. 59.

59. Eric Dunning, "Sport as a Male Preserve: Notes on the Social Sources of Masculine Identity and Its Transformations," in *Quest for Excitement: Sport and Leisure in the Civilizing Process*, ed. Norbert Elias and Eric Dunning (New York: Basil Blackwell, 1986), pp. 267-83.

60. Todd Crosset, "Masculinity, Sexuality and the Development of Early Modern Sport," in *Sport, Men, and the Gender Order*, p. 53.

61. Michael Kimmel, "Men's Responses to Feminism at the Turn of the Century," *Gender and Society* 1, no. 3 (1987): 261-83.

62. Stanley D. Eitzen and George H. Sage, *Sociology of North American Sport*, 4th ed. (Dubuque, Iowa: Wm. C. Brown Publishers, 1989).

arose that boys and men, and especially Christian boys and men, would become too womanly, since many of the qualities associated with being Christian were those traditionally associated with being female. Consequently, concerned church leaders alert to wider social norms began to "shift their emphasis from what they saw as 'feminized' values such as meekness, humility and submissiveness to a new set of 'manly values.'"[63] The concept of "muscular Christianity" provided the ideological link among sport, religion, and the endorsement of hegemonic masculinity.[64]

Muscular Christianity assumes that a person's physical shape has religious significance because "the body is the temple of God." Physical prowess is equated with moral strength,[65] and a strong and healthy-looking body is often taken as a sign that a person exercises self-control and discipline. As we embody gender, so we are also assumed to embody our faith. At the turn of the century this concept was used to promote sports as a means of making religion more attractive to males.[66] According to Michael Kimmel, "the image of Jesus was transformed from a beatific, delicate soft-spoken champion of the poor into a muscle-bound he-man whose message encourages the strong to dominate the weak."[67] Many church leaders began to incorporate sports programs into church activities in order to attract males and especially teenagers. But by doing this without constructing different practices in and meanings for sport, church leaders implicitly endorsed secular hegemonic masculinity. Consequently, athletic participation and prowess became too strongly equated with manliness, even in many Christian communities.

During this historical period the lines between women's and men's activities also began to blur, thus eliminating visible evidence of social differences between men and women. This was problematic because the dominant form of masculinity required men to have power and privilege based on their difference from women, and thus men needed ways to

63. Jay J. Coakley, *Sport in Society,* 4th ed. (St. Louis: Times Mirror/Mosby College Publishing, 1990), p. 357.

64. For an in-depth examination of the historical combination of sport and religion, see the *British Journal of Sports History,* Special Issue 1, no. 2 (1984).

65. Whitson, "Sport in the Social Construction of Masculinity."

66. Coakley, *Sport in Society;* and Eitzen and Sage, *Sociology of North American Sport.*

67. Kimmel, "Baseball and the Reconstitution of American Masculinity, 1880-1920," p. 59.

"prove" such difference (and superiority). Sport provided a natural way to shore up this base of difference and power. Since the strongest man is usually stronger than the strongest woman, sport seems to offer visible "proof" of the biological superiority of males and to give credence to a biologically ordained masculinity.[68] This is in fact the very function that competitive sport has assumed. It provides men with a visible way of validating their difference from women, a difference that is often translated into natural superiority. Today sports such as men's football and basketball that draw countless spectators are used to give visible proof of the "natural" superiority of men.

"Naturalizing" Superiority

According to Michael Messner, "The rise of football as America's number one game is likely the result of the comforting clarity it provides between the traditional male power, strength, and violence and the contemporary fears of social feminization."[69] The meaning that we give to this apparent male physical superiority may seem to be quite natural or even inevitable. However, that it is in many ways a social construct becomes evident when we look at the dynamics of race in sport. On the average, black men outperform white men in football and basketball. However, that physical superiority is rarely seen to be a reason for black dominance in society in general. Instead, whites often erroneously construe that superiority to mean that blacks are more physical than intellectual, and that they are therefore unable to function well in business and leadership positions. It could be argued that the same reasoning should be applied to all men in sports, that their physical "superiority" over women should be interpreted to mean that men are more brawn than brain and therefore should not hold business or leadership positions. Obviously that has not happened. We have constructed other meanings for this male superiority — meanings that support male dominance within a white-dominated North American society.

---

68. Birke and Vines, "A Sporting Chance." The unstated hegemonic process often prevents us from asking, Why is strength better than shortness or slightness in body build?

69. Messner, "The Life of Man's Seasons: Male Identity in the Life Course of a Jock," in *Changing Men*, p. 54.

Consequently, athletics has become the activity of choice for proclaiming one's endorsement of hegemonic masculinity, especially for boys and young men. It is no wonder that Michael Jordan of the Chicago Bulls is one of the biggest heroes of teenage boys in grades eight through twelve, and that 6.6 percent of twelfth-grade males use steroids to add bulk to their bodies.[70]

The congruence between being big and strong and being hegemonically male in the U.S. also explains why "Just say no" campaigns against steroid use or random testing for such use may have little effect on boys and young men. They see the advantages and privileges that are associated with this form of masculinity, and they are willing to take health risks to achieve them. The earlier-quoted comments from young men about their bodies showed that they have a very clear grasp of these advantages. They admire media strong men like Hulk Hogan, Rambo, and Conan the Barbarian, all of whom use their size to dominate and to be violent. As long as bigness translates into male superiority, drug use is likely to continue. Saying "no" to drugs may be construed as saying "no" to hegemonic masculinity, a difficult thing for young boys to do without social support. To combat such drug use, we have to transform our current definition of hegemonic masculinity.

Although men's sport is certainly marked by race and class lines, it can still serve as a context for male bonding because of its gender-exclusive nature. In sport boys and men not only train and compete together but also travel, eat, and engage in recreation together.[71] When women are present, they are in supporting roles — as mothers who wash uniforms, as waitresses, as cheerleaders and fans. Men not only compete together as athletes but also go to all sorts of athletic competitions together. In addition, they watch televised sports events together in bars and at home. Watching football together on Thanksgiving, New Year's Day, and Super Bowl weekend has almost become a male tradition.[72]

70. Anastasia Toufexis, "Shortcut to the Rambo Look," *Time*, 30 January 1989, p. 78; and K. A. Fackelmann, "Male Teenagers at Risk of Steroid Abuse," *Science News*, 17 December 1989, p. 391.

71. Donald Sabo and Joe Panepinto, "Football Ritual and the Social Reproduction of Masculinity," in *Sport, Men, and the Gender Order*, pp. 115-26.

72. In his article entitled "The Men's Cultural Centre: Sports and the Dynamic of Women's Oppression/Men's Repression" (in *Sport, Men, and the Gender Order*, pp. 31-44), Bruce Kidd calls the stadiums built for men's sports "men's cultural centres." He decries the fact that while women's crisis centers are under-

The exclusion of women as active participants from these events marks sport as a male activity, and therefore — since it has "masculine" sanction — enables males to show a certain degree of emotion and affection for each other. Whether playing sports or watching them, men can touch each other in ways that might be considered inappropriate outside of the athletic arena — indeed, that might quickly be labeled as homosexual. Thus sport provides a safe context in which males can show a certain amount of physical and emotional expressiveness.[73]

The majority of adult men are not college athletes or members of professional sports teams, but there are ways they can show their approval of hegemonic masculinity and their own embodiment of it. First, they can point to their own past athletic success in high school or college, or show an avid interest in current sport events, or coach a Little League team; if they're wealthy, they can even buy an athletic team. Second, in their daily work they can portray and value the same qualities that are associated with athletically nuanced masculinity: toughness, aggressiveness, and competitiveness. Their goal should be to win maximum profits, increased power, and/or promotion. Donald Trump is — or rather, was — an example of such a hegemonic male. As with sport, when we applaud such economic success, we are strengthening hegemonic masculinity.[74] However, even men such as Donald Trump do not do their work in public settings with 100,000 people present and millions more watching on television. This occurs *only* in sport. Thus in our culture it is in the sports arena where most of the collective and public affirmation of hegemonic masculinity occurs.

Sport plays a large part in validating males not only in the secular world but in the Christian subculture as well. To varying degrees Chris-

funded, prime land, money, and other resources are used for stadiums built by men, primarily for male profit and enjoyment. By contrast, if we built centers where, say, only Anglo-Americans could play, there would be much protest.

73. The nature of this expressiveness is, however, limited in scope. Athletes may hug each other and pat each other on the buttocks, but they may not admit to fear or to compassion for opponents, nor may they open up very much to each other emotionally.

74. Obviously class and gender relations intersect. In her article entitled "Sport and Social Change: Socialist Feminist Theory" (*Journal of Physical Education Recreation and Dance* 59 [1988]: 50-53), Cathy Bray has argued that the structures within which sport and business operate are created by capitalism, while the preparation and selection of people for those structures is a function of gender relations as well as of race/ethnic relations.

tian groups have used men's football and/or basketball to gain visibility. Think, for example, of the sports programs of Oral Roberts University, Calvin College, Texas Christian University, Southern Methodist University, Notre Dame University, and Georgetown University. Thanks to the emphasis that the media places on sports, we probably know more about the sports programs of these institutions than we do about their academic programs. Sport has also been used as a means to recruit Christian converts. In programs such as Athletes in Action and the Fellowship of Christian Athletes, Christian athletes witness to their beliefs through their actions on the court and their testimonies off the court. The primary audience targeted for this approach has been young men.[75]

Since the male near-monopoly on sports acts as a central mechanism for maintaining hegemonic masculinity in wider North American society,[76] there is no reason to believe that sport does not function similarly in the Christian colleges and universities just mentioned, as well as in Christian high schools. If sport in these institutions does *not* serve to reinforce the current nature of the gender relations system, then why do women's teams at these institutions receive considerably less attention than the teams of their male counterparts? Why do men's football and/or basketball games at these institutions draw the largest crowds? Possibly the promotion of this masculine image is a way for such institutions and their members to show that male Christians are manly, that they are not feminized by religion, and that they are hegemonically masculine — that is, that they are naturally superior to women.

Using Sport to Endorse Hegemonic Masculinity

At the Individual Level

Let's go off on a side track for a moment and talk about the meaning of all this for males at the personal level. Identifying "athlete" with "maleness" and even with "being a Christian" may seem to be a positive equation. However, it can make a male athlete personally dysfunctional. A good athlete gets a great deal of attention for his athletic accomplish-

75. Coakley, *Sport in Society*.
76. Connell, *Gender and Power*; and Brittan, *Masculinity and Power*.

293

ments from his peers, his family, and the community — more attention for this activity, on average, than for any other type of activity he might undertake.[77] This occurs in Christian circles in part because the Christian male athlete exemplifies hegemonic masculinity combined with muscular Christianity. But psychologically, such an athlete risks equating athletic identity with personal and Christian identity.[78] A Christian athlete may proclaim each win as "a victory for Christ" and receive a great deal of approval from the Christian community both for the win and for attributing the win to God. To receive this adulation, however, the athlete must perform consistently well and regularly achieve success. Given these dynamics, his faith and his athletic performance may become tightly interwoven in unhealthy ways.[79] How often do we hear an athlete label a loss or a poor performance as a victory for God? Failure to make a team, being cut from a team, or experiencing decreased performance may make an athlete feel inadequate as a Christian. He may believe that if God is on his side, his performance will be better and he will reach all his goals. If his success proves that he is a "good" Christian man, what does poor performance or being cut from the team prove?

And even a good performance is not enough. Unfortunately, in most sporting arenas you are only as good as your last game. Thus establishing one's identity is a constant struggle, a struggle that then begins anew when the athlete retires from sport. The wedding of "athlete" to "male" may make this retirement a painful experience, especially if it is the unexpected result of team cuts or injuries. The athlete who has worked since age eight in an arena where he has received much praise and recognition, where he has usually been introduced as an athlete, now at age twenty-two or so has to establish his identity in other ways, something that nonathletes have begun to do about a decade earlier. Michael Messner has documented how difficult that process can be.[80] The intensity of the game, the glory of the achievements attained, and the adulation of the crowd and community have given the athlete experiences that may make the rest of his life seem rather flat. By age

---

77. Messner, "The Meaning of Success: The Athletic Experience and the Development of Male Identity," in *The Making of Masculinities: The New Men's Studies*, ed. Harry Brod (Boston: Allen & Unwin, 1987), pp. 193-210.

78. Eitzen and Sage, *Sociology of North American Sport*.

79. Ibid. See also Frank Deford, "Religion in Sport," *Sports Illustrated*, 19 April 1976, pp. 88-102.

80. Messner, "The Meaning of Success."

twenty-one he has had his peak life experiences. Clearly, sport can be a somewhat dysfunctional experience for the athlete. How can he prove his maleness once he must leave his primary identity behind?

Obviously, then, the greater the equation of masculinity with athletics, the greater the chances that long-term and/or intensive participation in sport may be a dysfunctional experience for the male athlete. We need to explore how we contribute — wittingly or unwittingly — to that process in the Christian community, particularly in our schools and colleges.

At the Societal Level

At the societal level, combative sport strengthens the equation of aggression with physical strength, domination, and power. In sport men play the roles of both victims and perpetrators. They actively construct meanings around acts of violence and aggression.[81] Giving and taking pain are violent acts that are not usually associated with women. Accordingly, refusing to give pain or to take a "hit" on the playing field elicits female-associated putdowns: "You're a sissy," "You're playing like a bunch of girls," "You're a wimp," and so on. Men who engage in violent acts confirm our society's view of hegemonic masculinity, and what athletes do in combative sports tends to glorify violence; in fact, television's use of slow replays makes violent acts look graceful. In addition, combative sports may normalize violence for the many males who as spectators identify with the athletes. The young boys who were quoted in the previous chapter illustrate the point. When they were asked what they would do if they woke up and discovered they were girls, a number of them said that they would do violent things. It may be no coincidence then that the United States, which has more combative sports than any other society, also has the highest incidence of homicide and sexual assault,[82] and finds its shelters for battered women full after football playoff games.[83] Eugene Bianchi and Rosemary Ruether comment on the football phenomenon:

81. Michael Messner, "When Bodies Are Weapons: Masculinity and Violence in Sport," *International Review for the Sociology of Sport* 25 (1989): 203-20. See also Gilmore's *Masculinity in the Making.*
82. Peggy Reeves Sanday, "Sociocultural Context of Rape: A Cross Cultural Study," *Journal of Social Issues* 37, no. 4 (1981): 5-27.
83. Laura Fraser, "SuperBowl Violence Comes Home," *Mother Jones,* January 1987, p. 15.

In the football spectacle the role of woman in our society is clearly defined against the masculine criteria of value. The important action is male dominated; women can share only at a distance in a man's world. . . . Ultimately they [women] are his bunnies, his possessions for pleasure and service. . . . Yet football, by its very calculated violence, makes sensitive attunement to one own's body hard to achieve. The vicious body contact is the opposite of gentle touching and loving gesture. . . . Thus the sport depicts an unhealthy polarity towards women.[84]

The exclusive nature of sport tends to stimulate a misogynist and homophobic climate, which at its extreme becomes culturally conducive to rape and gay bashing. Jim Bouton, for example, describes how baseball players talk about "shooting beaver" (a reference to women's pubic hair), and G. Fine shows that the banter of Little Leaguers is peppered with derogatory comments about females and gays.[85] Donald Sabo and Joe Panepinto show how coaches encourage this behavior, "motivating" their players when their play is less than stellar by making such statements as "Go home and play with your sisters," "Start wearing silk panties," and "You're playing like a bunch of girls [or "pussies"]," and by doing things like hanging a bra in the locker of a boy whose play isn't considered tough enough.[86] A recent report indicates that male athletes (and fraternity members) are more involved in sexual assault, especially gang rape, than any other group of men.[87]

Little has been written about how Christian men and boys are taught to respond to this code of violence currently associated with masculinity. But what do we observe? In contact sports few of the Christian college teams mentioned earlier seem to turn the other cheek.

84. Bianchi and Ruether, *From Machismo to Mutuality: Essays on Sexism and Woman-Man Liberation* (New York: Paulist Press, 1976), p. 60.

85. Bouton, *Ball Four* (New York: Dell, 1971); Bouton, *I'm Glad You Didn't Take It Personally* (New York: Dell, 1972); Timothy J. Curry, "Fraternal Bonding in the Locker Room: A Pro-feminist Analysis of Talk about Competition and Women," *Sociology of Sport Journal* 8 (1991): 119-35; G. Fine, *With the Boys: Little League Baseball and Pre-adolescent Culture* (Chicago: University of Chicago Press, 1987).

86. Sabo and Panepinto, "Football Ritual and the Social Reproduction of Masculinity."

87. Beverly Lowy citing Gerald Eskenazi in "Rape Is Not a Sport," *On the Issues* 17 (1990): 4; Kathleen Hirsch, "Fraternities of Fear: Gang Rape, Male Bonding, and the Silencing of Women," *Ms.*, September/October 1990, pp. 52-56.

Many Christian boys and men respond the same way as other males to taunts about their masculinity: by fighting. We suspect that violent or rough play by Christian athletes is often justified by a legalistic appeal to "the rules of the game." If an action is allowed by those rules or the referee doesn't see it, then it's legal. This justification ignores the cultural and often sub-Christian meanings given to acts of violence in sport.

The Bible points us toward community, toward the sharing of resources, and toward an ethic of nonviolence. But little is known of the extent to which Christian men and boys experience and resolve the dissonance between the message of the Bible and the current definition of hegemonic masculinity in American society. This is an issue that should be explored, and it is particularly important that men explore it together. As long as Christians endorse society's idea of hegemonic masculinity (which is grounded in a view of gender relations character-ized more by dominance and subordination than by equality and mutu-ality), then this masculinity will also manifest itself in the life of Chris-tians in various ways, including the ways in which we use the body.

Some people may think that the ideas associated with hegemonic masculinity cannot be challenged because they are so deeply embedded in American society. But examples of challenges to hegemonic masculin-ity already exist. Women contest hegemonic masculinity by participating in team sports, by being strong and moving with self-confidence. Alan Klein points out that gay male bodybuilders challenge the idea that "strong" and "large" are synonymous only with male heterosexuality.[88] Perhaps the time has come for Christian men to challenge the current form of hegemonic masculinity as well, by developing a masculinity that is more consonant with the command to serve one another with love and to live by the fruits of the Spirit. Galatians 5:22 describes these fruits as love, joy, peace, patience, kindness, generosity, faithfulness, gentleness, and self-control. To this list the apostle James adds the following: we are to be peace-loving, considerate, mutually submissive, full of mercy and good works, impartial, and sincere. This does not mean that we neces-sarily have to abolish sport; but we do have to shape it differently and create other meanings for it. Sport could be used for self-mastery, cre-ativity, and building the skills of cooperation, something that, we are pleased to note, happens at certain Christian summer camps for children.

88. Klein, "Pumping Irony: Crisis and Contradiction in Body Building Sub-culture," *Sociology of Sport Journal* 3, no. 1 (1986): 3-23.

We can move the language of sport away from the language of military power and conquest and toward the language of creativity, cooperation, and camaraderie. We can increase the number of coed opportunities in all sports and playing positions, and challenge the sexism and heterosexism that exist in male-defined sports in the mainstream.

Those who think change is impossible should not forget that we are created to be responsible agents in the world. White, middle-class males who are privileged because of their gender, race, and class can use that power and privilege to bring about change. With God's grace we *can* create other meanings for sport and masculinity.

CHAPTER 10

Whatever Happened to the Fig Leaf?
Gender Relations and Dress

"Il faut souffrir pour être belle."
("One must suffer in order to be beautiful.")

JAMES LAVER

F emale and male, we are born into the world. Most bodies are dis- tinctly sex-marked by penis or labia. And as soon as the pediatric nurses cover our heads with pink or blue knitted caps, we begin to take on gender. Our *sex* is determined by our genital equipment, but *gender* is something we acquire through enculturation. What a given culture defines as feminine or masculine may vary, but each culture does define gender, and each human being insinuates her or his unique self into a gender category.

In any given culture, males are expected to adopt the trappings of hegemonic masculinity — what Brian Wren, a Christian poet, hymn-

---

The primary author of this chapter is Helen Sterk.

299

writer, and thinker, calls "masculinity as we know it."[1] A "real man" may wear long skirts (in Saudi Arabia), short skirts (in Scotland), or suits with pants and jackets (in Western industrial countries). By contrast, what distinguishes a "real woman" is her difference from and complementarity to a "real man." This does not mean that there is a hegemonic femininity which neatly balances hegemonic masculinity. Hegemonic femininity would mean femininity defined by powerful women in relation to the world, and it would be equal in weight to hegemonic masculinity. Such femininity, as we saw in the chapter on critical theory, does not exist. What does exist is femininity as defined *in relation to* "masculinity as we know it." Robert Connell, a theorist on the role of power in gender relations, calls this "emphasized femininity,"[2] but we prefer the term "privileged femininity," since privilege implies a value granted (in this case by hegemonic masculinity) and held in relation to that other, more valuable granting power. (See Chapter Eight for a more complete discussion of the terms "hegemonic masculinity" and "privileged femininity.")

In Western culture, size is supposed to be a key distinction between femininity and masculinity. Bigness and space belong to the masculine, constriction to the feminine. According to the feminist theorist Susan Brownmiller, as a woman *enacts* femininity, she learns to "accept the handicap of restraint and restriction, and to come to adore it."[3] Femininity not only makes women seek to embody smallness, symmetry, fragility, and smooth grace; it also, in Brownmiller's words, makes men "appear more masculine by contrast; and, in truth, conferring an extra portion of unearned gender distinction on men, an unchallenged space in which to breathe freely and feel stronger, wiser, and more competent, is femininity's special gift."[4] As women enact femininity, they reinforce men's sense of their own masculinity. Conversely, men's playing out of masculinity emphasizes femininity's boundaries.

The symbolic expression of gender may be embodied in the rituals

1. Wren, *What Language Shall I Borrow? God-Talk in Worship: A Male Response to Feminist Theology* (New York: Crossroad, 1990).
2. Emphasized femininity is performed especially for men and is structured on recognition of and adjustment to male power. See Robert Connell's *Gender and Power: Society, the Person and Sexual Politics* (Stanford: Stanford University Press, 1987), pp. 183-88.
3. Brownmiller, *Femininity* (New York: Simon & Schuster, 1984), p. 86.
4. Ibid., p. 16.

of etiquette or in novels and essays, "expert" medical opinion, conversation and gossip, theology, or social-scientific theory. In whatever form, symbolic expression becomes culture's playing field for gender definition and management. Norms of propriety are communicated at varying levels of enforcement: the phenomenon of a man preceding a woman through a door no longer attracts the shocked glares it would have around the turn of the twentieth century. Such norms also exhibit different levels of importance: for example, for some people, examining God's feminine aspects may be more important than debating what sort of birth experience women should have in urban hospitals. But whether marginal or central to gender definition, each type of symbolic expression adds material and form to what it means to be a woman or a man in a given culture.

In this chapter, we will consider just one symbolic means of gender expression: the fashionably clothed, "properly" proportioned human body. We will show how the fashion and body shape deemed appropriate for men and for women can affect a person's self-presentation, and at the same time how they can limit or enhance one's ability to be a social agent. First, we will discuss what fashion is and how it operates. Then we will show how fashion has operated in specific cultures, especially in Western culture in the nineteenth and twentieth centuries. Finally, we will suggest ways in which fashionable clothing could enhance rather than restrict the agency of both women and men.

Defining the Fashion System

According to Roberta Pollack Seid, author of *Never Too Thin*, "Clothing is simultaneously a material object, a social signal, a ritual, and a form of art."[5] Although clothing is intimately related to fashion, the two are not synonymous.

Just as gender differs from sex, so fashion differs from clothing. If clothing could be thought of as a kind of language, then our everyday wear would be like *conversation*, something we employ for reasons of utility, mood, and personal expression. Ethnic costumes, such as Native American dress or Irish traditional dress or even "Sunday best" dress,

---

5. Seid, *Never Too Thin: Why Women Are at War with Their Bodies* (New York: Prentice Hall Press, 1989), pp. 42-43.

would constitute the language of *ritual,* used to bind community members together. Fashion, however, is *rhetorical:* it is purposive, goal-oriented, and worn as a display of relative social power.

In Western culture, social power is still associated with hegemonic masculinity. Secondary power is then remanded to certain women in the form of privileged femininity. In our culture, hegemonic masculinity might be epitomized by the pre-fall Donald Trump, who was successful, wealthy, competitive, ruthless, famous, impeccably dressed, and able to discard one female trophy for another. Such characteristics image twentieth-century American masculinity at its secular zenith; below it fall levels of "subordinate masculinities," all accorded less value than the Trump variety. Not every male, simply by virtue of maleness, fits into the category of hegemonic masculinity. Yet all males know the standard. In Western culture it is taught to them through news broadcasts, office gossip, periodicals such as *Fortune* and *Time,* television shows such as *Dallas,* and films such as *Wall Street.*

Similarly, women learn the contours of privileged femininity by absorbing the ideals of white Western culture, including ideals about how women should dress. Fashion, as decreed first by the royal courts and later by designers, forms one part of the ideal for women's dress. "Fashion," especially "high fashion" or *haute couture,* aims its appeal specifically at women. While men may dress well, it is not considered masculine to be very fashionable. But to the extent that women, or their husbands or lovers, can afford it, women are expected to conform to current fashion, which changes from season to season. Fashion, then, is a matter of *money* and *time.* And given the efficiency of the mass media, women can learn about fashion changes as soon as they are unveiled by the designers — mostly male — of Paris, Tokyo, and New York.

From the fourteenth through the eighteenth centuries, fashion originated in the royal courts — either with the queen or with the king's mistresses[6] — and was communicated to women of lower ranks by word of mouth, by dressmakers' dolls clothed in the latest style, or, later, through pictorial volumes such as *Godey's Lady's Book.* Today, fashion is decreed by design houses and perpetuated by the endorsement of the rich. It then filters down to ordinary women through film images (e.g., Diane Keaton in *Annie Hall* or Faye Dunaway in *Network*), television

6. James Laver, *Letter to a Girl on the Future of Clothes* (London: Home & Van Thal, Ltd., 1946), p. 32.

images (e.g., Candice Bergen in *Murphy Brown*), and fashion magazines (*Vogue, Harper's Bazaar,* and *Elle,* to name a few). By the time Sears or J. C. Penney features a "look," you can be sure it is no longer on the cutting edge of fashion.

To be in fashion requires money and a serious desire to play the feminine game. Women who engage in high fashion do so not just for fun but for high stakes: securing the favorable attention of a hegemonic male. Women generally do not dress for themselves; they dress to attract the kind of men whose social position is reflected in the image these women choose to portray.

Hence a woman who opts *out* of the fashion system shows by her clothes that she refuses to align herself with a gender system defined around "masculinity as we know it." She opens herself up to charges of being at best an "ugly feminist" and at worst a "dyke." Men, however, are not so clearly vulnerable. True, a man who dresses in old clothes may be seen as less than hegemonically male, since he apparently ranks low in the financially determined status system. But he will not be judged automatically as unattractive to women. In fact, just the opposite might be true: some women find a frumpy male professor endearing. And here is why: men dress to show their relative position in the world of money and/or social status, while women dress to show their relation to the world of men. A frumpy male professor wins women's admiration because of his position in a respected profession; a frumpy female professor attracts men's curiosity or scorn — not admiration — because she is defined first and foremost as a woman, not as a respected professional. Only secondarily might the female frump be seen as dressing to indicate her professional rather than her personal, feminine status.

James Laver, a British museum curator with a passion for the nuances of fashion, suggests three principles that affect human dress: *utility, hierarchy,* and *seduction.*[7] Of the three, utility has the least effect on what people actually wear. If utility mattered, women cooking over open fires would not have worn long dresses in past centuries, nor would British soldiers have worn red uniforms that heightened their visibility on the battlefield. A man, writes Laver, dresses according to the *hierarchy principle,* not only to befit his position in the world but also to signal that high status to women. A woman, on the other hand, dresses according to the *seduction principle,* which has one of two goals: to appeal to men in

7. Laver, *Modesty in Dress* (London: Heinemann, 1969).

the highest possible category of masculinity (if the woman is unat-
tached) or to reflect her man's status (if the woman is attached). The
seduction principle operates most strongly when women are very dependent on men economically. The mid-to-late nineteenth century is a
clear case in point. According to Laver, when women have their own
money and define themselves on their own terms rather than in relation
to masculinity, "unexpectedly" their dress becomes "very plain; straight
in line, simple in decoration, and pale in color."[8] As examples Laver cites
the "dress code" of certain independent women at the turn of the
nineteenth century and in the early twentieth century.

But for the most part, fashion — that is, dress whose purpose is to
indicate class and gender — reflects the hegemonic masculinity of its
time. High fashion began in the late fourteenth century when the first
stirrings of the Renaissance began to undermine the church's hold on
culture. At this time, the courts of France and Burgundy became more
prominent, thus affording a performance stage for women and men
hoping to attract the king's attention. In the centuries since, women have
chosen their dress with only slightly varying intent — to attract the
attention of gorgeous aristocrats (14th-17th centuries), to attract the
attention of the more wealthy members of the bourgeoisie (17th-19th
centuries), to attract the attention of the men of the gentlemanly class
(19th and early 20th centuries), and, currently, to attract the attention
of the wealthy, powerful men of the commercial class.[9] As the basis of
male power and wealth shifts (from inherited title to worldly success),
as relative male prosperity shifts (from boom to bust times), and as the
stage for displaying hegemonic masculinity shifts (from court to battlefield to politics to business), so shifts fashion.

Thus, far from being trivial, fashion deserves our careful attention,
for it tells us much about the state of gender relations at any given time:
the current definition of masculinity, the control exerted over femininity
by current hegemonic masculinity, the amount and type of resistance
against fashion that is allowed, and the power of women to define
themselves. Fashion can act as a focus for understanding the complex
interplay of function and status and religious and cultural forces as these
contribute to the construction of gender.

8. Laver, *Letter to a Girl on the Future of Clothes*, p. 28.
9. Ibid., p. 16.

304

Fashion Trends in Western Culture: A Brief History

Pre-fashion

Prior to the fourteenth century, female and male dress differed very little. For example, the shape and style of Egyptian men's and women's costumes were similar, and the long, graceful, pleated tunics of kings and queens resembled those worn by the slaves, differing only in the amount of ornamentation and the quality of the material. Middle Eastern dress, while it was made of heavier material and covered the body more completely, was similar for men and women. Priestly or kingly status was marked by added decoration, such as a breastplate or a crown. No particular body type was favored by this sort of dress: tall, short, fat, lean — all looked about equally attractive. (For a more contemporary example of this leveling of attractiveness, think of Indian women wearing their saris.)

As this 12th-century frieze shows, female dress differed little from male dress — both were loosely draped over the body.

305

However, by the time of the first-century Greeks, one body type had emerged as ideal, one that exemplified a "golden mean" between the extremes of fat and thin. In sport contests, men competed naked, displaying those ideal forms. Clothing, as far as we can tell from the drapery on statues, flowed in graceful folds from the shoulder and was caught up by a belt at the waist. The style was essentially the same for both men and women. The only women who dressed in unusually fine clothes and tried out new ways of dressing were the *hetarae*, or concubines, "who, in spite of their social prestige, were outside the pale of respectability."[10] Wives, generally secluded at home, cultivated their appearance for their husbands, not for public viewing. Attracting public attention was considered shameful, so wives dressed as inconspicuously as possible on the rare occasions when they entered the public arena.

The Romans of the fourth and fifth centuries valued a body type similar to the Greek ideal. However, they attained that body type through destructive behavior that provided the desired outward effects rather than seeking inward *sophrosyne*, or disciplined moderation. Vomitoriums located just outside feasting places allowed the Romans to eat well past the point of satiation.[11] The Romans, like the Greeks, wore unisex garments. Roman women supplemented their draperies with jewelry and cosmetics, but like Greek women they hid the shape of their bodies. Men wore specialized costumes for war, but otherwise dressed in long draped tunics, like the Greeks.

Throughout most of the Middle Ages, clothing for high-status men and women consisted of long, straight-from-the-shoulder garments that indicated status by the richness of the material rather than by cut or variation in style. Peasants, slaves, soldiers, and children dressed functionally, in plain tunics, cut short to allow freedom of movement. There was still little sex differentiation by costume.

The Emergence of Fashion

With the coming of the fourteenth century, trade between societies expanded and brought with it the opportunity for travel. The power of

10. Laver, *Modesty in Dress*, p. 28.
11. Seid, *Never Too Thin*, p. 46.

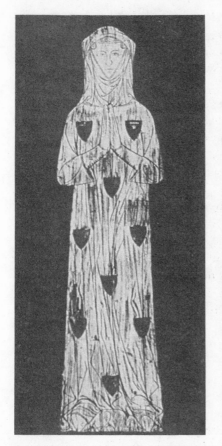

"Before and after." The rubbing on the left illustrates the asexual dress of
the 14th century. The rubbing on the right shows the onset of "fashion," in
which women's physical differences from men are emphasized.

the church began to be muted. And then came fashion. Brass rubbings
of the period show a swift, radical transformation in women's dress.
Noblewomen no longer wore the loose, straight, high-necked tunic of
previous times; their dress changed in cut, line, and ornamentation.
Within a few short years the neckline dropped, the torso became clearly
defined by means of a stiffened bodice, and the headdress became taller.
According to James Laver, the baring of the female bosom to the male
gaze was emblematic of cultural receptivity to the new ideas of the

307

In the 15th century, men wore clothing that accentuated their sexual parts (tights and codpieces), and women dressed in clothing that emphasized and eroticized their bellies.

Renaissance.[12] As mentioned earlier, the Renaissance made the court more important as a public stage. Women began to vie with each other for the attention of the king. Failing to achieve that, they settled for outdoing each other and perhaps gaining the attention and protection of a well-placed male courtier. By the same token, male fashion reflected a desire to attract the attention of *powerful women of the court* as well as the king. Consequently, men wore short tunics that displayed colorfully covered legs and well-turned calves. Thus, during this period, men and women alike dressed according to *both* the seduction *and* the hierarchy principle. As long as women had power and status of their own in the courts, it was to men's advantage to attract them.

By the fifteenth century, erotic attention had descended to the female *belly*, a fact that will probably surprise most twentieth-century readers. Fashionable waistlines crept up the rib cage to allow the display of a gently sloping stomach, the contours of which suggested a five-

12. Laver, *Modesty in Dress,* p. 29.

The full ruff and high collar of this outfit emphasize Elizabeth I's power and status. *(National Portrait Gallery, London)*

month pregnancy. Fifteenth-century paintings of female nudes also showed this look, as did the paintings of Jan Van Eyck: he frequently featured narrow-shouldered, full-bellied women. While women's bodies were covered from bosom to toes, men's legs remained in view. The late fifteenth to early seventeenth centuries could be considered the heyday of the "gorgeous male," whose costume marked his place in court. Male dress was noteworthy at this time for the way its cut, padding, and decoration increased *male size*. Enormous sleeves, puffed caps, large-toed shoes, and padded codpieces added to men's stature and width. This pattern of "bodily expansion" is normal for male dress, says Susan Brownmiller. While women often suffer bodily constraints for the sake of beauty, men rarely endure physical pain solely to look handsome.[13]

Elizabethan-era fashion is noteworthy for two things: the phenomenon of the ruff and the curious shape its clothes gave to the female torso. Although the ruff typically was worn by men, some women wore

13. Brownmiller, *Femininity*, p. 35.

it too. Its stiff width around the neck limited head movement and made wearing a wig next to impossible. Perhaps because of its obvious lack of function, the ruff was meant to indicate the social status of its wearers. Portraits of Queen Elizabeth I suggest the problems a female monarch faced in wearing an article of high-status male dress. There are at least two pictures of her wearing a ruff: in one, her ruff encircles her neck entirely, riding atop a high-necked dress; in the other, her ruff covers her shoulders and back but is cut away in front to reveal a low décolletage. The second version softens her claim to status and emphasizes her sex at least as much as her power. Perhaps Elizabeth I found that this compromise neutralized criticism against her "unwomanly" possession of power.[14] If so, she was not unlike contemporary powerful

The cutaway ruff and low décolletage of this ensemble play up Elizabeth I's womanliness. *(National Portrait Gallery, London)*

14. Indeed, the Scottish Reformer John Knox wrote his treatise entitled *First Blast of the Trumpet against the Monstrous Regiment of Women* in part to criticize the reign of Elizabeth I. Nearly everyone agreed that it was against divine law for women to rule men, but no English theologians of the day knew quite how to answer

women such as Margaret Thatcher and Patricia Schroeder, both of whom wear self-consciously feminine dress for public appearances.

Elizabethan dress also emphasized women's torsos in a way quite unlike that of today's clothes. Elizabethan women's dresses, which were as broad at the waist as they were under the arms, made the torso cylindrical. While this wasn't a particularly comfortable style, this type of dress suited a wide variety of female shapes. A stiff cylinder atop a wide, long skirt gave both large and small women the same silhouette, albeit in different diameters. In the eighteenth century, however, this silhouette changed significantly: then it became fashionable to wear dresses that made the torso look like a triangle set on its point atop a bell-like skirt.

The eighteenth century also saw an accelerated *rate* of change in women's fashions. Below the newly narrowed waist, women's skirts became either very wide and shallow (supported by a device called a "pannier," not unlike an ironing board in size and shape) or alternately quite deep and narrow-hipped, with a bustle on the buttocks. Gender differences in dress became quite pronounced during this century: men's clothes changed little, while women's dress varied dramatically. Over the years, men's clothing became (and remained) plainer and closer-fitting.

Several cultural and economic factors contributed to this divergence of men's and women's fashions. First, there was a change in popular perception, backed by medical pronouncements, of woman's

---

Knox, except to say that, in a fallen world, compromises (e.g., the occasional ruling queen) sometimes need to be made. At the same time, however, no theologian wanted to go into print and offend Elizabeth by defending her rule as nothing but the "lesser of two evils." In the words of C. S. Lewis, "No book more calculated to damage the Protestant cause could have been written. . . . No one wanted the thing to be said, yet no conscientious doctor could answer it in the resounding style which alone would satisfy Elizabeth. No woman likes to have her social position defended as one of the inevitable results of the Fall." See Lewis's *English Literature in the Sixteenth Century, Excluding Drama*, vol. 3 of The Oxford History of English Literature (Oxford: Clarendon, 1954), pp. 199ff. Lewis himself agreed with the view that any situation involving women's authority over men was to be viewed as a regrettable and temporary compromise with the Fall, and neither a creational nor an eschatological ideal. For a further analysis, see Gilbert Meilaender's book entitled *The Taste for the Other: The Social and Ethical Thought of C. S. Lewis* (Grand Rapids: William B. Eerdmans, 1978). See also Chapter Twelve in this volume.

The gender mores of the 18th-century upper class were exhibited through an extravagant emphasis of a woman's hair, breasts, waist, and hips. *(Picture Collection, The Branch Libraries, The New York Public Library)*

sexuality. Until the eighteenth century, women were generally seen as lustful, sensual creatures with sexual appetites equal to or even stronger than men's. During the eighteenth century, however, women's sexuality came to be seen as nonexistent. In a departure from previous times, the female orgasm was no longer considered necessary for the conception of a child; now it was often seen as evil.[15] (Later, in the nineteenth century, women's "voluptuous spasms" were positively to be avoided, since they were said to impede conception and "even cause sterility."[16]) In effect, women's bodies ceased to function for their own pleasure and became more and more the sexual vessels of men. Consequently, a woman could display her body in "innocent seductiveness," since she

15. Seid, *Never Too Thin,* p. 55.

16. Harvey Green, with the assistance of Mary-Ellen Perry, *The Light of the Home: An Intimate View of the Lives of Women in Victorian America* (New York: Pantheon Books, 1983), p. 132.

was presumed to have no sensual feelings of her own.[17] In addition, at this time middle-class values began to overtake court values. Since men no longer dressed for prestige in the royal court, their clothing became plainer. At the same time, arranged marriages were being phased out, so women needed to attract marriage proposals, marriage being their only route to any sort of status and security. Dieting appeared for the first time as a social institution in the eighteenth century; it was aimed at getting women to adapt their bodies to fit fashion rather than vice versa. And after the eighteenth century few male nude figures appeared in art. Instead, women became prominent subjects of male scrutiny and male ownership.

The Democratization of Fashion

In the nineteenth century men's dress went through a series of subtle evolutions, finally arriving in the 1880s at the basic line and look still current today. The first major shift was away from knee breeches to long trousers. After the turn of the nineteenth century, upper-class adult males no longer appeared in short pants. Trousers had two sources: the *sans culottes* of the French Revolution and sportswear. Originally worn by peasants, *sans culottes,* or long trousers, soon became a visual statement of support for democracy. As such, they worked their way — through a gradual process of formalization — into men's sportswear, then into day and evening wear. This is a common pattern, according to James Laver. "All male garments begin by being 'sport clothes,'" he points out. "They then become informal day wear, then evening wear. Push them a stage farther and they become the dress of servants or functionaries. The men's tailcoat has been all these things."[18] The informal garb originally worn to play at sports or make a political statement culminated in the convention of long trousers as the only acceptable public fashion for Western men. Other articles of male clothing also changed during the nineteenth century. Men's hats went from top hats to trilbies (soft felt hats with indented crowns),[19] and ties mutated from cravats and neck-

17. Seid, *Never Too Thin,* p. 55.
18. Laver, *Modesty in Dress,* p. 44.
19. In *Modesty in Dress,* James Laver notes the coincidence of tall hats with periods of female subservience to men — e.g., the Puritan and Cavalier eras — and

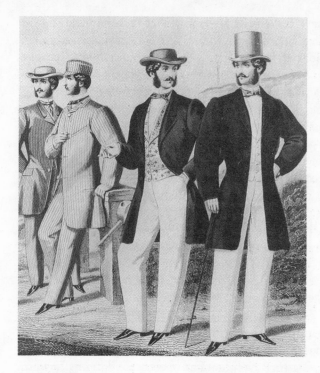

By the end of the 19th century, men's dress had reached the style still worn (with a few variations of cut and tailoring) today.

cloths to bow ties and finally to long ties.[20] By the end of the nineteenth century, the fundamental elements of today's male hierarchical principle in dress had been established: trousered suit, wide-shouldered jacket, low hat, and long tie — all of which subtly announce male strength and sexual power.

Women's dress in the nineteenth century did *not* reflect a single

flattened hats with times of female emancipation: the late 1800s, the early 1900s, and the late twentieth century (pp. 121-22). I would suggest, however, that men's hats, whatever their size, carry vestigial power in their reference to the king's crown or at the least to a soldier's helmet.

20. Like Sigmund Freud, James Laver associates men's ties with the phallus. To support his point that the tie is a sexual symbol, he presents examples of young men wearing loud ties or ties with naked women on them, clergy wearing either white ties or no ties at all, and the "roars of laughter" that greeted the snipping off of a man's tie in a Paris nightclub. The tie also represents the phallus as a symbol of power. Consider the "old school tie" and the prevalence of long ties over bow ties. See Laver's *Modesty in Dress*, p. 124.

pattern. The century opened with the short-lived, comfortable Empire style of dress, similar in look to the dress of the fifteenth century. But this was quickly replaced with a regression to the seventeenth-century silhouette of an inverted triangle set on a voluminous skirt. This silhouette was strictly maintained by the corset, an undergarment made of cotton and reinforced with slim stays of whalebone or steel that fitted tightly from a woman's breasts to her hips. Through the mechanics of corsetry, a woman's waist could be laced down to as little as sixteen inches.[21] This tiny waist was in marked contrast to the broad, ground-sweeping skirt, a contrast that emphasized the ways in which women were anatomically different from men. The small waist supposedly guaranteed virginity, while the broad hips promised fertility. Furthermore, the corset and wide skirt combined to impede women's mobility, effectively imprisoning them in their clothes. Uncomfortable as some articles of men's clothing may have been — the shirts with their high, tight collars and ties — the generally loose fit of men's jackets and trousers allowed free movement compared with the restrictions of women's clothing. In this way men's and women's clothing powerfully suggested their respective places in the social order.

Westerners look to the old Oriental practice of foot-binding with horror, disturbed by the little hooves it gave Oriental women and aghast at the limits they placed on women's ability to walk. Yet the corset, which placed women in far more danger, is glossed over as an interesting bit of nineteenth-century trivia. Unlike foot-binding, the tight lacing of corsets interfered with *all* the vital functions of a woman's body. In his book entitled *The Light of the Home,* Harvey Green lists among the results of corseting "broken ribs, collapsed lungs, weakening of abdominal walls (therefore necessitating the use of forceps when delivering a baby), neurasthenia, and an inverted or prolapsed uterus."[22]

Yet wearing corsets was hardly optional for women in nineteenth-century America, unless they had no aspirations to higher social status, because the corseted look helped win a successful man. Accordingly, girl babies were tightly swaddled, and, as soon as they could stand, little girls were laced into child-sized corsets by their mothers. An advertisement for "Good Sense" children's corsets aimed the following message at mothers: "Your child must be kept healthy or she cannot be beautiful.

21. Laver, *Modesty in Dress,* p. 112.
22. Green, *The Light of the Home,* p. 120.

315

Nineteenth-century advertisements such as this encouraged mothers to buy corsets for their little girls. Why? For reasons of health, beauty, and good sense! *(Courtesy of The Strong Museum, Rochester, New York)*

Sensible mothers buy Good Sense corset waists."[23] These corsets came in sizes to fit every female person from infant to adult.

As nineteenth-century girls matured into young women, their corsets became tools for expressing sexuality, another variation on the idea of "innocent seduction." An exceedingly narrow waist of the "double handspan" of twenty inches or less was a next-to-impossible achievement for a woman who had borne a baby. Thus a very narrow waist purportedly proclaimed a woman's virginity, while the less-narrow but still corseted waists of older women who had borne children recalled this virgin ideal. However, as women aged, considerable leeway was

23. Ibid., p. 44.

316

While corsets enabled women to whittle their waists down to a handspan,
they exacted a cruel price from women's bodies.

granted on waist size. While young women were expected to have a
waist of twenty inches or smaller, women in their thirties could have
waistlines as ample as thirty-six inches without causing undue comment.[24]

Different corsets to wear while sleeping, while pregnant, while
playing sports — all were available to nineteenth-century women. It
seems the only time a woman could avoid wearing a corset was while
taking a bath. According to the sports sociologist Kathleen McCrone,
The Lancet, a prominent British medical journal, "cited cases of women
who courted death by wearing corsets during gymnastic exercise and
pregnant women who had to be advised to loosen their stays and when

24. Seid, *Never Too Thin,* pp. 66-67.

in labor to remove them."[25] Women even wore specially-adapted corsets while playing golf. Indeed, the Royal Worcester Boneless Sport Corset Company claimed in advertisements that "their product would be worth at least three strokes a round and that uncorseted golfers risked losing control of their hips."[26] In addition to corsets, women tennis players wore a bustle and several petticoats under their clothes. "As long as lady players wore corsets and skirts approaching the ground," McCrone notes, "the degree of proficiency achievable remained limited — a fact that was conveniently forgotten when the innate superiority of the male game was extolled."[27] Later, observers would denigrate the ability of women swimmers, ignoring the heavy dresses they had to wear that quickly became waterlogged. They also downplayed the excitement of women's cricket and soccer, refusing to recognize the significant impediment to excellence provided by women's cumbersome dress.

People from non-Western cultures found it difficult to reconcile the corset with eighteenth- and nineteenth-century claims about Western women's freedom. Lady Mary Wortley Montague, wife of the English ambassador to Turkey in the late eighteenth century, notes the non-Western perception of corsets in this story:

> One of the highest entertainments in Turkey is having you to their baths. When I was introduced to one, the lady of the house came to undress me. . . . After she had slipped off my gown and saw my stays she was very struck at the sight of them, and cried out to the other ladies in the bath: "Come hither and see how cruelly the poor English ladies are used by their husbands. You need boast indeed of the superior liberties allowed you when they lock you up thus in a box."[28]

How could Western women be free, asked these non-Western observers, when they were so physically bound?

Not every aspect of nineteenth-century dress curtailed women's agency or their ability to make personal decisions about clothing. As we have noted, women were not free to discard their corsets, but they could

---

25. McCrone, *Playing the Game: Sport and the Physical Emancipation of English Women, 1870-1914* (Lexington, Ky.: University of Kentucky Press, 1988), p. 218.
26. Ibid., p. 236.
27. Ibid., p. 234.
28. Lady Montague, cited by Leila Ahmed in "Western Ethnocentrism and Perceptions of the Harem," *Feminist Studies* 8 (Fall 1982): 525.

loosen their stays and take the corsets off at night. But this was a paltry freedom at best—and in many other ways women were imprisoned by their clothing. Women could not usually shorten their skirts at will, even though long, voluminous skirts posed a fire hazard when close to cooking fires or wood stoves. Women's "limbs" were never to be seen in public; they were too obviously related to women's sexuality, so even in domestic settings they remained fully covered. This phenomenon was closely related to the nineteenth-century "cult of true womanhood," which held that women were not so much embodied humans as they were pure, ministering angels who provided men with a "haven in a heartless world."[29] Kathleen McCrone writes,

> As the image of ideal womanhood became increasingly "sacred," dress designers—almost exclusively male—deliberately sought to check unladylike activities and to compel women to conform to the passive

Cooking over an open fire posed risks to a long-skirted woman. *(Picture Collection, The Branch Libraries, The New York Public Library)*

29. Susan Strasser, *Never Done: A History of American Housework* (New York: Pantheon Books, 1982), p. 181.

319

lifestyle that was the hallmark of gentility. The design of female clothing thus became more confining and discordant with anatomical realities, and permitted women only a distant acquaintanceship with their own bodies.[30]

What McCrone fails to note is that it was *rich* women who wore the immobilizing high fashion of the day. These women had servants who dressed much more simply in order to do any manual labor that was necessary.

Nonwealthy women adapted the look of high fashion and "made do" within the limits of their means and/or dressmaking skills. For example, women might ease the close fit of a bodice or add hand-crocheted cuffs and collar for a dressier look or simplify a bustle to suit their taste and budget. This personal adaptation of high fashion by nineteenth-century women is often ignored by critics of fashion. Today's women must submit to the tyranny of standard sizes — a size 14 is a size 14, no matter if the woman whom the size fits in the waist or the bust is 5'11" or 5'2", and rare indeed is the store that offers women free alterations. By contrast, nineteenth-century women wore custom-made clothes, whether they sewed for themselves or hired a dressmaker. Among other sources, *Godey's Lady's Book* illustrated current looks that women adapted to their individual tastes by choosing a different color, material, sleeve style, bodice treatment, or trim than that shown. In this respect personal choice in clothing was more possible then than it is now, and less consensus existed on what type of body was "best." No matter what a woman's girth, her corset would smooth out the bulges, and her clothes, made to her measurements, would fit her.

These marks of agency or small liberties are admittedly subtle, given the overall discomfort caused by clothes that were tight on the top, fully belled on the bottom, and heavy. A typical winter ensemble could weigh up to thirty-seven pounds, nineteen pounds of which hung from the waist.[31] However, around 1850, Amelia Bloomer made an attempt to reform women's dress with an alternative that was named after her. And given the prevailing norms of dress, the inverted line of the bloomer

---

30. McCrone, *Playing the Game*, p. 217.

31. Barbara Ehrenreich and Deirdre English, *For Her Own Good: 150 Years of the Experts' Advice to Women* (Garden City, N.Y.: Doubleday-Anchor Books, 1978), p. 98.

costume — whose top hung from the shoulders in an A-line to mid-calf and whose bottom was a modest pair of trousers — seemed not only odd but scandalous, even perverse and sexually dangerous. It could be worn without a corset (making one a "loose" woman instead of "straitlaced"), and it revealed for the first time in Western history that women actually had two legs! The Western world was not yet ready for the bloomer costume. As McCrone explains, it was "condemned out of hand by fashion consultants and general opinion as ridiculous, monstrous, outrageous, unnatural, unwomanly, unhealthy, immoral and ugly, and by

The bloomer costume was seen as scandalous because it revealed women's legs (albeit well covered) for the first time in the history of Western fashion. *(Picture Collection, The Branch Libraries, The New York Public Library)*

321

some doctors who warned, vaguely, that trousers would cause a dangerous increase in bodily heat and threaten health and morals."[32]

The intensity of negative public opinion against the bloomer
costume reflected the extent to which hegemonic masculinity had a hold
over and was concerned about female dress. Masculinity, it seemed,
would be called into question if women were free to wear clothing
designed for their own comfort and pleasure. Elizabeth Cady Stanton's
experience underscores this point. When this prominent advocate of
women's suffrage wore the bloomer costume, public opinion turned
against both her and her husband. When her husband ran for political
office, her clothing became an election issue. "Some good Democrats,"
Stanton wrote to a friend, "said they would not vote for a man whose
wife wore the Bloomers."[33] The account of this incident does not say
whether Stanton's husband won or lost the election, but it does note that
Stanton wore the bloomer costume for only two years. She finally gave
in to social pressure and resumed the dress of privileged femininity.
Other feminists, such as Anna Howard Shaw, agreed that it was better
to dress in line with current norms; that way those campaigning for
women's rights would be better able to focus audience attention on their
arguments rather than on themselves.[34]

By the century's end, the dress of privileged femininity and the
dress of hegemonic masculinity were exemplifying the interplay of
these two principles rather than enhancing individual personalities. The
rich dressed to display male wealth and its ability to protect female
leisure, and this became the standard to which the less-wealthy generally
aspired. In *The Theory of the Leisure Class* Thorstein Veblen observed that
this period was known for the twin vices of conspicuous consumption
and conspicuous leisure.[35] Men's financial strength was displayed not
only in the houses and furnishings they could buy but also in the lives
of "ease" they could guarantee their wives. In effect, they advertised
their wealth on their wives' bodies: the dress of privileged femininity

32. McCrone, *Playing the Game,* p. 221.
33. Stanton, cited by Elisabeth Griffith in *In Her Own Right: The Life of Elizabeth Cady Stanton* (New York: Oxford University Press, 1984), pp. 71-72.
34. Anna Howard Shaw, *The Story of a Pioneer* (New York: Harper & Brothers, 1915), p. 260; see also McCrone's *Playing the Game,* p. 222.
35. Veblen, *The Theory of the Leisure Class* (1899; rpt. New York: Random House, 1934).

had a high, ruffled neckline, tight armholes, and a heavy, bustled skirt, and was undergirded by a corset, a camisole, a pair of knickers, and rustling layers of petticoats. No woman wearing this kind of clothing could walk at more than a strolling pace, let alone do strenuous work.

However, a minority of these women yearned for mobility, and the advent of the bicycle provides an interesting example of how sport influenced not only men's fashion but women's as well. Women eagerly took to cycles as soon as they became available. At first they piloted tricycles (adapted from the man's high-wheeler), which accommodated their large skirts. However, as the two-wheeler was refined, women and men began to ride similar bicycles. Men wore clothing relatively well-suited to the activity: trousered suits and caps or bowler-style hats. Women, on the other hand, initially wore their street clothes for cycling, as they did for every other sport they pursued — archery, golf, croquet, target practice. But the wind generated by a moving bicycle made street wear a distinct hazard. Women then coped by using heavier material in their skirts, by sewing lead weights into the hems, or by attaching loops

Rich women displayed their husband's wealth on their bodies. Ornate clothing that immobilized women was perceived as the ultimate in fashion. *(From Illustrated Sporting and Dramatic News, 1875)*

Left: While still cumbersome, this biking costume allowed more mobility for women than did their normal streetwear. *Right:* Female modesty was well preserved by this 19th-century bathing costume. *(Bathing costume from National Gallery of Art, Washington, D.C.)*

to the hems through which they would slip their feet before placing them on the pedals.[36] Eventually, however, biking costumes for women were designed. All were cumbersome, but each featured a skirt with less material than the usual dress worn on the street, a jacket, and some kind of cap. In *The Light of the Home*, Harvey Green describes the "londonderry" biking costume as follows:

> Made of gray-green hopsack — a coarse, loosely woven fabric of cotton or wool — the coat had long, full sides which formed a kind of

36. McCrone, *Playing the Game,* p. 239.

skirt when riding. This was worn over full knickerbockers and with either a skirt or double-breasted "cloth" (wool) or leather vest. In addition, the well-dressed woman also wore leggings, a hat, doeskin gloves, and a pair of broad, low, rubber-soled cycling shoes which had first come on the market in 1891. A bicycle belt, from which hung a small, leather purse, completed the outfit.[37]

By the early 1900s, women cyclists had pared down their costumes to bloomers, blouses, and vests. Despite these strides, women's owning and using bicycles was a strongly contested matter. "Experts," especially in medicine, expressed the same reservations about cycling that they had previously held about women riding horses astride rather than sidesaddle,[38] reservations centering on women's health and modesty. Moreover, nineteenth-century male medical opinion held that the source of both women's health and their maladies lay mainly in their reproductive systems.[39] Combined with this was the widespread medical and lay opinion that women should not experience orgasm, not through intercourse and certainly not through masturbation. They were not supposed to yield to pleasures of the flesh. Consequently, women's riding bicycles, going where they pleased and when and with whom they pleased, called their morals into question, especially considering which part of female anatomy met the bicycle's saddle!

Harvey Green writes about physicians Thomas Lathrop and William Potter, who "posited that the bicycle inevitably promoted immodesty in women, and could potentially harm their reproductive organs." By leaning forward a bit, women could "beget or foster the habit of

37. Green, *The Light of the Home*, p. 163.
38. Susan Brownmiller has observed that a sidesaddle kept a woman's legs together and thus "pleasurable contact between groin and saddle was deftly avoided" (*Femininity*, p. 190).
39. Ehrenreich and English explain that nineteenth-century doctors "'discovered' that female functions were inherently pathological." Menstruation (and lack of it), childbirth, and menopause were all occasions of ill health. (See *For Her Own Good*, pp. 99-100.) Harvey Green quotes the prevailing opinion of nineteenth-century physicians regarding women's constitution: "Women's reproductive organs are preeminent. They exercise controlling influence upon her entire system, and entail upon her many painful and dangerous diseases. They are the source of her peculiarities, the center of her sympathies and the seat of her diseases. Everything that is peculiar to her springs from her sexual organization" (*The Light of the Home*, p. 115).

masturbation,"[40] which was to be avoided at all costs. These experts insisted that masturbation was extremely harmful to women, claiming that it "destroys mental power and memory, it blotches the complexion, dulls the eye, takes away strength, and may even cause insanity. . . . No habit is more tyrannical than the dominion of unrestrained sexual desire."[41] These arguments anticipate those later leveled against women's participation in competitive long-distance running; the claim was that running would damage the uterus and ovaries. Given that women's reproductive organs are well protected by a natural girdle of bone, muscle, and fat, while men's reproductive organs hang outside their bodies, reproduction-based arguments against *women* undertaking strenuous sports miss the obvious! These arguments also recall those raised when some women stopped wearing bras in the 1960s, arguments that stressed potential damage to women's breasts.[42] What emerges in this whole debate is the power of hegemonic masculinity to define what is "proper" for women.

The evolution of women's dress in other sports follows the pattern of apparel change in golf, tennis, and biking. Initially women either covered themselves completely (as they did when they wore dress-like bathing suits) or wore slightly modified street wear (e.g., shooting and archery costumes). Organized team sports such as cricket required odd compromises in public dress. From the neck up, women's cricket wear echoed male norms of dress (tie, stiff collar, straw boater), while from the neck down it adhered to female norms (blouse, long skirt, corset).[43]

40. Green, *The Light of the Home*, p. 159.

41. Quoted in Green, *The Light of the Home*, p. 132. To be fair, we should note that at this time severe warnings about the consequences of masturbation were also leveled at men.

42. Brownmiller gets a bit short with the male members of the media who protested women's bralessness: "It was as if men had come to believe that taking off a brassiere somehow was their right and privilege" (*Femininity*, p. 45).

43. This phenomenon repeated itself when women entered the male-dominated field of secretarial work, too. As the field became dominated by women, their secretarial dress became more "feminine." See Farar Elliott's "Men and Women: Costume, Gender, and Power," *Off Our Backs*, December 1989, pp. 8-9. The business suits many women wear today reflect the same schizophrenia — male-style jackets paired with short skirts or sarong skirts.

Twentieth-Century Fashion

The twentieth century brought few changes in hegemonic male attire. Like Reason itself, it seems, male dress remained stable. Lapels and ties might narrow or widen, pant cuffs might come and go, but the standard suit of jacket and trousers remained. But like Nature herself, women's fashions changed with practically every season. The century opened with a new, more relaxed silhouette for women's dress, similar to the brief-lived Empire style of the fifteenth and eighteenth centuries. About the same time women received the vote, however, the so-called hobble skirt came into vogue, a new attempt to restrict women even as they gained new freedom. Gone were the crinolines and corsets of the nineteenth century; this time the point of constriction was the *knees* rather than the

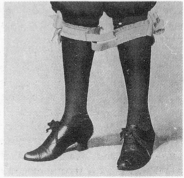

Hobble skirts and hobble garters (below) limited the movement of "emancipated women."
(Picture Collection, The Branch Libraries, The New York Public Library)

327

waist. To achieve the mincing, small-footed steps deemed essential to the hobble-skirt style, some women even resorted to wearing knee shackles.

With the 1920s came female emancipation and another revision of women's sexuality. A wife could be erotic again, the object of her husband's rather than her children's desire, his companion rather than their mom.[44] At the same time, the idea of "innocent seduction" waned. For the first time in Western history, dresses exposed women's bare legs! Clothing styles also began to bare women's arms with increasing frequency as women's dress lost the covered look. However, as if fashion were only able to focus on one erogenous zone at a time, breasts and hips "disappeared" in the 1920s even as arms and legs were highlighted. Breast binders and dieting took care of any appearance of mature womanliness. The image of woman as potential or actual mother began to evolve into that of woman as perpetually young, slim, and sexy.

During both world wars, fashion took a back seat to more serious matters. The hegemonic, war-defined men of the Western world battled each other while men of subordinate masculinities and almost all women stayed home. Men at war dressed in military costume, designed for utility and display of rank. Women dressed simply, in part because of the demands of their wartime work and in part because the men whom women dressed for were no longer there. During World War II, women's dress even allowed breasts to keep their natural shape; hemlines were knee-length (functionally short and swingy), and women's pants started to become acceptable.[45]

However, when the war was over, the surviving soldiers were home again, and cloth rationing was finished, the fashion industry began producing and promoting women's clothes that required more material. Christian Dior introduced a "New Look" that resurrected the 1850s silhouette of cinched waist and wide hips, although it was somewhat more compressed and streamlined than the earlier look.

A virtual cult of femininity flowered in the 1950s and 1960s. The

44. Seid, *Never Too Thin,* p. 42.
45. See Sherna Berger Gluck's book entitled *Rosie the Riveter Revisited: Women, the War, and Social Change* (Boston: Twayne Publishers, 1987). "Rosie" was the popular name given to the Women's Ordinance Workers ("W.O.W.'s") who replace drafted American men in the factories and shipyards in order to make the planes, ships, and ammunition needed during World War II.

Left: By the 1920s, women's legs came out of hiding while their breasts disappeared. *(Vogue, April 1926) Right:* After World War II, Dior's "New Look" returned fashion to the 19th-century silhouette of narrow, virginal waist and wide, fertile hips. *(© 1992 ARS, New York/ADAGP, Paris)*

industrial work women had ably taken on during the war became reserved for men only, as did most other work that was well paid. Whether they liked it or not, whether or not they had husbands and/or children, women were told in no uncertain terms to stay home. As the film *Rosie the Riveter* shows so well, the postwar cultural media united to tell women that the men had returned to take control, and that women's job was to support them. Magazines that during the war had praised day-care centers now ran psychoanalytically influenced articles on the psychological trauma posed for children by wage-earning mothers. No longer did magazines print recipes for meals that could be assembled in thirty minutes or less; these were replaced by menus that took entire days to prepare. Women were expected to marry, go home, and become full-time wives and mothers.

Fashion reinforced this message. Men's suits featured broader

329

shoulders and wider pants, effectively increasing the illusion of the wearers' size. Hats, which made men look taller, became an expected accessory of the business suit. Women's dresses again emphasized their anatomy: circle-stitched bras pointed the breasts out,[46] tight waists emphasized virginal spaces to be filled, and the look of broad hips under immense skirts hinted at women's fecundity. Excluded from the waged economy, placed in a position of total financial dependence, separated from other women by the layout of tract-house suburban communities,[47] middle-class women wore clothing that proclaimed their difference from men to an extreme not seen since the late 1800s, which was the height of the "true womanhood" cult.

In the mid-to-late twentieth century, several factors prodded both women's and men's fashion toward change, if not progress. First, reliable methods of birth control (such as the pill, the diaphragm, and the IUD) became widely available to women, and both popular and religious opinion (with the exception of that of Roman Catholicism) sanctioned their use. Women finally had the option to delay childbirth indefinitely, forever if they wished, and still be sexually active. This granted women a measure of self-determination previously out of their reach.

Second, the popularity of individual and team sports for women increased to an extent not known since the heyday of the bicycle. Women athletes such as Mary Dekker, Nadia Comaneci, Mary Lou Retton, Althea Gibson, Chris Evert, Florence Joiner, and Wilma Rudolph became role models for both young and adult women. Volleyball, basketball, and field hockey grew in importance, aided by Olympic coverage. This athletic revival gave women a new sense of strength and personal agency.

Third, in the 1960s the feminist movement resurfaced for the first time since the battle for women's suffrage (see also Chapter Three).

46. Susan Brownmiller sees breasts with "their emblematic prominence and intrinsic vulnerability" as "the chief badge of gender" (*Femininity*, p. 40). How breasts are molded or displayed in fashions indicates women's concerns about their relationship to men. Past fashions include the shelf-like monobosom, bound breasts, circle-stitched-bra breasts, "natural" breasts, underwired breasts, sports-bra breasts, and no-bra breasts, among others. All emphasize the breasts' sexual appeal to men. The only kind of breast that is taboo in Western culture is the milk-filled mother's breast, especially if it is being used in public.

47. Delores Hayden, *Redesigning the American Dream: The Future of Housing, Work and Family Life* (New York: W. W. Norton, 1984).

330

The miniskirt elicited a variety of public responses, including
scowls of disapproval. *(© Diana Mara Henry, Carmel, CA)*

Coalescing around the Equal Rights Amendment and beginning with an
emphasis on equality under the law for women, it continued to find ways
to affirm the value of all women, whether as paid or unpaid workers, as
individuals married or single, childless or childbearing. A sense of
women's intrinsic, self-defined value began to pervade the media through
magazines such as *Ms., Savvy, Essence, Lear's, Mirabella,* and so on. The
same theme has been developed in television shows such as "Murphy
Brown," "Roseanne," and "Designing Women," in movies such as *Steel
Magnolias,* and in the feminist mystery novels of Amanda Cross, Sue
Grafton, and Sara Peretsky, among others.

And finally, women began to return to the waged work force, many
out of economic necessity, since fewer and fewer men earned a "family
wage," while more and more women were either divorced, unmarried,
or on their own as single mothers. Others worked for pay because they
wanted to and saw no reason why their male partners could not learn to
share household responsibilities.

Business clothing worn by women in the late twentieth century

331

reflects the recency and ambiguity of their entry into what was previously an almost all-male domain. Just as nineteenth-century women who played team sports adapted their dress to an uneasy mix of masculine above the waist and feminine below, so twentieth-century women joining the business world adopted this half-and-half look.[48] In the 1970s women heeded John T. Molloy's advice in *The Woman's Dress for Success Book*[49] by dressing as if they were "men in skirts." Women's suits followed the same norm as men's: they were offered in a narrow range of colors (navy, gray, or black) and fabrics (plain or pin-striped, no plaids, and only natural fibers). Only the floppy bow tie and below-the-knee-length skirt betrayed their sex. In an odd compromise between the hierarchy principle and the seduction principle, women's dress clearly marked them as "little" or pseudo-men.

But more recently business women have begun to define for themselves what is appropriate work wear. Although the suit remains first choice, more women are wearing dresses. Even so, many recently designed suits for women continue to show a feeling of being out of place in a world defined purely by hierarchy. Male clothing norms are referenced from the waist up by a suit jacket; female attire is referenced from the waist down in either a longer or a shorter skirt and high heels.

The Tyranny of Physical Perfection

With the blurring of boundaries of public and domestic worlds (see also Chapters Twelve and Thirteen), designers were unable to develop a single seduction principle for women's dress. The nineteenth-century woman was simply supposed to run the domestic sphere and reflect her husband's status, but this is no longer the case. Consequently, modern fashion cannot determine a single look and let it evolve, as the dresses of the nineteenth century did through variations on skirt width that maintained the emphasis on the narrow torso. Women simply do not buy whatever designers decree anymore, and no single style reigns for any fashion season, so minis, midis, maxis, chemises, peasant looks, and

48. Elliott, "Men and Women," pp. 8-9.
49. Molloy, *The Woman's Dress for Success Book* (New York: Warner Books, 1977).

Above: The Molloy syndrome: a trio of women "dressed for success." *(© Diana Mara Henry, Carmel, CA)*
Left: Menswear with a twist: Today many women are wearing more body-conscious clothes and accessorizing them with greater individuality.

ethnic costumes come and go. What *has* come and remained is one ideal body type.

The woman of the late twentieth century can wear what she wishes. Indeed, partly because she still does not occupy a hegemonic position, she can experiment with her dress in ways not possible for men aspiring to or possessing hegemonic status. But her *face* must remain youthful and her *body* must remain young-looking and thin. In the late twentieth century, fashion's focus for women has shifted from clothing to the body itself.

Like the nineteenth-century experts, twentieth-century experts — both medical and lay — line up to tell women what their bodies should look like. But this time women are not warned away from trousers and laced up into stays. Instead, they are warned away from fat. Certainly there are a number of sound medical reasons for a woman's maintaining a healthy weight. But much of the modern emphasis on weight has had more to do with style than with health. In the nineteenth century, extra weight, at least on older women and men, was prized as stored "force," and "heavy" referred to a feeling of fullness after eating, not to one's weight.[50] In the twentieth century, however, the Metropolitan Life Insurance Company (MLIC) introduced *weight charts*. These were based on the self-reports of rich white men of northern European extraction, reports which were then adapted and applied to women. The charts first listed "average" weights, later "ideal" weights, and finally "desirable" weights, each progressively lighter.[51] At the same time, the MLIC standards ignored the harmful effects of constant dieting — for example, the stress placed on heart muscle by constant weight gain and loss. They also ignored studies showing that women who remain at a stable (even though high) weight are at a lower health risk than those who lose and gain weight in a cyclical fashion.[52]

Then Covert Bailey wrote a book called *Fit or Fat?* that introduced a new way to define what it means to be overweight — through analyzing the proportion of body fat to lean tissue. Like the MLIC, Bailey imposed a scale on the human body rather than allowing the body to suggest a scale. Studies show that the average twenty-year-old woman has 28.7 percent body fat; the average sixty-year-old woman, 41.5 percent. The

50. Seid, *Never Too Thin*, pp. 76, 69.
51. Ibid., pp. 97, 117, 118.
52. Ibid., pp. 290-93.

pattern for men is quite different: the average twenty-year-old man has 11 percent body fat; the average fifty-year-old man, 25.8 percent.[53] Yet in Bailey's formulation all women, no matter what their age, were to have no more than 22 percent body fat, and men no more than 15 percent. His own study of "thousands" of men and women "had revealed that most men averaged 23 percent, most women 36 percent."[54] Both percentages fall short of Bailey's ideal, yet women's average fat percentage is significantly higher than men's average fat percentage. Consequently, women would find it harder to meet Bailey's standards than men. (And, of course, it's not clear where Bailey's "ideal" ratings of fat to lean came from in the first place.)

While experts told women to lose weight, the mass media united to present one ideal female face and form — that of a 25-year-old northern European white woman who was thin, fit, and unwrinkled. Little girls' Barbie dolls, designed with picture-perfect faces, ample breasts, tiny waists, slim hips, and long legs, eased them into familiarity with this look. Advertisements aimed at older women by products such as Oil of Olay and Erase continued to remind them of the ideal. And women who failed to achieve the ideal body type didn't even have corsets to cinch themselves in; girdles remained available, but women were encouraged instead to sculpt their bodies with exercise or surgery. Moreover, women of color found almost no representatives of themselves in the popular media. Since the message given was that they could not even begin to compete, they were reminded of their distance from privileged femininity. This was also the case for women who were physically challenged, older, short, or stocky. In recent years this has begun to change somewhat, but for the most part women are still presented with a virtually unattainable physical "ideal."

In the past, before the advent of truly mass media, the game of fashion was played most seriously by the rich. Poorer folk may have adorned themselves or worn the costume of "Sunday best," but they did not engage in the conspicuous consumption and waste of changing fashion. One reason, of course, was lack of money, but another was simple lack of access to current information. *Godey's Lady's Book* might be several months to a year or more behind the latest fashion by the time

53. Ibid., p. 175.
54. Covert Bailey, *Fit or Fat?* (Boston: Houghton Mifflin, 1978), quoted by Seid in *Never Too Thin,* p. 175.

middle- or lower-class dressmakers saw a copy, and there were far fewer visual media at that time than there are now. Today, anyone with the spare change it takes to buy a *Chicago Tribune* can learn what was done in Paris yesterday. And even if that information does not affect immediate wardrobe choices, it still prods the desire to attain the new perfections shown. More importantly, the advertising is ubiquitous — in newspapers, in magazines, on billboards, in films, and on television. It no longer matters if one is rich or poor; the constant pitch to buy is made to everyone, and the same goods, however pricey, are promoted to all economic classes. Reebok athletic shoes, for example, which can cost seventy-five dollars and up, are pitched to rich and poor alike. In the face of social expectations that equate such items with success, attractiveness, and desirability, it is very hard for a poor person to live contentedly without such things, as we learn from the accounts of inner-city youngsters who kill each other for a pair of those same Reeboks.

In response to this relentless emphasis on appearance, twentieth-century women adapt themselves, insofar as they can, to what Roberta Seid calls the "new modesty." This standard allows the female body to be seen, but it must now be free of "unwanted" body hair, fat, cellulite, and wrinkles. It must also be perfectly formed with medium-sized, firm breasts, a narrow waist, and trim hips.[55] Since few women can approach that ideal without effort, the 1980s and 1990s have seen a boom in fitness clubs, which have become a new meeting place for hegemonic males and privileged females. This same era has also given us stomach stapling, face lifts, tummy tucks, intestinal shortening, mouth wiring, liposuction (major surgery, done under general anesthesia, which sucks out fat deposits in areas like the thighs), breast implants (which may migrate sideways or even become attached to the rib cage),[56] and every diet plan and weight-loss center imaginable.

55. Ibid., p. 216.
56. Early in 1992, the Food and Drug Administration held hearings on silicon breast implants that revealed woefully inadequate medical and scientific research on both the short-term and the long-term effects of these implants on women's bodies. This is a significant problem, since over two million women have had implants inserted into their bodies, and about 130,000 women a year seek implants (Nicholas Regush, "Toxic Breasts," *Mother Jones,* January/February 1992, p. 26). These hearings brought to light not only the lack of rigorous research on the effects of implants but also Dow Corning's actual suppression of data on adverse effects. As a result, women whose implants were causing serious health complications and

The Complicity of the Church

We would expect this relentless focus on weight and appearance to be criticized and corrected by Christianity, since in many ways it works against the Christian concept of the body as God's temple. But religious authors have rushed to capitalize on weight-reduction programs for women. Seid notes the explosion of Christian diet books and aids that hit the market in the 1970s:

> Prayer-Diet clubs of the 1950s gave way to Overeaters' Victorious, the Workshop in Lenten Living, the 3D (for Diet, Discipline, and Discipleship), and the Jesus System for Weight Control. There were Frances Hunter's *God's Answer to Fat — Lose It!* (1976), Joan Cavanaugh's *More of Christ and Less of Me* (1976), and C. S. Lovett's chillingly titled 1978 book, *Help, Lord — The Devil Wants Me Fat!* [57]

In 1990, the Christian women's magazine *Virtue* reinforced the secular values of thinness, youth, and beauty for women. While *Virtue* chose a pleasant-looking, "grandmotherly" woman as its "Woman of the Year," it did not allow her face to appear on its cover. Instead, the cover featured a young, thin, blonde model next to the "Woman of the Year" teaser, implying that the younger model was in fact the winner. If the magazine had been sincerely endorsing values other than those of the marketplace, the real winner would have been pictured on the cover. Inside, among articles that encouraged marital love, solid family life, and hospitality, *Virtue* gave fashion hints that assumed the secular model of womanhood and told readers how to achieve it.[58]

Sadly, the points of resistance to current fashion that do exist come from the secular world, not from within mainstream or evangelical Christianity. Indeed, for many people, church is one more stage for the display

---

the doctors who treated them often failed to recognize the implants as the culprit (Boston Women's Health Book Collective, "Comment on Breast Implants," *Ms.,* March/April 1992, p. 39). The outcome of the FDA hearings is that a temporary moratorium has been placed on silicon implants.

57. Ibid., p. 168. We have also come across weight-loss aids in Christian bookstores that feature titles like "Firm Believer" and slogans such as "He must increase, but I must decrease" (a pointed but contextually warped reference to John 3:30).

58. Jan M. McLaughlin, "Clothes That Flatter," *Virtue,* January/February 1990, pp. 46-48.

of status. Men wear the business suits that serve so well to mark their place in the world, while their wives wear clothing that indicates and flatters their husbands' position. Even working-class men "dress up" in hegemonic male fashion for church attendance, with their wives taking on the complementary dress of privileged femininity. Single women copy the married women, unless they wish to remain single, in which case they dress to suit themselves. Single men also wear the standard male uniform, unless they have no aspirations to leadership within the church. Children are dressed by their parents to suit not only prevailing peer norms but also their parents' social position. For resistance to current fashion tyranny, we have to look outside the church.

Points of Resistance to the Tyranny of Fashion

Recognizing the wisdom of appealing to more than ideals of style and beauty, the secular marketplace is now diversifying product lines, advertisements, and physical types. *Harper's Bazaar* now carries ads for larger-sized women's clothing, such as Spiegel's "For You" line. (However, it places these ads in the fashion magazine's "back of the bus" — after the editorial section.) Keds, the sneakers that baby-boomers wore as children, are now targeting that same group in their adult years. One recent ad shows a woman playing with her baby: she sets him on her lower legs, using them like a seesaw; the caption reads, "Keds introduces weight-lifting shoes." Another ad pictures a couple walking along the railroad tracks; the caption reads, "Keds introduces track shoes." The final ad in the series of three reads "Keds introduces mountain climbing shoes"; the accompanying photo shows a group of women and men making a gymnastic pyramid by kneeling on each other's backs. Unlike many ads for Nikes and Reeboks, these ads imply relational values rather than competition and personal advancement. And the recent media success of the fat and assertive Roseanne Arnold indicates a deep vein of desire for another way to talk about, and be, a woman.

Men, too, are resisting the uniform. Some now wear pink or purple shirts, more colorful accessories, pleated, baggy trousers, and minimally tailored jackets — to work. Some wear a counter-hegemonic tie such as the bow tie; some wear no tie, if their workplace managers will allow it. Off the job, they often dress to please not only themselves but also their female partners, wearing neon colors, shorts, sweaters, and so on. But still no skirts!

Fashioning the Future

This analysis of the gendered system of fashion is not meant to suggest that all of us, male and female, should attire ourselves in neutrally colored unisex clothing that obscures the gender of its wearers, or that all emphasis on fitness and weight is skewed and inappropriate. Far from it. We were meant to take care of our bodies, and we were not meant to live without expressing our creativity, our relations to others, or our joy in the diversity of the creation that God has given to us. But, just as surely, the Creator did *not* intend for us to be slaves to culturally mandated, ideal body types, or to live in the tyrannical grip of clothing whose main purpose is to display our wealth and position (if we are male) and our seductive capacities (if we are female). The frantic pursuit of fashion and physical perfection inhibits us as builders of God's kingdom because it takes undue time and attention and because it reinforces sex and class divisions. It is just another bar in the cage described in our discussion of the social construction of gender (see Chapter Eight). So, to return to the opening remarks of this chapter, clothing as *rhetoric* is to be avoided.

What that leaves us with is the language of *conversation* and *ritual* in our clothing choices. The clothing we wear should express our individual personalities, our freely chosen relations with others, and our membership in communities of mutual commitment. Wearing something we have made or that someone has made for us speaks of self-nurture and of the nurture of others. Wearing the gift of clothing from another person enhances the idea of clothing as conversation. Sharing clothing, lending it to friends and relatives, is another option. One of us shares with her husband a passion for large, heavy, hooded sweatshirts bearing a university or college logo. (They give each other these sweatshirts as gifts in a size they both can wear.) Others could refuse in simple ways to dress according to the norms of hegemonic masculinity and privileged femininity. For example, when dressing for occasions that typically "require" powerful (or rhetorical) clothes, such as speaking in public, conducting an interview, or working at a high-status job, men could choose to wear sweaters instead of blazers, and women could opt for pants instead of skirts. We could also adapt qualities of the ethnic costumes worn by our forebears. These choices and others could help to pry loose the grip of hegemony and privilege that is reflected in fashion.

339

CHAPTER 11

How Shall We Speak?
Language and Gender Relations

F aith Martin, a Christian feminist in the Reformed Presbyterian
Church, tells the following anecdote in her book *Call Me Blessed*:

> I'm the kind who cannot remember a joke long enough to tell it to the
> family at dinner. But here is one I heard over five years ago and have
> not forgotten: "When God created men, he rested. Then God created
> woman, and since then neither God nor man has rested."
>
> I was able to remember this joke so easily because it wasn't a joke
> — it was an insult, and I have no trouble remembering insults. Of
> course I laughed at the time because the speaker meant to be funny,
> not unkind. But beneath the joke lay a hidden message that lingered
> and stung: God and men share a common problem — women.[1]

Martin had this experience recently, but this kind of diminishment
of women has a long history. In 1880, Reverend Anna Howard Shaw was

1. Martin, *Call Me Blessed: The Emerging Christian Woman* (Grand Rapids: William B. Eerdmans, 1988), p. 105.

The primary author of this chapter is Helen Sterk. Douglas Schuurman contributed significantly to the section entitled "Silencing through Religious Language."

340

ordained in the Methodist Protestant Church. Her ordination examination proceeded with vigor verging on heat. One elder stood up and quoted 1 Timothy 3:2: "Now a bishop must be above reproach, married only once, temperate, sensible, respectable, hospitable, an apt teacher." How, he asked Ms. Shaw, could she be the husband of one wife? In response, she asked him if he was married. "No," was his answer. Then how, she asked him, could *he* claim to be the husband of one wife? "And," she continued, "you know the plain teaching of this passage is that an elder must live a life in decent, moral order, *not* that an elder must be male."[2]

A century later, Gretchen Gaebelein Hull, an elder in the Presbyterian Church (U.S.A.), tells the story of her participation in a denominationally appointed group that met to discuss women's ordination. Gaebelein Hull was the first (and at that time only) woman appointed to the denomination's executive council. Early in the meeting one minister commented, "Trying to address the problem we have in our denomination with women's ordination is like a man climbing on the back leg of an elephant, intent on rape. How does he start? Where does he begin?"[3] Gaebelein Hull was stunned into silence by this minister's assumptions — that he could proceed like a male talking exclusively to males, that she should adapt herself to his terms, and that a bestial simile of this kind was appropriate in this or any other context. She waited for the executive director to rebuke the speaker, but he did not. Later she approached the director to tell him of her reaction. The director failed to see the comment as offensive and essentially advised Gaebelein Hull that if she couldn't stand the heat, she should stay out of the kitchen.

Each of these stories reflects an aspect of women's relationship to language. In the first, Faith Martin is told a joke that denigrates her sex and thus her. She laughs to be polite, but remembers the incident as humiliating, not humorous. In the second, Anna Shaw resists the male elder's crude attempt to silence her by challenging him to accept 1 Timothy 3:2 as a call for all church leaders to lead a moral life. In the third, Gretchen Gaebelein Hull finds her presence in an all-male gathering effectively neutralized by the men's assumptions that she will not (and should not) take offense at a sexual analogy that compares the challenge of the women's ordination

2. Gaebelein Shaw, *The Story of a Pioneer* (New York: Harper & Brothers, 1915), p. 126.
3. Hull, *Equal to Serve: Women and Men in the Church and Home* (Old Tappan, N.J.: Fleming H. Revell, 1987), p. 43.

issue to a man trying to rape an elephant. In each case, women are assumed to be on the margins of language. This is generally the case in all uses of language in English-speaking culture. Male voices speak the dominant idiom; women's choices are to adapt, to be taken over, or to resist an idiom not of their own making.

This chapter tells stories of gender relations as reflected in one particular language: the English language used in middle-class homes, schools, churches, and public places. While such a focus may seem narrow, the "strategies of reclamation" we will see practiced by women in these situations may parallel the strategies of other groups whose experience has been muted by a dominant group's language, lexicon, and grammar. (For case studies of women's reclamation of power in the Third World, see Chapter Fourteen.)

Action through Language

How does language work? One view of language is that words simply mirror reality. According to this view, language is first a human tool that "names what is." Accordingly, accurate communication is both possible and usual and is wholly determined by the speaker's intention. This concept of communication assumes that meaning is a "package" that one person presents to another. Consider the example of a minister known by a member of our team. In a worship committee meeting, this minister resisted the suggestion that he had offended a church member by his use of sexist language in the pulpit. He did not, he maintained, *give* offense. If offense occurred, it was *taken,* not given. He assumed that since he had not intended to denigrate women, he in fact had not done so. (It is quite likely that the men involved in the situations described at the beginning of this chapter would have replied similarly to their women critics.)

What this minister failed to realize is that meaning is not simply identical with the speaker's intention. In her book entitled *Metaphorical Theology,* Sallie McFague observes that "the total interpretive situation of a text is a complex triad of speaker, text, and hearer in which many possibilities are present for misunderstandings, differences of opinions, varying interpretations, and revisions of previous interpretations."[4] And

4. McFague, *Metaphorical Theology: Models of God in Religious Language* (Philadelphia: Fortress Press, 1982), p. 56.

342

if one considers the spoken word to be a kind of text, then that "text" also takes on meaning from its context, including the time, the place, and the history of the relationship between speaker and hearer. The text also takes meaning from the type of speech it represents — sermon, lecture, conversation, and the like.

For example, if the supposed offense had happened during a casual conversation between strangers rather than during the presentation of a sermon by a minister to his parishioners, its meaning would probably differ significantly. A conversation's norms allow for give-and-take. If a conversational partner finds a particular comment offensive, she or he can say so. Furthermore, strangers have no established relationship that requires respect, trust, and nurture. Such is not the case when a pastor addresses a congregation. For one thing, the congregants remain mute during a sermon. But more importantly, congregants deserve a pastor's consideration and respect as persons who equally image God. So, yes, a minister can very well give offense even without intending it.

The point is that communication involves, at the very least, a triad of speaker, message, and hearer. More specifically, it involves an interaction of these elements within simultaneous contexts — the interpersonal, the social, and the cultural. One person in relation with another who desires to understand and be understood will negotiate meaning by listening not just to the other's words but for the other's intentions and by asking questions whenever purposes seem opaque or ambiguous. This person will also take turns speaking — exchanging the positions of speaker and hearer.

This understanding of communication assumes that humans act on each other through speaking as well as by direct physical means. Raised in an era that tried to reduce everything to brute matter, many of us were taught that "sticks and stones can break my bones, but names can never hurt me." But our actual experience — as well as the Bible's witness to the power of speech — tells us otherwise. In fact, humans may well act on each other more through language than through any other means. Among other things, language conveys law, social policy, interpersonal attitudes, education, scientific theories, and religion. Through language we communicate our attitudes and beliefs and encourage others to do as we wish.[5]

5. See, for example, James 3:5-10: "How great a forest is set ablaze by a small fire! And the tongue is a fire. The tongue is placed among our members as a world of iniquity; it stains the whole body, sets on fire the cycle of nature, and is itself

We have said that the quality of any given speech act depends on the speaker's intention, the message itself, and the hearer's reception of the message. No one element alone determines what sort of act it is. All three together — though perhaps message reception is a slightly more significant factor than message intention — create the action. Speakers must realize that their words take on a relatively independent life once uttered or written. This is especially true if a fairly impersonal relationship, one devoid of helpful contextual cues, exists between speakers and hearers or between writers and readers. At the same time, hearers and readers must recognize that meaning is not only what they perceive but also what the message implies and the speaker intends.

Anyone who has carefully crafted a letter understands the three-way interaction of the writer's intentions, the words and format chosen, and the way the reader will interpret the letter. For example, if someone is writing a letter to apply for a job, he or she highlights his or her skills. A good application letter shows that an applicant understands how his or her talents match the job's demands. By contrast, someone composing a letter to a friend can write more informally, less strategically, and in more personal, intimate terms. In either case, a good letter-writer needs to visualize the reader and speak in terms appropriate to the relationship. And a good reader needs to attend closely to the letter itself while trying to understand the writer. The letter is an index to the relationship between reader and writer.

Not only letters but all communications reflect human relationships. The way a person speaks — how, where, how long — can be analyzed to show the assumptions held by that person. (The anecdotes introducing this chapter illustrate this point clearly.) Particularly important to our purposes are the ways in which people commonly speak or refrain from speaking can be analyzed to uncover cultural assumptions about gender.

Seeing speech as a kind of action can help us work through some extremely thorny issues concerning both past and ongoing effects of

---

set on fire by hell. For every species of beast and bird, of reptile and sea creature, can be tamed and has been tamed by the human species, but no one can tame the tongue — a restless evil, full of deadly poison. With it we bless the Lord and Father, and with it we curse those who are made in the likeness of God. From the same mouth come blessing and cursing. My brothers and sisters, this ought not to be so." For a full discussion of the theory that language is action, see J. L. Austin's *How to Do Things with Words,* 2d ed. (Cambridge: Harvard University Press, 1975); and John Searle's *Speech Acts: An Essay in the Philosophy of Language* (1969; rpt. Cambridge: Cambridge University Press, 1978).

language on gender relations. In what follows we will focus on two general speech actions that have affected the way women and men see themselves in relation to each other. These actions are, first, the defining of "human," "man," and "woman," and, second, the silencing of women's voices, especially women's expression of their own experiences. In both cases we will uncover assumptions about who is assumed to be the speaker and who the hearer, uncover some of the ways in which these assumptions lead to a "man-made language," and finally show how women can reclaim positions as speakers, with men and other women as hearers.

How Naming and Defining Shape Gender Relations

Naming and defining are two of the most powerful acts of human speech. When something is named, it takes on a fuller reality. It can be talked about. It has presence. For instance, until sexual harassment was named, it was not considered to be real. But after it was named, policies to curtail it were easier to institute. The name provided a way to think about it and gave greater precision of definition to other terms as well. While "flirting" may be harmless, "sexual harassment" is not. The name allows people to see sexual harassment as a method of male dominance, the purpose of which is to harm (mostly) women, and thus as a phenomenon best recognized and named by women. Naming sexual harassment and defining it as harmful to women is a graphic example of how language not only reflects but also shapes gender relations.

There are three basic naming terms that have an impact on the construction of gender relations: *human, man,* and *woman.* Key questions in determining the nature of gender-specific speech acts include the following: Who decides the content and value of these names? And what effect do the resulting definitions have on gender relations?

Defining "Human Being"

What is human? According to one source, "Intromission and ejaculation are universal human behaviors."[6] Even passing attention to the message

---

6. Albert Scheflen, quoted by David Graddol and Joan Swann in *Gender Voices* (New York: Basil Blackwell, 1989), p. 110.

345

reveals that the implied speaker is male and the implied hearer is also male. Women do not appear at all in this reference to "universal human behaviors." This is no isolated instance. Until recently, when feminist consciousness made it impossible for publishers and readers to erase women from the category or to make their inclusion at best ambiguous, "human" effectively meant "male" and "man" meant "human."

Dale Spender devotes an entire book to such instances of man-made and man-centered language. Two of her examples come from the writings of psychologist Erich Fromm and biologist Loren Eiseley from the 1950s and '60s. According to Spender,

> [Fromm wrote] that man's "vital interests" were "life, food, access to females, etc." Loren Eiseley implied [man-centeredness] when he wrote of man that "his back aches, he ruptures easily, his women have difficulties in childbirth. . . ." If these writers had been using *man* in the sense of the human species rather than males, they would have written that man's vital interests are life, food, and access to the opposite sex, and that man suffers backaches, ruptures easily, and has difficulties giving birth.[7]

In a similar vein, Mary Daly, a feminist theologian, quotes a male theologian as follows:

> To believe that God is Father is to become aware of oneself not as a stranger, not as an outsider or an alienated person, but as a son who belongs or a person appointed to a marvelous destiny, which he shares with the whole community. To believe that God is Father means to be able to say "we" in regard to all men.[8]

This theologian may well have intended to include everyone, women and men alike, in his description of God's embrace. Unfortunately, his choice of language effectively hinders women readers from feeling as if they are part of God's people. While a woman could see God as her heavenly Father and therefore feel intimately familiar with God, it is somewhat more difficult for a woman to name herself as a "son." To do so, she would have to translate what "son" would mean in her case. She

7. Spender, *Man-Made Language*, 2d ed. (London: Routledge & Kegan Paul, 1985), p. 155.

8. Daly, *Beyond God the Father: Toward a Philosophy of Women's Liberation* (Boston: Beacon Press, 1973), p. 20.

could, for example, be a son of God if she understands "son" to mean "heir," a legitimate child of God. A woman reader could envision herself as a "person appointed to a marvelous destiny," to use the theologian's phrase. However, even a woman adept at translating male into female terms and deciding whether she is included *this* time will find it challenging to puzzle out a way in which she can be a "he" who belongs with the "we" of "all men." Daly wryly concludes that "she cannot belong to *this* without assenting to her own lobotomy."[9] At the very least, such mental gymnastics tend to wear a person out!

Further examples can be added to these two. Contemporary authors now write in gender-neutral language, by and large. But while their language does not overtly equate "man" with "human," its effect often remains the same. If words like *human* or *person* are used but still mean *man*, as close attention to the subtext will often show, then women are still excluded. For example, just before the Gulf War began in 1991, one American news magazine queried, "Who wants to fight a war to defend the Arabs' right to treat their women like camels?"[10] No doubt the writer of that rhetorical question was trying to be feminist, but the very structure of the sentence implies that no Arab persons are women! In another pointed criticism of this kind of masculinist subtext, political scientist Susan Moller Okin questions the assumptions undergirding current calls to return to the communal values and traditions of a culture. We agree with the many contempory male writers who are beginning to recognize the hazards of rampant individualism in our culture and who call for a resurrection of "communal values."[11] But Okin rightly points out that if cultural conceptualizations of "tradition" and "humanity" do not include concerns historically associated with women — such as developing and maintaining relationships and bearing and raising children — readers will have difficulty seeing women as contributing

9. Ibid.

10. Quoted in "Conventional Wisdom Watch," *Newsweek*, 2 December 1990, p. 6.

11. These include the following: Robert N. Bellah et al., *Habits of the Heart* (Berkeley: University of California Press, 1985), and *The Good Society* (New York: Alfred A. Knopf, 1991); Alasdair MacIntyre, *After Virtue: A Study in Moral Theology*, 2d ed. (South Bend: University of Notre Dame Press, 1984), and *Whose Justice? Which Rationality?* (South Bend: University of Notre Dame Press, 1988); John Rawls, *A Theory of Justice* (Cambridge: Harvard University Press, 1971); and Michael Walzer, *Spheres of Justice* (New York: Basic Books, 1983).

meaningfully either to tradition or to humanity.[12] (See also Chapter Thirteen.)

These examples show that when a masculine perspective frames the naming and defining of words like "human" and "person," women are not automatically assumed to be included. Indeed, women have had to work to be recognized as human, even when it could have been politically expedient for men to include them. Reverend Olympia Brown, a suffragette and the first woman minister to be ordained in the United States, addressed herself to President Woodrow Wilson's 1914 statement "that human rights are preeminent above all other claims." She asked, "Does that not mean the rights of women?"[13] The recent contemporary struggle over the Equal Rights Amendment also illustrates women's need to challenge unspoken gender-laden assumptions about "humanness" and "personhood" in political documents such as the U.S. Constitution.

Similarly, an excerpt from the form for Public Profession of Faith in one Protestant denomination reads as follows: "*Minister:* (after individuals have professed their faith): 'In the name of our Lord Jesus Christ, I now welcome you to all the privileges of full communion. I welcome you to full participation in the life of the church. I welcome you to its responsibilities, its joys and its suffering.'" These words are addressed to newly professing members of both sexes, despite the fact that in the denomination in question, women can be neither elders nor pastors. In what sense, then, are they being welcomed into *all* of the church's privileges and into *full* participation in the church's life? How is the average teenaged woman who is professing her faith along with her peers in front of the church to understand and act upon this highly ambiguous message?[14]

Defining "Woman" and "Man"

Dictionaries are repositories of cultural definitions. Dictionary definitions are supposedly denotative, or factual, and therefore value-neutral.

12. Okin's argument refers particularly to Alasdair MacIntyre's treatment of tradition and humanity in *After Virtue*. See her book entitled *Justice, Gender, and the Family* (New York: Basic Books, 1989), p. 60.

13. Charlotte Cote, *Olympia Brown: The Battle for Equality* (Racine, Wis.: Mother Courage Press, 1988), p. 152.

14. See the form titled "Public Profession of Faith," *Psalter Hymnal* (Grand Rapids: CRC Publications, 1987), p. 964.

But in the case of gender definitions, clear values emerge. Being a human is synonymous with being a man, while being a woman is being *only* a woman at best, and being subhuman at worst. For example, according to *Webster's Ninth New Collegiate Dictionary*, the first definition of man is "a human being; especially an adult human being." The first definition of woman is "an adult female person." What is even more telling, however, is the cultural value ascribed to the masculine over the feminine. "Mannish" is defined as "resembling or suggesting a man rather than a woman," a seemingly value-neutral definition. However, "womanish" is defined not only as "characteristic of or suitable for a woman" but also as "unsuitable to a man *or to a strong character of either sex*" (our emphases). A strong woman, then, would be insulted by being called womanish but perhaps complimented by being called mannish. These definitions, along with the definitions of *masculine, feminine, effeminate, manly,* and *womanly,* illustrate the positive regard that maleness enjoys in American culture, as well as the position of power inherent in the masculine perspective.

Dictionary definitions are only one index of the relative value a culture gives to women and men. Historically, many men's writings have defined women as at best sentimentally moral and at worst perniciously destructive to men. The early church fathers defined women as less worthy than men, more prone to evil, and in greater need of salvation. In the early days of the church, Jerome, Augustine, and John of Chrysostom defined women as sexual temptresses (downplaying the fact that men could also seduce women). Because of women's likeness to Eve, whom many construed to be the first sinner, women were believed to bear unique guilt in God's eyes.[15] In Philo of Alexandria's story of the fall from Paradise, "Mind corresponds to man ... the sense to woman; and pleasure encounters and holds parley with the senses first, and through them cheats with her quackeries the sovereign mind itself."[16] Philo's statement associates reason with man and sensuality with woman, and assumes that sensuality poses a grave danger to male rationality. During the Middle Ages, Aristotle's view of women as "misbegotten males" colored people's ideas about women. Along with Aristotle, Aqui-

15. Mary Daly, *The Church and the Second Sex* (New York: Harper & Row, 1968), chap. two.

16. Brian Wren, *What Language Shall I Borrow? God-Talk in Worship: A Male Response to Feminist Theology* (New York: Crossroad, 1990), p. 33.

nas believed that the father was the active principle in procreation and therefore should be loved more. (The mother's womb, on this account, were merely the soil in which the male-generated fetus grew.) Women, according to Aquinas, had no rightful public voice and so could only be hearers of the Word as spoken by men. What women heard, of course, kept them under men's rule.

In modern times, the patriarchal mind-set continues to value women less than men. Brian Wren, a Reformed British minister and hymn writer whose feminism informs his understanding of men, argues that patriarchal thinking is marked both by a desire for control and by a scorn for all that is womanly.[17] Given the cultural value of "masculinity," a man will strive to avoid being called effeminate while a woman might see her own "manly resolve" as something to be valued. Women and men alike can be captured by this mind-set and can internalize its terms of human value: maleness is good and powerful, while femaleness is less than and subordinate to maleness.

This view of the sexes is maintained not only by the denotative and connotative meanings of language but also by institutions such as the family, the legal system, the school system, and various social systems and their policies. But the cultural privilege enjoyed by masculinity need not necessarily be the result of an intentional conspiracy by males. Since, as David Graddol and Joan Swann point out, the majority of social structures "are controlled and run by men rather than women, it follows that the ideas which they promote will serve the interests of men, not because of any conspiracy or malevolent interest, but simply because important decisions about the expected behavior of women will be [made] by men and will reflect men's assumptions and values."[18] And any women allowed into power will affirm these male assumptions and values or risk losing power. In this way, women become men's accomplices. (See also Chapter Eight.)

In order to live in a patriarchal world, women learn to translate hidden messages adeptly. When are women included in speech references and when are they not? What do men think about women, and how can women use this knowledge to gain a modicum of power over their own destinies? And what is women's potential? Can women be human? Sallie McFague sums up the dilemma neatly: "The patriarchal model oppresses

17. Ibid., pp. 11-13.
18. Graddol and Swann, *Gender Voices*, p. 143.

women as much by what it does *not* say about women as by what it *does* say. What it does say defines her as inferior; what it does not say leaves her without alternatives."[19] This is life on the margins. When the very language available for women and men reflects masculine assumptions about life and value, women will find themselves on the periphery or excluded altogether. This is one reason why women may limit themselves to subservient positions in public and domestic life. Lacking the *language* of options, women may find it difficult to *perceive* options.

Reclaiming Humanity for Women

The acts of naming and defining *humanity, men,* and *women* are indeed foundational. "In the name of" gender, people will go to war, cut their hair, paint their faces, speak out, cook dinner, mow the lawn, choose to work in a day-care setting, and sue for alimony. Human action is given legitimacy and direction in large part through the words we use. If women are excluded from cultural definitions of humanity, then women are denied (and deny to themselves) the full range of actions available to persons. In this section we attend to the work women have done and are doing to claim the term *human* for themselves, thereby becoming the speakers rather than merely the receivers of the speech acts of naming and defining.

It is hard work for women to argue that they are human. To do so, women must cross the grain of their culture and their own socialization. For one thing, they need to assume the role of *speakers* in a culture that casts them primarily as *listeners.*[20] For another, they have to learn to put their needs first, and in white, Western culture women are socialized to put others' needs before their own. Feminist theologians suggest that the traditional understanding of pride as the besetting *human* sin rings false with women's experience.[21] They argue that women tend to *undervalue* rather than *overvalue* themselves, making excessive self-effacement a

19. McFague, *Metaphorical Theology,* p. 150.

20. Phyllis M. Japp, "Esther or Isaiah?: The Abolitionist-Feminist Rhetoric of Angelina Grimke," *Quarterly Journal of Speech* 71 (August 1985): 335-48.

21. Barbara Hilkert Andolsen, "Agape in Feminist Ethics," *Journal of Religion and Ethics* 9 (Spring 1981): 69-83; and Margaret Farley, "Love as Mutuality," in *Woman: New Dimensions,* ed. Walter Burkhardt (New York: Paulist Press, 1975), pp. 51-70.

351

woman's besetting sin. (See also Chapters Six and Twelve.) Finally, if it is true that women are cast in the role of hearers rather than speakers, it seems reasonable that women would find it easier to *hear* and *accept* prevailing cultural definitions of humanity than go against the grain and create new, womanly definitions.

A woman with no access to a public vehicle of expression, such as a lecture, sermon, essay, novel, or poem, has little opportunity to change her culture's definitions of women as less than fully human. Nineteenth- and twentieth-century women who first resisted the "cult of domesticity" have spoken and written of the price they paid for their actions. Women who felt a call to ministry implicitly demanded that they be seen as human. Some, such as Olympia Brown and Anna Howard Shaw, succeeded because they refused to even recognize, much less accept, cultural limitations on their talent. But not all were able to do so. A close friend of Reverend Brown's, Reverend Phoebe Hanaford, left her pastorate because of the treatment she received from her male parishioners. A single eloquent sentence records the reason for Reverend Hanaford's exit from her church: "For some women, the pain was too deep."[22] And Virginia Woolf, in *A Room of One's Own*, made clear the cost women could pay for even trying to write and publish in the early part of this century. In 1929 the definition of woman did not include the exercise of a public voice. "One can measure the opposition that was in the air to a woman writing," Woolf observes, "when one finds that even a woman with a great turn for writing has brought herself to believe that to write a book was to be ridiculous, even to show oneself distracted."[23] However, unless women write and tell stories of their own experiences, their names and definitions will be lost to humanity.

Men as well as women suffer when language excludes women except as framed by the perspectives of men. Unless women are given public voice, men will never know what women know about women or how women perceive men. Woolf uses the technique of reversal to show the dimensions of this problem:

> Suppose, for instance, that men were only represented in literature as lovers of women, and were never the friends of men, soldiers, thinkers, dreamers; how few parts in Shakespeare could have been

22. Cote, *Olympia Brown*, p. 122.
23. Woolf, *A Room of One's Own* (1930; rpt. San Diego: Harvest/HBJ Book, 1957), p. 66.

allotted to them; how literature would suffer! . . . Literature would be incredibly impoverished, as indeed literature is impoverished beyond our counting by the doors that have been shut upon women.[24]

The 1991 Senate confirmation hearing of Clarence Thomas gives a clear example of the contemporary problems that develop when male decision makers try to come to terms with women's perceptions. The outrage of American women over the treatment of Anita Hill led to the registration of ten million women voters and an increase in the number of women who ran for and were elected to political office. (There were two women in the Senate; now there are six.)

Our cultural view of *masculinity* is informed by men speaking and writing about themselves and their experiences. So, too, our cultural view of *femininity* is shaped by men speaking and writing about their experience of women. And not least, our understanding of *humanity* is determined by men's speaking and writing. Until women speak and write with authority, cultural conceptions of men, women, and humanity will be but pale ghosts of reality.

Fortunately, women now are articulating and publishing their own definitions and descriptions of life, of children, women, and men, and of the relations among them. This book is one part of an effort to add women's messages to the cultural stock of knowledge. However, neither men nor women are automatically docile listeners to messages spoken and written by women and expressive of women's assumptions. New speakers and new messages meet with great resistance. The stories of the nineteenth- and twentieth-century campaigners for women's rights, even the limited right to vote, show the cultural resistance that existed and may still exist, resistance that stands as an obstacle to hearing women's voices. In the nineteenth century female suffragists were not only cast as women of dubious morals; they were cast as no women at all — which, indeed, they were not, according to the cultural definitions of the day. In March 1917, Reverend Olympia Brown, then eighty-two years old, marched with fellow suffragists outside President Woodrow Wilson's White House, protesting the denial of the vote to women. Men gathered to taunt them. "Go back home and take care of your children," they jeered, and "You don't need to vote. We do that for you."[25] Some

24. Ibid., p. 87.
25. Cote, *Olympia Brown*, p. 1.

men jumped into the picket line, ripping up banners and snapping poster handles, snarling, "You women belong in the home, not out here mixing in politics."[26] Then the men pushed down some of the marchers. Up drove police officers, who arrested and handcuffed not the men but the women, on President Wilson's orders. Clearly, although these women had the physical characteristics of womanhood, their refusal to act according to cultural norms of femininity cost them the privilege of being treated like women. The force and vehemence of these words and actions show how deeply threatened these men felt and how shallow their chivalry could be.

Not only men but some women, influenced by masculine definitions of *citizen,* opposed extending the vote to women. The poet and essayist Charlotte Perkins Gilman wrote "The Anti-Suffragettes," published in 1897, in order to expose and criticize women who opposed granting women the right to vote. "Fashionable women in luxurious homes . . . have all the rights they want," she claimed, as do "successful women who have won their way" and "religious women of the feebler sort" and "ignorant women — college-bred sometimes" as well as "selfish women — pigs in petticoats" and "more's the pity, some good women, too." In the final verse of this poem Gilman expressed her despair about women who accept masculine limits:

And out of these has come a monstrous thing,
A strange, down-sucking whirlpool of disgrace,
Women uniting against womanhood,
And using that great name to hide their sin![27]

Even within contemporary Christian circles, where all people should be cherished as image bearers of God, resistance often greets women's attempts to speak their own names and definitions. One Reformed Protestant minister, Steve Schlissel, attacks feminists, both female and male, by saying, "How long will we tolerate those divisive ones who deny that these [issues of headship and women's ordination] are confessional matters. . . . Let us rise with one voice and show them the door."[28] And William Addie, attacking Christian feminism in a book

26. Ibid.
27. Gilman, "The Anti-Suffragettes," in *The World Split Open,* ed. Louise Bernikow (New York: Vintage Books, 1974), pp. 224-26.
28. Steve M. Schlissel, "Hugen's Best Shot: A Blank," *Christian Renewal,* 26

entitled *What Will Happen to God?* concludes that "the more powerful the Christian feminism movement becomes, the more abundant will be the Church's bitter harvest of division, anger, suspicion, and all uncharitableness."[29] The force of these words suggests the deep threat that these men feel at the prospect of transformed gender relations.

But although some women align themselves with a patriarchy which assumes that women must be mute, others speak out. Currently, work done by Carol Gilligan in psychology and by Sara Ruddick in philosophy, as well as work done by others in history, literature, and the sciences, reclaims humanity for women.[30] In *In a Different Voice,* Gilligan analyzes the ways women carry out mature moral decision-making. She finds that they are more likely than men to balance the needs of the self with those of significant others, and argues that we will not have a

---

December 1988, p. 14. Compare this statement to one made in 1860 by Albert Bledsoe Taylor, a pro-slavery professor at the University of Virginia: "The history of interpretation furnishes no examples of more violent perversions of the sacred text than are to be found in the writings of the abolitionists. They seem to consider themselves above the Scriptures: and when they put themselves above the law of God, it is not [surprising] that they should disregard the laws of men" ("Liberty and Slavery, or Slavery in the Light of Moral and Political Philosophy," in *Cotton Is King,* ed. E. W. Elliot [1860; rpt. New York: Negro University Press, 1969], pp. 379-80).

29. Addie, *What Will Happen to God?*(London: Photobooks [Bristol] Ltd., 1984), p. 155.

30. For discussions in the context of psychology, see Carol Gilligan's *In a Different Voice: Psychological Theory and Women's Development* (Cambridge: Harvard University Press, 1982); Gilligan et al.'s *Making Connections: The Relational Worlds of Adolescent Girls at Emma Willard School* (Troy, N.Y.: Emma Willard School, 1989); and *How Schools Shortchange Girls,* AAUW Education Foundation and National Education Association, 1992. For a discussion in the context of philosophy, see Sara Ruddick's *Maternal Thinking: Toward a Politics of Peace* (New York: Ballantine Books, 1989). For a discussion in the context of history, see Caroline Bynum's *Holy Feast and Holy Fast: The Religious Significance of Food to Medieval Women* (Berkeley: University of California Press, 1987). For discussions in the context of literature, see *The World Split Open* and *The Norton Anthology of Literature by Women,* ed. Sandra Gilbert and Susan Gubar (New York: W. W. Norton, 1985). For a discussion in the context of political science, see Susan Moller Okin's *Justice, Gender, and the Family.* For a discussion of the work women have done in their homes, see Susan Strasser's *Never Done: A History of American Housework* (New York: Pantheon Books, 1982). For a discussion in the context of rhetoric, see Karen A. Foss and Sonja K. Foss's *Women Speak: The Eloquence of Women's Lives* (Prospect Heights, Ill.: Waveland Press, 1991). This is, of course, just a sampling of the work being done.

355

full understanding of human morality until women's morality is studied *on its own terms.* In her book entitled *Making Connections,* Gilligan focuses on adolescent girls, and discovers that in childhood girls do not fear giving full voice to their opinions. In adolescence, however, they mute their opinions rather than risk being disliked. Not until quite a bit later in their development, if at all, do they risk expressing authentic ideas as women. Philosopher Sara Ruddick uses the perspective and voice of the mother to speak about war. Ruddick feels that unless motherly thinking, whether by females or males, is incorporated into theories about war, "humanity" will not be fully represented in those theories. (See Chapter Twelve for a more detailed elaboration of these theories.)

The arguments made by these women and by others like them are crucial to a full understanding of what it means to be human. Until psychology and philosophy recognize the distinctive development of women, they remain disciplines that are theoretically and practically impoverished. An analogous impoverishment exists in other academic fields, as well as in life beyond the academy. If women's and men's experiences are not articulated by women to the same degree that both are now articulated by men, then human experience itself is greatly diminished. The concept of humanity can be enriched only by expanding it to incorporate women's perspectives. Indeed, authentic self-definition by all marginal groups is crucial to a full conception of humanity. Drawing an analogy between women as a group and black people, Sister Sandra Schneiders says,

> One of the most revolutionary things we can do is change language. When blacks said, "No, we're not negroes; we're blacks," the white establishment's initial response was, "Blacks, negroes, what's the difference?" . . . But blacks said, "We'll name ourselves." At that point blacks claimed their own identity, and whites had to learn to respond to that identity.[31]

Now Jesse Jackson and other leaders advocate the term *African-American.* As with the change from *negro* to *black,* this name change met with ridicule

---

31. "God Is More Than Two Men and a Bird," interview with Sister Sandra M. Schneiders, *U.S. Catholic,* May 1990, p. 24. The common African-American practice of selecting unusual first names for sons and daughters (Rashida, Denea, Drametrius, and Pashon are among the ones we've noted) may also reflect a healthy determination to "name ourselves" in the face of a family history impoverished by slavery and by the imposition of English names by slave owners.

and even opposition from the white male power structure. Such opposition indicates whose voices are presumed authoritative and whose are suspect in this culture. Yet who has more right to the action of naming than the people being named?

Elsewhere in this book, we discuss the necessity of including women's definitions of work, spirituality, history, and family. We show that women's perspectives often differ from men's. In this chapter we have seen that women, more than men, have been placed in the position of listeners to messages rather than speakers and shapers of them. If a full understanding of humanity is to be achieved, women and men need to institute a flexible interchange of the positions of hearer and speaker.

How the Silencing of Female Experience Shapes Gender Relations

The second major speech act having to do with gender is that of silencing. Of course, simply defining who is human, man, or woman functions to silence certain aspects of human experience, because it suggests that men can appropriately name their own as well as women's and humanity's nature. However, women's voices are directly and indirectly rendered mute in several other ways. Direct silencing is achieved by placing physical constraints on women's expression. Indirect silencing is achieved by declaring certain topics (such as sex, pregnancy, birth, and nursing) off-limits to public expression by women. Further, women are indirectly silenced through lexical and grammatical means, through conversational control, and through the restriction of religious expression to male terms. Let us look at each of these in turn.

Direct Silencing of Women's Voices

In *The Devil's Dictionary*, Ambrose Bierce defined woman as "the animal which can be taught not to talk."[32] Historical records are full of ways in which women were taught, quite directly and sometimes physically, not to talk. Aristotle counseled women to be silent, to save their energy for their children because "children evidently draw on the mother who

32. Bierce, *The Devil's Dictionary* (1911; rpt. New York: A. & C. Boni, 1935).

357

carries them in the womb, just as plants draw on soil."[33] (We are reminded of later arguments, extending into the nineteenth century, against women pursuing higher education: the mental stress of study, they were told, might render their wombs barren.) In 1687, Abbé Fénelon defined a good woman as one who "spins, confines herself to her household, holds her tongue, believes and obeys."[34] In colonial America, a woman who was not silent might be lashed to a ducking stool and held under water, publicly gagged, or even fitted with "branks," an iron frame that encased a woman's head with a sharp metal bit for her mouth.[35]

In the nineteenth century, although women were admitted to some American colleges and universities, they were not permitted to engage in debate, either with men or among themselves. The early suffragists Lucy Stone and Reverend Olympia Brown both faced such unreasonable restrictions. In 1837, Lucy Stone began attending Oberlin College. "Although permitted to attend classes with men, she was not allowed to read her own papers in class or participate in debates," Kathleen Jamieson points out. "When she fulfilled the requirements to graduate, she learned that she could write her own commencement address but not deliver it."[36] (We are reminded of a recent woman graduate from a Reformed seminary who in her graduating year won a prize for writing the best student sermon but was not allowed to preach it in a church within her own denomination.) Facing similar restrictions at Mount Holyoke College in 1854, Olympia Brown and some other young women started a literary society in which they could practice public speaking. After they had attained some proficiency, they were visited by a committee of teachers, who listened silently to a debate and left. Subsequently Brown was told to disband the society or face expulsion. When she asked why, she was told that it made her "too independent" and that since she and her sister had argued opposite sides of an issue in the debate, that meant that either they opposed each other or that one of them was speaking convictions which were not her own — both of which were "inexcusable" for young ladies.[37]

In higher education in this century, it is rare to see such obvious

33. Aristotle, quoted by Kathleen Hall Jamieson in *Eloquence in an Electronic Age* (New York: Oxford University Press, 1988), p. 68.

34. Fénelon, quoted by Jamieson in ibid., p. 68.

35. Ibid.

36. Jamieson, *Eloquence in an Electronic Age*, p. 69.

37. Cote, *Olympia Brown*, p. 30.

silencing. Nevertheless, impediments to the speech of women students remain in effect. Research in American colleges and universities has shown that both male and female professors tend to call on male students more often. In addition, professors question male students more thoroughly, insisting that they attempt an answer. Professors also tend to make more direct and longer eye contact with male students. Furthermore, they interrupt female students more often than male. The combined effect of these actions tends to reduce women's vocal participation in their own education.[38]

Less obvious ways have also been used to silence women's voices. In her book entitled *The Writing or the Sex? or, Why You Don't Have to Read Women's Writing to Know It's No Good,* Dale Spender recounts story after story of how women's writing was kept from publication, or if published, kept from critical praise.[39] In particular, Spender presents evidence of Leo Tolstoy's usurpation of his wife's work in *War and Peace* and of F. Scott Fitzgerald's emotionally threatening theft of his wife Zelda's life experiences. Although traditionally credited simply with being Count Tolstoy's transcriptionist, Sonya Tolstoy (besides bearing her husband thirteen children and running their household) deciphered her husband's torturously small handwriting, cleaned up his literary structure and style, published his books, and argued with the state censor about questionable passages. Spender argues that if anyone other than a wife had done this work, the individual would have gotten recognition at least, perhaps even acknowledgment as co-author.[40]

---

38. R. M. Hall and B. R. Sandler, *The Campus Climate: A Chilly One for Women?* (Washington: Project on the Status and Education of Women, Association of American Colleges, 1982). See also *How Schools Shortchange Girls,* AAUW Education Foundation and National Education Association, 1992.

39. Writes Spender, "I concluded that the values being ascribed [to talk] were based on the sex and not the talk. . . . When men 'gossip' it is called something different. The same thesis applies to the written word and has a distinct counterpart in the novel. . . . From Jane Austen to Barbara Cartland — and despite all the dramatic diversity in between — there is the implication that *all* women's writing is romance, in much the same way that all women's talk is gossip. And a content analysis of the writing cannot possibly support such a classification scheme. Look at the domestic melodramas of Thomas Hardy, at the romances of D. H. Lawrence. Clearly when men write romance it's called something different" (*The Writing or the Sex? or, Why You Don't Have to Read Women's Writing to Know It's No Good* [New York: Pergamon Press, 1989], p. 21).

40. Ibid., p. 167. There is also a large body of literature in experimental social

When F. Scott Fitzgerald was working on *Tender Is the Night,* his literary treatment of Zelda's mental instability, Zelda was working on a novel of her own, on "the story of myself versus myself."[41] As Spender tells the story, Scott considered Zelda's experience his property to exploit and threatened to destroy her work unless she gave up writing about her experiences with psychiatry. She installed a double lock on her study door, but still desiring his companionship, she sought a compromise. In response, he demanded that she stop writing fiction, and commanded, "If you write a play, it cannot be a play about psychiatry, and it cannot be a play laid on the Riviera, and it cannot be a play laid in Switzerland, and whatever the idea is, it will have to be submitted to me."[42] Zelda never authored a psychiatric novel and Scott did publish *Tender Is the Night,* which is strongly based on Zelda's experiences.

Other more obvious forms of direct silencing can readily be found. For example, all-male or mostly male legislative bodies routinely make policies affecting women's lives. The U.S. Congress, state legislatures, church ruling groups, administrators in higher education, and corporate trustees and managers decide how people will live, worship, and work. Yet very few of these bodies can claim proportional representation of women. Occasionally women are invited to speak to these groups on issues of direct female concern, but they do so on the terms clearly set by the male authorities. Particularly poignant are cases of men setting policy on the issues of women's reproduction, sexual harassment, and whether women will even be admitted as members into these legislative groups.

Another but less visible form of direct silencing occurs in much medical research. Women were not included as subjects in certain studies

---

psychology which shows that the very same "product" (e.g., a graduate school application, an essay, an art portfolio, a career resumé) receives, on the average, a different (and more negative) evaluation if it is said to belong to a woman (e.g., "Joan T. MacKay") as opposed to a man (e.g., "John T. MacKay"). Male evaluators are more likely to make such a distinction than female evaluators. For a review of the pertinent literature, see Barbara S. Wallston and Virginia E. O'Leary's "Sex Makes a Difference: Differential Perceptions of Women and Men," in *Review of Personality and Social Psychology,* vol. 2, ed. Ladd Wheeler (Beverly Hills, Calif.: Sage Publications, 1981), pp. 9-41.

41. Quoted by Spender in *The Writing or the Sex?* p. 191.
42. Quoted by Spender in ibid., p. 191.

on the effects of overweight,[43] heart disease,[44] and cholesterol levels.[45] Nevertheless, the results of these studies were generalized from the all-male test groups to women. The reasons given for this omission vary from inconvenience and oversight to the difficulties of controlling for the effects of women's monthly hormonal fluctuations. But no matter what the reasons are, potential for real harm exists when women are excluded from medical research. If diagnosis and treatment of women patients are carried out on the basis of male norms, treatment may be inadequate, and unexpected side effects may well occur. Conclusions about *human* biology and functioning based on exclusively male test groups necessarily will be faulty. We need to affirm women's humanity and safeguard their well-being by including them in all medical research on humans.

While women have often been directly silenced, such silencings can at least be pinpointed and revealed as pernicious. The exposure of direct-silencing practices has made it rare to hear someone advocate women's public silence. While men in some quarters may devoutly desire such silence, no longer can they exclude women without anticipating protest. In many circles, overt sexism is as little tolerated as overt racism. Yet just as covert racism continues to plague American culture, so does covert sexism. It appears in the *indirect* silencing of women's voices,

43. Roberta Pollack Seid, *Never Too Thin: Why Women Are at War with Their Bodies* (New York: Prentice Hall Press, 1989), p. 118.

44. Research on heart disease has been conducted almost exclusively on men, the consequence being that doctors do not know with any certainty what sorts of diagnoses and treatments are appropriate for women. Studies show that "cardiologists are more likely to prescribe a bypass for a man while he is still healthy enough to withstand the procedure. But for a woman, they may delay making the same recommendation until she is sicker." The result is that a higher percentage of women than men die immediately after bypass surgery. Further, one study found that "40% of men who had an abnormal stress test got an angiogram, but only 4% of the women did." This lack of diagnostic work may contribute to women's deaths from heart disease ("Bypassed Women," *American Health*, October 1990, p. 16).

45. Research on women and cholesterol levels is virtually nonexistent. The research that has been done shows a far less clear correlation between cholesterol levels and heart disease in women than in men. The "magic number" of 200 as a safe cholesterol level is specific to men. As a result, women are being diagnosed and treated as if they were men, although health-care providers have no understanding of the effect of hormones on cholesterol levels. See Richard Trubo's "Cholesterol Gap: Lack of Studies Leaves Women Wondering," *American Health*, January/February 1990, p. 16.

361

conversations, and stories. Let us look at some of these more subtle ways of rendering women mute.

Indirect Silencing of Women's Voices

As the preceding section shows, women's silence has historically been seen as normative. Only when they broke that silence did any obvious muzzling have to occur. Speech was assumed to be a male prerogative. For women, the cultural assumption was that speech simply was not a regular option. In a culture dominated by masculinity, the powers of language to name, to characterize, and to categorize have been largely denied to women.

Anthropologists Edwin Ardener and Shirley Ardener have named women a "muted group." In their research they found women's muting particularly apparent in public discourse. Lacking access to public arenas, women cannot enter into meaning-creating dialogue with each other or with men. As a result, dominant meanings are male-influenced and not only exclude womanly interpretations but also downgrade the value and validity of those interpretations when they are offered.[46]

The implications of women's muted status are far-reaching, and woven into the very warp and woof of gender relations. Cheris Kramerae has carried out the most sustained research program on muted-group perspectives in the field of communication. In her theorizing, three key assumptions emerge: first, that women's perception of the world differs from men's due to the gendered division of labor; second, that a masculine system of perception dominates language due to men's control of available cultural power; and third, that women must translate their perceptions into male terms in order to function in society.[47] Not only does women's muting affect their ability to enact the cultural role of speaker; it also stunts men's potential for enacting the cultural role

46. See the following: Edwin Ardener, "Some Outstanding Problems in the Analysis of Events," paper presented at the Association of Social Anthropologists' Dicennial Conference, 1973; Edwin Ardener, "The 'Problem' Revisited," in *Perceiving Women*, ed. Shirley Ardener (London: Malaby Press, 1975), pp. 19-28; and Shirley Ardener, *Defining Females: The Nature of Women in Society* (New York: John Wiley, 1978).

47. Kramerae, *Women and Men Speaking: Frameworks for Analysis* (Rowley, Mass.: Newbury House, 1981), p. 3.

of listener. As a result, communication and culture itself are impoverished.

In the next several sections we will explore just a few of the ways in which masculine cultural hegemony has muted women's voices. First, we will analyze some of the lexical and grammatical means by which women are silenced; next we will briefly discuss topics rendered taboo by male standards about what is appropriate; then we will see how conversation itself is controlled by male norms; and finally, we will focus on a particular form of public expression — namely, religious discourse.

Lexical and Grammatical Silencing There is an abundance of names in the English lexicon for an overly talkative woman — gossip, magpie, shrew, scold, nag, harpy, harridan, fishwife, termagant, bitch, and virago, to name just a few. How many names are there for a man who talks too much? Other than "interminable bore" (and this is a label that can be applied to a woman as well as a man), there are very few. And "interminable bore" carries none of the vituperative power suggested by *virago, bitch,* and *harpy.* Consider also that there are 220 English terms to describe a sexually promiscuous woman and only 20 to describe a sexually promiscuous man.[48] Contrast, too, the connotative distinction between the terms. A man might be a stud, a Lothario, a rake, a gigolo, or a Don Juan, while a woman might be a slut, a whore, a nympho, or a cunt. Given the definition of the speech act we developed earlier in this chapter, we can ask who is doing the naming and who is receiving the names. In both these examples, note that the male terms generally have more positive connotations than the female terms. Persons naming *themselves* are not likely to choose names with negative connotations. So we are led to conclude that this naming has been done largely from a masculine perspective rather than a feminine one.

A woman living in a culture that has so many negative names for her speech and her sexuality soon learns the value of silence and muted behavior. The burden of having these names applied to her may be greater than she wishes to bear, so rather than risking public ridicule and losing what little influence her "appropriate" femininity allows, she may well choose silence. After all, her silence is usually rewarded, while her speech and overt behavior may be punished. Women learn this lesson early in life, and as a result they often cooperate with their own muting.

48. Graddol and Swann, *Gender Voices,* p. 110.

Even this brief look at the lexical resources of the English language shows that words have been sounded by masculine voices. Feminine voices have not added many new words or affected many meanings and usages.[49] Only recently have some small shifts begun to occur. To highlight this point, let us look at the use of *man* as a generic noun for humans and the use of *he* as a generic pronoun for humans.

In 1975, the theologian Paul Jewett wrote a book on gender called *Man as Male and Female.*[50] In it he set forth a view of the sexes as needing each other for completion, as being complementary, equally human, and equally image bearers of God. Although in his discussion Jewett treats women and men evenhandedly, his use of the term *man* nevertheless points to a serious lexical problem. Jewett decided to use the word *Man* with a capital "M" whenever he meant "human" or "person," and *man* with a small "m" whenever he meant "male person." Given the resources of the English language, which has several adequate terms for referring to both male and female (such as *human, human being, person*), Jewett's word choice weakens the argument of his book. Every time the reader reads "Man," a translation process has to take place. Does *this* "Man" refer to males only, males and females, or some sort of supermale? Male readers may not notice this process of translation; after all, no matter what the context, they are included. But as pointed out earlier in this chapter, women may *appear* to be included in a given use of the term *man* yet actually be excluded. So whenever the term is used, men do not need to translate, whereas women do.[51]

49. For a fuller documentation of this point as well as an extensive bibliography for further reading, see *Language, Gender and Society*, ed. Barrie Thorne, Cheris Kramarae, and Nancy Henley (Rowley, Mass.: Newbury House, 1983).

50. Jewett, *Man as Male and Female: A Study in Sexual Relationships from a Theological Point of View* (Grand Rapids: William B. Eerdmans, 1975).

51. When we say "men do not need to translate," we mean that the particular men who have power do not need to figure out whether they themselves are included. But historically, when hegemonic men have wished to exclude both women and nonhegemonic males from the so-called generic "men," they show that they are quite adept translators. Consider the Declaration of the Rights of Man, adopted by the National Assembly of France in 1789, and the statement that "all men are created equal" in the American Declaration of Independence. In both cases, "man/men" appears to be inclusive. But in the eighteenth century, Mary Wollstonecraft had to write her *Vindication of the Rights of Woman* (London, 1792) precisely because the male liberals of her era read "man" as "male" (indeed, *white, propertied* male) when it came to granting the franchise. The American women's suffrage movement and

In choosing *Man* as a label for generic humanity, Jewett, no doubt unintentionally, reinforced male superiority. Notice that this shows the value of seeing communication as a speech act including at least the three elements of message, intention, and reception. We know from his explicit statement and overall treatment of the subject that Jewett *does* respect women and men equally, so his intention was to use an inclusive term, showing honor to each. He tried to control the meaning of his word usage by clarifying in his first chapter that *man* would mean a male person and *Man* would mean all humans. But just saying something does not make it so. The word *man* is not completely under Jewett's control. Readers *may* read it with his caveat in mind, but Jewett's intention cannot guarantee that the reader's connotative understanding of the word will be what he intends. The word *man* does have a heavily loaded cultural meaning and value. Capitalizing the word does not reduce or eliminate that loading. In fact, it strengthens the force of the word. If *man* is male, then *Man,* some readers will infer, must be supermale. So capitalizing *man* may have a boomerang effect, achieving just the opposite of Jewett's intention. Male readers would not be confused by his use of *Man,* but female readers would have to intensify the translation process they always go through when they come across *man.* Does *this* use of *man* include women or not?

Even so, Paul Jewett's book is extremely valuable for biblical feminists. It illustrates, albeit painfully, how even the best-intentioned male can be taken over by what Brian Wren calls the two main characteristics of Western masculinity — desire for control and disdain for women. Jewett felt he could control the meaning of this word by specifying its boundaries. But it is not possible to control a language owned by an entire culture. Perhaps Jewett could control a brand-new term whose denotation he specified. But his choice of the term *Man* when *person* or *human* was available suggests a residual disdain for women.

Similar problems surround the use of *he* as a generic pronoun. Again, if pressed, speakers will maintain that they mean *she* as well as

---

the black civil rights movement were needed for the same reason: the male writers of the Declaration of Independence (and later the Constitution) simply took for granted that "all men" was to be translated as "all white, propertied men." Indeed, the hurdles that must be surmounted to register as a voter in the United States (in contrast to other Western democracies, where state or city employees do door-to-door registration) suggest that this attitude has not completely disappeared.

he when they use *he*. We recall the times that team members spoke to various church gatherings during our research year together. One of our team members got a positive response to almost every issue she raised — women's place in the professions, the need for shared housework and parenting, and so on. However, when she questioned whether *he* was actually a generic term, she met with great resistance. In fact, *women* led the resistance, saying such things as, "We know we're included. It's tradition. Why must we change even our language?"

Several answers are possible. First, language is malleable and always open to change. As new meanings are validated through common use, they are incorporated. New technologies, for example, need new names. Similarly, new behaviors and relations need new names. And old terms such as *gay* or *dumb* or *ass*, when no longer accepted as having the meaning they once did, have to change. Second, contrary to what many people think, the generic *he* is *not* the result of "natural" tradition; that is, it did not emerge as a generic referent through common use. In fact, in the older tradition, *they* was used as a generic singular or plural (e.g., "Each student should stay at their own desk"). However, in 1746 grammarian John Kirkby codified the first rules of English grammar in his "Eighty-Eight Grammatical Rules." Rule number twenty-one said, "The male gender [is] more comprehensive than the female," thus instituting the use of the so-called generic *he*.[52] However, ordinary people continued their idiomatic practice of using *they* to refer to either singular or plural antecedents. According to Dale Spender, "The male grammarians, who were incensed with the 'misuse' of *they*, were instrumental in securing the 1850 Act of Parliament which legally insisted that *he* stood for *she*."[53]

Today, even though women and men claim to know that *he* stands for both *he* and *she*, communication research has not borne out that claim. A 1979 study "found that both men and women rarely judged sentences which contained the generic 'he' to refer potentially to women. What is more, even sentences which contained a predominantly female antecedent (e.g., 'A nurse must frequently help his patients out of bed') were not judged as potentially referring to a female nurse."[54] Study after study bears out the fact that readers will impute maleness to *he* and will

---

52. Spender, *Man-Made Language*, p. 148.
53. Ibid., p. 150.
54. Mackay and Fulkerson, quoted by Graddol and Swann in *Gender Voices*, p. 151.

recognize potential for femaleness only if the word used is sex-neutral — for example, *chair* rather than *chairman*, *athlete* rather than *sportsman*, or *police officer* rather than *policeman*.[55] Students asked to elaborate on a sentence that uses *he* write about male subjects much more often than students responding to a sentence using *they*, a finding which has been corroborated in a review of fourteen laboratory studies. One researcher checked to see whether students actually intended *she* when they wrote *he*:

> [The researcher] asked subjects to complete sentence fragments that contained people in "male-oriented roles," "female-oriented roles," and "neutral roles" and found little evidence to suggest that college students used *he* in a generic sense, either in writing or in speech. Instead, they seemed to imagine a particular gender for the protagonists and use an appropriate sex-specific pronoun.[56]

"He/man" language is not gender-neutral and is not generic for humankind. However, its terms are short, easy to use, and familiar. Coming up with appropriate alternatives requires considerable thought, because it means new messages must be created that do not rely on sexist clichés. Male and female speakers must realize that he/man language is part of a patriarchal idiom that implicitly denigrates women by removing them from view. This denigration encourages women's silence and their complicity in their own marginalization. New terms might include sex-neutral ones such as *person, human, created ones, people*, and *humankind*. Speakers and writers can also alternate female with male pronouns. And they can use *they* as a generic singular pronoun, harking back to a tradition of the people rather than the impositions of grammarians. They might even use *female*-specific terms predominantly in an effort to bring balance into our cultural conception of humanity. According to Brian Wren, the Christian man should consider the present era as the time to say of woman, "'She must increase, and I must decrease.'"[57]

Language is always evolving. Many women and men no longer accept lexical gaps and sexist gaffes as natural and necessary. Increasingly, people recognize the need to expand language to include women.

55. Ibid. See also Wendy Martyna's "Beyond the 'He/Man' Approach: The Case for Non-Sexist Language," *Signs* 5 (1980): 482-93.

56. Graddol and Swann, *Gender Voices*, p. 151.

57. Wren, *What Language Shall I Borrow?* p. 226.

Handbooks such as Casey Miller and Kate Swift's *Handbook of Nonsexist Writing* and Bobbye Sorrels's *The Nonsexist Communicator* suggest concrete alternatives to exclusive language.[58] Moreover, few publishers of textbooks and scholarly journals accept sexist language in their publications anymore. Work continues at the level of published discourse to expand the domain of what is "human" to include women.

Women themselves are adding new words to the English language and redefining old ones. Suzette Haden Elgin has developed a womanly language called Laadan ("the language of those who perceive") in her science fiction. In this language there are many words denoting various kinds of pregnancy (e.g., *lewidan,* meaning first-time pregnancy, and *lalewida,* meaning joyfully pregnant), words for a woman's first menstruation, and words for completed menopause. Responding to women's sensitivity to human relations, Laadan has at least eight words denoting love: for example, *ad* refers to the respectful love felt for one not liked and *ashon* to the love felt for someone related not by blood but by the heart.[59]

Several new dictionaries redefine old terms in new ways, recasting language in women's terms. Of them, Mary Daly's *Webster's First New Intergalactic Wickedary of the English Language* plays most imaginatively with language. A self-named "webster" (a webster, Daly explains, is "a woman whose occupation is to Weave, esp. a Weaver of Words and Word-Webs"),[60] Daly reclaims and redefines derogatory terms applied to women and women's work. For example, a spinster is "a woman whose occupation is to Spin, to participate in the whirling movement of creation; one who has chosen her Self, who defines her Self by choice neither in relation to children nor to men; one who is self-identified; a whirling dervish, spiraling in New/Time Space."[61] Daly also coins derogatory terms for feminine qualities and "types" prized within Western culture. A *fembot,* for instance, is "a female robot: the archetypal role

58. See Miller and Swift's *Handbook of Nonsexist Writing* (New York: Lippincott & Crowell, 1980); and Sorrels's *Nonsexist Communicator* (Englewood Cliffs, N.J.: Prentice-Hall, 1983). See also the appendix on nonsexist writing guidelines in *Constructing and Reconstructing Gender,* ed. Linda Perry, Lynn Turner, and Helen Sterk (Buffalo, N.Y.: State University of New York Press, 1992).

59. Elgin, *A First Dictionary and Grammar of Laaden* (Madison, Wis.: Society for the Furtherance and Study of Fantasy and Science Fiction, 1988).

60. Daly, *Webster's First New Intergalactic Wickedary of the English Language,* ed. Jane Caputi (Boston: Beacon Press, 1987), p. 178.

61. Ibid., p. 167.

model forced upon women throughout fatherland: the unstated goal/end of socialization into patriarchal womanhood: the totaled woman."[62] In like manner, *A Feminist Dictionary* redefines selected concepts within women's realities (e.g., "fat," which is defined as "a substance in the form of energy stored; essential to the preservation of life and health among humans — but presented to contemporary Western women as a mortal enemy. . ."), laying bare the often unspoken dynamics within language's connotations, dynamics that give normative force to names.[63] In two ways — through creating *new* language and recasting *old* language — women are adding their understandings of the world to our culture's stock of knowledge.

Silencing Women by Making Certain Topics Taboo Women find themselves in quite a different relation to the English language than do men. As we have noted, they must play a "guessing game" with generic male nouns and pronouns (and some other terms as well) in order to decide whether or not they are included. Moreover, until recently women were denied access to public forums, the places where cultural meanings and values are established. If women had feelings other than the ones masculine discourse attributed to them, they were able to express their resistance to the limitations placed on them only to a few close friends, or perhaps in a diary or journal. Even experiences peculiar to females, such as their experiences of sex, pregnancy, birth, nursing, and menstruation, were talked about by men rather than women.

A very troubling example of the phenomenon of men giving voice to women's experiences is found in the recent case of Archbishop Weakland of Milwaukee, Wisconsin. In the summer of 1990, Archbishop Weakland met with several groups of Catholic women and asked them about their experiences with and feelings about abortion. He listened carefully and incorporated what the women had said in later talks he gave on the topic. Nothing he said denied any Roman Catholic teaching

62. Ibid., p. 198.

63. Cheris Kramarae and Paula A. Treichler, along with Ann Russo, *A Feminist Dictionary* (Boston: Pandora Press, 1985), p. 154. Those who see such exercises as needless overkill or simply defensive game-playing might recall that the Arctic Inuit have some dozen or more words to describe snow (in contrast to our paltry three or four). Most people see this as a creative, adaptive, and justified elaboration of a unique experience rather than a waste of words. Why then should we consider women's unique elaboration of our own language to be anything less?

on abortion. Yet, in the fall of 1990, the Pope prohibited a Swiss university from giving Weakland an honorary doctorate simply because he had solicited women's views on this topic. According to the Vatican, women's views had nothing to do with church policy on abortion, and Weakland should not have listened to, much less asked for, women's opinions.[64]

Women have also been denied a public forum for speaking about other experiences that many of them share, such as running a household, cooking, and cleaning. In pointed disregard for gender partnership, male speakers have appropriated female experience, interpreted it to fit their perspectives, and fed that message back to women, who have generally adapted themselves to the message. If women could not adapt gracefully and flawlessly, they pretended as best they could.

The moment-to-moment details of our foremothers' lives are largely lost to us. The available historical and literary accounts speak of women primarily as mothers, wives, sisters, or lovers, and occasionally as queens or some other history-making "exception." If Victorian novels written by men were our only source of information about late-nineteenth-century women, we might conclude that they were all wan and listless, had to be carried about by servants, made endless social calls on other women, and whiled away time in idle conversation until male lovers appeared. But increasingly women's voices are expressing women's experiences. Works such as *Quilters*, a recent play that highlights the strengths and resourcefulness of pioneer women, remind us that women helped each other give birth, participated in each other's marriages, and tenderly assisted in the burial of each other's dead.[65] *Women of the West* features extracts from women pioneers' journals that vividly illustrate their courage and strength (e.g., a woman gave birth during a rest stop and then bundled back into the wagon).[66] Susan Strasser's history of housework, *Never Done*, tells us that the typical middle-class woman of

64. For a description of the situation with Archbishop Weakland, see "Bishop Defends His Views on Abortion," *Chicago Tribune*, 24 November 1990, sec. 1, p. 4, and "Vatican Apologizes to Bishop," *Chicago Tribune*, 30 November 1990, sec. 1, p. 11. For a complete discussion of the archbishop's conversations with women, see "Listening Sessions on Abortion," a special issue of the *Catholic Herald*, 24 May 1990.

65. Molly Newman and Barbara Damashek, *Quilters* (New York: Dramatists Play Service, 1986).

66. Cathy Luchetti and Carol Olwell, *Women of the West* (St. George, Utah: Antelope Island Press, 1982).

the nineteenth century hauled four hundred pounds of water each wash-day.[67] Male accounts of women's lives simply do not capture the vivid reality of women's experiences.

Marian Glastenbury observes that there is no housework done in literature written by men. "Men don't want to have to admit how hard women have to work," she reasons. "It ruins their image as the chivalrous sex: It raises awkward questions about the ostensible weakness of women — and strength of men. And it certainly lends support to the premise that women have a genuine grievance."[68] Another thing not mentioned by male authors is the weight of the layers of clothing actually worn by the delicate, leisured ladies of the nineteenth century: a typical winter costume weighed thirty-seven pounds, nineteen of which hung from the waist![69] (See also Chapter Ten.) Again, male perspectives blunt the reality of women's experience.

Even on more intimate topics a male perspective continues to shape the messages. A vivid example in American culture is the way in which sexual intercourse has been named to exclude women's experience. Many popular terms for naming intercourse, such as *screwing* and *rooting*, highlight phallic action. And what is mere "foreplay" to a man could be the total event to a woman. A woman's lack of response to male-defined sexual activity is called "frigidity," but "reluctance" might more accurately capture the nature of the response from the woman's point of view. Freud labeled a woman's clitoral orgasm as less "mature" than a vaginal orgasm. Forceful penetration of an unwilling woman is called "rape," but this word effectively neutralizes the unique terror of the event,[70] since it is applied indiscriminately to any act of willful force (e.g., "the rape of the earth"). In this context, a fact cited earlier bears repeating: in 1977 the English language contained over 200 words, largely derogatory, for a sexually promiscuous woman, but only 20, largely laudatory, for a promiscuous man.[71]

Pregnancy and birth are physical experiences that only women can

---

67. Strasser, *Never Done: A History of American Housework* (New York: Pantheon Books, 1982).

68. Glastenbury, quoted by Spender in *Man-Made Language*, p. 118.

69. Barbara Ehrenreich and Deirdre English, *For Her Own Good: 150 Years of the Experts' Advice to Women* (Garden City, N.Y.: Doubleday–Anchor Press, 1978), p. 98.

70. Spender, *Man-Made Language*, pp. 177ff.

71. Graddol and Swann, *Gender Voices*, p. 110.

have. However, even though men cannot conceive, carry, or give birth to babies, it is their perspective, and not women's, that governs discourse about these events. Adrienne Rich decries the patriarchal thought and language patterns that have encouraged women to "recoil from female biology" rather than to see "our physicality as a resource."[72] In blunt and powerful detail, she explains how women's experience of birth has been taken over from female midwives and managed by male physicians, thereby alienating women from an experience fully and rightfully theirs.

Unless a woman seeks out a midwife, she may find her pregnancy treated as something akin to a disease, with doctors, books, and manuals advising her about its accompanying symptoms. "Amniocentesis," "Caesarean section," "ultrasound," and "Rh incompatibility" may become familiar terms. She may even be told she has an "incompetent cervix." (Somehow we doubt we will ever hear of an "incompetent penis.") But she may never know just how other women experience the painful privilege of birth unless she has close women friends or relatives that she can talk with. (One of our team members, who was carrying her first child when she and her husband pastored a rural church, was told by a woman farmer in the congregation that giving birth was a little like "trying to pass a watermelon." In retrospect, she found the description very apt!) Having given birth, a woman may feel confused and even guilty about the sexual response she may experience when nursing her baby, especially if she reads only medical doctors' reports and not the literature of La Leche League. And a woman will not be prepared for the pain of rock-hard, engorged breasts unless she talks with other women who have borne babies. Worse still, she may not get advice on how to relieve that pain unless she talks to another woman. A male doctor simply cannot know the feeling.

The preceding observations are not intended to downplay the positive achievements of modern obstetrics, gynecology, and pediatrics. Women who might otherwise have died in childbirth *have* benefitted from the invention of forceps, the development of Caesarian-section techniques, and the improvement of birth-related sanitation. But the "technologization" of birthing and of other womanly functions has stifled the voice of women's *own* experiences of such events and often rendered women passive and silent about their own needs and prefer-

72. Rich, *Of Woman Born: Motherhood as Experience and Institution* (New York: W. W. Norton, 1976).

ences as they live with their bodies. Literature about women, by and large, has not taken up these topics that are so personally meaningful for women. We find little about the details of ordinary life as experienced by our foremothers. Stories of women's coming of age with the onset of menstruation are absent. We read a lot about men's wars and about men's first sexual experiences, but little about birth or about how different women became pregnant and how they felt about it.[73] In literature, Dale Spender observes, "Women labor between the lines, children are born outside the pages, and rare even is the record of women's responses to such a momentous occasion."[74]

Since little in literature or public speech attends to the experiences common to most women, the public perception is that these experiences do not count. What counts is largely what can be named and what can be spoken of. But making menstruation, pregnancy, birth, nursing, and menopause taboo topics or subjects of no account robs women of shared knowledge and men of the possibility of understanding, in part, the powerful forces that gave them life. When women's physical experiences are repressed, our view of human life is incomplete.

Women are now sharing and writing and speaking about their own experiences, naming them in ways that are at odds with traditional, male-defined ways. Support groups grow out of women's need to share experiences, check perceptions, and give credibility to their own pleasure or pain. Groups for incest survivors and rape survivors allow women to express their feelings of violation and rage. Groups for women who have had abortions or who cannot get pregnant allow women to feel a sense

---

73. *Books in Print* for spring 1990 lists close to a hundred books on birth. Three seem to offer women's words on birth: K. C. Cole's *What Only a Mother Can Tell You about Having a Baby* (Berkeley: Berkeley Publishers, 1986); Sheila Kitzinger's *Giving Birth: How It Really Feels* (New York: Noonday Books, 1989); and Nancy Sorel's *Ever since Eve: Personal Reflections on Childbirth* (Oxford: Oxford University Press, 1984). Several pay particular attention to fathers' feelings and comments on pregnancy and birth — for example, Cecilia Worth's *Birth of a Father: New Fathers Talk about Pregnancy, Childbirth and the First Three Months* (New York: Worth/McGraw, 1988); Jack Heinowitz's *Pregnant Fathers: Making the Best of the Father's Role before, during, and after Childbirth* (Englewood Cliffs, N. J.: Prentice-Hall, 1982); and H. A. Brant's *Childbirth for Men* (Oxford: Oxford University Press, 1985). "Pregnant fathers" and "childbirth for men" — the language of these titles is mind-boggling! Only by turning childbirth from a physical act done by women into a cultural metaphor and then stretching that metaphor to the limit can one imagine "pregnant fathers."

74. Spender, *The Writing or the Sex?* p. 115.

of control over their reproductive life or at least less isolation in the wake of its associated experiences. La Leche League gives women a forum in which to share information and experience mutual support during the sometimes problematic, yet pleasurable, time of nursing.

More and more books challenge the medical establishment's assumption that male-defined techniques are invariably the best ones for bringing life into the world. Among the books that treat women's birthing experience sympathetically and use their language are these: *Silent Knife* by Nancy Wainer Cohen and Lois J. Estner, which focuses on how women felt about having Caesarean sections and how they managed to have vaginal births after Caesarean sections; *Of Woman Born* by Adrienne Rich, which is a historical account about how and why the control over birthing slipped from women's hands into men's tools; and several of Sheila Kitzinger's books — including *Giving Birth: How It Really Feels*; *The Experience of Childbirth*; *Birth at Home*; and *Your Baby Your Way*.[75]

These very physical topics, having directly to do with women's sexuality, are paradigmatic cases of topics that need to be addressed by women who have experienced them. But by no means are these the only topics on which women need to be heard. In other chapters of this book we argue forcefully for including women's views and experiences of — among other things — history, religion, psychology, and general embodiment. The garden of culture remains stunted if only one kind of gardener nurtures its growth.

Conversation as a Means of Silencing We note, however, that a masculine bias in general and males in particular still dominate the terms of conversation, whether between two persons or in a group. In conversation, masculine bias largely determines topic choice, the perspective taken on the topic, the role of interruptions, and the place and means of conversation. This bias indirectly silences women as they talk with men, depriving both women and men of women's perspectives. Let us look at some of the evidence for this male biasing of conversation.

Communication research on gender has found that women and

75. Cohen and Estner, *Silent Knife: Caesarean Prevention and Vaginal Birth after Caesarean* (South Hadley, Mass.: Bergin and Garvey, 1983); Rich, *Of Woman Born*; and Kitzinger, *Giving Birth: How It Really Feels* (New York: Noonday Books, 1989); *The Experience of Childbirth* (Harmondsworth: Penguin, 1984); *Birth at Home* (New York: Oxford University Press, 1979); and *Your Baby Your Way* (New York: Pantheon Books, 1987).

men differ in their understanding of conversation's goal. Women tend to see conversation as a cooperative effort, marked by give-and-take, questioning, listening, and extending the conversational points made by their partners. Men tend to view conversation as competitive, marked by attempts to control the topic. Men often talk until another conversational partner interrupts, interrupt to regain the floor, and make certain that their own points are made. Linguist Deborah Tannen calls women's conversational language "rapport talk," the point of which is to make interpersonal connections and to nurture relationships. She calls men's conversational style "report talk," which is used "primarily [as] a means to preserve independence and negotiate and maintain status in a hierarchical social order."[76] As you may have guessed, when women talk with women and men talk with men, their conversational goals often mesh. However, when women and men talk together, the conversations are noticeably asymmetric. In fact, many women cooperate with men's drive to compete.

The result is that women tend to support men in conversation. One researcher uses the term "relational work" to describe the effort women expend in mixed-sex conversation. Women's job in conversation is to get men to talk, to help them express emotion, and to situate the conversation in terms of the relationship. To accomplish these tasks, women ask questions, try to appear animated, and respond with nods or encouraging noises.[77] Even if a woman disagrees with a man's perspective, she tends to leave it unchallenged. Sally McConnell-Ginet has found that "if there is a difference between the man's world view and experience and those of the woman, then it is the man's that directs the entire discourse."[78] The woman does not necessarily *take on* the man's perspective. What happens is that her "experience and values never appear as assumptions in mixed-sex discourse."[79] So in conversation, as in public speech and in print, women's perspectives disappear in favor of men's.

One might think that at least when women *outnumber* men in conversational groups, the tendencies toward male dominance and female acquiescence would be diminished. But numbers do not always make a

76. Tannen, *You Just Don't Understand: Women and Men in Conversation* (New York: William Morrow, 1990), pp. 25ff.
77. Pamela Fishman, "Interaction: The Work Women Do," *Social Problems* 26 (1978): 397-406.
78. McConnell-Ginet, quoted by Graddol and Swann in *Gender Voices,* p. 171.
79. Ibid.

difference, as Dale Spender notes in a painfully humorous story about a workshop on sexism and education. Thirty-two women and five men were in attendance. The men dominated the discussion in style, content, and method. They objected to the use of "she" in reference to teachers, pointing to their own, male presence at the meeting and their feelings of exclusion. They shaped the content by declaring certain topics unimportant and urging the discussion on to topics they thought were important. And when they felt left out, they insisted on "getting back to the point: *their* point."[80] The men also protested women's "rambling" and insisted on a more linear, argumentative style of talk.

Seeing conversation as competitive rather than cooperative may lead men not only to dominate conversational style, content, and method, but also to interrupt. Studies have shown that men interrupt women up to 75 percent of the time — that is, of all interruptions counted in a conversation, up to 75 percent are initiated by men.[81] As a speech act, interruption indicates a presumption on the part of speakers that their point deserves to be heard over the point of the people already holding the floor. By interrupting, speakers impose their wills on others. Continued interruption may well create a cumulative effect, finally silencing a conversational partner through intimidation or sheer fatigue. Again, whether intimidation was *intended* is often immaterial to the quality and impact of the act. The nature of the act, as we have repeatedly emphasized, depends on the interaction among message, intention, and reception.

Another means of conversational control, potent but perhaps not as easily recognized, is masculine control of the places in which conversation may occur. This control may be exercised by the sheer numbers of men in a place, by excluding women either formally or informally, or by isolating women from each other.

80. Spender, *Man-Made Language,* p. 46.
81. C. West and D. H. Zimmerman, quoted by Graddol and Swann in *Gender Voices,* p. 78. Corroborating studies were completed by A. Esposito (1979) in research on preschool children and B. Eakins and G. Eakins (1976) in research on faculty meetings. C. West (1984) thought that status rather than gender influenced interruption patterns, but in a later study of doctors and patients, West "found that female patients were interrupted by male doctors, but also that female doctors were interrupted by male patients. She concludes that sex constitutes a 'superordinate status' so that no matter what professional level a woman achieves she is still treated like a woman" (Graddol and Swann, *Gender Voices,* p. 79).

For example, women may find it intimidating to speak up in a group in which they are outnumbered by men. Assigning only one woman to a policy-making committee of ten people effectively mutes her. Too often she is expected to speak not only for herself but also for "women in general." She also needs to speak much more often than any of the men in order to even approach a female-male balance in discussion, and this is generally impossible.

Many situations in which men greatly outnumber women occur without conscious intent on men's part. However, there are many other situations in which women are deliberately excluded, either formally or informally. Several members of the (all-male) Christian Reformed Church Synod of 1990 publicly highlighted women's exclusion from the discussion concerning their own future in the church.[82] But that so few of the 184 delegates noted the irony of such an exclusion indicates the depth of men's conviction that their voices are authorized to dictate the terms of gender relations. Other examples of the formal exclusion of women are male-only church councils, men's clubs, and men's sports.

Even more interesting, because of the subtlety by which it is enforced, is the informal exclusion of women from certain places *to* talk. Lana Rakow studied communication patterns in a small town in the Midwest. She found that men gathered to talk at the coffee shop and feed store, while women were discouraged from congregating in those (or any other) places. Sharp comments, glares, and rude jokes were enough to keep women off the men's turf. Women communicated with each other over the telephone, a means of communication that is ordinarily limited to two people. Rakow found that women who cannot speak in groups, women who are kept isolated, cannot generate shared meanings or bring to public consciousness their experience of life.[83]

Marilyn French's novel called *The Women's Room* illustrates how class and gender interact to impose isolation on women. When Moira, the book's main character, marries her doctor husband, he has yet to make his fortune, so they live in a small house with nearby neighbors. Moira becomes fast friends with her women neighbors, sharing homemaking and child-care

82. Audiotape of the deliberations of the Christian Reformed Church Synod, 18-19 June 1990. Tape available at the CRC's Stated Clerk's office, Grand Rapids, Mich.

83. Rakow, *Gender on the Line: Women, the Telephone, and Community Life* (Champaign: University of Illinois Press, 1992).

THE CULTURAL CONSTRUCTION OF GENDER RELATIONS

tasks with them and talking at length with them every day. But as her husband becomes wealthier, he and Moira move into progressively bigger houses, each with more property, until finally Moira lives in a big house on a hill surrounded by a moat of land, far from her old friends and isolated even from her new neighbors. All her energy is taken up by the furnishing and cleaning demanded by such a huge house.[84]

Susan Strasser tells a similar story of isolation in her history of women's domestic work. An unfortunate side effect of the technology that helped ease women's work load in the home was the increasing isolation of women in their homes. Kitchens became separate rooms rather than communal places where people gathered not just for meals but during food preparation and clean-up, as was the case in traditional farmhouses. Electric washing machines replaced porch washtubs; dryers replaced clotheslines. The informal conversation which used to accompany washday faded away, and women either dropped familiar conversation with neighbors or had to make an effort to continue talking with them during moments of leisure.[85]

The curtailing of such everyday, informal talk separates women from each other. While men continue to be able to get together in coffee shops and bars, at Rotary and Kiwanis meetings, women have lost what once was theirs. Dale Spender asks, "Why is it that one of the most salient features of our social organization has been the *isolation* of women?"[86]

But resisting masculine control of conversation is no simple matter of women talking more and men listening more. Those who advocate assertiveness training for women as a panacea do not recognize that assertiveness training teaches women male patterns of speech, thereby reinforcing the assumption that women will accommodate themselves to men's style. Furthermore, when women talk like men, it denies men the opportunity to learn what an authentic womanly style might be like, as well as the opportunity to adapt some of those patterns to their own speech. Those who simply advocate mutual sensitivity between conversational partners, as does linguist Deborah Tannen, ignore the cultural influences and power differentials affecting gender relations. (See also Chapter Eight.) Patterns of socialization are deeply ingrained and are not overcome simply by becoming aware of them. Conversations are

84. French, *The Women's Room* (New York: Simon & Schuster, 1977).
85. Strasser, *Never Done*, pp. 236-37.
86. Spender, *Man-Made Language*, pp. 106-7.

always situated in contexts. Forces outside the control of conversational partners rudely intrude, reducing the possibilities for new rules to struc- ture old patterns of talk.

Conscious effort must be made by people of extraordinary good- will, people whose motives are influenced by something other than traditional cultural mores. People who recognize the creational worth of every person, who recognize human equality before God's judgment and Christ's mercy, have reasons strong enough to break the forms that so harm human relationships. It is useless to appeal to American democratic values in trying to bring about openness between women and men. Too much power is held by men and too little by women for appeals to decency and politeness, or even equality and freedom, to make much permanent difference. Where power and greed are worshipped, gender or imbalance will be maintained.

Both women and men need to resist the evil influence of conver- sational silencers. Men need to welcome women into previously men-only groups and to listen quietly to the women who participate, taking their words seriously. Women need to take the risk of speaking out and of continuing to talk through interruptions. Women also need to seek the affirming company of other women. And both women and men need to pray for the grace and strength it will take to forge partnerships in communication.

Silencing through Religious Language The silencing of women's speech af- fects gender relations at all levels — at the level of self-awareness and self-esteem as well as at interpersonal and public levels. While costs are exacted at each of these levels, the costs exacted emotionally and spir- itually may be the most damaging. For no matter how a person is treated in the world at large, in church she or he should be treated as an image bearer of God as well as a sinner saved by grace.

Traditionally the church has been a haven for culturally marginal groups. Prior to the civil rights revolution of the 1960s, church was the one place where southern American black people were accorded dignity. In the outside world they may have been gardeners, chauffeurs, and maids; but inside the church, they were preachers, elders, deacons, and "mothers of the church."[87] Church members knew the deep satisfaction

87. Clifton Taulbert, *Once upon a Time When We Were Colored* (Tulsa, Okla.: Council Oak Books, 1989).

379

of authentic self-naming and self-definition. And if the stories of creation, salvation, the early church, and God's coming kingdom cannot provide grounds for cherishing the unique gifts and skills of every human being, nothing can. Thus, as we close this chapter about the influence of language and communication on gender relations, we will focus especially on the way that language about God shapes women's and men's religious experiences.

Traditional God-language often legitimizes and reinforces the oppression of women. In the words of a Reformed woman pastor, "Women still suffer, as they have in the past, the oppressive effects of stereotyping, of dehumanizing expectations, of confused and inferior self-images, of great odds when they try to make it in what is yet a man's world, of attacks on their femininity when they are too successful."[88] These things are part of women's experience — a part often legitimated by religious language — of control and dominance and headship. An agonizing number of women are victims of domestic or sexual abuse (one in four is a modest estimate), usually at the hands of men they knew and trusted.[89] Feminist criticisms of traditional, masculine God-language grow out of women's struggle with such realities.

Although it seems audacious, Mary Daly's infamous aphorism, "Since God is male, the male is God,"[90] accurately points to the social and psychological abuses of masculine God-language. According to Daly, the "symbol of the Father god, spawned in the human imagination and sustained as plausible by patriarchy, has in turn rendered service to this type of society by making its mechanisms for the oppression of women appear right and fitting. If God in 'his' heaven is a father ruling 'his' people, then it is in the 'nature' of things and according to divine plan and the order of the universe that society be male-dominated."[91] According to Sallie

88. Marchiene Rienstra, "God's Freedom for Women: Part I," *Reformed Journal*, September 1977, p. 11.

89. Susan Thistlethwaite estimates that one in two women is a victim of sexual or domestic abuse, usually at the hands of someone close to her (*Sex, Race, and God: Christian Feminism in Black and White* [New York: Crossroad, 1989], p. 24). The most conservative estimate is that one in six women are victims of sexual or physical abuse. See Mary Stewart Van Leeuwen's *Gender and Grace: Love, Work and Parenting in a Changing World* (Downers Grove, Ill.: InterVarsity Press, 1990). See also Calvin College Social Research Center, "A Survey of Abuse in the Christian Reformed Church" (Grand Rapids: Calvin College, 1990).

90. Daly, *Beyond God the Father*, p. 13.

91. Ibid. Rosemary Ruether likewise says, "Male monotheism reinforces the

McFague, male God-language creates a "mystification of roles" so that "the husband dominating his wife represents God 'himself.'"[92] The dominance of masculine names, similes, and metaphors for God slides all too easily into an idolatrous equation of God with men. Such idolatry perpetuates not only more blatant harms and injustices against women, but also more subtle forms of women's subordination to men. (See Chapter Six for a more detailed discussion of the relationship of feminist theology to the feminist critique of God-language.)

The effect of masculine God-language on women has received more attention than the effect of such language on men — and with good reason. Masculine terms for God are so taken for granted that it is hard to think about God at all without having them creep in. And yet, the Bible does not speak of God in exclusively male terms. God is spoken of as a mother — giving birth, suckling her young, fighting like a mother bear for her cubs, or gathering her chicks under her wing. Brian Wren notes that throughout the Bible, God is metaphorically said to have "a head, face, eyes, eyelids, ears, nostrils, mouth, voice, arm, hand, palm, fingers, foot, heart, bosom, and bowels" *as well as a womb*.[93] Nowhere in the Bible is God described as having male reproductive organs. In fact, the physical characteristics of women are given more metaphorical weight in the Bible than the physical characteristics of men! Jesus pointedly refers to himself as the Son of Humanity (the Greek word is *anthropos*, a more inclusive term than *aner*, meaning "male person").[94] And

social hierarchy of patriarchal rule through its religious system in a way that was not the case with the paired images of God and Goddess. God is modelled after the patriarchal ruling class and is seen as addressing this class of males directly, adopting them as his 'sons.' They are his representatives, the responsible partners of the covenant with him. Women as wives now become symbolically repressed as the dependent servant class. Wives, along with children and servants, represent those ruled over and owned by the patriarchal class. They relate to man as he relates to God. A symbolic hierarchy is set up: God-male-female. Women no longer stand in direct relation to God; they are connected to God secondarily, through the male. This hierarchical order is evident in the structure of patriarchal law in the Old Testament. . . . In the New Testament this hierarchical 'order' appears as a cosmic principle" (*Sexism and God-Talk: Toward a Feminist Theology* [Boston: Beacon Press, 1983], p. 53).

92. McFague, *Metaphorical Theology*, p. 19.

93. Wren, *What Language Shall I Borrow?* p. 103.

94. Nancy Hardesty, "'Whosoever Surely Meaneth Me': Inclusive Language and the Gospel," *Christian Scholar's Review* 17, no. 3 (1988): 231-40.

in Hebrew the word for spirit, *ruah,* is feminine, although when translated into Latin that word is rendered *spiritus,* a masculine noun.[95] Overall, interpreters of Scripture, such as theologians and ministers, have tended to neglect the feminine God-images that the Bible contains, while translators have made male what was either sex-neutral *(anthropos)* or feminine *(ruah).*

A key question to be answered is whether the biblical and traditional language for God naturally and inevitably leads to the oppression of women and the glorification of men, or whether these effects result from the human abuse of the biblical and traditional God-language. Evangelical feminists usually say that human abuse is the problem, showing how a "truly" biblical understanding of God resists such abuses.[96] They then use the biblical view to criticize contemporary and traditional Christian God-language. Thus Marchiene Rienstra concludes that women have experienced the Reformed doctrine of God as oppressively masculine. What has been ignored is the wealth of scriptural texts that describe God's omnipotence as all-conquering love; God's providence as the nurturing of creation; God's omnipresence as "enabling Presence in our lives; [God's] irresistible grace as a love which wins through a compelling force which does not destroy freedom; [God's] omniscience as his capacity for awareness [of] and ability to meet all needs and opportunities for loving; [God's] anger at sin as based upon the fact that sin destroys [God's] beloved children and creation."[97]

Written in 1977, Rienstra's description refers to God as "he." But notice, in the phrases quoted, what kind of "he" is being described! If human males had truly patterned their behavior after such a God, the debate about whether to call God "he" or "she" might never have become as heated as it has. As Rienstra compellingly argues, recasting God's power as enabling rather than overpowering strength is one way to reduce the idolatrous love of masculine God-language. Another is to give prominence to the feminine imagery already in the Bible, which will allow us to understand God more fully. After all, if *together* women and men image God (Gen. 1:27), then God should be understood not in

95. William E. Phipps, *Genesis and Gender: Biblical Myths of Sexuality and Their Cultural Impact* (New York: Praeger, 1989).

96. Hardesty, "'Whosoever Surely Meaneth Me,'" and *Inclusive Language in the Church* (Philadelphia: John Knox Press, 1987).

97. Rienstra, "God's Freedom for Women: Part II," *Reformed Journal,* November 1977, p. 26.

exclusively masculine or exclusively feminine terms but in terms embracing both.

Christians might consider what it could mean for our image of God and our relationship with God if we thought in the terms suggested in Isaiah 49:15: "Can a woman forget her nursing child, or show no compassion for the child of her womb? Even these may forget, yet I will not forget you." And let us attend to Isaiah 66:13: "As a mother comforts her child, so I will comfort you." Thinking of God's mothering may help to offset some of the negative connotative freight carried by the word "fathering." In contemporary American culture, "fathering" refers first and foremost to impregnating a woman. It does not carry with it the idea of continued, loving care that "mothering" does. In addition, *father* is a term that evokes fear in some women. Women victimized by incest or battering often point out that they are alienated by the idea of God as father. Indeed, Christian *males* who were raised by authoritarian, patriarchal fathers also confess that they have difficulty relating to God as a father figure.

If God is a spirit, as Jesus says in John 4:24 ("God is spirit, and those who worship him must worship in spirit and truth"), then to worship a "masculine" God does violence to God. Some suggest gender-neutral language for God as a nonsexist alternative. Brian Wren offers the term "Lover" as a possibility, with the assumption that the term will take on gender implicitly as each worshiper envisions a lover.[98] The Trinity, then, could be Lover, Beloved, and Mutual Friend, terms that emphasize relationship and mutuality. Sallie McFague suggests calling God both mother *and* father, but also thinking of God in terms of friendship. Just as one respects and cherishes a dear friend, one could respect and cherish God.[99] God would then be not just a God of power but a God who is involved in an ongoing, intimate relation with the believer.

But while there is much to commend in these suggested revisions, something of real value could be lost in the adoption of strictly gender-neutral language, and that is the *personhood* of God. We understand persons *as* gendered beings. Humans relate to each other not simply as "human" but as women and men. Male and female *together* constitute the image of God. So, in our quest to understand God as revealed in nature,

98. Wren, *What Language Shall I Borrow?* p. 210.
99. McFague, *Metaphorical Theology*, p. 178.

each other, and the Bible, we need to *expand* our repertoire of names for God. To cling to exclusively male names for God reveals more about our own fears than about God's nature.

Naming God may be the most awesome speech act human beings can attempt. It should not be done out of blindness or ignorance or arrogance. It should not be done by predominantly one kind of person. It should not be done on the basis of human values ascribed to gender — preferring masculine over feminine because of a disdain for what is feminine. Instead, this naming must grow out of a continual reading and rereading of the biblical text and an ongoing dialogue between believing women and men. Authentic naming of the God who incorporates and transcends both genders cannot be done only in terms of one gender. The image of God is too important to be reduced to metaphors drawn from only half the human race.

Speaking with Respect

For gender relations to reflect the kind of mutuality described in Genesis 1 and 2, before sin entered the world, and the kind of equality modeled by Christ, not only material and social conditions will have to change, but language also. Several conditions need to be met if women and men are to speak together in harmony.

First, we need seriously to explore the resources of biblical language. This requires translations such as the New Revised Standard Version, in which the translators have tried to capture the meaning of the original language.[100] If *human* is meant, *human* rather than *man* is used. For example, in Luke 17, Jesus gives his disciples guidelines for their relationships with each other. In the Revised Standard Version, his words are rendered this way: "Take heed to yourselves; if your brother sins, rebuke him, and if he repents, forgive him; and if he sins against you seven times in the day, and turns to you seven times, and says, 'I repent,' you must forgive him" (vv. 3-4). However, the New Revised Standard Version eliminates the exclusive nouns and pronouns: "Be on

100. For further commentary on the language and its effect on readers, see Carole R. Fontaine's article entitled "The NRSV and the REB: A Feminist Critique," *Theology Today* 68 (October 1990): 273-81; and Herbert G. Grether's "Translators and the Gender Gap," *Theology Today* 68 (October 1990): 299-305.

your guard! If another disciple sins, you must rebuke the offender, and if there is repentance, you must forgive. And if the same person sins against you seven times a day, and turns back to you seven times and says, 'I repent,' you must forgive" (vv. 3-4). This language allows both women and men to enter into the text. *Both* need to translate, to test whether *disciple, offender,* or *you* applies to them and people they know. The message is not overtly biased in favor of one gender over another.

While the New Revised Standard Version presents human language about humans in inclusive and relatively neutral terms, it leaves God-language (about God and spoken by God) in masculine terms. Jesus still refers to himself as "Son of Man" rather than "Son of Humanity." God remains "Father." However, even though this language is male, the neutral language used for human references yields a very positive benefit. It makes the female metaphors for God stand out more vividly and clearly. When less of the language in the Bible is overtly male, the references that are obviously gender-specific stand out in relief. And there is a clearer balance between male metaphors and female metaphors for God. The woman seeking her lost coin (Luke 15:8-10), the hen gathering her chicks (Luke 13:34), and the woman who mixes yeast into her bread dough (Luke 13:20) seem less like anomalies and more like legitimate expressions of God's nature.

Second, we need to structure public discourse in ways that feature women as speakers and men as listeners. In schools, women need to be represented as teachers, administrators, and board members at *all* levels, not primarily at the elementary level. In churches, women need to lead worship — praying, singing, playing instruments, and preaching. Men need to serve in the nursery, pour coffee, do dishes, and teach little ones. Women and men need to share leadership duties as well as service duties in the churches. Only by making these kinds of moves can Christians reduce the overwhelming masculinity of the church culture — a culture which assumes male control and which, intentionally or not, accords lesser value to women.

In more intimate gatherings, work must be done to enhance "communication partnership" between women and men. Men need to monitor their speech to see how much they talk, how often they talk, and how frequently they interrupt women. Women must resist the reflex temptation to function mainly as listeners and affirmers, the conversational roles traditionally accorded them. This resistance may especially mean speaking out on topics that women understand from experience, but about which men claim expertise only from observation. It may mean pointing out to men the nature and extent of their silencing behaviors. And it may mean taking the risk of being disliked and being called names.

These are just a few of the ways in which people can exert control over language. Language may be a structure into which we are born and acculturated, but it is also a structure created by humans. As such, it is one that humans can, and do, change. Such change signals new names, new assumptions, and new ways of relating to each other. Changing language can help to change practice.

PART IV

SOCIAL INSTITUTIONS AND GENDER RELATIONS

CHAPTER 12

Private versus Public Life:
A Case for Degendering

In 1955 Oxford Don C. S. Lewis published his *Mere Christianity*, a book on Christian apologetics, ethics, and theology that remains widely read to this day. In it Lewis devotes two pages to a defense of male headship in marriage. He reviews the standard arguments about the need for a tiebreaker when domestic disagreements arise, then goes on to explain why the person with that tiebreaking authority should be the male. The chief reason, he writes, is that "the relations of the family to the outer world — what might be called its foreign policy — must depend, in the last resort, upon the man, because he always ought to be, and usually is, much more just to the outsiders. A woman is primarily fighting for her own children and husband against the rest of the world. . . . She is the special trustee of their interests. The function of the husband is to see that this natural preference of hers is not given its head. He has the last word in order to protect other people from the intense family patriotism of the wife."[1]

---

1. Lewis, *Mere Christianity* (London: Collins–Fontana Books, 1955), p. 100. For a systematic analysis of Lewis's ideas on gender relations, see Gilbert Meilaender's

---

The primary author of this chapter is Mary Stewart Van Leeuwen.

In talking about "the family and the outer world," "family patriotism," and family "foreign policy," Lewis makes it clear that he accepted
his culture's mid-twentieth-century assumptions about the dichotomy
between "public" life and "private" or domestic life. It is also clear from his
words about a woman's "natural preference" and "special trustee[ship]"
that he regarded women as essentially fitted for the honorable but limited
sphere of domesticity. A woman's "intense family patriotism" is understandable and necessary, given her role as wife and mother. But it is up to
her husband, as the stronger and less parochial member of the couple, to
see that it doesn't exceed its rightful boundaries and result in injustice to
outsiders. With this brief natural-theological argument for male headship,
Lewis closes his chapter on Christian marriage.

The purpose of this chapter and the next is to take a closer look
at these assumptions about the private/public dichotomy — namely, that
women are somehow "naturally" fitted for the private sphere and men
for the public because each sex "naturally" possesses the moral and
cognitive capacities best suited to each domain. We will argue that
although there is a fair amount of evidence for what are sometimes
called "women's ways of knowing," these are neither uniquely female
(let alone rigidly determined by biology) nor suited only to the small-
scale intimacies of marriage, family, and friendship.

This is an important topic to include in a book on gender relations,
because for many people (in addition to Lewis) the public/private distinction has been descriptive not merely of what *is* but also of what
ought to be. Throughout history it has often been assumed that certain
classes of people (e.g., slaves, women, children, cloistered religious)
belong more properly to the private than to the public sphere. Sometimes
punishments have been imposed on members of such groups when they
have attempted to leave that sphere in anything except a token or temporary fashion. Conversely, the adult men whose role assignments have
been in the public sphere cannot spend too much time away from it
without having doubt cast upon their masculinity.

In this chapter we take "private" to refer to activities encompassing
domestic life and genital sexual activity, and "public" to refer to the
activities of the marketplace, the academy, and the political forum. These
definitions reflect the liberal, post-Enlightenment understanding of "pri-

---

book entitled *The Taste for the Other: The Social and Ethical Thought of C. S. Lewis*
(Grand Rapids: William B. Eerdmans, 1976), esp. chap. 4.

vate" and "public." We have chosen them because it is this liberal understanding that bears the brunt of the contemporary feminist critique.

We will begin with an overview of contemporary mainstream feminist critiques of the public/private split, building on material already presented in our earlier historical chapters. We will then deal with the feminist theological critique of that same dichotomy, which overlaps with the mainstream critique but grounds it in a biblical worldview. This will be an expansion of some themes that were introduced in our earlier theological chapters. In the following chapter we will look at some recent attempts by feminist thinkers to transcend the public/private dichotomy in ways compatible with the biblical vision of justice and *shalom* to which we committed ourselves at the beginning of this book.

Late Twentieth-Century Feminism and the Public/Private Dichotomy

We noted in Chapter Three that the "second wave" of feminism began in the Western, English-speaking world during the 1960s. This wave was predicated largely on traditional liberal political theory. Building on earlier feminist treatises such as Mary Wollstonecraft's *A Vindication of the Rights of Woman* (1792) and John Stuart Mill's *The Subjection of Women* (1869), liberal feminists held that women's subordination and oppression were the result of less-than-rational laws and customs blocking their entry into the so-called public world of the marketplace, the political forum, and the academy. Rectifying this, they concluded, would require only that women be recognized as men's social and intellectual equals and be granted the same civil rights and educational opportunities. It would not, however, require legal intervention or attitudinal change in the so-called private spheres of sexual and family life, which liberals have traditionally insisted should be exempt from state regulation. Liberals have generally held that sexual activity is nobody's concern except that of the consenting adults involved, and hence that the state has no business in the bedrooms of its people. And in company with many conservative Christians, classical liberal theorists have tended to see the family as a locus of "natural human affection" that would be dangerously weakened if subject to bureaucratic regulation.[2]

2. See Alison M. Jaggar's *Feminist Politics and Human Nature* (Totowa, N.J.:

391

Nor did liberal feminists think that justice for women would require that male-dominated public spheres be changed in any qualitative way to accommodate them. It did not occur to them that there might be differences in men's and women's cognitive, ethical, and managerial styles, let alone that women's styles might be superior in some ways, although you will recall that precisely such arguments were used by nineteenth-century "domestic feminists" to justify giving women the vote.[3] As we have noted in earlier chapters, liberal feminists often share the same class status as dominant males. Consequently, they have tended to accept hegemonic male norms for public life, arguing only for women's equal right to compete for access to the roles represented therein. To the extent that they have done so, their underlying rhetorical question has been, "Why can't a woman be more like a man?"[4]

In contrast to the liberal-feminist acceptance of the public/private split, there is a feminist cliché, also dating back to the 1960s, to the effect that "the personal is political." This pointed rejection of the classic liberal division between public and private life implies several things, depending on the type of feminist who invokes it. In Chapter Three, we noted that the phrase was originally coined by radical feminists. As such, it was meant to be a summary rejection of the privatization of family and sexual life. Radical feminists maintained that, far from assuring individual sexual freedom and the operation of natural human affections (as liberals had claimed), the public/private split simply reinforced the oppression of women. According to this view, because the public sphere is overwhelmingly peopled by politically and physically

---

Rowman & Allanheld, 1983), chaps. 3 and 7; and Rosemarie Tong's *Feminist Thought: A Comprehensive Introduction* (Boulder, Colo.: Westview Press, 1989), chap. 1. It should be noted that John Stuart Mill was an early (but unheeded) exception to the liberal tendency to exempt domestic relations from the requirements of justice and equal rights. He correctly perceived that if justice were not guaranteed between the sexes in the home, women could hardly profit from any legal reforms in the public sphere. See Susan Moller Okin's *Justice, Gender, and the Family* (New York: Basic Books, 1989), esp. chap. 1.

3. See, for example, Aileen S. Kraditor's *Ideas of the Woman Suffrage Movement, 1890-1920* (Garden City, N.Y.: Doubleday–Anchor Books, 1971), and Sheila M. Rothman's *Woman's Proper Place: A History of Changing Ideals and Practices, 1870 to the Present* (New York: Basic Books, 1978).

4. Jean Bethke Elshtain, *Public Man, Private Woman: Women in Social and Political Thought* (Princeton: Princeton University Press, 1981), p. 228.

powerful men, and the private sphere by correspondingly dependent women, men have been able to control women's sexual and reproductive capacities for their own purposes.[5]

Thus to radical feminists it is not just outdated laws and customs that account for women's subordination. It is rather a systemically pervasive patriarchy that begins in less visible spheres such as sexuality and family, from which it fans out to affect more visible spheres such as law, politics, religion, and the academy. These in turn reinforce men's control over women's bodies in a continuously vicious cycle. Universal in its scope while variable in its expression, patriarchy is said to have controlled women's sexuality to men's advantage through institutions as diverse as prostitution, pornography, rape, sexual harassment, battering, foot-binding, suttee, purdah, clitoridectomy, witch-burning, and reproductive technology. Because they see patriarchy as the root problem of which gender-biased laws are only one manifestation, many radical feminists conclude that "[this] system, characterized by power, dominance, hierarchy and competition . . . cannot be reformed but only ripped out root and branch. It is not just patriarchy's legal and political structures that must be overturned; its social and cultural institutions (especially the family, the church, and the academy) must also go."[6] Thus, in the radical feminist analysis, the personal is political because only as gender

5. Thus, in saying that "the personal is political," feminists are using the term *political* in the very broad sense of "being characterized by power relations," and not the more technical sense of "being a political (or government-like) institution" with a clearly articulated constitution, laws, and publicly debatable rules for operation. Feminists' use of the term *political* often seems to their critics to be so broad as to be meaningless, until one realizes that it is the systematic, domestic disempowerment of women, often in the guise of "protecting" family relations from crass intervention by the state, that is the target of the criticism implied in the assertion "The personal is political."

6. Tong, *Feminist Thought*, pp. 2-3. An early radical feminist statement equating women's biology with women's oppression is Shulamith Firestone's book entitled *The Dialectic of Sex: The Case for Feminist Revolution* (New York: William Morrow, 1970). More recent treatments include Susan Brownmiller's *Against Our Will: Men, Women, and Rape* (New York: Simon & Schuster, 1975); Andrea Dworkin's *Our Blood: Prophecies and Discourses on Sexual Politics* (New York: G. P. Putnam, 1981); Susan Schecter's *Women and Male Violence: The Visions and Struggles of the Battered Women's Movement* (Boston: South End Press, 1982); and Marilyn French's *Beyond Power: On Women, Men and Morals* (New York: Summit Books, 1985). For an extensive bibliography of sources as well as critiques of radical feminism, see Tong's *Feminist Thought*, pp. 278-82.

relations in more privatized domains are exposed to scrutiny and over-hauled will any public-domain changes be of lasting benefit to women.

The indivisibility of the private from the public, the "personal" from the "political," is conceived in still more complex terms by socialist feminists. As we saw in Chapter Three, socialist feminists can be regarded as somewhat chastened Marxists. They are convinced that the eradication of capitalism per se does little to improve the status and treatment of women, and have proceeded to revise and gender-permeate Marxist theoretical constructs. Of particular interest to our critique of the public/private dichotomy is Iris Young's use of the "gendered division of labor" as a unifying concept.[7]

Unlike classical Marxists, who focus on the means and relations of production in a gender-blind fashion, Young uses division-of-labor analysis to draw attention to the actual people who are involved in production. It is no accident, she asserts, that it is *men* who are seen as the permanent paid labor force and who more often give orders, do the humanly stimulating work, and get the better pay. By contrast, it is *women* who are treated as a reserve labor-pool and who more often take orders, do repetitive drudge work, and get the lower pay (or none at all if they are shifted back to homemaking). As Young sees it, capitalism and patriarchy are so thoroughly intertwined that each reinforces the other.

It is true, Young concedes, that a gendered division of labor pre-dated capitalism. But capitalism has dissolved what used to be a clearer economic partnership between men and women, "driving a wedge between the workplace and the home, sending men, as a primary workforce, out into the former and confining women, as a secondary workforce, to the latter," all the while retaining the right to shunt women back and forth between the two spheres as the efficiencies of profit-making dictate.[8] On the socialist-feminist account, the personal is indeed political, but both public-political and private-personal life are also permeated by

7. Young, "Socialist Feminism and the Limits of Dual Systems Theory," *Socialist Review* 10 (March-June 1980): 169-88.

8. This summary of Young's thought is found in Tong's *Feminist Thought*, p. 185. Young asserts that the economic marginalization of women is *essential* to capitalism, and supports her thesis by pointing out that as Third World nations are transformed into capitalist economies, their women move rapidly from the primary to the secondary work force. See also Ester Boserup's *Women's Role in Economic Development* (London: George Allen & Unwin, 1970). See also Chapters Four and Fourteen of this volume.

economics. Socialist feminism, as we have seen, aims to incorporate all three into its theorizing.

New Voices in the Debate:
Psychoanalytic and Philosophical Feminism

Our overview of feminist theory in Chapters Two and Three concentrated on liberal feminism, Marxist and socialist feminism, and relational and radical feminism (the latter being a descendant of nineteenth-century relational feminist thought). In this discussion, we add two recent feminist voices from the relational tradition — voices that we will label psychoanalytic and philosophical feminism. These are in the relational tradition inasmuch as each tries to grapple with gender relations per se, rather than reducing them to some other category of analysis, such as generic humanness (as in the liberal tradition) or the relations of production (as in the Marxist tradition). They are important to the present discussion because each includes a powerful critique of the way our society has assigned the private sphere largely to women and the public sphere largely to men, devaluing the moral and cognitive styles of women in the process.

Psychoanalytic Feminism: A Challenge to Freud

At first glance, readers might be tempted to say that "psychoanalytic feminism" is a contradiction in terms. After all, does not classical Freudian psychoanalysis proclaim that "anatomy is destiny," thus seeming to endorse a gendered view of the public/private dichotomy that most feminists deplore? Indeed it does, largely by locating the crossroads of gendered personality development in the resolution of the so-called Oedipus complex.

According to Freud, children around the age of three or four become sexually attracted to the parent of the opposite sex. Eventually, of course, they realize that marriage to the opposite-sex parent is out of the question, because the same-sex parent has already staked a claim. The young boy, according to Freud, resolves this Oedipal conflict by reluctantly identifying with his strong, distant, publicly involved father. This action reflects his unconscious hope that he can attract a woman

395

like his mother when he grows up. In identifying with his father, the boy also gains an acculturated, "masculine" gender identity. His sister, on the other hand, learns to identify with her homebound mother in the hope that she can grow up to attract a man like her father. In either case, Freud assumed, "anatomy is destiny." In a process Freud labeled "identification with the aggressor," the boy aspires to join his father as an active male in the public sphere, in part to assuage his fear that his father might castrate him for his sexual designs on his mother. His sister, by contrast, must continue to identify with the domestically oriented "passivity" of her mother if she is to become truly feminine as an adult.

Psychoanalytic feminism has mounted a challenge to classical Freudian theory not by denying the importance of the Oedipal period per se but by stressing what goes on beforehand, from birth to about age three. According to psychoanalytic feminists, this period, known as the stage of developing "object relations," is really the more important one for the development of both girls' and boys' gender identity.

In most cultures, children are cared for mainly by their mothers from birth to at least age three. However, as socialist feminists in particular have noted, the care of children by women has become much more specialized in our culture since the advent of the Industrial Revolution and the separation of men's waged work from women's domestic labor. "Parenting," in other words, has becomes almost exclusively identified with "mothering" in an isolated, domestic setting. Therein lies a major cause of troubled gender relations, according to psychoanalytic feminists.

Misogyny and Exclusive Mothering

That infant girls are nurtured by a same-sex caretaker and boys by an opposite-sex one is seen by psychoanalytic feminists as a reason for both the "reproduction of mothering" in women and the "reproduction of misogyny" in men.[9] Isolated in their domestic world both from the public

9. See in particular Nancy Chodorow's *Reproduction of Mothering: Psychoanalysis and the Sociology of Gender* (Berkeley: University of California Press, 1978). See also Dorothy Dinnerstein's book entitled *The Mermaid and the Minotaur: Sexual Arrangements and Human Malaise* (New York: Harper–Colophon Books, 1977); Jessica Benjamin's *Bonds of Love: Psychoanalysis, Feminism, and the Problem of Domination* (New York: Pantheon, 1988); Miriam M. Johnson's *Strong Mothers, Weak Wives: The Search for Gender Equality* (Berkeley: University of California Press, 1988); and Mary Stewart

realm and from the fathers who inhabit it, young children of both sexes inevitably bond and identify strongly with their mothers. However, roughly between ages two and three, children of both sexes develop a stable, cognitive awareness of gender distinctions. Having done so, little girls are able to remain comfortably attached to their primary caretaker: to grow up culturally "feminine," they need only do what they would do anyway — that is, stay close to and model the behavior of that caretaker. Boys, on the other hand, become gradually aware that this loved, seemingly powerful, and ever-present caretaker is "not like" themselves. And they also begin to grasp that they are expected to become like the male parent whom they very rarely see.

According to psychoanalytic feminists, because boys separate psychologically from their mothers just when gender identity is developing and when, at the same time, they have no regular access to a same-sex role model, they risk developing a less-secure gender identity than girls. That is to say, they are less certain than their sisters (who have an ever-present mother as a role model) that they have correctly "figured out" and begun to practice what it means to be culturally masculine. To compensate for this insecurity, men may develop an unconscious hostility toward "womanly" activities. And since child care is one of the activities most closely associated with women, it follows that these under-fathered men will have a deep psychological resistance to taking part in it — especially in industrialized societies that take for granted a strongly gendered public/private split. In this way, according to psychoanalytic feminist theory, men (and the women who cooperate with them) continue to reproduce the very conditions that undergird misogyny and defensive masculinity — namely, a gendered division of labor along public/private lines.[10]

Some psychoanalytic feminists have noted that people in preindustrial and especially hunter-gatherer societies make almost no dis-

Van Leeuwen's *Gender and Grace: Love, Work and Parenting in a Changing World* (Downers Grove, Ill.: InterVarsity Press, 1990).

10. Psychoanalytic feminism also theorizes about the effects of "exclusive mothering" on female personality. The positive side of this is the generally greater social and emotional sensitivity of women. The negative side is women's unconscious desire to reproduce the early, comfortable mother-daughter bond by investing too heavily in mothering others. See, for example, Chodorow's *Reproduction of Mothering,* Benjamin's *Bonds of Love,* Johnson's *Strong Mothers, Weak Wives,* and Van Leeuwen's *Gender and Grace.*

tinction between "public" and "private" life. Indeed, such people would probably not even understand the distinction, given the fluidity and minimal differentiation of their social roles. Such cultures also tend to be both more flexible about gender roles and less misogynous than ours. All of these characteristics are interconnected, according to psychoanalytic feminists. For if father absence and exclusive mothering contribute to men's misogyny, then increasing fathers' nurturant contact with children should decrease it. This has led some feminist anthropologists of a psychoanalytic bent to conclusions such as the following:

> Change [in our own society] must proceed in two directions. To begin with, it would seem imperative to integrate men into the domestic sphere, giving them an opportunity to share in the socialization of children, as well as the more mundane domestic tasks. What is more ... women's status will be elevated only when they participate equally with men in the public world of work.[11]

Evaluating Psychoanalytic Feminism

The strength of psychoanalytic feminism lies in its recognition that changes in gender relations are unlikely to occur only through rational discourse (as in liberal feminism) and/or through economically structured change (as in Marxist feminism). Gender relations are rarely negotiated on a strictly rational or a strictly economic basis. Unconscious feelings about "proper" masculine or feminine behavior and related feelings about one's own adequacy as a man or a woman inevitably enter into the equation, and these are rarely shifted by a mere call to "be rational," or even "to be fair." For most people a much deeper, more emotional kind of digging is needed, because such feelings, developed earlier in childhood than most of us want to acknowledge, rarely keep pace with our best intentions.

Psychoanalytic feminism, provided it does not become reductionistic, suggests at least one mechanism through which fallen gender relations reproduce themselves, and one reason for their tenacity among even well-intentioned adults. It also suggests one mechanism for change

11. *Women, Culture, and Society*, ed. Michelle Zimbalist Rosaldo and Louise Lamphere (Stanford: Stanford University Press, 1974), p. 14. For a report of research findings on the benefits of involved, nonauthoritarian fathering, see Kyle D. Pruett's *Nurturing Father* (New York: Warner Books, 1987).

— namely, the nurturant, equally involved parenting of children by both adult women and adult men. Granted, we may have to wait a generation to reap the full benefits of coparenting in the form of more egalitarian gender relations, because early emotional associations about what is "masculine" and "feminine" are not that easily changed in adults who were raised under the "parenting-equals-mothering" system. But without such changes on the emotional and behavioral level we will lack the necessary energy to implement what we know to be both rational and just in gender relations. Such slow, socially supported self-examination and self-correction is one goal of grass-roots feminist "consciousness-raising" and also of much feminist therapy. It can also be a goal of Christian prayer (both individual and corporate), Christian action, and Christian support groups for both men and women, if we care enough to make it so.

Epistemology and Ethics: Concerns of Philosophical Feminism

Epistemology is the area of philosophy concerned with how we acquire knowledge and decide what is true. Ethics, in its normative sense, is the area that studies criteria for deciding what is right or wrong to do. In recent years feminist philosophers, aided by psychologists, have focused on apparent differences in men's and women's styles of thinking and ways of making ethical decisions. For want of a better term, we are calling this stream of thought simply "philosophical feminism," with the understanding that it is really an interdisciplinary venture, and that philosophy itself includes much more than just ethics and epistemology. Philosophical feminism is a stream of thought that is very significant for the feminist critique of the public/private split.

In our discussion of psychoanalytic feminism, we spoke of the need to bring together thinking and feeling if we are to work for changes that can last. But traditional male (and liberal) discourse tends to separate these functions, assigning detached, rational thought primarily to the public, male-dominated social arena and empathetic feeling primarily to the female-dominated privacy of the home. In an earlier chapter, we noted that this privatization of the nonrational has also led to the marginalization of religion. Since religion consists of supposedly "nonrational" and "subjective" faith commitments, liberal (including liberal feminist) theorizing has tended to relegate it, along with sexuality, to the realm of purely private preference. The assumption is that religion, like emotion, has no bearing on public life, other than perhaps to shore up a view of rights and responsibilities that has been arrived at by purely "rational" public discourse.[12]

This, however, is a view that still presumes a neat separation of public, objective, "scientific" knowledge from the private, emotional, and religious functions — a view now questioned by both feminist and mainstream philosophers of science. Both groups hold that the conduct of science and philosophy does *not* take place in some detached realm of pure, publicly verifiable thought and observation, unaffected by one's social, emotional, and religious commitments, but that these inevitably interact with the more formal methods of one's discipline. By ignoring such considerations, liberals (including liberal feminists) not only silence and marginalize those who want their religious commitments to undergird all of life. They also marginalize those for whom the pursuit of truth takes place in intimate, small-scale relationships (such as families and friendships) rather than in the supposedly more detached, cerebral atmosphere of the public marketplace, the academy, or the political forum.[13]

12. The fact that "religion," "emotion," and "women" have all been relegated to the private domain in Western liberal thought may be one reason why women are seen as both more religious and more emotional than men. See Inge K. Broverman et al.'s "Sex-role Stereotypes: A Current Appraisal," *Journal of Social Issues* 28, no. 2 (1972): 59-78.

13. The beginnings of this "postmodern" debate on the nature of science go back to Thomas Kuhn's book entitled *The Structure of Scientific Revolutions* (Chicago: University of Chicago Press, 1962). A good critical evaluation of this debate can be found in Frederick Suppe's *Structure of Scientific Theories*, 2d ed. (Urbana, Ill.: University of Illinois Press, 1977). Accessible volumes written from a Christian standpoint include Del Ratzsch's *Philosophy of Science: The Natural Sciences in Christian Perspective* (Downers Grove, Ill.: InterVarsity Press, 1986); Nicholas Wolterstorff's *Reason within the Bounds of Religion* (Grand Rapids: William B. Eerdmans, 1976); and Mary Stewart Van Leeuwen's volume titled *The Person in Psychology: A Contemporary Christian Appraisal* (Grand Rapids: William B. Eerdmans, 1985). Feminist treatments include Evelyn Fox Keller's *Reflections on Gender and Science* (New Haven: Yale University Press, 1985); Sandra Harding's *Whose Science? Whose Knowledge? Thinking from Women's Lives* (Ithaca, N.Y.: Cornell University Press, 1991); *Feminism and Methodology: Social Science Issues*, ed. Sandra Harding (Bloomington: Indiana University Press, 1987); and *Women, Knowledge and Reality: Explorations in Feminist Philosophy*, ed. Ann Garry and Marilyn Pearsall (Boston: Unwin Hyman, 1989).

Respecting Women's Ways of Knowing

Philosophical feminists have been quite sympathetic to this "post-modern" and "postliberal" critique of objectivist epistemology. This is so because traditional views of "objectivity" and "reason" have been overwhelmingly associated with masculinity, leaving the impression that however women think, it certainly isn't reliable. In questioning such traditional stereotypes about "the man of reason" and "the woman of emotion," these critics, unlike liberal feminists, are not trying to make a case for women's ability to attain *male* standards of public rationality. They are instead trying to show the limitations of the latter and the strengths of previously undervalued "women's ways of knowing." According to traditional stereotypes, women cannot think coolheadedly and abstractly; they are always getting bogged down in personal relationships, in feelings, and in concrete details. "Reason" and "scientific objectivity" have thus been associated with the mind, the universal, the public, the tough-minded, and the male, whereas emotion and attention to detail (at the expense of the "big" picture) have been linked to the body, the particular, the private, the softheaded, and the female.

Furthermore, the domestication and sexual possession of women have a long history of being used as metaphors for scientific research and the control of nature. Male scientists speak of "disrobing" nature, "wooing," "conquering," and "subduing" her, "penetrating" her secrets and "taking possession" of "virgin" fields of inquiry.[14] This manner of speaking is often accompanied by the assumption that impersonal detachment, experimental control, and reducing what is studied to smaller and smaller components (as in physics) are the royal routes to reliable, scientific knowledge. A sensitivity to context, whether ideological, emotional, or ecological, is often regarded as unnecessary at best and conducive to substandard science at worst.

One philosophical feminist has contrasted this more typically "male" epistemology with that of Barbara McClintock, a Nobel prize-winning biologist who did most of her work (in maize genetics) away from the male-dominated academic world. McClintock spoke of "letting

14. For an expanded analysis of the history of these themes, see especially Keller's *Reflections on Gender and Science,* and also Genevieve Lloyd's *Man of Reason: "Male" and "Female" in Western Philosophy* (London: Methuen, 1984). See also the book by Mary F. Belenky et al. entitled *Women's Ways of Knowing: The Development of Self, Voice, and Mind* (New York: Basic Books, 1986).

the material speak to you" and allowing it to "tell you what to do next."
For her, the process of scientific discovery was facilitated not by staying
a detached observer determined to control the materials, but at least
sometimes by becoming "part of the system" and gaining "a feeling for
the organism."[15]

Feminist philosophers have also contrasted the commonly male
academic style of public, combative interaction with a more nurturant,
domestic, and flexible form of "maternal thinking." For example, philosopher Sara Ruddick points out that mothers (and, it should be noted,
she holds that "mothering" can be done by people of either sex) develop
a style of thought rooted in day-to-day interaction with a particular,
needful, ever-growing child. Echoing Barbara McClintock's comments
on her study of maize, Ruddick characterizes maternal thinking as "a
unity of reflection, judgment and emotion." Against the older concept
of thought as totally objective, value-free, and abstract, Ruddick asserts
(in the spirit of postmodern philosophy of science) that maternal thinking is "no more interest-governed, no more emotional, and no more
relative to a particular reality . . . than thinking that arises from scientific,
religious, or any other practice."[16]

Ruddick and her colleagues do not decry traditional "male"
epistemology per se. They are, after all, trained in that mode themselves.
But they do want to show that reliable knowledge emerges in a variety
of ways, and that there are not as many differences between the public,
"hardheaded" (usually male) scientist and the domestic, "softheaded"
(usually female) nurturer as we have been led to believe. Good scientists

15. These quotations from McClintock that Keller cites in *Reflections on Gender
and Science* are taken from her biography of McClintock entitled *A Feeling for the
Organism: The Life and Work of Barbara McClintock* (San Francisco: W. H. Freeman,
1983). Keller also appeals to psychoanalytic feminism to account for men's attraction
to objectification and detachment as modes of scientific inquiry. She suggests that
the same psychological forces that produce males' defensive separation of themselves from the "not-like-me" mother contribute to an exaggerated separation from
the materials they later study as scientists. The converse — that is, a sense of
connected "feeling for the organism" — would be more likely to hold for women,
who are usually nurtured by a same-sex parent from whom they need not separate
so unequivocally.

16. Ruddick, "Maternal Thinking," in *Women and Values: Readings in Recent
Feminist Philosophy,* ed. Marilyn Pearsall (Belmont, Calif.: Wadsworth Publishing Co.,
1986), p. 341. See also Ruddick's book entitled *Maternal Thinking: Toward a Politics
of Peace* (New York: Ballantine Books, 1989).

are both logical and intuitive, depending on the varying demands of their work. So are good mothers.

Respecting Women's Moral Judgments

Philosophical feminists also criticize male-associated ethical standards. One of their targets has been the view that moral development gradually advances beyond loyalty to a particular person or persons — for example, "My family [or "my country"], right or wrong" — to the adoption of more abstract, universal principles (e.g., "Life is more important than property," "Act only as you would wish others to act toward you in a similar situation," "Treat all people as ends, not means," etc.). Psychologist Lawrence Kohlberg claimed to measure such moral "maturity" by analyzing people's responses to hypothetical moral dilemmas. Suppose, for example, that an impoverished man's wife is dying of cancer and the druggist who has developed a medicine for its treatment is demanding an exorbitant price for it. Should the man steal the drug, or let his wife die?[17]

According to Kohlberg's original scheme of moral development, the most "mature" thinkers (mostly Western males) solve the dilemma by a quick application of a moral principle: for example, "Life is more important than property; therefore, the man is justified in stealing the drug." Women's judgments tend to be more circuitous and oriented around the particular people involved in the situation: "Couldn't we get the poor man and the druggist to sit down and talk? Better still, couldn't we get the druggist and *his* wife to meet the dying woman and her beleaguered husband? Then surely we could arrive at a mutually satisfying solution." And so on. In other words, women more than men try to preserve or enhance specific relationships in the process of making ethical decisions.

According to Kohlberg's original theory, however, this lack of abstraction was considered morally immature. Indeed, it seemed to confirm traditionalist ideas about women's unsuitability for public life: they were simply "too immersed in particularity to achieve the principled impartiality of mature moral beings."[18] At the beginning of this chapter

17. Kohlberg, *The Philosophy of Moral Development* (San Francisco: Harper & Row, 1981). Kohlberg's hypothetical dilemma concerning "Heinz" (the man with the dying wife) and the druggist is probably his most famous dilemma and the one most often cited by both those who support and those who oppose his theory.

18. Lorraine Code, "Experience, Knowledge, and Responsibility," in *Women, Knowledge and Reality*, p. 164.

403

we saw that C. S. Lewis, despite being a perceptive critic of his culture in many respects, appeared to agree with this view, and used it both as an explicit justification for husbandly headship and as an implicit argument for keeping women at home.

But to philosophical feminists, led by Harvard psychologist Carol Gilligan, it is hardly surprising that women score low on Kohlberg's scale, since he developed his original scheme of "human" moral development using only males. Moreover, his theoretical approach placed a low value on the very thing that is held to be women's moral strength — namely, their refusal to reduce an ethical conflict to abstractions and their determination to do justice to all of the concrete relationships affected by it. This is a morality of "care" or "responsibility," developed and reinforced in the intimate sphere of family and friendship, rather than a morality of abstract "rights," which (for better or worse) typifies public, male-dominated life. In the former, according to Gilligan (with anticipations of Sara Ruddick),

> moral problems arise from conflicting responsibilities rather than competing rights, and require for their resolution a mode of thinking that is contextual and narrative, rather than formal and abstract. This conception of morality as concerned with the activity of care centers moral development around the understanding of responsibility and relationships [rather than] the understanding of rights and rules. . . . The morality of rights differs . . . in its emphasis on *separation* rather than *connection*, in its consideration of the *individual*, rather than the *relationship*, as primary.[19]

What Is the Origin of Women's Thought and Morality?

Implicit in this philosophical feminist critique is the idea not only that child care should be gender-integrated (as in psychoanalytic feminism) but that gender-related cognitive styles should be revalued as well. Neither Ruddick nor Gilligan is recommending a wholesale rejection of more typically male epistemology and ethics. They are, however, demanding that more

---

19. Gilligan, *In a Different Voice: Psychological Theory and Women's Development* (Cambridge: Harvard University Press, 1982), p. 19 (our emphases). For a critical review of these two research traditions, see Owen Flanagan and Kathryn Jackson's "Justice, Care, and Gender: The Kohlberg-Gillian Debate Revisited," *Ethics* 97 (April 1987): 622-37.

typically female approaches be given their due. And such reforms are not just cast in terms of gender justice, adequate science, and adequate parenting. It is even said that the preservation of the planet may depend on the promotion of a more typically female epistemology and ethics, given that traditional male ways have been so highly correlated with warmongering and environmental pollution.[20] In all of this we can hear echoes of the "expediency argument" used by the "first wave" relational feminists (see Chapter Two). These feminists, you may recall, held that women's innate concern for family, morals, and peace would, through women's voting patterns, have a civilizing effect on brute male politics.

But unlike their nineteenth-century predecessors, most philosophical feminists are quick to deny that women's thinking and ethical styles are rooted in natural differences between the sexes. They point out that there has always been a "recessive" tradition in male-dominated philosophy which has questioned the devaluation of emotion and its separation from rationality.[21] They also note that the empirical correlation between one's sex and one's thinking style is far from perfect: there are men who think and who solve moral dilemmas more like the average woman, and vice versa. This suggests that socialization accounts for the sex-related trends more than biology does.[22]

This conclusion also has some cross-cultural support in that aspects of thinking considered "feminine" in our culture may be considered "masculine" in others. For example, in centuries past, male Chinese civil servants were expected to have a sensitive grasp of Chinese classical poetry in order to carry out their jobs well—a far cry from our own culture's image of the "rational bureaucrat." The Indian concept of *dharma*, or social duty, is also a very relational one, despite being associated more with men than women. Many philosophi-

---

20. See, for example, Ruddick's *Maternal Thinking* and also Jean Bethke Elshtain's *Women and War* (New York: Basic Books, 1987).

21. See, for example, Susan Bordo's *Flight to Objectivity: Essays on Cartesianism and Culture* (Albany, N.Y.: SUNY Press, 1987).

22. For further, more technical discussion of the "nature/nurture" debate regarding the origin of psychological sex differences, see Anne Faust-Sterling's *Myths of Gender: Biological Theories about Women and Men* (New York: Basic Books, 1985); R. C. Lewontin, Steven Rose, and Leon J. Kamin's *Not in Our Genes: Biology, Ideology, and Human Nature* (New York: Pantheon Books, 1984); Margaret W. Matlin's *Psychology of Women* (New York: Holt, Rinehart & Winston, 1987); and Mary Stewart Van Leeuwen's *Gender and Grace*.

cal feminists believe that in our own culture the most reliable predictor of "women's ways of knowing" is actually subordination and oppression — whether by sex, race, class, disability, or sexual orientation. As evidence of this, they point to similarities between traditional stereotypes of women (e.g., emotionality, intuitiveness, dangerous sexuality) and those that have been applied to other socially marginalized groups, such as blacks.[23]

Moving Away from "Muscular Christianity"

Philosophical feminism is not a full-blown theory about the origins of women's subordination and its cure. Like psychoanalytic feminism, it is perhaps best regarded as an approach that highlights particular features of gender roles and relations — in this case those having to do with thought and moral judgment. For Christians a particular value of these two streams of thought is the implicit permission they give men to care more openly and deeply about the concrete needs of persons, relationships, and the natural environment in which they live. We should note that the fruits of the Spirit listed in Galatians 5 — love, joy, peace, patience, kindness, goodness, faithfulness, gentleness, self-control — that are urged upon *all* believers have a peculiarly "feminine" ring to them. Indeed, when Frederick Nietzsche wrote his late nineteenth-century diatribe against Christianity, he specifically compared "weak," self-effacing Christian men to *women,* and flatly stated that neither were fit to be world-dominating "supermen."[24]

23. See, for example, Jean Baker Miller's *Towards a New Psychology of Women* (Boston: Beacon Press, 1976), and Anne Wilson Schaef's *Women's Reality: An Emerging Female System in a White Male Society* (San Francisco: Harper & Row, 1981).
24. Nietzsche, *The Anti-Christ,* trans. R. J. Hollingdale (London: Penguin, 1971). What follow are some of the things Nietzsche had to say about the relationship between "Christian" virtues and a lack of manliness:

What is good? All that heightens the feeling of power, the will to power, power itself in man. What is bad? All that proceeds from weakness. What is happiness? The feeling that power *increases* — that a resistance is overcome.... What is more harmful than any vice? Active sympathy for the ill-constituted and weak: Christianity. [Pp. 115, 116]

Christianity is called the religion of pity. Pity stands in antithesis to the tonic emotions which enhance the energy of the feeling of life: it has a depressive effect. One loses force when one pities.... Pity on the whole thwarts the law of evolution, which is the law of *selection.* It preserves what is ripe for destruction....

Of course, Nietzsche's portrait of the "meek Christian" is a very distorted one, since the biblical portrait of humanness includes, in addition to the fruits of the Spirit, both accountable dominion and a prophetic zeal for justice. Nevertheless, the New Testament call to imitate Christ by living self-sacrificially as peacemakers has been at odds with the cultural message we have been given about the association of masculinity with aggression, dominance, hardheadedness, and controlled emotion. At the same time, as we will show in the following section, Christian women have too often been told that it is neither Christian nor feminine to be other than endlessly self-sacrificing.

We would hope that both Christian commitment and biblical literacy might help people transcend such gendered dichotomies. But Christians are finite and flawed like everyone else, and thus are not exempt from cultural conditioning of their emotions and attitudes. As psychoanalytic feminists have reminded us, we do not easily shed deep, infantile feelings about what "real men" and "real women" should be like. Consequently, it is even possible that misogyny among Christian men is actually heightened by the association some of them may feel between being Christian and being "feminized."[25] If this is even remotely the case, then Christians of both sexes have good reason to support the efforts of philosophical and psychoanalytic feminists, who are working to increase everyone's appreciation and appropriation of women's ways of knowing. For these, in the final analysis, are not simply women's ways of knowing but rather qualities that the Bible calls all of us to cultivate if we are to become the full human beings God wants us to be.

Feminist Theological Critiques
of the Public/Private Split

These last observations lead naturally to the final part of this chapter. Thus far we have reviewed radical, socialist, and psychoanalytic feminist

---

Nothing in our unhealthy modernity is more unhealthy than Christian pity. [Pp. 118-19]

If a Christian wants to be "chosen of God," or "a temple of God," or "a judge of angels," then every *other* principle of selection, for example on the basis of integrity, intellect, manliness and pride . . . is simply "of the world." [P. 162]

25. For further discussion, see Van Leeuwen's *Gender and Grace,* chap. 6.

critiques of the public/private dichotomy, in addition to those mounted by feminist philosophers and psychologists working in ethics and epistemology. Absent so far has been any reference to a theological critique of the public/private distinction, partly because religion is still not taken very seriously in mainstream feminist discussions. To liberal feminists, as we have noted, religious conviction is merely part of the private sphere that they are trying to keep from mingling with matters of the public (but ideally gender-integrated) arena. According to this view, public discourse is based on generic human rationality rather than on subjective religious faith. To socialist feminists, who have generally retained the materialism and historicism of their Marxist days, religion is largely irrelevant because they believe that God does not exist and that both class and gender are social constructions resulting from the organization of the means of production.[26] Psychoanalytic feminists, while rejecting Freud's biological determinism, appear to have absorbed his atheism, couching it in humanist rather than materialist terms. Finally, most early radical feminists rejected religion as just one more manifestation of patriarchy in men and false consciousness in women, although later writers have explored the attractions of a totally woman-centered spirituality.[27]

There are obvious problems with the mainstream feminist marginalization, dismissal, or feminization of religion. As we have already noted, the liberal feminist privatization of faith ignores the challenge of postmodern epistemology, which asserts that a separation of "private" worldview from "public" rationality is not possible. The social-constructionist assumptions of many other feminists imply a value relativism which, if consistently applied, leaves no toehold for ethical pronouncements of any kind, feminist ones included. As we noted in Chapters Three and Four, if we believe only what we have been socially

26. Thus Alison Jaggar: "Mother Jones [an early organizer] is alleged to have said 'God almighty made the women and the Rockefeller gang of thieves made the ladies.' But God almighty did not make women and neither did Mother Nature. A traditional class analysis explains the transformation of some women and men into ladies and gentlemen. But only socialist feminism makes a serious attempt to explain how human beings continuously transform themselves into men and women" (*Feminist Politics and Human Nature,* pp. 148-49).

27. See, for example, Mary Daly's *Beyond God the Father: Toward a Philosophy of Women's Liberation* (Boston: Beacon Press, 1973); and *Womanspirit Rising,* ed. Carol Christ and Judith Plaskow (San Francisco: Harper & Row, 1979). See also Chapters Five and Six of this volume.

conditioned to believe, who is to say that an oppressively patriarchal worldview is any "worse" than a gender-egalitarian one? Both simply "are" the inevitable results of past learning. Finally, as we noted in our chapter on Reformed Christianity and feminism, a totally woman-centered spirituality easily slides into a feminist utopianism, which forgets that women are not exempt from sin simply by virtue of having suffered themselves. It is for these reasons, among others, that some Catholic, Protestant, and Jewish feminists have developed their own critique of the public/private dichotomy, mainly through the route of theological anthropology and ethics.[28]

Creation, Sin, and the Feminization of Agapic Love

The anthropological starting point for this critique is a revised reading of the doctrines of creation and sin. As we noted in our earlier, theological chapters, many feminist theologians hold that created human nature — both male and female — includes a paradoxical mix of freedom and dependence. That is, it includes a need for individual achievement on the one hand and social belonging on the other. They then go on to suggest that sin distorts these functions in ways that are usually *different* for women and men. Mediated through nature, nurture, or both, men's greater temptation (according to these theologians) is toward the misuse of freedom, resulting in selfishness, pride, and the illusion of self-sufficiency. Women, by contrast, are more prone to distort their relational side, which results in a dependence on others for self-identity and a passivity with regard to the development of self and vocation.[29]

Given these renderings of creation and fall, feminist theologians

---

28. In particular, see Valerie Saiving Goldstein's essay entitled "The Human Situation: A Feminine View," in *Womanspirit Rising,* pp. 25-42; Judith Plaskow's *Sex, Sin, and Grace: Women's Experience and the Theologies of Reinhold Niebuhr and Paul Tillich* (Washington: University Press of America, 1980); Barbara Hilkert Andolsen's "Agape in Feminist Ethics," *Journal of Religious Ethics* 9 (Spring 1981): 69-83; and *Women's Consciousness, Women's Conscience: A Reader in Feminist Ethics,* ed. Barbara Hilkert Andolsen, Christine E. Gudorf, and Mary D. Pellauer (San Francisco: Harper & Row, 1985). See also Van Leeuwen's *Gender and Grace,* chap. 2.

29. See especially Goldstein's "Human Situation" and Andolsen's "Agape in Feminist Ethics." See also Van Leeuwen's *Gender and Grace,* chap. 2.

find much to criticize in traditional, male-formulated Christian ethics. They argue that its stress on agapic or self-sacrificial love as the pinnacle of Christian virtue has simply exacerbated the differentially sinful tendencies of men and women.[30] It is not that the Christian call to agapic love is deemed illusory or wrong. But under the influence of male theologizing, it has become associated with the private rather than the public arena, and hence with female rather than male ethical imperatives. Reinhold Niebuhr has been singled out as a twentieth-century theologian who helped to promote these dichotomies. For even while he affirmed agapic love as the highest Christian virtue, grounding it in the atoning sacrifice of Christ, Niebuhr also took for granted the split between public and private spheres that characterizes advanced industrial society. And in a fallen world, he concluded, *agape* can be practiced with consistent success only in small-scale, private relationships, most notably in friendships and families. Niebuhr substituted justice as a working norm for public life, as the standard for maintaining a tolerable balance among the interests of competing groups — a justice that aims (as Kohlberg's theory also did) at equality and human freedom through the rational calculation of interests and rights.[31]

Nowhere did Niebuhr deal with the problematic fact that his public/private split was also a highly gendered one in Western society, thus effectively turning women into the agapic specialists and releasing men, in their largely public life, from agapic demands. The result, in theologian Barbara Andolsen's words, is that "women have too often found in practice that Christian self-sacrifice means the sacrifice of women for the sake of men.... Men have espoused an ethic which they did not practice; women have practiced it to their own detriment."[32] Andolsen also accuses Niebuhr of idealizing the so-called traditional family, which is in many ways a historical product of the Industrial Revolution. This family, as we have seen, is characterized by a commuter/wage-earner husband and an economically dependent wife who, in largely domestic isolation, has primary responsibility for the maintenance of the household and the upbringing of the children. In taking this to be normative, Niebuhr and

30. Particular targets of criticism include Anders Nygren's *Agape and Eros* (Philadelphia: Westminster Press, 1932); Reinhold Niebuhr's *Nature and Destiny of Man*, 2 vols. (New York: Charles Scribner's Sons, 1941 and 1943); and Gene Outka's *Agape: An Ethical Analysis* (New Haven: Yale University Press, 1972).

31. Niebuhr, *The Nature and Destiny of Man*, vol. 2.

32. Andolsen, "Agape in Feminist Ethics," p. 75.

his intellectual descendants failed to acknowledge the degree to which legal, economic, and cultural forces have helped dictate the actual shape of the family, thus rendering problematic the theoretical separation of public (hence male) ethics from private (hence female) ethics in the first place.[33]

Accompanying the elevation of the traditional, privatized family is often its romanticization. In *The Nature and Destiny of Man*, the two-volume treatise Niebuhr produced in the early 1940s, he seemed to assume that the family's intimate nature and reduced scale are sufficient to make it a reliable "haven in a heartless world." Indeed, in his work of a decade earlier, *Moral Man and Immoral Society* (1932), he was convinced that women had won a "complete victory" over the "vestigial remnants of male autocracy."[34] Yet half a century later it is clear that while home may be a haven to many men, it is often (as radical feminists keep pointing out) a dangerous place for women and children. The gender-neutral phrase "spouse abuse" turns out, demographically, to refer overwhelmingly to the abuse of women by male partners. And while the term *incest* technically covers the sexual abuse of children by women as well as men, it too turns out to refer mainly to the abuse of female children by male relatives. In North America it is estimated that physical abuse and sexual abuse each involve as many as one in four women in the general population and one in six women even in families that call themselves Christian.[35] Far from assuring the operation of

33. See Christine E. Gudorf's "Parenting, Mutual Love, and Sacrifice," in *Women's Consciousness, Women's Conscience*, pp. 175-91. Others who presume the normativity of the "traditional" family include Christopher Lasch; see his *Haven in a Heartless World: The Family Besieged* (New York: Basic Books, 1977). Similar tendencies are evident in Elshtain's *Public Man, Private Woman*. For a review and critique of conservative Protestant idealization of the industrial-era "traditional" family, see James Davidson Hunter's *Evangelicalism: The Coming Generation* (Chicago: University of Chicago Press, 1987), esp. chap. 5. See also Van Leeuwen's *Gender and Grace*, chap. 11.

34. Niebuhr, *Moral Man and Immoral Society* (New York: Charles Scribner's Sons, 1960), p. 46.

35. It should be noted that these estimates are always regarded as conservative, since the underreporting of abuse is judged to be high generally and to be particularly high in Christian circles. For sociological, psychological, and historical treatments, see Donald D. Dutton's *Domestic Assault of Women* (Boston: Allyn & Bacon, 1988); Lewis Okun's *Woman Abuse* (Albany: State University of New York Press, 1986); Florence Rush's *Best-Kept Secret: Sexual Abuse of Children* (Englewood Cliffs,

"natural human affection" by making an ethical separation between the public and the private, we have created a space for domestic violence unregulated by the extended family (long since nuclearized by industrialization), the extended community (long since fragmented by urbanization and geographic mobility), or the law.

The Call to Mutuality in All Spheres of Life

All of these problems, according to feminist theologians, have been exacerbated by the view that agapic love, grounded in the Atonement, is the paramount Christian virtue. Indeed, appeals to agapic love have frequently been used to excuse men's violent or sexually abusive behavior toward women. Victims are told, sometimes even by their pastors, that "Even if he is sexually eccentric or hot-tempered, it's your duty as a Christian to bear it, or at least to forgive and forget it." In more conservative Christian circles, a further qualifier may be added — namely, "It's your duty as a Christian *woman* to bear it." What was merely implicit in Niebuhr's neo-orthodox analysis — the effective feminization of the call to self-sacrifice — has been all but doctrinally enshrined in many conservative Protestant and Catholic circles.[36]

N.J.: Prentice-Hall, 1980); and Diana E. H. Russell's *Secret Trauma: Incest in the Lives of Girls and Women* (New York: Basic Books, 1986). For ethical and pastoral analyses, see Marie Marshall Fortune's *Sexual Violence: The Unmentionable Sin* (New York: Pilgrim Press, 1983); Karen Burton Mains and Maxine Hancock's *Child Sexual Abuse: The Hope for Healing* (Wheaton, Ill.: Harold Shaw, 1986); James Alsdurf and Phyllis Alsdurf's *Battered into Submission: The Tragedy of Wife Abuse in the Christian Home* (Downers Grove, Ill.: InterVarsity Press, 1989); and *Abuse and Religion: When Praying Isn't Enough*, ed. Anne L. Horton and Judith A. Williamson (Lexington: D. C. Heath, 1988). For a denominational survey (perhaps the first such to be undertaken) that shows prevalence rates of abuse in Christian homes to be similar to those in the general population, see "A Survey of Abuse in the Christian Reformed Church," done by the Calvin College Social Research Center (Grand Rapids: Calvin College, 1990). Although not accompanied by survey data, the U. S. Catholic Bishops' Statement entitled "When I Call for Help: A Pastoral Response to Domestic Violence against Women" (New York: U. S. Catholic Conference, 1992) is another example of a denominational response to abuse.

36. See, for example, Mains and Hancock's *Child Sexual Abuse* and Alsdurf and Alsdurf's *Battered into Submission*. C. S. Lewis routinely called all Christians to self-sacrifice, but held that women were mainly called to such sacrifice in the family sphere and men in the public sphere. Aside from this uncritical acceptance of the

The theological solution to this problem, according to feminist critics, is a regrounding of agapic love in the doctrine of the Trinity, leading to its redefinition as mutuality rather than self-sacrifice. These critics point out that all three persons in the Trinity are both active and receptive, giving and receiving in a life of perfect mutuality. In the eyes of many feminist theologians, the human paradigm for such a relationship is that of a successful friendship, in which self and other both give and receive without the need to designate one or the other party as "head." They also assert, however, that the practice of such "agapic mutuality" cannot be limited to small-scale relationships such as friendship and family, as Niebuhr maintained: "It must serve as a norm for political and economic life as well. . . . The present division between public and private has been possible largely because of women's essential sacrifice of themselves for the sake of other family members. Mutuality demands a reintegration of private and public life."[37] We will have more to say about possibilities for such reintegration in the following chapter.

At the same time, most biblical-feminist theologians are careful to avoid triumphalism in making mutuality and public/private desegregation their aim. They readily concede that in a world which continues to be distorted by evil, and in which we have both personal limitations and limited material resources, self-sacrifice will often be the most responsible Christian course of action. But, they maintain, because the idealization of sacrifice has often been used to victimize women and other marginal groups, it can no longer be considered "the self-evident Christian solution to every moral conflict."[38] If it is Christianly appropriate to anyone, they suggest, it is to those who have more rather than less power, as exemplified in the great opening hymn of Philippians 2.

---

public/private dichotomy, Lewis also failed to note the effects of Niebuhr's analysis, according to which self-sacrifice is mainly a private-sphere possibility and hence largely a female responsibility. For a more detailed analysis, see Meilaender's *Taste for the Other*. See also Chapters Five, Six, and Seven of this volume.

37. Andolsen, "Agape in Feminist Ethics," p. 79. See also Margaret Farley's "New Patterns of Relationship: Beginnings of a Moral Revolution," in *Woman: New Dimensions*, ed. Walter Burkhardt (New York: Paulist Press, 1975), pp. 51-70; Eleanor Humes Haney's "What Is Feminist Ethics? A Proposal for Continuing Discussion," *Journal of Religious Ethics* 8 (Spring 1980): 115-24; and Beverly Wildung Harrison's "New Consciousness of Women: A Socio-Political Resource," *Cross-Currents* 24 (Winter 1975): 445-62.

38. Andolsen, "Agape in Feminist Ethics," p. 80.

SOCIAL INSTITUTIONS AND GENDER RELATIONS

Nor are Christian feminists blindly idealistic about the potential of mutuality in the "best friends" mode. Sometimes, they concede, there will be conflicts of interest that do require an appeal to principle for their solution. But they suggest that some new criteria be employed. One is that basic human needs, both physical and psychological, should be met first, with the party in greater need having the *prima facie* claim over the other. Implicit in this criterion is the warning that no group, and especially not a socially dominant one, has the exclusive right to decide what *are* the essential needs of various others. Every party must have a respected voice in the discussion. A second criterion is that occasions of sacrifice should be "distributed" as equally as possible among all parties over time. For example, if a woman has worked at a boring job to put her husband through graduate school, it is only fair that he should restrain his ambitions at a not-much-later date so that she can pursue her own vocational vision.[39] Even so, Christian feminists conclude, all situations of sacrifice should be considered disruptions — even if unavoidable ones — of God's intended, creational *shalom*. In aiming, however imperfectly, for its restoration, "human beings should be dedicated to so providing for human needs and so diminishing oppression that situations calling for sacrifice are reduced to a minimum."[40] Whether or not such a recommendation can be implemented is one of our concerns in the chapter that follows.

Conclusion

This chapter has focused on a critique of the public/private dichotomy, a critique mounted in somewhat different forms by both secular and Christian feminists. Various feminists have argued, and we have agreed, that the public/private dichotomy, especially in its gendered form, is often artificial and dehumanizing — for both sexes, but particularly for

39. Indeed, it is not even clear that the order of a couple's vocational development should always favor the husband. Some of us know a very mature young man who concluded, when he and his wife completed their undergraduate studies, that it made more sense for him to support her through graduate school first. His reasoning was that when and if they had children, she was more likely to have to take time off from her public vocational pursuits, so it was only fair that she should get a head start in that area.

40. Andolsen, "Agape in Feminist Ethics," p. 80.

women, whose confinement to the private domain has resulted in a loss of power and a devaluation of what are more typically women's ways of knowing. At the same time, the cultural demand that men be active mainly in the public realm has created problems in the formation of the gender identity of young boys, and deprived men — including Christian men — of a sense of what it means to be a complete human being characterized by a unity of thought, emotion, and interpersonal attachment.

In the following chapter we will go from criticism to programmatic recommendations. Is the concept of "privacy" now completely outdated, or should it be retained in a new but radically degendered form? Likewise, are domesticity in general and the family in particular doomed to deconstruction, or are they also capable of re-emerging in a more just and less rigidly gendered form? Finally, is it possible to export what are more typically women's ways of knowing and valuing from the private to the public realm? Can we practice principled — and even biblical — justice in the domestic sphere and relational nurturance in the arena of public affairs? These are the questions on which we concentrate in the chapter that follows.

CHAPTER 13

Family Justice and Societal Nurturance: Reintegrating Public and Private Domains

As we saw in the last chapter, both secular and religious feminists have worked hard to break down the dualisms associating men with public life, abstract thinking, and justice-oriented ethics, and women with domestic life, concrete thinking, and particularistic loyalties. But what, we may now ask, do they propose to put in place of these dualisms? For it is one thing to argue that the ideology of gendered and separate spheres is damaging to women and men alike, and hence must go. It is quite another thing to assume that distinct spheres or levels of human activity and interaction — for example, the family — need not be retained at all, even in ungendered (or more justly gendered) form.

In the last chapter we noted that radical and socialist feminists lean toward a complete abolition of the public/private distinction. For these two groups, a major impulse behind the rallying cry "The personal is political" has been the desire to bring legal, psychological, and moral help to women and children victimized by the ideology of noninterference in the "naturally affectionate" domains of marriage and family. And this is an impulse we must continue to respect. Radical feminists are

The primary author of this chapter is Mary Stewart Van Leeuwen.

416

often castigated or ridiculed for exposing sexuality and family life to the harsh light of political (in the sense of "power") analysis. But their tenacious protests have begun to yield needed legal and social reforms. Gradually the "family secrets" of incest, child abuse, and wife battering are being recognized for the pervasive problems that they are. Gradually society is learning to support and re-empower rape victims rather than treating them as somehow responsible for their own victimization. More and more it is acknowledged that violent pornography, far from being harmless private entertainment, at the very least degrades women and at worst contributes to their sexual harassment, rape, and battering.[1]

However, many radical feminists have not attended to what might be lost in the process of making the "personal" so thoroughly "political." But a group of feminists whom we might describe as "chastened liberals" have begun to do so, and it is to some of their work that we now turn. We concentrate on two of their arguments: first, that both the concept and the practice of privacy are needful for healthy gender relations, albeit in forms different from traditional understandings; and second, that gender relations in the family can become more just without eliminating the family as a social institution. In the final part of the chapter we go on to examine the possibilities for enriching public life by opening it up to what we have called "women's ways of knowing." In the process we will note that despite its secular ring, the contemporary feminist call to restore justice to family life and caring nurturance to the public sphere is in many ways reflective of the biblical vision of *shalom.*

Giving Women the Privacy They Need

To begin with, some feminist theorists have pointed out that merely deconstructing the public/private dichotomy will not do, because such an exercise may well leave women with even *less* privacy than they had before.[2] The reason for this lies in an implicit assumption of the tradi-

1. For a survey of feminist debates on pornography, see Rosemarie Tong's *Feminist Thought: A Comprehensive Introduction* (Boulder, Colo.: Westview Press, 1989), chap. 4. For a (largely) sympathetic response by male feminists, see *Men Confront Pornography,* ed. Michael S. Kimmel (New York: Crown, 1990).
2. See, for example, Anita Brown's *Uneasy Access: Privacy for Women in a Free Society* (Totowa, N.J.: Rowman & Allenheld, 1988); Eloise Buker's "Politics As If Women Were Normal: Defending the Post-Feminist Polity," paper given at the

tional "gendered spheres" ideology — namely, that a properly domesticated woman exists primarily to serve all other members of her household. In the extreme case, she may have responsibility for every occupant
and every room of the house without being entitled to any truly private
time or space of her own. For example, the parents of one of our team
members recently retired after many years in the pastoral ministry. In
their newly acquired home, one room was set aside (as it had been in
every previous house they occupied) for the husband's study. But this
time a room was also set aside for the wife's "studio," as she called it. As
she guided visitors through the new house, she encountered great resistance to her use of the word *studio*; the visitors kept wanting to call
it her "sewing room," even though she planned to do much more than
just sew in it.

A century ago the British essayist John Ruskin exhorted women to
be "enduringly incorruptibly good; instinctively infallibly wise . . . not
for self-development, but for self-renunciation."[3] And even today, people
of both sexes often resist the idea of a woman cultivating an identity
other than that of being the caretaker of others. In a bold challenge to
these assumptions, British writer Virginia Woolf made this assertion in
1928 in *A Room of One's Own*: "It is necessary to have five hundred
[pounds] a year and a room with a lock on the door if you are to write
fiction or poetry."[4] Woolf, who had barely scraped together a living as
an odd-jobber before inheriting a legacy from a wealthy aunt, wanted to
show to a society that took for granted the natural inability of women
to write great works just how many social obstacles prevented them from
doing so.

Written over sixty years ago, Woolf's perceptive statement about
the human (not simply male) hunger for learning and creativity and the
obstacles preventing its satisfaction in women has become a recurrent
theme among feminists of all stripes. "Give us bread, but give us roses!"

Michigan State University conference "Revisioning Women in the Curriculum,"
April 1990; and Susan Moller Okin's *Justice, Gender, and the Family* (New York: Basic
Books, 1989).
    3. Ruskin, "Of Queen's Gardens," Lecture No. 2 of *Sesame and Lilies* (London:
A. L. Burt, 1871), p. 86.
    4. Woolf, *A Room of One's Own* (1929; rpt. New York: Harcourt Brace
Jovanovich, 1957), p. 109. See also Margaret Adams's essay entitled "The Compas-
sion Trap," in *Woman in Sexist Society: Studies in Power and Powerlessness*, ed. Vivian
Gornick and Barbara K. Moran (New York: Basic Books, 1971), pp. 401-16.

ran the refrain of an early American trade-union song penned by women. And in the 1940s, Dorothy Sayers, in her witty essay entitled "The Human-Not-Quite-Human," took a rare jab at the church for reinforcing the myth of women's naturally self-sacrificing character. She wrote,

> I think I have never heard a sermon preached on the story of Martha and Mary that did not attempt, somehow, somewhere, to explain away its text. Mary's, of course, was the better part — the Lord said so, and we must not precisely contradict him. But we will be careful not to despise Martha. No doubt, he approved of her too. We could not get on without her, and indeed (having paid lip-service to God's opinion) we must admit that we greatly prefer her. For Martha was doing a really feminine job, whereas Mary was just behaving like any other disciple, male or female; and that is a hard pill to swallow.[5]

Certainly it is not the case today that all sermons on this text (Luke 10:38-42) try to "explain away" Jesus' praise for Mary's desire to learn and his gentle rebuke of Martha's hyperdomesticity. But as we saw in our chapter on narrative and gender relations, there is still a general tendency to ignore or downplay scriptural accounts of women's extra-domestic achievements — even in Bible study materials specifically prepared for women!

With the re-emergence of organized feminism in the 1960s came echoes of Woolf's insistence on a woman's need for (and right to) a room of her own. In a much-reprinted essay entitled "The Politics of Housework," Pat Mainardi observes,

> If human endeavors are like a pyramid with man's highest achievements at the top, then keeping oneself alive is at the bottom. Men have always had servants (us) to take care of this bottom strata of life while they have confined their efforts to the rarefied upper regions. It is thus ironic when they ask of women — where are your great painters, statesmen, etc. Mme. Matisse ran a millinery shop so he could paint. Mrs. Martin Luther King kept his house and raised his babies.[6]

5. Sayers, "The Human-Not-Quite-Human," in *Are Women Human?* (Downers Grove, Ill.: InterVarsity Press, 1981), pp. 46-47.
6. Mainardi, "The Politics of Housework," in *Voices from Women's Liberation,* ed. Leslie B. Tanner (New York: New American Library, 1970), p. 339. Visual echoes of Mainardi's point appeared in Sally Swain's "Home Is Where the Art Is" (*Ms.,* April 1989, pp. 72-73). Swain created colorful caricatures of famous modern paint-

The message in all this is clear: radical feminism to the contrary, the personal (or private) domain cannot be made completely continuous with the public domain because women in particular have an unfulfilled need for personal privacy, with the discretionary time and space that this implies. Nor is this need limited to women who are full-time homemakers, since those who share the wage-earning burden with their husbands are still not, on average, repaid in kind by their husbands' taking on an equal share of domestic responsibilities. The result, according to the research of sociologist Arlie Hochschild, is that women in paid, full-time positions work the equivalent of a full month of eight-hour days per year more than their husbands. "These women," writes Hochschild, "talked about sleep the way a hungry person talks about food."[7]

Because of women's generally unsatisfied need for personal time and space, political theorist Susan Moller Okin speaks of challenging not the public/*private* dichotomy but only the traditionally gendered notion of a public/*domestic* split: "Both the concept of privacy and the existence of a personal sphere of life . . . are essential," she writes. They are essential for all persons, but at this time particularly for women if they are to have the time, energy, and space needed to exercise the intellectual, artistic, and other kinds of creativity they have wrongly been assumed to lack. Nor does such an analysis deny the need for a measure of *family* privacy. But, Okin adds, the sphere of private family life "can be just and secure only if its members are equals, and if those who must temporarily be regarded as unequal — children — are protected from abuse."[8]

Implied in Okin's assertion is a need for greater justice in family life. This is a serious theme in Okin's work — not because she disparages the work other feminists have done to highlight the relational virtues of this womanly sphere, but simply because she is convinced (as are we) that these virtues must rest on a prior substrate of justice if they are

---

ings, altered to show what the artists' wives were likely to be doing to support their husband's artistic work. Mrs. Toulouse-Lautrec appeared as a cancan dancer with a toilet brush attached to her foot, Mrs. Degas vacuumed the floor in an elegant ballet dress, a cubist Mrs. Mondrian mopped the floor, a bare-breasted, Tahitian-looking Mrs. Gauguin conducted a Tupperware party, and so on.

7. Hochschild, *The Second Shift: Working Parents and the Revolution at Home* (New York: Viking Press, 1989), p. 9.

8. Okin, *Justice, Gender, and the Family*, p. 128.

not to become vehicles for women's exploitation. Let us look more closely at this line of argument now. We will begin by clarifying what is meant by the term *justice*, not just in ordinary academic parlance but in biblical-theological terms, particularly as is affects gender relations. Then we will go on to discuss what we mean when we say that the affectional (or relational) ideals of family life must be built on a just foundation. That is, while ideally families should be more than "merely just," they should never be *less* than just toward all their members.

Justice in Philosophical and Biblical Perspectives

In his book *Crime and Its Victims,* lawyer Dan Van Ness — now director of the Christian agency known as Justice Fellowship — recalls that his youthful desire to be a lawyer began in the 1950s and '60s when he would watch *The Perry Mason Show* on television. Defender Mason's clients were always innocent people wrongly accused of a crime, and thanks to his matchless cross-examination skills, the true criminals were always exposed and Mason's clients were exonerated. At the end of each episode, the credits rolled across a background showing the symbol of the Greek goddess of Justice, with her blindfold, scales, and sword. The ideal was clear, says Van Ness: "Impartial Justicia, weighing the evidence and ready to impose judgment on the wrongdoer. Impersonal, objective, single-minded, relentless, fair."[9]

When he finally became a practicing lawyer, Van Ness found that the reality of the court system did not match the picture painted in the *Perry Mason* episodes:

> Not all defendants are innocent. Few attorneys are as skillful as Perry Mason. Many of our criminal cases seem to focus more on the technical rights of defendants than on the issue of guilt or innocence. Some guilty offenders are acquitted; innocent defendants are occasionally convicted. Victims are forgotten and angry. The goddess' blindfold sometimes appears to be preventing her from seeing the truth rather than enabling her to be impartial.[10]

9. Van Ness, *Crime and Its Victims: What We Can Do* (Downers Grove, Ill.: InterVarsity Press, 1986), p. 114.
10. Ibid., p. 114.

Van Ness is speaking about the ideals (and the miscarriage) of what is commonly called "retributive justice." He is also assuming, quite rightly, that justice is a profoundly social concept. In a universe inhabited by just one person, the concept of justice or fairness would be meaningless, at least on the human level. When we speak of justice, we are speaking of principles — however these are derived — that guide relations among human beings.

Retributive justice is invoked when persons violate the claims their society has on them by virtue of its laws — when, for example, they injure or steal from other people. In the world of Perry Mason, the principles and practice of retributive justice are clear-cut and, in the end, always congruent. In the real world, as Van Ness discovered when he became a lawyer, practice does not always match up with principle, and sometimes even the principles are questionable — for example, the principle in Western law that it is only "the state" which is offended when a crime is committed, and not the victim of the crime per se.[11]

But complex and inconsistent as it may be, retributive justice is often easier to agree about than what is called "distributive justice." While retributive justice concerns what happens when people violate their legal responsibilities *to* society, distributive justice has to do with the claims people have *on* society. It is concerned with what is "fairly ours" or what is "our due" as members of a given society. As with retributive justice, it is difficult to imagine the idea of distributive justice arising on an island inhabited by a lone person: by its very nature it has to do with the distribution of tangible (and intangible) goods *among* people. These goods include things like access to natural resources (e.g., land, air, water), protection from harm, disease, and starvation, and the opportunity to develop one's gifts and exercise a vocation. In what follows we will be talking largely about distributive justice, especially as it applies to gender relations. But we will occasionally refer to retributive justice and to a third form, contractual justice, which has to do with specific promises made between two or more parties, such as the warranty a seller provides a buyer guaranteeing a particular, well-functioning product in return for a particular price paid.

---

11. For a further explanation of the nature and historical development of "state-centered justice," see Van Ness's *Crime and Its Victims*, chap. 5.

Distributive Justice and Gender Relations

In a society that contained endless goods of the kinds just specified, or alternately, was made up of people who cared as deeply and consistently for everyone else as for themselves, distributive justice would be a meaningless concept. It is only when goods are at least somewhat scarce and people are inclined to compete for them that principles are needed for their just distribution.[12] What principles, then, do people apply, and how does the choice of them reflect beliefs about gender relations?

Political conservatives have sometimes invoked the principle of merit — either ascribed or achieved — as the best way to decide who gets what. Ascribed merit refers to qualities over which one has no control, such as the accidents of birth or geography. Aristotle, for example, was convinced that some people were simply "born" to be slaves by virtue of their stupidity, and many of our more recent ancestors believed something similar — namely, that race was the relevant test for slave or free status. Other kinds of ascribed merit are also part of the mix in the Western world. Theologian Lewis Smedes concedes that "many men believe that being born male confers on them certain prerogatives that women do not share. And most of us act as though our living in a country whose soil is rich and black means that we deserve to eat more than people who were born on white sand."[13]

For liberal feminists concerned with gender justice, the idea of ascribed merit (particularly on the basis of biological characteristics) as the basis for distributive justice is simply inadequate. What, then, about achieved merit — the notion that we "earn" access to certain things in

12. The eighteenth-century philosopher David Hume expressed this as follows: "If men were supplied with everything in the same abundance, or if *every one* had the same affection and tender regard for *every one* as for himself, justice and injustice would be equally unknown among mankind. Here then is a proposition which, I think, may be regarded as certain, *that 'tis only from the selfishness and confined generosity of men, along with the scanty provision nature has made for his wants, that justice derives its origin*" (his emphases). See his *Treatise of Human Nature* (1739-1740), ed. L. A. Selby-Bigge (Oxford: Clarendon Press, 1975), p. 495.

13. Smedes, *Mere Morality: What God Expects from Ordinary People* (Grand Rapids: William B. Eerdmans, 1983), p. 39. See also Brian Barry's *Theories of Justice* (Berkeley: University of California Press, 1989); Scott Gordon's *Welfare, Justice, and Freedom* (New York: Columbia University Press, 1980); John Rawls's *Theory of Justice* (Cambridge: Harvard University Press, 1971); and Elizabeth Wolgast's *Grammar of Justice* (Ithaca, N.Y.: Cornell University Press, 1987).

423

proportion to our individual achievements? This may be somewhat closer to the mark, provided that opportunities to achieve are equalized — a classically liberal feminist goal. At the same time, what we "deserve" on the basis of our achievements should be limited to the areas of life associated with those achievements. For example, our work as professors may entitle us to secretarial services; it does not entitle us to push ahead of our secretaries in the lunch line. And most people would agree that all of us justly deserve certain things regardless of achievement, simply because we are human beings — for example, protection from wanton attack, a minimally nourishing diet, and special medical help for those with physical handicaps.

Similar considerations rule out the idea of simply treating everyone equally as the basis for distributive justice, since some people need certain kinds of preferential treatment just to stay in the race to achieve. In a relational feminist analysis, this would sometimes apply to women — as in the argument for job-protected maternity leave. A socialist analysis of distributive justice is apt to go even further, invoking need as the most important criterion for deciding who gets what, in accordance with the Marxist principle "From each according to his abilities, to each according to his needs." According to socialist feminists, women lack and therefore deserve economic parity with men both in the waged workplace and at home. Along with their radical feminist sisters, socialist feminists might also insist that women need special legal protection from battering spouses, from rapists (and a legal system that trivializes rape), and from the consequences of the production and sale of pornography.

People also disagree on what constitutes the range of legitimate human needs deserving of society's resources. Are we speaking only of minimal biological survival needs, or also (as many feminists would insist) of what is needed for the full flourishing of persons — including such things as education, culture, leisure, respect, social fellowship, and the opportunity to pursue meaningful work? It seems that whether we settle on merit, equality, or need as our principle of distributive justice, we create as many problems as we solve.[14] How much can the biblical vision of justice help us to decide among these competing principles? And what will that vision suggest regarding justice in gender relations?

14. Smedes, *Mere Morality*, chap. 2.

Justice in Biblical Perspective

As we noted in Chapter Two of this book, the Old Testament words normally translated as *justice, righteousness,* and *peace* are closely bound up with each other. According to theologian Lewis Smedes, justice, in its Old Testament sense, is part of the larger biblical notion of righteousness, which in turn is part of the fullness of *shalom,* or peace. Certainly the Bible calls for fair weights and measures, for the poor of Israel to get an impartial hearing in the courts, and for widows and orphans to get enough to eat. These are examples, respectively, of what we have called contractual, retributive, and distributive justice. But these constitute only the "bottom line" of the biblical vision for society. Like the progressively larger sections of a telescope, biblical justice is meant to extend into righteousness, which in turn is to extend into the fuller vision of *shalom.* In the words of Lewis Smedes, "The prophets never demand less than justice, but they promise more. Nothing else is enough without justice; but justice is not enough by itself."[15]

Smedes goes on to make this observation about the Old Testament prophets:

> True justice is fulfilled, they believed, in righteousness. Justice and righteousness come in tandem, as in this much quoted word from Amos:
>
> > Let justice roll down like waters,
> > And righteousness like an ever-flowing stream (Amos 5:24).
>
> Amos was not envisioning two different things, justice and righteousness, rolling down the hillsides into the villages of Israel. He probably saw justice as one ingredient of righteousness. When people received their due, justice was done.... [But] righteousness goes beyond our ordinary sense of justice to a humanity made whole.... Righteousness exists where people care for their neighbors and befriend them, concerned not merely that they get their [material] due, but that their deepest personal needs are satisfied.[16]

Finally, what is implied in the biblical notion of peace, or *shalom?* In an earlier chapter we noted that to live in the *shalom* of God is fully

15. Ibid., p. 31.
16. Ibid., p. 30.

to *enjoy* life with God, with one's neighbors, with one's physical surroundings, with oneself. Smedes concurs: "*Shalom* is righteousness erupting in joy, the vibrancy of health, the creativity of love, the lust of living. In the biblical peace, people are both good and happy, and so have the perfect combination of *shalom* with righteousness."[17]

But for *shalom* to come about — for people to fully enjoy each other — reconciliation needs to occur; relationships need to be restored to their rightful pattern. Thus biblical justice as a component of *shalom* goes well beyond the contractual, distributive, and retributive justice which is the usual concern of ethicists, economists, and political theorists. According to Dan Van Ness, biblical justice "is far more than fair treatment and due process. It is also more than vindication of those who have been wronged and punishment of the wrongdoer. The full meaning of [biblical] justice is to establish once again the *shalom* that existed before [an] offense [took place]. *Justice is active and relational and it is redemptive in its intent.*"[18]

Applying Biblical Justice to Family and Gender Relations

How does all of this apply to our concern for justice in family and gender relations? It suggests, first of all, that while the distinction between an "ethic of justice" (mostly male, mostly public) and an "ethic of care" (mostly female, mostly private) may accurately describe a set of dualisms into which our society has lapsed, it is not a distinction that reflects the biblical vision of justice, righteousness, and peace. We have just seen that in this vision principled justice is meant to be a foundation for nurturing neighbor-love, or righteousness, which in turn is to lead to a state of *shalom* in which human reconciliation and renewal take place. And nowhere in the Bible is there any suggestion that "justice" is limited to the marketplace and other "public" arenas of activity, while "righ-

17. Ibid., p. 30. See also *The Faith That Does Justice: Examining the Christian Sources for Social Change,* ed. John C. Haughey, S.J. (New York: Paulist Press, 1977); Paul Marshall's *Thine Is the Kingdom* (Grand Rapids: William B. Eerdmans, 1987); Paul Ramsey's *Basic Christian Ethics* (New York: Charles Scribner's Sons, 1953); Nicholas Wolterstorff's *Until Justice and Peace Embrace* (Grand Rapids: William B. Eerdmans, 1983); and also the entries for *Sadeq* and *Shalom* in *Theological Wordbook of the Old Testament,* ed. R. Laird Harris et al. (Chicago: Moody Press, 1980).

18. Van Ness, *Crime and Its Victims,* p. 121 (our emphases).

teousness" is limited to the home — let alone that men are to be the primary purveyors of justice while women are to specialize in practicing righteousness. Those who would be members of God's kingdom, *whatever* their race, nationality, class, or gender, are called to weave a seamless web of justice *and* righteousness *and* peace throughout all areas of their personal and corporate lives.

Thus contemporary feminists are right to be critical of theorists and theologians who exempt domestic life from the requirements of justice. As we have already noted, the laws of ancient Israel recorded in Scripture reflect the need of all societies for standards of contractual, retributive, and distributive justice. However, taken as a whole the laws of the Old Testament existed less to protect the privileges of the strong than to guarantee justice for the weak, among whom women and children (and especially widows and orphans) are regularly included. Theologian Lewis Smedes notes that "the prophets were for the rights of everyone, rich as well as poor, but they do not worry about justice for the rich, who can take care of themselves. Besides, [the rich] tend to be so blinded by their selfishness that they cannot be trusted to honor the rights of poor people."[19] Lawyer Dan Van Ness adds that "the biblical concept of justice, far from being impartial, reflects a special concern for protecting vulnerable people from victimization by the powerful. It stems not from the image of a minor Greek goddess [the impartial Justicia, who in practice all too often ends up favoring those with power] but from the character of the one true God, Jehovah."[20]

Hence the Covenant Code (Ex. 20:22–23:23) and the book of Deuteronomy have specific legislation to ensure that the enslaved, the widowed, the orphaned, the poor, and the stranger are not exploited but instead are securely integrated into the economic and social life of Israel. To this list of vulnerable groups Jesus pointedly adds children, whose very vulnerability reflects the attitude required of anyone wishing to enter the kingdom of heaven (Matt. 18:1-5). No fewer than five times throughout the Gospels Jesus warns that these "little ones" (in the immediate context he is referring to children, but the image also pertains to other easily exploited groups) are God's special concern. Of those who cause them to stumble, he says, "It would be better for you if a great millstone were fastened around your neck and you were drowned

19. Smedes, *Mere Morality*, p. 31.
20. Van Ness, *Crime and Its Victims*, p. 121.

427

in the sea."[21] This warning is sounded not to replace grace with works in the economy of salvation but simply to show how important children and other vulnerable groups are in God's sight. If the "last" are to become "first" in God's kingdom (something that Jesus is recorded as affirming no fewer than six times in the Gospels), then those charged with their care must tremble at the thought of abusing their power, as must those who turn a blind eye to such abuse.

The Bible leaves us in no doubt about our need for the kind of justice that is especially sensitive to the socially less-empowered. From the Fall onward, human relationships, despite their continuing potential for goodness, have become permeated with sin. And the Bible is quite unsparing in its documentation of the results. From Cain's murder of his brother Abel (Gen. 4:1-16) to the Pharisees' self-serving neglect of elderly parents through a pseudoreligious sheltering of their assets (Mark 7:9-13), we are regularly exposed to the distortions wrought by sin in relationships for which God's unchanging intentions are justice, peace, and love. Sensitive to the fallenness of gender relations, the Scriptures present us with blunt accounts of rape, adultery, incest, and polygamy run wild (recall Solomon's 700 wives and 300 concubines). We are told of sins aimed at covering up previous sins — witness the account of Potiphar's wife playing the sexual victim after unsuccessfully trying to seduce Joseph. We are told of David's plot to murder the husband of Bathsheba, the woman he impregnated, and shown that David's violence and sexual sin find an intergenerational echo in his son Amnon's callous rape of his sister Tamar (2 Sam. 13).

The book of Judges twice contains the ominous statement that "In those days there was no king in Israel; all the people did what was right in their own eyes" (Judg. 17:6; 21:25). To illustrate the fruits of this lawlessness, the book includes an account of the rape of the Levite's concubine and its resulting brutal, tribal feud (Judg. 19–22), as well as the account of the sacrifice of Jephthah's daughter for the sake of her father's rash vow.[22] None of this is meant to portray God's intention for family and gender relations. It is rather the accurate portrayal of fallen men and women,

21. This concern of Jesus for vulnerable "little ones" is recorded in Matt. 18:6; Matt. 18:10; Matt. 18:14; Mark 9:42; and Luke 17:2.

22. For a further analysis of such biblical stories as they apply to gender relations, see Phyllis Trible's *Texts of Terror: Literary-Feminist Readings of Biblical Narratives* (Philadelphia: Fortress Press, 1984).

"warts and all," a portrayal that the apostle Paul confirms when he summarizes the sinful tendencies which beset Jew and Gentile alike: "There is no one who is righteous, not even one; there is no one who has understanding, there is no one who seeks God. All have turned aside . . . ; there is no one who shows kindness. . . . Their mouths are full of cursing and bitterness. Their feet are swift to shed blood; ruin and misery are in their paths, and the way of peace they have not known" (Rom. 3:10-12, 14-17).

Restoring Justice in the Family

Having examined both secular and biblical meanings of the term *justice*, as well as the Bible's clear message about our need for justice in all human relationships, let us now return to some contemporary feminist reflections on the family. By redrawing the boundary between the private and the public in the manner explained earlier, contemporary feminist theorists may seem to be claiming that "public" includes everything *except* the "room of one's own" — to be claiming, in other words, that no social institution rightly exists between the person as private individual and the person as public, state-regulated, state-involved citizen. This is a view taken by some Marxists and socialist feminists, but it is not the view of those we have called "chastened liberals." In general, these feminists are seeking to alter, not deconstruct, the inequitably gendered power relations of family life. Susan Okin effectively summarizes the agenda of these feminists:

> Most contemporary feminists, while critiquing the gender-structured family, have not attacked all varieties of family. . . . We refuse to give up on the institution of the family, and refuse to accept the division of labor between the sexes as natural and unchangeable. . . . The family is in no way inevitably tied to its gender structure, but until this notion is successfully challenged, and non-traditional groupings and divisions of labor are not only recognized but encouraged, there can be no hope of equality for women in either the domestic or the public sphere.[23]

The difference between Okin's stance and that of earlier liberal feminists shows in her insistence that the family *not* be viewed as a sphere

23. Okin, *Justice, Gender, and the Family,* p. 125.

429

of naturally gendered roles and affections exempt from legal or social regulation. This is a point on which virtually all feminists are now agreed. But Okin parts company from other feminists — particularly those who unreflectively criticize "male" styles of thought and ethical judgment — in her insistence that traditionally liberal notions of justice, far from being overimposed by men on everyone else, have been mistakenly underapplied to family life. What we need, she suggests, is not a forced choice between an "ethics of justice" and an "ethics of care" (as some feminists seem to suggest), nor a limiting of the latter to family life and the former to public life (as some male ethicists and theologians have assumed), but rather a greater concern for justice (particularly distributive justice) in family life and a greater concern for care in public life. Let us look at each of these themes in turn, noting even as we begin that such concerns are consonant with the biblical call to make the practice of justice, righteousness, and peace a "seamless web" in all areas of our lives, whether we are women or men.

Justice as a Necessary Condition of Care

In the previous chapter we summarized the feminist critique of justice-oriented ethics — of the notion that mature moral judgment requires people to abandon a (more feminine) appeal to specific human loyalties for a (more masculine) appeal to "universal" moral principles. However, despite the strong feminist argument for an "ethic of care" over a purely detached "ethic of justice," we also noted that some feminists came full circle, moving back to a form of principled ethics, even as they presented their case for an ethic of care. Specifically, we saw some feminist theologians conceding that an ethic of mutual care might still require an appeal to principle, particularly when personal goals conflict and the distribution of scarce resources (e.g., time, money, educational opportunity) must be negotiated. Such situations, they conceded, can occur even in relationships based on the mutuality of the "best friends" model. Thus, while insisting that self-sacrifice cease to be considered the automatic Christian solution to every interpersonal conflict (especially for women), these theologians conceded that, in a society with differing interests and only finite resources, sacrifice is often inevitable. They then went on to suggest some revised principles for a more just distribution of sacrifice.

This suggests a growing recognition among feminists that an ethic of justice, properly understood, may be compatible with or even essential to an ethic of care — a suggestion that is more fully developed by Okin in her book on justice in the family. It is interesting that Okin, while decidedly not claiming to be a Christian, prefaces her argument by admitting that mere justice, in the sense of all persons getting what is minimally their due, is not the highest ethical virtue. When we sincerely engage in acts of care — of benevolence, mercy, heroism, or self-sacrifice — whether unilaterally or mutually, we are certainly being much better than simply "just."[24] Nevertheless, these higher-order ethical virtues, the practice of which helps bind a community of persons together in a way that the practice of mere justice could not, still cannot exist without a foundational commitment to justice. This is particularly the case in family life, and Okin cites three reasons why.[25]

The first is that an ethic of care is both conceptually and practically dependent on an ethic of justice. To show how this is so, let's take an example not as gender-loaded as the traditional family — that of a religious order dedicated to founding schools and teaching in them. At its best, such a group might seem to embody ethicist John Rawls's definition of a situation in which justice concerns are irrelevant — namely, "an association of saints agreeing on a common ideal."[26] But conceptually and practically, justice is still an important foundation of this association. Let us suppose that each member of the group has taken a lifelong vow of poverty and charity. Does this preclude all conflict over goals or over the distribution of scarce resources? Perhaps within the order it does (although even here, decisions about what differing members *need* to subsist in "poverty" or act with "charity" may require an appeal to principles of distributive justice). But certainly to carry out its external mission, the order, unless it possesses infinite resources, will have to appeal to principles of justice constantly. Given a limited budget, should

24. This is perhaps why Jews have reserved the label of "righteous Gentile" for those non-Jews who risked their own lives to help rescue Jews from death in the Nazi-occupied Europe of World War II.

25. In constructing her argument, Okin acknowledges a debt to John Rawls's *Theory of Justice*; however, she is the one who did the work of extending Rawls's arguments to cover gendered institutions such as the family. She develops this application particularly in the first chapter of *Justice, Gender, and the Family*.

26. The definition is from Rawls's *Theory of Justice*, p. 129, but the example of the religious order is our own.

they open up a new school in one part of the inner city or improve an existing school in another? Should they retain the teaching of Latin for the college-bound few, or drop it in favor of technical courses for their more modestly endowed students? It is hard to see how an appeal to principles of distributive justice can be avoided, even in a group that comes theoretically as close as this one to being "an association of saints agreeing on a common ideal."

In the second place, Okin agrees with other feminists on this point: it is a dangerous exercise in romanticism to argue, as ethicists past and present have done, that because of its reduced scale and supposedly affectional basis, the family is a sphere of life in which justice need not operate. We have just seen that even in a voluntarily sacrificial, single-sex "association of saints agreeing on a common ideal," justice considerations continue to affect both internal operations and external mission. How much more must this be so in an institution — the family — where it has been the woman who takes a vow of "poverty and charity" as both she and her property are appropriated by her husband? For although in theory women are now equal in suffrage and before the law, in practice married women still labor under the residual effects of the ancient common law of coverture. Right up through to the twentieth century in the English-speaking world, this legal practice has enabled political theorists to remove family relations from the realm of justice by collapsing all distinctions of property and interests when two people marry.

What did the original law of coverture entail? If it had meant that when two people marry they are supposed to be so mutually committed that "what is his becomes hers, and what is hers becomes his," then we might indeed have some grounds — at least in theory — for removing family relations from the concerns of justice that regulate other social institutions. But in fact this common law did not institute mutual property-sharing between spouses, but rather transferred the wife's property, body, children, and legal rights to the husband, a principle whose legal and social effects have by no means completely disappeared.[27]

Thus, Okin points out, by concentrating in their theories on the sentimental "one flesh" aspect of coverture but neglecting the fact that this one flesh was in fact the person of the husband, political theorists

---

27. Hence the derivation of the term *coverture:* upon marriage the husband was presumed symbolically to "cover up" the wife, so that she no longer was "visible" as a separate person.

have been able to have their cake and eat it too — that is, to see the family as the sphere of idyllic, mutual affection and at the same time preserve male privilege within it.[28] And the residual legal ramifications of coverture are being dismantled only very slowly — witness, for example, the fact that only recently has the law ceased (in some places) to uphold the right of a husband to force his wife to have sexual intercourse. The residual psychological effects of coverture also continue to exert an influence, even on the minds of some women. For example, sociologist Miriam Johnson describes the case of a social worker trying to convince a rural woman of the need to press charges against her husband for having sex with his young daughter. The woman did not see the social worker's point, and finally responded in exasperation, "Well, so what? He's had sex with his daughter. She's his'n, ain't she?"[29]

A final reason for bringing an ethic of justice into family life has to do with the effects of its absence on children. Many political theorists and psychologists have stressed that the family is the crucible of early moral development and the place where, especially in the first few years of life, children form basic social attitudes. It is, at least potentially, a place where children can *learn* to be just, since a sense of justice requires shared social experience and the gradual acquisition of the ability to see things from others' points of view — particularly others who are important to the child yet are different from him or her in some ways. However, most of these theorists of moral development have placed insufficient stress on the specifically gendered inequities of family life. Reviewing the writings of political theorists such as Rousseau, Hegel, and Tocqueville, Okin demonstrates that "none of these theorists argued

---

28. This ethical sleight-of-hand is common to classically liberal political theory. Other theorists, even today, do not even bother to attempt such a compromise, but rather simply say that family relations at their best are, for biological or theological reasons, unjust (comparatively speaking, ungoverned as they are by the standards for justice operative in other spheres). Allan Bloom appears to espouse the former position — see his book entitled *The Closing of the American Mind: How Higher Education Has Failed Democracy and Impoverished the Souls of Today's Students* (New York: Simon & Schuster, 1987). For a critique of this stance, see Okin's *Justice, Gender, and the Family*, chap. 2; and also Mary Stewart Van Leeuwen's *Gender and Grace: Love, Work and Parenting in a Changing World* (Downers Grove, Ill.: InterVarsity Press, 1990), chaps. 3-5. C. S. Lewis leaned strongly toward the latter (theological) position.

29. Johnson, *Strong Mothers, Weak Wives: The Search for Gender Equality* (Berkeley: University of California Press, 1988), p. 168.

433

for just family structures as necessary for socializing children into citizenship in a just society":

> Though concerned with moral development, they bifurcated public from private life to such an extent that they had no trouble reconciling inegalitarian, sometimes admittedly unjust, relations founded upon sentiment within the family with a more just, even equalitarian, social structure outside the family. . . . All thought the family was centrally important for the development of morality in citizens, but all defended the hierarchy of the marital structure while spurning such a degree of hierarchy in institutions and practices outside the household.[30]

Again, this is not to say that justice is a sufficient condition for family life. Indeed, it is difficult to imagine anyone being a successful parent without having a strong tolerance for running not just one but several "extra miles" beyond mere distributive justice. This is especially the case when children are young and need large doses of benevolence, patience, and self-sacrifice from their caretakers. But when children see that most of these "extra miles" are being run by their mothers and other adult females rather than their fathers and other adult males, what lesson are they absorbing about the nature of distributive justice in the real world? Okin expresses the problem very cogently:

> What is a child of either sex to learn about fairness in the average household with two full-time working parents, where the mother does, at the very least, twice as much family work as the father? What is a

---

30. Ibid., p. 19. See also Elizabeth Fox-Genovese's *Feminism without Illusions: A Critique of Individualism* (Chapel Hill: University of North Carolina Press, 1991). As a historian, Fox-Genovese criticizes the liberal, individualist, male-defined tradition and notes some of the same contradictions in it that Okin does, particularly the tension between the political ideals of liberty and equality. "Once [property conditions] were taken into account, liberty and equality were not easily reconcilable, for equality among individuals could directly threaten the liberty of propertied individuals to exercise their rights freely. In the extreme case, the liberty of slave holders, defined as property holders, flatly contradicted the human equality of slaves, defined as property. The tension between liberty and equality acquired a special resonance for women [since most men] viewed either the liberty or equality of women as an unacceptable threat to the stability of families — and to the psyches of men whose autonomy depended upon unquestioning female support. . . . Historically, individualism for men has depended on the subordination of women" (pp. 67 and 123-24).

child to learn about the value of nurturing and domestic work in a home with a traditional division of labor in which the father either subtly or not so subtly uses the fact that he is the wage earner to "pull rank" on or to abuse his wife? What is a child to learn about responsibility for others in a family in which, after years of arranging her life around the needs of her husband and children, a [divorced] woman is faced with having to provide for herself and her children but is totally ill-equipped for the task by the life she agreed to lead, has led, and expected to go on leading?[31]

The answer to Okin's rhetorical questioning seems obvious: children raised in such settings will, regardless of any democratic rhetoric to the contrary, reach the same conclusion expressed in George Orwell's *Animal Farm:* "All animals are equal, but some animals are more equal than others."

To summarize Okin's argument: By denying the importance of justice to family life and cloaking the latter exclusively in the language of idealized affection, ethicists and political theorists have first of all neglected the extent to which an ethic of care necessarily presupposes an ethic of justice. Second, they have left the door open for the largely unregulated economic, physical, and sexual abuse of women and children. Finally, they have exposed children within families to dubious role-models of the justice they are expected to practice as adults in the larger world.

Many ethicists and political theorists are now willing to acknowledge the validity of the preceding criticisms. However, they remain concerned that by invoking "crude" justice in the family setting, we will diminish its potential for mutuality and love. "But," writes Okin (with echoes of the biblical vision of *shalom*), "why should we suppose that harmonious affection, indeed deep and long-lasting love, cannot co-exist with ongoing standards of justice?":

31. Okin, *Justice, Gender, and the Family,* pp. 22-23. Philosopher Merold Westphal, in his review of Okin's book, points out that single-parent families headed by women are the modern version of the widows and orphans of biblical times, and that Okin makes a strong case to demonstrate the systemic injustice they are suffering. See his essay entitled "Protecting Widows and Orphans," *Perspectives,* October 1991, p. 23. See also Lenore Weitzman's *Divorce Revolution: The Unexpected Social and Economic Consequences for Women and Children in America* (New York: Free Press, 1985). Weitzman found that, after divorce, women's average income *decreased* by 73 percent while men's *increased* by 42 percent.

We need to recognize that associations in which we *hope* that the best of human motivations and the noblest of virtues will prevail are, in fact, morally superior to those that are [merely] just only if they are firmly built on a foundation of justice, however rarely it may be invoked. . . . When we recognize, as surely we must, that many of the resources that are enjoyed within the sphere of family life — leisure, nurturance, money, time, and attention, to mention only a few — are by no means always abundant, we see that justice has a highly significant role to play. When we realize that women, especially, are likely to change the whole course of their lives because of their family commitments, it becomes clear that we cannot regard families as analogous to other intimate relations like friendship, however strong the affective bonding of the latter may be.[32]

Thus we can and should call the family — just as we call bodies of Christian believers — to go the "extra mile" beyond being merely just. But neither can be less than just in a world where pervasive depravity is mixed with creational goodness in all human institutions. Although Okin is not writing from a theological perspective, she clearly concurs:

[A] theory of justice must concern itself not with abstractions or ideals of institutions but their realities. If we were to concern ourselves only with ideals, we might well conclude that wider human societies, as well as families, could do without justice. The ideal society would presumably need no system of criminal justice or taxation, but that does not tell us much about what we need in the world we live in.[33]

---

32. Okin, *Justice, Gender, and the Family,* p. 32. It should be noted that at this point Okin is qualifying the feminist theologians' comparison of mutuality in marriage to mutuality in friendship, as discussed in the previous chapter. She says, in effect, that though we must surely aim to make such an analogy real, in a world where women have been socialized and regulated to be continuously self-sacrificing, we cannot expect to actualize the comparison simply by making it in theory. To make marriage truly analogous to the best examples of friendship will require the "degendering" of a host of practices and assumptions about who does what in family life. This degendering must occur not just on the theoretical level but also on the emotional, interpersonal, economic, and social-policy levels. This, as Okin's book makes clear, is going to take a great deal of effort and commitment from everyone. Power, once acquired, is only very reluctantly shared.

33. Ibid., p. 29. Note that this quotation shows a strong, if secularized, respect for the Calvinist doctrine of pervasive depravity. See also Fox-Genovese's *Feminism without Illusions,* p. 101.

Making the Public Realm a Sphere of Nurturance

We have just been discussing the contemporary feminist concern to bring justice into the family as a foundation on which affection must build, rather than expecting love alone to guarantee good family relations. We have also suggested that such a concern correlates with the biblical vision of *shalom* as an outgrowth of justice and love functioning in concert. But if the biblical vision requires both justice and love in family life, it also requires both in public life. If the family is to be characterized by justice as the substrate for nurturance, we also need to re-envisage our lives as citizens in terms of nurturance as the goal of justice. This is a theme currently being explored by philosophical feminists who wish to show the limits of more-traditionally-male modes of ethical thought and to extend more-typically-female modes of judgment from the domestic to the public realm. Let us look at some of their work now.

The Warrior versus the Nurturer

In her book entitled *Money, Sex, and Power: An Essay on Domination and Community*, political theorist Nancy Hartsock notes that a favored Western metaphor for citizenship has been that of the warrior.[34] From the time of the ancient Greeks through to present-day America, part of the male ideal of citizenship has been a willingness to die for the state. Analogously, part of privileged femininity has been the ideal of marrying and/or giving birth to a male warrior and "keeping the home fires burning" when the men are away at war. Eloise Buker, another political theorist, pursues the history of this metaphor. She notes that "the warrior image leads to a particular view of political action as risking one's life, to a view of the state as protector and to a view of politics as the management of conflict."[35]

This, of course, is a highly gendered picture of citizenship: warrioring is a traditionally male preserve. Moreover, the notion that ethical judgment is largely a case of solving disputes over individual rights is a way of thinking more typical of males than females, as we have noted

34. Hartsock, *Money, Sex, and Power: An Essay on Domination and Community* (New York: Longman, 1983).
35. Buker, "Politics As If Women Were Normal," p. 14.

frequently. Thus Buker proposes an alternative metaphor for citizenship — namely, the citizen as mother. In this vision, citizens, whether men or women, are committed to the task of nurturing, and public life is concerned primarily with creating and increasing opportunities rather than with protecting individual property rights in peacetime and demanding blind willingness to sacrifice lives in wartime. It is a vision of righteousness that involves "being with others and exercising responsibility for their welfare."[36]

At the same time, Buker notes, this model of citizenship does not preclude a concern for distributive justice — a concern that may even, as a last resort, have to be backed up by force. But its primary orientation is toward nurturing. Mere justice, when combined with the warrior metaphor, leads to a view of the community as being energized and controlled by its strongest members. But justice undergirded by a larger commitment to care measures the strength of a community by the capacity of all its members to maintain and develop mutually positive relationships.

A third theorist, Sara Ruddick (whose ideas we discussed in the previous chapter), believes that the kind of "maternal thinking" acquired in close parent-child (or other caretaking) relationships is essential to the development of "citizen nurturers." Growing children demand practices that guarantee their health and safety, enhance their growth, and develop their social skills. Accordingly, people who have primary responsibility for children (and perhaps other growing organisms as well) are apt to develop distinctive modes of thinking and valuing that will follow them into the public sphere — modes that stress the preservation of fragile life, a tolerance for developmental change, and resilience in the face of unpredictable events.

Maternal thinkers, in sum, develop what Ruddick calls a capacity for "attentive love." This is a stance that values and respects the experience of the other person, even though a third party may misunderstand, scorn, or patronize that experience. Ruddick believes that those who take this stance will, as they move into the public realm, be less apt to focus merely on individual rights and more apt to focus on what will enhance growth and a sense of belonging for everyone within the community.[37]

---

36. Ibid., p. 15. See also Robert N. Bellah et al.'s *Good Society* (New York: Alfred A. Knopf, 1991).

37. Ruddick, "Maternal Thinking," in *Women and Values: Readings in Recent*

The Limits and Potential of Maternal Thinking

Is this a utopian feminist vision — one that overrates both the goodness of "women's ways of knowing" and the possibility of transferring them to the public realm? Our answer to this question is both yes and no. It is certainly true that relational ways of thinking can become distorted. Feminist theologians, you will recall, have argued that in the wake of the Fall, men are strongly tempted to let their God-imaging, accountable dominion deteriorate into domination, both of the creation and of other people. By contrast, women's greater temptation is to let their God-imaging sociability, or relationality, become social enmeshment. As a result, women may try to preserve existing relationships no matter how unhealthy or unjust they have become. If this analysis is correct, then there are two equal and opposite dangers to watch for.

Nurturing Too Much or Too Narrowly

The first danger, in the words of a 1970s feminist, is that women will get caught in a "compassion trap."[38] Many women are already burdened by "double day" or "second shift" problems as they try to juggle waged work with family and household responsibilities. How much wearier will they become if they now feel obliged to do a large share of the "public nurturing" as well? Sociologist Miriam Johnson expresses this problem well:

> There is a danger for women in embracing maternal thinking if it means feeling that we must take care of everybody else in the world besides ourselves. [This] could be interpreted as calling upon women to mother not only children, but also everybody on earth and the earth itself. Surely there is a danger here of women becoming careworn with caretaking, while men continue to be cared for. Many women feel overburdened with caretaking already, especially poor women.[39]

This, of course, is precisely why we need to balance an appreciation of women's and men's sometimes-different styles of thought and

---

Feminist Philosophy, ed. Marilyn Pearsall (Belmont, Calif.: Wadsworth Publishing Co., 1986), pp. 340-51.
38. Adams, "The Compassion Trap," pp. 401-16.
39. Johnson, *Strong Mothers, Weak Wives,* pp. 31-32.

action with a recognition of their underlying capacity — not to mention the Bible's call — to think and act in similar, kingdom-enhancing ways. Johnson notes three good reasons why we should resist seeing maternal thinking as a "separate" female virtue that sets women apart from men. First of all, a balancing emphasis on gender similarity is needed to remind women that they may indeed care for themselves and not just endlessly sacrifice for others. "Ideally," Johnson writes, "women's caring is not an expression of sacrifice but a recognition of interdependence and an expansion of the self."[40] Expressed in terms of Jesus' summary of the law, if we are to love our neighbor as ourselves, then we are not fulfilling the spirit of the law if we fail to nurture ourselves adequately.

Second, a stress on gender similarity reminds us that although maternal thinking often comes easily to women, it is by no means the only kind of thinking they can and should do. Maternal thinking has certainly been undervalued and overly confined to domestic and other small-scale relationships in our society. But to say that all people should value and practice maternal thinking more is not to say that it should totally eclipse other modes of thought. As one of our team members once remarked, "Even if abstract thought has been a largely male preserve, it's much too valuable a tool to be left to men alone!"

Third, an appreciation of gender similarity reminds us that men too can think maternally. It is a kind of thinking that may come less easily to them, for a combination of reasons we may never fully disentangle. But the gradual increase in nurturant fathering shows that men can both learn to think maternally and profit from the closer personal relationships that result. Traditionally, Johnson notes, most men have valued maternal thinking only when women did it, and for men's benefit. "The next step," she writes, "is for men to prove that they value maternal thinking by learning to do it themselves."[41] Indeed, she points out, this process already began in nineteenth-century Britain and America under the influence of relational feminism, when husbands were exhorted to listen to their wives and let both their domestic and their public behavior be "civilized" by maternal virtues.

40. Johnson, *Strong Mothers, Weak Wives*, p. 32. See also Carol Gilligan's *In a Different Voice: Psychological Theory and Women's Development* (Cambridge: Harvard University Press, 1982), chaps. 5 and 6.
41. Ibid., p. 32. For an empirical study of couples living out a commitment to coparenting, see Diane Ehrensaft's *Parenting Together: Men and Women Sharing the Care of Their Children* (Champaign: University of Illinois Press, 1990).

But there are two dangers in overvalorizing maternal thinking: the danger (already mentioned) of expecting too broad an application of maternal thinking by women, which will make them experience "caretaker burnout," and the opposite danger of confining maternal thinking to too narrow a range of relationships. In the past, societies such as the pre–Civil War American South, Nazi Germany, and white South Africa have honored and supported women's roles as keeper of the home and transmitter of social values to the next generation. But in each case women, with men's encouragement, have nurtured their own families while effectively denying the full humanity of entire other groups of people — blacks or Jews, for example. Indeed, we see alarming traces of this kind of thinking in certain New Right groups, some of whom claim a Christian basis for their racial or other kinds of chauvinism.[42] It is not enough to be supported and honored as a maternal thinker if the scope of one's maternal thinking remains so narrowly focused that it ignores systematic injustice toward groups other than one's own.[43]

Of course, it is difficult to know just how to balance loyalty to kin, friends, and community with the call to promote justice, righteousness, and peace in the wider world. But in arguing for an integration of justice and care — in both men and women, and in both domestic and public life — we are affirming the biblical call to grapple with this difficulty in the nitty-gritty of historical existence. Indeed, two of us have family members who did just that in the Nazi-occupied Netherlands of World War II, women and men who joined the Dutch underground and helped to rescue Jews, at considerable risk to their own families and community. Although they understood the biblical mandate to care for their own families, they also embraced the wider meaning of biblical justice, with

42. See, for example, Rebecca E. Klatch's *Women of the New Right* (Philadelphia: Temple University Press, 1987); and Helen Zia's "Women in Hate Groups: Who Are They? Why Are They There?" *Ms.*, March/April 1991, pp. 20-27.

43. On the pre–Civil War American South, see Catherine Clinton's *Plantation Mistresses: Women's World in the Old South* (New York: Pantheon Books, 1983); and Elizabeth Fox-Genovese's *Within the Plantation Household: Black and White Women of the Old South* (Chapel Hill: University of North Carolina Press, 1988). On Nazi Germany, see Claudia Koonz's *Mothers in the Fatherland: Women, the Family, and Nazi Politics* (New York: St. Martin's Press, 1987). On South Africa, see Elaine Botha's "Voices from a Troubled Land," *Christianity Today*, 21 November 1986, p. 8 (in a special insert on South Africa).

its call to rescue and re-establish those who are being marginalized or persecuted. And, to invoke a more current example, all of us can point to friends and/or family members who continue to risk their own immediate social standing by publicly supporting our Christian feminism.

The Potential of Maternal Thinking

The preceding qualifiers should make it clear that we do not regard either maternal thinking or the women who do it as a panacea for all the world's ills. Nevertheless, there is some evidence that maternal values make a difference in the conduct of public citizenship. In the United States, for example, there is a consistent gender gap on the question of using state-supported force or violence. Whether or not they called themselves feminists, American women were more likely than men to have opposed the Vietnam War, and they remain more reluctant than men to approve of force as a means of quelling urban unrest.[44]

This is not to say that women have never been complicit in warmongering: throughout history they have adopted primary wartime roles ranging from nurses to concentration camp supervisors, and secondary roles ranging from cheerleaders to munitions makers.[45] But to the extent that women have had primary responsibility for raising children, they have also been susceptible to an "unheroic and irrational objection to the slaughter of their own children."[46] They have often recognized the

44. Keith T. Poole and L. Harmon Zeigler, *Women, Public Opinion and Politics* (New York: Longman, 1985), p. 6.

45. Mary Condren, "To Bear Children for the Fatherland: Mothers and Militarism," in *Motherhood: Experience, Institution, Theology*, ed. Anne Carr and Elisabeth Schüssler Fiorenza (Edinburgh: T. & T. Clark, 1989), pp. 82-90.

46. Mary O'Brien, *The Politics of Reproduction* (London: Routledge & Kegan Paul, 1981), p. 148. Kurt Vonnegut, Jr., captures this attitude in his novel *Slaughterhouse Five; or, The Children's Crusade* (New York: Dell, 1969), when he records the hostility of a friend's wife to his proposed book about the bombing of Dresden in World War II:

"You were just *babies* then!" she said.
"What?" I said.
"You were just babies in the war — like the ones upstairs!"
I nodded that this was true. We *had* been foolish virgins in the war, right at the end of childhood.
"But you're not going to write it that way, are you." This wasn't a question. It was an accusation.

senselessness of spending years bringing children to maturity, only to have them snatched away as cannon fodder by men who have invested much less in that process. Thus women are more reluctant than men to endorse violence as a solution to conflicting interests.

Likewise, women are more likely than men to favor policies that protect consumers, citizens, and the environment. Indeed, women's concerns for peace and environmental integrity converge in their fairly strong tendency to vote against the development and use of nuclear power. And despite the fact that women as a group are ranked in polls as more "conservative" and "traditional" than men in their overall attitudes, they also tend to vote favorably on such "socialist" issues as increased spending for public health, education, and welfare.[47] This tendency extends to younger women as well. A 1990 poll of 200,000 first-year college students in America indicated a renewed concern (largely dormant in the 1980s) for social problems and values among students of both sexes, but particularly among women. On the average, women respondents indicated a greater commitment than men respondents to "helping the less fortunate," "promoting racial understanding," "cleaning up the environment," and "participating in community action." As one commentator on this survey suggested, "Perhaps if we really want to encourage a 'kinder, gentler nation,' we should encourage women to participate more."[48]

"I — I don't know," I said.

"Well, *I* know," she said. "You'll pretend you were men instead of babies, and you'll be played in the movies by Frank Sinatra and John Wayne or some of those other glamorous, war-loving, dirty old men. And war will look just wonderful, so we'll have a lot more of them. And they'll be fought by babies like the babies upstairs."

So then I understood. It was war that made her so angry. She didn't want her babies or anyone else's babies killed in wars. And she thought wars were partly encouraged by books and movies.

So I held up my right hand and I made her a promise: "Mary," I said, "I don't think this book of mine is ever going to be finished. . . . If I ever do finish it, though, I give you my word of honor: there won't be a part for Frank Sinatra or John Wayne.

"I'll tell you what," I said. "I'll call it 'The Children's Crusade.'"

She was my friend after that. (Pp. 14-15)

47. Robert Y. Shapiro and Harpreet Mahajan, "Gender Differences in Policy Preferences: A Summary of Trends from the 1960's to the 1980's," *Public Opinion Quarterly* 59, no. 1 (1986): 42-61.

48. *U.S. News and World Report*, 18 March 1991, p. 12. See also the results of

Where might the further extension of maternal thinking into the public sphere lead in the future? That question cannot be given a definitive answer. There are no guarantees: human beings are too limited and too sinful to assure the complete realization of *any* social vision, no matter how positive. But various feminists have made concrete suggestions based on their own specialized interests and expertise, and it is with these and some of our own reflections that we close this chapter.

Attaining Concrete Justice for the Family

As we emphasized earlier, the development of nurturance in the public sphere cannot take place without the prior attainment of justice in the family. And, as we have also seen, justice in the family sphere requires not just goodwill and proper sentiment but also a commitment to legal, social, and economic change. Such commitment must include both a feminist and a Christian intolerance of domestic violence and sexual abuse, and a rejection of the underlying attitudes that lead to them — namely, the traditional notions of women and children as "property" and of the family as "beyond justice."

Church and state alike need to provide protection for victims of abuse, who are mostly women and children, as well as education in appropriate self-esteem and assertiveness. Also needed are discipline and re-education for perpetrators, who are overwhelmingly adult men. "We must not forget," warns philosopher Sara Ruddick, "that so long as a mother is not effective publicly and self-respecting privately, male presence [in the home] can be harmful as well as beneficial."[49]

But institutionalized responses to crisis situations represent only a beginning: ultimately we need to reduce the likelihood that such crises will occur in the first place. To this end we need legal, social, and economic incentives to facilitate women's economic security and men's greater commitment to hands-on family nurturing. The dismantling of sex-based job and wage segregation is essential to the first goal, and this will probably require adequate (and adequately enforced) antidiscrimi-

---

the 1990 poll of 200,000 first-year college students conducted in cooperation with the American Council on Education and the Higher Education Research Institute (UCLA).

49. Ruddick, "Maternal Thinking," p. 90.

nation and "comparable worth" legislation. Also essential to women's economic security are adequate medical coverage, job-protected leave when children are born (with better tax breaks and uninterrupted pension accumulation for those leaving the waged work force to raise children), and more flexibility in waged working hours and work location.[50]

Of course, the preceding proposals can also help men who desire to coparent their children and to arrive at a fairer division of domestic responsibility. We refer to such things as job-protected paternity leave, flextime in the waged workplace, and the opportunity to do a substantial portion of one's waged work at home. Where divorce does occur, there must be better enforcement of child-support payments and, where feasible, continued involvement of fathers in the nurture of their children.

But legal and economic change cannot work without fundamental attitudinal change. In Sweden, for example, generously paid parental leave is available for mothers and fathers alike, but thus far fewer than 15 percent of Swedish men take advantage of it.[51] Thus the church, the state, employers, and popular culture must combine forces to help men to see that nurturant parenting is a positive human virtue, not a less-than-masculine cop-out. And for men to become truly nurturant parents will take some relearning, given fatherhood's long-standing association in our culture with emotional distance and unquestioned authority. As Sara Ruddick points out, "It does women no good to have the power of

50. It should be noted that in the United States as of 1990, 34 million people were without health coverage of any kind, even though 11 percent of America's Gross Domestic Product was spent on health care. By contrast, Canada spent only 8 percent of its GDP on health care, and all of its citizens had equal coverage. The discrepancy is largely due to the administrative costs of having about 1500 different health insurance plans operating in the U.S., whereas Canada and other industrialized nations have a single health insurance system run by the federal and (where applicable) the provincial or state governments. Moreover, although the U.S. has the most advanced medical technology in the world, its infant mortality rate is among the worst in industrialized nations, largely because only those who can afford (quite expensive) individual health insurance or are fortunate enough to have job-related coverage have assured access to this technology. It should also be noted that, among industrialized nations, only the U.S. and South Africa still do not have job-protected parental leave mandated at the federal level for all citizens.

51. See *Equality between Men and Women in Sweden: Government Policy to the Mid-Nineties,* Summary of Government Bill 1987/88: 105 (Stockholm: Ministry of Labor, Division of Equality Affairs, 1988).

the Symbolic Father [as traditionally understood] brought right into the nursery."[52]

Bringing Nurturance into the Public Sphere

If we can bring justice back into the family on behalf of women and children, and if men can learn family nurturing skills, how then might the nurturing done by both men and women change the conduct of the public realm? More than one feminist has suggested a "social" as opposed to a "military" draft, with employers required to release workers for a minimum number of hours per year of approved community service. Employers are already obligated (in the United States) to release workers for jury duty and for military reserve service, and seem to accommodate both without undue disruption. Moreover, community service is already used as an alternative to the incarceration of nonviolent criminals, a scheme strongly promoted by Christian agencies such as Justice Fellowship.[53] Under a social draft, such community service would be extended to include all able-bodied adults. It would be especially geared to provide services to vulnerable people such as the young, the old, the poor, the physically challenged, and other marginalized groups.[54]

Even male writers have begun to support the diverting of military funds toward more nurturant goals. In a perceptive article titled "Manliness and Mother Earth," author Andrew Schmookler noted that while American leaders have always been ready to spend billions of dollars on vague, unconfirmed military threats, they routinely refuse to spend money on pollution control until the supposed environmental threat is confirmed beyond any possible doubt. "Why is it," Schmookler asks, "that when facing the 'Soviet threat' our conservative leaders insisted that we prepare for the 'worst-case scenario,' but when it comes to how we care for this living earth, they always assume the best and sneer at those who fear the worst?" The answer, he suggests, lies in our overattachment to the image of manliness modeled on the warrior:

52. Ruddick, "Maternal Thinking," p. 90.
53. For a further analysis, see Van Ness's *Crime and Its Victims.*
54. Buker, "Politics As If Women Were Normal"; and Ruddick, "Pacifying the Forces: Drafting Women in the Interests of Peace," *Signs* 8, no. 4 (1982): 471-89.

Preparing to fight our enemies is always manly. Nobody thinks it unmanly if a president spends billions for defenses against an exaggerated threat, or if a football coach prepares for a weak opponent as if it were strong. Showing concern about environmental dangers is another matter. . . . The remedy does not involve more action, but more restraint [and] real men in America are not supposed to accept limits. . . . It is one thing for a man to *guard* what is his own — that is the work of a warrior. It is another thing for a man to take care of what has been entrusted to him — that sounds a lot like women's work.[55]

Fortunately, Schmookler concludes, there is another ancient image of what a man might be, and that is the image of the "good steward," someone who can be trusted to take care of natural resources and people so that both may flourish. And, he warns, "until the good steward seems to us as manly as the vigilant warrior, our national security will be threatened by . . . the destruction our peacetime activities are wreaking on this planet."[56] Thus analysts of both sexes are beginning to agree that a new ordering of virtues is required if we are to nurture both the earth and its citizens adequately.

Toward a New Architecture of Gender

Other feminists have pointed out that both housing design and the design of public spaces must change if we are to nurture all persons adequately. As Dolores Hayden points out in her book entitled *Redesigning the American Dream*, millions of identical, self-contained suburban homes have been built over the past half-century with virtually no concern for energy conservation, access to public transit, racial integration, differing types of households, or varying child-care needs. The standard family was expected to have a male breadwinner who would commute by car to a job in the city, and a female homemaker who would be too anchored in domesticity to care about either waged employment or structured social and intellectual stimulation. To support the same suburban ideology,

55. Schmookler, "Manliness and Mother Earth," *Christian Science Monitor*, 3 October 1991, p. 19.
56. Ibid.

public spaces such as parks were sacrificed in order to create large, private lots for each household.[57]

There is a definite "architecture of gender" in the housing arrangements just described, one that has been gaining momentum ever since the inception of the nineteenth-century "cult of domesticity." Its underlying philosophy is that the ideal home is a privatized "haven" for a single nuclear family. It assumes further that the adult male will operate chiefly in the public sphere, and that his wife will care for the home and its occupants in a state of relative isolation and economic dependency. It also assumes that women will not, as a rule, leave the household, as Hayden explains:

> When nineteenth-century men (and women) argued that the good woman was at home in the kitchen with her husband, they implied that no decent woman was out in city streets, going places where men went. Thus, it was "unladylike" for a woman to earn her own living. Because the working woman was no *one* urban man's property (her father or her husband had failed to keep her at home), she was *every* urban man's property. She was the potential victim of harassment in the factory, in the office, on the street, in restaurants, and in places of amusement such as theaters and parks. . . . Men do not escape the problem. As husbands and fathers they share the stresses of the isolated houses and the violent streets they and their wives and children must negotiate. But rarely do men attribute the problems of housing and the city to the Victorian patriarchal views that reserved urban, public safety for men only.[58]

However, there is precedent for a very different architecture of gender — one that sees the home more as an "industrial machine," safely and efficiently connected to the public life of all of its members. For example, in 1943 the town of Vanport City was constructed on the Oregon coast to meet the needs of a diverse wartime labor force, including many of the female "Rosies" who replaced skilled male shipbuilders called up by the draft.[59] It consisted of federally subsidized

57. See Hayden's *Redesigning the American Dream: The Future of Housing, Work, and Family Life* (New York: W. W. Norton, 1984).

58. Ibid., pp. 209-10.

59. Ibid., chap. 1. See also Sherna Berger Gluck's *Rosie the Riveter Revisited: Women, the War, and Social Change* (Boston: Twayne Publishers, 1987).

housing designed for all types and sizes of households, including traditional families, single persons, single-parent families, and nonfamily groups wishing to share accommodations.

Housing units were designed for low maintenance and high energy efficiency, with affordable home-repair services available on short notice. Public transportation was designed to follow routes that would minimize the need for detours by parents dropping off or picking up children at schools or daycare centers. These same daycare centers functioned around the clock in order to accommodate parents working different shifts at the shipyards, and they included infirmaries for sick children, bathtubs for scrubbing children who hadn't had time to wash at home, and hot food services at the end of the day for parents who wished to pick up a low-cost casserole for dinner.

To promote the integration of children's school and home lives, the daycare centers were constructed with picture windows overlooking the shipyards, through which the children could watch the launching of ships that their fathers—or more likely their mothers—had helped build. By the end of World War II, Vanport City housed forty thousand people of white, African-American, Asian, and Hispanic origins, all living together in largely peaceful neighborhoods. After the war, however, much of the city was dismantled, and the rest was destroyed in a flood. Today, what was once the fifth-largest city in the northwest United States is now the site of a park.[60]

When team members discussed the Vanport City experiment, some of us thought it came close to being a feminist utopia, while others likened it more to a collective, bureaucratized rabbit-warren! Certainly it was designed to loosen the boundaries between domestic and public life, and such a move increases the risk that family uniqueness—in terms of values, traditions, and interpersonal bonding—will be weakened.[61] Nevertheless, Vanport City remains the United States' most visionary and successful attempt to shape a safe, sensible space for wage-employed women and their families. Its combination of government subsidies,

60. Ibid., pp. 11-12.
61. For an elaboration of this criticism, see Jean Bethke Elshtain's *Public Man, Private Woman: Women in Social and Political Thought* (Princeton: Princton University Press, 1981). However, it needs to be repeated that family "traditions" can include abusive, unjust, and authoritarian practices, and women in such situations might well be delighted to sacrifice some of the "privacy" and "family traditions" under cover of which they and their children have experienced abuse.

public amenities, and careful city planning made household life much more manageable in terms of scheduling, child care, and home maintenance, thus doing much to release women from the burden of the "double day."

Fortunately, there is a third option for integrating domestic and public space that avoids both the "suburban haven" and the "industrial machine" philosophies of housing. This is a view of the home as part of an "organic neighborhood" that includes transition areas between private and public spaces. One example would be a square of row houses surrounding a common courtyard. Another would be a downtown high-rise that includes not just apartments but also areas for shopping, eating, and recreation that open onto a common mall. One of our favorite examples is in Toronto: it is a church-sponsored group of housing units for the elderly that also shares space with a daycare center, a tearoom, and a Third World handicrafts outlet. Here young and old routinely benefit from each other's presence in a safe, organically unified space.

In such a design the barriers between public and private space become "semipermeable." In other words, household privacy is preserved while both public safety and human interaction are enhanced. But more is needed if we are to "domesticate" public space and make it a nurturing rather than a threatening environment. Where possible, home spaces, work spaces, and recreation spaces should be kept close to each other to avoid the "emptiness" of the after-hours city. Streets must become safer and friendlier for vulnerable commuters such as women, children, and the elderly.[62] Public spaces need to be designed on the assumption that children will normally be present, and that not just mothers will be caring for them. For example, we are pleased to note the gradual increase in public "baby-changing areas" accessible to adults of both sexes!

62. Safe access to public space is particularly difficult for older women in cities that operate in terms of a strongly gendered public/private dichotomy. A study done in the late 1970s of 82,000 Chicago widows, conducted by sociologist Helena Lopata, found that over half of them avoided going to public places and over a fifth did not even take the risk of making social visits to friends or relatives. See Lopata's essay entitled "The Chicago Woman: A Study of Patterns of Mobility and Transportation," in *Women and the American City*, ed. Catherine Stimpson et al. (Chicago: University of Chicago Press, 1981).

Conclusion

The challenge of this chapter has been to show that a healing of the highly gendered public/private split is both desirable and possible, particularly in terms of the biblical vision for justice, righteousness, and peace. By developing the meaning of that vision for human relations in general and for gender relations in particular, and by appealing to some recent feminist research, we have tried to show that so-called male concerns for justice should not and need not be limited to the public sphere, nor should so-called female concerns for relationality and nurturance be limited to private family life.

In the following chapters we will take some of these theoretical insights and apply them to concrete situations. In the next chapter we will focus on two Third World settings in which recent trends toward industrialization are causing a replay of some of our own problems associated with a highly gendered public/private split. In the chapters following we will return to the Western world and examine, among other things, the implications of the public/private dichotomy for gender relations in the domestic and waged-work arenas.

CHAPTER 14

Case Studies from India and Egypt in Class, Gender, and Survival

Today's American undergraduates, men and women alike, expect to "have it all" — marriage, children, career. Studies on nine different campuses have shown that highly career-oriented students are also interested in raising a family. One study conducted at the University of California, Berkeley, found that few women were willing even to consider marrying a man who was not committed to an equal division of domestic labor. But the women as well as the men interviewed at Berkeley still assumed that the wives' waged work would be optional, or at least interrupted, because women would bear primary responsibility for child raising. By contrast, all the women were "*absolutely* certain they wanted their future husbands to work continuously." Thus the author commenting on the studies concluded that while these Berkeley women may "talk career," they in fact "think job."[1]

A deep polarity seems to divide adult American women. Those

1. Anne Machung, "Talking Career, Thinking Job: Gender Differences in Career and Family Expectations of Berkeley Seniors," *Feminist Studies* 15 (Spring 1989): 35-58.

The primary author of this chapter is Margaret Koch.

committed to raising their own children and those committed to careers often find it difficult to talk to each other. Yet women in both groups experience some of the same ambivalence apparent in the responses from the young women from Berkeley. A woman knows that her undergraduate vision of having a career in the State Department and being the mother of four children is just not that easy. Homemaker mothers wonder if there is any way to be with their children after school and still be a recognized contributor to the larger society. And in offices across America, mothers, and some fathers, keep phone lines busy between 3:00 and 4:00 P.M. as they make sure their children have gotten safely home or to their after-school caretakers. These tensions, felt by both stay-at-home mothers and those in the marketplace, might produce occasions for dialogue. But more often they lead each group to try to muffle the other questions that persist inside themselves.

In this chapter we will see that the problems encountered by both sorts of women originate in a global historical phenomenon. As industrialization and commercialization have spread around the world, women's child-raising work has been radically separated from the work they do to support their families economically.[2] It is true that the work men have done in both areas has also undergone radical separation. But men have moved more rapidly than women into the waged workplace, leaving both domestic work and economic vulnerability to fall disproportionately on women. The usual solution of Western feminists is that of having *all* women orient themselves toward waged employment, as men have done. But voices from other quarters, concerned to defend "traditional" cultural values, continue to promote an image of women at home.

Neither side offers a convincing solution because each "solution" contains personal and social contradictions. More and more, feminists

2. In the last two decades scholars have produced a voluminous body of literature on the impact of "development" on women around the world. A brief bibliography organized by world regions can be found in Kathleen Staudt's "Women in Development: Courses and Curriculum Integration," *Women's Studies Quarterly* 14 (Fall/Winter 1986): 21-28. Annotated bibliographies, again organized by world regions, can be found in *The Cross-Cultural Study of Women: A Comprehensive Guide*, ed. Margot I. Duley and Mary I. Edwards (New York: Feminist Press, 1986). More recent scholarship, listed alphabetically by author, can be found in the bibliography of *Persistent Inequalities: Women and World Development*, ed. Irene Tinker (New York: Oxford University Press, 1990).

are realizing that the individualism and competition required for "success" in North America are poor substitutes for the nurturing and connectedness associated with women throughout history.[3] "Traditionalists," on the other hand, ignore the way old words and ways of thinking have acquired new meanings in industrialized, commercialized society. "Home" means something quite different when it denies rather than supports opportunities for making a living, and "work" done side by side with teenage sons or young daughters is quite different from work that can be done only outside the household.

This debate concerns Christians on two levels. On one level, Christians concerned about justice must attend carefully to the data on women's growing economic vulnerability. But on another level, Christian priorities require that economics should serve rather than rule the broader concerns of life. The polarization of this debate on gender and our own unreflective participation in the Western world's economically oriented individualism make it difficult to see the forest for the trees.

Accordingly, it is useful to step outside our own historical and cultural setting and into the lives of women in other parts of the world. The experience of women in South India and Cairo will serve as our starting point. These two settings, one rural and one urban, provide case studies through which we can understand better the dilemmas faced by women almost everywhere. Indeed, women's transformation into modern "housewives" may present more of a contrast in societies where women have historically been less closely identified with home and more active in long-distance trade. But the process we will observe has been experienced in some form by women in places as diverse as the coastal areas of Canada, the slums of Lagos, and the villages of Indonesia.

We will focus on women in Narsapur, India, and in Cairo, Egypt, beginning where they locate themselves — squarely within families. A major contribution of feminism has been its challenge to the myth of family harmony. It has shown that family relations are characterized by conflict as well as cooperation, individual self-interest as well as a concern for the group. Moreover, power imbalances between men and

---

3. See, for example, Linda Gordon's essay entitled "Why Nineteenth-Century Feminists Did Not Support 'Birth Control' and Twentieth-Century Feminists Do: Feminism, Reproduction and the Family," in *Rethinking the Family: Some Feminist Questions*, ed. Barrie Thorne and Marlyn Yalom (New York: Longman, 1982), pp. 40-53; and Sara Ruddick's *Maternal Thinking: Toward a Politics of Peace* (New York: Ballantine Books, 1989).

women in the larger society get reproduced in families and households. Nevertheless, while accepting these central feminist insights, we must see women where most see themselves: "within their families, in relation to men." It is here, according to Hanna Papanek, that we can "examine the processes of conflict and adjustment that [have] defined most women's experience."[4]

Our Egyptian and Indian case-studies will help us understand the changes brought about by modern commercialization and industrialization. We will see how women of different social classes have survived and realized personal goals despite changing social and cultural conditions. First, focusing particularly on lower-class women, we will see how men's and women's lives have diverged, and how power has tipped against women in the newly defined role of "housewife." Most of the world's women (and men) are poor and therefore *must* contribute to their family's economic as well as emotional well-being. Any Christian or feminist understanding must take this into account. Second, we will explore the responses of upper- and lower-class women to the liberal feminist antidote for women's domestic marginalization: namely, directing women to the waged economy in a way that encourages them to mimic men. Regardless of class, most Indian and Egyptian women refuse to embrace any solution that breaks the identification of women with family and home and requires them to pursue paid labor just the way men have. Some of their reasoning squares with Christian priorities, and some does not.

As social structures and cultural understandings change, women actively develop strategies that support their own and their daughters' interests. Such pragmatic strategies compromise the purity of any utopian vision; nevertheless, they show how real women press the bounds of social structures and cultural traditions in the service of their own perceived interests. Although some of these strategies are dangerous to women's long-term best interests, they nevertheless show that "work" and "family," so often polarized in Western thinking, must be taken together in any evaluation of efforts to attain gender justice. For most of human history, the mainstream of life has flowed through the home, and hence *work* and *family* had different (and more unified) meanings from those we apply today. Thus we must grapple with the meaning of

4. Papanek, "To Each Less Than She Needs, from Each More Than She Can Do: Allocations, Entitlements, and Value," in *Persistent Inequalities,* p. 171.

each term as well as the relationship between them if we are to understand and begin to move beyond the dilemmas women face in the modern world.

The Divergent Lives of Men and Women

In Narsapur

Around the town of Narsapur in southeast India, between 150,000 and 200,000 women produce handmade lace for European and American markets.[5] The industry began in the late nineteenth century when the widow of a Scottish missionary, Mrs. Cain, introduced the craft to poor Christian converts during a time of famine.[6] In the beginning their lace table-mats and doilies were sold through informal networks set up by Western missionaries and their contacts. All the income generated was returned to the lacemakers or invested in the purchase of more thread.

At the turn of the century, however, both lace production and marketing took quite a different turn. Two men reorganized the production of lace in the Narsapur region as an export business. The women, who once made and sold complete articles, were now assigned piecework — for example, one making only flowers, another only lace ribbons. Agents, at this point usually women, would then collect the pieces to be stitched together by others under the exporter's supervision. Piecework wages thus replaced income originally based on the sale of finished items. In the following decades, lace firms in the area multiplied to more than sixty as Hindus from the agricultural *jati* (subcaste) known as the Kapus became involved in production.

During the 1960s and 1970s another major change in the industry occurred as a result of changes brought about by the Green Revolution.

5. This account is based on an essay by Maria Mies entitled "The Dynamics of the Sexual Division of Labor and Integration of Rural Women into the World Market," in *Women and Development,* ed. Lourdes Beneria (New York: Praeger Publishers, 1982), pp. 1-28; and on Mies's book entitled *The Lace Makers of Narsapur: Indian Housewives Produce for the World Market* (London: Zed Books, 1982).
6. Details of the introduction of the industry are uncertain, though the broad outlines are clear. The "missionary wives," it should be noted, were clearly missionaries in their own right, however their sending congregations might have regarded them.

The cost of high-yielding varieties of seeds, fertilizers, and motorized irrigation systems pushed farmers to develop larger-scale, commercial operations. As a result, middle-level and rich Kapu farmers now had cash and the time to invest it. At the same time, the demand for cheap, handmade crafts was growing in places like the United States, Germany, and Australia. The lace industry, with its low wages, modest fixed-capital demands, and potential for export earnings, seemed an ideal investment. Thus male farmers, with the time and capital supplied by the Green Revolution, entered the industry as exporters and also replaced the female agents with male agents. The lace industry of Narsapur had begun with women's labor, organized and controlled by women. But as it grew into a more profitable business, men came to control the industry, with women supplying only the ill-paid labor. Women often crocheted six to eight hours a day for less than one-third of the official minimum wage for female agricultural laborers.

How did this happen? The lace industry was shaped by two forces, one economic and one cultural. First, local agricultural and craft production shifted away from subsistence activity toward commercial production for distant markets. Second, the industry was affected by shifting cultural assumptions about "proper" activities for men and women and for upper- and lower-class groups.

With regard to the first factor, recall that poor men and women who share the work of peasant agricultural labor have historically carried harsh burdens.[7] Work in such circumstances was certainly divided along gender lines, but it was hard for *everyone,* and rewards were few. Men had the clear advantage in certain kinds of social power, but protection for both men and women was secured by social networks of kinship and patron-client relationships. But processes begun under British colonial rule and carried through in the commercialization of agriculture gradually undermined these networks. Some households acquired more land and new capital resources to invest; other households lost the land by which both their men and women had previously produced a livelihood. Equally significant though less visible was the divergence of re-

7. For the general reader, it may be best to bypass the vast quantities of historical and social-science literature on the subject and read the moving fictionalized account of the transition from subsistence agriculture to commercialized life given in Kamala Markandaya's novel called *Nectar in a Sieve* (New York: Penguin–New American Library, 1982).

sources controlled by women and men. Men controlled the new wealth generated by some households because the Western colonial government in India, as elsewhere around the world, based its policies on the assumption that men were economically active and women economically dependent. Thus loans, technical expertise, and education were available almost exclusively to men,[8] a legacy that continues to this day. Men were drawn into emerging new economic opportunities, while women were left with only the shrinking resources of the home. And some of these women saw their resources shrink at the same time that their husbands and sons suffered diminished opportunity. Kapu women with hungry children, for example, felt pressure "to find ways and means to keep the household going."[9] These women increased their burdens by making more lace; but their men, many of them now without land or agricultural opportunity, often resisted looking for other kinds of work. Without land to farm, the work of fathers and their apprentice-sons disappeared, while women's domestic work increased.

Cultural assumptions also contributed to women's loss of control of the lace industry. The complex heritage of Hindu culture had always recognized the power of women.[10] But there was a deep ambivalence about this power, with its enormous potential to give and sustain life but also supposedly to create spiritual and social chaos. Woman's power had

8. Much historical work remains to be done in documenting the ways in which colonial governments and postcolonial "development" planners undermined the economic base of women through policies which assumed that women were not economically active. Examples include eroding women's property rights by replacing communal control of property with control by land titles registered in the names of individual men in Malaysia, opening opportunities for cash cropping for men in parts of Africa where women had historically done most of the agricultural work, and designing development projects for "households" without considering the ways in which women are given or denied access to productive resources. The outlines of this process are laid out in Ester Boserup's classic work, *Women's Role in Economic Development* (London: George Allen & Unwin, 1970), and in Barbara Rogers's book entitled *The Domestication of Women: Discrimination in Developing Societies* (London: Tavistock, Kogan Page, 1980).

9. Mies, "The Dynamics of the Sexual Division of Labor and Integration of Rural Women into the World Market," pp. 18-19.

10. Two helpful essays exploring Indian cultural understandings of the power of women are found in Doranne Jacobson and Susan Wadley's *Women in India: Two Perspectives* (New Delhi: Manohar, 1986). See as well *Women in Indian Society*, ed. Rehana Ghadially and Pramod Kumar (New Delhi: SAGE Publications, 1988), particularly the essay by Sudhir Kakar, "Feminine Identity in India."

two faces: the maternal power of the "benevolent, fertile bestower" and a sexual power which, if uncontrolled by men, became identified with the "malevolent, aggressive" powers of nature. Thus the sexuality and movement of younger women were often restricted, while senior women in kinship groups enjoyed substantial power and authority. In contrast to the recent Western emphasis on the need to protect women because they are assumed to be weak, Indian women were historically controlled far more out of fear of their strength.

Cultural practices also confined women to various forms of *purdah*, or seclusion (although this was more the case in northern India than in southern India). In addition, notions of ritual purity and pollution identified a rise in class status with an avoidance of manual labor. Thus, ironically, lower-class women enjoyed more freedom of movement while enduring poverty and hard labor. By contrast, upper-class women pursued an ideal according to which women of wealth and leisure stayed mainly at home. But as long as economic, social, and political activity centered on households and kinship networks, even the very restrictive *purdah* of the upper class did not necessarily make women economically unproductive or socially powerless.

We should note that neither in the traditional household of the poor peasant nor in that of the relatively wealthy landowner was there any role which approximated that of the Western "housewife." Whether as laborers in subsistence activities or as administrators of wealthier, extended households, Indian women contributed economically to their families' welfare. By bearing children, especially sons, they made what was considered the greatest contribution to the well-being of the household. Women were identified with the home, but the home, in turn, was a central social, economic, and emotional unit.[11] Now, however, the household no longer serves as a central economic or social locus. In today's world any cultural ideal that places the "good woman" at home while simultaneously devaluing manual labor leaves her both socially isolated and economically vulnerable.

The wealthier men who gained control of the lace industry in Narsapur replaced the female agents with male agents, whom they assumed were more mobile. At the same time, women who continued to

11. See, for example, the analysis of Veena Das in "Indian Women: Work, Power and Status," in *Indian Women: From Purdah to Modernity*, ed. B. R. Nanda (New Delhi: Vikas, 1976), pp. 129-45.

459

produce lace began to see themselves as *only* doing "housework," though they sandwiched a full workweek of crocheting in between such tasks as nursing babies, frying vegetables for meals, and gathering cow dung for fuel. The lace work often supplied much of the family's income, but neither women nor men equated it with the work of men, who earned cash outside the home. This unrealistic perception, reports Maria Mies, is still imposed on women and even endorsed by women who accept the culture's negative view of manual labor — and those who must do the work. In a curious way, this perception both overvalues and undervalues the work women do at home. For example, lower-caste women in Narsapur currently do most of the labor-intensive work of rice cultivation. But though agricultural and lace-making groups are in roughly the same economic class, and though women can earn substantially more by working in the fields, the lacemakers see themselves as superior to the rice workers because they work close to home and avoid heavy manual labor: "We Kapu women cannot work in the fields, only Harijan women do this work."[12]

Thus the old values of *purdah* and a scorn for manual labor persist, but their meaning and impact are now very different. As Mies points out, in a commercialized economy locked into a global economic network, "the social definition of women as housewives serves mainly to obscure the true production relations and to consolidate their exploitation, both ideologically and politically."[13] Some men move into "business" as agents or petty traders of products made by their wives. Others, economically supported by their wives after being marginalized in the larger society, resist taking work that threatens to demean them further. Yet in these new circumstances, women ironically see themselves as *more* dependent on men. A woman whose husband hawks her lace to tourists in Calcutta says, "I am dependent on his business; if he does not sell anything or if he does not send money, I have nothing."[14] The self-sacrifice of the good wife Sita in the Indian epic *Ramayana* has long set the ideal for a wife's service and obedience to her husband. But the lacemakers of Narsapur do *not* find themselves in a simple continuation of the "traditional" role of Indian women. In fact, they have been "devalued down" to that new cultural

12. Mies, "The Dynamics of the Sexual Division of Labor and Integration of Rural Women into the World Market," p. 16.
    13. Ibid., p. 15.
    14. Ibid., p. 22.

creation, the "housewife," who inhabits a similarly devalued domestic sphere. As we turn to our second case study, which focuses on the women of the traditional city quarters of Cairo, we will see a similar process taking place.

In Cairo

Cairo is among the world's oldest, largest, and most densely populated cities. And, as in New York, Calcutta, and Hong Kong, the gap between those at the top of society and those at the bottom is enormous. Among those near the bottom are the traditional urban women *(banat al-balad)* who live in the oldest parts of the city, whose economic activities, social relationships, and values still echo those of nineteenth-century Cairo.[15] In public these women set themselves apart by wrapping themselves in the large black square of fabric known as the *milaya-laff*.[16] The historic, multilevel stone row-houses that rise along the curving lanes have been broken into small apartments. Neighbors who live along a given lane share a common social world.

Like their husbands and fathers, women in this quarter have histori-cally worked in household-based shops or made crafts. Some have raised chickens, pigeons, or goats to eat and sell. Others have earned money as pawnbrokers or readers of tea leaves. Among the traditional women are the *mu-allima* (masters or chiefs), who direct large enterprises such as butcher shops and coffeehouses, or sell hashish and other merchandise in the markets. They may own property and pursue work entirely indepen-dent of their husbands. Both tough and coquettish, they are recognized and accepted within the community for their leadership abilities. Although full-fledged female *mu-allima* have been rare, women have attempted on a

15. A fine study of the social transformations experienced by Egyptian women during the nineteenth century is Judith Tucker's *Women in Nineteenth-Century Egypt* (Cambridge: Cambridge University Press, 1985).

16. This account of the *banat al-balad* is drawn from Sawsan el-Messiri's "Self-Images of Traditional Urban Women in Cairo," in *Women in the Muslim World,* ed. Lois Beck and Nikki Keddie (Cambridge: Harvard University Press, 1978), pp. 522-40, and Andrea B. Rugh's "Women and Work: Strategies and Choices in a Lower-Class Quarter of Cairo," in *Women and the Family in the Middle East: New Voices of Change,* ed. Elizabeth Warnock Fernea (Austin: University of Texas Press, 1985), pp. 273-88.

smaller scale to retain independent control of the resources they bring into a marriage or develop and earn during it. For in the words of an Egyptian proverb, "She who trusts men, trusts a sieve to hold water."[17]

Within the close quarters of these Cairo neighborhoods, women have not been segregated from men. The banter recorded by researcher Saswan el-Messiri in the 1970s even includes an eighteen-year-old woman's teasing of the oldest man in the community. She joked that "he was just the man she [dreamt] of since she felt young men were useless."[18] These urban women have seen themselves as quick-witted, "capable of playing with an egg and a stone at the same time" — without breaking the egg.[19] Yet they pride themselves on maintaining a "traditional" demeanor that stays within the accepted bounds of modesty and reserve, bounds that they see more "modern" women shamelessly violating.

While clearly active in a wide range of economic activities, the women of these city quarters still assume that a woman's primary work centers on family and household. Arabic cultural ideals have long emphasized the bond between mothers and sons, and many a young wife will attest to the actual power of this bond. Although difficult for Westerners to imagine, in many settings it is realistic for a woman, considering her entire life's course, to see caring for her children as a way of caring for herself. Mothers in traditional Cairo hope to inspire in their children sentiments such as a strong and loving loyalty, expressed in this message from a son to his mother:

> Now, mother, it's your turn, my mother. . . . I don't know what to say to you. First, your hands and feet I kiss. . . . I always, always miss you. I miss the times when I say, "Mother, give me my allowance," when I embrace you, I kiss you, I cause you trouble and suffering. . . . My mother, I don't know my feelings toward you. When I say, "my mother," tears burn in my eyes.[20]

When the support of one's birth family provides the best defense in marital negotiations and the love of one's children the best security for old age, it is difficult to draw a clear line between "personal" and "family" interests.

17. Quoted by Tucker in *Women in Nineteenth-Century Egypt*, p. 1.
18. el-Messiri, "Self-Images of Traditional Urban Women in Cairo," p. 525.
19. Ibid.
20. Halim Barakat, "The Arab Family and the Challenge of Social Transformation," in *Women and the Family in the Middle East*, p. 29.

In this Cairo subculture, femininity is indeed synonymous with household tasks and child care. But the different meaning associated with these tasks is illustrated by the strength and physical size of this culture's "ideal woman." Likewise, masculinity is synonymous with financial support. But unlike the Western male "breadwinner," the father in this culture supports his family not at a distance but in the hands-on training of his young sons, brothers, or nephews in a trade or craft.

However, since Anwar Sadat's ascent in the 1970s, the Egyptian economy has become increasingly oriented toward the global market. Inflation has risen exponentially, and the best income opportunities for lower-class women and men have come from abandoning the labor-intensive production of crafts in the traditional sector and moving into the service sector or foreign industry. Increasingly, people have taken work in government offices, in factories, or, as a last resort, in other people's households as servants.

But economically active women in the traditional quarters often resist taking work in the modern sectors. The rhythm of modern work denies them control of their day and threatens their ability to perform the "womanly responsibilities" in which are rooted both their personal identity and their prestige in the community. A woman's work, they feel, should take place within the accepted rhythm of family life. A woman should be able to market in the early morning, prepare the main family meal for midday, and gossip with neighbors in the evening. A job with regular industrial hours interrupts the pattern of such a life. It means that a woman must shop in the evening when the produce is wilted. Instead of enjoying an evening of banter, a government-employed woman must prepare the main meal for the next day. She carries a dramatically increased burden without social interaction, scheduling flexibility, or compensating moments of leisure.

While women take pride in caring for their families, the same cultural ideal requires men to support their wives and children financially. Since economically strong families enjoy status in the community, a woman can undermine her family's status by taking work outside the household that visibly advertises the family's economic need. Women have enjoyed respect for their generosity and cleverness in generating income in and around their family activities. But work in the modern sector pulls them in two different directions, creating a dichotomy between economic activity and family commitments.

In the face of economic threats to their quality of life and family status, it is not surprising that many lower-class women cling to the ideals of "producing many children, caring well for them, and managing the housework skillfully,"[21] with their men financially supporting them in a life of comfort and leisure.[22] Many simply state, "I don't have the time to work," which researcher Andrea Rugh interprets to mean that "they do not want the frantic pace of the employed woman's life."[23] From the work she did in 1981, Rugh also concluded that "in general, all jobs that blatantly display need are performed by women whose husbands are dead or have abandoned them and therefore are not present to incur shame, or they are performed by women whose husbands' inability to earn sufficient income is so devastatingly apparent that the point of shame has been passed. Such women have little community status to lose."[24]

Rising inflation and the decreasing profitability of traditional occupations have pushed men into taking jobs in the modern sector and even into migrant labor in the oil-rich Arab states. As a result, men and women increasingly move, quite literally, in "different worlds." Men encounter the values of individualism and consumerism, which run counter to those of their neighborhood. Moreover, fathers, instead of doing work in which children can share, are increasingly distanced from the daily routine of their children and household. And while the overall household income may increase, the money that women control to meet household needs actually declines.

In one study of household budgeting in a lower-class Cairo neighborhood, the families most likely to have continuous conflict over finances were those in which the husband worked in the modern sector.[25] Working as drivers for foreign companies, as barbers in hotels, or as

21. Rugh, "Women and Work," p. 279.

22. Saswan el-Messiri comments on the ambivalence that lower-class women feel toward upper-class "modern" women: "Though *bint al-balad* claims to disdain certain attitudes of upper-class women, she still aspires to the same material comforts that those women enjoy, wishes that her husband might provide them, and to some degree idealizes that situation" ("Self-Images of Traditional Women in Cairo," p. 536).

23. Rugh, "Women and Work," p. 278.

24. Ibid., p. 280.

25. Homa Hoodfar, "Household Budgeting and Financial Management in a Lower-Income Cairo Neighborhood," in *A Home Divided: Women and Income in the Third World,* ed. Daisy Dwyer and Judith Bruce (Stanford: Stanford University Press, 1988), pp. 139-40.

laborers in beer factories, these husbands moved in a world and generated an income that made them far less interdependent with their wives. Developing a taste for the foods sold in cafés, some ceased to eat regularly at home. They spent their money on Western-style clothes and subsequently concluded that it would be safer to send them to a launderette than to leave them with their wives on washday. As one wife put it, "You see how he spends his money. He eats chicken and kabob for lunch and dinner; we do not see meat more than once a week. He spends the rest of his time in cafes and cinemas, while we cannot leave the neighborhood from year to year."[26] Spending less and less time in the neighborhood whose traditional ways they come to scorn, these men, not surprisingly, spend less and less of their income at home and on the family. As a result, whatever the *ideal* may be about men supporting their families, lower-class women, given their reality, feel more pressure than ever to contribute economically to the family. As Homa Hoodfar commented in her study, "All the women . . . , although readily accepting the ideology of man the breadwinner, thought it necessary under the existing social order for a woman to have an income of her own to help provide a better life for her children and herself and to make her more of an equal partner in the eyes of her husband."[27]

The "Domestication" of Women

The changes in the lives of the Narsapur women and those in the old quarters of Cairo reflect the uniqueness of each culture and the different ways their households survive economically. A concern for ritual purity, combined with limited opportunities in the countryside, shapes the lives of the Hindu lacemakers in different ways from those of women in Cairo adhering to traditional roles. There the women enjoy the varied economic opportunities of the city but refuse to relinquish their claim on men's financial support in return for mothering. Nevertheless, the common, underlying pattern of change in Cairo and Narsapur has been repeated again and again around the world. The story might be that of a New England shoemaking household in the early nineteenth century or an African village moving from subsistence production to plantation

26. Ibid., p. 132.
27. Ibid., p. 142.

agriculture: as production becomes organized outside the household and driven by increasingly distant market forces, the gap widens between women's and men's worlds, and new forms of economic and social power favor men over women.

In both India and Egypt, economic changes have altered the meaning of the household as women's primary sphere. Indeed, the cultural ideal of man as breadwinner and woman as economically marginalized housewife is gaining ground throughout the (so-called) developing world. In much of Africa, women historically did most of the agricultural work and were also long-distance traders. But Western assumptions about breadwinning men and dependent women have affected both colonial government policy and local attitudes about gender roles.[28] Women in Indonesia were historically active in rice production and small-scale trading and often managed the family finances.[29] Yet in both Africa and Indonesia, the Western ideology of the housewife infuses contemporary school textbooks and advertising, even as women face socioeconomic realities similar to those of Cairo and Narsapur.

The housewife of modern commercial society, who spends her days isolated from the social and economic mainstream, is thus a historically recent creation.[30] Her Western version may have originated in the tradition of the fair damsel's need for a knightly protector. Her Indian version may have built on notions about womanly responsibility for the spiritual well-being of the family. Her Egyptian version may grow out of a cultural ideal that expects a father to provide financially for family members and a mother to care for them materially as well as emotionally. But in each case the conditions of modern commercialized, industrialized society have isolated the housewife in unanticipated ways from the

28. Claire Robertson and Iris Berger, *Women and Class in Africa* (New York: Africana Publishing Co., 1986).

29. See, for example, Gillian Hart's *Power, Labor, and Livelihood: Processes of Change in Rural Java* (Berkeley: University of California Press, 1986); Lenore Manderson's *Women's Work and Women's Roles: Economics and Everyday Life in Indonesia, Malaysia and Singapore* (Canberra: Development Studies Centre, Australian National University, 1983); and the essay by Hannah Papanek and Laurel Schwede entitled "Women Are Good with Money: Earning and Managing in an Indonesian City," in *A Home Divided*, pp. 71-98.

30. A classic study of the "housewife" in the West is Ann Oakley's *Housewife: High Value, Low Cost* (London: Allen Lane, 1974). An international overview is found in *The Domestication of Women* by Barbara Rogers.

main economic currents of society. Throughout the world, the ideology of the housewife, embraced by women as well as men, adds to the barriers and hardships faced by all but the most privileged.

The wide-ranging traditional activities that sustained households economically and emotionally were unquestionably divided along gender lines. But prior to commercialization and industrialization, the Western distinctions between public and private, between production and reproduction were largely irrelevant. It was the transition to a cash-based economy that produced practical consequences from such distinctions. The identification of women with the privatized domestic sphere and men with opportunities being created outside it spawned serious new disadvantages for women, both within the household and beyond it.

Individuality and Cooperation in the Family

People who live together in families have always had both common and individual interests. Romantic notions of complete household harmony appear on Hallmark cards and in mainstream social and economic analysis, while some feminists offer the opposite, cynical view that "the family is the one institution in which the oppressed shares a bed with the oppressor." The reality in most families lies somewhere between these extremes. Individuals in families do have much to gain from cooperation, but the pressure to make individual activities "take the form of being overly cooperative" often disadvantages those with less access to resources, who disproportionately tend to be women.[31]

Economist Amartya K. Sen has analyzed the "cooperative conflict" that characterizes most households. When members of the household want the same outcome, cooperation is possible. But when individuals feel they would be best served by different outcomes, the results of negotiation depend on the relative amount of power enjoyed by each party. (See also Chapter Eight.) Both economic resources (such as ownership and access to waged labor) and social resources (such as access to external and communal support systems) affect a person's bargaining position. Sen identifies three factors that either jeopardize or enhance an individual's position: (1) the "[post-]breakdown well-being response,"

31. Amartya K. Sen, "Gender and Cooperative Conflicts," in *Persistent Inequalities,* p. 147.

467

(2) the "perceived interest response," and (3) the "perceived contribution response." Commercialization and industrialization have weakened women's position with respect to each of these factors.

The first, the "[post-]breakdown well-being response," refers to the advantages enjoyed by the party who can best weather a "breakdown" in the relationship. If a total breakdown will seriously jeopardize one person's well-being, the solution agreed upon will probably be less favorable to his or (more usually) her well-being. For example, in Cairo and Narsapur, as elsewhere, if the marriage of a couple ends, the wife is more likely to be assigned care of the children. The cultural ideal may demand that the husband financially provide for the family, but in practice, when a marriage breaks down, it is the woman who assumes most of the physical and financial burdens of raising the children, a situation similar to that in the Western world. Divorce, widowhood, neglect, the migration of male labor — all contribute to making many women the primary earners of their households. In fact, according to statistics provided by the United Nations, nearly one-third of households around the world are headed by women.[32]

It can never have been easy for a woman to shoulder the entire burden of supporting a family. But when kinship networks are weakened and women progressively lose access to productive resources, their position becomes even more precarious. When a household had rice-producing land or a family business, the labor of a wife and her children could be used, however reluctantly, to increase production. But when a woman and her relatives are dependent on the wages of an adult male, a fixed economic "pie" must be divided into ever-smaller portions. In addition, women's traditional hedges against hard times, such as gold jewelry, have little value in a world where income depends on skills and mobility. Women have fewer opportunities than men to earn cash; they also have higher levels of illiteracy, fewer years of education, fewer capital resources, and fewer marketable skills. Without such assets to assist them in the global market economy, women face far greater risks than men if there is a marital breakdown. This is what Sen means when she says that women's post-breakdown well-being is reduced, while that of their spouses is enhanced.[33]

32. "Family Configurations in the Third World," slide and tape presentation available from The Glenhurst Collection of Women's History and Culture, St. Louis Park, Minnesota.
33. Although for somewhat different reasons, the post-marital-breakdown

Second, Sen suggests that what she calls a "perceived interest response" also sets the stage for marital advantage or disadvantage. Within a household, the person who does *not* separate individual interests from those of the group is likely to get the worse deal in a negotiated solution. For example, as the worlds of men and women diverge in Narsapur and Cairo, men become individual laborers or mobile entrepreneurs. From these activities they derive an identity emphasizing individuality and drive that helps them compete. But women, who have less access to the market and fewer pressures to compete economically as they adhere to the cultural ideal of "femininity," are less likely to see themselves as individuals. In her study of lower-class women in Cairo, Homa Hoodfar concludes, "Women did not and in fact often could not distinguish between their personal needs and those of the family."[34] But in an economy that is becoming increasingly commercial, this is a dangerous state of mind. The lacemakers of Narsapur cannot reverse the exploitation of their labor unless they see themselves as individuals who do income-generating "work." Lower-class women in Cairo may readily accept an ideology of man the breadwinner, but they know that for their family's welfare they too must earn an income, and that it must fairly reward the labor they invest.

The difference between men's and women's self-perceived interests can be seen in the way they spend their income. Research on lower-class families in Egypt shows that where women have control of household finances or have independent incomes, they try to save for durable goods (such as a stove) and school expenses. The income men control is more likely to be spent on personal or entertainment items. When a man controls the family income, a household is likely to own a television set before a gas stove that would substantially lighten the woman's work load.[35] Studies ranging from South India to Jamaica, Ghana, and Guatemala also show that women's income, far more than men's, is spent

well-being of Western women is, on average, also much worse than that of their husbands. The work of sociologist Lenore Weitzman shows that American men's standard of living goes up an average of 42 percent after divorce, while that of their ex-wives goes down an average of 72 percent. See Weitzman's book entitled *The Divorce Revolution: The Unexpected Social and Economic Consequences for Women and Children in America* (New York: Free Press, 1985).

34. Hoodfar, "Household Budgeting and Financial Management in a Lower-Income Cairo Neighborhood," p. 142.

35. Ibid., p. 137.

on everyday subsistence and nutrition. A positive correlation often exists between the size of the mother's income and the nutritional well-being of her children, but does not always exist between combined parental income and children's nutritional well-being.[36]

Finally, there is what Sen calls the "perceived contribution response," which refers to the fact that the person who is perceived to make the larger contribution to the group is likely to receive a more favorable outcome in household negotiations. In both Narsapur and Cairo, the value accorded to women's contribution to the household has declined in relation to the value accorded to men's contribution, even where women are the main supporters of the household. The reason for this is simple: men generate cash. Women do so less easily, and the work they do to raise children and support community life is valued less and less as a cash economy takes over. We have only to look at the lower birth rates of industrialized countries to see how children come to represent a drain on cash resources rather than a contribution to the household labor pool and insurance for their parents' old age.

Such shifts in value also extend to other areas of life as economic, social, and political arenas become more compartmentalized. The visiting and gossip that previously cemented the social fabric of a community are now seen as "wasting time." The fluid boundary between domestic and income-generating work in a family business or on a family farm hardens into a dichotomy between activities (usually male) that earn cash and the "shadow work" (usually female) that maintains the well-being of individuals and groups. Men's identification with their families is replaced by a primary identification with their waged work, now done at a distance from the home. And women's identification with subsistence-enhancing work declines as they are "domesticated" within a redefined "home." Thus men are perceived (however inaccurately) as contributing far more than women to the household's well-being.

In such settings, the life of the middle-class housewife can be held up as a "traditional" ideal only by ignoring the actual shape of women's lives in earlier periods. The creation of the Western "housewife" and the "domestication of women" worldwide are products of a unified

---

36. A number of recent studies are noted in the introductory essay in *A Home Divided*, p. 5. For commentary on South Asia, see, in the same volume, Joan P. Mencher's essay entitled "Women's Work and Poverty: Women's Contribution to Household Maintenance in South India," pp. 99-119.

process by which production is moved from the household into large-scale enterprises and oriented away from subsistence needs toward the demands of the market. This reorganization of family and work life radically shifts the terms according to which women must learn to survive.

The terms that govern men's lives also shift dramatically. According to the newly defined ideal of the "male breadwinner" many men are miserable failures, through no fault of their own. As the possibilities for work with family and community shrink, it is perhaps not surprising when men who cannot individually provide for their families simply stop coming home or "drink up" their paychecks. Men as well as women lose when their self-worth is measured by purely economic criteria. But those who fight for survival against the most frightening odds are usually women — women who must provide both economically and emotionally for their children in homes that now provide only marginal economic opportunities.

The Ideology of the "Housewife"

We have seen that societies which distance women from economic opportunity end up dramatically handicapping them. Our case studies on the lacemakers of Narsapur and lower-class women in Cairo show how economically damaging that ideology can be when it identifies women with a radically constricted home life. Christian concern for justice calls for a challenge to the economic marginalization of women and to the cultural ideals that make it especially hard for poor women to join their husbands in working to feed their families.

When Western feminists have viewed these problems, they have most often suggested that women, like men, orient themselves toward the market. Women, they insist, must simply enter the paid work-force, like men. The appeal of this solution is strong, for if women had the earning power of men, their "perceived contribution" might be higher and their vulnerability in the wake of marital breakdown might be no greater than that of their partners. A reorientation toward the market might help women to see their own interests as individuals and put them on firmer ground in household negotiations. Just as important, it might provide women with a base for insisting that men again share the nurture of the next generation and begin to share household work more equally.

Yet lower-class women in Cairo and Narsapur resist embracing this solution, preferring the continued identification of women with family. Western feminists have noticed this resistance, but most have attributed it to non-Westerners' predictably "lower" development of feminist consciousness.[37] Alternately, they have concluded that less enlightened cultures make the social costs of resistance so high that women *cannot* challenge the identification of women with family. But are these conclusions justified? Are women who maintain a primary identification with family either blinded by false consciousness or utterly powerless to effect change? Or do women sometimes *choose*, with good reason, to maintain their identification with family and home? More importantly, can women who maintain this identification somehow *improve* their negotiating position so that they will be less jeopardized by economic and social change?

Much scholarly work has been done to explore the transformation of public institutions as a result of both colonial (or neocolonial) rule and commercial, industrial reorganization. The interdisciplinary field known as "women in development" has begun to show how barring women from emerging public institutions has crippled them. However, the attempt to understand the effect of privatization on various traditional institutions has barely gotten underway. The institutions recast as "private" have varied by social context, but certainly family, sexuality, and religion have been among them. All three undergo transformation when "public" and "private" worlds are arbitrarily created. And the emerging historical record suggests that women not only get trapped in the so-called private sphere but also actively help to shape it.

Women of different classes relate in different ways to the ideology of the housewife. Economic as well as cultural differences separate the women who join Betty Friedan in rejecting that ideology from the poor Asian women studied by Hanna Papanek, who "fervently desire to be housewives."[38] The latter, having few individual economic prospects, may hope to claim a share of community resources on the basis of their social and familial contributions. As we will see subsequently, more

37. See also Chapter Four in this volume.
38. Papanek, "Low Income Countries," in *Women and Work in Fifteen Countries*, ed. Janet Farley (Ithaca, N.Y.: ILR Press, New York State School of Industrial and Labor Relations, Cornell University, 1985), p. 85.

privileged women may push beyond the confines of the household by hiding behind a "traditional" ideology but infusing it with new meaning. Nevertheless, both upper-class and lower-class women face serious dilemmas when they refuse to deal with industrial, commercial society on its own terms — terms which dictate that economic concerns are primary and that the individual is the basic human unit. Let's try to understand these dilemmas by returning to our two case studies and examining the responses of upper-class and lower-class women to the ideology of the housewife.

Privileged Women and the Ideology of the Housewife

Upper-class women in both India and Egypt have responded ambivalently to the emerging ideal of the housewife. As noted previously, both cultures, though patriarchal, recognized the substantial powers of women. Women from elite families often had considerable social power, particularly as they grew older. Thus when Indian men, educated to serve in the colonial bureaucracy, began to press their wives to adopt Western standards of education, dress, and social mobility, many women instinctively resisted. They were not anxious to alter their dress and enter the newly emerging Anglo-Indian "public" spaces, or to be recast as the marital soul mates idealized in romantic Western literature.[39] Although such resistance has often been painted as reactionary, it may in fact have been prophetic: elite women were not at all sure that their position would be better in the emerging social order.

It soon became clear, however, that if upper-class women in both India and Egypt were to maintain social power, they would need access to the public institutions being created under colonial rule. And although unhampered by the Western stereotype of the "helpless woman," both Indian and Egyptian cultures had strong barriers to women's freedom of movement in the larger society.[40] Feminists of both sexes in these cultures challenged these barriers, some echoing

39. Ghulam Murshid, *Reluctant Debutante: Response of Bengali Women to Modernization, 1849-1905* (Rajshani University, Rajshahi, Bangladesh: Sahitya Samsad, 1983).

40. The emotional power of this conflict in India is conveyed in a film by director Satyajit Ray (now out on video) called *The Home and the World,* based on the story by Nobel prize-winner Rabindranath Tagore (Ghare Bhaire, India: National Film Development Corporation of India, 1984).

473

the sentiments of Western reformers and some reworking the traditional ideals.[41] They debated the proper understanding of woman in the Islamic tradition and the appropriate role of women in a "modern" Egypt within the context of other concerns. These included Egyptian nationalism (in the face of French, Ottoman, and British domination) and Islamic reformism aimed at countering the humiliations inflicted on the Muslim world by a now-ascendant West. In India, a Hindu reform movement challenged institutions such as the dowry and the prohibition on widows' remarriage. In addition, women's participation in the Indian nationalist movement propelled them further into public life.

Since Egyptian upper-class women had the opportunity to travel and receive a Western education, they led the way in throwing off the veil and carving out new opportunities, first in philanthropy and then in the professions. Gradually, elite Indian families associated with British rule began to educate their daughters for the professions. As independence approached, the number of women enrolled in college swelled, rising from only 6,782 in 1937 to 201,304 in 1945.[42] Women from the traditional elites drew on the power of their families to challenge accepted social norms. Since the social and economic power of newly emerging elites derived increasingly from the colonial government, their members also gained freedom from local expectations. Moreover, they increasingly had the economic resources to prepare their daughters for "respectable" work. All of these factors help explain the substantial number of present-day women professionals in both countries. In Egypt, there are more women earning wages in the "professions" (which in

41. A brief overview of feminism and nationalism can be found in Kumari Jayawardena's *Feminism and Nationalism in the Third World* (London: Zed Books, 1986). Joanna Liddle and Rama Joshi's *Daughters of Independence: Gender, Caste, and Class in India* (New Brunswick, N.J.: Rutgers University Press, 1986) provides a basic history and bibliography of women's response to modern India. For Egypt, see Thomas Philipp's "Feminism and Nationalist Politics in Egypt" and Afaf Lutfi al-Sayyid Marsot's "The Revolutionary Gentlewomen in Egypt," in *Women in the Muslim World*, pp. 261-76 and 277-94; Soha Abdel Kader's *Egyptian Women in a Changing Society* (Boulder, Colo.: Lynne Rienner Publishers, 1987); and the account of Huda Sha'arawi, *Harem Years: The Memoirs of an Egyptian Feminist (1879-1924)*, translated, edited, and introduced by Margot Badran (London: Virago Press, 1986).

42. Mary Trembour, "Women in Education," in *Women and Work in India: Continuity and Change*, ed. Joyce Lebra, Joy Paulson, and Jana Everett (New Delhi: Promilla & Co., 1984), p. 109.

Egypt includes some clerical jobs) than in any other occupational category.[43]

President Sadat's "open door" policy created other opportunities for women of this class. In its wake, the capital and contacts of upper-middle-class women provided them with resources for opening various businesses, such as boutiques for imported goods and small hotels for tourists.[44] As far back as 1970, women made up 17 percent of all professionals in India, a very select elite in a country where, in the mid-1980s, men with degrees made up only 1 percent of the nation's population and 3 percent of urban males. According to recent government statistics, 82 percent of Indian women professionals come from families whose fathers are college graduates.[45]

In both countries, professional women enjoy advantages unavailable in the West. Living in child-oriented societies which simply assume that mothers will love their children, upper-class women may be under less pressure than Western women to "prove" that love by staying at home. Upper-class women also have access to abundant cheap help as they organize housework and arrange for the care of their children. Thus neither the upper-middle-class woman nor her family are required to make major sacrifices. In fact, the education and competence of a professional woman who still maintains a well-run household may enhance not only the economic well-being but also the social status of the entire family.

Given these social and cultural advantages, have these upper-class women overthrown cultural ideals that identify women primarily with children and home? As Indian and Egyptian women have entered the public work-force, cultural expectations *have* in some ways shifted. Many people follow Western fashions. A romantic match, rather than an arranged marriage, has become an increasingly acceptable means of finding a partner. Some men now play a minor role in what was once the fiercely guarded arena of women's authority: the running of the household.

But the basic identification of women with children and family

43. Alma T. Junsay and Tim B. Heaton, *Women Working: Comparative Perspectives in Developing Areas* (New York: Greenwood Press, 1989), p. 68.
44. Safia K. Mohsen, "New Images, Old Reflections: Working Middle-Class Women in Egypt," in *Women and the Family in the Middle East*, p. 58.
45. Liddle and Joshi, *Daughters of Independence*, pp. 124-25.

seems to be holding firm. In her classic study published in 1970, Rama Mehta concluded that the Western-educated Hindu woman not only rejected Western domestic values but also the Western concept of individualism.[46] While a middle-class woman might be admired and encouraged to use her education to supplement family income, the women themselves "aspired to incorporate those modern attitudes that improved the economic potential of their children and to reject those that reduced Hindu domestic discipline."[47] Studying privileged women in the city of Madras in southern India, anthropologist Patricia Caplan recently found that "it is only for a small minority of women, who have either exceptional abilities or who suffer economic misfortune, that it is considered legitimate to work."[48] The vast majority of women in the middle and upper-middle classes do not work for pay outside the home. And even among professional women there is little challenge to the ideal that glorifies women's self-sacrifice in the domestic arena. Caplan quotes these assertions from a professional women's magazine:

> Indian working woman's great strength lies in her psychological security which is related to her compliant nature. She accepts the family without question. . . . She likes to be needed and important to others. [The] Indian working woman adjusts herself to the life of her husband, helping him in all ways that she can. . . . She wants to be a perfect partner in mind and temperament.[49]

Some might say that these Indian women professionals need a huge dose of feminist consciousness-raising. But are there any other ways to explain this perspective? We can offer several explanations from within their own social context.

First, women of the upper classes may well be correct to perceive their personal well-being as rooted in the well-being of their families. This is true even if we consider only the economic and social factors that have most often concerned Western analysts. Kinship wealth and connections *do* provide crucial educational and occupational opportuni-

46. Mehta, *The Western Educated Hindu Woman* (Bombay: Asia Publishing House, 1970).

47. Ibid., p. 207.

48. Caplan, *Class and Gender in India: Women and Their Organizations in a South Indian City* (London: Tavistock Publications, 1985), p. 87.

49. Ibid., p. 194.

476

ties. Nuclear households may be replacing the extended family as the ideal or real residential unit, but one's place in society is still affected by the social position of one's father and mother, brothers and sisters, sons and daughters. We should note that this is probably far more true among American elites than is generally acknowledged. The most obvious example is that of the Kennedy family, whose name clearly opens many doors. In American politics, in the Junior League or the country club, even in Jamaican immigrant networks in a New York slum, one's personal well-being does depend to a degree on the well-being of one's family.

Thus, as long as the family is important in establishing the social position of individuals, women quite logically see themselves as doing important work when they act to maintain their family's social position. Hanna Papanek calls such activity "family status production work," which includes the following:

> unpaid assistance in the work of an earning member of the household, as in the "two-person career" of men in professional occupations . . . ; participation in children's schooling that directly assists the efforts of teachers or is linked to upward social mobility efforts; direct "status politics" in the community; and performance of religious rituals tied to family status in the community.[50]

In bureaucratized Western society there are only limited forms of "family status production work." But here too the woman who has time to invest in well-chosen political campaigns or the right charitable functions may augment the efforts of the wage-earning family members and translate her activities into political and/or social power for the entire group. As a slightly different example, one of our team members has a son who was a scholarship student at a somewhat elite prep school. He suggested to her that since the family was in no position to swell the endowment coffers of the school, she ought to volunteer her expertise as a gender-studies scholar in helping the school to implement its decision to become a co-educational institution. She gladly did so, largely because she approved of the motives and means behind the school's decision, but also because her son felt that her activity would enhance his own standing as part of the "school family." Those who have studied such indirect work in non-Western societies suggest that "women's with-

50. Papanek, "To Each Less Than She Needs."

477

drawal from paid work" should be seen "as not so much the end-product of mobility as a strategy for further mobility." Women's activities are not just a symbol of existing social status but also an instrument of upward social mobility.[51]

There is another reason for the continued identification of elite women with home and family. As domestic and public spheres move apart, privileged women experience the resulting tensions differently than do lower-class women. Lower-class women *need* to be economically active; privileged women may *choose* whether or not to be. Thus we find in late twentieth-century Madras the same phenomenon that was evident in Victorian England: elite women elaborating and elevating the domestic life.[52] In various ways this "cult of domesticity" transforms the economic, social, and political work once done in the household into a new kind of homemaking, which now emphasizes the mother as *teacher*.

This new vision of the housewife in India, as in many other countries, looks remarkably like the one created earlier in the West as it underwent similar changes. As economic forces begin to dominate public life, women use the now-diminished domestic space to keep alive a vision that affirms "care giving and nurturance, . . . values and needs denied and undermined by the fragmentation and impersonality fostered by capitalism."[53] We can better understand the strength of this determination to maintain social commitments not ruled by market forces when we contrast some aspects of Western society with the values of "traditional" cultures. University women in Egypt expressed the following sentiments:

> We disapprove of the behavior of Western women. They have abused their liberty. It's gone beyond the limits of decency. Here we could never accept such permissiveness. We would never accept the sight of women walking about on beaches with bare breasts, pornographic

---

51. Ibid., p. 168. See also Kamala Ganesh's "State of the Art in Women's Studies," *Economic and Political Weekly*, 20 April 1985, pp. 683-89; and Kalpana Bardhan's "Stratification of Women's Work in Rural India: Determinants, Effects and Strategies," in *Social and Economic Development in India: A Reassessment*, ed. Dilip K. Basu and Richard Sisson (New Delhi: Sage Publications, 1986), pp. 89-105.

52. Leonore Davidoff and Catherine Hall, *Family Fortunes: Men and Women of the English Middle Class, 1780-1850* (Chicago: University of Chicago Press, 1987).

53. Barrie Thorne, "Feminist Rethinking of the Family: An Overview," in *Rethinking the Family*, p. 19.

films, or allowing young people to have sexual relations outside marriage. The West really has no shame. Everything is disappearing. Our own society still respects certain values. We maintain our standards, our respect for the law and conventions, for our religion.[54]

So it is not just male-dominated culture that enforces women's identification with the home; women themselves often support a vision of personal integrity that is bound up with social relationships. Their concerns echo those identified by feminist historian Linda Gordon when she studied members of the North American New Right: "They fear a completely individualized society with all services based on cash nexus relationships, without the influence of nurturing women counteracting the completely egoistic principles of the economy, and without any forms in which children can learn about lasting human commitments to other people."[55] We may question the assumption that it is only women who can or should do such nurturing; nevertheless, as Gordon notes, these are things about which feminists, and, we would add, all Christians, should be deeply concerned. (See also Chapters One and Two.)

Yet this "woman's culture," dominated by privileged women and celebrating the image of the housewife, is not totally benign, because economic activity is optional only for the most advantaged of women. Women who have a choice about doing waged work and have ready access to child care and domestic help may indeed have no particular reason to challenge their identification with home and family. In fact, some have suggested that it is perhaps precisely *because* elite Indian women "never overtly challenge the ideals regarding womanhood that they are in fact able to deviate so considerably from them."[56] In such a situation, men's egos remain unthreatened, and lower-class women workers protect their privileged sisters from the stresses of the "double day." Elite women, who have the most social resources to oppose the ideal of woman as housewife and who in practice find ways to deviate from it, seem only seldom to have felt sufficient pain and frustration to actually challenge it. In both India and Egypt, only a tiny fraction of elite women are prompted to question the identification of women with family and home.

54. Zenie-Ziegler, *In Search of Shadows: Conversations with Egyptian Women* (Atlantic Highlands, N.J.: Zed Books, 1989), pp. 78-79.
55. Gordon, "Why Nineteenth-Century Feminists Did Not Support 'Birth Control' and Twentieth-Century Feminists Do," p. 50.
56. Caplan, *Class and Gender in India*, p. 97.

Patricia Caplan looks at the charitable work that middle-class and upper-class women now carry out in Madras and compares it with the activities and ideology of middle-class Christian philanthropists of the late nineteenth century. Caplan notes that while the middle-class philanthropists were elaborating a womanly ideal focused on home, children, and volunteer charities, the British census of 1851 showed that three-quarters of unmarried women from all classes were wage-employed. By 1865, one-third of *all* British women over age twenty-one were in the paid work-force.[57] Today, statistics from Third World countries consistently underrepresent women's economic activity. Like the work of the women in Narsapur and Cairo, it is often trivialized, but nevertheless remains important. The situation in India is reminiscent of that in mid-nineteenth-century England: most women need to do at least some paid work in order to support their families. Yet in their charitable activities privileged women often promote a domestic ideal that ignores the economic realities of their "more unfortunate sisters." Because the economic marginalization of poor women helps to supply cheap domestic labor, it is not in the interests of privileged women to bring it to light. Wealthy persons often establish day nurseries or give gifts to women they see as "ignorant, weak, needy and backward," but they rarely call these women "poor."[58] Like American advertisers, Indian advertisers use the image of the housewife in an attempt to make all Indian women, like their Western sisters, good consumers. One Indian feminist has noted that the image of the woman standing in her modern kitchen surrounded by appliances strikes most Indian women as nothing but an "insult to their poverty."[59]

Thus the ideology of the housewife must be separated from the personal strategies of women who choose a life without paid employment. The ideology of the housewife limits the economic opportunities of lower-class women, while at the same time it blinds privileged women to their own potential economic vulnerability. And indeed, women in India and Egypt are beginning to call attention to the dangers that may confront even women who are "comfortable" at home. For example, in

57. R. Basch, *Relative Creatures — Victorian Women, 1837-67* (London: Allen Lane, 1974).
58. Caplan, *Class and Gender in India,* p. 208.
59. *No Longer Silent,* a film on women in India, available from the International Film Bureau, produced by the National Film Board of Canada and CINE-SITA, 1987.

recent years, India has seen a growing number of "dowry murders."[60] Dowry, the payment made by a bride's family to a groom's family, has been technically illegal in India since 1961. However, in an increasingly consumer-oriented society, informal dowry costs have in fact risen. Women may now need an education in order to attract a husband who is a good provider, but the "perceived contribution" of even an educated woman has fallen. As Indian social identity is increasingly defined by what one owns, dowry often becomes a means of raising cash and getting consumer goods such as VCRs and motorcycles.

Concerned for their daughters' future well-being and anxious to avoid a reputation for stinginess, families strain to give as much dowry as they can. Sometimes it is not enough. In a startling number of cases, young brides whose families have quarreled with grooms' families over dowry have been set on fire over their cooking stoves and burned to death. After the fact, it is hard to prove whether the event was an accident, a suicide, or a murder. The groom is thus free to marry again — and receive a second dowry. One Indian sociologist estimates that in Delhi alone, dowry-related deaths rose from 421 in 1980-81 to 690 in 1983-84; between 1979 and 1985 there were 2,000 such deaths.

The distortions that result when Indian middle-class women accept the ideology of the dependent housewife can be seen in some responses to the murders. The feminist journal *Manushi* records the voices of neighborhood women who insist that one young victim must have killed herself. When protestors challenge this interpretation, the neighbors give these answers:

"How do we know? Nowadays, girls can't put up with the smallest thing — they get into a temper."

"Teach your daughters patience. Girls must learn to bear everything patiently."

60. See articles in the Indian feminist magazine *Manushi,* reprinted in *In Search of Answers: Indian Women's Voices from Manushi,* ed. Madhu Kishwar and Ruth Vanita (London: Zed Books, 1984), pp. 215-30; and Rehana Ghadially and Pramod Kumar's account entitled "Bride-Burning: The Psycho-social Dynamics of Dowry Death," in *Women in Indian Society.* A Western account is found in Wanda Teays's essay entitled "The Burning Bride: The Dowry Problem in India," *Journal of Feminist Studies in Religion* 7 (Fall 1991): 29-52. See also the account in the film *No Longer Silent.*

"What is it to do with us? Forget it."

"The one who had to die has died. What's the use of making a noise about it?"[61]

Middle-class women who raise these issues in India meet with the same sort of denial that Western feminists encounter when they expose domestic violence in our society. In both cases, commitment to and dependence on an idealized version of the interdependent family too easily slide into a denial of the real vulnerabilities surrounding women and others.

In Egypt and India, as in America, middle-class women are also vulnerable to job segregation and wage discrimination. Professional women in Egypt and India tend to be concentrated in female-dominated occupations.[62] Their teaching and clerical work are overwhelmingly at the lower end of the pay scale.[63] The waged labor of lower middle-class women in Egypt is also vulnerable to the forces of economics and migration. When men move out of jobs, women move in. But it is often when women need jobs most — that is, in a constricted economy — that they are least able to find work. So it is not only in homes but in offices that the perceived contribution of women is low. This occurs in offices partly because of the way in which women who try to juggle home and work are viewed. The head of a government research department in Egypt described the situation as follows:

> We hire the best people, both men and women, train them to be excellent researchers, then men get offers for other jobs in other ministries or at the university and the women are left. . . . Women are equally good if not better, but the image is still there that women are not serious and that to them the job is low priority. . . . They see the women worry about the house and send the janitors to buy things needed at home and say, "See, they cannot be serious about their work if all they can think about is . . . the best buy in the cooperative store

61. Manini Das, "Women against Dowry," in *In Search of Answers*, p. 225.

62. One study found that in Egypt, 59.3 percent of professional women are elementary or high-school teachers and 18.8 are in nursing or related medical professions. A mere 3.1 percent were in the physical and life sciences; 6.3 percent were in architecture or engineering; 3.1 percent were lawyers and judges. The number of women who were doctors, college teachers, artists, or authors was too negligible to report. See Alma T. Junsay and Tim B. Heaton's *Women Working*, p. 96.

63. Caplan, *Class and Gender in India*, p. 85.

today." Men do it, too, but we tend to view that as a sign of the man's responsibility and strength. Men are more subtle about it and do it with such authority that it somehow seems part of their jobs.[64]

Thus the relatively few Egyptian professional women who have made their way as equals in a man's world often pay a high price. When they dare to challenge the total identification of woman with home and family, they may come to feel, like Dr. Nawal el Sa'adawi, "estranged in [their] own country."[65]

Lower-Class Women and the Ideology of the Housewife

Like their nineteenth-century Western counterparts, many upper-class women in Egypt and India shape an acceptable life for themselves without challenging traditional notions of womanhood. But our case studies from Narsapur and Cairo suggest that lower-class women have pressing reasons to challenge the emerging ideology of the housewife. Nevertheless, many of these women are disinclined to challenge the identification of woman with home, even though this seriously disadvantages them both in the marketplace and in negotiations within the household. There are several possible reasons for this reluctance.

The first reason has to do with the nature of the jobs available to men and women of the lower classes. Work as a household servant often requires a long commute in unreliable transport to do an ill-paid, low-status job. Both agricultural laborers (the largest category of wage-earning women in India) and construction workers do backbreaking work. The construction industry is still labor-intensive, using few machines except in urban areas. Consequently, women construction workers "cut soil, carry cement, stones, bricks, mortar and water on their heads, crush bricks and mix concrete."[66] And the agricultural laborers, refuse sweepers, street vendors, and others who make up India's nonprofessional female work-force do only slightly lighter work.

On top of such demanding waged labor, one's own household work

---

64. Mohsen, "New Images, Old Reflections," p. 61.

65. el-Sa'adawi, *Memoirs from the Women's Prison* (London: The Women's Press, 1986), p. 2.

66. Chitra Ghosh, "Construction Workers," in *Women and Work in India,* p. 203.

remains to be done. A day in the life of Shantabai, a worker in the city market of Pune, looks like this:

> "Man's work is from sun to sun but women's work is never done." . . . She gets up at 2 a.m., walks a quarter mile to fetch water for the day, cooks a meal for her son. She herself drinks only a cup of tea, cleans up, and starts walking to the vegetable market at 3:30 a.m. Three other women accompany her. She uses the public latrine at the market because there is no latrine near her home. Work starts at about 4:30 a.m. and she is busy carrying loads, sorting and weighing produce, and so on till about 10 a.m. She has to wait till 1:30 or 2:30 in case her employer wants anything done. In any case, she is not paid until after 2 p.m. In the afternoon she has another cup of tea. Thus she has by 2 p.m. worked for almost 12 hours with only two cups of tea as nourishment. She then goes home, cooks and eats her lunch, and sleeps till 5:00 p.m. When her son comes home she has to start cooking the evening meal, do the washing and cleaning. She rarely goes to bed before 10:00 p.m. Then, less than five hours later, she has to start the routine all over again.[67]

Although the details vary, the "double day" worked by many Third World women is uniformly harsh. If a woman's husband has enough economic security that she needs to do only a little paid work to keep the family alive, she may well feel fortunate. Colleen Samuels, an Indian Christian feminist, has articulated the challenges faced:

> The Syro-Phonecian woman's pleading for her children is very much the pleading of our Indian women — pleading for crumbs of time — where they can spend more time with the family, to cuddle the little one or to brush the elder girl's hair and put some flowers in it. . . . A woman's needs cannot be separated from [those] of her family. The children's rice must be cooked, their diarrhoea or fever must be taken care of. Can a woman who leaves her hut at 7 a.m. and returns at 8 p.m. have time to be a mother and a wife and yet have time to be herself? This is not a "patching up" method but a realisation that a feminist must take the woman's family into consideration.[68]

---

67. Sulabha Brahme, "The Growing Burdens of Women," in *In Search of Answers*, p. 56.

68. Samuels, "Room To Be a Woman, To Be Human," *Transformation: An International Dialogue on Evangelical Social Ethics*, special issue with the title "Focus on Christian Feminism," April/June 1989, p. 1.

Given the realities of waged labor and domestic life, it should not surprise us if some working-class women choose not to do paid work when that becomes an option.

In India, the number of women engaged in agriculture, artisans' work, and petty trade has fallen with the decline of household-based economic activity, even as the number of professional women has increased.[69] Commercial farming has pushed women to the edges of the farm economy, where they mainly fill the seasonal jobs men are unwilling to consider. Industrialization has undercut the crafts that women traditionally have done. In India, as in the West, early industrialization often retained family patterns of participation — for example, in jute and textile production, and even on plantations.[70] But as this early form of factory production was abandoned and women were pushed out of agricultural production, the number of women in the waged labor force declined from 41.8 million in 1911 to 31.2 million in 1971, a dramatic absolute decline, since the population itself had risen steeply. From 1961 to 1971, "male and female populations increased by 25% and 24% respectively . . . and the number of men workers increased by 15.2% while women workers declined by 41.1%."[71] Although these statistics underrepresent the number of women engaged in cash-generating and other economically useful activities, they nevertheless demonstrate the marginalization of women's labor.

In all this we see that women who cannot find economically or personally rewarding waged work *do* have something to gain by emphasizing the value of the work they do at home. A poor working woman from the Indian slums may contribute about a third of her family's income. But if her husband is fortunate enough to get a salaried position, it makes economic sense for her to stay home and for him to take on

---

69. According to Sulabha Brahme, "The number of women employed in 'traditional' occupations — agriculture, artisan work and petty trade — declined from 34.44% of the total working population in 1911 to 17.35% in 1971" ("The Growing Burdens of Women," p. 49).

70. For accounts of early family-based factory life in the U.S., see Mary Ryan's *Cradle of the Middle Class: The Family in Oneida County, New York, 1790-1865* (Cambridge: Cambridge University Press, 1981); and Tamar Hareven's *Family Time and Industrial Time* (Cambridge: Cambridge University Press, 1982).

71. Mary Higdon Beech, "The Domestic Realm in the Lives of Hindu Women in Calcutta," in *Separate Worlds: Studies of Purdah in South Asia*, ed. Hanna Papanek and Gail Minault (Columbia, Mo.: South Asia Books, 1982), p. 123.

extra part-time work that will generate the same income that she could earn only in a full-time job. Thus the lower-class women studied by anthropologist Mary Beech often chose to have more children (rather than take on paid work) and to make a substantial contribution to family life through their work at home. Beech makes this observation: "Conscious of the indignities to which a lower class woman is exposed when she must work, and of the neglect of her children, the working class woman is proud of her status as the *barir grihini*, the 'lady of the house.'"[72] Homa Hoodfar's study of lower-class women in Cairo suggests that they have a similar perspective. Given the options of "modern" life, women would prefer to be supported by a man. But in the face of growing economic pressures, most think it best to have some independent income. Hoodfar also reports that many "expressed sympathy and pity for their husbands and for men in general because life was becoming more expensive and the burden of their responsibilities was greater. On the other hand, they occasionally commented ironically that, in the past, women had had to work far too hard, so now it was the men's turn."[73] Thus lower-class women embrace the ideology of the housewife not only because men and/or upper-class women foist it upon them but also because a woman who must both maintain a household and do ill-paid, physically demanding work simply has too much to do.

In his early work on Western capitalism and the family, Eli Zaretsky suggested that the separation of economic production from its household/family base, for all its negative impact, did justify the concept of leisure as well as "an ethic of pleasure and self-gratification previously unknown to a laboring class."[74] Thus a working-class woman may well view the possibility of domestic respite from the hard, tedious labor of survival as a remarkable liberation. Patricia Caplan found that when

72. Ibid., p. 125. The fact that professionally trained men can often earn more income in extra *part-time* work than their wives can earn in *full-time* work is a source of frustration to many Western feminists of both sexes. Although anxious to reintegrate fathers back into family life on a day-to-day basis (and to reintegrate mothers back into public life), many American couples find that it currently makes no "economic sense" (in terms of balancing the family budget) for a wife to engage in paid employment simply to enable her husband to spend more time at home.

73. Hoodfar, "Household Budgeting and Financial Management in a Lower-Income Cairo Neighborhood," p. 125.

74. Zaretsky, *Capitalism, the Family and Personal Life*, rev. ed. (New York: Harper & Row, 1986), p. 51.

poor Indian women of Madras could live in a rented hut or room on the income their husbands made as drivers or tailors, they generally did not enroll their children in the charity day schools in order to take on waged work. They wanted instead to stay home and give their children a head start on their education. As they saw it, investing their labor at home in this way promised to improve the quality of family life — at least in the long run — more than their taking on available jobs. However, in families that could maintain a middle-class life-style by combining the earnings of husband and wife, both often took paid jobs. These women reported that their greatest problem was "the double burden of paid work and household work."[75]

The lower classes as a whole are more economically vulnerable than the more privileged classes. But in both the lower and the upper classes, the vulnerability of women is relatively greater than that of men. The declining state of women in commercializing, industrializing India is seen most dramatically in the survival statistics for male and female children. In 1901 the ratio of women to men within the Indian population was 972 women to 1000 men, already somewhat alarming. By 1981, the figure was 935 women to 1000 men. There is dramatic regional variation in these figures, with survival rates for girls in southern India markedly higher.[76] Nevertheless, the cost of dowry and the cultural assumption that adult sons, not daughters, will care for aged parents contribute to the devaluation of girl children, who then receive, intentionally or not, poorer health care and nutrition.

The investment that lower-class women make in their children is to some extent based on a hope, rooted in an earlier social structure, that their children will later care for them. In pre-industrial societies, women's ability to bear the children who were the group's future was a recognized power, as both Indian and Egyptian cultures reflect. Indeed, Gerda Lerner's recent work shows how much even Western feminist consciousness has been rooted in the "sisterhood of motherhood."[77] And women feel they have good reason to hang on to a cultural norm that emphasizes

75. Caplan, *Class and Gender in India,* pp. 176-78.

76. Barbara Miller reviews the literature on the issue until 1986 in "Health, Fertility and Society in India: Microstudies and Macrostudies — A Review Article," *Journal of Asian Studies* 45 (November 1986): 1027-36.

77. Lerner, "The Emergence of Feminist Consciousness: The Idea of Motherhood," paper presented at the Berkshire Conference on Women in History, Rutgers University, 1990.

the mother-son bond over the conjugal bond, since a mother rooted in an ongoing blood lineage is in a far more secure position than a wife bound to a husband only by romantic attachment. Western culture's celebration of romance is bound up with its glorification of youth and independence. What it fails to see is that while the wife-husband link favors young women, enduring mother-child bonds favor older women, and, until recently, especially older women who have borne sons.

Christians affirm that human society reflects a relationality rooted in the very nature of the triune God. Hence they can hardly embrace a social vision that allows each person to do individual economic planning which ignores the care of others. Historically as parents have cared for children, so children have usually cared for parents. Yet as we say this, we must also acknowledge that in increasingly commercialized societies, parents are more often abandoned than cared for by their children. Fatima, from the Bulaq neighborhood of Cairo, poignantly expresses this loss as she speaks of a son now working in Saudi Arabia:

> Muhammad sent his wife three hundred pounds to buy a refrigerator. He tells me in the tapes, "May God cure you." . . . But I ask you, since when did words cure someone? Did Muhammad send me money? Even people not related to me, like yourself, if they see me sick would offer me money; shouldn't one's own son do as well? Why did I spend so much to get my son married if he doesn't even ask after me now?[78]

In an earlier social structure, women could reasonably assume the truth of the adage that "Husbands may come and go, but children remain."[79] Although this formerly safe assumption is now risky, women's continued attempts to establish a base of security through their children is not hard to understand.

In this section we have seen that many women around the world are disinclined to adopt the dominant Western feminist solution to women's marginalization at home. Their failure to embrace the solution of male-style waged work may inhibit the economic advancement of these women, and even reduce the survival chances of some. But they are understandably unwilling to embrace a solution that accepts the individualistic, economically driven orientation of the modern commer-

78. Evelyn Early, "Fatima: A Life History of an Egyptian Woman from Bulaq," in *Women and the Family in the Middle East*, p. 81.
79. Ibid., p. 77.

cialized economy. While the ideology of the housewife has been used to shame poor working women, the ideals of nurturing and community to which many women cling reflect positive human values. And it may also be said that mothering, however ambivalent an experience it may be, is potentially the most challenging and rewarding work most of the world's women will ever find.[80]

Life Strategies

American Women and Gender Strategies

Our case studies from southern India and Cairo illustrate how the lives of men and women diverge and domestic power shifts under the impact of commercialization and industrialization. In a nutshell, men have easier access to modern institutions, while the ideology of the housewife restricts women to a home setting of diminished economic significance. Yet women around the world are ambivalent about abandoning their identification with home, even though this identification poses increasing economic risks.

Industrialization and commercialization followed a somewhat different history in the West, a powerful consumer society that initiated these changes over two centuries ago. Yet the processes explored in this chapter are also part of the Western historical experience. We could just as easily have looked at the changes in New England shoemaking households as production moved into factories at the beginning of the

---

80. For many nonprofessonal women around the world, this point is simply common sense. It is made in feminist literature not only by Third World and black American women but also in various ways by some white, middle-class feminists. Linda Gordon makes the point in "Why Nineteenth-Century Feminists Did Not Support 'Birth Control' and Twentieth-Century Feminists Do," p. 50, and Mary Field Belenky and the other authors of *Women's Ways of Knowing: The Development of Self, Voice, and Mind* (New York: Basic Books, 1986) explore the way in which some poor, severely abused women have in fact acquired the beginnings of "self" and "voice" precisely through bonding with their own children. In *Maternal Thinking,* Sara Ruddick also comments on the feeling of competence many women develop as they learn to care for their children. These works, as well as Adrienne Rich's *Motherhood as Experience and Institution* (New York: W. W. Norton, 1976), show the beginnings of a feminist scholarly concern with what is, for many women, a central life experience.

nineteenth century, or at the strategies of women in American rural communities as commercial farming developed.[81] As the different cultural settings of Cairo and southern India gave distinct shape to the strategies of the women living there, so the responses of women in North American communities have varied. But the outlines of a major social change are common to all these stories.

In her recent work entitled *The Second Shift*, feminist sociologist Arlie Hochschild argues that the stresses a Western woman experiences from being both "housewife" and "working woman" have arisen because it is now "'the woman's turn' to move into the industrial economy." Hochschild takes seriously the ambivalence of Western women toward "home" and "work." She refuses to rank these women on a continuum between "enlightenment" (read "career-oriented") and "mystification" (read "home-oriented"). Instead, she suggests that in the complex milieu of contemporary American society, women pursue various strategies based on personal choice, available resources, and the possibilities they envision for themselves.

Their ambivalence about these choices and the pressures they experience in trying to live out their vision of the "ideal woman" echo the concerns of women from Narsapur to Cairo. Hochschild has found that the American woman, who has far more privileges and choices than most women around the globe,

> [sizes up] her education, intelligence, age, charm, sexual attractiveness, her dependency needs, her aspirations and . . . matches these against her perception of how women like her are doing in the job market and the "marriage market." What jobs could she get? What men? . . . Half-consciously, she assesses her chances — chances of an interesting, well-paid job are poor? Her courtship pool has very traditional men? She takes these into account.[82]

Whatever choices they make, all women experience the tensions of having been left behind economically while men's search for cash has moved them away from domestically oriented life, where women now

---

81. These processes can be seen in the fine studies collected in *To Toil the Livelong Day: America's Women at Work, 1780-1980*, ed. Carol Groneman and Mary Beth Norton (Ithaca: Cornell University Press, 1987).

82. Hochschild, *The Second Shift: Working Parents and the Revolution at Home* (New York: Viking Press, 1989), p. 17.

shoulder the caretaking burdens of two. Yet women continue to seize available opportunities to press social and cultural boundaries in their own interests. Some are as unsuccessful as the lacemakers of Narsapur. Some do in fact carve out new possibilities for themselves and those women who follow them. As we look at several of these strategies, the resourcefulness of women and the pitfalls that lie before them are equally clear.

Women in Egyptian Factories

In the 1960s, state-run Egyptian factories began to draw women into industrial production.[83] President Nasser's socialist-leaning government made an effort to create a protected factory environment that would be congenial to women workers. A measure of this policy's success is the reputation for respectability that women's factory work now enjoys, even among the working classes, and even though the original goals of free maternity benefits and on-site child care have only rarely materialized.

Throughout the world, factories are typically managed by men, even when the work force is overwhelmingly female. Because of this phenomenon, some have argued that women's factory work merely replicates the patriarchal hierarchy of the family. Moreover, there is little doubt that the underpaid factory labor of women around the world contributes to the comfort of consumers (mostly Western) even as it jeopardizes the workers' own long-term interests.

Nevertheless, women who work in Egyptian factories have found ways to make this experience work for them. In the first place, the pay they get is at least as good as that in other jobs, and their work in factories is generally less threatening to the status of their families than other kinds of employment would be (e.g., work that requires a woman to be dependent on another family or find herself in a compromising situation in another man's home as a maid). Most begin work as unmarried women, though many continue to work in the factories for ten to fifteen years after marriage. Others begin factory work as divorced or widowed women; in 1976 these two groups comprised 15 percent of all production workers in Egypt.

83. This account is based largely on Barbara Lethem Ibrahim's essay entitled "Cairo's Factory Women," in *Women and the Family in the Middle East,* p. 293.

Egyptian women who work in factories are not enamored of their work, but they are aware of its advantages. Barbara Lethem Ibrahim has interviewed a number of women in Cairo who work in factories. A woman named Soraya mused:

> "Working is hard, but not to work would be harder. The young girls here, they dream of getting married and brag that they will be able to quit. Of course all of us would prefer to stay home. They will find it the same as the rest of us. Salaries they can waste on new dresses and outings now will be needed for food and rent once they have families of their own. Quitting work is easy to talk about, hardly anyone can do it."[84]

Another woman named Hadiya commented, "Work strengthens a woman's position. She can command respect in her home and can raise her voice in any decision."[85] The power a woman actually enjoys may depend on the degree to which she controls her own earnings; even so, her perceived contribution is likely to rise, while her vulnerability in the event of a marital breakdown will decrease.

Thus women who earn a wage in the modern sector understand what their work contributes to their independence and individual interests, and they often enjoy a new measure of freedom, even to choose a mate. But, though this experience emphasizes their power as individuals, these women also begin to think about their problems collectively: "We are a tight group. . . . We defend each other's rights. If we see a fellow worker poorly dressed whose husband is taking her salary, we show her the unfairness of it and encourage her to ask for her rights."[86] Issues that are hard to discern when embedded in the emotional bonds of family now stand out more clearly. For example, it seems unfair that the promised on-site child-care has never materialized, so that one woman must spend two hours a day taking her child to and from a day nursery while another leaves her son with a school guard during the hour between her departure for work and the start of school. Meeting together at work on the terms of modern society, women begin to form alliances and make analyses that can help them challenge the status quo. Women in Bombay, India, have begun the same process, though with even less structural support.

84. Ibid., p. 297.
85. Ibid., p. 296.
86. Ibid, p. 299.

Mahila Mandel of Bombay

Many Indian women cannot wait until the dominant ideology gives them permission to leave their homes in search of the money they now need to survive. In the meantime, like the grass that grows through the sidewalk cracks, they discover ways to challenge cultural and social boundaries, as the following example illustrates.

In recent decades male migrants from rural India have flocked to the cities in search of work. The textile industry in Bombay employs thousands of these men, who live in the slums, often near relatives or members of their own caste. Women who live in the area have found that they can earn cash by feeding a group of sixteen to twenty workers in their homes for a fixed fee per month. But like the lacemaking of the women of Narsapur, the work of the individual "annapurna" (annapurna means "Goddess of Food") was rarely seen as "work," though it in fact paid for food for her own family.

In 1973, however, the attention of Prema Purav, a trade-union activist, was drawn to the annapurnas. During a 42-day textile strike, many annapurnas pawned their jewelry in order to feed the workers who could no longer pay for their meals. "I came to know the interest rates women were paying to buy grain," Purav commented. "Till then I had never looked at the problems of these women. The women, quietly, without any fanfare, were enabling the men to continue their struggle, encouraging them to hold out till their demands were met. And yet their own problems were never taken up."[87] Purav's first goal was to help the annapurnas purchase provisions without becoming indebted to grocers charging interest rates of up to 150 percent. A handful of women were organized to apply for a collective loan from a nationalized bank. Although each received an individual sum, they shared a collective responsibility to see that the entire loan was repaid. Within three years the initial group of fourteen women had grown to include approximately 5,000 women in the cooperative, which was known as the Annapurna Mahila Mandel (Women's Association). Group kitchens were organized

---

87. My account of the well-known Annapurna Mahila Mandel cooperative is drawn largely from material supplied by Glenhurst Publications in their video called "Annapurna Mahila Mandel: An Experiment in Grassroots Development for Women" (available from Glenhurst Publications, Inc., Central Community Center, 6300 Walker St., St. Louis Park, Minn. 55416).

where women could cook together and then distribute food to people in factories. Some women gained experience in administering the project, others in bookkeeping. Recently, a graduate with an MBA and experience with computers has been hired to expand the educational opportunities available to women working in the cooperative.

Although not without its drawbacks, the cooperative has effectively challenged both the social and the cultural barriers that make women's work so much more difficult. It counters social isolation and makes women's work visible *as work*. And it provides women some access to the networks that control resources in an industrial, commercial society. Both social esteem and self-respect grow as women come to be seen and come to see themselves as capable.

The Veiled Women of Cairo

Between the traditional urban women of Cairo and the small elite who share some Western cultural and economic values, there is a mass of women pushing ambivalently into the modern sector. That it is still thought to be more important for girls of this class to marry than to train for a job is evidenced in a 1980 study of one Cairo neighborhood, which found that the percentage of girls who never enter school is twice that of boys. However, the pressures of inflation and the possibility of employment in an office setting are shifting these traditional values.

As a result, increasing numbers of middle- and lower-class families are supporting their daughters' education.[88] Indeed, where families can use their connections to find good employment for their sons in the traditional sector, boys are more likely than girls to drop out of school. Families prefer business employment for their sons, since the bureaucratic positions to which education leads pay only a fixed salary with no hedge against inflation. Daughters are allowed to continue their education in order to take jobs that do not compromise their personal or family status, such as the impersonal, sex-segregated work of an office or a factory. But, according to Wedad Zenie-Ziegler, daunting "second shift" problems have often meant that waged work, "far from representing a chance to bloom and develop, means more servitude for women."[89]

88. Rugh, "Women and Work," pp. 285-87.
89. Zenie-Ziegler, *In Search of Shadows*, p. 82.

Those who cannot envision a household with domestic help are unlikely to embrace waged work wholeheartedly.

To have a husband and a happy family life are still the goals of most Egyptian women. But these goals have been complicated by the rise of consumerism. In addition to the problems created by the division of waged work from family life, there are those created by Western notions of romantic love and its accompanying standards of "attractiveness." As Safia Mohsen puts it, "While the old virtues of good reputation and family background still play an important role, the possession of cars, expensive clothes, and stylish hairpieces also has become important in the quest for a suitable husband."[90] Although a minimal amount of "dating" does sometimes take place, it is not socially acceptable for people of the opposite sex to build relationships outside of kinship networks. Thus there is often little opportunity for young people to explore personal qualities beyond appearance. Western fashion thus creates new problems for those with little money, problems any North American parent who has dressed a teenage daughter can readily appreciate.

To cope with these new pressures, many middle-class women adopted a new strategy during the 1980s. While continuing to work in the modern sector, they exchanged Western dress for the *hejab*, a full-length traditional garment that covers all of a woman's body and her hair, leaving only her face and hands exposed.[91] Egyptian feminists have echoed the horror expressed by Westerners over this shift.[92] Traditional dress seemed to hide a woman's beauty, restrict her movement, and presume the responsibility Egyptian culture has long put on women not to "tempt" men. And women who don the *hejab* do seem to reverse the courageous work of earlier feminists, who pushed for more liberal dress standards as they pressed for opportunities for women in education and employment. Yet women choose to wear the *hejab* for many reasons, not all of which can be labeled reactionary or antifeminist.

Putting on the *hejab* is for some women a matter of religious

90. Mohsen, "New Images, Old Reflections," p. 67.

91. The film titled *A Veiled Revolution* (1982), produced by Elizabeth Warnock Fernea, records a range of Egyptian women's perspectives on the issue (available from ICARUS Films, 200 Park Ave., South, Suite 1319, New York, NY 10003; tel. [212] 727-1711).

92. See, for example, Nawal el-Sa'adawi's opinion articulated in Angela Davis's "Egypt," in *Women: A World Report* (New York: Oxford University Press, 1985), p. 342.

495

conviction. According to the Quran, a woman's beauty is not for public display. Consequently, many women who do not veil themselves still express admiration for the convictions of those who do. Nationalism plays a further part in the rejection of Western dress. Wearing the *hejab* is also a way of stepping off the fashion merry-go-round on which many Western women are trapped. It proclaims a rejection of standards that value women primarily on the basis of their physical attractiveness. Others say that it is simply a practical form of dress. A media production engineer says, "I can bend down to look under a machine without worrying about what people can see."[93]

Some university women and lower-middle-class working women adopt the dress to express their continued commitment to the ideal that identifies home as women's primary sphere. University women feel that it gives them more freedom of movement with male students and colleagues. As one of them expressed it, "Since I [began wearing] the veil, I don't worry anymore. No one is going to accuse me of immorality or think that we were exchanging love vows. I feel much more comfortable now and do not hesitate, as I did before, to study with the men in my class or even walk with them to the train station."[94] For others, wearing the veil seems to provide an advantage over wealthier, Westernized women in the search for a husband. Wearing the veil advertises a commitment to modesty and a good reputation. Thus women can pursue education and jobs while allaying the ambivalence and insecurity many men feel about Westernized women. The *hejab* can also function as a kind of mask. As one researcher has noted, "It is impossible to guess the social class of a veiled woman. The *hejab* is a refuge. In other words, it is . . . a means of disguising poverty, of overcoming shame."[95]

In summary, although not without problems, the choice to dress in full-length traditional garb seems to be a phenomenon that cannot be reduced to merely an action that supports an attempt to marginalize or mystify women. Instead, it can be seen as one more ambivalent attempt by women in a concrete cultural and historical setting to negotiate the complex demands of work and family life. It does not, of course, challenge the underlying cultural assumption that women rather than men bear the responsibility for maintaining sexual purity. And to the extent

93. This is a comment recorded in *A Veiled Revolution.*
94. Quoted by Mohsen in "New Images, Old Reflections," p. 69.
95. Zenie-Ziegler, *In Search of Shadows,* p. 84.

that it represents an ideology which places the "ideal woman" in the home, it is likely to hurt many women. But to the extent that traditional dress allows women both to advertise their commitment to family and to be free to pursue the work they need and want, it is an understandable strategy for women to embrace.

Some Christian Observations

Throughout the modernizing world, the separation of paid work from family life has cost women dearly. Their ambivalence about joining the changing public sphere calls attention to the social losses that affect not only women but men and children too. When feminist theory encourages women to ignore these losses and instead to mimic a male economic agenda or to devalue relationships, it undermines the credibility of its own social critique. Christians too must attend not only to women's economic problems but also to the social losses that affect women as well as men, fathers as well as mothers.

The various strategies we have seen women adopting are far from ideal. Women who take paid jobs still feel the powerful pull of household responsibilities, but no equally pressing reality links men to domestic life, in which their forefathers were once rooted. A mother without food for her children must find work, but a man who is unconnected to his children may easily settle for some hours with his friends in a coffeehouse or bar. Justice and a commitment to human wholeness require men and women to work together in this struggle. But in fact, women are often left pleading for men's help while trying to overcome boundaries erected by culture and society. Christians may embrace a vision of kingdom *shalom*, but steps toward this vision are taken within concrete cultural traditions, actual family situations, and the terms of the workplace. As we evaluate strategies for attaining greater gender justice in our own industrialized, commercialized economy, several Christian observations are useful.

First, the tendency to create hierarchies based on status is endemic in a fallen world. Status symbols come in many forms, and we all tend to seek them out. Both having the time to care for one's own children and devoting oneself to a "meaningful career" can be used to enhance one's own position and devalue the work of other women, particularly those with fewer choices. Within Christian circles especially, "being

497

married" is itself a status marker, even though this does not square with the honor given to singleness in the New Testament. The Indian lacemakers' overidentification with the superior status of "housewife" has dramatically constricted their choices and vision, even as it has contributed to the devaluation of women who do agricultural labor. Thus the symbols we choose to identify our superior status may serve not only as ways to look down on others but as blinders that handicap ourselves.

Second, the ambivalence expressed by the women of Cairo and southern India toward the Western feminist solution of "waged work for women" is an implicit criticism of the individualistic, economic orientation of our society. It is extremely difficult, in the face of advertising and career pressures, to remember that "life is more than bread, and the body more than raiment." If Christians are right in affirming that people are more important than things, then no solution to women's problems will be adequate if it simply replicates the materialistic, consumeristic orientation of our larger society. And although the spheres of work and family are polarized in modern social practice, most women — and many men — plan for the future with both in mind. Consequently, the challenge facing us is to carry into public life the concern for nurturing and community that modern reorganization "leaves behind" in the private sphere, while at the same time not losing a concern for individual well-being in either the domestic or the public arena. (See also Chapter Thirteen.)

Third, to care about nurturing requires us to make certain that those who nurture are economically secure. But as economic life is pulled out of its traditional kinship and household networks, support for those who nurture begins to collapse. No amount of sentimental appreciation will make this frightening vulnerability go away. It is too easy to say, as even some Christian economists have, "There are values other than those of the market. Family life lies outside the narrow sphere of economics. To put a dollar value on such things would be to devalue them." But this perspective ignores the fact that in earlier societies, nurturers were given economic support through extended families and communities, whereas today that support is fast disappearing in our modern, commercialized society.

When we place such problems outside the realm of economic analysis, we fall short of a Christian vision for justice and social interdependence. To assume that women who are economically dependent on men *should* be secure simply ignores historical and sociological facts. Historically, all but a tiny fraction of the world's most privileged women — a group that includes many twentieth-century North American women — have had to make substantial contributions to their families' economic well-being. This basic fact of human life is unlikely to change. Consequently, finding ways to meet the human need for nurturing and community-building will require a reorientation of our individualistic, market-driven American way of thinking and living.

This will require a solid recognition of the nurturing, emotion-managing, and community-building work that women — and some men — do without remuneration. (Historically, when men have assumed such roles, they have gradually become recognized as professions. The traditional work of midwives, for instance, is now the carefully guarded guild of obstetricians, a group that is mostly male. Women in America have lost this work, and the tangible and intangible rewards that went with it.) Currently there is an imbalance that needs to be addressed. In a society where most economic opportunities must be pursued away from home, women cannot afford to carry both their own and men's share of domestic nurturing tasks. And neither productivity nor a truly human life can be maintained without the fulfillment of these tasks. Men must join in doing some of this work without pay, and women must be guaranteed the financial security needed to continue doing it.

Fourth, any ideology that celebrates a falsely ascribed weakness in women violates the Christian understanding of human beings as created in the image of God. Egyptian and Indian images of women's power remind us — at the same time that the controls erected against it may trouble us — that their strength is appreciated in settings other than our own. Our culture idealizes thin, childlike, inarticulate, and vulnerable women, though historically neither women nor their cultural symbols have resembled this ideal very much. Moreover, in a social setting that favors men economically, the ideology of the housewife, offered as a rationale for the protection of women, is as likely to be an invitation to their abuse.

Fifth, we must reject any prescription for women or men that debases the basic work of making hot meals, changing linens, and washing dirty feet and faces. These tasks would most likely have been part of the rhythm of life in the original, pre-fall creation. But no one group of persons should be left doing this work, with the result that they have no time for more creative, interactive activities. Women's lives have been diminished as they

499

have been buried in these tasks. Moreover, a "solution" that simply pushes this work onto another group — often other women — is likely to be just as unfair. A profound distortion occurs when individuals or groups see these tasks as mere tedium and pass them on to other persons — to wives, to servants, to slaves, to the mentally less fit. Rather than being recognized as a common denominator that unites us all, attending to these tasks becomes an indicator of low status, and those who can avoid them see themselves and their own tasks as more important.

Finally, we need to reject the thinking that sets "correct" feminist understanding against "womanly mystification," moving instead toward a consideration of the realities most women face. In the process, we may find ways of dealing with a big challenge faced by today's women: that of guiding their daughters toward an understanding of themselves and their place in the world. One of the most difficult things to face as one explores the damage done to women around the globe is the participation of mothers in the crippling of their daughters. The binding of women's feet and the performance of clitoridectomies, euphemistically called "female circumcision," have in fact been overseen by women. Why? For many mothers, fulfilling these social norms seemed essential to secure a place for their daughters within society. For some, sheer survival was at stake. For others, any hope of a better life hinged on fulfilling the norms of the ruling class.

For women, as for men, there is some comfort in the acceptance that results from adhering to social norms. Writing about the honor women and other dependents can experience in Bedouin society, Lila Abu-Lughod says, "What is voluntary is by nature free and is thus also a sign of independence. Voluntary deference is therefore the honorable mode of dependency."[96] The woman who voluntarily adheres to social norms receives at least a reflected honor. The silencing and attenuation that Carol Gilligan has noted in girls between the ages of eleven and sixteen seem to confirm this sort of social experience in our own culture: girls who have their own voices at age eleven have muted them by age sixteen in an attempt to fulfill social expectations and preserve their place in a network of relationships.[97]

96. Abu-Lughod, *Veiled Sentiments: Honor and Poetry in a Bedouin Society* (Berkeley: University of California Press, 1986), p. 104.
97. *Making Connections: The Relational Worlds of Adolescent Girls at Emma Willard School*, ed. Carol Gilligan et al. (Troy, N.Y.: Emma Willard School, 1989).

However a woman may have responded to social norms in her own development, she experiences the struggle anew with her daughter.[98] Daughters remind their mothers of the temptation, or necessity, to follow questionable social norms in order to get ahead. In China, binding a young girl's feet left her crippled for life, but failure to bind them closed off even more opportunities. A nineteenth-century working-class Chinese woman quoted her mother as saying, "A plain face is given by heaven but poorly-bound feet are a sign of laziness."[99] Who would marry a woman with big feet, especially when something could have been done to change them? Since most women want to marry and share their lives with families, those concerned for women cannot completely ignore a given society's mating rituals, even as they aim to challenge them. It was a telling moment when married feminists on our team admitted that the marriage vows they uttered fifteen or twenty years ago pandered to a quite traditional understanding of gender relations! This particular time in life impels people of both sexes toward conservative social norms: the period in which we start families is no time for excessive social experimentation — not if young and vulnerable lives are to be adequately nurtured.[100] Our society does not bind the feet of its young girls, but neither does it arrange secure marriages for them, nor will it allow them *not* to care whether they are cute or have dates. Are mother and daughter equally helpless in the face of such pressures?

An earlier generation of feminists, prepared to defy all social convention to secure justice for women, is now being ignored by young women who take for granted easy access to the marketplace and hence are more concerned about finding a mate. These young women, vulnerable to social pressures, are in need of more nuanced feminist understandings. Most young women have a deep need for affirmation from

98. Hanna Papanek has recently written on this process in terms of "secondary socialization." See "To Each Less Than She Needs, from Each More Than She Can Do," pp. 175-80.

99. Ida Pruitt, *A Daughter of Han: The Autobiography of a Chinese Working Woman* (Stanford: Stanford University Press, 1967), p. 22.

100. For example, in a recent issue of the avowedly countercultural *Utne Reader,* one writer defended his decision to move his family from the inner city to the suburbs and their better schools by noting that even parents who are social activists are rarely "willing to sacrifice their children to their social principles." See Joseph Nocera, "How the Middle Class Has Helped Ruin the Public Schools," *Utne Reader,* no. 41 (September-October 1990): 66-72.

their peers and a deep desire for a life partner. In this period of their lives they make decisions about work and marriage that will affect all their future choices.

If we can acknowledge the felt needs of young women for a family, a livelihood, and the opportunity to use their God-given abilities, we can strategize in ways that can be heard more widely. By sharing various life strategies through our own life stories, informed by theory and historical perspective, we can clarify the pitfalls of both economic and family life. We can hope, as we work with them, that both our daughters and our sons will maintain personal strength and integrity while finding their place in a society still in need of much change.

CHAPTER 15

Is Someone in the Kitchen with Dinah?
Gender and Domestic Work

A s children, some of us learned the American folk-song "I've Been
Working on the Railroad," a song whose somewhat mystifying lyrics
end with the following verse:

Someone's in the kitchen with Dinah,
someone's in the kitchen I know.
Someone's in the kitchen with Dinah
strumming on the old banjo.

An amalgam of a black railway workers' chorus and an earlier black
plantation melody,[1] this song dates back to a period when it was quite

---

1. *Long Steel Rail: The Railroad in American Folksong,* ed. Norm Cohen (Champaign:
University of Illinois Press, 1981), pp. 837-41. The part of the song beginning "I've
been working on the railroad" had its first known printing in 1894, while "Someone's
in the Kitchen with Dinah" appeared as an independent song as early as 1834. No one
seems to know how the two parts (a railway song and a domestic song) eventually got
put together. It is possible that "Someone's in the Kitchen with Dinah" was picked up
and sung by whites as an unfortunate sentimentalization of Southern plantation life.

The primary author of this chapter is Annelies Knoppers.

503

routine for "someone" to be in the kitchen helping the adult woman domestic worker, whether that worker was mistress of her own kitchen or working for someone else. It was only with the advance of industrialization in America that female homemakers began to be progressively more isolated in their housewifery. How that happened, what some of the consequences were, and what we might do about it are the topics of this chapter.

We noted in previous chapters that gender relations are structured in various ways: in the distribution of power, in the nature of interpersonal attraction, and in the division of labor. In this chapter we will especially focus on the last of these. The current division of labor in Western countries is well known: there is domestic work, which is associated primarily with women, and there is waged work, which has different associations for women than for men. We will explore the gendered division of labor by beginning with a brief historical overview, and follow with an examination of how the construction of domestic work contributes to the prevalent pattern for gender relations in white, middle-class culture. Gender relations in the waged work-force will be the topic of the following chapter.

In the long sweep of history, almost all work, whether done by women or men, has been domestic work — that is, related to the management and upkeep of home and family. Until recently, then, someone was almost always "in the kitchen with Dinah" — and usually doing something other than "strumming on the old banjo." By contrast, in today's monied economy there is paid labor, which is usually done away from the home, and domestic work, which, if done for one's family or one's self, is usually done by women, working alone and without pay. The majority of American women (66.9%) and men (85.5%) engage in paid work,[2] but generally women still carry the responsibility for domestic work. This dichotomy is very much a product of historical forces as well as of human agency. We will summarize the former as they relate to white, middle-class people in North America today. We focus first on unpaid domestic labor, because it has been, and still is, largely invisible

---

Nevertheless, our point in quoting it is still valid: before the advent of industrialization, domestic work was a much more cooperative endeavor, crossing both age and sex lines. See also James Field's *Book of World Famous Music: Classical, Popular and Folk* (New York: Crown Publishers, 1966), pp. 255 and 421-22.

2. "Working Women," *Newsweek*, 14 October 1991, p. 3.

in our industrialized, monetarized society. Our consideration of waged work continues in the following chapter.

Domestic Work in Historical Perspective

Prior to the Industrial Revolution, rural and small-town living was the norm.[3] Most work was done at or near the home, in company with one's dwelling partners. Tasks were assigned according to age, gender, and/or social status; nevertheless, cooperative interaction was the norm. In the American colonial period, cooking per se was "women's work" — but much of the prior preparation of tools and meat was men's work. Women scrubbed floors, but men made the lye cleanser that was essential to the task. Women spun linen, but only after the men had crushed the flax fibers. Women and girls cared for infants in cradles that men and boys assembled during long winter evenings. As historian Ruth Schwartz Cowan has noted,

> If an eighteenth century woman had attempted housekeeping without the assistance of a man . . . she would most likely have had markedly to lower her standard of living. . . . A similar fate would have befallen a man under the same circumstances had he tried to farm without the help of a woman. Small wonder that most people married and, once widowed, married again. Under the technological conditions that prevailed before industrialization, survival at even a minimally comfortable standard of living required [the cooperative effort of] adults (or at least grown children) of both sexes.[4]

Even the urban home was a site of production. It was a place where clothing was made, baked goods were prepared, and laundry was done for the family and sometimes for others. In other words, the home was a site for the production of goods and services as well as a place to live. Moreover, the average home, especially that of European settlers in North America, consisted of only one room with a turf or wooden floor, a few dishes, and a few sticks of furniture.[5] Consequently, little time

3. Susan Strasser, *Never Done: A History of American Housework* (New York: Pantheon Books, 1982).
4. Cowan, *More Work for Mother: The Ironies of Household Technology from the Open Hearth to the Microwave Oven* (New York: Basic Books, 1983), p. 25.
5. Ann Oakley, *Subject Women* (New York: Pantheon Books, 1981).

was diverted from productive activity to housekeeping. Working-class people were most likely to work away from their homes as day laborers and domestic servants. Black family members, often separated from each other by white slave-owners, worked (and often lived) away from their own homes.

The Industrial Revolution brought about many changes in Western society, including a more completely monetarized economy and a shift of ideas concerning what kinds of work were appropriate for each sex.[6] The Industrial Revolution shifted many forms of production away from the home and into factories, mills, and mines. Initially both women and men left home and worked for pay in these locations. As machines became more efficient, however, fewer workers were needed, resulting in a surplus of people wishing to work for pay. At the same time, the home, which used to be the site of reproduction *and* production, was reduced to being a place for reproduction and for the consumption of goods produced elsewhere. That is, goods were no longer made mostly in the home, but instead were bought outside the home for use inside. In addition, the rise of a monied economy meant that *making* a living was replaced by *earning* a living. The power of money — that is, of wages — accordingly increased, while unpaid domestic labor began to lose its status as an activity of value.[7] These conditions helped to reshape gender relations around issues of waged labor on the one hand and domestic labor on the other.

As the role of the home in production decreased and the importance of money and therefore of waged labor increased, working for pay outside the home became associated with hegemonic masculinity. While hegemonic masculinity was constructed around the idea of males as breadwinners, privileged femininity was associated with unpaid domestic labor and financial dependence. This "cult of domesticity" made it easy to see women as mere surplus workers in the waged work-force. Accordingly, they were the first to lose waged jobs as machines began to replace workers. The resulting association of paid work (and its value) with hegemonic masculinity became so entrenched that both "work" and "paid work" came to mean work done outside the home

6. The development and entrenchment of these ideas aptly illustrate how gendered practices are constructed, contested, and legitimated.

7. Meg Luxton, *More than a Labour of Love: Three Generations of Women's Work in the Home* (Toronto: The Women's Press, 1980).

— that is, outside "women's proper domain." (If unpaid labor had been valued more than waged work, as it was among the medieval monastics, then perhaps hegemonic masculinity would have been associated with domestic work, and that work would have higher status than it has today.)

Ironically, working-class women and black women continued to work outside the home, since the classism and racism embedded in the structure of waged work prevented working-class men and men of color from earning a "family wage" — that is, a wage adequate to support an entire family.[8] Nonprivileged women engaged in waged work, albeit for low pay and often in the homes of white, privileged women. If working-class women stayed home, they often took in ironing or boarders to make ends meet.[9] The cult of domesticity was thus very much a construction of the Western, white, middle class. Since this privileged group had access to the most resources and could therefore implement strategies to make its ideas stick, its ideology became dominant. According to this ideology, a man was a man if he supported his family — a persistent concept that has pervaded all classes. Even today, both in the Western world and in nations which are just beginning to industrialize, many working-class women describe their earnings as "supplemental income" so that their husbands can still feel that they are the breadwinners. (See Chapter Fourteen.)[10]

The ideology of male breadwinner/female homemaker thus pushed many white, middle-class women out of the paid work-force, made them economically dependent, and kept them isolated at home. This ideology was supported by the argument that women "naturally" possessed talents for domestic labor and raising children. Religious teaching helped make this work seem "natural," a manifestation of inherent female gifts. Catherine Beecher summarized this ideology when she said, "God made woman to do the work of the family,"[11] work that was equated with love as well as with piety. The emphasis on love as the motivating force was important in justifying the lack of pay for domestic work. It also helped forestall the suggestion that changing countless

8. Maxine Baca Zinn, "Family, Feminism, and Race in America," *Gender & Society* 4 (1990): 68-82.

9. Cynthia Fuchs Epstein, *Deceptive Distinctions: Sex, Gender and the Social Order* (New Haven: Yale University Press/Russell Sage Foundation, 1988).

10. Ellen I. Rosen, *Bitter Choices: Blue-Collar Women In and Out of Work* (Chicago: University of Chicago Press, 1987).

11. Beecher, cited by Strasser in *Never Done*, p. 186.

diapers at home was not much different from labeling countless bottles on an assembly line!

This ideology supported the idea that each family should have only one adult, male wage-earner. It seemed common sense then that he should earn a "family wage." This was possible in part because families were defined as consisting only of mother, father, and children, and were becoming smaller as the birthrate declined. The concept of male bread-winner/female homemaker was also used to justify the idea that when women *did* enter the waged work-force, they should earn less than men. As society changed under the impact of the Industrial Revolution, challenges to this ideology had to be either absorbed or coopted, so that it could stay intact.

For example, one would think that the invention of various domestic appliances would have given women more leisure time and hence the opportunity to engage in waged work. But while appliances helped to decrease the *drudgery* of domestic work, they did little to decrease its *amount*, since both the physical size of the middle-class house and the standards for its upkeep continued to rise. The arrival of appliances in the home also helped to isolate middle-class women socially, since such appliances tended to replace the hired women who used to assist with chores such as laundry and heavy cleaning.[12] The consumerism needed to sustain capitalism also played a role here. It helps to explain why these appliances became status symbols for single households instead of machines shared by several families. Mass production and mass consumption were the goals here.

In addition, the time saved by using these appliances was countered by changing cultural notions about "children's needs." Motherhood became a romanticized, full-time vocation, one that required attentive work carefully and intentionally done. A woman was rated a "good" mother only if she devoted a great deal of "quality time" to her children. Indeed, equipping homes with appliances was often justified on the grounds that using them for household chores would give mothers more time with their children. Little thought was given to the possibility that fathers would have to work harder and longer to be able to afford such appliances, thereby spending progressively less time with their children.

The new standard for mothering was reinforced in the early twentieth century by Freud's emphasis on the importance of the child's first

12. Cowan, *More Work for Mother.*

five years. But ironically, instead of this claim leading to an emphasis on professional child-care, it led to a greater emphasis on the importance of mothering. Whereas previously babies were expected to sleep most of the day, now they were to be talked to and taught various things, which of course required that mothers be available to them all day.[13]

The historically unique and privileged nature of this ideology received very little attention. Prior to the Industrial Revolution, mothering was not such a distinct vocational task, nor was it possible for working-class women of the early twentieth century to devote much time to it. Little thought was given to the needs of black or working-class children, whose mothers had so little time for the "distinct task" of parenting. Indeed, emphasizing the importance of "good mothering" could be used to reinforce class and race distinctions. White, middle-class women were seen as "good" mothers because they stayed at home, whereas working-class women who of necessity did waged work were by definition "inadequate" mothers. The problems of working-class youth could then be attributed to poor mothering. Even today, the rising rates of poverty, delinquency, and crime among blacks are often attributed in part to the high incidence of "single parenting" in the black community. As Maxine Baca Zinn points out, the hidden assumption here is that black mothers are not doing a "good" job.[14] She suggests that we see racism as the cause of these rising rates and that the problematic aspect of single-parent families is not so much lack of parenting as lack of resources. Single black women who parent often do so within a rich context of kinship and friendship networks, but also in a situation in which it is often very difficult to make ends meet. Thus attributing delinquency to inadequate parenting or mothering fails to take into account the class and race structure that favors a mothering style possible only for the white, middle-to-upper class. It also ignores the ideology that allows fathers of *all* classes to avoid nurturing contact with their children.

For the white middle class, then, the romanticization of mothering emerged through an emphasis on the needs of children, an emphasis on women's innate ability to mother, and the equation of motherly love with domestic labor. This romanticization obscured the low status and socially isolated nature of homemaking, its lack of pay, and the economic dependence of women on men.

13. Luxton, *More than a Labour of Love.*
14. Zinn, "Family, Feminism, and Race in America."

In an earlier chapter we noted that science has been used to buttress the ideal of slimness as an aspect of privileged femininity. Similarly, the importance of homemaking as a separate and distinct job was legitimated by its "scientification." Ellen Swallow Richards began to convert household work to a domestic science in the late nineteenth century, calling for a "science of right living" that was grounded in Pasteur's germ theory of disease. Infant mortality and various illnesses were attributed to lack of cleanliness in the home. Failure to keep a clean house was thus seen as a form of child abuse,[15] and standards of cleanliness became fused with ideas of moral purity. "Good" domestic workers kept their houses clean, while "bad" domestic workers were those who had homes infested with deadly dustballs. To this day, it is surprising how many Christians believe that the phrase "Cleanliness is next to godliness" is actually in the Bible!

"Home economics" gradually became an area of academic study that attempted to develop theories and strategies for "efficient" homemaking and child raising. According to its emerging standards, laundry had to be not just clean but whiter than white; clothes had to be ironed; housecleaning had to include daily, weekly, and yearly schedules; children had to be disciplined a certain way. Yet these methods, like the new household appliances, also created new tasks and higher standards for domestic workers. Small wonder, then, that one social historian has titled her history of the mechanization and scientification of housework *More Work for Mother*.[16] In addition, "efficiency" experts studied the kitchen, redesigned it to include appliances, and made it into an area separate from the living area. Again, consumerism based on capitalist ideology nurtured the demand for appliance-laden, separate-roomed kitchens as replacements for communal cooking and eating areas. The turn-of-the-century farm kitchen, in which at any given time various people might be cooking, conversing, knitting, or sleeping on the "day bed" behind the wood stove, became a rarity in the middle-class suburbs. This meant that domestic workers were often isolated, especially if there was entertaining to be done: elaborate food preparation meant being

15. Oakley, *Subject Women*.
16. Cowan, *More Work for Mother*. Similarly, the current push toward saving the environment also affects domestic workers: the wash must again be dried on the line to save electricity, cloth diapers must be washed (using disposables isn't "eco-friendly"), garbage must be sorted, and so on.

marooned in the kitchen.[17] Many hostesses know the irritation of missing parts of conversations held in the living room because they are busy preparing food in the kitchen!

The growth of home economics as a science and the increase in the number of its experts illustrate how contradictions in the construction of the gender system can be obscured by hegemonic ideals and forces. If women have "natural" or "innate" talents for homemaking, then why do they need advice on how to do it? Yet the existence of experts, backed up by "scientific" findings, ensures that women will conclude there is a "wrong" and a "right" way to do homemaking. As most readers will recognize, advertising for the consumption of products is built on this distinction. We are told that a given product will do its job better than any other. Some products even receive the Good House-keeping Seal of Approval.

The ideology of domesticity, although created primarily for and by the middle class, has become very pervasive, in part because of its appeal to "naturalness." It became — and still is — the dominant ideology about women in our culture, an ideology that has at times been at odds with reality. For example, during the Depression, married, middle-class women were criticized for working for pay; yet they increasingly did so in part out of economic need and in part because they wanted to.[18] Similarly, reformers who worked in the inner cities began to offer cooking classes for working-class women in order to teach thrift and nutrition. But given that both these women and their husbands were waged laborers, one might well wonder why both were not taught how to run an efficient, healthy home! It is also interesting to note that those Westerners who went to Third World countries (first as colonizers and missionaries and later as "experts" in development) promoted and encouraged women's domesticity, forgetting that the concept of "house-wife" was a middle-class construction of Western culture. (See Chapter Fourteen for a further discussion of this topic.)

In fact, in the early 1900s, middle-class women were the only large social group *not* regularly doing waged work. Instead, their work was usually invisible, unpaid domestic work. This group of women finally

17. Luxton, *More than a Labour of Love.*

18. Johanna Brenner and Barbara Laslett, "Gender, Social Reproduction and Women's Self-Organization: Considering the U.S. Welfare State," *Gender & Society* 5, no. 3 (1991): 311-33.

began to enter the paid labor force in large numbers in the 1950s and continue to do so today.[19] Their reasons for doing so paralleled those of women from other social classes.[20] Engaging in well-paid work often enhances women's self-esteem, increases their social opportunities, contributes to the stability of their living arrangements, and lessens their financial dependence on men. Like their male counterparts, women value a satisfying and well-paying job. This is important not only for psychological reasons but also for economic reasons. By "economic reasons" we do not mean the desire for luxury items such as a cottage or a boat, but simply the desire to be able to survive in comfort and dignity without welfare, to be able to have both "bread and roses."

In the 1950s, middle-class women were most likely to seek employment when their children were teenagers, a time when family expenses are highest.[21] Today things are significantly different. In households where both spouses are in the waged work-force, women contribute an average of 30 to 40 percent to the family income.[22] However, the number of women who are single householders jumped from 30.9 percent in 1969 to 46.2 percent in 1985. This is variously due to people staying single, to alternative living arrangements, to the death of spouses, and to divorce, with one in two American marriages now likely to end in divorce.[23] The phenomenon of the "displaced homemaker" is a reminder that married women are often dependent on the "good favor" as well as the health (physical and financial) of their husbands. Thus jobs for white, middle-class women can also be a hedge against future financial disaster, whether within the marriage or as a result of its breakup.[24] But even this hedge is a shaky one in

19. The entry of middle-class women into the waged labor force thus preceded the second wave of feminism; possibly it was one of the factors that gave rise to this wave of feminism.

20. Lesley Doyal, "Waged Work and Women's Well-Being," *Women's Studies International Forum* 13 (1990): 587-604.

21. Brenner and Laslett, "Gender, Social Reproduction and Women's Self-Organization."

22. Rebecca M. Blank, "Women's Paid Work, Household Income, and Household Well-Being," in *The American Woman, 1988-1989: A Status Report*, ed. Sara E. Rix (New York: W. W. Norton, 1988), pp. 79-122.

23. Jerry A. Jacobs and F. Furstenberg, "Changing Places: Conjugal Careers and Women's Marital Mobility," *Social Forces* 64, no. 3 (1986): 714-32.

24. Jacqueline Jones, *Labor of Love, Labor of Sorrow* (New York: Basic Books, 1985).

America: sociologist Lenore Weitzman found that divorced women's income declined an average of 73 percent while their ex-husbands' income rose an average of 42 percent.[25] And although women are usually granted physical custody of their children, only 20 percent of fathers pay child support regularly; 15 percent do so irregularly, and the remaining 65 percent pay nothing at all. Remarriage is also least likely for women with children, with the result that many single women are supporting not only themselves but also one or more offspring. In 1984, 34.5 percent of female-headed families had incomes below the poverty line; these families were 48 percent of all the poor families in the United States.[26] These data show why the pauperization of women and children is on the rise and indicate one of the reasons why many women engage in waged work.

But although economic considerations lead many women to enter the paid work-force, women have not benefitted economically from waged work as much as men have. In 1990 an American woman averaged 67 to 69 cents for every dollar a white man made.[27] This gendered wage allocation increases women's economic dependence on husbands, fathers, male employers, government bureaucrats, and other male figures; it also reflects a gendered division of labor in the waged workplace.[28]

In America, fully 80 percent of waged women workers are in female-dominated jobs or occupations. This phenomenon is called sex segregation of the work force. It is associated with a gendered wage gap, and it has created both social and economic inequality, as we will show in more detail in the following chapter. According to Heidi Hartmann, "the roots of women's present social status lie in this sex-ordered division of labor."[29] We will also argue that the roots of this gendered division

25. Weitzman, *The Divorce Revolution: The Unexpected Social and Economic Consequences for Women and Children in America* (New York: Free Press, 1985).

26. Lorraine Sorrell, "What Women Are Worth," *Off Our Backs* 20 (February 1990): 4, 29.

27. Ibid.

28. Researchers who have reviewed studies on wages have found that a third to a half of the gendered wage differential is due to the sex segregation of jobs. See F. Blau's "Occupational Segregation and Labor Market Discrimination," in *Sex Segregation in the Workplace: Trends, Explanations, Remedies,* ed. B. Reskin (Washington: National Academy of Sciences, 1984),pp. 117-43; and Jerry A. Jacobs's *Revolving Doors: Sex Segregation and Women's Careers* (Stanford: Stanford University Press, 1989).

29. Hartmann, "Capitalism, Patriarchy, and Job Segregation by Sex," *Signs* 1 (1976): 137.

of labor lie in women's social status, each factor contributing to the other in a mutually causal fashion.

One might argue that women's mere participation in paid labor suggests that waged work can no longer be associated solely with hegemonic masculinity. But because men avoid domestic work or make paid work their primary concern, this association has continued, supported by the enduring idea that women are responsible for domestic work. This work is done not only for husbands/partners and/or children; seventy percent of caregivers to the elderly are wives, daughters, or daughters-in-law.[30] Consequently, regardless of class and race, women who do paid work often end up working a "double day" or "second shift." That is, after their paid work is done, they go home to another round of work, this time unpaid. What accounts for this phenomenon? We continue our discussion by looking at contemporary domestic work and exploring why it continues to be women's responsibility.

The Nature of Contemporary Domestic Work

As we begin this discussion, we should keep in mind that the conditions of domestic work are shaped by factors other than gender as well. For example, if a household is on a very tight budget, then a domestic worker will have to be very frugal and creative in making ends meet. If the household's primary wage-earner is in a management or professional position, then the homemaker may have to entertain his colleagues in order to enhance his career. These examples — and many more could be cited — make it clear that domestic labor consists of many threads woven together in a complex, multicolored tapestry. Its various threads include those of class, race, religion, age, geographic location, and ethnicity. We will try to make visible some of these threads, especially those colored by gender.

Since most of the responsibility for domestic labor is still carried by women, we will refer to domestic workers as women in the following pages. In addition, our discussion will focus primarily on those who do domestic work in the context of a home where there is a husband and children. We do so because it is in the context of the "nuclear" family

---

30. *Circles of Care: Work and Identity in Women's Lives,* ed. Emily Abel and Margaret Nelson (Albany, N.Y.: SUNY Press, 1990).

that the division of labor for domestic work is most likely to reinforce the current shape of gender relations. It is that context which has been most visible and which is still the norm. We realize that there are many exceptions to this model: single people with or without children, homes that include aged parents, "blended families," and so on. Yet the shape of domestic labor both contributes to and contests the nature of gender relations in each of these kinds of arrangements as well. Every home requires domestic labor, and that work is most often the responsibility of women, whether or not they live in nuclear families and whether or not they engage in paid work.

What exactly is involved in domestic labor? Overall, domestic labor consists of managing a home and caring for the physical and emotional well-being of those who live there. It usually includes preparing meals and cleaning up after them, doing laundry, cleaning the house, and managing emotions in the process of caring for spouse, children, and others. It also includes shopping, entertaining, planning, time management, chauffeuring, home maintenance, and record-keeping. Domestic labor is often fragmented — that is, many activities must be done simultaneously, such as watching the children, rotating loads of laundry, and preparing dinner.[31] In addition, even in households where spouses share the work more equally, it usually is the woman who remains responsible for managing and coordinating all tasks.

The dominant/subordinate aspect of gender relations is reinforced through social practices in the home. For example, the schedule of the home often centers on the adult male's activities.[32] Meals tend to be scheduled at a time that is most convenient for him. And if he engages in leisure-time sports activities or in volunteer work that interferes with the meal schedule, then often a second meal is prepared for him. Similarly, the nature and location of his job often determine his wife's friendships and social life, especially with regard to friends who are entertained during evenings or weekends. She is more likely to serve and entertain his colleagues and their spouses than he is likely to entertain her colleagues and friends. Much of her work is done on his behalf.

---

31. According to Meg Luxton, this fragmentation is one reason why so many accidents occur in the home.

32. Rosemary Deem, *All Work and No Play? The Sociology of Women and Leisure* (Milton Keynes, U.K.: Open University Press, 1986); and Luxton, *More than a Labour of Love.*

Domestic labor is highly demanding yet without the kinds of perquisites and acknowledgments of worth that accompany a challenging waged job. One is often on call twenty-four hours a day, and the actual and potential work never ends. Lesley Doyal points out that domestic work is meant to be invisible: it only gets noticed when it is not done.[33] Ann Oakley reports that 75 percent of the women she interviewed found domestic work to be monotonous, and that they liked least the tasks which were most like those on an assembly line, such as ironing. They liked best those tasks that permitted creativity, such as cooking.[34] Overall, even though domestic work is invisible, it requires a great deal of problem-solving, creativity, and skills for which domestic workers get little recognition. Not only must they do many tasks simultaneously, but their work also requires a high level of responsibility, accompanied by isolation, economic dependence, and little affirmation.

These factors, coupled with the expectation that homemakers will also manage emotions and interpersonal tensions, make domestic work highly stressful, especially if a person is married and/or parenting. It is tiring and frequently frustrating, and often makes domestic workers feel trapped.[35] It is no wonder, then, that many women complain of chronic lethargy or fatigue.[36] For despite the fact that they work on their own and according to self-monitored schedules, domestic workers have very little time to call their own. In part, this lack of time is exacerbated by their not having a space of their own:

> The continued presence of household duties and obligations means that it is difficult for women to set aside time for leisure at times when others are relaxing which they can be sure will be uninterrupted. It is rare for women who live with others to have a space of their own for leisure, whereas men, and frequently children too if they do not simply leave the house, often have special places to go even in cramped housing conditions . . . where they are likely to remain undisturbed.[37]

33. Doyal, "Hazards of Hearth and Home," *Women's Studies International Forum* 13 (1990): 501-17.

34. Oakley, *Subject Women.*

35. Luxton, *More than a Labour of Love*; Oakley, *Subject Women.*

36. Luxton, *More than a Labour of Love*; Arlie Hochschild, *The Second Shift: Working Parents and the Revolution at Home* (New York: Viking Press, 1989).

37. Deem, *All Work and No Play?* p. 81.

In part, this lack of time or leisure is a result of the seemingly never-ending nature of domestic work. A therapist once told us of a husband who complained about his wife's lack of sexual interest. His wife replied that she would be more interested in lovemaking if it began in the kitchen with him doing the dishes! This therapist also observed that even when both husbands and wives engaged in waged work, most husbands still had time for sports (playing on the church team or in pickup games) and for doing volunteer work in the church and community. Meanwhile, wives generally had no time or energy for anything after the "double day" of waged work and domestic labor that many of them put in.

Domestic workers' reduced access to leisure is also related to their financial power, according to Rosemary Deem: "Money is one of the indices of who is in control of their lives and choices, and who is not. . . . Women who have little or no financial power may also have little control over their time, work and leisure."[38] Moreover, even when domestic workers engage in leisure activities such as watching TV, they also tend to work: they mend socks, iron, catch up on family correspondence, prepare vegetables, or mind the children.[39] Small wonder, then, that many domestic workers suffer from chronic fatigue.

Domestic labor is thus more than the mere sum of its activities: it is complex, demanding, invisible, and often contradictory. Meg Luxton catalogs the differences between waged labor and domestic labor:

> For most waged workers there is a distinct separation between their workplace and home, between their co-workers and their family, between their work and their leisure. They leave their homes each workday to go off to their jobs and return at the end of the workday to rest and relax. For housewives, whose work is based on marriage and parenting, such distinctions do not exist. Housewives are not employed — they work for their husbands and children. Their work is unpaid and performed in their family home. It is therefore both private and unseen. Because their work is rooted in the intense and important relationships of the family, it seems to be a "labour of love."[40]

As we noted earlier, the emphasis on domestic work as a labor of love helped to romanticize it and disguise the fact that it was a job without

38. Ibid., p. 94.
39. Luxton, *More than a Labour of Love*; Deem, *All Work and No Play?*
40. Luxton, *More than a Labour of Love*, p. 11.

517

pay. Let's examine the aspects of domestic work that allow it to be called a "labor of love."

Quite often this "labour of love" centers on the nurturing activities of women toward their husbands and/or children. Nurturing includes activities such as managing emotions (being affectionate, bolstering egos, arbitrating disputes, etc.) and trying to see the world through the eyes of another person. And such nurturing activities often do give domestic workers a sense of purpose and emotional fulfillment.[41] However, when Sally Cline and Dale Spender took a closer look at the way in which nurturance works in the lives of male-female couples, they found that women spent a great deal of time taking care of men emotionally (something we have already noted in a previous chapter).[42] They listened to their husbands, comforted, praised, and supported them, and looked out for them, even to the extent of making sure their husbands left for work properly clothed. They worked hard at "reflecting" the men — that is, making the men feel good about themselves. The authors compare the women's nurturing style to a looking glass that reflects the men as twice their natural size.

Of course, making someone feel wonderful is not necessarily a bad thing. But Cline and Spender found that reciprocal nurturing by the men was relatively rare. In fact, women had to get a great deal of their support and care from other women rather than from their husbands. This was true even in relationships that both husband and wife characterized as egalitarian. Thus, when we speak of the home as a place of nurturance, we must think of a place where it is primarily *men and children* who receive nurturance. Women, by contrast, often feel obliged to go to their female friends outside of the home to receive emotional care.

For many women the greatest source of enjoyment in domestic labor comes from the nurturing of children: for them, that task *is* labor done with love.[43] Yet the presence — or should we say omnipresence — of children tends to make domestic work a round-the-clock job, one that has no boundaries and one that others presume will be done with endless good grace, simply out of love and caring.[44] Moreover, caring

41. Ibid.; and Oakley, *Subject Women.*
42. Cline and Spender, *Reflecting Men at Twice Their Natural Size* (New York: Seaver Books, 1987).
43. Deem, *All Work and No Play?.*
44. Doyal, "Hazards of Hearth and Home."

for young children also creates tension because it interferes with house-keeping activities. How can you keep the house neat and tidy when you have two active preschoolers? As one mother explained, "I just figured my kids were more important than clean clothes and a tidy living room. So the house was always a pigsty."[45] Another mother put it this way: "I knew I had to choose — a clean house or time with my kids. I chose the kids but I went slowly mad in that messy house."[46]

Because of women's assigned responsibility for children, we often hold them responsible for how the children "turn out." Yet this expectation overlooks the fact that children, especially those of school age, spend less than half their waking time with their mothers.[47] In combination, they spend more time with peers, at school, and in front of the TV. Other adults also influence children, as does the father's presence/absence and the quality of his relationship with his wife and children. We therefore should not hold women solely responsible for how their children "turn out." When we engage in "mother blaming," we create a no-win situation for women who do domestic work.

Men and Domestic Work

In light of the preceding discussion, some men may protest that we are regarding only women as domestic workers. They may point out that they too do chores around the home and should receive recognition for that. We recognize that men do indeed engage in domestic work, including nurturing; yet even here there is a division of labor along gender lines. This division manifests itself both in the type of tasks done and in the amount of time spent on domestic work.

The type of domestic work a man generally does is quite different from what a woman usually does.[48] For example, men tend to take on the more pleasant tasks of child care: playing with the children, reading them bedtime stories, taking them places, watching and encouraging their participation in sports.[49] Women tend to do the more routine and

45. Cited by Luxton in *More than a Labour of Love,* p. 184.
46. Cited by Luxton in ibid., p. 184.
47. Ibid.
48. Hochschild, *The Second Shift.*
49. Deem, *All Work and No Play?*

mundane tasks, such as ensuring that the children are clean and properly dressed, that they get their homework and their chores done, and that discipline is maintained. Similarly, men are more likely to do tasks outside of the home, such as mowing the lawn, washing the car, or maintaining the exterior of the house. In contrast, women are more likely to do tasks inside the home such as cooking, cleaning, laundry, and household planning.

Although on the surface this may seem like an equitable arrangement, it ignores differences in the nature of the tasks. The types of chores done by men are more likely to be occasional ones that can be done at a time of one's own choosing, whereas those done by women are often routinized, daily tasks that must be done at specific times. Men therefore tend to have control over their domestic tasks, whereas time is more likely to control when women do theirs.[50]

The total amount of time spent on domestic work also varies. Studies show that on the average a married man works 11 to 15 hours per week at domestic labor, whereas a married woman works 33 to 55.4 hours.[51] This asymmetrical division of labor shows little variation by class or by participation in the waged work-force. Instead, it seems to be a direct function of current gender relations in our culture.[52] Why do men do so little domestic work? Let's first look at some commonsense perceptions and then use a critical-theory framework to suggest an alternative answer to this question.

Common Perceptions about Men and Domestic Work

If a woman's only job is that of full-time domestic worker, then one might argue that her spending three to five times the amount of time her husband spends on domestic tasks is an equitable arrangement. Her husband may not be able to spend more time on domestic chores since he is the breadwinner and comes home tired after a full day at his

---

50. Hochschild, *The Second Shift*.
51. Luxton, *More than a Labour of Love*; Hochschild, *The Second Shift*; John Robinson, "The Hard Facts about Hard Work," *Utne Reader* 38 (March/April 1988); and Heidi Hartmann, "The Family as the Locus of Gender, Class, and Political Struggle: The Example of Housework," in *Feminism and Methodology*, ed. Sandra Harding (Bloomington: Indiana University Press, 1987), pp. 109-34.
52. Deem, *All Work and No Play?*.

workplace. The plausibility of this argument is undermined, however, by the skewed division of labor that persists even when both spouses work outside the home. We would expect that the more hours a woman works for pay outside the home and/or the more she earns, the more time her husband will contribute to domestic chores. After all, in such a situation he is no longer the only breadwinner and thus no longer carries the total financial burden. Since that burden is shared, it stands to reason that the burden of domestic work will be shared as well. But Arlie Hochschild's study of married couples in which both partners were in full-time waged employment shows that this is not the case. Only in 20 percent of such households was the domestic work evenly divided. In the remaining households, women worked the equivalent of an extra month of 24-hour days per year. Hochschild calls this "extra" work — what in effect amounts to another job — the "second shift."

In addition, the logic behind the argument that husbands need to rest when they come home from waged work ignores the fact that homemaking wives have also been working the entire day. Aren't they equally entitled to a rest? If domestic work is valuable, then shouldn't it be counted as work, regardless of the fact that it is unpaid? Meg Luxton, author of *More than a Labour of Love*, describes one unusual working-class couple, both of whom worked full-time. He did waged work in a factory; she did unpaid domestic work in the home. During the day they both worked hard at their jobs, and when he came home, they shared the remaining work equally. The wife said, "I feel this way it's really fair. We both have our set work to do and then we split everything else down the middle. This way I feel like we live together in a partnership, not that I'm being supported by him or that I have to take care of him."[53] The husband realized that his wife's work was as valuable as his and that it was also *work*. He commented,

> It feels more co-operative this way. I feel like we both pull our weight. We both have about the same amount of work to do and we both get some time off. I really like feeling equally involved with the children. And because I do the work around the house, I know just how much she has to do, so I appreciate it. It feels better — sharing things.[54]

53. Cited by Luxton in *More than a Labour of Love*, p. 212.
54. Cited by Luxton in ibid., p. 212. See also Diane Ehrensaft's *Parenting*

We would all do well to emulate this couple!

In light of the preceding discussion, some may also argue that even when both husband and wife work full-time for pay, a husband cannot be as involved in domestic work as his wife is because his career is usually in a male-dominated area and is thus likely to pay more. Consequently, he may still have greater responsibility for the economic stability of the household than his wife does. But again, the earlier argument applies: Regardless of the nature and responsibility of one's job, both spouses *work*. In addition, if this reasoning were valid, one would assume that household chores would at least be evenly divided in marriages where wife and husband earn the same amount. But Hochschild has shown that this is not the case. Only 30 percent of the husbands who earned the same salary as their wives shared domestic work equally. And *none* of the husbands who earned *less* than their wives shared domestic work equally, let alone did more than 50 percent of it![55]

In addition, it is a questionable assumption that men experience more stress than women in the waged workplace. On the basis of her summary of the literature about such stress, Lesley Doyal concluded that women experience more stress than do men.[56] In fact, domestic *or* waged workers who are highly involved in supporting others experience more stress and burnout than those in executive positions, a point that we will discuss further in the following chapter.

Often linked with the assumption that men's jobs are more stressful is the idea that men's jobs take more time. Thus it is presumed that even if men are willing to do more domestic work, they simply don't have the time to do it. But this assumption is at odds with research showing that husbands actually have more leisure time and engage in more leisure activities than do their wives who also work full-time in the paid labor force.[57] If men have time to engage in leisure activities, surely they have time to do domestic work! In fact, as we showed earlier in this section, it is women who need more leisure time. The women interviewed by sociologists such as Rosemary Deem, Arlie Hochschild, and Meg Luxton

---

Together: Men and Women Sharing the Care of Their Children (Champaign: University of Illinois Press, 1987).

55. Hochschild, *The Second Shift.*
56. Doyal, "Waged Work and Women's Well-Being."
57. Deem, *All Work and No Play?.*

talked of being tired all the time, of never having enough sleep, and of having little or no time for leisure activities.

Some may appeal to the nineteenth-century assumption that women do more domestic labor because they have some innate ability for it. But if these skills are innately "feminine," then what explains the multitude of male experts, such as Dr. Spock and Dr. Brazelton, and the host of male pedagogues on TV telling women how best to clean their sinks? And why is it that when domestic tasks (with the exception of child care) become *waged* jobs, they are filled primarily by men—as in the case of dishwashers, cooks, janitors, pastors, licensed counselors, and so on?[58]

Others may appeal to the socialization perspective to explain men's minimal involvement in domestic work. They may argue that men simply have not *learned* to cook, sew, clean, or raise children. But Hochschild reviewed studies that examine the validity of such an argument and concluded that a man's socialization is only slightly related to the amount and kind of domestic work he does as an adult. In addition, if men, by virtue of their socialization, cannot do such things as cooking and cleaning, how do *non*married men survive? Some men may appeal to their faulty socialization simply as an excuse to escape domestic work! The flip side of this notion is that women are "properly" socialized to do domestic work. But we cannot assume that every woman is socialized to be a paragon of domestic skills. As noted earlier, the plethora of experts, advice and how-to books, cooking classes, and household hints printed in newspapers and periodicals indicate that women also have to learn the details of domestic labor.

Men's Agency and Domestic Work

As we have stressed in various chapters throughout this book, gender relations are constructed and reconstructed through hegemony and agency. Consequently, it should come as no surprise that men intentionally exercise agency to limit the time they spend on domestic work. Hochschild details some strategies that men use to avoid or minimize

58. Samuel Cohn, *The Process of Occupational Sex-Typing: The Feminization of Clerical Labor in Great Britain,* Women in the Political Economy series, ed. Ronnie J. Steinberg (Philadelphia: Temple University Press, 1985).

their participation in household tasks. She calls these "strategies of resistance." One such strategy is disaffiliation, or doing a task incompetently, such as shrinking clothes while washing them, burning food while making supper, breaking glasses while drying them, or buying the wrong products while shopping. The wives of such men are likely to conclude that doing the chores themselves is easier and less damaging than having their husbands do them.

A second strategy of resistance is what Hochschild calls "need reduction." The man who doesn't want to go to the grocery store says, "We don't need to shop; there's enough food in the house." The man who doesn't want to clean says, "We don't need to dust or vacuum. The house is clean enough as it is." Consequently, if the woman in this situation feels that shopping or cleaning needs to be done, she has to do it herself.

A third strategy consists of substitute offerings. That is, instead of actually doing domestic labor, men offer their wives various kinds of support. "If you can't do all the housework, let's hire a maid." They may affirm their wives' discipline of the children. They may buy "labor-saving" devices. They may encourage their wives to take adult education classes (as long as these don't interfere with domestic work). In these and other ways husbands obscure their neglect of domestic tasks by employing alternative support strategies.

A fourth strategy of resistance used by men, often in conjunction with substitute offerings, is selective encouragement. These men continually praise the domestic work done by their wives. "I couldn't do my work without the help of my wife" or "Jane is such a good mother" are commonly made comments. But these men use such praise to obscure the question of why they aren't working hard at parenting, or why they don't do more domestic labor and become experts at it themselves.

Women and Domestic Work

One may wonder why women continue to, in the words of Heidi Hartmann, "maintain a family life which is oppressive."[59] Why don't *they* act, exerting more pressure on men to increase their involvement in domestic

59. Hartmann, "The Family as the Locus of Gender, Class, and Political Struggle," p. 109.

work? Both Hochschild and Hartmann cite vulnerability as a primary reason. Since a woman generally earns less than a man, she is likely to need a husband and his goodwill for economic reasons. Moreover, a woman usually does not have the same background support as a man, support that would enable her to work long hours, to have a better-paying job, or even to put her career first. It is the rare woman who has a "two-person single career" — that is, a career which presumes a second person who takes care of her needs, the children, and the home so that she can concentrate on her waged job.[60] Finally, the statistics on the pauperization of women show that single women with children are disproportionately represented in the number of people living below the poverty line. Thus, despite its drawbacks, marriage — however inequitable it may be in some ways — may provide some women with short-term economic security. Accordingly, by choosing this option, women exercise agency. The security they gain with this option, however, is heavily dependent on both the altruism and the longevity of the husband, and as we indicated earlier, marriage no longer guarantees long-term financial security for women.[61] Consequently, many women may work a "double shift" as part of a larger implicit agreement or "bargain" made with their husbands, a bargain that reads something like, "I [the man] will pool my financial resources with you, but only as long as you don't demand a fair division of domestic labor between us."

Hochschild found that women whose household partners did a minor amount of the domestic work had another reason for putting up with this inequitable arrangement: gratitude. Since their husbands did more domestic work than *most* men, these women (as well as their husbands) saw this work as a gift and as evidence of the man's exceptionality, and so felt that they should be grateful for it. If, however, we compare the domestic work done by these men to that done by their female colleagues in the workplace, then their contributions seem obviously inequitable. Should women be grateful for inequity? And if women set the norms for domestic involvement, shouldn't we compare male workers to women workers rather than to other men?

60. Indeed, it could even be said that many white-collar male workers have a "three-person single career," since they have female helpers in the form of both their wives *and* their secretaries. In fact, secretaries are often jokingly referred to as "office wives."

61. Weitzman, *The Divorce Revolution.*

Another reason women may continue to do most of the domestic work is that home is usually the only place where they have some degree of control, where they are somewhat their own bosses, and where they can exercise agency that is not so circumscribed.[62] In the waged workplace, women may encounter the tyranny of unfair labor practices, sexual harassment, and the public devaluation of women and their work. By contrast, work in the home, although it involves many routinized tasks, is something over which women have some measure of control, and if they love and are loved by their children, they are able to nurture and sometimes to be nurtured.

In summary, then, many women assume responsibility for a great deal of domestic work because of economic vulnerability, gratitude, and the desire for a measure of independence and satisfaction in the work they do. Yet women often exhibit agency within such constraints. If they are full-time domestic workers, they can often follow *their* own schedule, at least when their husbands are out of the house. (This is perhaps the source of the misperception that full-time domestic workers have a great deal of leisure time. Perhaps *any* time that is not directly devoted to the husband is considered "leisure" time.) Many women also have a network of friends who offer advice and support and who reduce their isolation. In addition, these networks enable women to work collectively, doing things such as taking care of each other's children, shopping for one another, working together on heavy cleaning tasks, and car pooling.

Women also actively construct meanings about their presence or absence in the paid labor force. However, this agency is also constrained by structural forces, as Kathleen Gerson discovered. In a study of working-class and middle-class women, Gerson found that 90 percent of the women who were primarily domestic workers had previously experienced limited mobility in the paid labor force.[63] It seems that they regarded caring for children and a household as a relatively positive alternative to the frustrations they had experienced in their paid work. (Recall from the last chapter that working-class women in the Third

---

62. Strasser, *Never Done.*

63. Gerson, "What Do Women Want from Men?: Men's Influence on Women's Work and Family Choices," in *Changing Men: New Directions in Research on Men and Masculinity,* ed. Michael S. Kimmel (Newbury Park, Calif.: Sage Publications, 1987), pp. 115-30.

World often express similar sentiments.) These women knew, however, that their position as homemakers was financially precarious. Consequently, they assumed responsibility for most of the domestic labor. This allowed their husbands to have a "two-person single career," but it also made their husbands dependent on them to "keep the home fires burning." Ironically, it was also their own financial insecurity that made these women fight against policies which would make life easier for women in the paid labor force. They felt that as long as women encountered barriers in their paid work, it would be more difficult for their own husbands to reject the role of breadwinner. This strategy echoes that of the women interviewed by Ellen Rosen: by stressing that their own pay was only "supplemental" to that of their husbands, these working-class women sustained the "man-as-breadwinner" ideology.[64]

In contrast, Gerson found that women who worked full-time for pay had often begun their marriages with primarily domestic aspirations.[65] However, they later took work outside of the home for financial reasons, because their husbands were unable to bring home a "family wage." They also distrusted the long-term security of marriage and thus intended to be financially secure as a hedge against the future, a future made more secure if they received support from their bosses, usually male, in their quest for job advancement. Gerson concluded that choices about domestic work are often constrained choices and may pit women against women in their quest for security. Her study also shows how domestic and paid work influence each other in a dynamic and sometimes negative way.

As we have seen in the foregoing discussion, the norm of female domesticity persists — if not in practice, then at least as an ideal. This may in part be due to hegemonic factors related to the current structure of gender relations. With this in mind, let's use a critical theory framework to examine domestic work.

---

64. Rosen, *Bitter Choices.* A similar strategy underlies some women's opposition to divorce. Some women who picketed against more lenient divorce laws in Ireland in the 1980s displayed signs reading, "A woman who votes for easier divorce laws is like a turkey voting for Christmas!"

65. Gerson, "What Do Women Want from Men?"

Domestic Work from the Viewpoint of Critical Theory

Through the lens of critical theory, we see the home as a place where dominant meanings about gender get reproduced, challenged, and revised.[66] It is a place where both women and men are agents, but where the agency of women is often more circumscribed than that of men. In a predominantly monied economy, the dependence of women on men for financial security sustains male dominance on the structural level if not on the individual level. Capitalist owners who regard women as a surplus labor pool, husbands who do little or no domestic work, men who block women's advancement in the waged workplace, men who preach that a woman's place is in the home — all of these help to strengthen male dominance at the societal level. In addition, as we noted earlier, hegemonic masculinity is associated with waged work, and male dominance is sustained by this association of masculinity with paid work. If a man's masculinity is confirmed by his weekly paycheck, then why should he engage in additional, nonpaid work? This equation of masculinity with paid employment helps explain why unemployment is difficult for men even apart from the economic burden it imposes.[67]

This argument is not completely satisfactory, however. Men *do* engage in unpaid work — as school-board members, elders and deacons, fund-raisers, Boy Scout leaders, volunteer coaches, and so on. Doing unpaid labor is therefore not necessarily incongruent with hegemonic masculinity. Possibly, then, it is the *nature* of the unpaid labor and its positive or negative association with masculinity or femininity that determines the degree with which it is valued or devalued. If household work is associated with women, with dependence, *and* with unpaid and "unproductive" labor, then many men will not readily engage in it. Indeed, the failure of Western nations to include work done in the home in the calculation of the GDP (Gross Domestic Product) is indicative of society's general attitude toward the importance of this work.[68] This

66. See, for example, Deem's *All Work and No Play?* and Luxton's *More than a Labour of Love.*

67. Deem, *All Work and No Play?.*

68. For a more detailed analysis of this failure, see Marilyn Waring's book entitled *If Women Counted: A New Feminist Economics* (San Francisco: Harper & Row, 1989). It should be noted that many developing nations *do* include unpaid labor (as well as goods exchanged for barter rather than money) in the calculation of their gross domestic product.

attitude is also reflected in the difficulty women have in claiming domestic work on their job resumés as providing a worthy background for entry into the paid work-force. By contrast, activities such as being a Boy Scout leader, a church elder, or a school-board member usually enhance men's resumés.[69]

Possibilities for Change

A discussion of unpaid domestic work requires a discussion of waged work as well. But before we embark on that discussion, we want to mention briefly a few strategies for bringing about change with respect to domestic work. We do so with the full understanding that these changes depend on changes in the nature of waged work, and that both kinds of changes ultimately depend on a redefinition of hegemonic masculinity and privileged femininity in ways that diminish power differentials.

First, we need to value domestic work on a societal level. If it is truly valuable, then why not include it in the calculation of the GDP? Second, women need to be released from carrying the major responsibility for child care. If two people decide to have a child, then surely that child and its upbringing are the responsibility of both parents and/or other adults. Although little research has been done on fathers who "mother," Arlie Hochschild summarizes that research, pointing out that the more involved a father is with feeding, disciplining, and caring for his children, the better the children develop intellectually and emotionally.[70] Whether or not this enhanced development is a result of father-presence per se or merely of the involved presence of another adult is unclear at this time. It is possible that children need to bond with and receive sustained nurturing from more than one adult in order to develop in a holistic manner. Fathers and/or other adults besides mothers need to provide that nurturing for children. In many churches, congregations vow to share the responsibility for the upbringing of a child when it is

---

69. Obviously, celebrating Mother's Day annually does little to elevate the status of domestic work. Likewise, the celebration of Secretary's Day obscures the fact that clerical work is grossly underpaid.

70. Hochschild, *The Second Shift.* See also Ehrensaft's *Parenting Together* and Kyle Pruett's book entitled *The Nurturing Father* (New York: Warner Books, 1987).

baptized. We should begin to take that vow seriously by not allowing situations to develop where women are the primary caregivers of children. Perhaps we need to reclaim the idea of involved godparents as well.[71] The black community offers many examples of how kinship and friendship networks permit and encourage more than one adult to be involved in the raising of a child. Perhaps the white community needs to examine those examples and adapt them or even adopt them.

Men should provide nurture not only to children but to women and other men as well. Engaging in nurturance can be a very revolutionary and perhaps even scary prospect for many men. Those who say they don't know how to do it can develop the skill by learning from and "practicing on" women and children. If their wives are in the paid labor force, men will also need to make certain adjustments with respect to the management of emotions and nurturing, according to Meg Luxton:

> When women work a double shift, they let certain aspects of domestic labor go. It is often attention to the most invisible aspects which decreases first. Tension managing and catering to the husband's needs are often drastically reduced. . . . Women reeling under the strain of their double work load cannot provide the same attention, sensitivity and concern for their husband's needs as fulltime domestic workers can. Such husbands have to "fend for themselves" more often.[72]

Thus men need to take more responsibility for their own emotions and to share in the more general management of the family's emotions.

Third, if we wish to create a just and caring community, then men, in their caring for women and in their quest for justice, cannot continue to let women work a double shift. Men also need to do domestic work so that their wives can develop their gifts in the paid work world without feeling continually fatigued and overstressed. If we are to be responsible

71. Catholic theologian James Burtchaell offers the following observation on the intrinsically social task of child-raising: "Psychologists and the media have reminded us recently of the inadequacy of the one-parent home. But the church has always been aware that the *two-parent* home is inadequate. In many traditions, godparents are a part of the baptismal service; the family is thereby augmented by fellow believers who pledge themselves to help the neophyte grow in faith, and who stand as proxies for all those dozens of people that each of us needs, beside our family, to be able to make the journey from selfishness to love" ("Make Room for Baby," *Christianity Today*, 11 November 1991, p. 43).

72. Luxton, *More than a Labour of Love*, pp. 190-91.

stewards of creation, we need to make it possible for all people to use their gifts fully. The world is beset by problems: the dehumanization of labor, the destruction of the environment, persecution and oppression, and so on. Surely we need to employ the creativity and ideas of all people rather than just those of a privileged few. People should be assigned their tasks in paid and unpaid labor not on the basis of their gender, age, race, ethnicity, or class, but on the basis of their gifts. We need to provide a climate in which such gifts can be discovered and developed.

Men should also engage in domestic labor because each adult needs to be responsible for his or her own personal maintenance. Nonmarried persons who live together are quite capable of rotating chores, sharing responsibility for communal areas, and taking responsibility for their own upkeep without too many problems. We call this the "friendship model." Yet when people marry or have children, they often seem to fall back on the gendered division of labor described earlier. We therefore need to make greater use of the "friendship model" in the home if we are to achieve the goal of fairness in the division of domestic labor. This model should also apply to nurturing: women and men should equitably share responsibilities for nurturance in the family.

Both women and men need to take on their fair share of routinized and more occasional household tasks and other domestic responsibilities. It is even possible that women should do somewhat fewer tasks, since (as we saw earlier) they often experience more stress at the workplace than do men. Basically, each adult in a household should be able to manage every routine task, so that if one adult falls sick, goes away for a few days, or must work overtime, tasks are not neglected. No longer should a woman who is going away for a week have to spend extra energy cooking and freezing meals beforehand and then when she returns be faced with a mountain of laundry and a dirty house. In addition, if all members — including children as they are able — learn how to do each task, the traditional gendered division of labor will break down.

Men who take on a more equitable share of domestic labor need to be ready to assume a subordinate role at times. We have heard men who do some domestic work complain that it often has to be done according to the norms and schedules set by their wives. They want to do it their way and at their leisure. But as Hochschild points out, women often end up being the time managers in the household and thus often *do* know best when and how a task should be done.[73] Men need to recognize that their quest for their own norms and schedules is a struggle for control over a female-dominated job. When a woman begins a new job, she, like everyone else, has to follow company rules and schedules and be willing to learn from her manager. The situation is similar when a man takes on more household responsibilities: he needs to be willing to learn rather than immediately trying to take control and do it "his" way.

Fourth, every woman should have economic security and should be made aware of her vulnerability if she lacks it. The practical reality is simply that, in our society, women who do household labor without compensation are in extremely vulnerable positions, as a group called the Westchester Radical Feminists has pointed out:

> We [as wives] live in comfort only to the extent that our homes, clothing, and the services we receive feed and prop the status and egos of the men who support us. Like dogs on a leash, our own status and power will reach as far as our husbands and their income and prestige will allow. As human beings, as individuals, we in fact own very little and should our husbands leave us or us them, we will find ourselves with the care and responsibility of children without money, jobs, credit or power.[74]

One possibility for ensuring women's financial security is through payment for domestic work. Such payment may not necessarily have to be in the form of an hourly wage; it might also be given in the form of insurance benefits, a monthly government allowance, investments, and so on. Yet there is a troubling aspect to this solution of wages for domestic work: it reinforces both a gendered division of labor and the idea that women are the primary caregivers and domestic workers in our society. Women can gain a measure of financial security by working for wages outside the home. Obviously, the extent of this security depends on the degree to which women's and men's labor is equitably rewarded. This is a topic we will discuss in the next chapter.

Fifth, if we need other strategies for reorganizing domestic work, then perhaps we should look at those used by black families. Maxine

---

73. Hochschild, *The Second Shift*.

74. Westchester Radical Feminists, quoted by Catharine Mackinnon in *Toward a Feminist Theory of the State* (Cambridge: Harvard University Press, 1989), p. 270.

Baca Zinn has shown how blacks have a history of encountering situations which are then later faced by white, middle-class families. She says, "With respect to single-parent families, teenage childbirth, working mothers, and a host of other behaviors, Black families serve as barometers of social change and as forerunners of adaptive patterns that will be progressively experienced by the more privileged sectors of American society."[75] If we truly desire to change the situation, we can do so. We should bear in mind that our current gendered ideas about domestic work are relatively "new."

Semper reformanda is a motto coined in the context of the Reformation. It asserts that Christians can and should always be reforming themselves and their world. That reformation should embrace all of life, of which domestic work is an important component. In the following chapter we will consider ways of reforming gender relations in waged work settings, in the full recognition that domestic and waged work are inextricably linked.

75. Zinn, "Family, Feminism, and Race in America," p. 79.

CHAPTER 16

Pink, White, and Blue Collars:
Gender and Waged Work

In our society, as we saw in the last chapter, women are disproportionately responsible for domestic work. This happens for a variety
of reasons, many of which are related to the structure of waged labor.
In fact, domestic and waged work are intertwined in a way that often
privileges males. That is, collectively men use their engagement in paid
work to sustain hegemonic masculinity, even though they may do a
certain amount of domestic work. Yet women are not only responsible
for a great deal of domestic work; many of them also engage in paid
work. How then can men use paid work to strengthen hegemonic
masculinity and keep women in a subordinate position? To answer this
question, we need to explore how the dynamics of waged work give
meaning to gender and interact with the dynamics of domestic work.

We will first take a look at popular explanations for the sex segregation of jobs and occupations, and then take a second look at this
practice using a critical-theory framework. After examining the process
by which people are granted or denied entry into specific jobs, we will
focus on the workplace itself as a setting that creates and reproduces

The primary author of this chapter is Annelies Knoppers.

534

meanings about gender. We will close with some general suggestions for change, although we will be making specific suggestions throughout the chapter.

Although all societies practice a gendered division of waged labor, there is great cultural variety in the actual tasks assigned to women.[1] For example, while secretarial work is considered a woman's or "pink-collar" job in America, in Morocco it is an occupation dominated by men. While medicine is dominated by men in America, it is dominated by women in Russia. Regardless of culture, however, men's activities tend to be assigned greater social status and economic reward than women's. Women, being valued less than men, tend to be assigned to unpaid domestic work and low-paying jobs.[2] Overall, men predominate in the highest-paying, "white collar" and professional jobs in the United States. None of the five best-paid occupations for women pay as well as the top five for men. The lowest-ranking of these five occupations for women pays a median salary that is $14,500 lower than the lowest median salary for men. By contrast, women predominate in six of the eight lowest-paying kinds of work (employment as practical nurses, sewers and stitchers, child-care workers, hairdressers, nurses' aides, and health-care workers). The lowest-paying "blue collar" jobs for men pay a median of ninety dollars more per week than the lowest-paying of the female-dominated jobs (employment as workers in the food-service industry and farm workers). Child-care workers employed in private households are the most poorly paid of all, receiving only a median weekly wage of ninety dollars.[3]

The sex segregation of waged labor has a direct impact on a person's pay and thus on his or her ability to live above the poverty line.

1. Jerry A. Jacobs, *Revolving Doors: Sex Segregation and Women's Careers* (Stanford: Stanford University Press, 1989).
2. In the United States, for example, the highest-paid occupations for women and men tend to be in law. (In 1986, the median salary for women was $32,448; for men, $42,912.) The other four highest-paid occupations for women, from highest to lowest, are in engineering, computer science, medicine, and educational administration. The other four highest-paid occupations for men are employment as economists, airplane pilots and navigators, personnel and labor relations managers, and managers in marketing, advertising, and public relations. See Sara Rix's *American Woman, 1988-1989: A Status Report* (New York: W. W. Norton, 1988); and the Ministry of Labour document entitled *Equality between Men and Women in Sweden: Government Policy to the Mid-Nineties* (Stockholm, Sweden, 1988).
3. Ibid.

It is clear that, like men, many women need to work for pay. However, it is also clear that when women engage in waged work, they are likely to end up in female-dominated jobs. As statistics routinely show, these are the jobs that pay the least and yield weekly wages below the poverty line — examples include employment as retail sales workers, cashiers, workers in the food-service industry, and nursing aides.[4] Women thus need to have easier access to better-paying jobs, but currently those jobs are male-dominated. If we were to have had a fully integrated work-force in the United States in 1989, 59 percent of all women would have had to change jobs!

It is true that women have begun to enter male-dominated jobs in record numbers; what is less well known is the fact that women frequently *leave* male-dominated jobs. Jerry Jacobs found that only about half of the women who had entered male-dominated occupations could be found in those jobs ten years later, and that the women who left tended to move to female-dominated occupations. He concluded that there was a disproportionately high likelihood that women in nontraditional (i.e., male-dominated) jobs would make this change.

Although we will detail the reasons for and the results of this practice later on, at this point we can say in summary that besides being a graphic example of inequality in American society and a phenomenon that shapes the nature and power structure of the family as well as playing a large part in the pauperization of women, such "job channeling" also limits the use of women's talents and creativity within society. If Christians are to fulfill the cultural mandate, then they need to recognize the sinfulness of underusing, undervaluing, and underpaying women's talents.

Since sex segregation by job has its greatest negative impact on women, we will examine it in the following sections mainly from the viewpoint of women. However, men will also be visible, since the gendered division of labor is a key component in the current construction of gender relations.

4. Lorraine Sorrell, "What Women Are Worth," *Off Our Backs* 20 (February 1990): 4, 29.
5. Jacobs, *Revolving Doors.*

Individually Oriented Explanations:
Sex-Role Socialization Theory and Human Capital Theory

Why is there sex segregation? Why do women and men work in different jobs and occupations? Sex-role socialization theory and human capital theory both try to explain sex segregation in terms of gendered interests and choices. As we explained in an earlier chapter, sex-role socialization theory assumes that we learn what is appropriately gendered behavior in our childhood and adolescence from family, religious institutions, schools, peers, and the media. The assumption is that we have internalized these views by the time we reach adulthood, which leads us to choose certain occupations as a result of our acquired interests and skills.[6]

A second but similar theory sees wage differences as a result of differences in human capital, which in the paid work-world is usually defined by formal job qualifications such as experience and education.[7] This theory assumes that education plays a major role in determining one's location in the job market. The less experience and education one has, the lower the wages one can earn. Moreover, according to human-capital theory, people choose occupations on a rational, economic basis as they try to "maximize their utility." For example, Gary Becker, a Nobel prize-winning human-capital theorist, argues that sex-segregated work comes about because women *choose* careers in which few skills are needed (that is, minimal human capital) because they see such jobs as domestically advantageous: if women take time out to raise children, the skills required are not diminished very much.[8] According to human-capital theory, women are assumed to prefer jobs that do not penalize work interruptions by depreciating their skills, do not involve excessive overtime or travel, and are flexible in case of domestic emergencies. In addition, human-capital theory assumes that the traditional arrangement of the white, middle-class family is the result of a rational assessment

6. Cynthia Fuchs Epstein, *Deceptive Distinctions: Sex, Gender and the Social Order* (New Haven: Yale University Press/Russell Sage Foundation, 1988).

7. Mary H. Stevenson, "Some Economic Approaches to the Persistence of Wage Differences between Men and Women," in *Women Working: Theories and Facts in Perspective,* ed. Ann Stromberg and Shirley Harkess, 2d ed. (Mountain View, Calif.: Mayfield, 1988), pp. 87-100.

8. Becker, "Human Capital, Effort, and Sexual Division of Labor," *Journal of Labor Economics* 3 (1985): 533-58.

by both spouses of the job market, their individual child-raising responsibilities, and the gendered wage gap.[9]

For example, consider the real-life case of a couple, a counseling psychologist named John and a journalist named Jane, who had three young children. Much as Jane wanted to get back into journalism after being at home for several years with the children, the "rational" choice for balancing their budget was to have John do more after-hours counseling. After all, he could earn more by putting in those few extra hours than Jane, with her fewer and more outdated credentials, could earn in an entire week! Human-capital theory would laud this as both a "free" and a "rational" choice.

As this overview makes clear, both sex-role socialization theory and human-capital theory see sex segregation in the workplace primarily as a result of individual choice, in the context of previous socialization and/or of a free market system.[10] On this account, sex-segregation patterns could change only if changes in socialization practices were paralleled by changes in the labor market and/or the structure of the home and family.

A Critique of These Theories

Both these approaches explain sex segregation only in terms of individual, gendered interests and choices, thus overlooking other factors that may be operative. For example, socialization theory seems to suggest not only that we are "fixed" by our early childhood experiences but that we all absorb the same ideology and behavioral patterns. But from both a Christian and a critical-theory perspective, we are *actors*, not simply unreflective reactors. Even in our formative years we often critically reflect on our socialization, and our learning, evaluation, and self-transformation do not stop once we reach adulthood.

In fact, the overall contribution of early socialization to eventual

---

9. Epstein, *Deceptive Distinctions*.

10. Paula England and Lori McCreary, "Integrating Sociology and Economics to Study Gender and Work," in *Women and Work*, vol. 2, ed. Ann Stromberg, Laurie Larwood, and Barbara Gutek (Newbury Park, Calif.: Sage Publications, 1987), pp. 143-72; and Barbara Reskin and Heidi Hartmann, *Women's Work, Men's Work: Sex Segregation on the Job* (Washington: National Academy Press, 1986).

job choice seems to be minimal,[11] in part because changes in technology mean that jobs frequently change and new kinds of jobs are developed. For example, twenty years ago, jobs in "information management" and "fitness management" were virtually nonexistent; now they abound. In addition, Jerry Jacobs has shown that people's vocational aspirations tend to have short life-spans, and that variations in job structure require frequent adjustments in vocational goals.[12] Similarly, Kathleen Gerson did a study of women engaged in waged and domestic work and found that the decisions these women made concerning work were shaped more by their adult experiences than by their socialization as children.[13] Studies like these show that most people have very fluid career patterns or labor histories, much of which cannot be explained by childhood socialization.

Socialization and human-capital theories may partially explain occupational segregation, but they fail to explain why job segregation occurs even within occupations where we would expect otherwise.[14] As we pointed out in the last chapter, women do not dominate jobs that require skills traditionally associated with them; for example, women do not constitute the majority of professional counselors, elementary-school principals, short-order cooks, or child-care experts. And sex segregation occurs within major occupational groupings even when there are few if any gender differences in educational attainment.[15]

More specifically, although educational attainment may explain variation in wages among men, it fails to account for the gendered wage

11. Margaret M. Marina and Mary C. Brinton, "Sex Typing and Occupational Socialization," in *Sex Segregation in the Workplace: Trends, Explanations, Remedies,* ed. Barbara Reskin (Washington: National Academy Press, 1984), pp. 192-232; and Reskin and Hartmann, *Women's Work, Men's Work.*

12. Jacobs, *Revolving Doors.*

13. Gerson, "What Do Women Want from Men? Men's Influence on Women's Work and Family Choices," in *Changing Men: New Directions in Research on Men and Masculinity,* ed. Michael S. Kimmel (Newbury Park, Calif.: Sage Publications, 1987), pp. 115-30.

14. Samuel Cohn, *The Process of Occupational Sex-Typing: The Feminization of Clerical Labor in Great Britain,* Women in the Political Economy series, ed. Ronnie J. Steinberg (Philadelphia: Temple University Press, 1985); Janice Moulton and Francine Rainone, "Women's Work and Sex Roles," in *Beyond Domination: New Perspectives on Women and Philosophy,* ed. Carol C. Gould (Totowa, N.J.: Rowman & Allanheld, 1984), pp. 189-203.

15. Jacobs, *Revolving Doors.*

gap. For example, there are male-dominated jobs requiring little human capital (skill or training). These include jobs as farm workers, parking attendants, gas-station attendants, and custodians; in these jobs women comprise less than a third of the workers. Yet such jobs pay better than their low-skilled, female-dominated counterparts.[16] If education is the chief determinative factor, why aren't there more women in these male-dominated jobs? Analogously, if women-dominated jobs require as little skill as human-capital theory suggests, why don't these jobs have just as many unskilled men as women in them? Not all men begin their work in the labor force with acquired skills;[17] in fact, overall, women and men have similar levels of education. Yet this tends not to translate into unlimited access to jobs for women or into salaries that reflect their educational level.[18]

The human-capital perspective also assumes that women's absence from the labor market leads to a deterioration of skills. But some researchers have shown that only 3 percent of the wage gap can be accounted for by differences between men and women in work interruption.[19] In addition, we should not overlook the fact that men also interrupt their work for such things as leaves of absence, participation in military service, jury duty, and running for and holding political office. Yet rarely is it assumed that such an absence leads to a deterioration in a man's human capital; indeed, often the activities a man pursues during the absence are assumed to *enhance* his job resumé. Yet we might well ask this question of men who take time out for military service: For which jobs in the civilian work-force does learning to kill, to conduct warfare, and to endure physical intimidation really enhance one's human capital? Why would taking an academic leave of absence necessarily enhance one's skills more than taking a leave of absence to care for one's parents or children? The caregiving skills that one acquires while taking

16. Epstein, *Deceptive Distinctions;* and Rix, *The American Woman, 1988-1989.*

17. Cynthia Cockburn, *Machinery of Dominance: Women, Men and Technical Knowhow* (London: Pluto Press, 1985).

18. See, for example, the article by Annelies Knoppers et al. entitled "Gender and the Salaries of Coaches," *Sociology of Sport Journal* 6 (1989): 348-61; Jacobs, *Revolving Doors;* Cohn, *The Process of Occupational Sex-Typing;* and Moulton and Rainone, "Women's Work and Sex Roles."

19. M. Corcoran and G. Duncan, "Work History, Labor Force Attachment, and Earnings Differences between the Races and the Sexes," *Journal of Human Resources* 14 (1979): 3-20.

care of children or aging parents may be the kind of skills needed in the marketplace as well! The narrow definition of human capital fails to take into account the competencies acquired and the qualities developed in nonpaying jobs.[20]

In addition, the human-capital approach simply assumes a traditional family model in which women are the ones primarily responsible for domestic work. It ignores the possibility that the structure of the waged workplace is in part *responsible* for the division of labor along gender lines within a marriage. It also overlooks the possibility that different families may have different dynamics, and that not every woman has primary responsibility for the household.[21] Moreover, if it is women's household responsibilities that constrain their job choices, then why do women without children and women past early child-raising age still enter female-dominated occupations rather than the better-paying male-dominated occupations? These women will probably work full-time for pay until retirement and thus are "just as good a risk" as men. If employers truly preferred a stable labor force, as they claim to, they would hire women primarily from these two groups. Instead, when they hire women at all, they hire younger married and single women.[22]

Human-capital theory would lead us to expect that single women would be very much like men in terms of occupational attainment. But Patricia Roos has found that single women were just as likely as married women to be in female-dominated occupations.[23] The attainment pattern of never-married women is more like that of their married sisters than like that of men. Never-married women are like men in that they are likely to work full-time for pay, yet the kinds of work they tend to do link them to married women. Human-capital theory fails to explain these patterns.

Finally, human-capital theory seems to confer too much economic rationality on the labor market. If women can be paid less than men for comparable work in our profit-driven economy, why do employers per-

20. See Marilyn Waring's book entitled *If Women Counted: A New Feminist Economics* (San Francisco: Harper & Row, 1989).

21. Barrie Thorne, "Feminist Rethinking of the Family: An Overview," in *Rethinking the Family: Some Feminist Questions,* ed. Barrie Thorne with Marilyn Yalom (New York: Longman, 1982), pp. 1-24.

22. Cohn, *The Process of Occupational Sex-Typing.*

23. Patricia Roos, *Gender and Work: A Comparative Analysis of Industrial Societies* (Albany, N.Y.: State University of New York Press, 1985).

sist in favoring men for certain jobs? According to this theory, the choice made by John the psychologist and Jane the journalist are to be lauded as a result of rational consideration. However, for the couple involved (both of whom are gender egalitarians), it was a choice they made reluctantly and temporarily, with a lot of resentment toward the social forces that pushed them into it.

In summary, both sex-role socialization theory and human-capital theory explain sex segregation of the job market in terms of the interests and choices of the individual woman. Although these may function as a partial explanation of this phenomenon, they do not account for much of the gendered wage gap. Because both of these approaches are flawed, researchers have shifted away from these individually focused perspectives and have begun to focus more on the role played by societal structures. Two such structural approaches are the one proposed by Marxists and the one proposed by "organizational" theorists. We will summarize and evaluate these now, before returning to the critical-theory perspective that has helped us understand gender relations in previous parts of this book.

Structural Approaches

The Marxist Theory

The structural approach was initially grounded in Marxist thought. Its argument is that sex segregation in capitalist countries is more a function of the need for profit-making on the part of industries than it is of the interests and choices of women.[24] But although this perspective acknowledges the important role of capitalism in contributing to sex segregation, it seems to be unable to explain the existence of sex segregation of jobs in socialist countries. Moreover, public funding of both child care and domestic work in these countries has routinely been upstaged by industrial, military, and other budgets, leaving women with the continuing burden of the "second shift." Such developments strongly suggest

24. See Robert W. Connell's *Gender and Power: Society, the Person and Sexual Politics* (Stanford: Stanford University Press, 1987); and Jeff Hearn and Wendy Parkin's "Gender and Organizations: A Selective Review and a Critique of a Neglected Area," *Organization Studies* 4 (1983): 219-42.

that sex segregation is not merely a fallout of capitalism but a primary problem in itself. In addition, the Marxist approach stresses an economic determinism that privileges class above all other social relations. Accordingly, economic structure cannot be cast as the sole determinant of a gendered labor market.[25]

The Organizational Approach

By contrast, the approach based on an internal labor market or organization focuses on the structure of the workplace, rather than that of the economy as a whole, and on how this structure constrains individual choice and determines the work that various people end up doing. According to this view, wage differences across gender and race are based on one's position in the workplace. That is, women and minorities are kept in lower positions, and it is the location of those positions that plays a large role in determining both wage differences and work-related behavior.[26]

Those who use this organizational approach to study sex segregation and the gendered wage gap concentrate on hiring and firing practices, the influences of networks, the nature of a given job, available career opportunities, the distribution of power, and the ratio of women

25. A great deal of scholarly work has focused on the interaction of class and gender relations with respect to domestic and waged work. See, for example, Heidi Hartmann's "Capitalism, Patriarchy, and Job Segregation by Sex," *Signs* 1 (1976): 137-69; V. Nieva's "Equity for Women at Work: Models of Change," in *Sex Role Stereotyping and Affirmative Action Policy,* ed. Barbara Gutek (Los Angeles: UCLA Institute of Industrial Relations, 1982), pp. 125-227; Paula Rothenberg's "Political Nature of Relations between the Sexes," in *Beyond Domination,* ed. Carol Gould (Totowa, N.J.: Rowman & Allanheld, 1984), pp. 204-20; Sylvia Walby's *Patriarchy at Work: Patriarchal and Capitalist Relations in Employment* (Minneapolis: University of Minnesota Press, 1987); and Joan Acker's "Hierarchies, Jobs, Bodies: A Theory of Gendered Organizations," *Gender & Society* 4 (1990): 139-58. The scope of this book does not permit us to treat this topic here. However, we have stated throughout this book that forms of social relations interact, and in this discussion on work we make gender relations the most salient factor while fully acknowledging that class and gender as well as other social relations are mutually influential. Readers interested in this interaction are urged to consult the cited references.

26. Rosabeth Moss Kanter, *Men and Women of the Corporation* (New York: Basic Books, 1977).

to men in the work setting. Rosabeth Moss Kanter used this approach to show that gender-differentiated work behavior in a male-dominated organization was more a function of the worker's location in the organizational hierarchy than of his/her competencies or gender. She found that women were located in jobs that were significantly different from the jobs men typically occupied. In these jobs, women had shorter career ladders, fewer opportunities, limited access to resources and information, less autonomy in decision-making, and fewer same-sex colleagues.

According to the organizational approach, reducing gender differentiation in work behavior would most likely come about by restructuring the workplace along nonhierarchical lines and increasing the autonomy of workers. For example, workers would be given greater autonomy in decision-making, and administrators would become more accessible to workers and hold frequent staff meetings to share information. This in turn would lead to the empowerment of all workers. In addition, hiring plans would be implemented with the aim of balancing the gender ratio in various kinds of jobs.

The organizational approach is very helpful, since it shifts the explanation for sex segregation and the gendered wage gap from the individual to the organization. There is also evidence that structural effects are linked to work behaviors.[27] But the organizational approach fails to explain fully the dynamics of male domination and sex segregation of the workplace. Since it assumes that work behavior is shaped by a person's place in the hierarchy, gender-differentiated work behavior is reduced to a function of a gender-neutral structure — that is, the different locations of women (or men) in the organization.

There is evidence, however, that the power accompanying the organizational location of workers is anything but gender neutral.[28] In a review of the literature on tokenism, Lynn Zimmer has shown that being a token male in a female-dominated profession is in various ways quite different from and often more advantageous than being a token

27. A. Harlan and C. Weiss, "Sex Differences in Factors Affecting Managerial Career Advancement," in *Women in the Workplace*, ed. Phyllis Wallace (Boston: Auburn House, 1982), pp. 49-100; D. Izraeli, "Sex Effects or Structural Effects: An Empirical Test of Kanter's Theory of Proportions," *Social Forces* 62 (1983): 153-65; N. Toren and B. Kraus, "The Effects of Minority Size on Women's Position in Academia," *Social Forces* 65 (1987): 1096-1100.

28. Barbara Reskin, "Bringing the Men Back In: Sex Differentiation and the Devaluation of Women's Work," *Gender & Society* 2 (1988): 58-81.

female in a male-dominated profession.[29] For example, only 6 percent of all nurses are men, yet these men earn, on average, 10 percent more than women nurses. Only 2 percent of construction workers are women, yet these women earn, on average, 25 percent less than their male counterparts.[30] As this example shows, workers in a given job classification are seen not just as workers but as gendered individuals.

Organizational theory suggests that changing the gender ratio — that is, simply "adding more" of whichever sex is in the minority — will help to erase gender segregation. Intuitively this seems to make sense, and it is a solution advocated by many. But results indicate that it doesn't always work. An increase in the ratio of women to men in an occupation has often produced a positive change in *women's* attitude toward the job (which they now see as being "women friendly") but not in *men's* acceptance of women in that job.[31] For example, Christine Williams undertook a study of women in the Marine Corps and of men in nursing and found that male Marines were much less welcoming to women colleagues than women nurses were to male colleagues.[32] E. Marlies Ott has argued that men begin to resist the entry of women into an occupation when their number exceeds a certain percentage (between 20 and 40 percent). She suggests that at this point the increased competition for jobs may be a threat to male workers.[33] Although individual men may support and encourage token women, collectively men often "close ranks" in a hostile way when more women appear on the occupational scene.

A substantial change in the gender ratio in an occupation may not only engender resistance when women are the "new" workers; it may also be accompanied by an increase in the sex segregation of tasks or specialties *within* an occupation.[34] For example, women are entering

29. Zimmer, "Tokenism and Women in the Workplace: The Limits of Gender-Neutral Theory," *Social Problems* 35 (1988): 64-77.

30. "Odds and Trends," *Time* 136 (Fall 1990): 26.

31. See, for example, Izraeli's "Sex Effects or Structural Effects," and the article by Annelies Knoppers et al. entitled "Gender Ratio and Social Interaction among Coaches," *Sociology of Sport Journal* 9 (1992), forthcoming.

32. Williams, *Gender Differences at Work: Women and Men in Nontraditional Occupations* (Berkeley: University of California Press, 1989).

33. Ott, "Effects of Male-Female Ratio at Work," *Psychology of Women Quarterly* 13 (1989): 41-57.

34. William Bielby and James Baron, "Undoing Discrimination: Job Integration and Comparable Worth," in *Ingredients for Women's Employment Policy,* ed. Christine Bose and Glenna Spitze (New York: SUNY Press, 1987), pp. 211-29.

medicine and law in record numbers, yet within these fields women are likely to become pediatricians and family lawyers, while men are more likely to become surgeons and corporate lawyers. Similarly, the entry of women into real-estate sales has led to one largely female sales force that sells residential properties and another largely male sales force engaged in selling commercial real estate, which is more lucrative. Also, although women now make up 41 percent of all bakers (as compared to 25 percent in 1970), most women bakers are located in highly automated, lower-paying jobs. A. Stanley uses the "Hydra metaphor" to describe the phenomenon: "The Hydra metaphor is particularly apt, for whenever women enter a male trade, the work miraculously divides in two — along gender lines."[35]

Because of such findings, another major criticism of the structural approach to sex segregation is that it ignores the gendered nature of both organizational structures and the jobs within them.[36] For example, if we design a job on the assumption that those who fill it will give priority to waged work over domestic work and will have a backup person taking care of home and children as well as physical and emotional needs, then that job, as well as our concept of "worker," is gendered. Similarly, if jobs that require money management or power over others pay a great deal, while jobs that require caregiving pay little or nothing, then the structure of wages is gendered.

Up to this point we have reviewed theories that attempt to explain the gendered wage gap and sex segregation in terms of individuals (sex-role socialization and human-capital theories) or, alternately, in terms of structure (Marxist and organizational theories). Although each may give some insight into these gendered practices, our explanations are still incomplete. This may be so because they have failed to take into account the current nature of gender relations per se. Let us then examine the gendering of paid work through the lens of critical theory, which takes gender seriously as an independent category of analysis and does not try to reduce it or attach it to something else.

35. Stanley, "Gender Segregation in the Workplace: Plus ca Change," *NWSA Journal* 3 (1990): 641.
36. Joan Acker, "Hierarchies, Jobs, Bodies."

The Approach of Critical Theory:
The Pervasiveness of Gender

Those who use critical theory see organizations and the workplace as gendered and as places where we "do" gendering.[37] In other words, we reproduce, challenge, and at times revise dominant meanings about gender (as well as other social relations) in the workplace. According to this perspective, meanings about gender are embodied in every practice and process within a factory, firm, or organization. (We will use the term *organization* to refer to all three.)

In an earlier chapter we showed how males have appropriated sport for hegemonic masculinity and used it to help keep current gender relations in place. According to critical theory, a similar appropriation has occurred in waged work.[38] That is, if "paid work" is a characteristic that helps to define hegemonic masculinity, and if women engage in paid work, then a gendered, differentially waged division of labor and pay is needed to sustain that image of masculinity.[39] For example, the relative absence of women auto mechanics allows male auto mechanics to assume that their skills in this area are somehow innately superior to those of women. This assumption in turn helps to sustain hegemonic masculinity and keeps in place subordinate masculinities (those that don't share the requisite interests and/or mechanical skills necessary to hegemonic masculinity). Thus sex segregation, besides helping to explain the gendered wage gap, helps to maintain the ideology of male superiority, since it prevents women and men from competing with each other for the same jobs.

Sex segregation in the workplace is a dynamic process involving practices by both individuals and groups. Many of these practices are embedded in the workplace in a hegemonic way.[40] Let's begin to explore these multiple controls and processes by examining how we construct jobs and occupations. We will pay particular attention to those practices that keep women out of male-dominated work, since it is this work that pays the best.

37. For example, see Acker's "Hierarchies, Jobs, Bodies"; Williams's *Gender Differences at Work*; Cockburn's *Machinery of Dominance*; and Barbara Reskin and Patricia Roos's *Job Avenues, Gender Issues: Explaining Women's Inroads into Male Occupations* (Philadelphia: Temple University Press, 1990).
38. Cockburn, *Machinery of Dominance*, and Connell, *Gender and Power*.
39. Arthur Britton, *Masculinity and Power* (New York: Basil Blackwell, 1989).
40. Reskin, "Bringing the Men Back In."

The role played by gender in the construction of waged work should not be underestimated. To maintain any gendered division of labor, a society has to define positions or tasks as masculine or feminine and then find ways to enforce these definitions.[41] Social rules for the allocation of jobs by gender are found in almost all paid employment and in all industrial societies. Let us examine these "rules" as they exist in dominant North American organizations.

Gendered Structure

One factor associated with the gendering of waged work is that of complicity, which in turn is embedded in meanings given to organizational hierarchies.[42] For example, jobs associated with men are seen as more difficult, more important, and more complex than those that women do.[43] The creation of most organizational and occupational hierarchies is based on the assumption that jobs which require few and/or "simple" skills are situated at the bottom and those which require "complex" skills are situated at the top. Facilitating, nurturing, and managing multiple demands are defined as "simple" skills because they are believed to be skills that are innate, especially to women, and thus can be developed by anyone and require relatively little training. By contrast, "real skills" are those in which people must be trained or "credentialed." This credentialing, which means a greater investment in and by the worker, translates into more pay and higher placement in the formal job hierarchy.

Informal hierarchies in the workplace also serve to reinforce current meanings given to gender. When there are few clearly specified job ladders, employers may create an informal hierarchy among workers and obscure common interests by constructing clear gender boundaries.[44] In other words, gender boundaries can double as hierarchical boundaries. For example, gendered pay differentials can be used to keep male em-

41. Jacobs, *Revolving Doors.*

42. Barbara Reskin and Patricia Roos, "Status Hierarchies and Sex Segregation," in *Ingredients for Women's Employment Policy,* pp. 3-21.

43. Joan Acker, *Doing Comparable Worth: Gender, Class and Pay Equity* (Philadelphia: Temple University Press, 1989); Acker, "Hierarchies, Jobs, Bodies"; and Epstein, *Deceptive Distinctions.*

44. Jacobs, *Revolving Doors.*

ployees happy with their own (still relatively low) salaries, enabling employers to "buy the goodwill" of men.[45] Similarly, women may be undermined or put down by their male workmates with the tacit permission of managers. This gives men, who otherwise might feel powerless in the workplace because of low wages or limited autonomy, a certain degree of power. In addition, comments Jerry Jacobs, "male workers are likely to have more influence on keeping certain workers out than on other issues. Informal information is crucial to new workers; without it, women (or minorities) are effectively denied access."[46] It is possible that the desire to maintain hegemonic masculinity sometimes has even greater influence on male work behavior than their own economic self-interest!

In addition, our ideas about stress are often related to assumptions about hierarchy and gender. The common perception is that the jobs which are highest in the hierarchy, especially management positions, are those in which workers experience the most stress. Thus, if men dominate the top of the hierarchy and women the bottom, men must experience more stress than women and therefore deserve higher wages and greater sympathy. But this perception of stress is questionable, for in fact workers who have little control and few responsibilities (i.e., workers at "the bottom") tend to experience more stress than those with many responsibilities.[47] Why might this be so?

To begin with, the higher workers are in the managerial hierarchy, the more likely they are to have support staff to carry out the details of their responsibilities. By contrast, workers lower in the hierarchy must work on their own (although in practice they may assist each other, as when secretaries in a typing pool help each other out when one of them is facing a deadline). These workers also receive relatively little pay and thus experience the extra stress of trying to make ends meet. These conditions apply equally to women and men who are at or near the bottom of the job hierarchy. However, women in these jobs usually face two additional stressors: the risk of sexual harassment and primary responsibility for domestic work, as discussed earlier. Overall, as Lesley Doyal has shown, women in the work force experience more stress than

45. Ibid.
46. Ibid., p. 183.
47. Doyal, "Waged Work and Women's Well-Being," *Women's Studies International Forum* 13 (1990): 587-604.

their male counterparts of the same race and class.[48] We will return to issues surrounding stress in the workplace later.

Gendered Jobs

A second dynamic in the gendering of waged work is the making of assumptions about who will fill a job. As we noted earlier, male-dominated jobs are created on the assumption that the worker who fills them will give priority to waged work over domestic work and will have a backup person taking care of home and children as well as physical and emotional needs. It should come as no surprise, then, that men are deemed "best fitted" for those jobs. Robert Connell, for example, has argued that child care is an issue not about women but about men.[49] Men have control over the division of labor and have collectively decided not to engage in child care. This in turn has allowed them to keep most of the power in waged work settings. Men have made a similar decision about domestic work. Consequently, women have little choice but to take most of the responsibility for housework and child care.[50] By first creating jobs which assume that workers have few domestic responsibilities and then assuming that women will shoulder those responsibilities, employers can rationalize the practice of keeping women out of certain jobs.[51] This is not to suggest that employers consciously conspire to do this but rather that when our concept of workers is implicitly gendered, we will select workers for specific jobs accordingly.

Gendered Activities

A related factor that is used to maintain distinctions between male-dominated and female-dominated work and that may serve to keep women out of male-dominated jobs is the dominant meaning we give to the activity of the job itself.[52] The cultural and ideological value

48. Ibid.
49. Connell, *Gender and Power.*
50. Cockburn, *Machinery of Dominance.*
51. Jacobs, *Revolving Doors.*
52. Hearn and Parkin, "Gender and Organizations," p. 22.

attached to a specific job is often a function of the gender (as well as the race/ethnicity) of those who predominate in that job.[53] Hegemonic masculinity is enhanced through definitions of work that emphasize the association of certain jobs with the stereotypically masculine characteristics of males in a certain race and class.[54] It also benefits hegemonic masculinity to associate certain jobs with stereotypically feminine characteristics.

For example, if blue-collar work is seen primarily as work that requires a great deal of physical strength (rather than one requiring dexterity and coordination), and if such physicality is associated with hegemonic masculinity, then blue-collar work will be defined as "real men's work."[55] Similarly, if child care is seen primarily as a nurturing activity rather than one that requires a worker to lift and carry children, then the emphasis on nurturance means that child care will be associated with women. In white-collar work, masculinity cannot be expressed in a physical manner, so it is expressed through such things as aggression, rationality, stoicism, logic, and risk-taking, which are defined as male preserves.[56] By contrast, jobs such as that of flight attendant or receptionist are designed to combine certain technical skills with characteristics of privileged femininity. In addition to being technically competent, flight attendants must adhere to a standard for body weight, and receptionists may be hired as much for their appearance as for their job skills.

Robin Leidner did a study that graphically illustrates human agency in the creation of a gendered job. She studied two highly interactive jobs, fast-food service and insurance sales, and discovered that jobs which are very similar can be constructed so that the activity of one is more "appropriate" for women (fast-food service) and the other more "appropriate" for men (insurance sales). Both jobs require employees to be pleasant at all times and to adjust their mood to the demands of customers. This type of interaction is usually associated with females. Thus it is no wonder that girls and women are hired to work the service counters at McDonald's. However, the insurance salesperson is taught

53. Bronwyn Winter, "On Redefining Work," *Off Our Backs* 21 (May 1991): 1-2, 35.
54. Jacobs, *Revolving Doors.*
55. Note also that if blue-collar work is seen as "real men's work," then its association with hegemonic masculinity may compensate for its low monetary rewards, its dehumanizing and/or dangerous nature, and its lack of job mobility.
56. Jacobs, *Revolving Doors.*

to see that such deference is really "calculated," that the salesperson is really the one in control, and that nonresponse in the face of abuse is not "passivity" but a refusal to let someone else take control. By this reasoning, which stresses strategy and dominance, women are "ill-suited" for insurance sales and "well-suited" for fast-food service, while the reverse holds for men.[57]

If the actual activity of a job sustains an ideology of male dominance — that is, if it enables men to seem superior to women — then a large increase in the number of women filling that job will contest the status quo in such a way that the activity no longer legitimates hegemonic and other masculinities. Consequently, the entrance of women into a male-dominated job may result in that job becoming more associated with women than with men. Indeed, the job may lose status even though its gender ratio still favors men,[58] and it invariably loses status when the gender ratio tips in favor of women. For example, teaching and clerical work were originally male-dominated activities. They are now female-dominated, and their social status has declined accordingly. Law firms in which women are merely a large minority become known as "women's firms" and also tend to experience a drop in prestige.[59] Similarly, now that women are entering the medical profession in record numbers, doctors are becoming devalued in society.[60]

This dynamic may also affect wages. For example, the National Academy of Sciences reports that for every 1 percent increase of women in a male-dominated job, the median annual wage of the job drops forty-two dollars.[61] The same process also occurs when people of color enter a job traditionally dominated by white, hegemonic males. This is not to imply a simplistic causal connection. We still don't know the extent to which the decline in prestige of a job enables more women to enter it, or the extent to which the entry of women contributes to the declining prestige of a job. Possibly women (and minorities as well) are allowed to enter a job in record numbers when the social status and

57. Leidner, "Serving Hamburgers and Selling Insurance: Gender, Work, and Identity in Interactive Service Jobs," *Gender & Society* 5 (1991): 154-77.

58. Reskin and Hartmann, *Women's Work, Men's Work*; Reskin and Roos, "Status Hierarchies and Sex Segregation"; Bielby and Baron, "Undoing Discrimination."

59. Bielby and Baron, "Undoing Discrimination."

60. Reskin, cited by Chris Raymond in "Shift of Many Traditional Male Jobs to Women," *Chronicle of Higher Education*, 11 October 1989, p. A-4.

61. Sorrell, "What Women Are Worth."

wages of that job begin to slip, and their presence contributes to a further decline.

The Gendered Workplace

The gendering of waged work extends beyond gendered structures, jobs, and activities to workers and the workplace. Regardless of how people end up in a job or an occupation, they experience these dynamics of gender relations on a day-to-day basis in their workplace. Each workplace is a microcosm of meanings about gender, and in each workplace a work culture is formed that is often unique to the situation. Power in the workplace — that is, the ability to make one's own definitions dominant — is constantly negotiated and constructed. As a consequence, race, class, and gender relations that are based on negotiated power can be used to broker power on the job. We can illustrate several ways in which the workplace is gendered by looking at some everyday experiences.

Take this office scenario:

> When Joe comes into the office that morning, he stops by a colleague's office. When he sees that she's at her desk, he goes in and launches into a description of his son's first report card. After he has proudly revealed all the details, he stops by his secretary Jane's desk to recount the same story. While Joe is there, John stops by. Leaning against Jane's desk, John begins an animated conversation with Joe about the fate of their favorite baseball team. Later on, as Joe is working at his desk, Susan knocks on his door. She asks for permission to enter his office and asks if he has time to discuss a work-related problem. After she leaves, Jane knocks and asks if Joe can sign a few papers. When the signing is complete, she asks if she can leave early today to take her daughter to the doctor. Joe raises a fuss, gives her a lecture on responsibility, and in the end grants her permission with the understanding that this time is an exception.
>
> An hour later, as Joe walks past the secretaries' work-station, he frowns when he sees two secretaries standing there talking about the film they saw last night. "They should be working," he thinks, "not engaging in idle chitchat." When he arrives at his boss's office, Mary, the boss's secretary, tells him he'll have to wait a few minutes. To pass the time, Joe starts to tell Mary about his son's report card, but Mary clearly shows she isn't interested. "Wow, she's cranky!" Joe thinks to

himself. "If she keeps this up, we'll have to get rid of her. I need to see a smiling face, not a grouchy one!" When he enters his boss's office, he notices immediately that his boss is in a bad mood. In the ensuing conversation, Joe does everything he can to cheer up his boss, but without success. "He probably has a lot on his mind," Joe decides as he leaves.

When Joe returns to his office, he finds a message from his wife. She called to say that she had taken their baby daughter, Jill, to the doctor, who had attributed the baby's crankiness to an ear infection. So his wife had decided to take the afternoon off from her paid work to stay home with Jill.

This scenario shows how gender and class are part of everyday interactions in the workplace. Often men assume that they can enter the office of a female colleague or the work space of a secretary without asking for permission. Once there, they may engage in horseplay or idle chatter. Women, by contrast, must usually ask permission to enter the office of a male coworker, and if they have a discussion, it is likely to be work-centered.[62] It is also assumed that managers or bosses (usually male) can be cranky, but that secretaries (usually female) must always be polite and pleasant. Managers may talk with each other or with those "below" them about non-work-related subjects such as politics, sports, and family, but when secretaries talk about personal matters or their families, it is more likely to be seen as wasting time.[63] A male manager may not allow his female workers to take time off for child-care emergencies, or may be very stringent about the personal time he does allow them, but at the same time he may assume that his wife, who is also engaged in waged labor, will find a way to leave work when their own children need tending.

We could detail many more ways in which the workplace is gendered, such as in procedures for giving evaluations, granting promotions, and hiring and firing, but the scenario sketched here does an adequate job of making the basic point. Next we will explore the role that distorted heterosexuality plays in the negotiation of gendered

62. Jeff Hearn and Wendy Parkin, "Sex" at "Work": The Power and Paradox of Organization Sexuality (New York: St. Martin's Press, 1987).
63. Rosemary Pringle, Secretaries Talk: Sexuality, Power and Work (New York: Versco, 1989).

power. Since distorted heterosexuality plays a large role in the current nature of white, Western, middle-class culture, it should come as no surprise to the reader that gendered power in the workplace is often negotiated through sexual behavior.

Using Sexuality to Display Gendered Power in the Workplace

Prior to the televised hearings surrounding the selection of Clarence Thomas as a Supreme Court judge, most people may have associated sexuality in the workplace with sexual liaisons entered into by mutual consent.[64] Now many more people understand that they must include sexual harassment under the rubric of sexuality in the workplace. Yet sexuality in the workplace manifests itself in a myriad of other ways, many of which are very subtle. Take language, for example. Most metaphors used in business are either athletic or sexual in nature.[66] Think of the business-related terms that have sexual connotations, such as "seminal idea," "virgin territory," "market penetration," and "policy thrusts."[67]

Rosemary Pringle has also shown how male managers can use sexuality as a means of controlling or shaping the behavior of secretaries by requiring them to display behaviors associated with privileged femininity.[68] For example, a male manager may hire a secretary or receptionist on the basis of her appearance in order to ensure that the first contact that the client (usually male) has with the organization is a "pleasant" one. Similarly, through sheer numbers, men in a male-dominated occupation or job can be overtly hostile in a sexual way, and the net result is often a sexually demeaning work climate. For example, they may "sexualize" the workplace by posting female pinups, or they may tell sexual jokes that demean women and engage in other forms

64. When these liaisons occur under circumstances judged to be inappropriate, women are twice as likely to lose their jobs as men. See Hearn and Parkin's *"Sex" at "Work."*

65. For a thorough discussion of this topic, see Hearn and Parkin's *"Sex" at "Work."*

66. Barbara Gutek, "Sexuality in the Workplace: Key Issues in Social Research and Organizational Practice," in *The Sexuality of Organization,* ed. Jeff Hearn et al. (London: Sage, 1989), pp. 56-70.

67. Hearn and Parkin, *"Sex" at "Work."*

68. Pringle, *Secretaries Talk.*

of sexual behavior in order to remind women of the power they exercise as men.[69]

Explicit dress codes are another example of the management of sexuality. For those in female-dominated occupations such as nursing, food service, and airline service, mandatory dress codes are common. By contrast, dress codes in male-dominated workplaces are apt to be more implicit.[70] Women may seem to be allowed more variety in dress than males; nevertheless, the defining of dress codes, both stated and unstated, is usually done by men, and may be used to regulate the expression of women's sexuality by defining what is "feminine."

Often women are required to exhibit feminine characteristics and behaviors yet still do their work in a male-defined way. This creates a no-win situation for many women. For example, a woman lawyer at a large firm was told that she was not offered a senior partnership because she did not act in a "feminine" manner; her employers seemed to overlook the fact that she also brought the most business into the firm, and that doing so might have required her to exhibit the very kind of initiative and assertiveness they simultaneously condemned in her as "unfeminine." As it turned out, the U.S. Supreme Court ruled that the firm's action was illegal.[71]

Similarly, the norm of distorted heterosexuality often shapes behavioral interactions among women and men in the workplace. Males may behave inappropriately with women workers and colleagues because they are accustomed to seeing women primarily in the roles of mother, wife, child, or sexual partner. Nurturing and flirtation thus easily become the norm for interactions between women and men at work. In her study of secretaries, for example, Rosemary Pringle found that the most common mode of interaction between male bosses and female secretaries was one that resembled "institutionalized heterosexuality," a relationship

69. M. Swedlow, "Men's Accommodations to Women Entering Nontraditional Occupations: A Case of Rapid Transit Operative," *Gender & Society* 3 (1989): 373-87.

70. Hearn and Parkin, *"Sex" at "Work."*

71. Price Waterhouse vs. Hopkins, 109 S. Ct. 1775 (1989), cited by Martha Ertman in "Welcome to a World," *Off Our Backs* 21 (October 1991): 12-13. Ertman also argues that the law seems to be more interested in enforcing the responsibility to act like a man than the right to act like a woman. She cites a circuit-court decision that upheld the right of a company to fire a man for wearing a small gold-hoop earring on the grounds that Title VII does not protect "effeminacy."

in which the secretaries functioned as "office wives." By contrast, when women work for female bosses, the relationship changes from hetero-sexualized interest in the other to same-sex identification, or homosocial-ity.[72]

Even though the foregoing may seem obvious and may seem to imply a consistent pattern in the manner in which sexuality and ne-gotiated power interact, we often overlook the contradictions in the meanings given to sexuality within the workplace. For example, women are expected to engage in stereotypically heterosexual social rituals when they are at work. Yet with the exception of pregnancy, most of the uniquely female sexual states are ignored or rendered invisible in the workplace. Males may casually assume the right to attribute a woman's behavior to her premenstrual or menstrual state; but the same woman may *not* put a box of tampons next to the Kleenex box on her desk! Likewise, although skiing accidents may be a suitable topic for conver-sation, miscarriages and menopause are not. It seems that women are expected to act just like men in the workplace, yet still be attractively and invitingly feminine.

Since the norm for the workplace is distorted heterosexuality, men can safely be seen in the company of other men there. This bonding of men in the workplace is called the "old boys' network" or "male homo-sociality." Few people are suspicious of the amount of work time that men spend in the company of other men. Paid work, like sport, is so congruent with hegemonic masculinity that males within it can engage in homosocial activities that in themselves do not seem to sustain hege-monic masculinity in a visible manner. But all these activities, large and small, do in fact contribute to men's maintenance of power in the work-place.

Again, male homosociality in the workplace is not necessarily a bad thing, but it can often be problematic for women because male camaraderie provides a context for talk about job politics, sports, cars, and the pursuit of women, and so is by nature exclusionary.[73] Men engage in this camaraderie not only in all workplaces, from office build-ings to coal mines, but also in bars and other places after work. Jean Lipman-Blumen has argued that male homosociality occurs because all

72. Pringle, *Secretaries Talk*.
73. Barbara Gutek, *Sex and the Workplace* (San Francisco: Jossey-Bass, 1985); Jacobs, *Revolving Doors*.

men want to associate with the power held by hegemonic males.[74] It is the hegemonic males within a work setting who make the rules and who have the greatest power to reproduce the gender system in the workplace. If certain men are excluded from such groupings, it is not because of their gender but because they may represent a subordinate type of masculinity: they may be gay, black, immigrant, disabled, and so on.

Women, of course, also form homosocial groups in the workplace. However, there is a significant difference between male and female homosociality, just as there is a significant difference between hegemonic masculinity and privileged femininity. As Lipman-Blumen explains, "The two homosocial worlds usually are not equivalent nor symmetrical. The critical but surely not the only difference between the homosocial worlds of men and women is the control over institutional versus domestic or personal resources and the relative power each connotes."[75] For example, homosocial groups are linked to "old boys" or "old girls" networks. These tend to be informal and have the function of enhancing "sponsored mobility," which occurs when there is sharing of information about job vacancies and when network members are recommended for such jobs.[76] Mark Granovetter and Jeffrey Pfeffer have shown that informal networks tend to provide more accurate and more in-depth information about a job than do formal channels, such as posted notices or job descriptions in periodicals.[77] Consequently, those without access to such networks may not get the information they need to acquire a job or advance to a higher rank. Male homosociality in particular tends to create informal networks for passing along job information, excluding women in the process[78] and forcing them to count on less reliable, more formal channels such as advertisements and postings. This is another example of the power that white, hegemonic male workers have to exclude women.[79]

74. Lipman-Blumen, *Gender Roles and Power* (Englewood Cliffs, N.J.: Prentice-Hall, 1984).

75. Ibid., p. 185.

76. N. Lin and M. Dumin, "Access to Occupations through Social Ties," *Social Networks* 8 (1986): 365-86.

77. Granovetter, *Getting a Job: A Study of Contacts and Careers* (Cambridge, Mass.: Auburn House, 1974); Pfeffer, *Power in Organizations* (Marshfield, Mass.: Pitman Publishing, 1981).

78. K. Campbell, "Gender Differences in Job-Related Networks," *Work and Occupations* 15 (1988): 179-200; Angela Simeone, *Academic Women: Working towards Equality* (Hadley, Mass.: Bergin & Garvey Publications, 1987).

79. In *Deceptive Distinctions*, Cynthia Fuchs Epstein has argued that women

Male homosociality may in part be a reaction to the alienating kind of work that is typical of industrial capitalism[80] — a kind of "misery loves company" reaction to the lack of control over work conditions that typifies the lot of almost everyone not in a managerial or professional job. However, this by itself does not explain the exclusiveness of male bonding, since the excluded women are neither the cause of alienated work nor the beneficiaries of it. Overall, the homosocial bonding of men is a powerful influence in making job and occupational climates "chilly" for women. That such bonding can occur without weakening the norm of heterosexuality is also testimony to the strength of hegemonic masculinity.

Sexual Harassment in the Workplace

As the foregoing makes clear, part of the work climate or culture is constructed through meanings given to gender through sexuality. Sexual behavior in the workplace can become a way of reinforcing male power. A common channel through which this occurs is sexual harassment. According to Sue Wise and Liz Stanley, authors of *Georgie Porgie*, sexual harassment currently involves "sexual behaviors which represent unwanted and unsought intrusions by men into women's feelings, thoughts, behaviors, space, time, energies and bodies."[81] As is obvious from the definition, sexual harassment is not just confined to the workplace; it occurs in every sphere of life. We will, however, concentrate on how sexual harassment manifests itself in the workplace.

Sexual harassment includes a variety of actions used to assert one's power: frankly looking a person over; giving more subtle, suggestive looks; making unwanted sexual remarks and jokes; invading someone's personal space without permission; grabbing, pinching, or fondling someone; displaying pinups or sexist cartoons; and so on.[82] These actions are most often

---

have strong and powerful network ties only through the men in their lives. For example, women tend to enter Congress or to chair boards of corporations only after the death of husbands who held such positions.

80. Michael Kaufman, *A Framework for Research on Men and Masculinity*, paper presented at "Re-visioning Knowledge: Feminist Perspectives on the Curriculum," conference held at Michigan State University, 19-22 April 1990. The paper is forthcoming as an article in *Men's Studies Review*.

81. Wise and Stanley, *Georgie Porgie: Sexual Harassment in Everyday Life* (London: Pandora Press, 1987), p. 71.

82. Cockburn, *Machinery of Dominance*; Hearn and Parkin, *"Sex" at "Work"*; and

directed by men toward women. The context and manner of sexual harassment have partly to do with the gender ratio of the occupation or job in which it occurs. For example, Barbara Gutek and Bruce Morasch did a study of sexual harassment in which 66 to 74 percent of the women in male-dominated occupations reported receiving comments about their appearance, whereas only 58 to 63 percent of the women in female-dominated occupations reported receiving such comments.[83] Similarly, 14 to 20 percent of the women in male-dominated jobs reported being the target of insulting comments, looks, and gestures, but only 12 to 16 percent of the women in female-dominated jobs reported being the target of such behavior. In female-dominated jobs, sexual harassment tends to involve the power that accompanies differences in rank — for example, the power of a male manager over a female worker. If she refuses to go out with him or protests his sexualized treatment of her, he has the power to give her a poor job evaluation or even threaten her job security. Jeff Hearn and Wendy Parkin see such harassment as one way in which managerial men maintain social control.[84]

Gutek and Morasch attribute the difference in forms and frequency of sexual harassment in part to "sex-role spillover"; that is, a woman receives more attention in a male-dominated workplace because she presents a more obvious contrast to the male majority.[85] But it is also possible that sexual harassment is noticed more in male-dominated workplaces, whereas in female-dominated workplaces, such dominant/subordinate gender behaviors are embedded in a supposedly nongendered hierarchy and have become institutionalized, taken for granted, or ignored, and thus are not reported as frequently.[86] N. DiTomaso has likewise suggested that women who work in male-dominated jobs are more sensitive to sexual harassment than women who work in female-dominated jobs.[87] But even nonharassing sexual behavior can be a hindrance to women. According to

Barbara Gutek and Bruce Morasch, "Sex-Ratios, Sex-Role Spillover, and Sexual Harassment of Women at Work," *Journal of Social Issues* 38, no. 4 (1982): 55-74.

83. Gutek and Morasch, "Sex-Ratios, Sex-Role Spillover, and Sexual Harassment of Women at Work."

84. Hearn and Parkin, *"Sex" at "Work."*

85. Gutek and Morasch, "Sex-Ratios, Sex-Role Spillover, and Sexual Harassment of Women at Work."

86. Hearn and Parkin, *"Sex" at "Work."*

87. DiTomaso, "Sexuality in the Workplace: Discrimination and Harassment," in *The Sexuality of Organization*, pp. 71-90.

a study by Barbara Gutek and V. Dunwood, women regarded even remarks that were meant to be complimentary as insulting. By contrast, the same researchers found that men felt flattered by sexual overtures from women, and they reported few or no ill effects on their work as a consequence of sexually suggestive behavior.[88]

The popular belief that women want or use sexual behaviors in the work setting to achieve an advantage over others has often been used as an excuse to limit women's options in the workplace. Yet in her study of more than 1,200 workers, Rosemary Pringle found little evidence to support this stereotype. In fact, she discovered that men were more likely than women to say that they had used sexual behavior to gain an advantage in the workplace. Why do we tend not to "see" this? Because we stereotype hegemonic men as competent, productive, organizational beings who are asexual while on the job. In Pringle's words,

> Men can behave in a blatantly sexual way without it being identified. Playboys and harassers go largely unnoticed because "organizational man," goal oriented, rational, competitive, is not perceived in explicitly sexual terms. It is ironic that women are perceived as using sex to their advantage. They are much less likely to initiate sexual encounters and more likely to be hurt by sex at work.[89]

It seems that the hegemonic process has succeeded: because distorted heterosexuality pervades the entire concept of hegemonic masculinity, which in turn controls the workplace, "being sexual" on the job is so much a part of the atmosphere that we do not "see" it. As a result, it can be used to assert power. It is even possible that men who are accused of improper sexual behavior on the job may be convinced that the accusation is unjust, since they have no memory of engaging in such behavior—it simply passed unnoticed, much as other behaviors do that we consider routine or ordinary. According to Pringle, women are very much aware of sexual power structures and of the necessity to walk a fine line between principled resistance and pragmatic cooperation. They may indeed find the presence of men enjoyable much of the time, but they also know that they are being unjustly held responsible for drawing the line—that is, for controlling men's behaviors.

88. Gutek and Dunwood, "Understanding Sex in the Workplace," in *Women and Work.*
89. Pringle, *Secretaries Talk,* p. 94.

This gendered attitudinal difference toward sexual behavior explains why our definition of sexual harassment names "*unwanted* and *unsought* intrusions by men" as the distinguishing feature of sexual harassment.

As is obvious from this discussion, sexual harassment is an embedded evil in the workplace. It is an exercise in power that reflects distorted heterosexuality and detracts from the talents and energies that women bring to the workplace. The Bible is clear on the point that we must try to behave lovingly toward one another. Harassment, be it sexual or otherwise, is a far cry from expressions of mutuality. Men may be somewhat bewildered by this discussion. A businessman may ask, "Why can't I comment on the appearance of my women colleagues or secretaries? I'm only trying to be nice!" Or another may say, "If I can't make *any* comments, the workplace will be boring and colorless." Such men need to recognize that they have to let go of their own standards and listen to women. They need to realize that if a workplace becomes dull when all sexual harassment is eliminated, then it becomes dull only to men for whom sexual harassment is a means of exercising power, or for whom sexuality is a disproportionately important means of seeking pleasure.

How then can we reduce sexual harassment? Clear and explicit policies that strive to eliminate this behavior are a short-term solution. But these policies work only if they are enforced and give the benefit of the doubt to the victim. Men must listen and be sensitive to women in the workplace and elsewhere. They need to realize, for example, that if a woman laughs at a sexist joke, it doesn't necessarily mean she enjoys it. She may feel she has little real choice, because if she doesn't laugh, a man will typically tend to think that "she can't take a joke." If a woman says, "This is sexual harassment," then it is. In addition, men need to learn to distinguish between mutually consenting behavior and sexual harassment. Perhaps a helpful practical guideline would be for men to use the following questions to inform their behavior: Would I want important women in my life such as my mother, my sisters, my daughters, or my spouse to be treated this way? Would I want to see my remarks published in today's paper? If a man made similar remarks to *me* (or to another man), would I consider them simply an attempt to "add color" to the workplace?

Rules and policies alone, of course, cannot extinguish sexually harassing behavior, because powerful and seductive forces in society and the workplace encourage men not to relinquish it. Working-class men and men who belong to other subordinated masculinities may use such behavior to express their power and obscure the reality of their subordinated status. Privileged men may use sexuality to reinforce the power they already possess.[90] Sexual harassment in the workplace is obviously a symptom of a sin-filled desire to "do power." Policies and regulations can affect the ways in which that power is expressed, but they cannot eliminate the disease. Perhaps we can work, with God's help, toward the goal of a workplace that is characterized by the fruits of the Spirit.

Human Agency: Challenging, Resisting, Coping, and Reconstructing

Human agency is another factor that helps both to maintain and to challenge the nature of gender relations in the waged workplace. It should already be obvious that the gendering of hierarchies, jobs, workers, and the workplace does not "just happen." In part this gendering is the result of human agency. The analogy of the rope-tug game for social relations, which we explored in an earlier chapter, leads us to expect that when a subordinate group challenges dominant meanings, those for whom the dominant meanings supply privilege and power will react.

For example, when women enter jobs which for them are nontraditional, they contest male domination. This often leads to a "struggle" to legitimate the current nature of gender relations in other ways — for example, by redefining jobs or reconstructing male superiority in another dimension of the work world. If the gender ratio in a job begins to shift toward women, a variety of things may happen. Not only may wages be affected, but also men may move to adjacent jobs, set up barriers for women, routinize the skills involved or subdivide the job, or create a new job that has higher status than the previous one.[91] The reverse tends not to happen when men enter female-dominated occupations or jobs.[92] Take the study done by Christine Williams. She found that women who enter the Marine Corps, which is male-dominated, face greater barriers

90. D. Collinson and M. Collinson, "Sexuality in the Workplace: The Domination of Men's Sexuality," in *The Sexuality of Organization,* pp. 91-109.
91. Cockburn, *Machinery of Dominance.*
92. Epstein, *Deceptive Distinctions.*

and constraints than men who enter nursing, a female-dominated occupation. Male nurses are quick to receive supervisory posts and to work
in the more highly paid specialties. Women Marines, by contrast, have
been given access to only 20 percent of the available job titles, most of
which are clerical. Gender boundaries are also kept distinct by such
things as the requirement that women Marines must be feminine, especially when off duty, and by the practice of telling men not to act "like
a bunch of girls" when doing physical training. Thus, although the entry
of women into the Marines challenges meanings given to maleness, those
meanings are relegitimated in various ways. Conversely, women nurses
interviewed by Williams welcomed the entry of men into the nursing
ranks. They believed that the presence of men would increase the
profession's status and salaries.[93] By using this example, we do not mean
to imply that men are intentionally conspiring to make matters un-
pleasant for women in male-dominated jobs. The processes that exclude
women are highly complex. But we should not forget that we believe
we are active, responsible beings in God's world, and we can therefore
examine our own practices to ascertain the degree to which we as individuals and as groups help to sustain processes and practices in the
workplace that are not "women-friendly."

As noted, these processes and practices are complex. For example,
employers can use people's insecurities about gender to pit women and
men against each other. Doing so then makes it harder for men to realize
that they too may have a stake in equity and gender sensitivity in the
workplace. One would think that men with wives, daughters, and/or
mothers in the work force would already recognize the extent to which
discrimination and stereotypes hurt women (and, by extension, their
families) and would push for change in the workplace. There is little
evidence, however, to show that nonhegemonic males ally themselves
with women fighting for equity in male-dominated jobs. They are much
more likely to identify with the hegemonic males who control their own
work conditions.

It is not just male workers who exercise agency on behalf of the
status quo, but also men who manage industries, companies, and organizations. These men have much to gain by keeping the current shape of
gender relations in place, for it allows them to demand and receive
privilege. According to Barbara Reskin, "The dominant groups remain

93. Williams, *Gender Differences at Work.*

privileged because they write the rules and the rules they write enable them to continue to write the rules."[94] These rules can take the form of processes, informal policy action, and inaction. The way a job is constructed, the presence or absence of sexual harassment policies and child-care and parent-care leaves, the nature of the job climate — all of these and more are largely regulated by those who control companies, organizations, and industries. In general, hegemonic males can dictate the inclusion or exclusion of any type of worker to their own benefit. For example, the labor shortages in World War II led the government to pressure employers to hire women. After the war, however, the government reversed itself and pressured industries to hire the often-unskilled returning veterans, laying off even highly skilled women workers in the process.

Not all men, however, *are* hegemonic males. Many may feel they have little power in the workplace. This may be especially true of men who belong to "subordinated masculinities," who work in alienating or dehumanizing jobs. They may say that they "take" this stress in order to provide for their families, and that they are subject to greater stress than are women, whether at home or in the workplace. But such reasoning ignores certain factors. For one thing, women share physical risks in the workplace with their male coworkers.[95] For example, both women and men work in the electronics industry, which daily exposes them to chemical toxins. Both women and men work in agriculture, where they must cope with agrochemicals, poorly designed machinery, and hot sun. (Those warnings about skin cancer apply not only to sunbathers but also to people who work outdoors!)

This is not to say that nonhegemonic males do not experience stress. It is true that the responsibilities of the average male worker "subject him to a certain amount of stress, tension and pressure," according to Paula Rothenberg — but, as she points out, "the same may be said for the capitalist, whose endless attempts to extract more surplus value from the labor of his workforce no doubt lead to ulcers, alcoholism, and hypertension."[96] Our point is simply that *everyone* who works — male

94. Reskin, "Bringing the Men Back In," p. 60.
95. Doyal, "Waged Work and Women's Well-Being."
96. Rothenberg, "The Political Nature of Relations between the Sexes," p. 213. See also Kenneth Clatterbaugh, *Contemporary Perspectives on Masculinity* (Boulder, Colo.: Westview Press, 1990), chap. 6.

or female, hegemonically empowered or disempowered — experiences stress on the job, and that it does not justify sexist behavior. Christians are called to treat every person with dignity and respect, regardless of the stress under which they work. Some men may indeed be exploited by other men in the workplace, but when their status is compared with that of female colleagues and of families, it is clear that they enjoy a certain level of privilege. They need to recognize this privilege and use it in a stewardly and enabling way, rather than engaging in sexist behavior. The claim that men suffer in the workplace need not be discounted, but it should not be used as an excuse for creating an inhospitable climate for women workers or for demanding privilege with respect to domestic work in the homes they share with women partners.

Critical theory emphasizes that both the dominant group and the subordinate group employ agency. We have seen how men may use gender and sexuality as a "means of enabling them to 'do power.'"[97] But how are women demonstrating agency in response to this? They do so in many and various ways: by entering male-dominated jobs, by working under unfavorable circumstances, by challenging biased rules and procedures, and so on. Coping with sexual harassment is one way in which women show agency. In *Georgie Porgie: Sexual Harassment in Everyday Life*, Sue Wise and Liz Stanley identify four ways in which women might choose to cope with sexual harassment. First, women may try avoidance strategies, such as not going into the coffee room unless other women are present, taking work home rather than working late at the office, wearing clothes that may be less likely to elicit comments from male coworkers, and so on. Second, women may turn the harassment around so it works in their favor. For example, a women may dress or act a certain way to butter up a boss or supervisor — or, as Wise and Stanley put it, to hoist him by his own petard! The third strategy women use to cope with sexual harassment is letting a certain amount of harassment go by without reaction or comment. This functions as a survival strategy because it conserves energy: if women reacted to every form of sexual harassment they encountered, they could become chronically exhausted. Yet silence also takes its toll. Dr. Frances Conley, a prominent neurosurgeon at Stanford University, resigned after twenty-five years on the job because she was tired of working in a climate where sexual harassment was the norm. Although she returned because of the institution's

97. Wise and Stanley, *Georgie Porgie*, p. 64.

promise to be more vigilant about sexual harassment, much work still needs to be done before the climate at Stanford will be truly woman-friendly.

The fourth strategy is the most visible: it is reacting to the harassing behavior. Reactions may range from pleas to commands, from diplomatic requests to straightforward namings of the behavior. This last strategy is the riskiest. If sexual harassment is an exercise in male power, then calling attention to that behavior and contesting it means challenging that power. Often a woman has to trust that her superiors, usually male, will take her complaint seriously. As Anita Hill discovered when she challenged Clarence Thomas, this can be a very painful and disappointing process. But it can also be a very rewarding and empowering process — and it is necessary if women are to stem the tide of harassment.

Today it is not just women such as Anita Hill who are demonstrating agency in response to sexual harassment; so are all women who use their own strategies, as invisible as those strategies may seem, in order to be active rather than passive in the workplace.

Possibilities for Change

Thus far we have argued that an understanding of the labor market must include an awareness of how work gets gendered through our constructions and definitions of hierarchies, jobs, workers, and workplace, and through direct individual action. We have tried to show how each of these processes may contribute to a gendered division of labor, but in actuality they cannot be neatly separated. Instead, they interact in complex ways with each other and with current meanings attached to other social relations, such as race and class. These dynamics interact in the labor market in a myriad of ways, many of which still need to be explored. All need to be taken into account when we try to explain the experiences of women and men engaged in waged labor.

By now it should also be obvious that many social practices interact to bring about sex segregation in waged labor, and that these social practices have an impact on the meanings given to domestic work. Bringing about change may be a daunting task, because these practices are complex and interact with other forms of social relations. Yet we should not succumb to "the paralysis of analysis." Even people with reduced agency can bring about change at the individual level, and those with more power can do so at the organizational level. Those of us who come from a Reformed tradition should not be strangers to this call for a "reformation." In this case the reformation needs to occur in the workplace and in the nature of waged work. We close this chapter with reflections on several possibilities for beginning this reformation. But we must remember that these changes will mean little if they are unaccompanied by changes in the nature of current gender relations. As we argued earlier, human resources are wasted when we assign work on the basis of gender (as well as by race and class). If we are to be stewards of all that God has given us, we must change sin-tainted practices.

To begin with, both collectively and individually we need to examine our acceptance of hegemonic masculinity. As long as masculinity is based on showing superiority to and power over women, then what men do will always be judged as being more difficult and/or more important than what women do. If, however, we conceive of women and men working together in a mutually beneficial way, and if we value women culturally and ideologically and give them their material due, we can begin to overturn sex segregation. No longer should we associate masculinity with only paid work; rather, we should consider masculinity equally congruent with domestic work. We have begun to change our definition of privileged femininity, since many women now engage in waged work. We need to do the same for hegemonic masculinity.

We need to begin by assuming that every paid worker also has domestic responsibilities, and by designing jobs accordingly. Through our policies and actions, we need to support child raising and nurturing the well-being of children as well as other forms of domestic work. Having a "parent" track is not the answer, since that in effect blames individuals for having children rather than blaming the structure of jobs for creating parenting difficulties. Douglas Hall has summarized the research concerning men who take some responsibility for domestic work, and his overall conclusion is that men who take leave from the workplace to assume domestic responsibilities are seen as unambitious; consequently, most men do not apply for such leave.[98] Organizations have to examine their value systems and explore what is meant by being a "good" parent, a "good" worker, and a "good" career person. Employers need to make clear that they value and encourage good parenting by

98. Hall, "Promoting Work/Family Balance: An Organization-Change Approach," *Organizational Dynamics* 18 (Winter 1990): 5-18.

both sexes, and design jobs on the assumption that everyone is a working "caregiver"—if not of children, then perhaps of an aging parent or a disabled dependent.

Since men tend to have more power in the workplace, they need to be willing to take risks and press for company policies that make domestic and waged work more compatible rather than continuing to let women work a double shift. Governments and churches also need to become more "profamily" in the broadest sense of that term. Governments can show a profamily stance, for example, by giving tax breaks to companies and industries that design jobs on the assumption that all workers have household responsibilities. This may mean providing shorter workdays, flexible work schedules, day care, and/or family leave. Churches can do their part by calling companies to task, by pressing for profamily legislation, and by examining their own policies for workers, including overseas missionaries. Sunday school and adult education classes as well as sermons should teach congregations about the economic injustice of the status quo and about ways in which the family can become more supportive of women. We need to emphasize, among other things, the validity of the assertion that "Every working father is also a mother."

It is also important that we make provisions for adequate child-care in the paid workplace. We need to ascribe proper value to the care of children, as well as of parents and the disabled, so that the government is willing to subsidize it or provide incentives for companies to do so. This may mean higher taxes, but if we are to be truly a caring community, we must be willing to give more so that every person can live with dignity and self-respect. To implement this change, the government needs to make the welfare of children and families a high priority. A government that can spend billions of dollars on bailing out savings and loan institutions and on fighting in the Persian Gulf surely can support child care. If not, then the values of that government need to be assessed, criticized, and reordered.

At the managerial/organizational level, we can begin to implement change by enforcing both the letter and the spirit of statutes such as Title VII and the Equal Pay Act, which were designed to end blatant discrimination in the workplace. Companies could receive incentives such as tax breaks and positive publicity for a high retention of women and minorities in male-dominated jobs. Those in management positions could explore the extent to which their workplace is women-friendly by scrutinizing the behavior of men, including that of managers, to determine the extent to which power is brokered through sexuality and through gendered procedures such as hiring, firing, evaluating, mentoring, and promotion. They should strive to ensure that everyone is treated with dignity, respect, and friendliness. As managers they are responsible for modeling such behavior.

We must also examine the necessity and appropriateness of certain job-entry criteria and widen the pool of jobs with upward mobility to include women's jobs. Rather than asking "Why are there no women in this job? What's wrong with them?" we must ask, "What is wrong with this job or this workplace that so few women want — or are able — to be here?" At the same time, we must recognize that gender relations as currently constructed are very much entrenched. The interconnectedness of biased practices will increase the struggle. Changes in one social practice will be resisted in part because they will require changes in other social practices.[99]

We also need to discuss the ethos of the workplace and explore the extent to which hegemonic masculinity or the desire to "do power" sets the tone for interactions. Perhaps in order to flatten hierarchies we need to institute a model of friendship and cooperation in the workplace as well as in the home. Similarly, if the negative aspects of male bonding are to be lessened, then men need to see women as partners, as *people* worthy of camaraderie, respect, and dignity. Trying to lessen the distortions of heterosexuality might be a big step on the path to making the workplace a more humane place, a place where we can put our Christian ideals into practice.

We also need to explore ways of bringing about wage equity. The wage gap between women and men, which is too large to ignore, is a major contributor to the pauperization of women. Employing the concept of comparable worth is one way of closing the wage gap between male-dominated and female-dominated occupations.[100] In brief, the concept of comparable worth tries to redefine jobs in terms of their degree

---

99. For example, why do schools not mesh opening and closing time with those of the paid workplace? It may be because such synchronization would make it easier for women (who still are the primary child-care givers) to enter the waged work-force, and leave employers one less excuse for not hiring them.

100. For a summary of discussions on comparable worth, see Acker's *Doing Comparable Worth* and Jacobs's *Revolving Doors*.

of responsibility, the amount of training they require, and their complexity. So implementing comparable-worth policies in the area of unskilled labor would mean that unskilled workers would receive similar wages whether they worked in male-dominated or female-dominated jobs.

The implementation of comparable-worth policies may make female-dominated occupations more attractive to women (and even to men), and give dignity to such jobs. It could help to correct what Joan Acker sees as the fundamental misperception currently operative:

> Women's work is defined as inferior work, and inferior work is defined as work for women. Inferior work is often considered appropriate work for women by the same standards that define it as inferior, and by the same standards that define women's work as inferior work — its pay, status, interest or complexity, contacts with people, its relation to cleanliness or care of bodily needs.[101]

By recompensing work of equal value with equal pay, we may change this perception of women's work as inferior while enhancing the likelihood that women will have access to adequate financial resources. In a study of the implementation of comparable worth in Oregon, Acker found that it tends to give the most help to those at the bottom of the hierarchy — that is, it provides relief from poverty and makes certain skills socially visible, especially those associated with female-dominated jobs.[102] Acker suggests that a comparable-worth strategy is better than the traditional "family wage" approach, since comparable worth gives everyone, regardless of gender or race, a chance at a decent wage. The women factory workers that Ellen Rosen interviewed concurred.[103] But Acker cautions against seeing comparable worth as a panacea that will remove all sexism from the workplace. She points out that Sweden has a very small gender gap in wages, yet jobs that require caregiving are still devalued there, and most managerial jobs are held by males.

Discussions about wages should also include reflections on the global interconnectedness of work and consumerism. To what extent does our demand for "cheap" prices lead to the exploitation of women

101. Acker, *Doing Comparable Worth*, p. 41.
102. Acker, "Hierarchies, Jobs, Bodies."
103. Rosen, *Bitter Choices: Blue-Collar Women In and Out of Work* (Chicago: University of Chicago Press, 1987).

571

in free-trade zones or in Third World countries? Or, closer to home, if we employ someone to clean our house or take care of our children, do we pay that person as much as possible to help ensure that he or she makes a decent wage? Are such workers protected by social security and health-insurance plans? Are we willing to pay into those plans? Perhaps health care and pensions should be universally provided by the government so that all workers, regardless of their location in the labor force, will have adequate coverage.

But we also need to recognize that not all people can or should work for wages full-time throughout their lives. There may be times when certain individuals need to work part-time. This part-time status may allow them to do other valuable work such as providing care for others, volunteering in a nonprofit organization, and so on. These workers are, however, very vulnerable in terms of health insurance and pension plans, so provisions should be made to ensure that they are adequately covered.

Such changes can begin to reconstruct gender relations in many ways. First, if women are economically independent and/or have financial security, they no longer need to endure distorted heterosexuality and so can challenge it. They can see both marriage and singleness as viable choices, and they need not feel compelled to stay in a broken marriage sheerly for financial reasons. Second, if all men in marital relationships were willing to be "subordinate workers" in the home, then the boundaries between male dominance and female subordination would begin to crumble. These boundary changes need to be accompanied by greater humanization and a flattening of hierarchies in the workplace. This is especially crucial for working-class men, who may feel that home is the only place where they can exert some authority. If their subordination in the workplace is lessened, then perhaps they will not feel the need to dominate at home.

Obviously, as we stated earlier, changes in one sphere of life (such as the home) will affect and be resisted by practices in other areas of life (such as paid labor). The structure of both domestic work and waged work needs to be altered if women are to be relieved of the double day and if men are to nurture children and engage in domestic tasks. At the beginning of the previous chapter, we described how women and men used to work together at home, but how that changed when men's working lives began to be altered in revolutionary ways. Women are now caught up in similar revolutionary change. Perhaps we can come full

572

circle so that women and men work together in the paid labor force *and* in the home!

We close this chapter by looking at another society that has recognized the interconnectedness of waged and domestic work: Sweden. Currently, workers in that country can take time off with pay to engage in caregiving activities. Parental leave consists of twelve months (paid) away from the workplace, and parents can take simultaneous or sequential leaves. Those who have preschool children may work six-hour days without losing seniority or full-time benefits. Parents pay about 10 percent of child-care costs; the rest is subsidized by the government. These programs clearly indicate that the government supports coparenting by mothers and fathers. In an evaluative study of the impact of these programs, Phyllis Moen found an improvement in the well-being of Swedish women, including a lessening of fatigue. She also reported that Swedish fathers were more fatigued.[104] She attributed this "father fatigue" to the greater participation of men in child care and to the still prevailing ideal of "man the breadwinner." These results, coupled with those of Arlie Hochschild's study, which we cited earlier, indicate that policy change by itself addresses only symptoms. If these policies are not accompanied by a collective reconstruction of gender relations, then their impact is circumscribed. If hegemonic masculinity means that a male must continue to show he is male by engaging in different activities such as waged work in male-dominated jobs and sports, then gender relations will be continually adjusted so that males can show they are "masculine" whenever women cross gender boundaries. This "Hydra phenomenon" can be stopped only when we base gender relations on mutuality rather than on dominance and superiority. The Bible clearly gives us models for living in mutuality: we are to live by the fruits of the Spirit and to care for one another as bearers of the image of God. It will require a great deal of struggle and persistence on our part as we work toward models of living together that encourage mutuality. But just as the widow kept on searching for her lost coin (Luke 15:8-10), so we should persist in altering every pattern of distorted gender relations.

104. Moen, *Working Parents: Transformation in Gender Roles and Public Policies in Sweden* (Madison: University of Wisconsin Press, 1989).

CONCLUSION

CHAPTER 17

Still Living between the Times:
Realism and Hope about Gender Relations

W e have traveled over much ground since we began this volume
with Charles Dickens's comment about living in "the best of times
and the worst of times." We have introduced readers to many of the
forms that feminism has taken — in the previous century and in this
century, in the Western world and in the non-Western world, among
secularists and among Christians, including theologians, academics, and
lay persons. We have seen how narratives, especially alternative readings
of the creation narrative, can shape gender relations and in turn be
shaped by them. We have examined the ways in which language, dress,
and body image are used both to reproduce and to contest the status quo
in gender relations. We have challenged gendered assumptions and practices that are embedded in the modern Western dichotomy between
public and domestic life, and compared these with the survival strategies
of women in present-day India and Egypt. Finally, we have taken a
critical look at the shape of gender relations in domestic and waged
work within our own culture.

In Chapters One and Two we shared our vision for a Christian

All team members contributed to this chapter.

feminism, drawing on those aspects of liberal, relational, and socialist feminism that support the biblical vision of human beings as made in the image of God and of a society rooted in justice, righteousness, and peace. In subsequent chapters we traced how these three basic streams of feminism have branched out since the "first wave" of feminism in the nineteenth century. Liberal feminism has developed a more "chastened" form that acknowledges the problems of the public/private dichotomy and the strengths of "women's ways of knowing" (Chapters Twelve and Thirteen). Relational feminism has developed into various forms of radical feminism since the beginning of the "second wave" (Chapter Three), contributed to the development of psychoanalytic and philosophical feminism (Chapter Twelve), and found an echo in the concerns of feminist theologians and rhetorical analysts (Chapters Five and Six, Seven and Eleven).

In the twentieth century, nineteenth-century socialist feminism evolved into Marxist feminism, then into a revised socialist feminism that tries to give equal weight to economics and patriarchy in its analysis of women's oppression (Chapter Three). More recently, postmodern feminism has shown us the hazards of speaking too glibly about "the generic woman" unmodified by race, class, ethnicity, nationality, and other variables (Chapters Three, Four, and Fourteen). Finally, an approach based on critical theory has helped to produce a more dynamic picture of gender relations as constructed and contested by persons with agency and moral accountability (Chapters Eight, Nine, Fifteen, and Sixteen).

"I'm Not a Feminist, But . . ."

We began Part One of this book with an anecdote about a Christian student who scurried away from one of our team members when he discovered that she was prepared to call herself a biblical feminist. Was this student representative of Christians in general, and of Reformed and evangelical Christians in particular? Would he have walked away as quickly if he had been able to read this book before their encounter? How have feminist thought and activism actually affected Christians and others, and what effects can we realistically expect in the future? It is with a consideration of these kinds of questions that we wish to end our book on the challenge of gender reconciliation.

We begin with the observation that it is not just male, white, evangelical Christians who hesitate to call themselves feminists. According to Patricia Hill Collins, who specializes in African-American studies, black women intellectuals also hesitate to call themselves feminists. The reason for this, she suggests, is that when we accept a noun-style label for ourselves (such as "feminist," "socialist," "pacifist," etc.), we may feel we are committing ourselves to *just* that label and all that it implies, including pressure to separate from other groups with whom we might want to keep open the option of association. This may be one reason why so many people insist that they are *not* feminists, then go on to explain changes they want to see in gender relations in a way that reflects aspects of one or another stream of feminism! Thus, African-American women are concerned that if they adopt the feminist label, they will have to choose between solidarity with other women (regardless of their insensitivity to racial issues) and solidarity with African-American men (regardless of their insensitivity to gender issues). This dilemma was graphically illustrated — and much-commented on by the media — in the fall of 1991, when law professor Anita Hill leveled charges of sexual harassment against Clarence Thomas, a fellow African-American who was a nominee for the U.S. Supreme Court.[1]

Black theoretician bell hooks, to whose work we were introduced in Chapter Four, offers one solution to this dilemma: that people shift from statements such as "I am a feminist" to statements such as "I support the goals of feminism." Such a strategy, she suggests, could "serve as a way [people] who are concerned about feminism as well as other political movements could express their support while avoiding linguistic structures that give primacy to one particular group."[2] Patricia Hill Collins adds that even the standpoint of one's own particular interest group will be enriched by keeping its boundaries semipermeable, both linguistically and practically. Taking her own concern for black feminism as an example, she writes,

---

1. See Anita Hill's article entitled "The Nature of the Beast," *Ms.*, January/February 1992, pp. 32-33. See also chap. 9 of the book by Patricia Hill Collins called *Black Feminist Thought: Knowledge, Consciousness, and the Politics of Empowerment* (London: HarperCollins, 1990). It should be noted that another reason for black women's rejection of the term *feminist* (and the substitution of the term *womanist* by some) is the contention that the term *feminist* has in the past been too narrowly associated with a white, middle-class agenda.

2. hooks, *Feminist Theory: From Margin to Center* (Boston: South End Press, 1984), p. 30. See also chap. 2 of Collins's *Black Feminist Thought*.

Black women can produce [only] an attenuated version of black feminist thought separated from other groups. Other groups cannot produce Black feminist thought without African-American women. . . . But the full actualization of Black feminist thought requires a collaborative enterprise with Black women at the center of a community based on coalitions among autonomous groups. By advocating, refining, and disseminating Black feminist thought, other groups — such as Black men, white women, white men, and other people of color — further its development.[3]

Other women hesitate to call themselves feminists and support feminist causes because of the link that is regularly drawn between feminism and homosexuality. For example, many people who oppose the opening up of church offices to women claim that such a move will inevitably lead to the ordination of practicing homosexuals.[4] And when team-members' students are asked why they hesitate to call themselves feminists, many frankly confess that they are afraid that it would lead to accusations of being lesbian.[5] As we saw in our chapter on the gendering of the body, women athletes have had to cope with this kind of "scare tactic" for years. Indeed, in America the Ladies' Professional Golf Association has gone to great lengths to defend itself against such "guilty until proven innocent" insinuations — for example, by producing pin-up type calendars of some of its women athletes. As an antifeminist strategy, this kind of name-calling and fear-mongering is a classic example of the power that hegemonic groups have to make their ideas "stick."

3. Collins, *Black Feminist Thought,* pp. 35-36.
4. That the rates of physical, psychological, and emotional abuse tend to be highest among conservative, antifeminist, and homophobic Christians is, of course, rarely mentioned by such critics. For example, among members of the Christian Reformed Church in North America, there are two (unofficial) conservative newspapers, both of which are stridently antifeminist, antiabortion, and homophobic, but neither of which even made mention of the officially commissioned Synodical Report on Abuse from the time it was released in September 1991 until the time it was received by the 1992 Synod of the denomination. Since these publications purport to be concerned with "family values" and "taking the Bible literally," one would expect them to print strong editorials condemning sexual abuse in particular.
5. Some male students have confessed that being perceived as feminists leads to accusations from their peers that they are "pussy-whipped" (a stronger and more contemporary version of being "hen-pecked") and thus not fully masculine — that is, strong, independent, and in control of the women in one's life.

Where do members of our team stand on the issue? We do not think it is necessary to take a strong stand one way or the other on one's use of the label "feminist," though we are happy to be known as feminists. But we do agree with Patricia Hill Collins that the full development of feminist (including Christian feminist) thought requires both a sense of separate identity and selective cooperation with other groups. Throughout this book we have maintained and explained our identity as Christians pursuing God's mandate for justice, righteousness, and peace on earth. We believe and have tried to demonstrate that such an agenda is compatible with many aspects of feminist thought and less so with some others. We will try to summarize some of these tensions and compatibilities now, returning to our original, threefold distinction between liberal, relational, and socialist feminism.

Liberal Feminism Revisited

We have already noted that many people, Christians among them, say, "I'm not a feminist, but . . ." and then go on to endorse a surprising number of issues from one or another feminist agenda. Although we do not have systematic data on this phenomenon, we have found in our experience that such people are more likely than not to be endorsing various planks of the liberal feminist platform. Recall that classic liberal feminism emphasizes human rationality, autonomy, and individual rights. It also maintains a strict (but degendered) separation of private and public life, and holds that reforms in law, custom, and education are sufficient to bring women into the societal and economic mainstream of modern life. Thus when a person says, "I'm not a feminist, but . . . I believe in equal pay for equal work," or "I believe that a woman could make just as good a president as a man," or "I'm against gender stereotyping in the classroom," or "I believe that the state has no business in the bedrooms of its citizens" — then that person is more or less a supporter of liberal feminism.

Christians as "Closet Liberal Feminists"

Church historian Ruth Tucker notes that over the past century, Christians of both sexes, while usually not admitting it, have quietly begun to support more and more planks in the liberal feminist platform (the exceptions for some involve stances on abortion and homosexuality). During the nineteenth century, however, it was common for church authorities to argue that women should even be denied employment outside the home. Thus John James, a British Congregational minister, made these assertions in his book on female piety:

> Neither reason nor Christianity invites woman to the professor's chair, or conducts her to the bar, or makes her welcome to the pulpit, or admits her to the place of ordinary magistry.... The Bible gives her a place of majesty and dignity in the domestic circle: that is the heart of her husband and the heart of her family. It is the female supremacy of that domain, where love, tenderness, refinement, thought and feeling preside.[6]

This Christian endorsement of the cult of domesticity was compounded by a resistance in the early twentieth century to giving women access to birth control and to the voting booth. One well-known fundamentalist pastor, eulogizing a wife who died in her forties, praised her as "a woman who could never be induced to cast a vote at the polls, or participate in church work beyond home, prayer, and private devotions."[7] A church newspaper editor warned against the feminist promotion of birth control: "The new woman hates children," he wrote, "and is madly exerting her ingenuity in frustrating the ends of matrimony."[8]

Today, however, even Christian organizations that participate in the backlash against feminism do so in a context that implicitly concedes much to the liberal feminist agenda. For example, in its 1989 statement, the Council on Biblical Manhood and Womanhood reaffirmed male headship

6. James, quoted by Ruth A. Tucker in *Women in the Maze: Questions and Answers on Biblical Equality* (Downers Grove, Ill.: InterVarsity Press, 1992), p. 218. See also Dale A. Johnson's *Women in English Religion, 1700-1925* (New York: Edwin Mellen, 1983), p. 122. For a nineteenth-century Calvinist expression of this same view, see Abraham Kuyper's group of essays entitled *De Eerepositie der Vrouw* ("The Woman's Position of Honor") (Kampen, Netherlands: J. H. Kok, 1914), trans. Irene Konyndyk, unpublished manuscript, Calvin College, 1990.

7. William Bell Riley, "Mrs. W. B. Riley: In Memoriam," *Christian Fundamentalist* 5 (September 1931): 99.

8. Quoted by Alan Graebner in "Birth Control and the Lutherans," in *Women in American Religion*, ed. Janet Wilson James (Philadelphia: University of Pennsylvania Press, 1980), p. 231. See also Tucker's *Women in the Maze*, p. 218.

in church and home, but was notably silent regarding any biblical necessity for women to stay out of politics or waged work — despite its stated concern over "the increasing promotion given to feminist egalitarianism."[9] According to Ruth Tucker, evangelical antifeminist Beverly LaHaye "decries contemporary feminism, [but] enthusiastically embraces the feminism of an earlier generation. A political activist herself, she fervently pleads with her followers to get involved in the political process — not only in voting but in campaigning for particular causes. In her book *The Act of Marriage*, co-authored with her husband, she devotes an entire chapter to birth control, with no admonitions against it."[10]

Thus it seems that not a few contemporary Christians — and, in our experience, other "traditionalists" as well — are in many ways "closet liberals": they support many of the goals of liberal feminism while claiming to reject feminism per se. We point this out not because we believe that the agenda of classic liberal feminism is necessarily the one Christians *should* follow, but simply because both honesty and consistency require us to give credit where it is due.

The historical truth of the matter is that Christians have as often been followers as they have been leaders of reforms involving gender relations. Consequently, it is misleading at best and dishonest at worst to write as if the practices resulting from such reforms (women's access to birth control or the voting booth, for example) have been miraculously arrived at by Christians' astute theologizing and reading of Scripture. As we tried to show in Chapter Seven, our theologizing and biblical interpretation are heavily — even if not totally — conditioned by our place in time and space.[11] Accordingly, we need to acknowledge not only

9. Council on Biblical Manhood and Womanhood, "The Danvers Statement," *Christianity Today*, 13 January 1989, p. 41. This statement also calls husbands to "forsake harsh or selfish leadership and grow in love and care for their wives" (p. 41). It also states that "in all of life Christ is the supreme authority and guide for men and women, so that no earthly submission — domestic, religious, or civil — ever implies a mandate to follow a human being into sin." Such qualifiers suggest that this movement to "recover" biblical manhood and womanhood may in fact be an instance of what Judith Stacey calls "patriarchy of the last gasp." See her book entitled *Brave New Families: Stories of Domestic Upheaval in Late Twentieth Century America* (New York: Basic Books, 1990).

10. Tucker, *Women in the Maze*, p. 218. See also Beverly and Tim LaHaye's book entitled *The Act of Marriage: The Beauty of Sexual Love* (Grand Rapids: Zondervan, 1976).

11. For a thoughtful demonstration of this via a history of scriptural exegesis

our own blind spots of the past but also the help that God has seen fit to supply from any movement or group that works to remove the scales from our eyes.

Attractions and Hazards of Contemporary Liberal Feminism

As our discussion in Part One of this volume made clear, both the strengths and the weaknesses of liberal feminism stem from its stress on the autonomous rationality of individuals. In Chapter Two we noted that liberal thought began with a commitment to the dignity and freedom of human persons, in reaction to ideas such as the divine right of kings, the unquestioned authority of the church, and the power of the aristocracy. Although initially the "persons" championed by liberalism were only white, property-owning males, liberal feminism extended the argument to include women, thereby allowing them to "join the society" — that is, to enter into the public sphere (theoretically) on the same terms as men.[12]

In subsequent chapters we noted that liberal feminist reforms have indeed served to advance and protect the interests of middle-class, educated women, not just in the West but also in non-Western countries as, for better or worse, these embrace various aspects of modernity. These reforms have given such women both a political voice and a measure of economic independence which has allowed them to counteract the isolation and vulnerability that all too often are the consequence of the Western-style cult of domesticity. At the same time, however, liberal feminism has suffered from at least three recurring weaknesses.

First of all, it has tended to place too much faith in the capacity of human rationality to usher in a completely just society, as opposed to one in which some privileged women are allowed to join their hegemonic male counterparts in the public square. In such an arrangement, both non-privileged women (e.g., of different races and classes) and

---

relating to controversial social issues, see Willard Swartley's *Slavery, Sabbath, War, and Women: Case Studies in Biblical Interpretation* (Scottdale, Pa.: Herald Press, 1983).

12. This, of course, assumes that women are now constrained by nothing more than their own internal limitations in their attempts to act in the same privileged way as dominant males. As we pointed out in the chapter on gender relations that focused on critical theory, this ignores the powerful, informal restraints that continue to restrict the agency of "technically equal" but actually still subordinate groups.

privileged women caught up in the cult of domesticity still remain politically and economically vulnerable. Classic examples are the poorly paid women of color who become nannies for the children of upwardly mobile professional women and the full-time homemakers who because of their economic dependency on their husbands cannot easily leave their abusive marriages.

Second, the autonomous human rationality celebrated by liberal feminists has all too often turned out to be made in the image of Western, white males and has thus tended to ignore — or devalue in comparison with men's cognitive styles — the ways of knowing and relating that we described in Chapters Twelve through Fourteen. Because of the way women have been socialized for domesticity and child raising, these have come to be called "women's" ways of knowing in Western cultures. But we have argued that they are in fact essential to fully *human* knowing and relating, and that the lives of both women and men, in both domestic and waged-work settings, are impoverished by ignoring or denigrating them.

For example, in previous chapters we described the situation of a denomination in which many people have worked to open up church offices to women. But women working as pastors in denominations that have already cleared this hurdle warn that simply letting women "join the old boys' club" solves very little, for it assumes that the competence of women pastors and elders will be measured by their success in thinking and acting just like men. If male-dominated, overly hierarchical modes of church management remain in place, if church liturgies do not become woman-friendly, and if the real needs of ordinary women and their families continue to be trivialized or ignored, then the ordination of women turns out to be a questionable victory.[13]

The cross-cultural perspectives we explored in Chapters Four and Fourteen underline similar concerns: if feminist activism assumes that the individual is the basic unit of society, and if its success is measured only by the degree to which women act economically and politically like hegemonic Western males, then important familial, cultural, and religious networks are jeopardized. Non-Western feminists as well as women of color in the West readily concede the need to restructure gender relations within such networks. But most still wish to build their feminism upon them rather than apart from them.

13. For examples of feminist attempts to go "beyond mere ordination" in the reform of theology and liturgy, see Chapter Six of this volume.

Third, although there is now a "chastened" form of liberal feminism (which we described in Chapter Thirteen) that acknowledges the problems of the public/private split, liberal feminists still tend to see issues related to religion, sexuality, and child raising as private matters in which only individual choice needs to be legally protected. Sometimes this can lead to uncomfortable contradictions, as in the case of the liberal feminist woman who chooses to pay low wages to a woman of color who takes over her child-care tasks, relief from which allows her to be a full-time professional. As another example, one of us recalls asking members of a national coalition of liberal feminists if they would approve any restrictions on abortion. When they answered in the negative — invoking the liberal feminist argument about defending the privacy of women's reproductive choice — our team member then asked, "What about women who want to selectively abort only *female* fetuses? Should that too be a legally protected private choice?" Her only answer was a conspicuous silence that obviously masked tremendous internal conflict.

Thus, despite its rhetoric about advancing the autonomy and dignity of all individuals, liberal feminist practice lets many individuals fall between the cracks. Its chief beneficiaries, as we have seen in previous chapters, are already privileged women — and even their benefits are won at the expense of entering the so-called public sphere on terms set by hegemonic males. This is particularly the case in the United States, which, to the extent that it supports feminist goals at all, does so largely from a base of liberal feminist assumptions. Indeed, it is possible that liberal feminism has such great appeal in America because it reinforces the capitalist notion that individual entrepreneurship is really all that is needed for success. Both capitalist and liberal feminist rhetoric tend to ignore (and sometimes even deny) the existence of structural constraints that work against not just the mobility of women but that of entire classes and races in the society.

Relational Feminism Revisited

Perhaps inevitably, it was a European feminist living in America who decided to go public in her criticism of the assumptions of liberal feminism and their consequences. An economist born and trained in Britain, with considerable research experience in continental Europe,

586

Sylvia Hewlett began her professorial career at Barnard College in New York, shortly before she had the first of her three children in 1977, at the age of thirty-one. Since then, both her personal and professional concerns have led her to espouse a form of relational feminism that both hearkens back to the nineteenth century (in the sense that it places women's childbearing activities front and center) and looks approvingly at the family and social policies of contemporary European countries.[14]

One of Hewlett's main criticisms of American-style liberal feminism is that it has relegated childbearing and its attendant burdens largely to the realm of individual responsibility. "Up until the time I had children," she writes, "I was profoundly confident of my ability to find fulfillment in both love and work."[15] After the birth of her first child, however, she began to experience the limits of the liberal, individualistic model of feminism. Not wanting to turn the care of her first child almost completely over to others, and finding that the preschool program at Barnard catered largely to wives of full-time faculty members who wanted only a few hours a week of group playtime for their children, Hewlett compromised by having her child in her office with her for part of each day.

To her amazement, she found that despite the fact that she was teaching at a women's university supposedly dedicated to providing role models for its students, a number of people profoundly resented her for letting her "private" child-raising life overflow into her "public" professional sphere. If women professionals were to make it in a male-dominated world, the message seemed to be, then they would have to do it on traditionally male terms and fit family concerns into whatever spare time they could manage to find outside of their paid work. One of her colleagues even left a note on her desk that commented pointedly, "We, at Barnard, are not running a creche but a college."[16]

14. See Hewlett's books entitled *A Lesser Life: The Myth of Women's Liberation in America* (New York: William Morrow, 1986), and *When the Bough Breaks: The Cost of Neglecting Our Children* (New York: Basic Books, 1991). There are other relational, academic feminists who criticize what they perceive as America's overly uncritical adherence to the liberal feminist model. We mention Hewlett in particular because of the audience her books have attracted outside the academy, especially among policy experts and public-service foundations concerned with the future of social and family policy in America.

15. Hewlett, *A Lesser Life*, p. 18.

16. Hewlett, *A Lesser Life*, p. 22. For another example of an academic woman

European Feminism: A Better Brand?

After doing some demographic research, Hewlett confirmed that most American women professionals up through the 1970s had simply opted *not* to have children. Being, by and large, token women in male-dominated fields and living in a culture which assumes that the full-time waged worker will have a backup person tending matters on the homefront, Hewlett's women colleagues had found that professional pressures functionally ruled out the practicality of having children. Indeed, she observed, "These same women often tend to resent [waged] working mothers, viewing their struggles to bear and raise children as an illegitimate effort to have their cake and eat it."[17]

At the same time, Hewlett began to collect both anecdotal and systematic evidence on the outworking of a more relational concept of feminism in Europe. Comparing America with Britain, France, Italy, and Sweden, she found that despite differences among the latter four countries (e.g., traditionally Catholic versus secular welfare state), they were all "nations that have produced better conditions of life for a majority of their female citizens [than America has]."[18] Paid maternity leaves offered in conjunction with job protection are common, as are government-funded family allowances indexed to the age and number of children in a family. Publicly funded access to medical care is provided in all four of these European countries.[19] Part-time work with secure benefits is readily available for women, as are paid sick-leave days for times when dependent family members need special care at home. In the event

---

who tried (with limited success) to bring a child to work, see the introduction to Arlie Hochschild's *The Second Shift: Working Parents and the Revolution at Home* (New York: Viking Press, 1989).

17. Hewlett, *A Lesser Life*, p. 23. Many men, particularly working-class men, express similar sentiments about wage-working mothers "having their cake and eating it" — especially when (as in Britain, for example) paid maternity leave is affected. See Joyce Gelb's *Feminism and Politics: A Comparative Perspective* (Berkeley: University of California Press, 1989), chap. 6.

18. Hewlett, *A Lesser Life*, p. 16.

19. The United States and South Africa are the only Western industrialized nations which do *not* have socialized health-care schemes that cover all citizens. It is also worth noting that in France the government pays pregnant women for showing up for each prenatal checkup, because this practice helps prevent later, more costly interventions in the perinatal and postnatal period. See chap. 6 of Hewlett's *When the Bough Breaks*.

of marital breakups, a system that efficiently enforces fathers' responsibilities for child-care payments (and provides government supplements to cover uncollectible ones) also helps to forestall the pauperization of women.

In these (and other) European states, Hewlett concluded, women are able to fulfill both family and waged-work obligations without either "burning out" from stress or falling into unrelieved poverty. Also of interest is the fact that among European nations, there is little correlation between the leniency of abortion laws and the rate of abortion. The Netherlands, for example, has one of the most lenient abortion policies in Europe, yet it has one of the lowest rates of abortion among all industrialized nations. What keeps the rate of abortion low in such countries, according to Mary Ann Glendon, a Harvard legal scholar, is the presence of precisely the kind of welfare "safety net" just described. A woman with a problem pregnancy is much more likely to carry the fetus to term knowing that neither she nor the child will lack for medical care, that she is entitled to job-protected, paid maternity leave, that subsidized housing, good day-care, and a family allowance are forthcoming, and that the father of the child will be held financially accountable too.[20]

Hewlett acknowledges that the average wage of women still lags behind that of men in these western European democracies. But, she points out, this is compensated for by the reliability of their welfare safety net that provides benefits over the lifespan of their citizens, and especially the provisions made for mothers and young children. Western Europe, she concludes, is overall a better place to be a mother — or a child — than America is.[21] And even liberally inclined feminists tend to agree. Political scientist Joyce Gelb, in her comparison of American, British, and Swedish feminism, writes,

20. Mary Ann Glendon, *Abortion and Divorce in Western Law: American Failures, European Challenges* (Cambridge: Harvard University Press, 1987). Glendon, who is Catholic, is also convinced that America has adopted the wrong language of discourse in speaking about abortion "rights" and the "right to life." She points out that European nations are careful to avoid such language in crafting abortion legislation, preferring instead to affirm the sanctity of life while also acknowledging that sometimes (as in the decision to fight a war) one has to choose between the lesser of two evils. However, as noted above, this approach, when combined with a reliable welfare "safety net," actually results in a lower rate of abortion than that in most countries which have greater restrictions on abortion.
21. Hewlett, *When the Bough Breaks.*

It is undeniable that because of the largesse of the Swedish welfare state, benefits to single-female heads of household, to female members of the labor force, and to their children are far superior to those offered in ... the United States. ... [Among other things] generous family rent and maintenance allowances, paid parental and sick leaves, in addition to special subsidies for single parents, have created a system that provides a far higher standard of living, without stigmatization and without long-term dependency and work disincentives, than in the United States.[22]

The Limitations of European Relational Feminism

In Chapter Two we defined classical relational feminism in terms of its emphasis on women's rights *as women* — that is, principally in terms of their childbearing and/or nurturing tasks. Relational feminists then go on to make claims on society for women on the basis of these reproductive and caretaking contributions. According to such criteria, it is clear that the European democracies described by Hewlett, Glendon, and Gelb have embraced relational feminism both in principle and in practice. And to American women worried about escalating medical expenses, affordable child care, and the stresses of the double shift, the contemporary European embodiment of relational feminism is bound to seem very humane and attractive. But a closer look reveals that the advantages of relational feminism as presently practiced in Europe come at a price.

To begin with, women's political and social equality in these welfare states has lagged greatly behind their material security. In the comparative research she undertook in the 1980s, Joyce Gelb found that a far higher proportion of British and Swedish women, as compared with American women, perceived that men were still treated more favorably than women in politics and in the general customs and practices of their respective countries. Moreover, British and Swedish women are even more likely than their American counterparts to be doing waged work that is part-time, highly sex-segregated, and lower-paying and service-oriented, work that is an extension of their domestic skills.

This in turn perpetuates a traditional division of labor in the home.

22. Gelb, *Feminism and Politics*, pp. 207-8.

Comparative surveys show that household chores, cleaning, and child care are all more traditionally gendered in both Britain and Sweden than in the United States. (And, as we saw in Chapters Fifteen and Sixteen, the U.S. is hardly a model of gender equity in these areas itself; indeed, in telling the story of her struggles, Sylvia Hewlett says that she faced the apparent presumption that juggling waged work and domestic responsibilities was *her* problem, not her husband's.) Even in Sweden, with its strong policy commitment to gender-neutral parental leave, about 75 percent of new fathers still sign over their parental-leave privileges to the mothers of their children (who are then allowed to add these benefits to their own). And although higher education receives more state funding in Britain and Sweden, fewer students have access to it, and among those who do, the percentages of women are markedly lower than in the United States.[23]

Thus, in Joyce Gelb's words, "the data suggest that strong patterns of gender polarization and traditional sex role socialization persist even among the sons and daughters of the welfare state."[24] Indeed, both Gelb and Catherine East, another feminist scholar, have noted that the comprehensive "safety nets" provided for women and children in many European countries were not the result of feminist forces in the first place. Often they were the result of post–World War II urgencies: the need to rebuild nations both in material ways (hence the need for an expanded labor force) and in terms of population (hence the need for pronatalist social policies). Moreover, the fact that western European countries have more ethnically homogeneous populations than the United States, as well as parliamentary systems of government, has made it easier for such social policies to be implemented.[25]

23. Gelb, *Feminism and Politics*, chap. 6. In 1986, only 5 percent of British women held bachelor's or advanced degrees; the comparable figure for women in the United States was 20 percent. A report in the September 10, 1986, issue of the *Chronicle of Higher Education* (p. 26) documented that in the U.S., women made up 27 percent of university faculty members, whereas in Sweden and Britain the comparable percentages were 5 percent and less than 4 percent, respectively. (In America, however, women faculty are still disproportionately represented in the part-time and non-tenured ranks.)

24. Gelb, *Feminism and Politics*, p. 201.

25. In America, feminist groups have worked very hard for the passage of such things as a national family policy and "dependent care" legislation, only to have them vetoed by the president even after passage by Congress. This in turn allows both politicians and the media to act as if liberal feminist goals (e.g., career opportunity and mobility) are the only ones women really care about — which is inaccu-

Thus, social policies in western European welfare states do *facilitate* women's labor-force participation and undergird it with a generous safety net that reduces the risk of both poverty and the chronic "double day." But these policies do little to *expand* the possibilities available to women in a way that challenges a traditionally gendered division of labor. Catherine East offers this assessment:

> [In the latter approach,] characterized by commitment to affirmative action and widespread feminist consciousness, the United States (and even Britain, with a longer and somewhat more meaningful commitment to equal opportunity enactments) appear to have surpassed Sweden. . . . Swedish women have in fact not really left their homes; their major domestic responsibilities and very partial attachment to the labor force . . . [have] resulted in the continuing primacy of traditional sex roles in society. The extension of traditional women's roles into public-sector paid employment, and the existence of benefits that help support women's part-time [waged employment] status, may reinforce rather than change sex roles over the long run.[26]

From the viewpoint of the psychoanalytic feminists we met in Chapter Twelve, this entrenchment of traditional gender roles — however equitably funded — is a problem. You will recall that according to psychoanalytic feminists, it is in part the "reproduction of mothering" and the absence of fathers as co-caretakers of young children that help to reproduce misogyny, including a cultural tolerance, shared by both sexes, of abuse toward females of all ages. And indeed, Joyce Gelb concludes that despite the economic redistribution that Sweden has achieved, "issues of power sharing and male dominance have largely been left untouched."[27] Moreover, welfare systems based on relational

---

rate, but a striking example of the structuring of national consciousness by hegemonic groups. See Catherine East's "Critical Comments on *A Lesser Life: The Myth of Women's Liberation in America*," paper published by the National Women's Political Caucus, 1275 "K" Street, Suite 750, Washington, D.C., 20005.

26. Ibid., pp. 211, 213. Hewlett's comparative work also fails to document what happens to European women trying to become full-time waged workers after their children are grown. In the Netherlands, for example, it is almost impossible for such "re-entry" women over forty-five years of age to find jobs, since they are considered "unskilled." As a result, they often have little choice but to stay home and/or to rely on government assistance.

27. Gelb, *Feminism and Politics*, pp. 210-11. The psychoanalytic feminist argu-

feminist assumptions seem to assume that all women *will* become mothers. It is not clear how much protection such systems provide for the economic and social interests of persons who remain single.

American feminist groups are also characterized by a willingness to set aside ideological differences for the sake of pragmatic goals. In our historical survey in Chapter Two, we saw liberal and relational feminists forming these pragmatic coalitions in order to advance the cause of women's suffrage in the United States. Today, that same flexibility has led to nationwide legal and social attention to the issue of domestic violence. Coalitions for the support of battered women now exist in every state, and the past twenty years have seen the formation of about 1,200 shelters for women.[28] Although this "shelter movement" actually began in England — and exists embryonically in other European countries — it has been most successful in the United States, in part because even radical feminists have been willing to compromise ideological purity in order to facilitate funding, legislative changes, and better enforcement of existing laws where this issue is concerned.[29] By contrast, European progress in extending a better economic "safety net" to all women has not been matched by comparable attention to issues such as domestic violence and pornography, in part precisely because of the assumption of those in high places that traditional gender roles need not be challenged but merely more equitably funded.[30]

---

ment for coparenting has sometimes been criticized for its lack of systematic empirical evidence. This, however, has begun to accumulate, at least in the United States. See, for example, Diane Ehrensaft's *Parenting Together: Men and Women Sharing the Care of Their Children* (Champaign: University of Illinois Press, 1990).

28. Nevertheless, the United States still has a long way to go: its 1,200 shelters for helping abused women are still outnumbered by the 3,200 shelters that exist in the United States for abused animals. See Colman McCarthy's article entitled "Women Face Greatest Danger at Home," Washington Post Writers' Group, 22 January 1991 (as reprinted in the *Grand Rapids Press* of the same date).

29. See Elizabeth Pleck's *Domestic Tyranny: The Making of American Social Policy against Family Violence from Colonial Times to the Present* (New York: Oxford University Press, 1987). It is also possible that the greater attention paid by American feminists to domestic violence is in part due to the fact that America is simply a very violent country — for example, its homicide rate is among the highest in the world.

30. Gelb, *Feminism and Politics,* chap. 6. Gelb notes that in Britain there is a strong tendency for various feminist groups (radical and socialist especially) to splinter over issues of ideological purity. This has made British radical feminism in particular a much more localized and variegated movement. A positive result of this phenomenon is that group members feel very integrated and supported at the local

A Third Way?

Thus, if we are looking for a feminist utopia, what we seem to have so far are two less-than-perfect models in the Western world. In material and economic ways it is easier to be a woman raising young children in western Europe in the 1990s — but it is relatively easier to be a woman challenging traditionally gendered educational, political, and employment practices in the United States, even though gender equity is still far from being a fait accompli here. This is not to say that women in Europe, the United States, and elsewhere do not find ways to advance their own and their families' interests, whatever the official shape of gender relations may be. For example, our case studies from India and Egypt have shown that both elite and working-class women find ways to combine traditional, familial, personal, and economic goals, despite the historical, material, and cultural forces working against them. But it is clear from our survey of gender relations throughout this book that much remains to be done both nationally and internationally.

Is there any way that we can effectively combine or transcend the liberal and relational models of feminism? Is it possible to envisage a society in which some women's domestic comfort and job mobility are not bought at the expense of others' continuing poverty, or at the cost of a chronic "double day" for themselves? Conversely, is it possible to have a society in which decent economic support for women does not come at the cost of maintaining traditional gender stereotypes and a traditionally gendered division of both domestic and waged labor? Our Calvinist sensibilities make us cautious about asserting final solutions in a world still broken by sin and inhabited by people who cannot see around corners. Nevertheless, we conclude with some suggestions for "next steps" as we face the task of gender reconciliation.

Socialist Feminism Revisited

Thus far in this final chapter we have compared the outworkings of liberal and relational feminist emphases in North America and Europe,

---

level and have a clear idea of what they stand for. A negative result is that nationwide legal and policy reforms, which by their nature require intergroup cooperation and compromise, occur more slowly in Britain than in the United States.

respectively, and found both in some ways wanting. But what about the third major stream of feminism — namely, socialist feminism — about which we spoke at the beginning of our volume? What has its line of descent been, and how, if at all, has it aided gender reconciliation?

In Chapter Two we pointed out that, unlike the nineteenth-century liberal and evangelical reformers, socialist-feminist thinkers aimed their critique squarely at the structural problems of emerging industrial, capitalist society. According to their analysis, women would be free only when the entire society was radically restructured, from its economic base up.[31] In the twentieth century, we have seen some of the outworking of this position in the European welfare states previously described: extremes of wealth and poverty *have* been greatly reduced in these nations, including the particular forms of poverty to which women with young children are susceptible. However, as we have shown, this change has occurred without adequate challenge to male political, professional, and social hegemony in these countries — a challenge better (although by no means perfectly) mounted in the United States.

To understand why this is so, we need to look briefly again at the evolution of socialist thought. By about 1900, the early forms of socialism we described in Chapter Two had split into two streams of classical Marxism. There was a revolutionary stream, which stressed the violent overthrow of capitalism either by the masses or by a vanguard communist party, and a more evolutionary stream, which stressed the democratic attainment of communism through the ballot box and the trade-union movement. The revolutionary stream of this thought led to the Russian Revolution of 1917 and the succeeding seventy years of

---

31. For an unusual nineteenth-century attempt to undergird social democratic reforms with an analysis based on a Reformed Christian worldview, see Abraham Kuyper's *Het Sociale Vraagstuk en de Christlijke Religie* ("The Social Problem and the Christian Religion") (Amsterdam: J. A. Wormser, 1891), translated by Dirk Jellema as *Christianity and the Class Struggle* (Grand Rapids: Piet Hein, 1950), and by James Skillen as *The Problem of Poverty* (Grand Rapids: Baker Book House, 1991). However, although Kuyper was unusually sensitive to the problem of class exploitation, he was much less attuned to problems of gender relations, and in fact joined other turn-of-the-century Christian leaders in buying unhesitatingly into the cult of domesticity for women. See his group of essays entitled *De Eerepositie der Vrouw* ("The Woman's Position of Honor"). See also Mary Stewart Van Leeuwen's analysis of these essays entitled "Abraham Kuyper and the Cult of True Womanhood," paper given at the 25th Anniversary Conference of the Institute for Christian Studies, Toronto, June 1992.

communist rule of the Eastern bloc. The evolutionary stream of thought led, among other things, to the various forms of democratic socialism practiced in western European welfare states. In both kinds of thought, however, there has been a strong tendency toward economic reductionism — that is, toward seeing the attainment of justice (including justice in gender relations) in purely economic terms.

However, around 1920 a third stream of socialist thought — a kind of "Western Marxism" — arose out of the earlier two streams, but it was also critical of both. Two of the key figures in this movement were the Hungarian György Lukács and the Italian Antonio Gramsci.[32] We noted in Chapter Eight that much of our critical-theoretical analysis of hegemony and of the dynamic between persons as "culturally constructed" and "culturally critical" originates in Gramsci's thought. Where that thinking parts with both revolutionary and evolutionary socialism is in its emphasis on the importance of hegemony (and hence potential resistance to it) throughout *all* of social life. Gramsci insisted that it was not just the economic and political hegemony of capitalism that held society in its thrall, but equally the working of hegemonic forces in art, popular culture, the intellectual life, and all other forms of social relations. Philosopher Lambert Zuidervaart offers this comment:

> The socioeconomic transformation [Gramsci] seeks would involve more than the transfer of political or economic power from the upper classes. It would involve the overthrow of an integral form of class rule which exists . . . also in active forms of experience and consciousness. For this to happen, an alternative hegemony, a new predominant practice and consciousness, must be created. Because art and other forms of culture play important roles in human practice and consciousness, developing alternative cultural programming is crucial for socioeconomic transformation.[33]

In our chapters on narrative, body image, dress, language, and work, we have tried to apply this holistic, critical analysis to gender relations. The thrust of our approach has been that since the fallout of broken

---

32. For a further treatment of these figures, see Raymond Williams's *Keywords* (London: Flamingo, 1983).

33. Zuidervaart, notes on Marx and Marxism, Calvin College Philosophy Department, Grand Rapids, Mich., 1992. See also Antonio Gramsci's *Selections from the Prison Notebooks* (London: Lawrence & Wishart, 1971).

gender relations affects all aspects of human social life, it can be rectified only by close examination and reform of all of them, taken both separately and together. It is not just in law, politics, or economics that hegemonic masculinity and privileged femininity are constructed and resisted: the same processes are at work in the language we speak, the forms of worship we use, the clothing we wear, the stories we tell each other, and the domestic and waged work we do.

Again, this is not to say that human beings are nothing but victims of the forces at work in all of these areas. Throughout this volume we have also tried to stress that people in general — and women in particular — both accept and strategically transcend the limitations placed upon them. In theological terms, they are both created beings constrained by natural and social contexts, and agents made in the image of a personal, transcendent God who freely acts. Our point in covering the many topics we have is simply this: because no part of life is exempt from the brokenness of gender relations, there are no "quick fixes," no compartmentalized repairs that will solve the problems we face. Activity by activity, sphere by sphere, we need to question what has been taken for granted and learn to carry out our kingdom-building tasks in ways that reflect justice, righteousness, and peace in gender relations.

Beyond Critical Theory to Biblical Shalom

Practitioners of critical theory have as their vision the release of human beings from all forms of domination.[34] The strength of this approach, and our reason for drawing on it frequently in this book, lies in its capacity to analyze shortcomings in the current social order — shortcomings usually taken for granted as "just the way things are" — in light of a vision of how things should be. For many critical theorists, however, the normative vision of how things should be is one of individual autonomy — albeit of a much more radical and inclusive kind than that put forth by traditional liberal theory. By contrast, our normative vision, which we laid out in Chapter One, is one of biblical *shalom*, which Nicholas Wolterstorff defines as "the human being dwelling at peace

34. See, for example, Jürgen Habermas's *Knowledge and Human Interests*, trans. Jeremy J. Shapiro (Boston: Beacon Press, 1971).

in all his or her relationships: with God, with self, with fellows, with nature."[35]

Biblical *shalom,* as we affirmed in Chapter Thirteen, certainly assumes conditions of social justice in which human beings no longer oppress each other. But it does not stop there, as Wolterstorff explains:

> Shalom in the first place incorporates right and harmonious relationships to *God* and delight in [God's] service. . . . Secondly, shalom incorporates right, harmonious relationships to other *human beings* and delight in human community. Shalom is absent when a society is a collection of individuals all out to make their own way in the world. . . . Thirdly, shalom incorporates right, harmonious relationships to *nature* and delight in our physical surroundings.[36]

The interpersonal dimension of *shalom* requires that we begin to see and implement power in a more radically biblical way. Practical theologian James Newton Poling defines power as "the ability to act in effective ways with the objects and people that make up our perceived world." He also acknowledges that "to the extent that people or institutions deprive a person of the power to live, that person is rendered powerless and her life is limited." Yet, he continues, we are mistaken to think of power, in its most normative sense, as simply a one-way effect that individuals have on others.[37]

Human power is inherently relational: it depends on connections among persons and on the institutions and ideas that they have in common. Accordingly, says Poling, power is better understood as "the energy of the relational web itself . . . the ability to sustain internal relationships and increase the power of the relational web as a whole."[38] Under conditions of God's *shalom,* this web of relationships is benevolent: it is a "win-win" situation in which the individual and the network enhance each other's creativity and undergo continuous, positive reciprocal transformation. By contrast, theologian Bernard Loomer defines the abuse of power as the presumption that one can affect

---

35. Wolterstorff, *Until Justice and Peace Embrace* (Grand Rapids: William B. Eerdmans, 1983), p. 69.

36. Ibid., p. 70 (author's italics).

37. Poling, *The Abuse of Power: A Theological Problem* (Nashville: Abingdon, 1991), p. 24.

38. Ibid., p. 24.

others with minimal effect on one's self. He goes on to sketch the social consequences of such abuse:

> As long as one's size and sense of worth are measured by the strength of one's capacity to influence others, as long as power is associated with the sense of initiative and aggressiveness, and passivity is indicative of weakness or a corresponding lack of power, then the natural and inevitable inequalities among individuals and groups become the means whereby the estrangements of life become wider and deeper. . . . We tend to trample on or remain indifferent to those people whom we feel we can safely ignore.[39]

The preceding paragraphs focus on the reform of power on the interpersonal level, which is of course very important: individual and interpersonal attitudes must certainly change if we are to bring about gender reconciliation. But at the group level, as we have stressed in previous chapters, power also involves the ability to impose meanings that are accepted by both dominant and subordinate groups regardless of their empirical accuracy. For example, when we accept the standard, 1950s-type American family as "traditional" (when in fact it is quite a late arrival on the historical scene), or when non-Western women accept the Western equation of "woman" with "housewife" (even though it is economically impossible for them to become only housewives), then the power of hegemonic groups to "make their definitions stick" is confirmed. Throughout this book we have tried to help readers become more aware of such struggles to control definition, and in the process to give them alternative "lenses" through which to view gender relations.

Thus, in various chapters we have attempted to make visible the taken-for-granted distortions of power that affect gender relations. We have tried to show that change is needed in many areas and on many levels: economic and linguistic, theological and familial, national and international. And both large and small transformations are needed, from changes in major societal structures to changes in the personal decisions we make about our bodies and how we clothe them. Our aim has been not to set ourselves apart as more virtuous than our readers, but rather to share the insights that our different disciplines and our interdisciplinary work together as Christian scholars can contribute to the cause of gender reconciliation.

39. Loomer, "Two Conceptions of Power," *Criterion* 15 (1976): 12.

Final Thoughts

One of the first steps that has to be taken in reforming any institution is to understand that things have not always been the way they are now. Our recurring historical emphasis — on the development of feminism, on the history of gendered language, dress, theology, and work — has hopefully helped readers toward this goal. But a second and even more vital step is learning to listen to the oppressed. If we are to overcome beliefs and practices that are at odds with the biblical vision of *shalom* for gender relations, we need to listen, as undefensively as possible, to those who are hurting. In Nicholas Wolterstorff's words,

> [We need] to listen to those who because of their social background or goals or sympathies see the situation differently than we do. It is especially important that we, who see history from the topside, listen to those who see it from the underside: Gentiles listening to Jews, Jews to Palestinians, men to women, rich to poor . . . North Americans to South Americans, the First World to the Third.[40]

We hope that our inclusion of cross-cultural case studies and critiques of Western feminism, along with our selective appeal to critical theory, has sensitized our readers to listen in the way that Wolterstorff describes. Certainly in our year together as a team, each of us learned to listen more acutely and receptively as we struggled to understand each others' backgrounds, goals, and sympathies. If we have helped our readers to do likewise — and thereby helped them to become effective agents of gender reconciliation — then we will consider our efforts well rewarded.

In the course of writing this book together, we also confirmed that we are part of an ongoing quest for gender reconciliation that stretches far back into history. While at times we were discouraged by the gap that still looms between our goal of gender reconciliation and the present state of gender relations, just as often we found ourselves amazed and gratified by the quantity and quality of gender-related scholarship we were able to draw on, by the excitement and encouragement of others on behalf of our work, and by real, positive changes taking place in the world at large. As Christian feminists, we accept this ambiguity that comes from living "between the times." Nevertheless, we look forward in hope to the *shalom* of a new heaven and a new earth, in which all things — and all relationships — will be made new.

40. Wolterstorff, *Until Justice and Peace Embrace*, p. 176.

BIBLIOGRAPHY

Works Cited in Chapter 1

Bonavoglia, Angela. "Sacred Secret." *Ms.*, March/April 1992, pp. 40-45.

Calvin College Social Research Center. "Survey of Abuse in the Christian Reformed Church." Grand Rapids: Calvin College, 1990.

Carnes, Patrick. *Don't Call It Love: Recovery from Sexual Addiction.* New York: Bantam, 1991.

Christ, Carol, and Judith Plaskow, eds. *Womanspirit Rising.* San Francisco: Harper & Row, 1979.

Faludi, Susan. *Backlash: The Undeclared War against American Women.* New York: Crown Publications, 1991.

Fiorenza, Elisabeth Schüssler. *In Memory of Her: A Feminist Theological Reconstruction of Christian Origins.* New York: Crossroad, 1985.

Furnish, Victor P. *Moral Teachings of Paul: Selected Issues.* Rev. ed. Nashville: Abingdon, 1985.

Greeley, Andrew. "Priestly Silence on Pedophilia." *New York Times,* 13 March 1992, p. A-15.

The Heidelberg Catechism. Grand Rapids: CRC Publications, 1975.

Horton, Anne L., and Judith A. Williamson. *Abuse and Religion: When Praying Isn't Enough.* Lexington, Mass.: D. C. Heath, 1988.

Jhally, Sut. "Dreamworlds: Desire/Sex/Power in Rock Video." Amherst, Mass.: Dept. of Communications videocassette, University of Massachusetts, 1990.

601

Kuhn, Sarah, and Barry Bluestone. "Economic Restructuring and the Female Labor Market: The Impact of Industrial Change on Women." In *Women, Households, and the Economy*, ed. Lourdes Benaria and Catharine R. Stimpson. New Brunswick, N.J.: Rutgers University Press, 1987.

Kuyper, Abraham. *Lectures on Calvinism.* Grand Rapids: William B. Eerdmans, 1975.

Leo, John. "Sexism in the Schoolhouse." *U.S. News and World Report,* 9 March 1992, p. 22.

Psalter Hymnal of the Christian Reformed Church in North America. Grand Rapids: CRC Publications, 1987.

Ruether, Rosemary Radford. *Sexism and God-Talk: Toward a Feminist Theology.* Boston: Beacon Press, 1983.

Russell, Diane E. H. *Secret Trauma: Incest in the Lives of Girls and Women.* New York: Basic Books, 1986.

Segal, Phillip. "Elements of Male Chauvinism in Classical Halakhah." *Judaism: A Quarterly Journal of Jewish Life and Thought* 24 (Spring 1975): 226-44.

Steinfels, Peter. "Inquiry in Chicago Breaks Silence on Sex Abuse by Catholic Priests." *New York Times,* 24 February 1992, pp. A-1, A-8.

Strauss, Murray A., and Richard Gelles. "Societal Change and Change in Family Violence from 1975 to 1985 as Revealed by Two National Surveys." *Journal of Marriage and the Family* 48 (August 1986): 465-79.

Swidler, Leonard. *Biblical Affirmations of Women.* Philadelphia: Westminster Press, 1979.

————. *Yeshua: A Model for Moderns.* New York: Sheed & Ward, 1988.

————, and Arlene Swidler, eds. *Women Priests: A Catholic Commentary on the Vatican Declaration.* New York: Paulist Press, 1977.

Synod of the Christian Reformed Church in North America. Taped proceedings of sessions held at Calvin College, Grand Rapids, Mich., 18 June 1990.

Trible, Phyllis. *God and the Rhetoric of Sexuality.* Philadelphia: Fortress Press, 1978.

Verhey, Allen. *The Great Reversal: Ethics in the New Testament.* Grand Rapids: William B. Eerdmans, 1984.

Works Cited in Part I

Ahmed, Leila. "Feminism and Feminist Movements in the Middle East— A Preliminary Exploration: Turkey, Egypt, Algeria, People's

Democratic Republic of Yemen." *Women's Studies International Forum* 5, no. 2 (1982): 164.

————. "Western Ethnocentrism and Perceptions of the Harem." *Feminist Studies* 8 (Fall 1982): 520-31.

Alsdurf, James, and Phyllis Alsdurf. *Battered into Submission: The Tragedy of Wife Abuse in the Christian Home.* Downers Grove, Ill.: InterVarsity Press, 1989.

American Association of University Women. "Shortchanging Girls, Short-changing America." AAUW, January 1991.

Amos, Valerie, and Pratibha Parmar. "Challenging Imperial Feminism." *Feminist Review* 17 (July 1984): 3-19.

Amott, Teresa, and Julie Matthaei. "Comparable Worth, Incomparable Pay." *Radical America* 18 (September/October 1984): 21-28.

Banks, Olive. *Faces of Feminism: A Study of Feminism as a Social Movement.* New York: St. Martin's Press, 1981.

Barrett, Michele, and Mary McIntosh. *The Anti-Social Family.* London: New Left Books, 1982.

Beneria, Lourdes, and Martha Roldan. *The Crossroads of Class and Gender: Industrial Homework, Subcontracting, and Household Dynamics in Mexico City.* Chicago: University of Chicago Press, 1987.

Bhavnani, Kum-Kum, and Margaret Coulson. "Transforming Socialist Feminism: The Challenge of Racism." *Feminist Review* 23 (June 1986): 86.

Bloom, Allan. *The Closing of the American Mind: How Higher Education Has Failed Democracy and Impoverished the Souls of Today's Students.* New York: Simon & Schuster, 1987.

Bonhoeffer, Dietrich. *Life Together.* Trans. John W. Doberstein. London: SCM Press, 1954.

Boserup, Ester. *Women's Role in Economic Development.* London: George Allen & Unwin, 1970.

Brabazon, James. *Dorothy L. Sayers: A Biography.* New York: Charles Scribner's Sons, 1981.

Bulbeck, Chilla. *One World Women's Movement.* London: Pluto Press, 1988.

Caldwell, Lesley. "Feminism and 'The Family.'" *Feminist Review* 16 (April 1984): 88-96.

Carby, Hazel V. "White Woman Listen! Black Feminism and the Boundaries of Sisterhood." In *The Empire Strikes Back: Race and Racism in 70s Britain,* ed. by the Centre for Contemporary Cultural Studies, pp. 212-35. London: Hutchinson, 1982.

Caulfield, Mina Davis. "Imperialism, the Family, and Cultures of Resistance." *Socialist Revolution* 20 (October 1974): 67-85.

Christ, Carol P., and Judith Plaskow, eds. *Womanspirit Rising*. San Francisco: Harper & Row, 1979.

Cixous, Helene. "Castration or Decapitation?" *Signs* 7, no. 1 (1981): 41-55.

Clark, Kelly J. *Return to Reason: A Critique of Enlightenment Evidentialism and a Defense of Reason and Belief in God*. Grand Rapids: William B. Eerdmans, 1990.

Combahee River Collective. "A Black Feminist Statement." In *This Bridge Called My Back*, ed. Cherrie Moraga and Gloria Anzaldua, pp. 210-18. New York: Kitchen Press, 1984.

Costa, Mariarosa Dalla, and Selma James, eds. *The Power of Women and the Subversion of Community*. Bristol, U.K.: Falling Wall Press, 1972.

Cott, Nancy F. "Feminist Theory and Feminist Movements: The Past Before Us." In *What Is Feminism? A Re-examination*, ed. Juliet Mitchell and Ann Oakley, pp. 49-62. New York: Pantheon Books, 1986.

————. *The Bonds of Womanhood: "Woman's Sphere" in New England, 1780-1835*. New Haven: Yale University Press, 1977.

————. *The Grounding of Modern Feminism*. New Haven: Yale University Press, 1987.

Daly, Mary. *Gyn/Ecology: The Metaethics of Radical Feminism*. Boston: Beacon Press, 1978.

————. *Pure Lust: Elemental Feminist Philosophy*. Boston: Beacon Press, 1984.

Das, Veena. "Indian Women: Work, Power, and Status." In *Indian Women: From Purdah to Modernity*, ed. B. R. Nanda, pp. 129-45. New Delhi: Vikas, 1976.

Davidoff, Leonore, and Catherine Hall. *Family Fortunes: Men and Women of the English Middle Class, 1780-1850*. Ed. Catharine R. Stimpson. Chicago: University of Chicago Press, 1987.

Dworkin, Andrea. *Our Blood: Prophecies and Discourses on Sexual Politics*. New York: G. P. Putnam, 1981.

————. *Woman Hating: A Radical Look at Sexuality*. New York: E. P. Dutton, 1974.

Edmond, Wendy, and Suzie Fleming, eds. *All Work and No Pay*. London: Power of Women Collective and Falling Wall Press, 1975.

Ehrenreich, Barbara. *The Hearts of Men: American Dreams and the Flight from Commitment*. Garden City, N.Y.: Doubleday-Anchor, 1984.

Eisenstein, Sarah. *Give Us Bread, But Give Us Roses: Working Women's Consciousness in the United States, 1890 to the First World War*. Boston: Routledge & Kegan Paul, 1983.

Eisenstein, Zillah. *The Radical Future of Liberal Feminism*. New York: Longman, 1981.

Emecheta, Buchi. "Education — United States." *Women: A World Report.* New York: Oxford University Press, 1985.

————. *Joys of Motherhood.* New York: Braziller, 1979.

Engels, Dagmar. "The Limits of Gender Ideology: Bengali Women, the Colonial State, and the Private Sphere, 1890-1930." *Women's Studies International Forum* 12, no. 4 (1989): 425-37.

Engels, Frederick. *The Origin of the Family, Private Property and the State.* 1884; rpt. New York: International Publishers, 1972.

Fiorenza, Elisabeth Schüssler. *In Memory of Her: A Feminist Theological Reconstruction of Christian Origins.* New York: Crossroad, 1985.

Firestone, Shulamith. *The Dialectic of Sex: The Case for Feminist Revolution.* New York: William Morrow, 1970.

Fortune, Marie Marshall. *Sexual Violence: The Unmentionable Sin.* New York: Pilgrim Press, 1983.

Fox-Genovese, Elizabeth. *Feminism without Illusions: A Critique of Individualism.* Chapel Hill: University of North Carolina Press, 1991.

Friedan, Betty. *The Feminine Mystique.* New York: W. W. Norton, 1963.

Gerson, Judith M., and Kathy Peiss. "Boundaries, Negotiation, Consciousness: Reconceptualizing Gender Relations." *Social Problems* 32 (April 1985): 317-31.

Gilder, George. *Men and Marriage.* Gretna, La.: Pelican Publishing, 1987.

Gordon, Linda. "Why Nineteenth-Century Feminists Did Not Support Birth Control and Twentieth-Century Feminists Do: Feminism, Reproduction and the Family." In *Rethinking the Family: Some Feminist Questions,* ed. Barrie Thorne and Marilyn Yalom, pp. 40-53. New York: Longman, 1982.

Hamner, Jalna. "Men, Power and the Exploitation of Women." *Women's Studies International Forum* 13 (1990): 443-56.

Hancock, Maxine, and Karen Burton Mains. *Child Sexual Abuse: The Hope for Healing.* Wheaton, Ill.: Harold Shaw, 1986.

Hartmann, Heidi. "Capitalism, Patriarchy, and Job Segregation by Sex." *Signs* 1 (1976): 137-69.

Hartsock, Nancy. "Foucault on Power: A Theory for Women?" In *Feminism and Postmodernism,* ed. Linda Nicholson, pp. 163-64. London: Routledge & Kegan Paul, 1990.

————. *Money, Sex, and Power.* New York: Longman, 1983.

Hewlett, Sylvia Ann. *A Lesser Life: The Myth of Women's Liberation in America.* New York: William Morrow, 1986.

Heyzer, Noeleen, ed. *Daughters in Industry: Work Skills and Consciousness of Women Workers in Asia.* Kuala Lumpur: Asian and Pacific Development Center, 1988.

Hochschild, Arlie. *The Second Shift: Working Parents and the Revolution at Home.* New York: Viking Press, 1989.

hooks, bell. "Racism and Feminism: The Issue of Accountability." In *Ain't I a Woman: Black Women and Feminism.* Boston: South End Press, 1981.

————. *Feminist Theory: From Margin to Center.* Boston: South End Press, 1984.

————. *Talking Back: Thinking Feminist, Thinking Black.* Boston: South End Press, 1989.

Irigaray, Luce. *This Sex Which Is Not One.* Trans. Catherine Porter. Ithaca, N.Y.: Cornell University Press, 1985.

Jaggar, Alison M. *Feminist Politics and Human Nature.* Totowa, N.J.: Rowman & Allanheld, 1983.

Jaquette, Jane. "Women and Modernization Theory: A Decade of Feminist Criticism." *Women's Studies Quarterly* 15 (Fall 1986): 267-84.

Jayawardena, Kumari. *Feminism and Nationalism in the Third World.* London: Zed Books, 1986.

Jennett, Christine. "The Feminist Enterprise." In *Three Worlds of Inequality: Race, Class and Gender,* ed. Christine Jennett and Randall G. Stewart, pp. 361-78. Melbourne: Macmillan, 1987.

————, and Randall G. Stewart, eds. *Three Worlds of Inequality: Race, Class and Gender.* Melbourne: Macmillan, 1987.

Johnes, M. G. *Hannah More.* Cambridge: Cambridge University Press, 1952.

Keller, Evelyn Fox. *Reflections on Gender and Science.* New Haven: Yale University Press, 1985.

Kelly, J. N. D. *Early Christian Doctrines.* London: A. & C. Black, 1958.

Kerber, Linda K. "Separate Spheres, Female Worlds, Women's Place: The Rhetoric of Women's History." *Journal of American History* 75 (June 1988): 9-39.

Kishwar, Madhu, and Ruth Vanita, eds. *In Search of Answers: Indian Women's Voices from Manushi.* London: Zed Books, 1984.

Klein, Patricia, et al. *Growing Up Born Again: A Whimsical Look at the Blessings and Tribulations of Growing Up Born Again.* Old Tappan, N.J.: Fleming H. Revell, 1987.

Kollontai, Alexandra. *Selected Writings of Alexandra Kollontai.* Translation and foreword by Alix Holt. Westport, Conn.: Lawrence Hill & Co., 1977.

Kraditor, Aileen S. *The Ideas of the Woman Suffrage Movement, 1890-1920.* Garden City, N.Y.: Doubleday-Anchor Books, 1971.

————, ed. *Up from the Pedestal: Selected Writings in the History of American Feminism.* New York: Quadrangle/New York Times Book Co., 1968.

Kristeva, Julie. *Revolution in Poetic Languages.* Trans. Leon Roudiez. New York: Columbia University Press, 1984.

Kuyper, Abraham. *Lectures on Calvinism.* 1931; rpt. Grand Rapids: William B. Eerdmans, 1976.

Lazreg, Marnia. "Feminism and Difference: The Perils of Writing as a Woman on Women in Algeria." *Feminist Studies* 14 (Spring 1988): 97.

Lloyd, Genevieve. *The Man of Reason: "Male" and "Female" in Western Philosophy.* London: Methuen, 1984.

Lorde, Audre. "The Master's Tools Will Never Dismantle the Master's House." In *This Bridge Called My Back: Writings by Radical Women of Color,* ed. Cherrie Moraga and Gloria Anzaldua, pp. 98-106. New York: Kitchen Press, 1983.

———. "An Open Letter to Mary Daly." In *Sister Outsider,* pp. 66-71. Trumansburg, N.Y.: The Crossing Press, 1984.

Lovibond, Sabina. "Feminism and Postmodernism." *New Left Review,* November/December 1989, p. 12.

MacKinnon, Catharine. *Feminism Unmodified: Discourses on Life and Law.* Cambridge: Harvard University Press, 1987.

Marshall, Paul. "Individualism, Groups and the Charter." Unpublished manuscript, Institute for Christian Studies, Toronto, 1987.

Marx, Karl. *A Contribution to the Critique of Political Economy.* 1859; rpt. New York: International Publishers, 1972.

Mehta, Rama. "From Purdah to Modernity." In *Indian Women from Purdah to Modernity,* ed. B. R. Nanda, pp. 113-28. New Delhi: Vikas, 1976.

———. "Purdah among the Oswals of Mewar." In *Separate Worlds: Studies of Purdah in South Asia,* ed. Hanna Papanek and Gail Minault, pp. 139-63. Columbia, Mo.: South Asia Books, 1982.

———. *Inside the Haveli.* New Delhi: Arnold Heineman, 1977.

Millett, Kate. *Sexual Politics.* Garden City, N.Y.: Doubleday, 1970.

Minh-ha, Trinh T. "Difference: 'A Special Third World Women Issue.'" *Feminist Review* 25 (March 1987): 5-22.

———. *Woman, Native, Other: Writing Postcoloniality and Feminism.* Bloomington: Indiana University Press, 1989.

Minow, Martha. "Learning to Live with the Dilemma of Difference: Bilingual and Special Education." *Law and Contemporary Problems* 48, no. 2 (1984): 157-211.

Mitchell, Ella Pearson, ed. *Those Preachin' Women: Sermons by Black Women Preachers.* Valley Forge, Pa.: Judson Press, 1985.

Mitchell, Juliet. *Psychoanalysis and Feminism.* New York: Vintage Books, 1974.

Moraga, Cherrie, and Gloria Anzaldua, eds. *This Bridge Called My Back: Writings by Radical Women of Color.* New York: Kitchen Press, 1983.

Moschkovich, Judit. "— But I Know You, American Woman." In *This Bridge*

Called My Back: Writings by Radical Women of Color, ed. Cherrie Moraga and Gloria Anzaldua, pp. 79-85. New York: Kitchen Press, 1983.

Mullen, Shirley. "Women's History and Hannah More." *Fides et Historia* 19 (February 1987): pp. 5-21.

Murshid, Ghulam. *Reluctant Debutante: Response of Bengali Women to Modernization, 1849-1905.* Rajshahi University, Rajshahi, Bangladesh: Sahitya Samsad, 1983.

Nash, June, and Maria Patricia Fernandez-Kelly, eds. *Women, Men, and the International Division of Labor.* Albany, N.Y.: SUNY Press, 1983.

Offen, Karen. "Defining Feminism: A Comparative Historical Approach." *Signs* 14, no. 1 (1988): 119-57.

Ogunyemi, Chikwenye Okonjo. "Womanism: The Dynamics of the Contemporary Black Female Novel in English." *Signs* 11, no. 11 (1985): 63-80.

Okin, Susan Moller. *Justice, Gender, and the Family.* New York: Basic Books, 1989.

Palmer, Phyllis Marynick. "White Women/Black Women: The Dualism of Female Identity and Experience in the United States." *Feminist Studies* 9 (Spring 1983): 151-70.

Pankhurst, Richard. "Anna Wheeler: A Pioneer Socialist and Feminist." *The Political Quarterly* 25 (April-June 1954): 132-43.

Phongpaichit, Pasuk. "Bangkok Masseuses: Holding Up the Family Sky." *Southeast Asia Chronicle* 78 (1984): 15-23.

————. *Rural Women of Thailand: From Peasant Girls to Bangkok Masseuses.* Geneva: International Labour Office, 1981.

Piercy, Marge. *Woman on the Edge of Time.* New York: Fawcett–Crescent Books, 1976.

Piper, John, and Wayne Grudem. *Recovering Biblical Manhood and Womanhood: A Response to Evangelical Feminism* (Westchester, Ill.: Crossway Books, 1991).

Ratzsch, Del. *Philosophy of Science: The Natural Sciences in Christian Perspective.* Downers Grove, Ill.: InterVarsity Press, 1986.

Reagon, Bernice Johnson. "Coalition Politics: Turning the Century." In *Home Girls: A Black Feminist Anthology,* ed. Barbara Smith, pp. 356-68. New York: Kitchen Table/Women of Color Press, 1983.

Register, Cheri. "Motherhood at Center: Ellen Key's Social Vision." *Women's Studies International Forum* 5 (1982): 599-610.

Reiter, Rayna, ed. *Toward an Anthropology of Women.* New York: Monthly Review Press, 1975.

Remick, Helen, ed. *Comparable Worth and Wage Discrimination: Technical Possi-*

bilities and Political Realities. Philadelphia: Temple University Press, 1984.

Rich, Adrienne. *Of Woman Born: Motherhood as Experience and Institution*. New York: W. W. Norton, 1976.

Rosaldo, Michelle Zimbalist, and Louise Lamphere, eds. *Woman, Culture, and Society*. Stanford: Stanford University Press, 1974.

Rothman, Sheila M. *Woman's Proper Place: A History of Changing Ideals and Practices, 1870 to the Present*. New York: Basic Books, 1978.

Rowbotham, Sheila. "What Do Women Want? Women-Centered Values and the World as It Is." *Feminist Review* 20 (June 1985): 49-69.

Ruddick, Sara. *Maternal Thinking: Toward a Politics of Peace*. New York: Ballantine, 1989.

Ruether, Rosemary Radford. *Sexism and God-Talk: Toward a Feminist Theology*. Boston: Beacon Press, 1983.

Russell, Diana E. H. *The Secret Trauma: Incest in the Lives of Girls and Women*. New York: Basic Books, 1986.

Sayers, Dorothy. *Are Women Human?* Downers Grove, Ill.: InterVarsity Press, 1971.

Scott, Hilda. *Working Your Way to the Bottom*. London: Pandora Press, 1984.

Scott, James. *The Moral Economy of the Peasant: Rebellion and Subsistence in Southeast Asia*. New Haven: Yale University Press, 1976.

Scott, Joan Wallach. "Deconstructing Equality-versus-Difference: or, The Uses of Poststructuralist Theory for Feminism." *Feminist Studies* 14 (Spring 1988): 33-50.

Sen, Gita. "Women Workers and the Green Revolution." In *Women and Development*, ed. Lourdes Beneria, pp. 1-28. New York: Praeger, 1982.

Sha'arawi, Huda. *Harem Years: The Memoirs of an Egyptian Feminist*. Translated, edited, and introduced by Margot Badran. London: Virago Press, 1986.

Smith, Ruth L., and Deborah M. Valenze. "Mutuality and Marginality: Liberal Moral Theory and Working-Class Women in Nineteenth-Century England." *Signs* 13, no. 2 (1988): 277-98.

Spelman, Elizabeth V. "What Women Are Worth." *Off Our Backs* 20 (February 1990): 4, 29.

—————. "Woman as Body: Ancient and Contemporary Views." *Feminist Studies* 8 (Spring 1982): 109-31.

—————. *Inessential Woman: Problems of Exclusion in Feminist Thought*. Boston: Beacon Press, 1988.

Spence, Jonathan. *The Gate of Heavenly Peace: The Chinese and Their Revolution, 1895-1980*. New York: Viking Press, 1981.

Spender, Dale, ed. *Feminist Theorists: Three Centuries of Key Women Thinkers.* New York: Pantheon, 1983.

Stacey, Judith. "Are Feminists Afraid to Leave Home? The Challenge of Conservative Pro-family Feminism." In *What Is Feminism? A Re-examination,* ed. Juliet Mitchell and Ann Oakley, pp. 208-37. New York: Pantheon Books, 1986.

Stack, Carol. "Sex Roles and Survival Strategies in an Urban Black Community." In *Woman, Culture, and Society,* ed. Michelle Z. Rosaldo and Louise Lamphere, pp. 113-28. Stanford: Stanford University Press, 1974.

Stanton, Elizabeth Cady, et al., eds. *The Original Feminist Attack on the Bible: The Women's Bible.* 1898; rpt. New York: Arno Press, 1974.

Steady, Filomina Chioma, ed. *The Black Woman Cross-Culturally.* Cambridge, Mass.: Schenkman Publishing, 1981.

Stites, Richard. *The Women's Liberation Movement in Russia: Feminism, Nihilism, and Bolshevism, 1860-1930.* Princeton: Princeton University Press, 1978.

Storkey, Elaine. *What's Right with Feminism.* Grand Rapids: William B. Eerdmans, 1986.

Tanner, Nancy. "Matrifocality in Indonesia and Africa and among Black Americans." In *Woman, Culture, and Society,* ed. Michelle Z. Rosaldo and Louise Lamphere, pp. 150-56. Stanford: Stanford University Press, 1974.

Thorne, Barrie, with Marilyn Yalom, eds. *Rethinking the Family: Some Feminist Questions.* New York: Longman, 1982.

Tinker, Irene. *Persistent Inequalities: Women and World Development.* New York: Oxford University Press, 1990.

Tong, Rosemarie. *Feminist Thought: A Comprehensive Introduction.* Boulder, Colo.: Westview Press, 1989.

Trible, Phyllis. *God and the Rhetoric of Sexuality.* Philadelphia: Fortress Press, 1978.

Valenze, Deborah M. *Prophetic Sons and Daughters: Female Preaching and Popular Religion in Industrial England.* Princeton: Princeton University Press, 1985.

Van Leeuwen, Mary Stewart. "Psychology's Two Cultures: A Christian Analysis." *Christian Scholar's Review* 17 (June 1988): 406-24.

————. "Selective Sociobiology and Other Follies." *Reformed Journal* 38 (February 1980): 24-28.

————. *Gender and Grace: Love, Work and Parenting in a Changing World.* Downers Grove, Ill.: InterVarsity Press, 1990.

Verhey, *The Great Reversal: Ethics in the New Testament.* Grand Rapids: William B. Eerdmans, 1984.

Walker, Alice. "One Child of One's Own: A Meaningful Digression within the Work(s)." In *The Writer on Her Work*, ed. Janet Sternburg, pp. 133-34. New York: W. W. Norton, 1980.

————, ed. *I Love Myself When I Am Laughing—A Zora Neale Hurston Reader.* New York: Feminist Press, 1979.

————. *In Search of Our Mothers' Gardens.* New York: Harcourt Brace Jovanovich, 1984.

Wallace, Michele. "A Black Feminist's Search for Sisterhood." In *All the Women Are White, All the Blacks Are Men, But Some of Us Are Brave: Black Women's Studies,* ed. Gloria T. Hull, Patricia Bell Scott, and Barbara Smith, pp. 5-12. New York: Feminist Press, 1982.

Waring, Marilyn. *If Women Counted: A New Feminist Economics.* San Francisco: Harper & Row, 1989.

Wolgast, Elizabeth H. *Equality and the Rights of Women.* Ithaca, N.Y.: Cornell University Press, 1980.

Wollstonecraft, Mary. *A Vindication of the Rights of Woman.* 2nd ed. Ed. Carol H. Poston. New York: W. W. Norton, 1975.

Wolterstorff, Nicholas. "On Christian Learning." In *Stained Glass: Worldviews and Social Science,* ed. Paul Marshall, Sander Griffioen, and Richard Mouw, pp. 56-80. Lanham, Md.: University Press of America, 1989.

————. *Reason within the Bounds of Religion.* Grand Rapids: William B. Eerdmans, 1976.

————. *Until Justice and Peace Embrace.* Grand Rapids: William B. Eerdmans, 1983.

Zetkin, Clara. *Reminiscences of Lenin.* New York: International Publishers, 1934.

Zizoulas, John D. *Being as Communion: Studies in Personhood and the Church.* Crestwood, N.Y.: St. Vladimir's Seminary Press, 1985.

Works Cited in Part II

Achtemeier, Elizabeth. "Female Language for God: Should the Church Adopt It?" In *The Hermeneutical Quest,* ed. Donald G. Miller, pp. 97-114. Allison Park, Pa.: Pickwick Publications, 1986.

————. "The Impossible Possibility: Evaluating the Feminist Approach to the Bible and Theology." *Interpretation* 42 (January 1988): 45-57.

Andolsen, Barbara Hilkert. "Agape in Feminist Ethics." *Journal of Religious Ethics* 9 (Spring 1981): 69-83.

Ansell, Nicholas John. "'The Woman Will Overcome the Warrior': A

Dialogue with the Feminist Theology of Rosemary Radford Ruether." Master's Thesis, Institute for Christian Studies, Toronto, 1990.

Augustine, Saint. *On Christian Doctrine.* Trans. D. W. Robertson, Jr. Library of Liberal Arts, no. 80. Indianapolis: Bobbs-Merrill Educational Publishing, 1958.

Baldwin, Claude-Marie, trans. "Marriage in Calvin's Sermons." In *Calviniana: Ideas and Influence of Jean Calvin,* vol. 10, Sixteenth-Century Essays and Studies, ed. Robert Schnucker, pp. 121-31. Kirksville, Mo.: Sixteenth-Century Journal Publications, 1988.

Barth, Karl. *Church Dogmatics.* Trans. G. W. Bromiley. New York: Charles Scribner's Sons, 1956.

Bettelheim, Bruno. *The Uses of Enchantment.* New York: Alfred A. Knopf, 1976.

Bloesch, Donald G. *Is the Bible Sexist?* Westchester, Ill.: Crossway, 1982.

Boesak, Allan. *Black and Reformed: Apartheid, Liberation and the Calvinist Tradition.* Ed. Leonard Sweetman. Maryknoll, N.Y.: Orbis Books, 1984.

Bratt, James D. *Dutch Calvinism in Modern America: A History of a Conservative Subculture.* Grand Rapids: William B. Eerdmans, 1984.

Brown, Francis, S. R. Driver, and Charles A. Briggs. *The New Brown-Driver-Briggs-Gesenius Hebrew and English Lexicon.* Peabody, Mass: Hendrickson Publishers, 1979.

Brueggemann, Walter. *The Bible Makes Sense.* Winona, Minn.: Saint Mary's Press, 1985.

Calvin College Social Research Center. "A Survey of Abuse in the Christian Reformed Church." Grand Rapids: Calvin College, 1990.

Calvin, John. *Calvin: Institutes of the Christian Religion.* Ed. John T. McNeill. Trans. Ford Lewis Battles. Philadelphia: Wesminster Press, 1960.

Campbell, Cynthia. *Theologies Written from Feminist Perspectives: An Introductory Study.* New York: Office of the General Assembly of the Presbyterian Church (U.S.A.), 1987.

Christ, Carol P., and Judith Plaskow, eds. *Womanspirit Rising.* San Francisco: Harper & Row, 1979.

Clark, Elizabeth, and Herbert Richardson, eds. *Women and Religion: A Feminist Sourcebook of Christian Thought.* New York: Harper & Row, 1977.

"Classis Chatham Appeals Decision of 1984 Synod re Women in Office." Protests and Appeals, *Acts of Synod,* pp. 511-44. Grand Rapids: Board of Publications of the CRC, 1985.

Clouse, Bonnidell, and Robert G. Clouse. *Women in Ministry: Four Views.* Downers Grove, Ill.: InterVarsity Press, 1989.

"Committee on Headship in the Bible, Report 33." *Acts of Synod*, pp. 282-376. Grand Rapids: Board of Publications of the CRC, 1984.

Cooper, John. "God Is Not Father and Mother." *The Banner*, 30 April 1990, pp. 8-11.

Coppes, Leonard J. "Adam." In *Theological Wordbook of the Old Testament*, vol. I, ed. R. Laird Harris, Gleason L. Archer, Jr., and Bruce K. Waltke, p. 10. Chicago: Moody Press, 1980.

Crites, Stephen. "The Narrative Quality of Experience." In *Why Narrative? Readings in Narrative Theology*, ed. Stanley Hauerwas and L. Gregory Jones, pp. 65-88. Grand Rapids: William B. Eerdmans, 1989.

Daly, Mary. "The Qualitative Leap beyond Patriarchal Religion." *Quest* 1 (1974): 1-21.

———. *Beyond God the Father: Toward a Philosophy of Women's Liberation*. Boston: Beacon Press, 1973.

———. *The Church and the Second Sex*. New York: Harper & Row, 1968.

Douglass, Jane Dempsey. "Women and the Continental Reformation." In *Religion and Sexism: Images of Woman in the Jewish and Christian Traditions*, ed. Rosemary Radford Ruether. New York: Simon & Schuster, 1974.

———. *Women, Freedom, and Calvin*. Philadelphia: Westminster Press, 1985.

Elwell, Walter A., ed. *Evangelical Dictionary of Theology*. Grand Rapids: Baker Book House, 1984.

Engel, Mary Potter. "Tambourines to the Glory of God: From the Monarchy of God the Father to the Monotheism of God the Great Mysterious." *Word and World* 7, no. 2 (1987): 153-66.

Fee, Gordon, and Douglas Stuart. *How to Read the Bible for All Its Worth*. Grand Rapids: Zondervan, 1982.

Fiorenza, Elisabeth Schüssler. *Bread Not Stone: The Challenge of Feminist Biblical Interpretation*. Boston: Beacon Press, 1984.

———. *In Memory of Her: A Feminist Theological Reconstruction of Christian Origins*. New York: Crossroad, 1985.

Fisher, Walter. *Human Communication as Narration: Toward a Philosophy of Reason, Value, and Action*. Columbia, S.C.: University of South Carolina Press, 1987.

Frye, Northrop. *The Great Code*. New York: Harcourt Brace Jovanovich, 1982.

Gilligan, Carol. *In a Different Voice: Psychological Theory and Women's Development*. Cambridge: Harvard University Press, 1982.

"God Is More Than Two Men and a Bird." Interview with Sandra M. Schneiders. *U.S. Catholic*, May 1990, pp. 20-21.

Goldberg, Michael. "God, Action, and Narrative: *Which* Narrative? *Which*

613

Action? *Which* God?" In *Why Narrative? Readings in Narrative Theology,* ed. Stanley Hauerwas and L. Gregory Jones, pp. 348-65. Grand Rapids: William B. Eerdmans, 1989.

Goldstein, Valerie Saiving. "The Human Situation: A Feminine View." In *Womanspirit Rising: A Feminist Reader in Religion,* ed. Carol P. Christ and Judith Plaskow, pp. 25-42. San Francisco: Harper & Row, 1979.

Gronbeck, Bruce. "Communication and Community: Mythic Conceptions of Self and Society." Paper delivered at Central States Communication Association Conference, Detroit, 1990.

Gustafson, James M. *Ethics from a Theocentric Perspective,* vol. 1: *Theology and Ethics.* Chicago: University of Chicago Press, 1981.

Gutiérrez, Gustavo. *Theology of Liberation: History, Politics and Salvation.* Maryknoll, N.Y.: Orbis Books, 1973.

Hardesty, Nancy. "'Whosoever Surely Meaneth Me': Inclusive Language and the Gospel." *Christian Scholar's Review* 17, no. 3 (1988): 231-40.

————. *Inclusive Language in the Church.* Philadelphia: John Knox Press, 1987.

Harrison, Beverly Wildung. "Human Sexuality and Mutuality." In *Christian Feminism: Visions of a New Humanity,* ed. Judith L. Weidman, pp. 141-57. San Francisco: Harper & Row, 1984.

————. "Keeping Faith in a Sexist Church: Not for Women Only." In *Making the Connections: Essays in Feminist Social Ethics,* ed. Carol S. Robb, pp. 206-34. Boston: Beacon Press, 1986.

————. "The New Consciousness of Women: A Socio-Political Resource." *Cross-Currents* 24 (Winter 1975): 445-62.

————. "Sexism and the Language of Christian Ethics," in *Making the Connections: Essays in Feminist Social Ethics,* ed. Carol S. Robb, pp. 22-41. Boston: Beacon Press, 1986.

Hauerwas, Stanley. *A Community of Character: Toward a Constructive Christian Social Ethic.* Notre Dame: University of Notre Dame Press, 1981.

————, and L. Gregory Jones. *Why Narrative? Readings in Narrative Theology.* Grand Rapids: William B. Eerdmans, 1989.

"Hermeneutical Principles Concerning Women in Ecclesiastical Office, Supplement-Report 31." *Acts of Synod,* pp. 491-94. Grand Rapids: Board of Publications of the CRC, 1978.

Jamieson, Kathleen Hall. "The 'Effeminate' Style." In *Eloquence in an Electronic Age,* pp. 67-89. New York: Oxford University Press, 1988.

Keil, C. F., and F. Delitzsch, eds. *Commentary on the Old Testament,* vol. I. Trans. James Martin. Grand Rapids: William B. Eerdmans, 1983.

Kuyper, Abraham. "The Woman's Position of Honor." Trans. Irene Konyndyk. Unpublished manuscript, Calvin College, 1990.

————. *Christianity and the Class Struggle.* Trans. Dirk Jellema. Grand Rapids: Piet Hein Publishers, 1950.

————. *Lectures on Calvinism.* 1931; rpt. Grand Rapids: William B. Eerdmans, 1976.

————. *Women of the Old Testament.* 6th ed. Trans. Henry Zylstra. Grand Rapids: Zondervan Publishing Co., 1934.

Lerner, Gerda. *The Creation of Patriarchy.* New York: Oxford University Press, 1986.

MacIntyre, Alasdair. "The Virtues, the Unity of a Human Life, and the Concept of a Tradition." In *Why Narrative? Readings in Narrative Theology,* ed. Stanley Hauerwas and L. Gregory Jones, pp. 89-110. Grand Rapids: William B. Eerdmans, 1989.

————. *After Virtue: A Study in Moral Theory.* Notre Dame: University of Notre Dame Press, 1980.

McFague, Sallie. *Metaphorical Theology: Models of God in Religious Language.* Philadelphia: Fortress Press, 1982.

————. *Models of God: Theology for an Ecological, Nuclear Age.* Philadelphia: Fortress Press, 1987.

McKim, Donald D. "Hearkening to the Voices: What Women Theologians Are Saying." *Reformed Journal* 35 (January 1985): 7-10.

Michelson, Alvera. "An Egalitarian View: There Is Neither Male nor Female in Christ." In *Women in Ministry: Four Views,* ed. Bonnidell Clouse and Robert G. Clouse, pp. 173-206. Downers Grove, Ill.: InterVarsity Press, 1989.

Morris, Leon. "Adam." In *Evangelical Dictionary of Theology,* ed. Walter A. Elwell, p. 10. Grand Rapids: Baker Book House, 1984.

Mouw, Richard J. *The God Who Commands.* Notre Dame: University of Notre Dame Press, 1990.

Munro, Winsome. "Women, Text and the Canon: The Strange Case of 1 Corinthians 14:33-35." *Biblical Theology Bulletin* 18 (January 1988): 24-29.

Okin, Susan Moller. *Justice, Gender, and the Family.* New York: Basic Books, 1989.

Olthuis, James H. "On Worldviews." In *Stained Glass: Worldviews and Social Science,* ed. Paul Marshall, Sander Griffioen, and Richard Mouw, p. 29. Lanham, Md.: University Press of America, 1989.

Outka, Gene. *Agape: An Ethical Analysis.* New Haven: Yale University Press, 1972.

Ozment, Steven. *When Fathers Ruled: Family Life in Reformation Europe.* Cambridge: Harvard University Press, 1983.

Pagels, Elaine. *Adam, Eve, and the Serpent.* New York: Random House, 1988.

Palmer, Parker. "Keynote Address." Proceedings of the Conference on Communication and Christianity. Marquette University, Milwaukee, Wisconsin, June 1990.

Pleck, Elizabeth. *Domestic Tyranny: The Making of American Social Policy against Family Violence from Colonial Times to the Present.* New York: Oxford University Press, 1987.

Ramsey, Paul. *Basic Christian Ethics.* New York: Charles Scribner's Sons, 1953.

"Report of the Committee to Study Headship." *Agenda and Acts of Synod,* pp. 309-49. Grand Rapids: Board of Publications of the CRC, 1990.

Rienstra, Marchiene. "God's Freedom for Women" (Parts 1, 2, and 3). *Reformed Journal* 27 (September 1977): 11-14; (October 1977): 19-23; and (November 1977): 26-29.

Robb, Carol S., ed. *Making the Connections: Essays in Feminist Social Ethics.* Boston: Beacon Press, 1986.

Ross, Mary Ellen. "Feminism and the Problem of Moral Character." *Journal of Feminist Studies in Religion* 5 (Fall 1989): 47-64.

Ruddick, Sara. *Maternal Thinking: Toward a Politics of Peace.* New York: Ballantine Books, 1989.

Ruether, Rosemary Radford. "A Religion for Women: Sources and Strategies." *Christianity and Crisis,* 10 December 1979, pp. 307-11.

————. *New Woman/New Earth: Sexist Ideologies and Human Liberation.* New York: Seabury Press, 1975.

————. *Sexism and God-Talk: Toward a Feminist Theology.* Boston: Beacon Press, 1983.

————. *Womanguides: Readings toward a Feminist Theology.* Boston: Beacon Press, 1985.

————. *Women-Church: Theology and Practice of Feminist Liturgical Communities.* San Francisco: Harper & Row, 1986.

Russell, Letty M. "Feminist Critique: Opportunity for Cooperation." *Journal for the Study of the Old Testament* 22 (1982): 54-66.

————, ed. *Feminist Interpretation of the Bible.* Philadelphia: Westminster Press, 1985.

————. *Human Liberation in a Feminist Perspective—A Theology.* Philadelphia: Westminster Press, 1974.

Scanzoni, Letha, and Nancy Hardesty. *All We're Meant To Be.* Waco, Tex.: Word Books, 1974.

Schnucker, Robert V., ed. *Calviniana: Ideas and Influence of Jean Calvin.* Vol. 10, Sixteenth-Century Essays and Studies. Kirksville, Mo.: Sixteenth-Century Journal Publications, 1988.

Schuurman, Douglas. "The Great Reversal: Ethics and the New Testament
— A Critical Assessment." *The Calvin Theological Journal* 23 (November
1988): 222-37.

—————. *Creation, Eschaton, and Ethics: The Ethical Significance of the Creation-Eschaton Relation in Emil Brunner and Jürgen Moltmann.* New York: Peter
Lang Press, 1991.

Smit, D. J. "What Does 'Status Confessionis' Mean?" In *A Moment of Truth:
The Confession of the Dutch Reformed Mission Church,* ed. G. D. Cloete
and D. J. Smit, pp. 7-32. Grand Rapids: William B. Eerdmans, 1984.

Soelle, Dorothee. *To Work and To Love.* Minneapolis: Augsburg, 1984.

Spencer, Aida Besancon. *Beyond the Curse: Women Called to Ministry.* Nashville:
Thomas Nelson Publishers, 1985.

Stanton, Elizabeth Cady, et al., eds. *The Original Feminist Attack on the Bible:
The Women's Bible.* New York: 1898; rpt. New York: Arno Press, 1974.

Stob, Henry. *Ethical Reflections: Essays on Moral Themes.* Grand Rapids: William
B. Eerdmans, 1978.

Storkey, Elaine. *What's Right with Feminism.* Grand Rapids: William B. Eerdmans, 1986.

Swartley, Willard M. *Slavery, Sabbath, War, and Women: Case Issues in Biblical
Interpretation.* Scottdale, Pa.: Herald Press, 1983.

"Synodical Studies on Women in Office and Decisions Pertaining to the
Office of Deacon, Minority Report II, Report 32." *Acts of Synod,* pp.
525-31. Grand Rapids: Board of Publications of the CRC, 1981.

Taylor, Mark Kline. *Remembering Esperanza: A Cultural-Political Theology for
North American Praxis.* Maryknoll, N.Y.: Orbis Books, 1990.

Tennis, Diane. *Is God the Only Reliable Father?* Philadelphia: Westminster Press,
1985.

Thistlethwaite, Susan. *Sex, Race, and God: Christian Feminism in Black and White.*
New York: Crossroad, 1989.

Tolbert, Mary Ann. "Protestant Feminists and the Bible: On the Horns of
a Dilemma." *Union Seminary Quarterly Review* 43, no. 14 (1989): 1-17.

Tong, Rosemarie. *Feminist Thought: A Comprehensive Introduction.* Boulder,
Colo.: Westview Press, 1989.

Trible, Phyllis. "Depatriarchialism in Biblical Interpretation." *Journal of the
American Academy of Religion* 41 (March 1973): 30-48.

—————. *God and the Rhetoric of Sexuality.* Philadelphia: Fortress Press, 1978.

Troeltsch, Ernst. *The Social Teaching of the Christian Churches.* Trans.
O. Wyon. 2 vols. New York: Harper–Torchbooks, 1960.

Tucker, Ruth A. *Daughters of the Church: Women and Ministry from New Testament Times to the Present.* Grand Rapids: Zondervan, 1987.

Van Leeuwen, Mary Stewart. *Gender and Grace: Love, Work and Parenting in a Changing World.* Downers Grove, Ill.: InterVarsity Press, 1990.

van Wijk-Bos, Johanna W. H. *Reformed and Feminist: A Challenge to the Church.* Louisville: Westminster/John Knox Press, 1991.

Walzer, Michael. *The Revolution of the Saints: A Study in the Origins of Radical Politics.* Cambridge: Harvard University Press, 1965.

Wolters, Al. *Creation Regained: Biblical Basics for a Reformational Worldview.* Grand Rapids: William B. Eerdmans, 1985.

Wolterstorff, Nicholas. "On Christian Learning." In *Stained Glass: Worldviews and Social Science,* ed. Paul Marshall, Sander Griffioen, and Richard Mouw, pp. 56-80. Lanham, Md.: University Press of America, 1989.

————. *Until Justice and Peace Embrace.* Grand Rapids: William B. Eerdmans, 1983.

A Woman and Her World. Grand Rapids: CRC Publications, n.d.

"Women in Ecclesiastical Office, Supplement-Report 39." *Acts of Synod,* pp. 514-94. Grand Rapids: Board of Publications of the CRC, 1973.

"Women in Ecclesiastical Office, Supplement-Report 46." *Acts of Synod,* pp. 57-94. Grand Rapids: Board of Publications of the CRC, 1975.

"Women Suffrage in Ecclesiastical Meetings, Supplement 19." *Acts of Synod,* pp. 308-15. Grand Rapids: Board of Publications of the CRC, 1957.

Wren, Brian. *What Language Shall I Borrow? God-Talk in Worship: A Male Response to Feminist Theology.* New York: Crossroad, 1990.

Works Cited in Part III

Adams, Carol J. *The Sexual Politics of Meat: A Feminist-Vegetarian Critical Theory.* New York: Continuum Publishing Co., 1990.

Addie, William. *What Will Happen to God?* London: Photobooks (Bristol) Ltd., 1984.

Aguero, E., F. Bloch, and D. Byrne. "The Relationships among Sexual Beliefs, Attitudes, Experience, and Homophobia." *Journal of Homosexuality* 10 (1984): 95-107.

Ahmed, Leila. "Western Ethnocentrism and Perceptions of the Harem." *Feminist Studies* 8 (Fall 1982): 520-31.

Allis, Sam. "What Do Men Really Want?" *Time,* Special Issue 136 (Fall 1990): 80-82.

Alsdurf, James, and Phyllis Alsdurf. *Battered into Submission: The Tragedy of Wife Abuse in the Christian Home.* Downers Grove, Ill.: InterVarsity Press, 1989.

Andolsen, Barbara Hilkert. "Agape in Feminist Ethics." *Journal of Religious Ethics* 9 (Spring 1981): 69-83.

Ardener, Edwin. "Some Outstanding Problems in the Analysis of Events." Paper presented at the Association of Social Anthropologists' Dicennial Conference, 1973.

Ardener, Shirley. *Defining Females: The Nature of Women in Society.* New York: John Wiley, 1978.

Ashcroft, Mary Ellen. *Temptations Women Face: Honest Talk about Jealousy, Anger, Sex, Money, Food, Pride.* Downers Grove, Ill.: InterVarsity Press, 1991.

Austin, J. L. *How to Do Things with Words.* 2d ed. Cambridge: Harvard University Press, 1975.

Bailey, Covert. *Fit or Fat?* Boston: Houghton Mifflin, 1978.

Bart, Pauline B., and Patricia H. O'Brien. *Stopping Rape: Successful Survival Strategies.* New York: Pergamon Press, 1985.

Bellah, Robert N., et al. *Habits of the Heart.* Berkeley: University of California Press, 1985.

Bennet, Roberta, et al. "Changing the Rules of the Game: Reflections Toward a Feminist Analysis of Sport." *Women's Studies International Forum* 10, no. 4 (1987): 369-80.

Bernikow, Louise. *The World Split Open.* New York: Vintage Books, 1974.

Bianchi, Eugene, and Rosemary R. Ruether. *From Machismo to Mutuality: Essays on Sexism and Woman-Man Liberation.* New York: Paulist Press, 1976.

Bierce, Ambrose. *The Devil's Dictionary.* 1911; rpt. New York: A. & C. Boni, 1935.

Birke, Lynda, and Gail Vines. "A Sporting Chance: The Anatomy of Destiny?" *Women's Studies International Forum* 10, no. 4 (1987): 337-48.

"Bishop Defends His Views on Abortion." *Chicago Tribune,* 24 November 1990, sec. 1, p. 4.

Boutilier, Mary, and Lucinda San Giovanni. *The Sporting Woman.* Champaign, Ill.: Human Kinetics Books, 1983.

Bouton, Jim. *Ball Four.* New York: Dell, 1971.

————. *I'm Glad You Didn't Take It Personally.* New York: Dell, 1972.

Bray, Cathy. "Sport and Social Change: Socialist Feminist Theory." *Journal of Physical Education, Recreation and Dance* 59 (1988): 50-53.

Brittan, Arthur. *Masculinity and Power.* New York: Basil Blackwell, 1989.

Brittan, Dana. "Homophobia and Homosociality: An Analysis of Boundary Maintenance." *Sociological Quarterly* 31 (1990): 423-39.

Brod, Harry, ed. *The Making of Masculinities: The New Men's Studies.* Boston: Allen & Unwin, 1987.

Broverman, Inge K., et al. "Sex-role Stereotypes: A Current Appraisal." *Journal of Social Issues* 28, no. 2 (1972): 59-78.

Brown, Laura. "Lesbians, Weight and Eating: New Analyses and Perspectives." In *Lesbian Psychologies: Explorations and Challenges,* ed. Boston Lesbian Psychologies Collective, pp. 294-309. Champaign, Ill.: University of Illinois Press, 1987.

————. "Women, Weight, and Power: Feminist Theoretical and Therapeutic Issues." *Women & Therapy* 4 (Spring 1985): 61-71.

Brownmiller, Susan. *Femininity.* New York: Simon & Schuster, 1984.

Brumberg, Laura. *Fasting Girls.* Cambridge: Harvard University Press, 1988.

Bynum, Caroline Walker. *Holy Feast and Holy Fast: The Religious Significance of Food to Medieval Women.* Berkeley: University of California Press, 1987.

"Bypassed Women." *American Health,* October 1990.

Calvin College Social Research Center. "A Survey of Abuse in the Christian Reformed Chruch." Grand Rapids: Calvin College, 1990.

Caputi, Jane, and Diana Russell. "'Femicide': Speaking the Unspeakable." *Ms.* September/October 1990, pp. 34-37.

Carrigan, Tim, Robert Connell, and John Lee. "Hard and Heavy: Toward a New Sociology of Masculinity." In *Beyond Patriarchy: Essays by Men on Pleasure, Power, and Change,* ed. Michael Kaufman, pp. 139-92. Toronto: Oxford University Press, 1987.

————. "Toward a New Sociology of Masculinity." In *The Making of Masculinities: The New Men's Studies,* ed. Harry Brod, pp. 63-100. Boston: Allen & Unwin, 1987.

Chapkis, Wendy. *Beauty Secrets: Women and the Politics of Appearance.* Boston: South End Press, 1986.

Charles, Nickie, and Marion Kerr. "Food for Feminist Thought." *Sociological Review* 34 (August 1986): 537-72.

Chernin, Kim. *Fat Is a Feminist Issue.* London: Women's Press, 1981.

Clatterbaugh, Kenneth. *Contemporary Perspectives on Masculinity: Men, Women and Politics in Modern Society.* Boulder, Colo.: Westview Press, 1990.

Coakley, Jay J. *Sport in Society.* 4th ed. St. Louis: Times Mirror/Mosby College Publishing, 1990.

Cohen, Nancy Wainer, and Lois J. Estner. *Silent Knife: Caesarean Prevention and Vaginal Birth after Caesarean.* South Hadley, Mass: Bergin & Garvey Publishers, Inc., 1983.

Cohn, Samuel. *The Process of Occupational Sex-Typing: The Feminization of Clerical Labor in Great Britain.* Women in the Political Economy series, ed. Ronnie J. Steinberg. Philadelphia: Temple University Press, 1985.

Cole, K. C. *What Only a Mother Can Tell You about Having a Baby.* Berkeley: Berkeley Publishers, 1986.

Connell, Robert W. *Gender and Power: Society, the Person and Sexual Politics.* Stanford: Stanford University Press, 1987.

Cote, Charlotte. *Olympia Brown: The Battle for Equality.* Racine, Wis.: Mother Courage Press, 1988.

Crosset, Todd. "Masculinity, Sexuality and the Development of Early Modern Sport." In *Sport, Men, and the Gender Order: Critical Feminist Perspectives,* ed. Michael A. Messner and Donald F. Sabo, pp. 45-54. Champaign, Ill.: Human Kinetics Books, 1990.

Curry, Timothy J. "Fraternal Bonding in the Locker Room: A Pro-feminist Analysis of Talk about Competition and Women." *Sociology of Sport Journal* 8 (1991): 119-35.

Daly, Mary. *Beyond God the Father: Toward a Philosophy of Women's Liberation.* Boston: Beacon Press, 1973.

————. *The Church and the Second Sex.* New York: Harper & Row, 1968.

————. *Webster's First New Intergalactic Wickedary of the English Language.* Ed. Jane Caputi. Boston: Beacon Press, 1987.

Deford, Frank. "Religion in Sport." *Sports Illustrated,* 19 April 1976, pp. 88-102.

Diamond, Nicky. "Thin Is the Feminist Issue." *Feminist Review* 10 (1985): 45-64.

Dunning, Eric. "Sport as a Male Preserve: Notes on the Social Sources of Masculine Identity and Its Transformations." In *Quest for Excitement* by Norbert Elias and Eric Dunning, pp. 267-83. New York: Basil Blackwell, 1986.

Ehrenreich, Barbara, and Deirdre English. *For Her Own Good: 150 Years of the Experts' Advice to Women.* Garden City, N.Y.: Doubleday-Anchor, 1978.

Ehrlich, Carol. "The Reluctant Patriarchs." In *For Men against Sexism: A Book of Readings,* ed. Jon Snodgrass, pp. 141-45. Albion, Calif.: Times Change Press, 1977.

Eitzen, Stanley D., and George H. Sage. *Sociology of North American Sport.* 4th ed. Dubuque, Iowa: Wm. C. Brown Publishers, 1989.

Elgin, Suzette Haden. *A First Dictionary and Grammar of Laadan.* Madison, Wis.: Society for the Furtherance and Study of Fantasy and Science Fiction, 1988.

Elliott, Farar. "Men and Women: Costume, Gender, and Power." *Off Our Backs,* December 1989, pp. 8-9.

Evans, Mary. "The Problem of Gender for Women's Studies." *Women's Studies International Forum* 13 (1990): 457-62.

Fackelmann, K. A. "Male Teenagers at Risk of Steroid Abuse." *Science News,* 17 December 1988, p. 391.

Farley, Margaret. "Love as Mutuality." In *Woman: New Dimensions,* ed. Walter Burkhardt, pp. 51-70. New York: Paulist Press, 1975.

Fine, Gary. *With the Boys: Little League Baseball and Preadolescent Culture.* Chicago: University of Chicago Press, 1987.

Fishman, Pamela. "Interaction: The Work Women Do." *Social Problems* 26 (1978): 397-406.

Fontaine, Carole. "The NRSV and the REB: A Feminist Critique." *Theology Today* 68 (October 1990): 273-81.

Foss, Karen A., and Sonja K. Foss. *Women Speak: The Eloquence of Women's Lives.* Prospect Heights, Ill.: Waveland Press, 1991.

Fraser, Laura. "Superbowl Violence Comes Home." *Mother Jones,* January 1987, p. 15.

Freedman, Rita. *Beauty Bound.* Lexington, Mass.: D. C. Heath, 1986.

French, Marilyn. *Beyond Power: On Women, Men and Morals.* New York: Summit Books, 1985.

————. *The Women's Room.* New York: Simon & Schuster, 1977.

Frieze, Irene, et al. *Women and Sex Roles: A Social Psychological Perspective.* New York: W. W. Norton, 1978.

Frye, Marilyn. *The Politics of Reality.* Freedom, Calif.: Crossing Press, 1983.

Gilligan, Carol. *In a Different Voice: Psychological Theory and Women's Development.* Cambridge: Harvard University Press, 1982.

————, et al. *Making Connections: The Relational Worlds of Adolescent Girls at Emma Willard School.* Troy, N.Y.: Emma Willard School, 1989.

Gilman, Charlotte Perkins. "The Anti-Suffragettes." In *The World Split Open,* ed. Louise Bernikow, pp. 224-26. New York: Vintage Books, 1974.

Gilmore, David D. *Manhood in the Making: Cultural Concepts of Masculinity.* New Haven: Yale University Press, 1990.

Gluck, Sherna Berger. *Rosie the Riveter Revisited: Women, the War, and Social Change.* Boston: Twayne Publishers, 1987.

"God Is More Than Two Men and a Bird." Interview with Sister Sandra M. Schneiders. *U.S. Catholic,* May 1990, pp. 20-24.

Goldstein, Valerie Saiving. "The Human Situation: A Feminine View." In *Womanspirit Rising: A Feminist Reader in Religion,* ed. Carol P. Christ and Judith Plaskow, pp. 25-42. San Francisco: Harper & Row, 1979.

Graddol, David, and Joan Swann. *Gender Voices.* New York: Basil Blackwell, 1989.

Gramsci, Antonio. *Selections from the Prison Notebooks.* London: Lawrence & Wishart, 1971.

Green, Harvey. *The Light of Home: An Intimate View of the Lives of Women in Victorian America.* New York: Pantheon Books, 1983.

Grether, Herbert G. "Translators and the Gender Gap." *Theology Today* 68 (October 1990): 299-305.

Griffin, Susan. "Rape: The All-American Crime." *Ramparts* 10 (September 1971): 26-35.

————. *Rape: The Power of Consciousness.* San Francisco: Harper & Row, 1979.

Griffith, Elisabeth. *In Her Own Right: The Life of Elizabeth Cady Stanton.* New York: Oxford University Press, 1984.

Hall, R. M., and B. R. Sandler. *The Campus Climate: A Chilly One for Women?* Washington: Project on the Status and Education of Women, Association of American Colleges, 1982.

Hamner, Jalna. "Men, Power and the Exploitation of Women." *Women's Studies International Forum* 13 (1990): 443-56.

Hardesty, Nancy. "'Whosoever Surely Meaneth Me': Inclusive Language and the Gospel." *Christian Scholar's Review* 17, no. 3 (1988): 231-40.

————. *Inclusive Language in the Church.* Philadelphia: John Knox Press, 1987.

Hayden, Dolores. *Redesigning the American Dream: The Future of Housing, Work, and Family Life.* New York: W. W. Norton, 1984.

Hirsch, Kathleen. "Fraternities of Fear: Gang Rape, Male Bonding, and the Silencing of Women." *Ms.,* September/October 1990, pp. 52-56.

Hsu, L. K. George. "Are the Eating Disorders Becoming More Common among Blacks?" *International Journal of Eating Disorders* 6 (1987): 113-24.

Hubbard, Ruth. *The Politics of Women's Biology.* New Brunswick, N.J.: Rutgers University Press, 1990.

Hull, Gretchen Gaebelein. *Equal to Serve: Women and Men in the Church and Home.* Old Tappan, N.J.: Fleming H. Revell, 1987.

Hunt, Mary. "Food, Glorious Food." *Waterwheel* 2, no. 3 (1989): 1.

Jamieson, Kathleen Hall. *Eloquence in an Electronic Age.* New York: Oxford University Press, 1988.

Japp, Phyllis M. "Esther or Isaiah?: The Abolitionist-Feminist Rhetoric of Angelina Grimke." *Quarterly Journal of Speech* 71 (August 1985): 335-48.

Jewett, Paul K. *Man as Male and Female: A Study in Sexual Relationships from a Theological Point of View.* Grand Rapids: William B. Eerdmans, 1975.

Kanter, Rosabeth Moss. *Men and Women of the Corporation.* New York: Basic Books, 1977.

Kaufman, Michael. "The Construction of Masculinity and the Triad of Men's Violence." In *Beyond Patriarchy: Essays by Men on Pleasure, Power, and Change,* ed. Michael Kaufman, pp. 1-29. Toronto: Oxford University Press, 1987.

————. "A Framework for Research on Men and Masculinity." Paper presented at the conference entitled "Re-visioning Knowledge: Feminist Perspectives on the Curriculum," Michigan State University, East Lansing, Mich., 19-22 April 1990.

Kidd, Bruce. "The Men's Cultural Centre: Sports and the Dynamic of Women's Oppression/Men's Repression." In *Sport, Men, and the Gender Order: Critical Feminist Perspectives*, ed. Michael A. Messner and Donald Sabo, pp. 31-44. Champaign, Ill.: Human Kinetics Books, 1990.

Kimmel, Michael. "Baseball and the Reconstitution of American Masculinity, 1880-1920." In *Sport, Men, and the Gender Order: Critical Feminist Perspectives*, ed. Michael A. Messner and Donald Sabo, pp. 55-66. Champaign, Ill.: Human Kinetics Books, 1990.

————. "Men's Responses to Feminism at the Turn of the Century." *Gender and Society* 1, no. 3 (1987): 261-83.

Kitzinger, Sheila. *Birth at Home.* New York: Oxford University Press, 1979.

————. *The Experience of Childbirth.* Harmondsworth: Penguin Books, 1984.

————. *Giving Birth: How It Really Feels.* New York: Noonday Books, 1989.

————. *Your Baby Your Way.* New York: Pantheon Books, 1987.

Klein, Alan. "Pumping Irony: Crisis and Contradiction in Body Building Subculture." *Sociology of Sport Journal* 3, no. 1 (1986): 3-23.

Knoppers, Annelies. "Androgyny: Another Look." *Quest* 32, no. 2 (1980): 184-91.

Kramerae, Cheris. *Women and Men Speaking: Frameworks for Analysis.* Rowley, Mass.: Newbury House, 1981.

————, and Paula A. Treichler, with Ann Russo. *A Feminist Dictionary.* Boston: Pandora Press, 1985.

Lakoff, Robin, and Raquel Scherr. *Face Value: The Politics of Beauty.* Boston: Routledge & Kegan Paul, 1989.

Laver, James. *Costume and Fashion: A Concise History.* London: Thames & Hudson, 1969.

————. *Letter to a Girl on the Future of Clothes.* London: Home & Van Thal Ltd., 1946.

————. *Modesty in Dress.* London: Heinemann, 1969.

Lenskyj, Helen. *Out of Bounds: Women, Sport and Sexuality.* Toronto: Women's Press, 1986.

Lewis, C. S. "Membership." In *Fern-seed and Elephants and Other Essays on Christianity,* pp. 19-20. London: Collins, 1975.

————*English Literature in the Sixteenth Century, Excluding Drama.* Vol. 3 of The Oxford History of English Literature. Oxford: Clarendon, 1954.

————. *God in the Dock: Essays on Theology and Ethics.* Ed. Walter Hooper. Grand Rapids: William B. Eerdmans, 1970.

"Listening Sessions on Abortion." *Catholic Herald,* Special Issue, 24 May 1990.

Lowy, Beverly. "Rape Is Not a Sport." *On the Issues* 17 (1990): 4.

Luchetti, Cathy, and Carol Olwell. *Women of the West.* St. George, Utah: Antelope Island Press, 1982.

McCrone, Kathleen E. *Playing the Game: Sport and the Physical Emancipation of English Women, 1870-1914.* Lexington, Ky.: University of Kentucky Press, 1988.

McFague, Sallie. *Metaphorical Theology: Models of God in Religious Language.* Philadelphia: Fortress Press, 1982.

MacIntyre, Alasdair. "The Virtues, the Unity of a Human Life, and the Concept of a Tradition." In *Why Narrative? Readings in Narrative Theology,* ed. Stanley Hauerwas and L. Gregory Jones, pp. 89-110. Grand Rapids: William B. Eerdmans, 1989.

McLaughlin, Jan M. "Clothes That Flatter." *Virtue,* January/February 1990, pp. 46-48.

Mains, Karen Burton, and Maxine Hancock. *Child Sexual Abuse: The Hope for Healing.* Wheaton, Ill.: Harold Shaw, 1986.

Martin, Emily. *The Woman in the Body: A Cultural Analysis of Reproduction.* Boston: Beacon Press, 1989.

Martin, Faith. *Call Me Blessed: The Emerging Christian Woman.* Grand Rapids: William B. Eerdmans, 1988.

Martyna, Wendy. "Beyond the 'He/Man' Approach: The Case for Non-Sexist Language." *Signs* 5 (1980): 482-93.

Meilaender, Gilbert. *The Taste for the Other: The Social and Ethical Thought of C. S. Lewis.* Grand Rapids: William B. Eerdmans, 1978.

Messner, Michael. "The Life of Man's Seasons: Male Identity in the Life Course of a Jock." In *Changing Men: New Directions in Research on Men and Masculinity,* ed. Michael S. Kimmel, pp. 53-67. Newbury Park, Calif.: Sage Publications, 1987.

————. "Masculinities and Athletic Careers: Bonding and Status Differences." In *Sport, Men, and the Gender Order: Critical Feminist Perspectives,* ed. Michael Messner and Donald Sabo, pp. 97-108. Champaign, Ill.: Human Kinetics Books, 1990.

————. "The Meaning of Success: The Athletic Experience and the Development of Male Identity." In *The Making of Masculinities: The New Men's Studies,* ed. Harry Brod, pp. 193-210. Boston: Allen & Unwin, 1987.

————. "Sport and Male Domination: The Female Athlete as Contested Ideological Terrain." *Sociology of Sport Journal* 5 (1988): 197-211.

————. "When Bodies Are Weapons: Masculinity and Violence in Sport." *International Review for the Sociology of Sport* 25 (1989): 203-20.

————, and Donald F. Sabo, eds. *Sport, Men, and the Gender Order: Critical Feminist Perspectives.* Champaign, Ill.: Human Kinetics Books, 1990.

Meulenbelt, Anja. *De Ziekte Bestryden, Niet de Patient: Over Siksisme, Racisme en Klassisme.* Amsterdam: Van Geenep, 1986.

Miller, Casey, and Kate Swift. *The Handbook of Nonsexist Writing.* New York: Lippincott & Crowell, 1980.

Miller, Jean Baker. *Towards a New Psychology of Women.* Boston: Beacon Press, 1976.

Millman, Marcia. *Such a Pretty Face: Being Fat in America.* New York: W. W. Norton, 1980.

Mishkind, Marc, et al. "The Embodiment of Masculinity: Cultural, Psychological and Behavioral Dimensions." In *Changing Men: New Directions in Research on Men and Masculinity,* ed. Michael S. Kimmel, pp. 37-52. Newbury Park, Calif.: Sage Publications, 1987.

Molloy, John T. *The Woman's Dress for Success Book.* New York: Warner Books, 1977.

Nelson, James B. *Embodiment: An Approach to Sexuality and Christian Theology.* Minneapolis: Augsburg Publishing House, 1978.

Newman, Molly, and Barbara Damashek. *Quilters.* New York: Dramatists Play Service, 1986.

Office for Sex Equity in Education. "Influence of Gender Role Socialization upon the Perceptions of Children." Michigan Department of Education, Lansing, Mich., 1989.

Okin, Susan Moller. *Justice, Gender, and the Family.* New York: Basic Books, 1989.

Olrich, Tracy. "The Relationship of Male Identity, Mesomorphic Image and Anabolic Steroids in Body Building." Unpublished thesis, Department of Physical Education and Exercise Science, Michigan State University, East Lansing, Mich., 1991.

Perry, Linda, Lynn Turner, and Helen Sterk, eds. *Constructing and Reconstructing Gender.* Buffalo, N.Y.: State University of New York Press, 1992.

Pharr, Suzanne. *Homophobia: A Weapon of Sexism.* Inverness, Calif.: Chardon Press, 1988.

Phipps, William E. *Genesis and Gender: Biblical Myths of Sexuality and Their Cultural Impact.* New York: Praeger Publishers, 1989.

Plaskow, Judith. *Sex, Sin, and Grace: Women's Experience and the Theologies of Reinhold Niebuhr and Paul Tillich.* Lanham, Md.: University Press of America, 1980.

Pollitt, Katha. "Georgie Porgie Is a Bully." *Time,* Special Issue 136 (Fall 1990): 24.

Pronger, Brian. *The Arena of Masculinity: Sport, Homosexuality, and the Meaning of Sex.* New York: St. Martin's Press, 1990.

Rakow, Lana. *Gender on the Line: Women, the Telephone, and Community Life.* Champaign: University of Illinois Press, 1992.

Rawls, John. *A Theory of Justice.* Cambridge: Harvard University Press, 1971.

Regush, Nicholas. "Toxic Breasts." *Mother Jones,* January/February 1992.

Rich, Adrienne. *Of Women Born: Motherhood as Experience and Institution.* New York: W. W. Norton, 1976.

Rienstra, Marchiene. "God's Freedom for Women" (Parts 1, 2, and 3). *Reformed Journal* 27 (September 1977): 11-14; (October 1977): 19-23; and (November 1977): 26-29.

Rosen, Lionel, et al. "Pathogenic Weight Control Behavior in Female Athletes." *The Physician and Sportsmedicine* 14 (January 1986): 79-83, 86.

Rothenberg, Paula. "Teachable Truths: Connecting Race, Gender, Class." *Feminist Teacher* 3: 1-3.

Ruddick, Sara. *Maternal Thinking: Toward a Politics of Peace.* New York: Ballantine Books, 1989.

Ruether, Rosemary Radford. *Sexism and God-Talk: Toward a Feminist Theology.* Boston: Beacon Press, 1983.

Sabo, Donald. "Sport, Patriarchy and Male Identity: New Questions about Men and Sport." *Arena Review* 9 (1985): 1-30.

————, and Panepinto, Joe. "Football Ritual and the Social Reproduction of Masculinity." In *Sport, Men, and the Gender Order,* ed. Michael A. Messner and Donald Sabo, pp. 115-26. Champaign, Ill.: Human Kinetics Books, 1990.

Sage, George. *Power and Ideology in American Sport: A Critical Perspective.* Champaign, Ill.: Human Kinetics Books, 1990.

Sanday, Peggy Reeves. "Sociocultural Context of Rape: A Cross Cultural Study." *Journal of Social Issues* 37, no. 4 (1981): 5-27.

Schuiteman, Jayne. "Self-Defense Training and Its Contributions to the Healing Process for Survivors of Sexual Abuse." Ph.D. Dissertation, Michigan State University, 1990.

Searle, John. *Speech Acts: An Essay in the Philosophy of Language.* 1969; rpt. Cambridge: Cambridge University Press, 1978.

Seid, Roberta Pollack. *Never Too Thin: Why Women Are at War with Their Bodies.* New York: Prentice Hall Press, 1989.

Shaw, Anna Howard. *The Story of a Pioneer.* New York: Harper & Brothers, 1915.

Smart, Carol. *Feminism and the Power of Law.* New York: Routledge, 1989.

Snodgrass, Jon, ed. *For Men against Sexism: A Book of Readings.* New York: Times Change Press, 1977.

Sorel, Nancy. *Ever since Eve: Personal Reflections on Childbirth.* Oxford: Oxford University Press, 1984.

Sorrels, Bobbye. *The Nonsexist Communicator.* Englewood Cliffs, N.J.: Prentice-Hall, 1983.

Spence, Janet T., and Robert L. Helmreich. *Masculinity and Femininity: Their Psychological Dimensions, Correlates, and Antecedents.* Austin: University of Texas Press, 1978.

Spender, Dale. *Man-Made Language.* 2d ed. London: Routledge & Kegan Paul, 1985.

————. *The Writing or the Sex? or, Why You Don't Have to Read Women's Writing to Know It's No Good.* New York: Pergamon Press, 1989.

Steinem, Gloria. *Outrageous Acts and Everyday Rebellions.* New York: Holt, Rinehart & Winston, 1983.

Steiner-Adair, Catherine. "The Body Politic: Normal Female Adolescent Development and the Development of Eating Disorders." In *Making Connections: The Relational Worlds of Adolescent Girls at Emma Willard School,* ed. Carol Gilligan, Nona P. Lyons, and Trudy J. Hanmer, pp. 162-83. Troy, N.Y.: Emma Willard School, 1989.

Strasser, Susan. *Never Done: A History of American Housework.* New York: Pantheon Books, 1982.

Swartley, Willard M. *Slavery, Sabbath, War, and Women: Case Issues in Biblical Interpretation.* Scottdale, Pa.: Herald Press, 1983.

Szekely, Eva Aniko. *Never Too Thin.* Toronto: Women's Press, 1988.

Tannen, Deborah. *You Just Don't Understand: Women and Men in Conversation.* New York: William Morrow, 1990.

Taulbert, Clifton. *Once upon a Time When We Were Colored.* Tulsa, Okla.: Council Oak Books, 1989.

Thistlethwaite, Susan. *Sex, Race, and God: Christian Feminism in Black and White.* New York: Crossroad, 1989.

Thompson, E. H., C. Grisanti, and J. H. Pleck. "Attitudes toward the Male Role and Their Correlates." *Sex Roles* 13 (1985): 413-27.

Thorne, Barrie. "Gender . . . How Is It Best Conceptualized?" Unpublished paper, Sociology Department, University of Southern California, 1980.

————. "Girls and Boys Together . . . But Mostly Apart: Gender Arrangements in Elementary Schools." In *Relationship and Development,* ed. W. Hartup and Z. Rubin, pp. 167-84. Hillsdale, N.J.: Lawrence Erlbaum Associates, 1986.

628

————, Cheris Kramarae, and Nancy Henley, eds. *Language, Gender and Society.* Rowley, Mass.: Newbury House, 1983.

Trubo, Richard. "The Cholesterol Gap: Lack of Studies Leaves Women Wondering." *American Health,* January/February 1990.

Van Itallie, Theodore, M.D. "Health Implications of Overweight and Obesity in the United States." *Annals of Internal Medicine* 103, no. 62 (1985): 983-88.

Van Leeuwen, Mary Stewart. *Gender and Grace: Love, Work and Parenting in a Changing World.* Downers Grove, Ill.: InterVarsity Press, 1990.

Veblen, Thorstein. *The Theory of the Leisure Class.* 1899; rpt. New York: Random House, 1934.

Wallston, Barbara S., and Virginia E. O'Leary. "Sex Makes a Difference: Differential Perceptions of Women and Men." In *Review of Personality and Social Psychology,* vol. 2, ed. Ladd Wheeler, pp. 9-41. Beverly Hills, Calif.: Sage Publications, 1981.

Walzer, Michael. *The Revolution of the Saints: A Study in the Origins of Radical Politics.* Cambridge: Harvard University Press, 1965.

Weitzman, Lenore. *Sex-Role Socialization.* Palo Alto, Calif.: Mayfield Publishing Co., 1979.

Whitson, David. "Sport in the Social Construction of Masculinity." In *Sport, Men, and the Gender Order,* ed. Michael A. Messner and Donald Sabo, pp. 19-29. Champaign, Ill.: Human Kinetics Books, 1990.

Wise, Sue, and Liz Stanley. *Georgie Porgie: Sexual Harassment in Everyday Life.* London: Pandora Press, 1987.

Wollstonecraft, Mary. *A Vindication of the Rights of Woman.* 2d ed. Ed. Carol H. Poston. New York: W. W. Norton, 1975.

Woolf, Virginia. *A Room of One's Own.* 1930; rpt. San Diego: Harvest/HBJ Book, 1957.

Wren, Brian. *What Language Shall I Borrow? God-Talk in Worship: A Male Response to Feminist Theology.* New York: Crossroad, 1990.

Works Cited in Part IV

Abu-Lughod, Lila. *Veiled Sentiments: Honor and Poetry in a Bedouin Society.* Berkeley: University of California Press, 1986.

Acker, Joan. "Hierarchies, Jobs, Bodies: A Theory of Gendered Organizations." *Gender & Society* 4 (1990): 139-58.

————. *Doing Comparable Worth: Gender, Class and Pay Equity.* Philadelphia: Temple University Press, 1989.

Adams, Margaret. "The Compassion Trap." In *Woman in Sexist Society: Studies in Power and Powerlessness,* ed. Vivian Gornick and Barbara K. Moran, pp. 401-16. New York: Basic Books, 1971.

Alsdurf, James, and Phyllis Alsdurf. *Battered into Submission: The Tragedy of Wife Abuse in the Christian Home.* Downers Grove, Ill.: InterVarsity Press, 1989.

American Association of University Women. "Shortchanging Girls, Short-changing America." AAUW, January 1991.

Andolsen, Barbara Hilkert. "Agape in Feminist Ethics." *Journal of Religious Ethics* 9 (Spring 1981): 69-83.

——, Christine E. Gudorf, and Mary D. Pellauer, eds. *Women's Consciousness, Women's Conscience: A Reader in Feminist Ethics.* San Francisco: Harper & Row, 1985.

Barakat, Halim. "The Arab Family and the Challenge of Social Transformation." In *Women and the Family in the Middle East,* ed. Elizabeth Warnock Fernea, pp. 27-48. Austin: University of Texas Press, 1985.

Bardhan, Kalpana. "Stratification of Women's Work in Rural India: Determinants, Effects and Strategies." In *Social and Economic Development in India: A Reassessment,* ed. Dilip K. Basu and Richard Sisson, pp. 89-105. New Delhi: Sage Publications, 1986.

Barry, Brian. *Theories of Justice.* Berkeley: University of California Press, 1989.

Basch, R. *Relative Creatures — Victorian Women, 1837-67.* London: Allen Lane, 1974.

Becker, Gary S. "Human Capital, Effort, and Sexual Division of Labor." *Journal of Labor Economics* 3 (1985): 533-58.

Beech, Mary Higdon. "The Domestic Realm in the Lives of Hindu Women in Calcutta." In *Separate Worlds: Studies of Purdah in South Asia,* ed. Hanna Papanek and Gail Minault, pp. 110-38. Columbia, Mo.: South Asia Books, 1982.

Belenky, Mary Field, et al. *Women's Ways of Knowing: The Development of Self, Voice, and Mind.* New York: Basic Books, 1986.

Bellah, Robert N., et al. *The Good Society.* New York: Alfred A. Knopf, 1991.

Benjamin, Jessica. *The Bonds of Love: Psychoanalysis, Feminism, and the Problem of Domination.* New York: Pantheon Books, 1988.

Bielby, William, and James Baron. "Undoing Discrimination: Job Integration and Comparable Worth." In *Ingredients for Women's Employment Policy,* ed. Christine Bose and Glenna Spitze, pp. 211-29. Albany, N.Y.: SUNY Press, 1987.

Blank, Rebecca M. "Women's Paid Work, Household Income, and Household Well-Being." In *The American Woman, 1988-1989: A Status Report*, ed. Sara E. Rix, Women's Research & Education Institute, pp. 79-122. New York: W. W. Norton, 1988.

Blau, F. "Occupational Segregation and Labor Market Discrimination." In *Sex Segregation in the Workplace: Trends, Explanations, Remedies*, ed. B. Reskin, pp. 117-43. Washington: National Academy of Sciences, 1984.

Bloom, Allan. *The Closing of the American Mind: How Higher Education Has Failed Democracy and Impoverished the Souls of Today's Students.* New York: Simon & Schuster, 1987.

Bly, Robert. *Iron John: A Book about Men.* Reading, Mass.: Addison-Wesley, 1990.

Bordewich, Fergus M. "India: Dowry Murders." *Atlantic Monthly,* July 1986, pp. 21-27.

Bordo, Susan. *The Flight to Objectivity: Essays on Cartesianism and Culture.* Albany, N.Y.: SUNY Press, 1987.

Boserup, Ester. *Women's Role in Economic Development.* London: George Allen & Unwin, 1970.

Botha, Elaine. "Voices from a Troubled Land." *Christianity Today,* 21 November 1986, special insert on South Africa, p. 8.

Brahme, Sulabha. "The Growing Burdens of Women." In *In Search of Answers: Indian Women's Voices from Manushi*, ed. Madhu Kishwar and Ruth Vanita, pp. 49-62. London: Zed Books, 1984.

Brenner, Johanna, and Barbara Laslett. "Gender Social Reproduction and Women's Self-Organization: Considering the U.S. Welfare State." *Gender & Society* 5, no. 3 (1991): 311-33.

Brittan, Arthur. *Masculinity and Power.* New York: Basil Blackwell, 1989.

Broverman, Inge K., et al. "Sex-role Stereotypes: A Current Appraisal." *Journal of Social Issues* 28, no. 2 (1972): 59-78.

Brown, Anita. *Uneasy Access: Privacy for Women in a Free Society.* Totowa, N.J.: Rowman & Allanheld, 1988.

Brownmiller, Susan. *Against Our Will: Men, Women, and Rape.* New York: Simon & Schuster, 1975.

Buker, Eloise A. "Politics As If Women Were Normal: Defending the Post-Feminist Polity." Paper given at the Michigan State University conference entitled "Revisioning Women in the Curriculum," April 1990.

Calvin College Social Research Center. "A Survey of Abuse in the Christian Reformed Church." Grand Rapids: Calvin College, 1990.

Campbell, K. "Gender Differences in Job-Related Networks." *Work and Occupations* 15 (1988): 179-200.

Caplan, Patricia. *Class and Gender in India: Women and Their Organizations in a South Indian City.* London: Tavistock Publications, 1985.

Chodorow, Nancy J. *The Reproduction of Mothering: Psychoanalysis and the Sociology of Gender.* Berkeley: University of California Press, 1978.

Christ, Carol P., and Judith Plaskow, eds. *Womanspirit Rising: A Feminist Reader in Religion.* San Francisco: Harper & Row, 1979.

Cline, Sally, and Dale Spender. *Reflecting Men at Twice Their Natural Size.* New York: Seaver Books, 1987.

Clinton, Catherine. *The Plantation Mistresses: Women's World in the Old South.* New York: Pantheon Books, 1983.

Cockburn, Cynthia. *Machinery of Dominance: Women, Men and Technical Know-how.* London: Pluto Press, 1985.

Code, Lorraine. "Experience, Knowledge, and Responsibility." In *Women, Knowledge and Reality: Explorations in Feminist Philosophy,* ed. Ann Garry and Marily Pearsall, pp. 157-72. Boston: Unwin Hyman, 1989.

Cohn, Samuel. *The Process of Occupational Sex-Typing: The Feminization of Clerical Labor in Great Britain.* Women in the Political Economy series, ed. Ronnie J. Steinberg. Philadelphia: Temple University Press, 1985.

Collins, Patricia Hill. *Black Feminist Thought: Knowledge, Consciousness, and the Politics of Empowerment.* London: HarperCollins, 1990.

Collinson, D., and M. Collinson. "Sexuality in the Workplace: The Domination of Men's Sexuality." In *The Sexuality of Organization,* ed. Jeff Hearn et al., pp. 91-109. London: Sage, 1989.

Connell, Robert W. *Gender and Power: Society, the Person and Sexual Politics.* Stanford: Stanford University Press, 1987.

Cowan, Ruth Schwartz. *More Work for Mother: The Ironies of Household Technology from the Open Hearth to the Microwave.* New York: Basic Books, 1983.

Daly, Mary. *Beyond God the Father: Toward a Philosophy of Women's Liberation.* Boston: Beacon Press, 1973.

"The Danvers Statement." *Christianity Today,* 13 January 1989, pp. 40-41.

Das, Manini. "Women against Dowry." In *In Search of Answers: Indian Women's Voices from Manushi,* ed. Madhu Kishwar and Ruth Vanita, pp. 222-27. London: Zed Books, 1984.

Davidoff, Leonore, and Catherine Hall. *Family Fortunes: Men and Women of the English Middle Class, 1780-1850.* Chicago: University of Chicago Press, 1987.

Davis, Angela. "Egypt." In *Women: A World Report.* New York: Oxford University Press, 1985.

Deem, Rosemary. *All Work and No Play? The Sociology of Women and Leisure.* Milton Keynes, U.K.: Open University Press, 1986.

Dinnerstein, Dorothy. *The Mermaid and the Minotaur: Sexual Arrangements and Human Malaise.* New York: Harper–Colophon Books, 1977.

DiTomaso, N. "Sexuality in the Workplace: Discrimination and Harassment." In *The Sexuality of Organization,* ed. Jeff Hearn et al., pp. 71-90. London: Sage, 1989.

Doyal, Lesley. "Hazards of Hearth and Home." *Women's Studies International Forum* 13 (1990): 501-17.

———. "Waged Work and Women's Well-Being." *Women's Studies International Forum* 13 (1990): 587-604.

Duley, Margot I., and Mary I. Edwards, eds. *The Cross-Cultural Study of Women: A Comprehensive Guide.* New York: Feminist Press, 1986.

Dutton, Donald D. *The Domestic Assault of Women.* Boston: Allyn & Bacon, 1988.

Dworkin, Andrea. *Our Blood: Prophecies and Discourses on Sexual Politics.* New York: G. P. Putnam, 1981.

Dwyer, Daisy, and Judith Bruce, eds. *A Home Divided: Women and Income in the Third World.* Stanford: Stanford University Press, 1988.

Early, Evelyn. "Fatima: A Life History of an Egyptian Woman from Bulaq." In *Women and the Family in the Middle East: New Voices of Change,* ed. Elizabeth Warnock Fernea, pp. 76-83. Austin: University of Texas Press, 1985.

Ehrensaft, Diane. *Parenting Together: Men and Women Sharing the Care of Their Children.* Champaign: University of Illinois Press, 1987.

el-Messiri, Sawsan. "Self-Images of Traditional Urban Women in Cairo." In *Women in the Muslim World,* ed. Lois Beck and Nikki Keddie, pp. 522-40. Cambridge: Harvard University Press, 1978.

Elshtain, Jean B. *Public Man, Private Woman: Women in Social and Political Thought.* Princeton: Princeton University Press, 1981.

———. *Women and War.* New York: Basic Books, 1987.

England, Paula, and Lori McCreary. "Integrating Sociology and Economics to Study Gender and Work." In *Women and Work,* vol. 2, ed. Ann Stromberg, Laurie Larwood, and Barbara Gutek, pp. 143-72. Newbury Park, Calif.: Sage Publications, 1987.

Epstein, Cynthia Fuchs. *Deceptive Distinctions: Sex, Gender and the Social Order.* New Haven: Yale University Press/Russell Sage Foundation, 1988.

Equality between Men and Women in Sweden: Government Policy to the Mid-Nineties (Summary of Government Bill 1987/88). Stockholm: Ministry of Labor, Division of Equality Affairs, 1988.

"Family Configurations in the Third World." Slide and tape presentation available from The Glenhurst Collection of Women's History and Culture, St. Louis Park, Minnesota.

Farley, Margaret. "New Patterns of Relationship: Beginnings of a Moral Revolution." In *Woman: New Dimensions,* ed. Walter Burkhardt, pp. 51-70. New York: Paulist Press, 1975.

Faust-Sterling, Anne. *Myths of Gender: Biological Theories about Women and Men.* New York: Basic Books, 1985.

Fernea, Elizabeth Warnock, producer. *A Veiled Revolution.* Film released in 1982 and available from ICARUS Films, 200 Park Ave., South, Suite 1319, New York, NY 10003.

Firestone, Shulamith. *The Dialectic of Sex: The Case for Feminist Revolution.* New York: William Morrow, 1970.

Fortune, Marie Marshall. *Sexual Violence: The Unmentionable Sin.* New York: Pilgrim Press, 1983.

Fox-Genovese, Elizabeth. *Feminism Without Illusions: A Critique of Individualism.* Chapel Hill: University of North Carolina Press, 1991.

————. *Within the Plantation Household: Black and White Women of the Old South.* Chapel Hill: University of North Carolina Press, 1988.

French, Marilyn. *Beyond Power: On Women, Men and Morals.* New York: Summit Books, 1985.

Ganesh, Kamala. "State of the Art in Women's Studies." *Economic and Political Weekly,* 20 April 1985, pp. 683-89.

Garry, Ann, and Marilyn Pearsall, eds. *Women, Knowledge and Reality: Explorations in Feminist Philosophy.* Boston: Unwin Hyman, 1989.

Gerson, Kathleen. "What Do Women Want from Men?: Men's Influence on Women's Work and Family Choices." In *Changing Men: New Directions in Research on Men and Masculinity,* ed. Michael S. Kimmel, pp. 115-30. Newbury Park, Calif.: Sage Publications, 1987.

Ghadially, Rehana, and Pramod Kumar, eds. *Women in Indian Society.* New Delhi: SAGE Publications, 1988.

Ghosh, Chitra. "Construction Workers." In *Women and Work in India: Continuity and Change,* ed. Joyce Lebra, Joy Paulson, and Jana Everett, pp. 201-11. New Delhi: Promilla & Co., 1984.

Gilligan, Carol. *In a Different Voice: Psychological Theory and Women's Development.* Cambridge: Harvard University Press, 1982.

————, et al., eds. *Making Connections: The Relational Worlds of Adolescent Girls at Emma Willard School.* Troy, N.Y.: Emma Willard School, 1989.

Goldstein, Valerie Saiving. "The Human Situation: A Feminine View." In *Womanspirit Rising: A Feminist Reader in Religion,* ed. Carol P. Christ and Judith Plaskow, pp. 25-42. San Francisco: Harper & Row, 1979.

Gordon, Linda. "Why Nineteenth-Century Feminists Did Not Support 'Birth Control' and Twentieth-Century Feminists Do: Feminism, Reproduction and the Family." In *Rethinking the Family: Some Feminist Questions,* ed. Barrie Thorne and Marilyn Yalom, pp. 40-53. New York: Longman, 1982.

Gordon, Scott. *Welfare, Justice, and Freedom.* New York: Columbia University Press, 1980.

Gornick, Vivian, and Barbara K. Moran, eds. *Woman in Sexist Society: Studies in Power and Powerlessness.* New York: Basic Books, 1971.

Granovetter, Mark. *Getting a Job: A Study of Contacts and Careers.* Cambridge, Mass.: Auburn House, 1974.

Groneman, Carol, and Mary Beth Norton, eds. *To Toil the Livelong Day: America's Women at Work, 1780-1980.* Ithaca: Cornell University Press, 1987.

Gudorf, Christine E. "Parenting, Mutual Love, and Sacrifice." In *Women's Consciousness, Women's Conscience: A Reader in Feminist Ethics,* ed. Barbara Andolsen et al., pp. 175-91. San Francisco: Harper & Row, 1985.

Gutek, Barbara. "Sexuality in the Workplace: Key Issues in Social Research and Organizational Practice." In *The Sexuality of Organization,* ed. Jeff Hearn et al., pp. 56-70. London: Sage, 1989.

————. *Sex and the Workplace.* San Francisco: Jossey-Bass, 1985.

————, and Bruce Morasch. "Sex-Ratios, Sex-Role Spillover, and Sexual Harassment of Women at Work." *Journal of Social Issues* 38, no. 4 (1982): 55-74.

————, and V. Dunwood. "Understanding Sex in the Workplace." In *Women and Work: An Annual Review,* vol. 2, ed. A. Stromberg et al. Newbury Park, Calif.: Sage, 1987.

Hall, Douglas T. "Promoting Work/Family Balance: An Organization-Change Approach." In *Organizational Dynamics* 18 (Winter 1990): 5-18.

Haney, Eleanor Humes. "What Is Feminist Ethics? A Proposal for Continuing Discussion." *Journal of Religious Ethics* 8 (Spring 1980): 115-24.

Hareven, Tamar. *Family Time and Industrial Time.* Cambridge: Cambridge University Press, 1982.

Harlan, A., and C. Weiss. "Sex Differences in Factors Affecting Managerial Career Advancement." In *Women in the Workplace,* ed. Phyllis Wallace, pp. 49-100. Boston: Auburn House, 1982.

Harris, R. Laird, et al., eds. *Theological Wordbook of the Old Testament.* Chicago: Moody Press, 1980.

Harrison, Beverly Wildung. "The New Consciousness of Women: A Socio-Political Resource." *Cross-Currents* 24 (Winter 1975): 445-62.

Hart, Gillian. *Power, Labor, and Livelihood: Processes of Change in Rural Java.* Berkeley: University of California Press, 1986.

Hartmann, Heidi. "Capitalism, Patriarchy, and Job Segregation by Sex." *Signs* 1 (1976): 137-69.

———. "The Family as the Locus of Gender, Class, and Political Struggle: The Example of Housework." In *Feminism and Methodology,* ed. Sandra Harding, pp. 109-34. Bloomington: Indiana University Press, 1987.

Hartsock, Nancy. *Money, Sex, and Power: An Essay on Domination and Community.* New York: Longman, 1983.

Haughey, John C., S.J., ed. *The Faith That Does Justice: Examining the Christian Sources for Social Change.* New York: Paulist Press, 1977.

Hayden, Dolores. *Redesigning the American Dream: The Future of Housing, Work, and Family Life.* New York: W. W. Norton, 1984.

Hearn, Jeff, and Wendy Parkin. "Gender and Organizations: A Selective Review and a Critique of a Neglected Area." *Organization Studies* 4 (1983): 219-42.

———. *"Sex" at "Work": The Power and Paradox of Organization Sexuality.* New York: St. Martin's Press, 1987.

Hewlett, Sylvia Ann. *When the Bough Breaks: The Cost of Neglecting Our Children.* New York: Basic Books, 1991.

Hochschild, Arlie. *The Second Shift: Working Parents and the Revolution at Home.* New York: Viking Press, 1989.

Hoodfar, Homa. "Household Budgeting and Financial Management in a Lower-Income Cairo Neighborhood." In *A Home Divided: Women and Income in the Third World,* ed. Daisy Dwyer and Judith Bruce, pp. 120-42. Stanford: Stanford University Press, 1988.

Horton, Anne L., and Judith A. Williamson. *Abuse and Religion: When Praying Isn't Enough.* Lexington: D. C. Heath, 1988.

Hume, David. *Treatise of Human Nature* (1739-1740), ed. L. A. Selby-Bigge. Oxford: Clarendon Press, 1975.

Hunter, James Davidson. *Evangelicalism: The Coming Generation.* Chicago: University of Chicago Press, 1987.

Ibrahim, Barbara Lethem. "Cairo's Factory Women." In *Women and the Family in the Middle East,* ed. Elizabeth Warnock Fernea, pp. 293-302. Austin: University of Texas Press, 1985.

Izraeli, D. "Sex Effects or Structural Effects: An Empirical Test of Kanter's Theory of Proportions." *Social Forces* 62 (1983): 153-65.

Jacobs, Jerry A. *Revolving Doors: Sex Segregation and Women's Careers.* Stanford: Stanford University Press, 1989.

————, and F. Furstenberg. "Changing Places: Conjugal Careers and Women's Marital Mobility." *Social Forces* 64, no. 3 (1986): 714-32.

Jacobson, Doranne, and Susan Wadley. *Women in India: Two Perspectives.* New Delhi: Manohar, India, 1986.

Jaggar, Alison M. *Feminist Politics and Human Nature.* Totowa, N.J.: Rowman & Allanheld, 1983.

Jayawardena, Kumari. *Feminism and Nationalism in the Third World.* London: Zed Books, 1986.

Johnson, Miriam M. *Strong Mothers, Weak Wives: The Search for Gender Equality.* Berkeley: University of California Press, 1988.

Junsay, Alma T., and Tim B. Heaton. *Women Working: Comparative Perspectives in Developing Areas.* New York: Greenwood Press, 1989.

Kader, Soha Abdel. *Egyptian Women in a Changing Society.* Boulder, Colo.: Lynne Rienner Publishers, 1987.

Kanter, Rosabeth Moss. *Men and Women of the Corporation.* New York: Basic Books, 1977.

Kaufman, Michael. *A Framework for Research on Men and Masculinity.* Paper presented at the conference "Re-visioning Knowledge: Feminist Perspectives on the Curriculum," Michigan State University, East Lansing, Mich., 19-22 April 1990.

Keller, Evelyn Fox. *A Feeling for the Organism: The Life and Work of Barbara McClintock.* San Francisco: W. H. Freeman, 1983.

————. *Reflections on Gender and Science.* New Haven: Yale University Press, 1985.

Kimmel, Michael, ed. *Men Confront Pornography.* New York: Crown, 1990.

Kishwar, Madhu, and Ruth Vanita, eds. *In Search of Answers: Indian Women's Voices from Manushi.* London: Zed Books, 1984.

Klatch, Rebecca E. *Women of the New Right.* Philadelphia: Temple University Press, 1987.

Knoppers, Annelies, et al. "Gender and the Salaries of Coaches." *Sociology of Sport Journal* 6 (1989): 348-61.

————. "Gender Ratio and Social Interaction among Coaches." *Sociology of Sport Journal* 9 (1992).

Kohlberg, Lawrence. *The Philosophy of Moral Development.* San Francisco: Harper & Row, 1981.

Koonz, Claudia. *Mothers in the Fatherland: Women, the Family, and Nazi Politics.* New York: St. Martin's Press, 1987.

Kraditor, Aileen S. *The Ideas of the Woman Suffrage Movement, 1890-1920.* Garden City, N.Y.: Doubleday-Anchor Books, 1971.

Kuhn, Thomas. *The Structure of Scientific Revolutions.* Chicago: University of Chicago Press, 1962.

Lasch, Christopher. *Haven in a Heartless World: The Family Besieged.* New York: Basic Books, 1977.

Leidner, Robin. "Serving Hamburgers and Selling Insurance: Gender, Work, and Identity in Interactive Service Jobs." *Gender & Society* 5 (1991): 154-77.

Lerner, Gerda. *The Creation of Patriarchy.* New York: Oxford University Press, 1986.

Lewis, C. S. *Mere Christianity.* London: Collins–Fontana Books, 1955.

Lewontin, R. C., Steven Rose, and Leon J. Kamin. *Not in Our Genes: Biology, Ideology, and Human Nature.* New York: Pantheon Books, 1984.

Liddle, Joanna, and Rama Joshi. *Daughters of Independence: Gender, Caste, and Class in India.* New Brunswick, N.J.: Rutgers University Press, 1986.

Lin, N., and M. Dumin. "Access to Occupations through Social Ties." *Social Networks* 8 (1986): 365-86.

Lipman-Blumen, Jean. *Gender Roles and Power.* Englewood Cliffs, N.J.: Prentice-Hall, 1984.

Lloyd, Genevieve. *The Man of Reason: "Male" and "Female" in Western Philosophy.* London: Methuen, 1984.

Lopata, Helena. "The Chicago Woman: A Study of Patterns of Mobility and Transportation." In *Women and the American City,* ed. Catherine Stimpson et al., pp. 158-66. Chicago: University of Chicago Press, 1981.

Luxton, Meg. *More than a Labour of Love: Three Generations of Women's Work in the Home.* Toronto: The Women's Press, 1980.

Machung, Anne. "Talking Career, Thinking Job: Gender Differences in Career and Family Expectations of Berkeley Seniors." *Feminist Studies* 15, no. 1 (Spring 1989): 35-58.

MacKinnon, Catharine. *Feminism Unmodified: Discourses on Life and Law.* Cambridge: Harvard University Press, 1987.

Mainardi, Pat. "The Politics of Housework." In *Voices from Women's Liberation,* ed. Leslie B. Tanner, pp. 336-42. New York: New American Library, 1970.

Mains, Karen Burton, and Maxine Hancock. *Child Sexual Abuse: The Hope for Healing.* Wheaton, Ill.: Harold Shaw, 1986.

Manderson, Lenore. *Women's Work and Women's Roles: Economics and Everyday Life in Indonesia, Malaysia and Singapore.* Canberra: Development Studies Centre, Australian National University, 1983.

Marina, Margaret M., and Mary C. Brinton. "Sex Typing and Occupational

Socialization." In *Sex Segregation in the Workplace: Trends, Explanations, Remedies*, ed. Barbara Reskin, pp. 192-232. Washington: National Academy Press, 1984.

Markandaya, Kamala. *Nectar in a Sieve*. New York: Penguin–New American Library, 1982.

Marshall, Paul. *Thine Is the Kingdom*. Grand Rapids: William B. Eerdmans, 1987.

Marsot, Afaf Lutfi al-Sayyid. "The Revolutionary Gentlewomen in Egypt." In *Women in the Muslim World*, ed. Lois Beck and Nikki Keddie, pp. 277-94. Cambridge: Harvard University Press, 1978.

Matlin, Margaret W. *The Psychology of Women*. New York: Holt, Rinehart & Winston, 1987.

Mehta, Rama. *The Western Educated Hindu Woman*. Bombay: Asia Publishing House, 1970.

Meilaender, Gilbert. *The Taste for the Other: The Social and Ethical Thought of C. S. Lewis*. Grand Rapids: William B. Eerdmans, 1976.

Mencher, Joan P. "Women's Work and Poverty: Women's Contribution to Household Maintenance in South India." In *A Home Divided: Women and Income in the Third World*, ed. Daisy Dwyer and Judith Bruce, pp. 99-119. Stanford: Stanford University Press, 1988.

Mies, Maria. "The Dynamics of the Sexual Division of Labor and Integration of Rural Women into the World Market." In *Women and Development*, ed. Lourdes Beneria, pp. 1-28. New York: Praeger Publishers, 1982.

———. *The Lace Makers of Narsapur: Indian Housewives Produce for the World Market*. London: Zed Books, 1982.

Miller, Barbara. "Health, Fertility and Society in India: Microstudies and Macrostudies — A Review Article." *Journal of Asian Studies* 45 (November 1986): 1027-36.

Miller, Jean Baker. *Towards a New Psychology of Women*. Boston: Beacon Press, 1976.

Moen, Phyllis. *Working Parents: Transformation in Gender Roles and Public Policies in Sweden*. Madison: University of Wisconsin Press, 1989.

Mohsen, Safia K. "New Images, Old Reflections: Working Middle-Class Women in Egypt." In *Women and the Family in the Middle East*, ed. Elizabeth Warnock Fernea, pp. 56-71. Austin: University of Texas Press, 1985.

Moulton, Janice, and Francine Rainone. "Women's Work and Sex Roles." In *Beyond Domination: New Perspectives on Women and Philosophy*, ed. Carol Gould, pp. 189-203. Totowa, N.J.: Rowman and Allanheld, 1984.

Murshid, Ghulam. *Reluctant Debutante: Response of Bengali Women to Modernization, 1849-1905.* Rajshani University, Rajshani, Bangladesh: Sahitya Samsad, 1983.

Napier, Augustus Y. *The Fragile Bond: In Search of an Equal, Intimate, and Enduring Marriage.* New York: Harper & Row, 1988.

Niebuhr, Reinhold. *Moral Man and Immoral Society.* New York: Charles Scribner's Sons, 1960.

————. *The Nature and Destiny of Man.* 2 vols. New York: Charles Scribner's Sons, 1941 and 1943.

Nietzsche, Frederick. *The Anti-Christ.* Trans. R. J. Hollingdale. London: Penguin, 1971.

Nieva, V. "Equity for Women at Work: Models of Change." In *Sex Role Stereotyping and Affirmative Action Policy,* ed. Barbara Gutek, pp. 125-227. Los Angeles: UCLA, Institute of Industrial Relations, 1982.

Nocera, Joseph. "How the Middle Class Has Helped Ruin the Public Schools." *Utne Reader,* no. 41 (September/October 1990): 66-72.

No Longer Silent. Film produced by the National Film Board of Canada and CINE-SITA, 1987; available from the International Film Bureau.

Nygren, Anders. *Agape and Eros.* Philadelphia: Westminster Press, 1932.

Oakley, Ann. *Housewife: High Value, Low Cost.* London: Allen Lane, 1974.

————. *Subject Women.* New York: Pantheon Books, 1981.

"Odds and Trends." *Time* 136 (Fall 1990): 26.

Okin, Susan Moller. *Justice, Gender, and the Family.* New York: Basic Books, 1989.

Okun, Lewis. *Woman Abuse.* Albany: State University of New York Press, 1986.

Orwell, George. *Animal Farm.* London: Penguin Books, 1951.

Ott, E. Marlies. "Effects of Male-Female Ratio at Work." *Psychology of Women Quarterly* 13 (1989): 41-57.

Outka, Gene. *Agape: An Ethical Analysis.* New Haven: Yale University Press, 1972.

Papanek, Hanna. "To Each Less Than She Needs, from Each More Than She Can Do: Allocations, Entitlements, and Value." In *Persistent Inequalities: Women and World Development,* ed. Irene Tinker, pp. 162-84. New York: Oxford University Press, 1990.

————, and Laura Schwede. "Women Are Good with Money: Earning and Managing in an Indonesian City." In *A Home Divided: Women and Income in the Third World,* ed. Daisy Dwyer and Judith Bruce, pp. 71-98. Stanford: Stanford University Press, 1988.

Pearsall, Marilyn, ed. *Women and Values: Readings in Recent Feminist Philosophy.* Belmont, Calif.: Wadsworth Publishing Co., 1986.

Pfeffer, Jeffrey. *Power in Organizations.* Marshfield, Mass.: Pitman Publishing, 1981.

Philipp, Thomas. "Feminism and Nationalist Politics in Egypt." In *Women in the Muslim World,* ed. Lois Beck and Nikki Keddie, pp. 261-76. Cambridge: Harvard University Press, 1978.

Plaskow, Judith. *Sex, Sin, and Grace: Women's Experience and the Theologies of Reinhold Niebuhr and Paul Tillich.* Lanham, Md.: University Press of America, 1980.

Poole, Keith T., and Harmon Ziegler. *Women, Public Opinion and Politics.* New York: Longman, 1985.

Pringle, Rosemary. *Secretaries Talk: Sexuality, Power and Work.* New York: Versco, 1989.

Pruett, Kyle D. *The Nurturing Father.* New York: Warner Books, 1987.

Pruitt, Ida. *A Daughter of Han: The Autobiography of a Chinese Working Woman.* Stanford: Stanford University Press, 1967.

Ramsey, Paul. *Basic Christian Ethics.* New York: Charles Scribner's Sons, 1953.

Ratzsch, Del. *Philosophy of Science: The Natural Sciences in Christian Perspective.* Downers Grove, Ill.: InterVarsity Press, 1986.

Rawls, John. *A Theory of Justice.* Cambridge: Harvard University Press, 1971.

Ray, Satyajit. *The Home and the World.* Film and video produced by the National Film Development Corporation of India, Ghare Bhaire, India, 1984.

Reskin, Barbara. "Bringing the Men Back In: Sex Differentiation and the Devaluation of Women's Work." *Gender & Society* 2 (1988): 58-81.

———, and Heidi Hartmann. *Women's Work, Men's Work: Sex Segregation on the Job.* Washington: National Academy Press, 1986.

———, and P. Roos. "Status Hierarchies and Sex Segregation." In *Ingredients for Women's Employment Policy,* ed. Christine Bose and Glenna Spitze, pp. 3-21. Albany, N.Y.: SUNY Press, 1987.

Rix, Sara. *The American Woman, 1988-1989: A Status Report.* New York: W. W. Norton, 1988.

Robertson, Claire, and Iris Berger. *Women and Class in Africa.* New York: Africana Publishing Co., 1986.

Robinson, John. "The Hard Facts about Hard Work." *Utne Reader* 38 (March/April 1990): 70.

Rogers, Barbara. *The Domestication of Women: Discrimination in Developing Societies.* London: Tavistock, Kogan Page, 1980.

Roos, Patricia. *Gender and Work: A Comparative Analysis of Industrial Societies.* Albany, N.Y.: State University of New York Press, 1985.

Rosaldo, Michelle Zimbalist, and Louise Lamphere, eds. *Women, Culture, and Society.* Stanford: Stanford University Press, 1974.

Rosen, Ellen. *Bitter Choices: Blue-Collar Women In and Out of Work.* Chicago: University of Chicago Press, 1987.

Rothenberg, Paula. "The Political Nature of Relations between the Sexes." In *Beyond Domination: New Perspectives on Women and Philosophy,* ed. Carol Gould, pp. 204-20. Totowa, N.J.: Rowman & Allanheld, 1984.

Rothman, Sheila M. *Woman's Proper Place: A History of Changing Ideals and Practices, 1870 to the Present.* New York: Basic Books, 1978.

Ruddick, Sara. "Maternal Thinking." In *Women and Values: Readings in Recent Feminist Philosophy,* ed. Marilyn Pearsall, pp. 340-51. Belmont, Calif.: Wadsworth Publishing Co., 1986.

————. "Pacifying the Forces: Drafting Women in the Interests of Peace." *Signs* 8, no. 4 (1982): 471-89.

————. *Maternal Thinking: Toward a Politics of Peace.* New York: Ballantine Books, 1989.

Rugh, Andrea B. "Women and Work: Strategies and Choices in a Lower-Class Quarter of Cairo." In *Women and the Family in the Middle East: New Voices of Change,* ed. Elizabeth Warnock Fernea, pp. 273-88. Austin: University of Texas Press, 1985.

Rush, Florence. *The Best-Kept Secret: Sexual Abuse of Children.* Englewood Cliffs, N.J.: Prentice-Hall, 1980.

Russell, Diana E. H. *The Secret Trauma: Incest in the Lives of Girls and Women.* New York: Basic Books, 1986.

Ryan, Mary. *Cradle of the Middle Class: The Family in Oneida County, New York, 1790-1865.* Cambridge: Cambridge University Press, 1981.

Samuels, Colleen. "Room To Be a Women, To Be Human." In *Transformation: An International Dialogue on Evangelical Social Ethics* (special issue with the title "Focus on Christian Feminism"), April/June 1989, p. 1.

Sayers, Dorothy. "The Human-Not-Quite-Human." In *Are Women Human?* Downers Grove, Ill.: InterVarsity Press, 1981.

Schaef, Anne Wilson. *Women's Reality: An Emerging Female System in a White Male Society.* San Francisco: Harper & Row, 1981.

Schechter, Susan. *Women and Male Violence: The Visions and Struggles of the Battered Women's Movement.* Boston: South End Press, 1982.

Sen, Amartya K. "Gender and Cooperative Conflicts." In *Persistent Inequalities,* ed. Irene Tinker, pp. 123-49. New York: Oxford University Press, 1990.

Sha'arawi, Huda. *Harem Years: The Memoirs of an Egyptian Feminist (1879-*

1924). Translated, edited, and introduced by Margot Badran. London: Virago Press, 1986.

Shapiro, Robert Y., and Harpreet Mahajan. "Gender Differences in Policy Preferences: A Summary of Trends from the 1960's to the 1980's." *Public Opinion Quarterly* 59, no. 1 (1986): 42-61.

Simeone, Angela. *Academic Women: Working towards Equality.* Hadley, Mass.: Bergin & Garvey Publications, 1987.

Smedes, Lewis. *Mere Morality: What God Expects from Ordinary People.* Grand Rapids: William B. Eerdmans, 1983.

Sorrell, Lorraine. "What Women Are Worth." *Off Our Backs* 20 (February 1990): 4, 29.

Stanley, A. "Gender Segregation in the Workplace: Plus ca Change." *NWSA Journal* 3 (1990): 640-45.

Staudt, Kathleen. "Women in Development: Courses and Curriculum Integration." *Women's Studies Quarterly* 14 (Fall/Winter 1986): 21-28.

Stevenson, Mary H. "Some Economic Approaches to the Persistence of Wage Differences between Men and Women." In *Women Working: Theories and Facts in Perspective,* ed. Ann Stromberg and S. Harkess, 2d ed., pp. 87-100. Mountain View, Calif.: Mayfield, 1988.

Strasser, Susan. *Never Done: A History of American Housework.* New York: Pantheon Books, 1982.

Strober, M. "Toward a General Theory of Occupational Sex Segregation: The Case of Public School Teaching." In *Sex Segregation in the Workplace: Trends, Explanations, Remedies,* ed. Barbara Reskin, pp. 144-56. Washington: National Academy Press, 1984.

Suppe, Frederick. *The Structure of Scientific Theories.* 2d ed. Urbana, Ill.: University of Illinois Press, 1977.

Swain, Sally. "Home Is Where the Art Is." *Ms.,* April 1989, pp. 72-73.

Swedlow, M. "Men's Accommodations to Women Entering Nontraditional Occupations: A Case of Rapid Transit Operative." *Gender & Society* 3 (1989): 373-87.

Thorne, Barrie. "Feminist Rethinking of the Family: An Overview." In *Rethinking the Family: Some Feminist Questions,* ed. Barrie Thorne with Marilyn Yalom, pp. 1-24. New York: Longman, 1982.

Tinker, Irene. *Persistent Inequalities: Women and World Development.* New York: Oxford University Press, 1990.

Tong, Rosemarie. *Feminist Thought: A Comprehensive Introduction.* Boulder, Colo.: Westview Press, 1989.

Toren, N., and B. Kraus. "The Effects of Minority Size on Women's Position in Academia." *Social Forces* 65 (1987): 1096-1100.

Trembour, Mary. "Women in Education." In *Women and Work in India: Continuity and Change*, ed. Joyce Lebra, Joy Paulson, and Jana Everett, pp. 100-125. New Delhi: Promilla & Co., 1984.

Trible, Phyllis. *Texts of Terror: Literary-Feminist Readings of Biblical Narratives.* Philadelphia: Fortress Press, 1984.

Tucker, Judith. *Women in Nineteenth-Century Egypt.* Cambridge: Cambridge University Press, 1985.

Van Leeuwen, Mary Stewart. *Gender and Grace: Love, Work and Parenting in a Changing World.* Downers Grove, Ill.: InterVarsity Press, 1990.

————. *The Person in Psychology: A Contemporary Christian Appraisal.* Grand Rapids: William B. Eerdmans, 1985.

Van Ness, Dan. *Crime and Its Victims: What We Can Do.* Downers Grove, Ill.: InterVarsity Press, 1986.

Walby, Sylvia. *Patriarchy at Work: Patriarchal and Capitalist Relations in Employment.* Minneapolis: University of Minnesota Press, 1987.

Walzer, Michael. *Spheres of Justice.* New York: Basic Books, 1983.

Waring, Marilyn. *If Women Counted: A New Feminist Economics.* San Francisco: Harper & Row, 1989.

Weiztman, Lenore. *The Divorce Revolution: The Unexpected Social and Economic Consequences for Women and Children in America.* New York: Free Press, 1985.

Williams, Christine. *Gender Differences at Work: Women and Men in Nontraditional Occupations.* Berkeley: University of California Press, 1989.

Wise, Sue, and Liz Stanley. *Georgie Porgie: Sexual Harassment in Everyday Life.* London: Pandora Press, 1987.

Wolgast, Elizabeth H. *The Grammar of Justice.* Ithaca, N.Y.: Cornell University Press, 1987.

Wolterstorff, Nicholas. *Reason within the Bounds of Religion.* Grand Rapids: William B. Eerdmans, 1976.

————. *Until Justice and Peace Embrace.* Grand Rapids: William B. Eerdmans, 1983.

Woolf, Virginia. *A Room of One's Own.* 1929; rpt. New York: Harcourt Brace Jovanovich, 1957.

"Working Women." *Newsweek,* 14 October 1991, p. 3.

Young, Iris. "Socialist Feminism and the Limits of Dual Systems Theory." *Socialist Review* 10 (March-June 1980): 169-88.

Zaretsky, Eli. *Capitalism, the Family and Personal Life.* Rev. ed. New York: Harper & Row, 1986.

Zenie-Ziegler, Wédad. *In Search of Shadows: Conversations with Egyptian Women.* Atlantic Highlands, N.J.: Zed Books, 1989.

Zia, Helen. "Women in Hate Groups: Who Are They? Why Are They There?" *Ms.,* March/April 1991, pp. 20-27.

Zimmer, Lynn. "Tokenism and Women in the Workplace: The Limits of Gender-Neutral Theory." *Social Problems* 35 (1988): 64-77.

Zinn, Maxine Baca. "Family, Feminism, and Race in America." *Gender & Society* 4 (1990): 68-82.

Works Cited in Chapter 17

Collins, Patricia Hill. *Black Feminist Thought: Knowledge, Consciousness, and the Politics of Empowerment.* London: HarperCollins, 1990.

"The Danvers Statement" (issued by the Council on Biblical Manhood and Womanhood). *Christianity Today,* 13 January 1989, p. 41.

East, Catherine. "Critical Comments on *A Lesser Life: The Myth of Women's Liberation in America.*" Paper published by the National Women's Political Caucus, 1275 "K" Street, Suite 750, Washington, D.C., 20005.

Ehrensaft, Diane. *Parenting Together: Men and Women Sharing the Care of Their Children.* Champaign: University of Illinois Press, 1990.

Gelb, Joyce. *Feminism and Politics: A Comparative Perspective.* Berkeley: University of California Press, 1989.

Glendon, Mary Ann. *Abortion and Divorce in Western Law: American Failures, European Challenges.* Cambridge: Harvard University Press, 1987.

Graebner, Alan. "Birth Control and the Lutherans." In *Women in American Religion,* ed. Janet Wilson James. Philadelphia: University of Pennsylvania Press, 1980.

Gramsci, Antonio. *Selections from the Prison Notebooks.* London: Lawrence & Wishart, 1971.

Habermas, Jürgen. *Knowledge and Human Interests.* Trans. Jeremy J. Shapiro. Boston: Beacon Press, 1971.

Hewlett, Sylvia. *A Lesser Life: The Myth of Women's Liberation in America.* New York: William Morrow, 1986.

———. *When the Bough Breaks: The Cost of Neglecting Our Children.* New York: Basic Books, 1991.

Hill, Anita. "The Nature of the Beast." *Ms.,* January/February 1992, pp. 32-33.

Hochschild, Arlie. *The Second Shift: Working Parents and the Revolution at Home.* New York: Viking Press, 1989.

hooks, bell. *Feminist Theory: From Margin to Center.* Boston: South End Press, 1984.

Johnson, Dale A. *Women in English Religion, 1700-1925.* New York: Edwin Mellen, 1983.

Kuyper, Abraham. *De Eerepositie der Vrouw* ("The Woman's Position of Honor"). Kampen, Netherlands: J. H. Kok, 1914; trans. Irene Konyndyk, unpublished manuscript, Calvin College, 1990.

—————. *Het Sociale Vraagstuk en de Christlijke Religie* ("The Social Problem and the Christian Religion"). Amsterdam: J. A. Wormser, 1891. Translated by Dirk Jellema as *Christianity and the Class Struggle* (Grand Rapids: Piet Hein, 1950), and by James Skillen as *The Problem of Poverty* (Grand Rapids: Baker Book House, 1991).

LaHaye, Beverly, and Tim LaHaye. *The Act of Marriage: The Beauty of Sexual Love.* Grand Rapids: Zondervan, 1976.

Loomer, Bernard. "Two Conceptions of Power." *Criterion* 15 (1976): 12.

McCarthy, Colman. "Women Face Greatest Danger at Home." Washington Post Writers' Group, 22 January 1991.

Pleck, Elizabeth. *Domestic Tyranny: The Making of American Social Policy against Family Violence from Colonial Times to the Present.* New York: Oxford University Press, 1987.

Poling, James Newton. *The Abuse of Power: A Theological Problem.* Nashville: Abingdon, 1991.

Riley, William Bell. "Mrs. W. B. Riley: In Memoriam." *Christian Fundamentalist* 5 (September 1931): 99.

Stacey, Judith. *Brave New Families: Stories of Domestic Upheaval in Late Twentieth Century America.* New York: Basic Books, 1990.

Swartley, Willard. *Slavery, Sabbath, War, and Women: Case Studies in Biblical Interpretation.* Scottdale, Pa.: Herald Press, 1983.

Tucker, Ruth A. *Women in the Maze: Questions and Answers on Biblical Equality.* Downers Grove, Ill.: InterVarsity Press, 1992.

Van Leeuwen, Mary. "Abraham Kuyper and the Cult of True Womanhood." Paper given at the 25th Anniversary Conference of the Institute for Christian Studies, Toronto, June 1992.

Williams, Raymond. *Keywords.* London: Flamingo, 1983.

Wolterstorff, Nicholas. *Until Justice and Peace Embrace.* Grand Rapids: William B. Eerdmans, 1983.

Zuidervaart, Lambert. Notes on Marx and Marxism. Grand Rapids: Calvin College Philosophy Department, 1992.

INDEX

Abraham, 163, 185, 189, 192, 196
Abu-Lughod, Lila, 500
Achtemeier, Elizabeth, 141-43, 145, 161-
    62, 164
Acker, Joan, 571
Adam, 185, 189-90, 200, 207, 211-12, 218
Addie, William, 354-55
Ahmed, Leila, 84, 93
Allis, Sam, 245
Amos, Valerie, 80
Andolsen, Barbara, 170, 410
Anthony, Susan B., 41
Aquinas, Thomas, 350
Ardener, Edwin, 362
Ardener, Shirley, 362
Aristotle, 349, 357-58, 423
Astor, Lady, 274
Augustine, Saint, 349

Bailey, Covert, 334-35
Banks, Olive, 31
Bart, Pauline, 284
Barth, Karl, 161, 177
Becker, Gary, 537
Beech, Mary, 486
Beecher, Catherine, 507

Beneria, Lourdes, 71
Bettelheim, Bruno, 186
Bhavnani, Kum-Kum, 80-81
Bianchi, Eugene, 295-96
Bierce, Ambrose, 357
Bloesch, Donald, 161-62
Bloomer, Amelia, 320
Boesak, Allan, 124, 156-57, 158
Bonhoeffer, Dietrich, 26
Bouton, Jim, 296
Brazelton, T. Berry, 523
Brown, Laura, 271, 272-73, 276, 279, 284-
    85
Brown, Olympia, 348, 352, 353, 358
Brownmiller, Susan, 300, 309
Brueggemann, Walter, 194
Brumberg, Laura, 271, 281
Buker, Eloise, 437-38
Bulbeck, Chilla, 87
Bush, George, 237
Butler, Josephine, 36

Calvin, John, 119, 133-35, 137, 141, 159,
    163-64, 172, 176, 179-80, 182, 219
Campbell, Cynthia, 177
Caplan, Patricia, 476, 480, 486

647